AT THE LIMITS OF JUSTICE

Women of Colour on Terror

Edited by Suvendrini Perera and Sherene H. Razack

The fear and violence that followed the events of September 11, 2001, touched lives all around the world, even in places that few would immediately associate with the global War on Terror. In *At the Limits of Justice*, thirty contributors from six countries explore the proximity of terror in their own lives and in places ranging from Canada and the United States to Jamaica, Palestine/Israel, Australia, Guyana, Chile, Pakistan, and across the African continent.

In this collection, female scholars of colour – including leading theorists on issues of indigeneity, race, and feminism – examine the political, social, and personal repercussions of the war on terror through contributions that range from testimony and poetry to scholarly analysis. Inspired by both the personal and the global impact of this violence within the War on Terror, they expose the way in which the war on terror is presented as a distant and foreign issue at the same time that it is deeply present in the lives of women and others all around the world.

An impassioned but rigorous examination of issues of race and gender in contemporary politics, *At the Limits of Justice* is also a call to create moral communities that will find terror and violence unacceptable.

SUVENDRINI PERERA is a professor in the Department of Communication and Cultural Studies at Curtin University.

SHERENE H. RAZACK is a professor in the Department of Social Justice Education at the Ontario Institute for Studies in Education, University of Toronto.

At the Limits of Justice

Women of Colour on Terror

EDITED BY SUVENDRINI PERERA
AND SHERENE H. RAZACK

UNIVERSITY OF TORONTO PRESS
Toronto Buffalo London

ISBN 978-1-4426-4825-8 (cloth)
ISBN 978-1-4426-2600-3 (paper)

Library and Archives Canada Cataloguing in Publication

At the limits of justice : women of colour on terror / edited by
Suvendrini Perera and Sherene H. Razack.

Includes bibliographical references and index.

ISBN 978-1-4426-4825-8 (bound). – ISBN 978-1-4426-2600-3 (pbk.)

1. Terrorism – Social aspects. 2. Violence – Social aspects. I. Perera, Suvendrini, editor II. Razack, Sherene, editor

HV6431.A8 2014   303.6'25   C2014-902892-X

This book has been published with the help of a grant from the Federation
for the Humanities and Social Sciences, through the Awards to Scholarly
Publications Program, using funds provided by the Social Sciences and
Humanities Research Council of Canada.

University of Toronto Press acknowledges the financial assistance to its
publishing program of the Canada Council for the Arts and the Ontario Arts
Council, an agency of the Government of Ontario.

University of Toronto Press acknowledges the financial support of the Government of Canada through the Canada Book Fund for its publishing activities.

Contents

Section Six: Theorizing (at) the Limits of Justice

List of Illustrations

Acknowledgments

The editors would like to thank the Social Sciences and Humanities Research Council and the Researchers and Academics of Color for Equality (RACE) network for grants to fund the workshop for which the papers in this collection were prepared. We would like to thank Nashwa Salem for her extraordinary research and organizing contributions to the workshop and to the preparation of the manuscript for publication. Without her deep commitment to the ideas of the project and her capacity to research and organize, the workshop would not have been the success that it was. Sherene Razack thanks the Ontario Institute for Studies in Education of the University of Toronto, and Suvendrini Perera thanks the School of Media, Culture, and Creative Arts at Curtin University for institutional resources in support of the workshop and the book. We would like to thank the following for permission to reproduce parts of previously published materials:

Anna M. Agathangelou. "Anxieties of Global Empire: Politics of Visibility Epistemologies and 'Terror.'" In *Knowing Al-Qaeda: The Epistemology of Terrorism*, ed. Christina Hellmich and Andreas Behnke. 29–56. Burlington: Ashgate, 2010.

Denise Ferreira da Silva. "To Be Announced: Radical Praxis or Knowing (at) the Limits of Justice." *Social Text* 31(1) (2013): 43–62.

Inderpal Grewal, "Outsourcing Patriarchy: Feminist Encounters, Transnational Mediations, and the Crime of 'Honour Killings.'" *International Feminist Journal of Politics* 15(1) (2013): 1–19.

Teresa Macias. "'Tortured Bodies': The Biopolitics of Torture and Truth in Chile." *International Journal of Human Rights* 17(1) (2013): 113–32.

Malinda S. Smith, ed. *Securing Africa: Post-9/11 Discourses on Terrorism.* Burlington: Ashgate, 2010.

Omeima Sukkarieh. "Mori Cards: The Body Bags Installation." *Somatechnics* 1(1) (2011): 134–7.

Omeima Sukkarieh. "Unsewing My Lips, Breathing My Voice: The Spoken and Unspoken Truth of Transnational Violence." *Somatechnics* 1(1) (2011): 124–33.

Nicole Watson. "The Northern Territory Emergency Response – Has it Really Improved the Lives of Aboriginal Women and Children?" *Australian Feminist Law Journal* 35 (2011): 147–63.

AT THE LIMITS OF JUSTICE

Women of Colour on Terror

Introduction. At the Limits of Justice:
Women of Colour Theorize Terror

SUVENDRINI PERERA AND SHERENE H. RAZACK

This anthology began in response to a documentary aired in Britain on Channel 4 that showed shocking – and in our experience unprecedented – levels of terror against civilians. The images had been recorded as trophy shots and battlefield memorabilia by the victors in the final battle between the Sri Lankan state and the separatist Liberation Tigers of Tamil Eelam (LTTE).[1] In the wake of that documentary, we, as academics in the global North, began to ask a series of questions about how to respond to such scenes of horror, especially when international institutions and our own governments were silent. This official silence was all the more striking because it contrasted so strongly with the pervasive discourses and representations of violence of the global "War on Terror." Terror seemed to be both nowhere and all around us. To examine these issues with a range of scholars sharing similar concerns, we organized a workshop in Toronto, Canada, titled "Violence in a Far Country: Women Scholars of Colour Theorize Terror." This volume is the outcome of that workshop.

The workshop's title was intended to provoke reflection on the complexities of articulating relations of distance and proximity. For us as convenors, and for many of the contributors to this volume, our origins and histories, as well as our racialized and gendered positioning in our current locations, connect us to places that are popularly conceived as the ground, source, or locus of terror. At the same time, as academics of the global North (Canada, Australia, Israel/Palestine, Europe, the United States), most of us write from locations seen as outside or remote from terror, that is, from places whose own historical and continuing practices of terror – invasion, occupation, colonialism, imperialism, militarism, racism – have been disowned, displaced, or dismissed as aberrations.

Yet for indigene and settler, for colonized and colonizer, for migrant and refugee, violence is *not* a far country; nor is it so for those of us who inhabit one or more of these locations. It was from a consciousness of these shared complexities of location, rather than any form of simple identification, that our workshop took shape. What emerged during it was a recognition of solidarity and, somewhat unexpectedly, an exhilarating sense of collaborative purpose grounded in the politics of our specific emplaced and embodied relations to terror.

The title of this volume remains focused on the complexities of distance and proximity, the near and the far, but it also points to shared conditions and possibilities of working against spatialized relations of terror and against the limits of (in)justice:

> *I was giving birth, but living death at the same time ... promising my unborn to reach the hospital, and have her in Jerusalem, bil Quds ya habibti bil Quds* [in Jerusalem, my love, in Jerusalem].
>
> *I wanted to have Eiman* [her baby] *in Jerusalem. I promised myself I would never deny my children this privilege ... not because of the medical insurance Jerusalemite ID holders have, and not because of the blue ID, but because I can't see my kids suffer ... I could not let them inherit suffering ... although we Palestinians have already inherited suffering.*   (Shalhoub-Kevorkian, this volume)

In her chapter "Terrorism and the Birthing Body in Jerusalem" in this volume, Nadera Shalhoub-Kevorkian meticulously details how "the occupied body that has inherited suffering due to historical injustice in an occupied *time* and *space*" is caught in a constrictive "geography of fear and within an archaeology of constant uncertainty." Yet the force of her repeated and profoundly ironic invocation, *"in Jerusalem, my love, in Jerusalem,"* signifies as an opening in the geography of entrapment; it is an avowal and a promise that suffering's limits will be circumvented. Taking inspiration from this story of living, knowing, and acting at the extremities, against the limits, the title of this volume also references a passage in Denise Ferreira da Silva's chapter: "Knowing at the limits of justice must start before, but facing the beyond of, representation ... Knowing at the limits of justice is at once a kind of knowing and doing, it is a praxis, one that unsettles what has become but offers no guidance for what has yet to become."

This volume clearly positions itself within the genealogy of women of colour feminism in the global North, beginning with the landmark anthology *This Bridge Called My Back: Radical Writings by Women of*

Color, edited by Gloria Anzaldúa and Cherríe Moraga (1981). As Jody Melamed writes, the lasting achievement of that anthology was to "constitute women of color as a community of friendship and solidarity, a political movement and a subject position," with the latter understood as unstable and processual, "subject to changing empirical possibilities and epistemological tendencies."[2] Subsequent anthologies (*Feminist Genealogies, Colonial Legacies, Democratic Futures,* ed. M. Jacqui Alexander and Chandra Talpade Mohanty; and *Colonize This! Young Women of Color on Today's Feminism,* ed. Daisy Hernandez and Bushra Rehman, to name only two) mark the institutional space that women of colour feminists have made for the praxis of knowing and doing at the limits of justice as well as the continually unsettled and shifting nature of that project.

Drawing on these histories, this volume is defined by the often overlooked geopolitical, psychic, and sociocultural repercussions of the War on Terror and its expanding spatial and temporal effects. Our understandings of *terror* are shaped and delimited by this now decade-long war, even in those chapters that do not address it directly. In our initial invitation we asked our contributors to consider the following questions:

How do we name, remember, and respond to atrocity and terror?
How do narratives and spectacles of violence and terror take shape in diverse regions, disciplines, and forums, and how they travel from one domain to another?
How we might transform these responses into a collective politics for social and political action, to reshape what Arundhati Roy describes as the unequal geographical distribution of suffering and violence?

The volume embodies our responses to, and distinctive articulations of, these questions in relation to our specific contexts. Inevitably, then, it speaks in many accents: the contributors inhabit distinct and sometimes clashing political and theoretical positions and deploy different languages; and the genres represented range from poetry, testimony, and life writing to scholarly essays. We do not try to homogenize these voices or to unify them within a singular framework. All chapters, however, are attempts to work through the effects of what Andrea Smith names, in the US context, as three distinct but still interrelated logics: "(1) slaveability/anti-black racism, which anchors capitalism; (2) genocide, which anchors colonialism; and (3) Orientalism, which anchors war."[3] This volume is held together by a shared project of identifying the workings of these violent logics at the global and local levels as well as by our collective commitment to "critique and something else."[4]

Knowledge Production and/in the War on Terror

At the Limits of Justice provides a space for Indigenous women and women of colour academics to reflect on our own particular dilemmas as they produce knowledge on the topic of terror. Sometimes this leads to unexpected insights, connections, and juxtapositions. In the context of Canadian First Nations peoples, Robina Thomas writes: "For some reason, I never thought about my work with former residential school students as an act of witnessing violence and terror." Her chapter proceeds to explore how public knowledge about these experiences of terror is produced as well as the dilemmas and responsibilities of bearing witness to them.

A problem we face as racialized women is that each time we encounter hegemonic discourses on terror, and attempt to circulate critical counter-narratives, we are seen not as academics who have carefully researched an issue, but rather as persons with a personal and therefore partial and non-objective analysis. The ethical issues involved in doing our work loom large. For example, as critical scholars we want to preserve a space for noting the destructive impact of exclusionary and fundamentalist ethno-religious or nationalist forces, be they Hindu, Christian, or Muslim. By engaging in a critique of our own communities of origin, however, we provide ammunition for those who are anxious to affirm Christian and white Western superiority. The stakes are high, as Sherene Razack suggests in her chapter on the torture of Omar Khadr as a child in Bagram and Guantanamo prisons. Scholars play a central role in knowledge production in the War on Terror. For example, in Khadr's case, Michael Wellner, a psychologist, testified that Khadr was an unrepentant and violent jihadist, a psychological status assessed in terms of his religiosity and his character and supported by ideas about Muslims being predisposed to violence. Narratives about the innate cultural inferiority of Muslims have gained a new respectability through the work of scholars and experts who take an openly extreme anti-Muslim position and whose texts are widely circulated in the media. Native informants – that is to say, scholars from Muslim cultures – are much in demand as they provide apparently privileged insights into their own communities. In this climate, if, for example, we critique the ideological leanings of Khadr's family as evident in their media interviews, then we open the door for the legal argument that Khadr comes from a family of terrorists and therefore is likely to pursue a violent agenda. Indeed, a key media strategy that has had an impact on legal processes is precisely to juxtapose "bad" Muslims with "good" Muslims, the latter being those who attest to the innate cultural failings of their religion and of their communities. Not a day goes by without someone being feted in the media for writing from an "insider" position on the violence of Muslim men and the inherent misogyny of Quranic texts.

This volume examines the ethical-political dimensions and dilemmas of producing narratives/knowledge of terror vis-à-vis one's own racialized and gendered positioning and North/South asymmetries of power. Gender is an important component of our approach. Extreme sexual violence features prominently in regimes of terror. However, the violence in women's lives is often uncoupled from the wider contexts of terror in which they live. For example, in the West, there has been a general interest in "honour killings" in the Middle East and South Asia but less interest in the numbers of women and children who are dying from state-sponsored violence or from the violence of war and occupation, and still less interest in the relationship between those two forms of violence. We are particularly alert to how this dynamic has produced and sustained an indifference to the human suffering of both men and women in the global South. In her chapter, Inderpal Grewal tracks the emergence and seemingly uncritical acceptance of the category "honour killing" while examining how productive that term is in both the North and the South and while attending to the very real violence against women.

The question of how we are to foster moral communities that reject multiple sources of violence and terror is a pressing one. To answer it, it is imperative to consider the discursive and representational means through which violence and terror gain social approval. In this endeavour, the idea that narratives travel across regions and institutional sites has received little attention. Significantly, there has been little critical reflection among scholars about their own difficulties and complicities in researching violence and terror, and this is especially the case among women scholars of colour, whose origins and histories in the South and location in the global North operate in specific ways to constrain what can be written. By emphasizing questions about how narratives circulate and our moral responsibility as scholars, we hope to fill a serious gap in anti-violence studies. As we collectively insist that the dehumanization of our communities must end, we need to grapple with the many layers of our implication in violence.

Organization of the Volume

This book has six sections, each with an introduction that outlines its key concerns and topics. These introductions were prepared by graduate students at various universities in Toronto who participated in the workshop. They offer here their own reflections on the principal ideas and theoretical directions underpinning the chapters. We hope these introductions will be particularly useful for students and teachers who use this book as a course text.

The title of Section One, "Mundane Terror / (Un)Livable Lives," borrows a term from Shalhoub-Kevorkian's chapter about the birthing body in Jerusalem. "Mundane Terror" beautifully encapsulates the unspectacular ways in which terror (de)forms day-to-day lives in places marked by everyday violence, from Canada and the United States to Palestine. Robina Thomas's "Violence and Terror in a Colonized Country" begins by placing the experiences of residential school survivors in the context of colonial terror and violence. As Thomas shows, this violence remains part of the ongoing war against First Peoples even as the state repeatedly attempts to assert its own innocence through mechanisms such as the current inquiry into residential schools. Sherene Razack's chapter on how Canadians came to accept the detention and torture of a Canadian teenager as necessary in the War on Terror reminds us that our moral sensibilities are shaped through everyday acts of watching the national news or reading a newspaper. Sunaina Maira's "Surveillance Effects" examines another form of warfare at home, "the domestic war on terror" that is being waged in particular against young Muslim Americans. This form of domestic war, she argues, is a flexible "technology of nation making" that approaches its subjects as bodies to be "preserved and protected as well as monitored, contained, repressed, or removed, if necessary through violence." Andrea Smith's chapter, "The Biopolitics of Christian Persecution," turns to another form of mundane violence, one that has been largely invisibilized – the violent psychic and material structures that underpin American evangelical Christianity. "On the global stage," she points out, "the Christian persecution movement positions [white] evangelical Christians in the United States in the place of the oppressed Third World Christian, allowing white evangelism to disavow its complicity in creating conditions of oppression through the export of US capitalist exceptionalism." The logic of US evangelical Christianity calls for the sustaining of a permanent crisis that licenses its own tactics of everyday warfare.

The chapters in Section Two, "Violence in a Far Country," explore the intersections of and conjunctions between multiple forms of violence against women, as well as their transnational ramifications across diverse sites and locations in the broader context of the War on Terror. Amina Jamal's "Collateral Violence" juxtaposes the stories of two Pakistani women: Aasia Bibi, a forty-five-year-old Christian who was sentenced to death for making derogatory remarks about the Prophet Mohammed, and Aafia Siddiqui, an American-based scientist of Pakistani origin charged with shooting a US Marine in Afghanistan. Through the very different public stories told of these two women, Jamal considers how violence against women "is indirectly but deeply inflected by contestations over the state's enlistment in the global militaristic and counter-terrorism project." Similarly, in "Outsourcing Patriarchy," Inderpal Grewal explores the accretions of a transnational public understanding around the term "honour killing" and "the process through which powerful circuits of knowledge produce hegemonic meanings through which other possibilities, struggles, and violence remain submerged." Nadine Naber's "Diasporas of Empire" explores the convergence of imperial and domestic war for diasporic Arab women in the United States. Her subjects' lives, Naber argues, "are constituted by the same military violence" as "those in the countries targeted directly by bombs or bulldozers." For Naber's interlocutors, "military violence (bombs, bulldozers, etc.) and gendered-racial violence in the United States" are "moving parts of the same imperial present and take place within the same spatial-temporal context." In the final chapter in this section, Meyda Yeğenoğlu considers whether global violence against women can be thought of in the same terms as the response to terrorism: "What is it that prevents us from imagining a 'war on domestic violence' that is of comparable scope to the 'War on Terror'?"

Questions about the ethics, aesthetics, and politics of memory and the ways in which we remember the terror of small, obscure wars thread together the contributions in Section Three, "Terror and the Limits of Remembering." Merlinda Bobis's chapter, "Weeping Is Singing," was complemented at the Toronto workshop by the author's live performance *River, River*. In both her performance there and her chapter here, Bobis interweaves "water–body–story–song" in a retelling of the counter-insurgency campaign carried out by the Philippine army in Bobis's hometown of Bikol at the southern tip of Luzon, the largest island in the Philippines. So that her story of the deep losses of an unknown local war can "be heard in the public space," Bobis "offered what is most private: my own body. I had to perform the story, and the weeping became a singing: a militant dirge." Honor Ford-Smith's chapter explores memorializations of violent confrontations between Jamaican street gangs and the Jamaican state across domestic and diasporic spaces and temporalities. Both the marking and the forgetting of that memory are critical to how gendered and racialized ideologies about violence are reproduced, circulated, and resisted. Ford-Smith discusses a diversity of genres and forms – vigils, mural making, street protests, theatre – as performances of memorialization. Alissa Trotz's chapter, "'Lest We Forget,'" is concerned with memory and terror in another small place. Fifty years after racialized violence swept what was then British Guiana on the eve of independence, Trotz explores how that violence is remembered and layered onto the present as it "maps itself onto contemporary landscapes laid bare by over three decades of neoliberally driven structural adjustment programs." "'Tortured Bodies,'" Teresa Macias's chapter on the Truth Commission in Chile, considers how memory, state violence, and reparative or transitional justice relate to one another. Macias explores how the production of tortured bodies by the Truth Commission serves as evidence of "the nation's capacity to overcome." She identifies a structural continuity between the torturing state that imprints its violence on recalcitrant bodies and the contemporary state that "requires biopolitical corporeal technologies that render the tortured body minutely and intimately known now for the purpose of producing a national truth about torture." The chapter resonates in important ways with the questions posed by Thomas and Razack elsewhere in the volume regarding the making of a "national truth about torture"; it also engages with questions posed in Section Four on the links among humanitarianism, terror, and state power.

The chapters in Section Four, "Thinking Humanitarianism / Thinking Terror," examine how humanitarian logics are deployed to complement and reinforce security logics. When does humanitarianism function as another face of terror? The state's disowning of its own violence and the perpetration of violence through discursive and institutional processes of humanitarianism are at the heart of Nicole Watson's chapter, "From the Emergency Response to Stronger Futures?" Watson considers the state's intervention, after the declaration of a state of emergency, in Aboriginal communities in Australia's Northern Territory. The stated aim of the intervention, to end chronic child sexual abuse in the communities, involved putting in place a range of biopolitical measures (compulsory health checks, bans on pornography and alcohol, quarantining of welfare funds) designed to protect children and women. Yet as Watson argues, such actions *for their own good* can be placed against a series of historical interventions that "in the name of protecting Aboriginal women invariably resulted in a binary that simultaneously rendered their rights invisible and subjected them to excessive regulation." Sedef Arat-Koç's chapter, "Power in/through Speaking of Terror," turns to the politics of humanitarian intervention in very different circumstances, those of "the Kurdish question" in Turkey. Here, Arat-Koç argues, the discourse of humanitarian intervention claims to address and condemn the violence of state sovereignty, but it does so by replacing it with imperial sovereignty. This has the effect of "stripping the recipients of humanitarianism of political subjectivity, reducing them to bare life," and "eliminating the space for political agency and democracy." Malinda S. Smith's chapter views the War on Terror from an "African-centred perspective." It asks us to remember a moment of radical possibility that exceeded humanitarian orthodoxies – the September 2001 Durban anti-racism conference that was subsequently overwhelmed by the upheaval of 9/11. From this vantage point, Smith reassesses the widespread understanding of the latter as an epochal moment that "changed the world forever." In the final contribution in this section, "Humanitarianism as Planetary Politics," Miriam Ticktin stretches the frame to consider the paradox of humanitarianism's expanding frontiers, such that, even as they bring more domains of non-human biological life into humanity's purview, they render others as monstrous or invisible. Ticktin probes the limits and boundaries of this expanding humanitarianism and asks: "Which lives does it newly recognize, and which lives does it cast aside?"

The chapters in Section Five, "Terror Circuits," consider interconnected visual, geopolitical, and affective economies of terror, tracking how they interpellate and implicate diverse subjects even while they interact with counter circuits, events, and temporalities. In "Visual Colonial Economies and Slave Death in Modernity," Anna Agathangelou, through a series of visual images of Osama Bin Laden, traces how an "objectified (and eroticized) portrayal of Bin Laden is essential to the consolidation of a powerful US subject" and indicative of how "global empires" and "contemporary regimes of visuality" are constitutive of each other. In this way, she argues, "visual technologies are used as appropriating methods of the 'other' ... to quench the global desire for forces that open up spaces with the potential for the creation of new value" and to transmute "differences forcefully ... into new raw material." Suvendrini Perera's chapter, "Viewing Violence in a Far Country," turns to another set of key visual images of the War on Terror – the trophy photographs of Iraqi prisoners at Abu Ghraib prison. Perera argues that while much has been written about the Abu Ghraib photographs' domestic impact in the United States, their global effects remain unmapped: "How does Abu Ghraib as a cluster of practices, images, discourses, and technologies reappear and resound as it expands across diverse geographies and temporalities?" She discusses the Abu Ghraib images in the context of the trophy photographs from the Sri Lanka killing fields and the "Kony 2012" campaign. Sunera Thobani's chapter, "Fighting Terror," turns to cinematic representations of monstrous others, examining the role these representations play in "shaping the hegemonic form of Western masculinity that has emerged as dominant through the 'War on Terror.'" It asks: "How have feminists engaged with hegemonic constructs of the monstrous nature of the 'enemies' of the 'West'?" Through a discussion of "Islamophobic visual logics" encountered in scenes from popular films such as *Kandahar* and *Osama*, Thobani seeks to "problematize the dominant feminist narrative of women being 'used' to serve what are defined as essentially masculinist interests by interrogating whether these women – including the feminists among them – are also not served by such 'masculinist' interests, as well as those of the imperialist state."

The chapters in Section Six, "Theorizing (at) the Limits of Justice," expose the limits of what Asma Abbas refers to as "the ontological or epistemological terms that have been at play so far"; they also address questions of love and its intimacy with terror. Abbas, "In Terror, in Love, out of Time," enjoins that "a contemporary, relevant, anticolonial politics must address the modes of love ... inaugurated by the colonial and liberal projects in collusion with capital [and] explore where that has settled in each of us; and ... inquire into the ways we are intimate with terror." She argues that locating "political possibility for lives continually, and increasingly, forced to confront not merely incidences of destruction but their very political subjectivities cast in the form of destruction and violence" involves attending to their "forms of sensuous life," in particular, those "that erupt as the form called terror colludes with the forms of love." Her chapter engages in particular with the work of Nadeem Aslam, who "along with other South Asian writers ... can hold the murder and the love together, for there is no choice not to." Denise Ferreira da Silva's "Radical Praxis or Knowing (at) the Limits of Justice" also seeks to "contemplate another horizon." Silva begins, in the wake of the 2011 urban revolts in Britain, by staging an "invented exchange" about "slavery, blackness, and violence." Her chapter does not claim to offer any program or explanation of the revolts by deploying "our dear social categories" or the "the tools of racial knowledge." Rather, she proposes another form of thinking "at the limits of justice":

> Thinking the limits of justice does ... require a plan of sorts, a certain procedure, but one not committed to resolving the conditions it exposes into more effective measure, grid, or account ... Knowing the limits of justice, nonetheless, is an ethical-political praxis, it acknowledges all the effects and implications as well as the presuppositions informing our accounts of existing with/in one another. Knowing at the limits of justice, as an ethico-political praxis, requires onto-epistemological accounts that begin and end with relationality (affectability) – that do no more than to anticipate what is to be announced, perhaps, a horizon of radical exteriority, where knowing implicates affection, intention, and attention.

The section concludes with just such another "onto-epistemological account," Omeima Sukkarieh's extraordinary "Unsewing My Lips, Breathing My Voice":

> Why are you crying so much?
> *Because I have lost happiness.*
> Where?
> *Across the sea somewhere.*
> Then why don't you go find it?
> *Because I can't swim.*
> Does happiness know that you're looking for it?
> *I don't know, but it threw me in the water in the first place and left me to drown.*
> Then why do you want to find it?
> *Because my sorrow is lonely without it.*   (Sukkarieh, this volume)

Traversing the spaces between Palestine, Iraq, and Australia, Sukkarieh speaks from the place of the citizen and the migrant, the stateless and the refugee. In a contribution that cuts across the generic conventions and cherished categories that separate theory, critical analysis, testimony, and poetry, she deploys a range of voices directly to address the terror of transnational violence, call it to account, and contemplate its cessation.

We close this introduction with a return to the spatialized limits of justice, on the shores of an impassible ocean: the site of the border, the checkpoint, and the customs inspection. These have become all too familiar to subjects registered as suspect on multiple counts in the era of the War on Terror. Here, as the lesbian Sri Lankan–Canadian poet Leah Lakshmi Piepzna-Samarasinha writes, our lives, our papers, our queer-shaped baggage with its dubious emanations, our loves and solidarities, are all open to violent scrutiny and interrogation, liable to confiscation, subjected to the arbitrary terror of the border:

> What if every time we crossed a border we never made up
> and they started up with
> *Why do you have a Qur'an in your bag*
> *Have you ever been on welfare?*
> *Where is your husband? Why aren't you travelling with him?*
> We could start asking them questions,
> important ones, like
> *How do you touch your child*
> *with the same hands that ripped open*
> *my bags, my Quar'an, my stories?*
> *What if we could bring them to that long beige place*
> *And make them unlock all the ones who didn't make it through?*
> Leah Lakshmi Piepzna-Samarasinha, "Restorative Justice"[5]

Piepzna-Samarasinha's poem does not speak of fear or capitulation at the border; rather, it considers the possibility of staging a counter-interrogation, one that would ask the really important questions of the interrogators themselves, before ending with a hope of an even more radical overturning for "all the ones who didn't make it through." For those ensnared in in the terror of the checkpoint, the poem poses a series of daring (im)possibilities – questions that we take also as ethical imperatives at the limits of justice: "*What if …?*"

NOTES

1 "Sri Lanka's Killing Fields," Channel 4, UK, http://srilanka.channel4.com.
2 Melamed, *Represent and Destroy*, 104.
3 A. Smith, "Indigeniety, Settler Colonialism, White Supremacy."
4 da Silva, in this volume.
5 Piepzna-Samarasinha, *Consensual Genocide*, 63.

SECTION ONE

Mundane Terror / (Un)Livable Lives

1 Introduction to Section One

LAURA KWAK

The power of violence lies not so much in its death-making function but in its generative force: its management of life. This is not at all to discount the destructiveness of terror but rather to contextualize how violence makes itself the rule. The chapters in this section illustrate how it is through the bureaucratic governance over life that violence reinvigorates liberal democracy, remakes nations, reinscribes binaries, and renarrates mythical stories about a clash of civilizations. By paying attention to circuits of knowledge and cartographic strategies that weave stories about the dangers out there threatening us in here, the authors of this section's chapters demonstrate how some stories become known as truth, how a lie becomes a law, and how a nation establishes its innocence.

These chapters facilitate discussion about the broken promises of liberal democracy and the impossibility of social justice under global capitalism. They emphasize the contradictions of modernity that imagine some nations as free by disparaging other lands as always already conquerable. They compel us to interrogate the violence that produces some bodies as living through other bodies, which are made "torturable" and are imagined as always already dying. The authors examine the politics of producing knowledge about violence as well as the subjects that emerge out of pedagogies of terror – subjects that are exalted but also subjects that have been obscured and cast out. In doing so, they reveal a shadow archive of empire, scaffolded by torture and by narrative renderings of sameness/otherness. In what follows, I highlight three themes that emerge from these texts: (1) violence as rule, (2) the naming of terror, and (3) bearing witness as a political act.

Violence as Rule

The chapters in this section reveal how the residential school system in Canada, military checkpoints in Israel/Palestine, and Guantanamo Bay in Cuba are just some of the spaces that have opened up in circumstances where the state of exception[1] has become the rule. When violence is rule, the elimination of certain bodies, marked outside the modern, becomes mundane. The state of emergency[2] then distracts the public from the excesses of power located in bureaucracies. We learn from the authors that when scenes of violence, however appalling, become productive in the geopolitical and socio-economic grid of the everyday, those scenes become un-appalling, or normalized. In fact, the contradictions of so-called democracy are experienced acutely in the daily lives of men, women, and children who have been stripped of their humanity and reduced to harbingers of terror. The contributions in this volume address these processes of disciplining – called biopolitics[3] and/or necropolitics[4] – that overdetermine which bodies are included or excluded. When death or the making of death acts as the foundation for life, massacres become vital to the project of empire. Part and parcel of such a project is then to continuously create the conditions that render some bodies suitable for death while simultaneously insisting that those conditions emerge naturally. Those bodies are reduced to bare life as the sovereign[5] suspends the law through the law itself. The colonial machinery then comprises all facets of the social, economic, and political and flexes its muscles at the micro, meso, and macro levels. Seemingly neutral institutions such as schools then participate in the circulation of knowledge that normalizes violence as rule.

The Naming of Terror

The geopolitics and chrono-logics of the enlightened West continue to be shaped by Orientalist[6] imaginaries that arrest certain bodies in their racial biology and chemistry, thereby rendering them permanently outside the modern. Terror as epistemology (a) (un)makes gendered and racialized subjects of terror and (b) reinstalls the myth of American exceptionalism and Canadian benevolence. The authors demonstrate that terror is narrated by other names that serve to justify violence against certain bodies. For instance, the violence of residential schools comes to be known as improvement; imprisoning children and restricting women's bodies as security; surveilling Arab, Afghan, and South Asian

Americans as patriotism; and ongoing wars of genocide as fighting for religious freedom. Terror reproduces the binary of subjects who need to be protected against those subjects that need to be surveilled, contained, and removed. More astutely, though, the chapters reveal how the politics of resistance have become increasing complex now that dissent is regulated through the separation of the radical from the moderate. Who becomes an adjudicating subject in times of war? And who renders torture possible? How are *some* others invited to participate in these projects on the condition that they participate in the exclusion of *other* others? Racial logics are alive and well when entrance into civility is facilitated through liberal participation in imperial governance. Part of that project has always been to disavow gendered and racial oppression; this is governing through liberation, producing for the subjected the principles of their own subjection.

The West profits from its own manufacture of the conditions of global inequalities even while presenting itself as global guardian of human rights and guarantor of freedoms. For instance, the ills of sexism, racism, and homophobia supposedly flourish only "there" and not "here." Thus, the West takes on the burden of "humanitarianism" or rescuing women and children from the premodern enemy. This allows the United States, Canada, and other aligned powers to tell a story of innocence, disguising imperial interventions for liberal democracy through the language of human rights. Stories of violence are circulated as stories of good people doing good work. Wars and peacekeeping missions are then technologies of nation and empire building and are not only about protecting people and land but also, to a significant degree, about ideological securitization.

Bearing Witness as a Political Act

These chapters on narratives of torture and spectacles of terror make connections that are not supposed to be made. Thomas bears witness to legacies of systemic violence inherited by the residential school system. Shalhoub-Kevorkian bears witness to the suffering of pregnant Palestinian women who must endure military checkpoints. Razack bears witness to the politics that narrate a child as a terrorist in order to justify torture against him. Smith bears witness to the complexities and contradictions of Christian persecution movements as they intersect with American exceptionalism. Together, these contributors cast a light on the shadow of law, thereby challenging its authority. In this way, bearing witness becomes not only a powerful political act but also a reason to act for a world yet to be. In bearing witness to the interior lives of those cast out and to what Shalhoub-Kevorkian calls the "everydayness of their annihilations," these chapters recover the humanity of the tortured and terrorized. When law is ensconced in violence and shapes the parameters of justice we consider (im)possible, it is vital to stay with the abject bodies and unarchived stories. They return our focus to brown and black bodies that have been marked, tortured, and folded into difference. Bearing witness is then a critical methodology that returns to the violence of the law itself and thereby contests the very powers that make life out of death. In other words, these essays bear witness to the limits of justice when it is under law's relentless authority that life is made (un)livable for some.

NOTES

1 Agamben, *State of Exception.*
2 Benjamin, "Theses on the Philosophy of History."
3 Foucault, *Society Must Be Defended.*
4 Mbembe, "Necropolitics."
5 Agamben, *State of Exception.*
6 Said, *Orientalism.*

2 Violence and Terror in a Colonized Country: Canada's Indian Residential School System

ROBINA THOMAS

Introduction

These past few months have been really interesting for me. For some reason, I never thought about my work with former residential school students as an act of witnessing violence and terror. It was not until I received an e-mail from Dr Sherene Razack asking me to participate in the "Violence in a Far Country" workshop that I stopped to reflect on this research. Since then, I have been trying to determine my own particular dilemma in producing knowledge on the topic of terror. What do I have to contribute to this very important topic? Through my life-long commitment to understanding residential schools and the impact of those institutions on Indigenous people, I have heard horror stories that include sexual, physical, spiritual, and emotional abuse. But still, what about producing knowledge on that topic? Although I have never thought about my work as an act of witnessing violence and terror, the impact on me has been, and continues to be, traumatizing. I have listened to stories that have numbed both my body and my spirit. I have spent countless sleepless nights tossing and turning trying to make sense of these unbelievable and unimaginable stories. It took me years to be able to pick up my graduate thesis "Storytelling in the Spirit of Wise Woman: Experiences of Kuper Island Residential School" without bursting into tears.[1] Just picking up the document brought back all the embodied memories I carry from doing that research.

After sitting with these thoughts and contemplating my role in researching and writing about acts of violence and terror, a number of things became abundantly clear. First, colonization, in and of itself, is incredibly violent. That being so, any topic that relates to Indigenous people in Canada is rooted in violence and terror. This violence and terror has not stopped, as is evident in the ongoing Truth and Reconciliation Commission.[2] And finally, despite all the violence and terror, as an Indigenous person who was honoured to be called to "witness" these stories of residential school experiences, I have a responsibility to speak out. This chapter is one way to do that and to make visible the violence and terror of residential schools, most of which has been systematically hidden from Canadians.

Dedication

Before I go any further, I will introduce myself and "stand up" (honour) two of my mentors, who themselves lived through the violence and terror that constituted the residential school system.

My Hul'qumi'num name is Qwul'sih'yah'maht (my English name is Robina Thomas). I am a member of Lyackson First Nation located on Valdez Island, one of the Gulf Islands near Vancouver Island. Through my Grandmother I have Snuy'ney'muxw (Nanaimo) First Nation ancestry, and through my Grandfather, that of the Skwah of the Sto:lo people living in Chilliwack. Because I carry a traditional name, I am required to share who I am and where I am from. And because our old people are worried that once we work our way into academe we will lose our way, I introduce myself this way.

I had the honour and privilege of spending many hours with former residential school students. Seletze and Tsaqwuasupp are two people who taught me the integrity of storytelling. We shared intimate moments, hours, and days discussing residential school experiences. They taught me what residential schools were really like. They taught me how living though violence and terror plays out in our lives as we move away from those institutions. They taught me about honesty and integrity in a way I previously would not have been able to comprehend. They taught me how to live with a good mind and spirit (*uy'skwuluwun*) by sharing their stories selflessly; they hoped those stories would allow others to share their own and begin to live their lives in healthier, happier ways – or, as they say, free their souls.

Seletze Delmar Johnnie (1946–2012)
Seletze was born and raised in Khenipsen, one of the Cowichan tribes in Duncan, BC. He was one of the most generous people I have ever met. Delmar was a loving husband, father, an artist, a role model, and a storyteller. The teachings of his Elders were a sacred part of his

own personal transformation. In the 1980s, Delmar was one of the first former Kuper Island Residential School students in the Duncan area to speak publicly about his abuse. After years of living with the horrific secrets of the abuses he suffered in residential school, he decided it was time to speak out and let go of the dark secret he had carried his whole life. His disclosure was out of sheer selflessness – he wanted to inspire others to release their own residential school secrets (more appropriately, nightmares) and learn to live a life full of love. By spirit, Seletze was a trickster. He learned to share and heal through the power of laughter and love. As a renowned Coast Salish artist, Seletze very generously mentored many young artists. Yet if you spoke to these artists, most would acknowledge that what they learned was far beyond art: Delmar taught them to live with a good mind and heart – *uy'skwuluwun.*

Tsaqwuasupp Art Thompson (1948–2003)
… was the spirit of regeneration … He was a man who made the hero's journey from disconnection, fear and pain, facing and defeating demons all along the way. As we knew him, he stood as the most powerful carrier of his people's heritage and their most sensitive and dignified voice. When you met Tsaqwuasupp in person, you were drawn into his strength as a Ditidaht man. It was a remarkable strength, all the more effecting because you sensed its profound connection to the deepest roots of his people's experience – all of his nation's pains, the joys, the sufferings and the triumphs congealed in the living existence of one man. This life of dignity had not been an inheritance; it was fought for with blood and tears and sacrifice, and recovered out of the ashes of a life fire nearly destroyed by what his people did inherit: abuse, violence and drugs. If there ever was a person who embodied the spirit of a warrior reborn and who taught us how dignity can be recovered, it was this man.[3]

I dedicate this paper to Seletze and Tsaqwusupp. And to all of those who live or lived with memories of violence and terror every day of their lives – my hands go up to you with respect – *huy ch q'u siem* (thank you, respected people) for sharing your lives and stories with me.

Violence and Terror in a Colonized Country

Any writing about Indigenous people in Canada will be a story of violence and terror. Colonization is violent. In Canada, in particular, the residential school policy, which legislated children out of their families and communities, and which forced them to speak English and pray to a foreign god, was violent to the point of being genocidal. Judy Baca contends: "My point is: if you deny the presence of another people and their culture and you deny them their tradition, you are basically committing cultural genocide."[4] In this way, residential schools were clearly an attempt at cultural genocide. Children were not only denied their culture and traditions but also sexually, physically, spiritually and mentally abused on a routine basis. For example:

In 2001, a report issued by the Truth Commission on Genocide in Canada maintained that the mainline churches and the federal government were involved in the murder of over 50,000 Native children through the system. The list of offences committed by the church officials includes murder by beating, poisoning, hanging, starvation, strangulation, and medical experimentation.[5]

Despite reports such as this and the earlier Royal Commission on Aboriginal People (RCAP, 1996), my experience as a university educator has been that the residential school story remains virtually unknown. Ella Shohat believes that denying and distorting the history of the colonized is necessary if that colonization is to continue.[6] Colonizers who acknowledged the violent nature of colonization would be unable to avoid accountability for their actions. Indigenous people know that no one in Canada has truly been held accountable. Yes, some individual staff who violated and abused young Indigenous children have been held accountable, but what about governments and churches that implemented these policies? A few pathetic individuals have been held accountable through our legal system, but the grand narrative – that Canada, as a country, in partnership with churches, implemented a residential school policy that abused thousands of children – remains to be told.

These distorted and denied stories include those of abused Indigenous children. Delmar was haunted his whole life by his experiences at Kuper Island Residential School. He was a mere child when his abuse began:

I hated the infirmary. I was in there and I was in so much pain from the beating. This Nun came in and she was going to make a man out of me. I could stand the beatings. I could stand the beatings, but I couldn't stand being sexually abused.[7]

I remember, like it was yesterday, the evening Delmar shared this painful experience. More than remember – I carry this experience both in my spirit and in my body. As I type this, I am brought back to that moment. I feel a sickness so deep in the pit of my stomach that I can feel nothing else. I am numb. And I cry. How could this have happened to someone I love so much? Who else has this happened to? How many more were/are there?

A few years later I was asked to support my cousin and his family while he testified in federal court. Art was suing Canada and the United Church of Canada for the abuse he endured in the Port Alberni Residential School. His case was unique in that his testimony went uncontested, as he had been offered a settlement. He agreed to the settlement only if he was able to testify, uncontested, and have his story documented. His hope was that the documentation would offer support to other residential school victims seeking justice through the legal system.

Art began his testimony by sharing his lineage, both matrilineal and patrilineal. He shared the lines of chieftainships, dances, songs, and names. In this, he included knowledge of both the Ditidaht and Quw'utsun' (Cowichan) language and culture. These stories began to shed light on the rich and various options that would have been available to him had the residential school experience not taken him from his family and community and shattered his world.

For two days, Art recounted the innumerable abuses he endured during his years at the Port Alberni Residential School. After a few hours in the courtroom, I began gently tapping my face, not out of nervousness, but to check that I was in fact conscious and that what I was hearing was not a horrible nightmare. And for the second time in my life – the first being when I heard Delmar's story of sexual assault – I was forced to ask my Spirit to sit beside me and allow this process to be a mental one. The story was so violent and unreal that I knew my Spirit needed protection. I wondered then, if my Spirit needed to be protected, what about Art and Delmar, their wives, mothers, children, families? And what happened to the Spirits of the thousands of children who had been forced by the Canadian government to attend those institutions?

One of the offenders named in Art's court case had already been sentenced. During the sentencing, Judge John Hogarth had stated: "As far as the victims of the accused in this matter are concerned, the Indian Residential School system was nothing but a form of Institutionalized

Pedophilia, and the accused, as far as they are concerned, being children at the time, was a sexual terrorist."[8]

As I tried to make sense of the story I was witnessing, I looked around the courtroom. To my left was Art's mother, Ida. Aunty Ida was sitting on the bench, sobbing and gently rocking back and forth in a semi-fetal position. What could she possibly be thinking, a mother, as she listened to a son disclose unimaginable abuse endured at the hands of the State and the Church? In front of me sat Art's wife Charlene. She too sat, head down, sobbing. On either side of her, also sobbing, sat their daughters. The courtroom was full of family there to support Art and his journey to heal. They all sat silently, each gazing ahead with a look of disbelief, sadness, and pain. Residential school happened to our families and continues to affect our families to this day.

I have offered snippets of two peoples' stories – there are thousands more. And as you can see from them, they have impacted generations of Indigenous people. Both Art and Delmar claimed that an important part of their healing was telling their stories in order to free their souls.

The Truth and Reconciliation Victoria Event

I would be remiss not to mention Canada's ongoing Truth and Reconciliation Commission (TRC).[9] On 11 June 2008, Prime Minister Stephen Harper issued an apology to former students of residential schools. That apology and the court-approved Indian Residential Schools Settlement Agreement (the largest class action settlement in Canadian history) were the impetus for Canada's TRC, whose main goal is to bring about reconciliation between Indigenous and non-Indigenous Canadians through a process of truth telling. This seems like a good place to point out that, as Verna St Denis puts it, "colonization and marginalization of Indigenous people is not just an Indigenous story, but also the story of Canada."[10] I could not agree more. Yes, the colonization of Indigenous people is part of the Canadian story, and Justice Murray Sinclair agrees; but I am not convinced that the TRC will enable Indigenous and non-Indigenous Canadians to move forward in a reconciliatory relationship. First, in the Canadian context, "reconciliation" implies a false equivalency between Indigenous people and settlers.[11] Simply by Canada implementing a TRC, will Indigenous people and settlers arrive at an agreement to live in peace? This is very patronizing: Launch a TRC so that Canada can claim it has reconciled with former students of the residential school system and put that dark secret to bed once and for all? My view is that the TRC, like RCAP, is just one more tool for Canada to show "its willingness to engage in fair and respectful dialogue with Aboriginal people."[12] Amber Dean contends that reconciliation must include both political action and support for those who have been harmed.[13] In the context of Canadian reconciliation, political action has been completely omitted. And just as with RCAP, once the mandate has been achieved and the recommendations have been made, the report will be shelved, with no meaningful change implemented.

Despite my scepticism, and perhaps as an example of how flawed the TRC actually is, I feel obligated to mention the commission in a chapter that focuses on the experiences of residential school survivors. I will begin by sharing a few stories, which validate my concerns about national reconciliation, from a regional TRC event in Victoria (13–14 April 2012).

The last residential school closed in 1990 (Gordon Residential School), yet the legacy of them is alive and well. Knockwood recalls viewing the charred remains of Shubie (the Indian Residential School at Shubenacadie, Nova Scotia): "I thought about how many of my former school mates, like Leona, Hilda, and Maimie, had died premature deaths. I wondered how many were still alive and how they were doing, how well they were coping, and if they were still carrying the burden of the past on their shoulders like I was."[14]

Tragically, this "burden of the past" was a piece of Canadian federal policy. Chrisjohn and Young refer to the Canadian federal policy as a piece of "colonial machinery."[15] As long as the machinery is oiled, serviced, and maintained, it will continue to function exactly as it was intended. It appears that in the Canadian context, our "colonial machinery" is in pristine shape, because the "burden of the past" continues to play itself out in incredibly violent ways. One example of this colonial machine is the TRC. Over two days, it held a multitude of workshops and forums. For the purposes of this chapter, I will discuss only two of these events: the "Commissioners' Sharing Panel," where former students of Canada's residential school system were invited to publicly share their experiences (or stories) of those institutions; and the "Statements of Reconciliation," where non-Indigenous people were able to come forward and express publicly their views, feelings, and/or opinions about residential schools and reconciliation.

I sat in on only one of the sharing panels because I knew that listening to the stories would be excruciatingly painful. Even though I have made it a life goal to understand residential schools, I still find it difficult to listen to stories of abuse over and over again – especially ones about residential schools, because they are the stories of the young ones, the most vulnerable in our society, those whom we as adults are supposed to protect. And hundreds of those children were my family members. But out of respect for all former students, I felt obliged to witness at least one sharing panel and honour the stories they shared. This was also important because these stories are supposedly the cornerstone of the TRC – truth telling. Perhaps this is one of the most troubling aspects of the TRC: Why do former victims of the residential school system have to give public testimony in order for Canada to be able move forward in the spirit of "reconciliation"? What an ass-backward system! What is it about a child being sexually or physically violated that needs to be publicly disclosed? Abuse is abuse. And where is the story of the violators? What are they publicly disclosing? Dean contends that the public sharing (or what she calls public mourning) of such horrors is "inadequate when not accompanied by political commitments to recognize and redress the ways that injustices of the so-called past continue to shape the present in very concrete ways.[16]

For many former residential school students, the TRC is too little too late. They do not feel that the TRC has anything to offer them. Yet for others, sharing their stories is part of a healing journey. Many former students find a great sense of validation in being able to publicly "speak out" about their experiences – perhaps it gives them a place to leave the past behind. I will never take away from someone's personal growth and their personal healing journey; my concern is that the stories of former students amount to only half the story – they are the stories of the survivors' experiences. If we are sharing our common experiences, where is the other story, the one that implicates Canada and the churches? Stories untold.

From the opening to the closing ceremonies, the buildings bustled with media. Yet at the end of the day, little was written about the TRC event. Mostly what got picked up was the horror – the abuse (physical, emotional, sexual) passed on from generation to generation, the violence and the addiction and all of the unbecoming behaviours that stem from these. Stories told. Roger Simon refers to these stories as the "too bad, so sad syndrome."[17] What he means is that non-Indigenous people can hear the stories of suffering, pain, and violence and in a very illogical way confirm their humanitarianism because they feel bad about the other's pain. But these folks never move beyond feeling bad. They fail to look for the counter-story that will implicate Canada – and ultimately them as Canadians – by examining the ways they have been privileged through myriad colonial policies in Canada, including the residential school policy.

Nothing was written that actually held Canada accountable for implementing genocidal policies. Nothing was written that focused on churches that hired pedophiles and violent human beings who then had access to more than 150,000 Indigenous, Métis, and Inuit children.[18] I read nothing that acknowledged that residential schools were part of a deliberate policy whose primary goal was genocide, or at the very least assimilation. Remember here that residential schools were founded in 1920 by legislation that made it mandatory for children to attend them – in effect, children were legislated out of the care of their families. And remember, finally, that officials such as the police, Indian Affairs personnel, and health care workers knew of the abuse that was taking place in those institutions from the day they opened and failed to protect those children. What about the 50,000 Indigenous children Smith refers to who never returned from those institutions? What happened to them?[19] Who will ever tell their stories? Stories untold.

No, the "bad things happen to bad people" story is a much more sensational one, and that is the one the media chose to pick up. In fact, that story supports what Chrisjohn and Young refer to as the "standard account."[20] At the only Statements of Reconciliation forum I attended, an Oblate from the Christie Residential School in Tofino, BC, shared this account perfectly. He declared he was attending the TRC to share his truth. He began his statement by saying that he was twenty-one years old when he was sent to Christie to take on the position of supervisor of the senior boys. At that time, he claimed, there were around 120 First Nations students who had been "sent by their parents for the purpose of attending school." The six Sisters, he believed, were "highly educated and committed" and "loved and cared for the children." "What I experienced over the six years I was at Christie Residential School," he said, was a staff who tried to "provide, as much as possible, a safe, loving environment for the children attending Christie School." He went on to claim that the school was not perfect, but "no living situation is perfect." He added that putting 120 students together for twenty-four hours a day, ten months of the year, was definitely problematic, but he believed there was no other viable way to educate students from remote communities. So, it seems that the problem stemmed from putting the students together. Another story told. The power of words: the "problem" was putting children together. What does putting children together have to do with caregivers abusing them? If the church knew this was problematic, why did they not stop it? Another story untold. As this Oblate was sharing his statement of reconciliation, former students in the crowd were yelling "this is a truth and reconciliation commission, tell the truth. We never sent our children to those schools." I saw many former students weeping uncontrollably. Of all the stories I have listened to, this Oblate's bullshit has been by far the most violent and emotionally and spiritually abusive. I stood at the back of the room, stunned. All I could picture were the faces of thousands of children – innocent children who were compelled by federal law to attend those institutions. How dare he? How *dare* he blame the children? This TRC event made it clear to me that the violence has not stopped. I also know that we are nowhere near "sharing the burden of the past."

Nearly thirty years after the last residential school officially closed it doors, we continue to hear these "untrue" stories being put forward as truths. Even more important is that these stories themselves are abusive and violent. This Oblate's story highlights the TRC's contradictions: in one room we have former students sharing their stories in the spirit of reconciliation and in the hope of having their abhorrent experiences at residential schools validated, and in the next room another story is being shared that negates the whole process. How is reconciliation ever to occur if we cannot even find a beginning point from which to start a truthful process? And let us not forget that denial is a very violent act upon the denied.

Cherokee writer Thomas King asks: "Do the stories we tell reflect the world as it truly is, or did we simply start off with the wrong story?"[21] The standard account of residential schools is definitely the faulty one, because it is like magic – *poof* – a myth that transforms violence, terror, and abuse into a story about good intentions, good hearts, and good people – a feel-good story to say the least. So, the story goes, if residential schools were about good, then – as suggested by the Oblate – it must be that the Indigenous students were bad, and we all know that bad things happen to bad people. My own contention is that "we simply start[ed] off with the wrong story" because the right story is almost unthinkable. As humans, we listen to these stories and question human nature; we wonder how evil can seep so deep into people's souls that they are capable of becoming violent, abusive pedophiles. I believe the atrocity that was residential schools is so unbelievable that most Canadians opt to hold on to the nice Canadian peacekeeper myth; in doing so, they completely deny the experiences of former residential school students. The TRC is hoping to bring forward the truthful stories regarding residential schools and "help set our spirits free and pave the way to reconciliation."[22] But allowing statements of reconciliation such as the one made by the Oblate from Christie will not pave that way. At best, it will support the status quo:

> We believe that "when the truth comes out" … the system will set things right. We believe history is also about justice, that understanding history will enlighten our decisions about the future. Wrong. History is also about power. In fact history is mostly about power. It is the story of the powerful and how they became powerful, and then how they use their power to keep them in positions which they can continue to dominate others. It is because of this relationship with the power that we have been excluded, marginalized and "othered."[23]

If the colonizer's story of the residential school system came out, Canada would be implicated in it because residential schools were a government policy with assimilation (or genocide) as one of its intended goals. That policy forcibly removed children from their families and homes and placed them in the hands of "caregivers" who abused them on a daily basis. And all the while for fifty years, officials who knew of the abuse turned a blind eye. Secrets kept – stories untold.

Stories Told

So why continue sharing stories? Why do I continue to place myself in situations where the stories I am bringing forward are completely dismissed? Why do I open up my mind and spirit only to have it shut down? I must speak out, because, as I stated at the beginning, I have a responsibility to be a voice for the voiceless. But just as the questions I pose are complicated and often conflicting, and despite my responsibility to speak out, I am always troubled about sharing stories. I always fear "documenting" our stories because I wonder, will the voices be heard? And, more importantly, *how* will the voices be heard? Will the stories be edited? Traditionally storytelling was purposeful. Is there a purpose in putting forward these very tragic stories?

***Uy'skwuluwun* (To Be of a Good Mind and Spirit)**

In the Coast Salish culture, at all major events in the Thi'lelum (Big House) we have a custom of paying "witness." Representatives from different communities are called upon to "witness" the event. When you are asked to witness an event, your name is announced and you are asked to stand up so that you can be publicly acknowledged. Witnessing is a significant responsibility because you are now accountable to everyone in attendance, as well as to the various communities they come from, to remember all the details of the evening. In years to come, if you have any questions or concerns about what took place at that particular event, you can always go to one of the witnesses. Witnesses will remember the details of the event because they were called upon to take up the responsibility for remembering. This highly sophisticated process of witnessing continues to be central to our traditional ceremonies. I believe that when someone shares a story with you, it is equivalent to being asked to "witness" an event. As academics and researchers, we are responsible to the storytellers because we have "witnessed" their stories.

Snuy'uy'ul is the Hul'qumi'num word for our fundamental teachings or our ways of knowing and being. One of the many teachings of *snuy'uy'ul* is *nutsa maat*. *Nutsa maat* teaches us that we are all one. It does not mean that we are the same; it means that collectively we are a whole. *Nutsa maat* teaches us that we are all connected and that as such we are responsible to one another. Because we are, we should be more concerned with the collective than with ourselves. Delmar and Art exemplified this teaching by openly and honestly sharing their horrific stories of abuse, hoping it would give others who had suffered at residential schools the necessary strength to speak out and face their demons. Both men were selfless in speaking out for the collective well-being, not just of their former classmates but of all Indigenous people.

In the past, we were taught to always speak for those who could not speak for themselves. This included the young ones, and the hurt or injured ones. It also included those who were afraid to speak as well as those who could not because they had journeyed to the other side.

I learned this lesson the hard way. I was asked to speak on a residential school panel a number of years ago. Because I had done my master's thesis on Kuper Island, this particular group invited me to participate and share my expertise. I looked at the list of other folks who had been invited, and I declined because one of them was my late cousin Art. Art had become a prominent critic of residential schools as well as an advocate for survivors of that system. Later he called me to ask why I had declined the offer to sit on the panel. I told him, "I never went to residential schools, I do not have firsthand experience, my knowledge is through my research and because you are speaking from firsthand experience on the panel I thought it only appropriate that I decline." He laughed. "Chicken shit," he said. I asked, "Why?" He said, "Robina, you were given those stories for a reason – it is now your responsibility to speak for those who are either voiceless or have gone on to the other side." I presented on the panel with my cousin and have never forgotten his words. I needed to speak for those people who cannot do it for themselves. This is a teaching of *nutsa maat*.

Conclusion

I continue to struggle with the contradictions that writing about violence and terror raise for me. For this chapter, I focused on Canada's residential school system as one example of writing about violence and terror. However, any topic that focuses on the experiences of Indigenous people in a colonized country will be just as violent. For example, had I written about Indigenous children in care, I would have discussed how more than half of all children in care are Indigenous even though we make up around 4 per cent of the Canadian population.[24] Or I could have discussed how there are nearly six hundred disappeared and presumably dead Indigenous women in Canada.[25] Or how despite the deplorable overcrowding on reserves, our land has been stolen in order to create resource-rich land bases for settlers. All of these stories are incredibly violent and are rooted in the impact of colonization. But despite how difficult it is, I will continue to write about these things because that is my responsibility. If we as academics do not speak out and start to problematize the great Canadian myth, who will?

To write about Indigenous experiences is to write about violence and terror. I have never been able to separate those experiences from my spirit. I have never been able to write about abuse, violence, and terror apart from who I am as a human being. *Nutsa maat* – we are all one. I get angry, I scream, I cry, I pray. And then I remember those who cannot speak. We must continue to speak out. The only way I can draw strength to nurture my body and spirit is through prayer and asking for guidance and direction from the *Ta't Mustimuxw* (ancestors). Our teachings and the fact that I have been given the privilege and honour of "witnessing" survivors' stories are what gives me the strength to speak out and not forget.

Thomas King refers to himself as a "hopeful pessimist." He says that none of the stories he has told will change the world, but he continues to write, hoping that someday they will.[26] I too must be a hopeful pessimist, because I have a profound sense of responsibility to the stories. Delmar once told me that every time someone who attended residential school dies, so does that person's story, and Canada and the churches look more innocent. I cannot be a part of making Canada and the churches look innocent. May I always hold on to their stories and continue to "speak out." May I always draw strength from their teachings when I become weary and am too tired to speak. May I always remember, stories remembered – stories told.

NOTES

1 Thomas, *Storytelling*.
2 A valid fear of many people is that the Truth and Reconciliation Commission is a diversion from Indigenous peoples' goal of sovereignty because it focuses on individual harms. Due to the scope of this paper, I am unable to address this concern directly. For a more thorough discussion of it, see Simon, "Towards a Hopeful Practice of Worrying."
3 Alfred, "My Grandmother," 1.
4 Baca, "Our People Are the Internal Exiles," 256.
5 A. Smith, *Conquest*, 40.
6 Shohat, "Sephardim in Israel," 44.
7 Cited in Thomas, *Storytelling*, 78.
8 Cited in Nuu-chah-nulth Tribal Council, *Indian Residential Schools*, viii.
9 For more information on the Truth and Reconciliation Commission, visit http://www.trc.ca.
10 St Denis, "Foreword," vii.
11 Alfred, "Colonial Stains on Our Existence," 8.
12 Anderson and Denis, "Urban Native Communities and the Nation," 62.
13 Dean, "Public Mourning," 186.
14 Knockwood, *Out of the Depths*, 132.
15 Chrisjohn and Young, "Among School Children," 2.
16 Dean, "Public Mourning," 183.
17 Simon, "Towards a Hopeful Practice of Worrying,"133.
18 http://www.trc.ca.
19 A. Smith, *Conquest*.
20 Chrisjohn and Young, "Among School Children."
21 King, *The Truth about Stories*.

22 http://www.trc.ca.
23 L.T. Smith, *Decolonizing Methodologies*, 34.
24 Blackstock, "Why Addressing the Over-Representation," 1.
25 http://www.nwac.ca.
26 King, *The Truth about Stories*, 92.

3 Terrorism and the Birthing Body in Jerusalem

NADERA SHALHOUB-KEVORKIAN

The past three days were the worst days of my life ... having the baby under such stress, needing to catch a bus while experiencing the pain of severe contractions, knowing that I might have the baby on the bus ... I had contractions, bad ones; I was dying from fear, pain, *ruo'b* [terror] ... real terror ... holding on to my bag ... as if the bag can carry the pain, crying my body in silence, wanting to go back to my house ... to have the baby there ... but then, the baby would end up without an ID, undocumented, unsecured, displaced ... *mhahshata* [displaced] all her life ... I really had the worst days of my life ... I was giving birth, but living death at the same time ... and I stopped myself from giving birth ... hanging onto my bag, squeezing it, promising my unborn to reach the hospital, and have her in Jerusalem, *bil Quds ya habibti bil Quds* [in Jerusalem my love, in Jerusalem].

I made it. I wanted to have Eiman [her baby] in Jerusalem. I promised myself I would never deny my children this privilege. Not having them in Jerusalem – not because of the medical insurance Jerusalemite ID holders have, and not because of the blue ID, but because I can't see my kids suffer. I told myself that I could not let them inherit suffering ... although we Palestinians have already inherited suffering ... I can't see my kids suffer more from being alone, away from their cousins, family, grandparents, land, home and schools.

I took the bus, alone, because my husband was stopped on our way to the bus ... The Israeli soldiers were checking the area, and he was stopped and delayed for five hours ... so, I went on, I was in pain, took the bus, and came to the hospital alone ... I did not think, just took the bus, passed the checkpoint ... showed them my ID, waited in pain until they allowed the bus to go through, took a taxi to the hospital, and I had her ... Thank God she was healthy ... But, I am tired, still anxious, upset and agitated.

You asked me how I feel? I will ask you ... do you know anyone in the world, anyone that suffered like us Palestinians? Do you know any pregnant woman that needs to cross checkpoints, ride a bus, leave her kids alone under the mercy of them throwing tear gas bombs, under their *majassat el muraqabeh* [surveillance devices] that are surrounding our area ... to make sure the new baby is born in Jerusalem ... for only if she is born here can she survive their terror, otherwise, she will be dead ... yes, dead ... like all those who are unable to reach their homes ... like all those who are deprived of even seeing their beloved ones, just like when you are physically dead ... My sister can't come to Jerusalem ... my sister can't come visit my sick father in her own house ... I will never do this to my own children ... You might think I am crazy ... but, it is better to take the bus, wait at the checkpoints, be humiliated on the way, be threatened by their rifles, be worried and scared ... It is better to go through all this, than ending up having a child that is undocumented, unrecognized and most of all deprived of his family, his support, his *eizwi* [extended community's support] ... What do I feel? I feel tired, happy, sad, terrorized by their policies and threats... but I also feel like I did it. (Aida, twenty-nine years old)

Aida's words portray the reality of the inheritance of suffering among Palestinians. They express her feelings of living in fear and terror. Her fears and anxieties – both as a woman on the verge of giving birth and also after giving birth – are physical and psychological manifestations of the treatment of Palestinian women bound by the politics, geopolitics, biopolitics, and sociocide of military occupation.

The invasion of the occupied body that has inherited suffering due to historical injustice in an occupied *time* and *space,* in a state of mundane terror, in which hegemonic knowledge production has situated Aida and her newborn in a geography of fear and within an archaeology of constant uncertainty, is the overarching concern of my argument. Aida's words do not reflect solely her own intimate and individual fears and worries (feeling terrorized at a critical moment in her life, as she is about to bring another life into her world); her testimonial addresses larger issues that surround the inscription of power onto the Palestinian woman's birthing body, during contractions and in moments of birth in the occupied Palestinian territories (OPT).

Birth in Jerusalem, the military occupation's insolence, insolence within which a dominant Israeli narrative about Palestinian "terrorism" is crafted, insolence towards Palestinians' everydayness, in its minute details, finds itself carved on women's pregnant bodies. Discussing

Israeli domination over Palestinian women's pregnant bodies is a way of raising and addressing how one can narrate what is unspeakable and unacknowledged and how this unspeakability and acknowledgment shape the categories of exclusion and inclusion in which colonial racism is embedded.

I contend that the production of knowledge involving the narration of Palestinians' Otherness as terrorists (as inscribed on women's pregnant bodies and psyches so that this inscription is circulated across borders) is embedded in a global politics of denial, a politics that denies Palestinian women the right to safe birthing and indeed to full citizenship.[1] I focus on the case study of birth in Jerusalem, looking closely at this inscription on women's bodies and lives, with all the domineering actions of Israeli colonial racism, in order to argue that the unseen and unacknowledged Israeli practices, laws, and modes of domination – as demonstrated in Aida's narrative, in her act of riding a bus while having contractions, in her willingness to face a military checkpoint when in labour, in her ability to carry her birthing body with a psychological determination that refuses to normalize suffering – are not solely made up of fixed and finite sets of regulations. Those practices, laws, and modes are the interchanging and malleable conditions of racism, for they combine both fixed and fluid elements, turning racial violations of women's bodies and lives into mobile, fluid, mercury-like racism. They are technologies of oppression at one moment and technologies of protection at another. I argue that such state terrorism is fused into familiar everyday practices, justified by the need to prevent "criminality" and through technologies of hegemonic knowledge production such as Israeli statistical practices, which we compare below to Palestinian ones. This state terrorism is prevalent and legal and is conducted in the name of "security" and "protection."

In listening to Aida's voicing of her ordeal and her discussion of "birth" in Jerusalem – both as material reality for a given woman at a specific time, and as a conceptual event not just for Palestinian women in the region, but also within the power nexus that surrounds them – we have to take into account the various economies of birth that are prevalent in the Occupied Territories. What complicates such a discussion is that its physical and conceptual aspects meet on a middle ground where the psyche and the body must inevitably be discussed in tandem. In the testimonials of various Palestinian women discussed in this chapter, the body space, the physical space, and time, become implicated in their experiences; ironically, time comes to be conceptualized in their words as a place/space of timelessness, an eternity of waiting and wishing for an end to the multiple assaults on their daily lives. Days, months, and moments merge together in a confluence of suffering that is so continuous that the measurement of time becomes meaningless – indeed, nothing short of impossible.

Aida's testimonial and those of the other women in this chapter raise new questions as to the nexus of issues that should inflect our understanding of birth in conflict zones. Her words call attention to the ways in which power comes to be exercised over the corporeal body of the pregnant woman and – as I argue in this chapter – over her psyche as well. How can we understand, for example, an ostensibly material issue such as surveillance, executed materially – let us say for the sake of argument, although there are many other ways – through the "checkpoint," when the constant fear associated with the ever-shifting dynamics of the checkpoint and the emotional residue of that fear seep into the very mind and body of the subject? In other words, the material reality of the checkpoint and the resulting induced fear become psychological realities as well.

This chapter will travel to a new place by examining pregnancy and birth under military surveillance in Jerusalem. It will focus on the extent to which the colonizing state and its institutional apparatus of practices, policies, and knowledge production mobilize, produce, and maintain a state of institutionalized fear regarding the pregnant mother and the newborn Palestinian child even while producing the mother and the newborn child in a state of otherness – born as terrorists and criminals, as unwanted entities. Such violations are clearly substantiated by the voices of birthing Palestinian women.

Coming to Know Birthing Women

To examine birth in Jerusalem, one needs to explore how relations of power and their epistemic violence are inscribed on the body, on life, and in the everyday decisions women make. One needs to trace that body as it moves through space, living out the everydayness that I mentioned above in the midst of conflict. Childbirth is a particularly fecund area (no pun intended) for exploring the ways in which birth and death are intimately connected to the body in ways that are both obvious and less apparent. Since the body is also intimately and already connected to space and time, it is critical to explore how power relations manifest themselves in matters of childbirth and the body in a context of military occupation.

While conducting a study on the politics of everydayness in Jerusalem, in part through interviews with Jerusalemite men and women,[2] I interviewed pregnant women and realized how little I knew about their ordeals, fears, and hardships as Palestinian women living in a militarized zone controlled and administered by the Israeli regime. Knowledge production about the conditions in which Palestinian women give birth took a sharper turn when Hannan, one of the members of the research team, shared her ordeal:

> My daughter was born seventeen months ago, and I still dream that I lost her while at the checkpoint. I still wake up crying, wondering whether I was denied entry to the hospital, and I still await my mother who was not able to join me when I was giving birth. I live the trauma of childbirth every time I see a pregnant woman, and tell myself that I do not want to have more kids, I do not want to go through that same feeling and experience again.

Hannan's words, the anxiety she exhibited while sharing her ordeal, and her insistence on studying birth in Jerusalem prompted me to commence this study in an effort to produce bottom-up knowledge based on Palestinian women's narratives.

The primary data provided in this chapter, the narratives of the women themselves, come from thirty-seven interviews conducted with individual women between June 2011 and February 2012. Birthing mothers were interviewed while they were in the hospital following the birth of their child and during the first two years of the child's birth. The author conducted the first twenty-seven interviews. After realizing that most interviewees discussed their dreams and nightmares, the author approached an experienced social worker and asked her to conduct an additional ten interviews to validate the results and the interviewing mode of the author, and to make sure her mode of interacting had not affected women's narratives or their modes of sharing their birthing stories.

Because of security issues, some of the data and details have been changed to protect confidentiality and prevent reprisals against the interviewed women. All names are pseudonyms, but the ages of the women have been retained. In some cases, due to the sensitivity of the area studied, I have refrained from using the data collected so as ensure the safety and security of the interviewed women, their families, and their communities. The interviews explored how birthing women experience the psychic trauma inflicted by the Israeli regime of power. The narratives those women shared bring the psychological into the arena of challenges to colonial legacies, in that they invented forms of anti-colonial resistance at the time of giving birth. I engage with women's birthing experiences in an attempt to open up new spaces for listening to, sharing, and producing counter-hegemonic knowledge. However, the methodology used – empathic listening to women's narrations of their ordeals – means that in order to repair what the humiliation of Israeli militarism and colonialism have broken, there must be a reconnection with women's practices of survival through acknowledgment of their truths and by allowing the power of their powerlessness in moments of giving birth to illuminate and legitimize the processes through which colonized women resist oppression and so recover their humanity.

"Every Palestinian Child Is a Potential Terrorist"

A report written by a delegation of British lawyers on the treatment of Palestinian children under Israeli military law, published in June 2012, noted that "it may be that much of the reluctance to treat Palestinian children in conformity with international norms stems from a belief, which was advanced to us by a military prosecutor, that every Palestinian child is a 'potential terrorist.' Such a stance seems to us to be the starting point of a spiral of injustice."[3] Spirals of injustice and the limits of justice influence all aspects of life under military occupation and reconstruct the politics of everydayness. The political, economic, and symbolic effects of militarization can be clearly found in the various testimonies of the Palestinian birthing women who were interviewed for this chapter, including Ghaida, a young Palestinian woman interviewed two days after having her first son:

> Because I was pregnant, I felt that the soldiers on the checkpoints wanted to humiliate and torture me more. My story with the soldiers on the checkpoint is a long story, but during my pregnancy they behaved in a more aggressive and nasty manner ... On Wednesday, while I was trying to reach my doctor after I discovered some blood spots ... and was worried that I was about to have the baby before time ... I was delayed for two hours at the checkpoint ... in the heat, with all the people in the crowd ... and when I managed to reach the checkpoint's window the soldier asked me to pass through the X-ray ... Believe me, they made me pass through the X-ray ...

and I did, for I knew that I was not risking my baby's health; he was about to be born and so nothing would now cause any defects ... But, they then decided that I couldn't cross the checkpoint because my passing permit was not "an original" – so they claimed. I got very upset, very hurt, and had tears in my eyes, but had no time to cry; I just sat for three minutes and thought about a way out ... They delayed me, made me so anxious and tired, and treated me like a criminal; they prevented me from reaching the hospital when I was in dire need just to see a doctor and make sure I was not losing my son ... all this while I was alone, for my mother could not get a permit, and my husband was already in Jerusalem awaiting me in the hospital ... I ended up sneaking in like a thief, and had no other choice but to take a taxi to help me reach the hospital without any delay. My destiny was in their hands, and with my fears, loneliness, confusion – for this is my first pregnancy and first child, and I suffered from severe anxiety, mainly in the last days of my pregnancy and before giving birth. I had no other choice but to hold back my tears and my anger, and go to the hospital by the bypass roads. I called my brother, and he helped me ... He called a taxi for me, it came, picked me up, and hurried me to the hospital. The baby was healthy, he was born ten minutes after I arrived at the hospital; but, I am not. I am tired from all that happened, I am tired from being afraid, alone, anxious, and upset all the time, from feeling perceived and treated like a criminal who could never prove that she is innocent. I made it, and my baby is healthy ... but why this torture, why can't I be treated as a human being, why can't I have my baby under normal conditions and not under such horror, why am I perceived to be a criminal? A terrorist? (Ghaida, twenty-one years old)

Ghaida's words suggest that Israelis read the Palestinian birthing body and the unborn or just-born Palestinian child as a potential terrorist who should be mistrusted, checked, and racially profiled. Ghaida portrays how she was treated like a criminal and made to feel unwanted and unwelcomed – factors that exacerbated her fears of losing her newborn while she was struggling to reach the hospital to give birth. Her testimonial reflects darkly the words of the Israeli military prosecutor who claimed that every Palestinian child is a potential terrorist. Through her description, we sense her anxiety, we hear her voice mixed with pain, and we see her tears and her shivering body as she remembers the agony of facing the Israeli soldiers. Ghaida held her two-day-old son in her arms as she continued her story:

I was carrying him inside me [i.e., while still pregnant], as if holding him in my arms, when they were talking to me in Hebrew, telling me that I couldn't pass the checkpoint. I was very stressed out, could not hold back tears. I even called the female soldier over to put her hand on my belly in order to prove that I am carrying a baby, not an animal; a baby, not a terrorist; a baby, not a bomb. I thought that, as a woman, she would feel with me, and would at least read the medical report I showed her and so allow me to cross, but she refused. She was filled with disgust from even looking at me, let alone touching me, and they both, the male and female soldiers, screamed "Rohi rohi min hon" [go, go from here]. At that point, I felt totally shocked … and stopped talking, crying, thinking or responding … I went into a deep, very deep silence [she stopped narrating for two or three minutes] … Then I started talking to myself … and God … in a loud voice, "Mish adri ya Rabbi" [I can't take it, God]. I felt like a criminal wandering in the streets, not knowing what to do, where to go … what to think or what to say? … This is it.

And in this way she ended the sharing of her story. Her clear detection of the soldiers' power to inscribe injustice on her birthing body, through their power to prevent her from reaching the hospital, moved her birthing body to the periphery, to a no-man's-land. Such a periphery was not simply geographical but also human and political. Her birthing body and her narrative became peripheral to the knowledge and recognition of those in power. The inscribed injustice and imposed trap of her birthing body and soul aimed at turning her into an object of knowledge in a manner that denied her humanity. The colonial knowledge both enabled the inscription of "here is a terrorist" on her birthing body and was produced by that inscription. By situating her in a space of non-existence, while inscribing their power over her birthing body, the soldiers not only trapped her body/life/feelings but also turned her voice into an unheard one and her experience into an unseen, unwanted, and non-existent one. Her testimony shows how the Israeli epistemic violence that portrays Palestinians as criminal terrorists works hand in hand with the colonial logic of eliminating the colonized by preventing Palestinian babies from being born in Jerusalem, for they do not want Palestinians in Jerusalem. Yet Ghaida refused to accept the soldier's logic as the only logic in power. She refused to abide by their reading of her birthing body – as the body of a criminal, a filthy entity that cannot be touched, believed, or even looked at. Their hegemonic epistemic violence – their portrayal of her as a filthy criminal, and their treatment of her unborn as a potential terrorist – was challenged by her total silence. Ghaida's words and acts of resistance told a different story than the hegemonic one. Her birthing body and her body language made a different argument, an argument that challenged the occupier's trap.

Applying Frantz Fanon's analysis in *The Wretched of the Earth*, we can see that Ghaida's traumatic memory, her actions and agency, challenged the colonizers' language when it framed her as a criminal terrorist, but this did not liberate her nor did it help her escape the violence of colonization. The violence and trauma she experienced have created fractures in her memory of birthing her first child; her ways of narrating her experience and producing knowledge about her ordeal are desperate attempts to make sense of her memories and transcend them so that they do not paralyse her through the fear they inspire. To make sense of her memories, Ghaida insisted on sharing the complexity of her contradictory condition and the psychological apparatus she encountered. To that end, she discussed the violence she faced as a birthing woman while also sharing the way she resisted this dishonour, humiliation, and demonization. The moments of humiliation and injustice she suffered were calcified by her deep silence about that unarticulated, disremembered, and traumatic experience.

Key features of Ghaida's narrative (the colonizers' control over the ability of the colonized to give birth in a safe space, in Jerusalem; their attempts to portray Palestinian newborns as a demographic threat, as potential terrorists, as unwanted entities; their constant surveillance of Palestinians) represent what Fischbach refers to as "rule by record."[4]

The Israeli CBS (Central Bureau of Statistics) and the JIIS (Jerusalem Institute for Israel Studies) have reported that the total population on the Palestinian side of Jerusalem is 283,900, while PCBS (Palestinian Central Bureau of Statistics) reports 382,041. This discrepancy extends to live births of Palestinians: CBS and JIIS report 8,299, while PCBS reports 3,042, less than half the Israeli number. Moreover, when looking at crude birth rates, CBS and JIIS report 29.6 per 1,000 while PCBS reports 8. This has led CBS and JIIS to report that the natural increase per 100 is 27.2, while the PCBS reports it as 0.7.

The two data sets tell different stories: one suits the Israeli narrative that Palestinians are a demographic threat because of their a high rate of population growth. The CBS and JIIS data support the construction of a colonial "imagined geography" that portrays Palestinians as a "demographic threat," as "targets," and as "savages." Meanwhile, statistical reports produced in the Occupied Territories, including East Jerusalem, describe the shadow that colonial formations have cast over Palestinians' intimate biosocial ecologies as well as the power politics that seep into knowledge production.

The notion of Palestinian terrorists not yet born has been embedded in Israeli statistics in ways that violate Palestinian women's right to give birth in safe conditions. By expanding military checkpoints, excluding Palestinians from some sections of the city, and changing their status from being part of Jerusalem neighbourhoods to being excluded from them, and by restricting Palestinians' access to their own hospitals, doctors, and families, colonial power "counts" unwanted Palestinians in a manner that erases them. The numbers indicate attempts to tell a story that serves the colonial agenda, colonial logic, and colonial imagined geographies, to change geography and reconstruct history.[5] The figures shared are performative in the sense that they produce the effects they count.

The contested numbers are central to my argument, for they cut into the very fabric of Palestinian existence and contribute directly to a production of knowledge that destroys Palestinian women's chances of experiencing safe pregnancy and delivery. This analysis poses questions about what the numbers hide. What is embedded in this Israeli control over the social fabric of everyday life, birth, and death? In *Orientalism*, Edward Said points out that behind the archives of the colonizers, just as behind the statistics of the occupiers in our case study, we find racial ideologies and hierarchies. The occupiers and their bureaucrats are obsessed with the intimate details of who is sleeping with whom, who is marrying whom, who is giving birth, and whose children will be recognized, or not.

These findings challenge how statistics are being used. Data are being manipulated to serve ideology, policy, and power holders. In the demographic–political environment of Jerusalem, to what extent does this game of numbers generated by statisticians play a role in public policy? Given that the two sides disagree over their numbers – the Israelis are arguing that the Palestinian population is growing more quickly than the Palestinians themselves contend – what is at stake from the Israeli perspective? How are the statistics generated by the colonizers useful in gathering public support for policies to control the birthing Palestinian body?

Time and Space

> I am twenty-nine years old, from Silwan [a small village in Jerusalem];
> originally I was from Eizareyyeh [about a ten-minute drive from Silwan].
> I have four girls and just had my first baby boy. I actually had two miscar-
> riages, because I am always worried about being caught by the soldiers
> while visiting my family in Eizareyyeh ... You know, I do not have a blue
> ID [the colour of ID that Jerusalemites carry] ... I did not visit any doctors
> or go for medical check-ups while pregnant ... I fear ... fear being caught by
> the soldiers ... My reality [has] changed so much ... everything changed ...
> I don't know what is going on any more ... The rules and laws change
> every day... The world keeps on changing ... Life [has] changed ... I used to
> commute from Silwan to Eizareyyeh easily, sometimes twice a day while
> engaged ... There is nothing I can do about it now ... I could cry, get de-
> pressed, go crazy ... Nothing will change … I feel so sick, so weak, so pow-
> erless ... If I walk from here – I mean by foot – I could reach my parent's
> house in less than forty minutes ... If I could only show Bash-shar [her son]
> to my parents ... I [feel] choked ... totally choked ... tired from living in this
> *khan'aa* [suffocation] ... They do not want us.... (Haya, twenty-nine years
> old, interviewed three months after the birth of her son)

Haya's words reflect the politics behind the reading of the previous
statistics. Her voice is similar to Aida's, with which I opened this chapter. She speaks of feeling isolated and rejected. In comprehending her
plight, she speaks of her family home being a forty-minute walk away.
But that is now an impossible distance because of how the colonists
have delineated the space of the Occupied Territories. Within the statistics and within time and space, the colonists have found it necessary to
reconfigure, reimagine, and overwrite Palestinian geography.

Colonial manipulations that count the number of Palestinians who
can remain residents of Jerusalem directly account for and implicate
Haya's body as well, situating that body in specific articulations of
space, place, and time. Here, Haya's body must also be understood as
the body of a woman who has just given birth (the same dynamics hold
true for a woman who is about to give birth). This is a political topog-
raphy based on an ongoing counting and accounting for even the most
subtle population shifts. The methodologies and ideologies underpinning such an accounting praxis are readily verifiable by examining official Israeli documents that discuss demographics.

Given that Haya is a Palestinian birthing woman, neither her body nor her space in her occupied home can escape her condition on the margins, while her time cannot settle for anything less than a politics of continuity and survival. Such a politics has no place and no meaning unless the colonized space, her subjectivities, and time of her home and homeland are all historicized. Her knowledge, like her voice, refuses to hide behind the "urgencies" of the materialism of those in power. Her voice requires us to listen carefully to those who survived their own sociocide and the everydayness of their annihilation. Her voice urges us to realize that time and space have bestowed on the birthing women subjectivities cast in the form of deep-seated violence and agony – subjectivities that attempt to destroy the psychological and social harmony and fabric of Palestinian society. Haya's narrative offers a new sensorium for understanding the everyday spatial and temporal politics of birthing women, a political sensorium that rejects suffering and sociocide and that is less comfortable with the politics of numbers, a politics whose aim is to serve the Israeli surveillance regime and its "scientific," "academic" followers.

Bureaucracy and Administration of Terror over Life and Birth

Violence against Palestinian women during pregnancy and while giving birth, and against children born or unborn, is inflicted through the transposition and control of space and through the bureaucracies of military occupation. The following narrative offers a glimpse into the procedures of the Israeli security regime – a regime that, besides upholding the military apparatus, produces the knowledge that justifies narrating Palestinians as terrorist Others.

Administrative controls shape the Palestinian community and its unborn and newborn children as terrorists. This nomenclature and its political and demographic implications justify monitoring the movements of Palestinians. Indeed, it is what allows the occupiers to shape at will the apparatus of military and population control. The bureaucratic system is perhaps the most pervasive part of the occupation regime; it is what has enabled the occupiers to trap, haunt, and suffocate Palestinian society. This bureaucracy, however, usually does not pose a direct threat to life and the physical body; rather, it denies Palestinians their rights as well as the proper conditions for life. Below, Raeda describes how her newborn baby was created in what Giorgio Agamben would call "bare life," a human life stripped of its humanity and rights in the state of exception, because the militarized Israeli sovereign power has used law to suspend law itself:[6]

> My ID is a West Bank ID, but my parents and grandparents are from Jerusalem. We are all from Jerusalem; but as you know, before it was normal to move from one area to another, but now Israel has drawn borders and we live outside the Jerusalem border. But, we never cared; it is all Jerusalem to us. These are borders they drew, but it never affected us. In 1996, I got married to my husband who had an Israeli ID, and my ID was a West Bank ID. We applied twice for family reunification, so that we would all have the same ID cards and wouldn't need to apply for a permit to come from my parent's house to my own house, or to my in-laws place, but we got rejected twice ... We did not care because we always found a way to move about, we always managed to reach our home, our families ... But, over the years, the permit and checkpoint system became harsher, and I started experiencing real problems: the inability to reach a doctor, to participate in a family funeral, to meet my kids' teacher or go to their school, to join my family during the birth of a child or for weddings, and much, much more ... our stories never end ...
>
> Last year, I was pregnant and had my child in the Al-Hilal hospital [in Jerusalem]. While I was pregnant, everybody was warning me that the child would not be recognized. He was born on May 15th, the day of the Nakba commemoration ... as if I needed additional Nakbas. Arrests were taking place everywhere around me. They viciously arrested many people and used tear gas in our area without mercy ... My female neighbour was dragged across the street in a disrespectful manner ... I was extremely scared because not only was I pregnant, I also carry a West Bank ID ... Only God knows how I reached the hospital [she became tearful when she said this] on that day ... But, thank God [crying] ... I had my son in the hospital, but under these conditions ... and he was healthy and beautiful ... I was happy that they gave us a document stating that I gave birth to my son in Jerusalem.
>
> This document needs to be approved by the Israeli authorities in order to attain a legal birth certificate. We were anxious for three months waiting for the *kushan* [the actual birth certificate]. Two weeks after my delivery, my husband was arrested and became a security prisoner. For three months I was denied a birth certificate for my son, Amar. I went to the Israeli National Insurance office, where they usually approve birth certificates. They refused, telling me that "his father is a terrorist," which means that my son is a terrorist. This is revenge. "Amar does not deserve a birth

certificate," they told me. I started begging them for a birth certificate for Amar; I was told that I should go to the Ministry of Internal Affairs ... and I went to the Ministry of Internal Affairs. The Ministry wanted proof that I lived in Jerusalem. They wanted my *arnona* [i.e., property tax documents], so I got it for them. Then they asked for papers and bills paid to the water company, proof that I pay the TV and electricity bills. The problem was that our house, having been the dwelling place of a suspected "terrorist" and us being the family of a security prisoner, the house was now physically blocked off, sealed up, you know that this is what they do to the houses of security prisoners. The house was sealed in cement, but I had to find the *arnona* bills and papers. I explained that since the house is sealed and I no longer live in it, but live in a small room with my in-laws, I no longer pay *arnona* ... They drove me crazy; they kept on saying that they had confidential information that we do not live in Jerusalem, they had confidential information that Amar was not born in the hospital ... And how can a woman like me counter their use of confidential security information ... So, I kept on insisting; I got them pictures of me and Amar leaving the hospital after his birth ... They went back to *arnona* papers ... and I found the old *arnona* papers to get the birth certificate; but they came up with new requests, now they wanted the phone bill, and I have no phone at home ... How can I have a home phone when I do not have a home anymore? For the past eleven months, my son has not been recognized and has no medical insurance, and every time he gets sick, I am worried about his survival ... My son won't be able to enrol in schools in Jerusalem, he won't be able to move, or go to be with his uncles or aunts; he will suffer as I am suffering ... he will be as trapped and persecuted as I am.

Raeda's narrative, her racialized position as she circulates through the borders and boundaries drawn by the Israeli security apparatus, created a strong sense of uncertainty and unrecognizability in her, with devastating social, economic, educational, and political consequences.

The bureaucracies of occupation, as reflected in the permit system that tied up Raeda and Amar, and as apparent in the many bureaucratic regimes used to stifle Palestinian women, create an institutionalized dysfunctional apparatus based on the racialized positioning of Palestinian families and communities. Race-oriented bureaucracies and bureaucratic rules unleash harsh violence against birthing in Jerusalem. The resulting administrative practices, as related by the various interviewees, demonstrate that the Israeli occupation relies heavily on shifting "security" rules, hierarchies, and ever-changing colonial bureaucracies that raise the level of uncertainty in the lives of the occupied. As Raeda put it:

> Everything is confidential, as if they have secrets ... and each time they uncovered one small detail, nothing is clear, so our lawyer was guessing ... and she is Jewish ... we were all guessing.

This "certainty of randomness" and state of non-recognition, a result of the production of knowledge (such as demographics) and the mobilization of practices, policies, and laws based on that knowledge and maintained through the bureaucratic regime, generates Palestinian otherness. This regime has created a state of institutionalized fear of Palestinian newborns in part by depicting the newborn child as a terrorist in the making.

Raeda's voice invites us to investigate the inner workings of the Israeli bureaucracy's power over Palestinian women's birthing bodies and lives. Her voice allows us to comprehend how the fluid apparatus of the military bureaucracy operates. It reveals how the basic organizing foundations of such a regime are grounded in its very dysfunctionalities – for example, by defining her as a West Banker and her husband as one who holds an Israeli ID when both live in the same area, belong to the same family, go to the same schools, shop in the same markets, pray in same place, and so on. And this divide-and-rule policy – a policy that counts one as a member of an acknowledged community and the other as unacknowledged and unrecognized – has been transferred to their children; two of Raeda's daughters have been granted Israeli ID, yet the newborn son has been rejected and so is "unrecognized." These power games of the dysfunctional yet well-calculated and neatly orchestrated regime are embedded in a racialized colonial system of control that goes beyond limiting Raeda and Amar's possibilities for planning their lives. Such racial hierarchies and bureaucracies are based on a colonial model and are used as a "non-violent" weapon to control racialized subjects.

Raeda's narrative allows us to understand how colonial bureaucracies maintain control. It helps us comprehend how such bureaucracies are reproduced and legitimized every time Palestinians use them; their capacity to inscribe power over women's bodies is further strengthened by their very ineffectiveness. This latter phenomenon – which arises through the construction of children, pregnant women, and entire Palestinian communities as security threats and hence as people and communities to be feared – leads to the denial of basic living conditions, of safety and security during pregnancy and while giving birth.

Concluding Remarks

The voices of Palestinian women shared here reveal a regime of control over birthing in Jerusalem. Women's narrations of their birth experiences told a distinct story. Their birthing bodies made an argument that challenges the hegemonic securitized one. Palestinian women's narrations explained how such persecution increased women's suffering and how what happens to them in spaces of marginality and in erased times and histories is deeply inscribed on women's psyches, bodies, and lives.

Said in his 1978 discussion of Orientalism and imagined geographies points to the ways in which imagined geographies create multiple partitions between "the same" and "the other." In listening to women's birthing narratives, we see clearly how constructions of the other and the imagined geographies of Palestinian birthing women produced an archive, a discourse, that allows us to see new things through the narratives of pregnant women. It reveals the colonial structure that implies that Palestinian pregnant women and their unborns and newborns are "threats," "terrorists," and "dangerous" others. The production of Palestinian women as the other not only implies imagined geographies that carry colonial histories – as Derek Gregory would argue – but also performs precarious spaces and lives that carry within them the likelihood of reproducing and reaffirming the colonial dispossession of the Palestinian people.

As I argue, the Israeli regime, its political authorities and its bureaucrats, use birth in occupied Jerusalem to control, trap, haunt, harass, humiliate, and terrorize birthing mothers. The power and concomitant randomness of the classifications, decisions, and reactions to birthing have generated severe psychosocial hardships among the women but also agency and resilience. Setting aside these women's strong sense of persecution, the certainty of arbitrary treatment has done much to create a racialized official system of control. In a context where Palestinians, even when seeking the help of family, their community, lawyers, human rights organizations, and other professionals, are unable to contest evidence based on "secret security" information, birthing demarcates belonging and non-belonging and creates a distinction between the norm and the exception, the wanted and the unwanted, the human

and the non-human. The discretionary power of the Israeli secret services, the security justifications that are confidential but have the power
to delay or prevent the registration of a child as a living entity, and
the radicalized positioning of the Palestinian family as a terrorist one,
together create a space of a near-total lack of control and complete uncertainty. Furthermore, the fluid borders and boundaries add to the
overwhelming sense of uncertainty and exacerbate injustices inflicted
on Palestinian birthing. Fears of the Palestinian birth rate, the invisibility and liminality of birthing, and the everydayness of suffering, all
of these added to the bureaucracy and administration of "terror," have
resulted in endless exhaustion.

Fearing the unborn Palestinian as the Palestinian birthing woman
emerges as reproduced through the logic of liminality, invisibility, and
hyper-visibility of Israeli numbers and the re-creation of the randomness of uncertainty, created a new state terror and criminality rational-
ized by the state's colonial ideology. The birthing Palestinian woman
and her unborn or newborn child are naked lives that encounter their
nakedness and extreme vulnerability in their quotidian existence while
being transformed into criminals and security threats. Their restricted
temporalities at the time of birthing and their lives under emergency
conditions as declared by the colonial state, in "security spaces" that are
insecure, point to a complex unheard and unacknowledged violence.

It is crucial to note that the moment of inscribing the birthing woman
in such a way as to make her unrecognizable or imperceptible by the
colonial regime lays the foundation for the articulation of "terror" and
of "terrorism" and its politics and production of fear. Colonial constructions of birth in occupied Jerusalem are necropolitical as Achille
Mbembe has defined it: "a generalized instrumentalization of human
existence and the material destruction of human bodies and population." Such constructions seek to justify the continuation of colonial aggression.[7] As facets of the imperceptibility of the birthing Palestinian
woman's naked life, her suffering and her existence are necropolitical
performances that assault "bare life" and maintain sovereign power.
Mbembe's definition of necropolitics helps us understand how colonial
control exercises sovereignty over birthing bodies and mortality "to define life as the deployment and manifestation of power."[8]

Rendering perceptible that which is imperceptible requires uncovering, expanding, disturbing, and deviating from the hegemonic confines of terrorism. Leaving Palestinian women in a "secured" space of

"emergency" renders them extremely vulnerable to having more violence committed against them.

Historically, we Palestinian women were seldom invited to participate in discourse and knowledge production, even when we were its topic. This chapter is a first step towards the critical unearthing of the truths of birthing in Jerusalem. To produce such knowledge based on women's voices and ordeals is to take a long step towards ownership of one's story and oneself as a Palestinian woman. Birthing Palestinian women's ways of living, knowing, and seeing their ordeals and their birthing experiences tell a story that should not be denied expression and a space in the history and future of knowledge production.

In my work as a traumatologist I have learned that one way to address traumatic memories is by engaging with them through a return to the sites of violation. The modes of return – as were portrayed here by the women's narratives of birthing – involve remembering acts of struggle, pain, agency, silence, and so on, across time, space, and place, while relying on women's voices and capacities to describe the characteristics of their suffering and/as power, as new routes to survival.

The narratives shared in this chapter and the knowledge they reflect are stories of birthing women who are crying out against injustice and telling of a reality and truth otherwise unknown. Those narratives constitute the return of the voice to the site of a violation that muted voices and silenced speech. Writing about this violation reveals the human suffering, and this writing is guided by those who experienced it so that they can help heal the wounds. Returning to the site of trauma by writing about it, by exploring, understanding, and questioning it, has – I hope – for the birthing women, started the process of rebuilding the violated home and finding a rooted destination against the certainty of randomness. For Palestinian women, both the home and the body are sites of violations. Women's narratives, and the knowledge produced by their own voices, have brought back a sense of home, a home that allows birthing women to revisit sites of violation and to articulate miseries that have been denied a voice. For colonized subjects in general, exposing hidden experiences and histories of violence through acts of sharing and writing – even in those moments of silence while narrating their histories – helps peel away heavy layers of current colonial experience and silenced memories as they engage in the project of articulating knowledge that can reclaim their rights and thereby challenge hegemonic distortions and racialized politics.

NOTES

1 Said, *Orientalism*; Gregory, *The Colonial Present*.
2 Shalhoub-Kevorkian, *Trapped Bodies and Lives*; Shalhoub-Kevorkian, "Trapped."
3 *Children in Military Custody*.
4 Fischbach, *Records of Dispossession*. See also Zureik, Lyon, and Abu-Laban, *Surveillance and Control*.
5 Said, *Orientalism*; Gregory, *The Colonial Present*.
6 Agamben, *Homo Sacer*; Agamben, *State of Exception*.
7 Mbembe, "Necropolitics," 14.
8 Mbembe, "Necropolitics," 12.

4 The Manufacture of Torture as Public Truth: The Case of Omar Khadr

SHERENE H. RAZACK

Introduction

Torture is a powerful pedagogy, teaching each of us who we are in the nation and in the human community. Torture does its work as narrative, a story of power written both on the body and on the social body. Scarry reminds us that during torture, the torturer becomes voice. The torturer is civilization; he or she transcends the body, while the tortured becomes reduced to body, to the guttural sounds of pain.[1] It is perhaps obvious to point out that torture terrorizes. That is, regimes of terror rely on torture to communicate to the tortured, the torturer, and all others, where power lies. More than this, torture obeys the principle that human life is not sacred and as such, it nurtures the seed of terror and helps it to blossom into a structuring principle. Slow and careful, bureaucratized and diligent, torture makes the dream of terror into a reality. We can also put this another way: Torture, announced as for the purpose of extracting vital information, is the violence that coats itself in law, providing the "proof" of criminality (the confession) that is law's alibi for violence.

In this chapter, I explore how torture comes to be a public truth in democratic regimes. How is torture written on the social body? How does a practice that is so extreme come to be seen as a necessary part of our everyday world, a world in which even the spanking of children is regarded as grievous harm? I have elsewhere turned to Todorov, who observes that torture is a cancer that can metastasize, spreading through the social body even among those who thought themselves immune,[2] and to Marnia Lazreg, writing of the torture of Algerians by the French during the Algerian War of Independence, who shows how torture provided the French with a source of social integration that united the government and the military and turned the state into a militaristic institution.[3] Along the same lines, I suggest that torture as practised today by liberal democratic states in the West (often aided by elites in the East) unites the West against the East, turning the globe into a militarized zone. In joining the United States, as a nation that tortures, or that is able to render others to be tortured, Canada's entry into the club of white nations can be secured. Individual white Canadians are then scripted as civilized peoples of European origin who must rely on torture to defend themselves from the barbarity of Muslims. As the story of the torture of Muslims circulates in the West, energizing some citizens and providing them with a heightened sense of their own racial superiority, it performs a psychic violence on those of us too easily racially identified with the tortured, reminding us of our own precarious status in the political community. In both instances, torture lays the groundwork for terror.

On 15 July 2008, Canadians watched on the national news a few minutes of a 2003 interrogation of Canadian Omar Khadr over four days at Guantanamo Bay by the Canadian Security and Intelligence Service (CSIS).[4] The Supreme Court ordered the release of the videotape to Khadr's Canadian legal team, who hoped the tapes would spur an outcry and increase calls for his repatriation. As day one of the interrogation begins, we see a young boy whose face lights up when the CSIS agent genially begins with, "I guess we're the first Canadians you've seen in a while." Omar smiles and replies, "I've been requesting the Canadian government for a while." By day two, Omar realizes that CSIS is there not to help him but to interrogate him. The sixteen-year-old has told his Canadian interrogators that he has been tortured and has asked them to protect him from the Americans.[5] He shows them his wounds. Australian scholar Joseph Pugliese has written about the devastating moment during the interrogation when a weeping Omar says he has lost his eye, his feet, and everything. His interrogator coolly informs him that he still has them, and he admonishes him to get his act together. Pugliese comments on the scene, pointing out the victim of torture who experiences his body as fragmented and lost, and the interrogator who is indifferent to the suffering youth and who insists there has been no harm.[6] When the interrogators leave the room, we see a young boy crying out in Arabic for his mother, and sobbing uncontrollably. Khadr's cries are simply absorbed into "a legal Black hole of unrelieved trauma and affliction."[7]

Canadians would come to learn that Omar Khadr had been subjected to sleep deprivation for long periods, used as a human mop to wipe up his own urine, shackled and bound in stress positions for long periods, and hooded to simulate suffocation. He had also been psychologically tortured – threatened with rape, the destruction of his family, and the prospect of never returning to Canada. All of this was in addition to a host of other physical tortures, especially at moments when he had been severely wounded. Only fifteen when he was captured, Khadr was first taken to Bagram prison and tortured (an American soldier once stationed at Bagram testified about specific practices at Khadr's trial).[8] He was later shipped to Guantanamo, where he was imprisoned for ten years. He has not been treated according to the Geneva Convention or the Optional Protocol of Child Soldiers; information obtained under torture was used during his trial; he has been detained in solitary confinement for a very long time; hearsay evidence has been allowed against him; his lawyers have not had full access to information, nor have they enjoyed full access to their client.[9] On 25 October 2010, Khadr changed his not guilty plea to guilty in exchange for a transfer to a Canadian prison. He was shortly thereafter sentenced to forty years for war crimes, with the actual sentence limited to eight more years. On 29 September 2012, despite concerted efforts by the Canadian government to delay his return, Khadr finally came home. He has begun serving the remaining years of his sentence in solitary confinement in a maximum security prison.

Overall, Canadians expressed little outrage on viewing the videotape of the interrogation or on learning that Khadr had been subjected to sleep deprivation torture for three weeks prior to being questioned again by CSIS in 2004. When details surfaced that cast profound doubt on the American claim that Khadr had thrown a grenade that killed an American soldier and wounded another, there was still little discernible sympathy for Khadr, either from the public or from the government. For a country that has for a very long time imagined itself to be kinder, gentler, and more humanitarian than its southern neighbour, this is puzzling, especially when one considers that all other Western countries have repatriated their citizens from Guantanamo and that Khadr was a child when first detained. Today, Canadians remain sharply divided on this issue. One poll reports that 81 per cent of Canadians are unhappy that Khadr is back in Canada.[10]

Khadr's case cries out for an analysis of how – by what discursive and representational means, including myth making – torture is made acceptable and normal in a democracy. How is the moral community that accepts torture created, maintained, and resisted? Canadian responses to Omar Khadr have been along two lines, both of which may be characterized as blood narratives. That is to say, each storyline, although it has contradictory goals, relies on the idea that values are innate – carried, that is, in the blood. Here let us consider Arendt's notion of race thinking, which is a structure of thought that divides the world into the deserving and the undeserving according to descent. In race thinking, values are inheritable traits.[11] The first narrative line, and the one held by the Conservative government of Stephen Harper, is that Khadr is a terrorist and that Muslim terrorists never change. They pose a threat to the West and must be contained at any cost. I contend that this line of thinking is a powerful biological narrative that scripts all Muslims as a race of people who carry the seeds of disloyalty, fanaticism, and violence in the blood; this in turn justifies their eviction from the legal and political community.

Those who have been uneasy about the first line of argument have tried to understand Khadr as a child soldier and demanded his repatriation on this basis. Advocates of this second line of argument soon find themselves caught in a humanitarian current that demands innocent Third World children who are in need of rescue by an enlightened West. The figure of the child has been of crucial importance to the West's construction of itself as humanitarian. For all his advocates try, Khadr cannot be easily seen as a child deserving of rescue. He was never the wronged child, and now, as a grown-up, he is even more easily cast out of the national community as the terrorist monster whose capacity for violence is innate and permanent. The child soldier narrative has been the weaker position as evidenced not only by the fact that the first line has prevailed in Parliament but also by the fact that the Canadian public has not been outraged about Khadr's detention, trial without fundamental rights, and torture.

The difficulty of saving Omar as a child soldier lies in a paradox. If it is our civility that prompts us to save him – our commitment, that is, to humanitarianism and the rule of law – it is hard to ignore that the West has not in fact treated him humanely nor has it included him in the rule of law. It is the West (the United States, with the approval and participation of Canada) that has detained him under cruel conditions, tortured him, and violated his fundamental rights.[12] The child soldier narrative thus runs aground when it has to confront *who* has been uncivilized. The child soldier narrative depends for its coherence on the idea that we must save children from the brutality of their own cultures, cultures we imagine to be the very opposite of our own and geographically in a far country; thus, it requires that we maintain a geographic as much as a racial difference between ourselves and the child to be saved.

In sum, we reconcile ourselves to the cries of a boy locked up in Guantanamo through these two blood narratives. The first, dependent on the figure of the Muslim as innately pre- and anti-modern, allows us to defend ourselves with the centuries-old colonial line that the natives only understand force and that we can deal with them in no other way. They carry the seeds of violence in their blood, a latent capacity from which we must protect ourselves, and the danger is nowhere more acute than in the body of the child. The second, in its appeal to our inherent civility, that is to say, our goodness, keeps us fully focused on imperial sentiments about our capacity to save the Third World's children. We need not confront how we have violated Khadr's rights and bodily integrity. Each narrative enables white citizens to feel that they are the normative citizens who must defend themselves against racialized groups or who must engage in saving children of colour who are salvageable. It is not surprising that such narratives populate both the evening news and the daily business of legislative committees. As I show below, both travel freely between these domains, shaping the moral sensibilities of all Canadians even while scripting some of us as less Canadian than others. Most of all, torture as an everyday practice prepares us for sustained terror.

Part One: Stained Blood

A Story about Gentlemen Soldiers and Girls with Down Syndrome

In her book *Modern Inquisitions: Peru and the Colonial Origins of the Civilized World*, Irene Silverblatt turns to Hannah Arendt, who sought an explanation for the rise of fascism in Europe and for the way that apparently civilized peoples turn to barbarity.[13] Arendt found the answer in nineteenth-century European imperialism. In *The Origins of Totalitarianism*, she identifies race thinking and shows how it became bureaucratized in nineteenth-century European imperial projects. At the heart of race thinking is the idea that character and culture are inheritable traits; imperial nations possessed an innate capacity for rationality, for example, that naturally positioned them as superior to those whose lands they were conquering. The conquered, in turn, possessed none of the traits that might equip them for modernity. For Arendt, European nationalisms were forged in these histories of imperialism and were distinguished by the race thinking that ran through them.[14]

Silverblatt finds the race thinking Arendt described for the nineteenth century much earlier, in the Spanish Inquisition of the seventeenth century. Making a compelling case that the Spanish Inquisition was a modern bureaucracy (rather than the premodern entity it is often presumed to be), she stresses that even as the accused were often tortured and had few legal rights, the inquisition "appealed to reason and to the public good, to the necessities of national security, to the mysteries of the state" as it went about the task of determining whether Spain's new Christians (those presumed to be descendants of Jews and Muslims) secretly practised their faith and were disloyal to the state.[15] Inquisitors drew upon the idea that "blood carried stains, and that stains could determine character traits, intelligence, political rights, and economic possibilities."[16] Loyalty was in the blood, and the inquisitors looked for signs of its presence in the life practices of the accused.

In my own study of Muslims in Western law and politics, I drew on Arendt and Silverblatt to show that an imperial and inquisition-like pattern of thinking persists today in security hearings, where Muslim men detained without charge and without full legal rights face a court that seeks to establish whether they will engage in terrorism against the state.[17] Arendt's race thinking is evident in these hearings when Muslims, Islamic extremists, and terrorists are all collapsed into one category and are imagined to share cultural and social characteristics (of fanaticism and a commitment to violence) that are innate. Importantly, people of European origin are also imagined to share innate social and cultural characteristics, such as civility and rationality; and as Arendt argued, ideas about the innate inferiority of one group are simultaneously ideas about the superiority of another.

In security hearings, a number of markers indicate that the accused is an Islamic extremist who possesses the latent capacity to be violent. These range from whether the detainee had been to Afghanistan in the 1980s to fight against the Russians, to whether the detainee acts too normally (thereby indicating the presence of a sleeper cell). In Adil Charchaoui's case, for instance, the fact that he owned a pizza parlour and was also a graduate student revealed that he was trying to pass for normal. Evidence of religious practice (from praying five times a day to going to Afghanistan to participate in Jihad) is evidence of possessing an "ideological repertoire" that includes a commitment to violence.[18] Most importantly, the Islamic extremist never changes. If the detainee went to Afghanistan in the 1980s, he is likely to go again. If he believed in Jihad against the Soviets, he is likely to believe in Jihad against America.

As in the Spanish Inquisition, such blood discourses thrive in a legal environment of secret evidence, detention without charge, and diminished standards of proof.[19] In the absence of proof, psychology has to do a great deal of work in the security hearing. The task is to pin down belief and to extrapolate a latent commitment to violence that will never fade. The psyche thus becomes the privileged site of investigation, and here race has an important role to play. Orientalist notions of monster terrorists who possess an inborn rage and hatred of the West guide the court in determining who is and who is not dangerous. The Orientalist child carries the seeds of disloyalty in his psyche, a latent capacity for violence that can erupt at any time. He is never a normal child.

Omar Khadr's Psyche

Omar Khadr's sentencing turned on whether he was an unrepentant and violent jihadist, a psychological status assessed in terms of his religiosity and his character. For the defence, prison guards at Guantanamo testified that they believed Khadr was a good kid who was not at all an extremist – an opinion shared by two other psychologists. But it was the testimony of the state-appointed psychiatrist, Michael Welner, that counted and that continues to structure media and Canadian government responses. Indeed, Canada gave as its official reason for delaying Khadr's transfer until September 2012 that it had not seen the videotape of Welner's seven-hour interview and had formally requested an unredacted report in order to make the final decision about his repatriation.[20] As the media reported, the United States was angered by the implication that Canada had been duped into signing an agreement to transfer Khadr without full possession of the facts. Michelle Shephard of the *Toronto Star*, who has been reporting on Khadr for several years, noted that Canadian officials had been present in the courtroom when the video and Welner's reports were discussed in various pre-trial hearings.[21] The move by the Canadian government to insist on viewing Welner's interview effectively focused the public's attention on Welner's psychiatric assessment. When *Maclean's*, Canada's national magazine, broke the news that it had obtained exclusive access to the released tape, and presented Welner's views in detail, Canadians were primed to accept that Khadr presented a textbook case of the terrorist psyche.[22]

Asked to offer an opinion of Khadr's "risk of dangerousness as a violent jihadist," Welner conducted a seven-hour interview with him, augmented by media interviews with the Khadr family and information obtained from guards and interrogators.[23] Having no prior experience in assessing "jihadists," Welner consulted with Danish psychologist Nicolai Sennels. Well known in Europe for his racist views of Muslims, Sennels believes that "massive inbreeding within the Muslim culture during the last 1,400 years may have done catastrophic damage to their gene pool."[24] Muslims, he contends, are genetically unable to integrate into European society and possess an inborn capacity to be violent. As I have shown in *Casting Out*, this biological view of Muslim degeneracy has gained currency in European courts and parliaments, often in as openly racist a form as Sennels's, but also at times disguised as moderate arguments about Muslim *cultural* incapacity to integrate.[25] Welner was unable to read Sennels in Danish and relied instead on a telephone conversation with him. Sennels's study of criminal Muslims particularly impressed Welner, who testified that he appreciated the study's therapeutic aspects and Sennels's interest in rehabilitation – an odd impression of Sennels, given his widely publicized belief that Europe should halt Muslim immigration since they will always be unable to integrate. When challenged by the defence about Sennels's racist views and his inexperience (Sennels was only thirty-three), Welner would only respond that he still admired the psychiatric work Sennels did.[26]

Welner's conclusion that Khadr was highly dangerous was based on several observations. First, he felt that Khadr showed no remorse, a conclusion he drew from information obtained from Khadr's interrogators and also from Khadr's own belief that he had been wronged. Second, although he acknowledged that Khadr was charming and comfortable with everybody, he concluded that Khadr had not become Westernized at Guantanamo. Instead he had become a more religious Muslim (understood here as non-Western). He had studied the Quran and had taken no initiative to undertake "secular" studies.[27] Counselling seldom worked with religious Muslim subjects, Welner declared, invoking Sennels, because radicalism was experienced as "spiritual beliefs."[28] When challenged by Khadr's defence, that Khadr had said he memorized the Quran because there was little else to do, and that he had tried to study the books that Canadians had sent to him but found it too hard to tackle some subjects unaided, Welner merely maintained that Khadr was not acculturated. In fact, for Welner, Khadr's reading of Harry Potter (and other popular novels) showed that he refused to reflect seriously on his life and instead lived a fantasy life.[29] It followed that Khadr was religious and therefore (according to Sennels) a poor candidate for deradicalization. Welner explained to the court that someone who memorized the Quran and who was called to lead prayers (precisely because he had memorized the Quran) was unlikely to drop his Jihad against the West.

There were many moments during Welner's testimony when inconsistencies, inaccuracies, and outright lies emerged, but these did little to undermine Welner's (and ultimately the court's) conclusion that Khadr was likely to engage in violent jihadist activity because of his religious inclinations and because of his family roots. As with the security certificate detainees, whose innate capacity for violence was interpreted through signs of religiosity as well as signs of being too "normal" (exhibiting Western behaviour), Khadr could not in fact win at his trial. Any characteristic he exhibited (avid reader of Harry Potter novels, keen student of the Quran) could be enlisted to support Welner's opinion that he was a violent jihadist. If Khadr appeared otherwise, he was merely awaiting the opportunity to go on Jihad.[30] Welner's professional opinion is reproduced in Canadian newspapers whenever Khadr becomes newsworthy,[31] and his "sound bites" from the trial – notably, where he states that Khadr is full of rage, is not remorseful, and is "al-Qaeda royalty"[32] – continue to circulate in both journalistic and political narratives.[33] Few journalists share columnist Thomas Walkom's assessment that Welner condemned Khadr for being an observant Muslim, for hoping to see his siblings again, for being upset that he was in Guantanamo, for reading novels by Danielle Steele and J.K. Rawlings, for leading prayers, and for behaving courteously.[34]

The Khadr Family

Given the importance of the idea of an enemy who is diseased and beyond redemption, breeding terrorists, Omar Khadr's family became of central importance to his case, and in this, they did not fail to deliver him up to those already prepared to accept the idea of tribal, premodern, intrinsically violent Muslims. Welner, for example, was heavily influenced by the media interviews he saw of the Khadr family, interviews that made clear to him that the Khadr clan was deeply committed to Jihad, hated the West, and looked to Omar to realize their dreams.[35] Interpreting Omar Khadr's reluctance to demonize his father as proof that he shared his father's commitment to al-Qaeda, Welner prefigured one of the key reasons the Minister of Public Safety, Vic Toews, gave for why he had serious concerns about repatriating Khadr. "Mr. Khadr idealizes his father," he declared in a press release upon Khadr's return.[36] The Canadian public developed their ideas through the same media interviews of the Khadr family, and these narratives, working in concert with the idea of the terrorist psyche, combined to limit any possibility that Khadr might be seen to be a child soldier and thus someone whom it was possible to rehabilitate.

It is revealing to track *how* narratives about the terrorist psyche circulate from the media to law and politics and back again and to reflect on the work they collectively do in building a moral community that finds torture acceptable. For instance, a specific interview with Omar's mother Maha and sister Zaynab travels to the House of Commons and to a parliamentary subcommittee and shapes discussion there. Scholars, lawyers, advocates, and politicians draw on the same news story, never reflecting critically on its assembly and deriving from it a sense of themselves as moral actors. Television, Evelyn Alsultany reminds us, mediates the War on Terror. It does so through "simplified complex representations," where representations of good Muslims serve to remind us of our tolerance while representations of bad Muslims repeat that the violence of Muslims is nevertheless carried in the blood. Muslim/ Arab violence is always irrational violence, having neither a history nor a context.[37] Simplified complex representations appear to complicate representations (although they keep all Muslims within a discussion of the War on Terror) yet continue to install the idea that some groups are deserving of torture. They do so largely through appeal to the idea that the West confronts a persistent and overwhelming Muslim threat. The Khadr family is framed, and frames itself, in ways that confirm a threat from a medieval and barbaric culture and people.

Media narratives keep our gaze on the terrorist psyche and the biological/social degeneracy of Muslims. The media present these narratives as spectacle, rarely offering a context in which to consider the simplistic, inarticulate, and extremist religious positions of Khadr family members. (One example is Zaynab's belief that the Quran requires Muslims to learn to ride horses so as to fight in Jihad.) In the most frequently played interview, Maha and Zaynab Khadr, wearing niqabs in which only their eyes are visible, both convey in belligerent tones that they are proud of Omar for putting up a fight. His sister Zaynab asks the interviewer belligerently what he would do in similar circumstances, if three of his friends were killed. The Americans killed three of Omar's friends and Omar killed an American soldier, she tells the interviewer, ending with "big deal." Both mother and sister indicate that they do not accept the values of the West (including homosexuality), and they explain at length their belief that Muslim land must be defended at any cost.[38]

It is critical to consider the impact of this interview with various viewers. Staged as a dramatic re-enactment of religious conservatism, and of Muslims as irrational and extreme, and replayed for the next eight years whenever there was coverage of the Khadr case, this interview more than earned its keep by inciting intense feelings of Western racial superiority.[39] However sympathetic the coverage of Omar Khadr's case, the impression remains that he comes from a hateful and extremist clan. Even when Maha Khadr responded with devastation to the interrogation tapes in which her son Omar cried for her, these earlier interviews, when replayed, worked to demonize her. If one is tempted to ask, "Why didn't evidence of Omar's dysfunctional and hateful clan operate to position him as a child to be saved?"' (as perhaps we might save a child who had been abused by his family),[40] the answer lies in how we have come to consider the figure of the Muslim terrorist as an anti-modern figure who carries the seeds of violence and disloyalty in the blood. Put simply, the child is as much a threat as the adult, and now, of course, the child Omar Khadr has become an adult. It is risky to bring him home, given that he carries disloyalty in his blood.

In November 2008, when the Canadian media speculated about whether the newly elected Barack Obama would indeed close Guantanamo, and when several opposition MPs began a campaign to repatriate Omar, the CBC showed once again its stock footage of the Omar Khadr story, including shots about his torture and possible innocence.[41] The program also ran footage of the interviews with Maha and Zaynab, and it included an interview with Layne Morris, an American soldier injured in the firefight, who, although he did not see Khadr throw the grenade, believed that he ought to be either executed or jailed for life. Morris emphasized what he described as the Khadr family's disdain for Western values and observed that they had never retracted their words. Omar could still become a suicide bomber, he suggested, and it was certain that the family would influence Omar profoundly. In the spirit of neutrality, the documentary included a psychiatrist from the Centre for Addiction and Mental Health who declared that his hospital was ready to rehabilitate Khadr. An expert in deradicalization suggested that Khadr was salvageable, and an Imam assured Canadians that Muslims were ready to guide Khadr in religious training that was not extremist. The problem of deradicalizing the terrorist psyche, however, given the clear evidence of a pathological family, would have left Canadians in doubt as to whether repatriating Khadr was a good idea.

"Can Muslims be deradicalized?" became the question of the day in the media, as it was in the trial at Guantanamo. It was taken for granted that the problem was not the specifics of Omar Khadr's case but the problem of Muslims in general and the violence they carry in their genes. Welner and Sennels may simply be the most dramatic about Muslim degeneracy, but their starting point – that the problem is the uniqueness of the Muslim terrorist psyche and a fatal Muslim incompatibility with modern life – is widely shared and produced. Harsh, unfeeling, simplistic women in niqab draw us frame by frame into a clash of civilizations between an enlightened West and a tribal, premodern East. If we have come to think of the problem of Omar Khadr as centrally about what to do with a "Muslim jihadist," there is little place in this optic for the torture of a child or for the illegality of Guantanamo. The story of Muslim pathology effectively blocks the violence of the West, securing Western innocence.

From the Media to the Legislature Where Not all Child Soldiers Are Equal

Torture as narrative is very much about performance. We have to "feel" Muslim pathology and white civilizational superiority and become energized by them. Law, media, and politics are domains in which there is a regular trafficking of narratives that aim to produce these specific emotional responses. Together they form a "hegemonic field of meaning."[42] Parliamentary subcommittee discussions and House of Commons debates frequently refer to media stories, and the media build their own narrative of Omar Khadr through interviews with politicians. It is not simply that the narratives flow from one domain to another, however; they also write a particular story of power on the social body as they circulate. The cumulative thrust of the message across these multiple domains is a powerful one that generates national feeling and simultaneously evicts others from national community.

The work of circulating knowledge about Muslim pathology is conducted at several legislative sites.[43] A particularly productive place is the Subcommittee on International Human Rights, which reports to the Standing Committee on Foreign Affairs and International Development.

Here the story of Muslim pathology meets its mirror opposite, white civility, and they dance an intimate pas de deux. Parliamentary sub-committees typically reflect the political agenda of the majority Conservative government, although they are all-party committees. The geopolitical lines of the subcommittee are thus drawn around human rights infringements in the Muslim world (e.g., those involving Iran, and the Copts in Egypt). These issues take their place alongside the problem of anti-Semitism and China/Canada and Cuba/Canada relations. Omar Khadr rose to the top of the subcommittee's agenda in March 2008 when an opposition MP (Wayne Marston, NDP) pointed out its urgency, since his hearing at Guantanamo Bay was scheduled for June 2008. The sub-committee allocated $39,200 to study the case and began its deliberations by hearing from Lieutenant Commander William Kuebler, Khadr's military counsel.

It is significant that Kuebler began his presentation with what he described as the offensive public comments of Maha and Zaynab Khadr, which by then had been aired on television. He stated that Canadians were right to be offended by remarks that "impugn Canadian values and express sympathy for our common enemies."[44] He thus immediately installed what others would be using to evict Khadr from the category child or citizen – namely, that he came from a terrorist family. Declaring that he blamed the family for the harm that had befallen his young client, he did his best to offer the committee images of a boy wrongfully involved in armed conflict.[45] He testified that Canadians should be angry at the family and should not focus on the illegality of Guantanamo. Insisting that Omar was a wronged child, Kuebler tried to leave the committee with images of the child Omar who longed to see *Lord of the Rings* and the Canadian Rockies. Under international law, Kuebler reminded the committee, child soldiers were protected and ought to be rehabilitated. He stressed that even if Canada were to try Omar, there would still be a legal obligation to consider his age and to rehabilitate him.

The child soldier argument immediately ran into difficulties when Conservative MP Jason Kenney asked: "Are you drawing analogies between his case and the child soldiers of Sierra Leone?"[46] For the Conservative members of the subcommittee, not all child soldiers were equal. When organizations such as Amnesty International and the Canadian Coalition for the Rights of Children reiterated Canada's obligation to consider Khadr a child soldier, and when opposition MPs described Khadr as "a dutiful son," the Conservative refrain was always the same: Khadr had killed an American "medic." (Speer was typically always named in full. It made little difference that when he was killed, he was acting in the capacity of a soldier of an elite fighting force and not as a medic.) The former chief prosecutor of the international war crimes tribunal of Sierra Leone told the subcommittee that he believed that no child under the age of fifteen can commit a war crime. David Crane's passionate advocacy on behalf of child soldiers rested, however, on his argument that the violence in Africa was "beyond description," carried out with a degree of savagery that the committee would have to imagine in Khadr's case. But the rehabilitation of Omar Khadr was not something that Conservative members could believe in. It was not as if Khadr could be compared to Ismael Beah, insisted Conservative MP David Sweet.[47] Khadr had no family (and of course no country) to help him escape the contamination of his blood.

Gentleman Soldiers and Girls with Down Syndrome

The racial thrust of blood narratives requires a tabloid style of performance, best illustrated in the exchange between well-known general Roméo Dallaire, who tried to warn the UN of the impending genocide in Rwanda and who became an advocate for child soldiers, and Jason Kenney, today a prominent minister in the Harper cabinet. Dallaire offered the position that Canada's role in the world was to follow the rule of law and to go to countries like Sierra Leone to help them establish democracies. Canada had lost credibility by refusing to bring Khadr home. But during the hearings, this human rights argument, which relies heavily on the idea of Canadian civility, ran smack into the notion that some people are too savage to deserve human rights. As Mokhtari reminds us, under the Bush administration "the United States created the categories of *terrorist, enemy of the United States,* and *enemy of freedom and human rights* as categories to which any strict application of human rights norms were inappropriate."[48] Conservative politicians in Canada hold fast to this idea, which requires them to constantly draw a colour line between dangerous Muslim men and civilized Europeans.

> HON. ROMÉO DALLAIRE: My position is that the minute you start playing with human rights, with conventions, and with civil liberties in order to say you're doing it to protect yourself – and you are going against the fundamentals of those rights and conventions – you are no better than the guy who doesn't believe in them at all.
> HON. JASON KENNEY: So would you contest the fact that this category of people is responsible for things such as capturing and beheading

innocent civilians, and in one instance recently, capturing teenage girls
with Down's syndrome, strapping them with suicide belts and sending
them into a child's pet market in Baghdad, and calling for the destruction
of all the Jewish people? Would you contest that these are some of the
tactics and aspirations of the terrorists to whom you referred?

HON. ROMÉO DALLAIRE: I notice you just threw in the last one there to give
yourself a whole context.

First of all, it is the same as those adults who use child soldiers in
Rwanda, Sierra Leone, Burundi, Uganda, Sudan, Darfur, and Sri Lanka.
In so doing, it is the child soldier who is being used, and we are using
illegal means to try them.

HON. JASON KENNEY: So is it your testimony that al-Qaeda strapping a
14-year-old girl with Down's syndrome and sending her into a pet
market to be remotely detonated is the moral equivalent of Canada's not
making extraordinary political efforts for a transfer of Omar Khadr to
this country? Is that your position?

HON. ROMÉO DALLAIRE: If you want it in black and white, then I'm only
too prepared to give it to you: absolutely. You're either with the law or
you're not with the law. If you wish to fiddle with the law and say, well,
we're going to go a bit this way and we're going to go a bit this way, then
fine. But in the process of what we are looking for, you're either guilty or
you're not. You're either a child soldier or you're not.

If you like, you can use the extreme scenarios under which I'm articulating my position, which is that you are not allowed to go against those
conventions, and if you do, you are going down the same road as those
who absolutely don't believe them at all.[49]

It is of course easy to see the geopolitical agenda that underpinned
Jason Kenney's comments. It was an anti-Muslim agenda with support for Israel at its core. Equally apparent in Kenney's images of
girls with Down syndrome and pet markets in Baghdad was what
Francois Debrix has called the tabloid realist style. Those images
were part of a false story first circulated by the US military.[50] They
were later retracted; nevertheless, they were circulated not just by
Kenney but by uncritical Canadian news reports on the Dallaire/
Kenney exchange. To this day, it remains hard for a researcher to uncover that the Kenney story was false; to do so, one must track down
little-known blogs.[51]

Debrix explains that the tabloid discursive style of truth telling is
overly simplistic, sensationalist, fear inducing, and reliant on images
and cartographical representations meant to help Americans visualize

threats. Tabloid realism has now become tabloid imperialism, "a matter of deploying vivid gruesome, real, or factual situations and so-called events, and, more importantly, of attaching those phenomena to larger-than-life and ideationally superior reasons, rationalizations, and ideologies, so that Americans could not just fear or panic, but also could hate, abject, dehumanize, and agonize over life and death."[52] Kenney insisted at every turn that Muslims sink to the lowest levels of depravity; against these images, it was impossible to consider Omar Khadr as we would a child soldier of Sierra Leone. Kenney secured for himself an ethical space by arguing that we could not deal with Omar Khadr through the rule of law, given the extent of Muslim depravity.

Tabloid realism depends on race thinking in exactly the way Arendt named. It presents both white civility and Muslim degeneracy as inheritable traits. Arendt noted in detail European thinkers who saw the liberal democratic state as the crowning achievement of European civilization and as an outcome of a superior rationality. Occluding the violence that makes the modern state, this Occidentalist view underpins the racial fault line embedded in global geopolitics today, as Fernando Coronil has argued.[53] Such a view is fully apparent in the presentation to the committee made by Howard Anglin, a Canadian lawyer working in Washington. Already known for articles on his blog arguing that the Geneva Convention must be suspended when dealing with militant Islamists, given their "depravity"[54] (he was subsequently appointed as Jason Kenney's chief of staff, a position he holds today), Anglin defended Guantanamo's military commissions as entirely lawful. In true tabloid fashion, he argued, "Everyone agrees that the detention of a fanatical and zealous enemy desirous of martyrdom imposes a new challenge for traditional and often anachronistic military and legal procedures."[55] The Geneva Convention "really conveyed a *Hogan's Heroes* sort of detention camp of gentleman soldiers. Whatever you want to say about Mr. Khadr, he is not a gentleman."[56] One wants to remind Anglin of the millions of Soviet prisoners of war killed by the Germans during the Second World War and the new levels of European barbarism that war reached; the historian Timothy Snyder has shown that by the end of 1941, the largest group of victims in occupied Poland were neither Jews nor Poles but Soviet prisoners of war.[57] It is not fact that matters, however, but feeling. As with the media narratives of the Khadr family, narratives about Western law must incite warm feelings of civilizational belonging.

Anglin seemed anxious to display his European pedigree. Noting (with no small degree of pompousness) that Khadr was surely a dutiful son, he elaborated that

> there is always something noble about sons – in this case a family of sons – standing up for their patrimony and for their father's beliefs. This sentiment is nobly and memorably represented in the Oath of the Horatii, the great classical painting by Jacques-Louis David, in which three sons swear to defend Rome against the Alba Longa. Unfortunately, if we're going to be Rome in that analogy, the Khadrs are the Curiatii and not the Horatii. He chose the wrong side and I think it's appropriate to take that into consideration in the context of being a most dutiful son.[58]

Leaving the committee with his knowledge of Latin, Anglin concluded, "You might say he's a boy of 15, but unfortunately the law says he is a soldier at 15. *Dura lex sed lex* is an old proverb."[59] It was hard to disturb his flow of images and his extravagant rhetorical gestures declaring Europeanness to be civility and lawfulness. The opposition members of the subcommittee tried to do so by reminding him that the US Supreme Court had ruled in *Hamdan* that military commissions were illegal. They argued that Khadr had been tortured. Anglin responded that the military commissions had since been improved and that these facts simply proved that the United States was in fact a civilized country and not "a country that holds kangaroo courts or show trials."[60]

The second witness, Naresh Raghubeer – the only "brown" witness and thus well suited for his role of native informant – also testified to the subcommittee as simply someone with a human rights agenda. He represented a group known as the Canadian Coalition for Democracies, which has strong anti-Muslim politics and a strong Hindu Right orientation. (The group supports India's right to Kashmir, a pro-Israel stance, and an end to all humanitarian assistance to Palestinians, and it regularly attacks Muslim Canadian public figures who are critical of these politics.) Raghubeer simply repeated the argument that Khadr had been treated well and that he had a right to consular access. (Conservative Members of Parliament would repeat these words almost verbatim in Parliament for several years.) He suggested that the Canadian government should go after the Khadr family and address the priming of hatred in Canadian homes. Khadr's family had primed him for martyrdom. Using the Arabic word "shahid" for martyr, and thereby indicating his expertise on Muslims, Raghubeer followed the tabloid script to a T. When asked what Khadr was alleged to have done, Kenney replied on Raghubeer's behalf: "What did he do? I gather he joined al-Qaeda, which is an international terrorist organization dedicated to creating an 8th century caliphate, an extreme Muslim dictatorship and to killing Jews and Americans and allies of the United States. I think that's what he did."[61] Locating the Khadr firmly within a terrorist family, and making repeated reference to the CBC's interview with Maha and Zaynab Khadr, Raghubeer recommended that Parliament ban the teaching of terror.

The House of Commons subcommittee was unable to overcome its political differences. It concluded that Omar Khadr should be considered a child soldier and that he should have the protection of the Optional Protocol. It recommended that his release be sought and his reintegration facilitated. In a dissenting opinion, the Conservative MPs warned that taking Khadr up as a victim would have implications for Canada's stance on terrorism. The Conservative committee members complained that Anglin had been particularly disregarded. They repeated his argument that the conditions of the War on Terror called for a departure from normal rules. Khadr posed a risk and was sure to re-establish ties with his family. While it may be that these Conservative narratives were drowned out by the opposition members of the subcommittee, as a majority government, the Conservatives have been easily able to stay the course in the House of Commons. From the moment of its election in 2006 to the present day, the Conservative government has been impervious to opposition calls for Khadr's repatriation, replying in formulaic terms whenever Khadr's case is brought up in the House of Commons. Rarely does the government feel compelled to depart from its stock three-line response: he faces serious murder charges for killing a medic; he is being treated humanely; and Canada respects the legal processes of the United States.[62]

Part Two: Civility in the Blood – A Story about the Child Soldiers of Africa

Canadians have prided themselves on their defence of child soldiers, and politicians often recall that Canada played a key role in pushing for the Optional Protocol on Child Soldiers, signed by sixty states in February 2007, which protects children under eighteen from being recruited by armed groups and which enjoins states to rehabilitate such children.

As the protocol's principles note, child soldiers who commit crimes are victims.[63] Child soldiers have featured strongly in the national imagination. Canadians, like Americans, have been taken with the story of former Sierra Leone child soldier Ismael Beah, whose memoir *A Long Way Gone* has garnered international praise. By the time Beah was thirteen years old, he had been involved in several heinous acts (Omar Khadr was twelve when his family took him to Afghanistan). Canadians have likewise been drawn to the story of Michel Chikwanine, a former child soldier from Congo who now lives in Canada and who was nominated by Free the Children founders Craig and Marc Kielburger for inclusion in the group of the next generation of leaders. Thousands of Canadian schoolchildren have heard Chikwanine's story of being abducted by rebel soldiers and forced by them to kill his best friend.[64]

If it is impossible to underestimate the importance of emotion in tabloid realism – the invocation, that is, of eighth-century caliphates, gentlemen soldiers of Europe, and children with Down syndrome who are forced to become suicide bombers, and the supporting political idea that the West has a political obligation to keep Muslim barbarism in check wherever it is assumed to live, it is also evident that the child soldier line must tap into the same wellspring of racial feeling when it comes to Western humanitarianism. Dallaire, for example, stresses that we are a civilized nation with an obligation to help the Third World into democracy. When he gave a speech in Montreal to this effect, a member of the audience who suggested that we might also examine our own consumption was dismissed by Dallaire for attempting to refocus the discussion on Western privilege; indeed, he was booed by the audience, as Ezra Winton reported on his blog.[65] It seems that we insist on having our child soldiers without a side dish of critical self-reflection about our supposed civility.

Scholars have been rightly critical of the focus on the child in human rights discourses, noting, for example, that it evades issues of economic inequality between the North and the South and positions Western activists as the saviours of Third World children. As David Jefferess has put it, "the 'protection' of the child is a self-consolidating project for the (Western) adult."[66] Jefferess points out that there is a particular problem in valorizing Western child-activist figures such as Craig Kielburger, founder of the Canadian organization Free the Children, in that the Western child is positioned as able to be both a child and a child activist, travelling the world saving children, something few children can do. The Third World child is rendered voiceless in these arrangements, and it is through that child that the Western child activist achieves personhood. Here we might note the same hierarchical arrangement that operates in torture: the tortured becomes body and the torturer voice; the former is annihilated, the latter is born out of torture.

Craig Kielburger has written of a chance encounter he once had with Omar Khadr in 1996 when he was thirteen and Khadr nine. Kielburger was travelling through South Asia learning about child labour. He was due to meet then Prime Minister Jean Chrétien, who was also travelling through South Asia. The Khadr family was waiting to meet the prime minister that day in order to plead their case for the release of Ahmed Khadr, then being held by the Pakistanis. Kielburger remembers exchanging a few words with Omar about being from the same neighbourhood in Toronto. Recalling the boy who liked comics, Kielburger commented on the different paths they had since travelled:

> Weeks later, I returned home to a firestorm of media attention. Many asked how I had accomplished so much at such a young age. Years later when I learned that the boy I met in Pakistan allegedly killed an American soldier in a firefight in Afghanistan, I wondered if anyone asked him that question. It dawned on me that people thought my 13 year old self did something kids shouldn't be capable of doing. But, when Omar was pushed into weapons training at 10, apparently he should have known better. Really though, the two of us are products of our environment. Omar is just being punished for his.[67]

Although he offers passionate support for Omar Khadr, we can immediately see how Kielburger is caught in the very construct Jefferess writes about. In seeing them both as simply children, Kielburger does not begin with the fact of his own privilege of traveling the world at 13. He cannot imagine that the differences between himself and Omar have to do with race and class, among other things. In Kielburger's world, where children are either white saviours able to travel the world or Black children in need of rescue, Omar is neither. He is of the First World but he is not white. Further, he is alleged to have killed an American Medic, a crime which columnist Rosie DiManno opined was particularly heinous to her given that she had spent time on the ground with Canadian troops in Afghanistan and knew intimately the dangers they faced.[68] Presumably, regardless of age, to kill a Canadian is not to be equated with the killing of an African. In these ways, Khadr cannot offer his saviours the rush of feeling that comes with saving.[69]

Teaching (about) Terror

A Muslim child is not readily accessible as an innocent victim of his own culture, as are African children. It is not the Orientalist child who must be protected; it is we who must be protected from him. Small wonder that Omar Khadr deeply troubles humanitarian discourses of the child. These difficulties are evident in the classroom activities that Free the Children prepares for Canadian schools. Schoolchildren are presented with scenarios in which they are encouraged to imagine themselves as living in an African country plagued with civil war and unrest. The scenarios always involve living in a village. Either a child soldier returns to his village and is welcomed back in a ceremony at which one of his former victims is also present, or he is seized from his village and escapes from his captors months later. Children are encouraged to explore the difficulties of reintegration into the village. The lesson plan suggests an extension where the class might consider the case of Omar Khadr, but one can immediately foresee the pedagogical difficulties of the situation. Tellingly, the lesson plan does not ask the children to imagine themselves in Omar's position, as it did with the other examples. Since the student is imagined as white and as poised to save African children, Khadr's case as a child from a suburb of Toronto would be beyond their imagination. It would surely be a pedagogical feat for white schoolchildren to think that their own country refuses to support them. Instead, the children are invited to discuss whether Omar Khadr is a child soldier at all, why Canada is resisting his return, and whether he would be accepted "once again." It is highly unlikely that Canadian schoolchildren can negotiate the treacherous waters of monster terrorists equipped only with discourses about children's rights. In this sense, Canadian schools are one more site for the reproduction of torture narratives as they concern Muslims.

Liberal discourses of the child soldier, I have been arguing, rely on a civilizational divide that cannot in the end bear the weight of the Muslim child. We believe in child soldiers to the extent that they confirm our own Western superiority. Human rights discourses have a built-in civilizational or colour line in which it is presumed that the West is the guardian of human rights whose challenge it is to instruct the non-West in civility. As several scholars, including myself, point out, this renders the violence of the West invisible. It is this fatal flaw of human rights discourses that we see when child soldier discourses fail to marshal Canadian support to repatriate Omar Khadr. As in the school lessons prepared by Free the Children, Canadians have little pedagogical help that would enable them to see Omar as a deserving child. To see him as a victim of torture would require that Canadians examine their relationship to the United States and to the family of white nations that wage the "War on Terror." Most have been unwilling to do this, and few politicians are prepared to risk the political consequences of doing so. Sentimental narratives of child soldiers must then suffice in its stead. They help us affirm our civilizational superiority even in the moment of critique. They do not help Omar Khadr.

Conclusion

Omar Khadr haunts the nation. He represents the dangerous possibility that we have been uncivilized, acquiescing to lawless zones where torture is permissible, and abandoning a child to his fate. We keep his ghost at bay through wild talk about monster terrorists, through sentimentality about child soldiers. Our melancholic attachment to Omar Khadr spells his doom. We need our terrorists carrying the seeds of fanaticism in their blood and no more so than when they are children and youth. Equally, we need our child soldiers in grass huts in Africa. These are constructs through which white Canadians come to understand their own racial superiority. When we torture or approve of torture, the public truth we will not give up is the idea of white superiority and the violence it requires and produces. It is frightening to think how easily blood narratives are bloodthirsty narratives.

Torture is now a public truth in many ways in Canada. The government has directed Canada's spy agency CSIS to use information that may have been extracted through torture in cases where public safety is at stake. The story, as columnist Thomas Walkom pointed out, was back page news in most newspapers.[70] Prior to this, the Canadian government prorogued Parliament rather than reveal its involvement in rendering Afghan detainees to torture.[71] We have several celebrated cases of Canadians who were tortured with the complicity and active assistance of the Canadian government, the best known of these being that of Maher Arar, who is also the only Canadian who has received compensation from the Canadian government but who is still banned from the United States. It is hard to find evidence that Canadians have noticed the increasing material involvement of their state in the torture of its own citizens. Against this backdrop, an energetic tabloid realism continues apace, with a daily reminder of Muslim degeneracy, as other papers in this workshop discuss, and with a regular instalment of European civility. If we follow these blood narratives, tracing the kinds of normative citizens they produce, and if we consider the social integration that their cumulative impact achieves, we will come to torture as practice and as truth.

NOTES

The author thanks Nashwa Salem and Louise Tam for extraordinary research assistance and Gada Mahrouse and Leslie Thielen Wilson for important conversations.

1 Scarry, *The Body in Pain*, 57.
2 Todorov, *Torture and the War on Terror*, 61.
3 Lazreg, *Torture and the Twilight of Empire*, 121.
4 "Excerpts as CSIS interviews Omar Khadr in February 2003," *The National*, CBC, 15 July 2008, http://www.cbc.ca/mrl3/8752/news/features/khadr-video.wmv.
5 *You Don't Like the Truth: 4 Days Inside Guantánamo*, dir. Luc Côté and Patricio Henríquez Montreal, QC: Les Films Adobe, 2010), DVD. This documentary is also available on TVOntario's website, accessed 7 June 2012 at http://ww3.tvo.org/video/164241/you-dont-truth-4-days-inside-guantanamo.
6 Pugliese, "Apostrophe of Empire," 14.
7 Pugliese, "Apostrophe of Empire," 15, citing G.F. Fletcher, "Black Hole in Guantanamo Bay," *Journal of International Criminal Justice* 2 (2004): 121–32.
8 Damien Corsetti, an American soldier stationed at Bagram in 2002, in *You Don't Like the Truth*.
9 Corsetti, in *You Don't Like the Truth*.
10 Yahoo Canada poll, 1 October 2012.
11 Arendt, *The Origins of Totalitarianism*, 158–84.
12 With respect to the torture of Omar Khadr, Canadian legal decisions have been as follows. In 2006, after the United States finally charged Khadr with murder, he sought disclosure in Canada of the records of "interviews" that Canadian officials (CSIS) had conducted at Guantanamo. In 2008, the Supreme Court ordered disclosure of these records ("interviews" is the word that appears in a Supreme Court summary). At this point, it was made clear that when CSIS interviewed Khadr in 2003, they were aware he had been subjected to a form of sleep deprivation known as the "frequent flyer program." Khadr then sought judicial review of the Canadian government's policy and decision not to seek his repatriation.

In April 2009, Federal Court judge James O'Reilly ruled that the prime minister was required to press the United States for the return of Khadr to Canada. The government appealed this decision and lost in the Federal Court of Appeal. It then appealed to the Supreme Court of Canada. Finally, on 29 January 2010, the Supreme Court overturned lower court orders to repatriate Khadr even though it agreed that Khadr's human rights had been violated and were still being violated by Canadian officials. The court ruled that the government must have the final say in how it implemented its foreign policy, and it refused to compel the Harper government to repatriate Khadr. As this Canadian legal history reveals, Canada responded to Khadr by acknowledging that his constitutional rights had been violated but stopping short of ordering his repatriation.

13 Silverblatt, *Modern Inquisitions.*
14 Arendt, *The Origins*, 206.
15 Silverblatt, *Modern Inquisitions*, 15.
16 Silverblatt, *Modern Inquisitions*, 25.
17 Razack, *Casting Out.*
18 Razack, *Casting Out*, 41.
19 Detainees are non-citizens and can be deported after a judge reviews the government's case against the detainee in a secret hearing at which neither the detainee nor his counsel is present. The minister need only satisfy the court that there is a possibility that the person is a terrorist or a member of a terrorist organization. In February 2007, the Supreme Court of Canada ruled that secret evidence was unconstitutional and required Parliament to amend the secrecy rule. At present, specially appointed advocates review the secret evidence. The court, however, neither condemned indefinite detention nor regarded it as cruel and unusual punishment. Detainees still do not have the unqualified right to see evidence that is held against them. Few cases have stood up to even this slight change in the rules; four of the men have now been released under various conditions. My analysis of the detention hearings reveals the circulation of ideas about Muslims.
20 Minister of Public Safety, Press Release: "In the Matter of Omar Ahmed Khadr and the *Internationl Transfer of Offenders Act*," 28 September 2012, Ottawa.
21 Shephard, "Canada Not 'Duped' to Take Khadr."
22 Friscolanti, "The Secret Khadr File."
23 See *United States v Omar Ahmed Khadr* (26 October 2010), ISN 0766 (Office of Military Commissions, Guantánamo Bay) (Testimony, Dr Michael Welner), 4361, 4395–6.
24 Sennels, "Muslim Inbreeding."

25 Razack, "Racism in the Name of Feminism," in Casting Out, 107–44.
26 See *United States v Omar Ahmed Khadr*, 4492–539.
27 See *United States v Omar Ahmed Khadr*, 4406–7.
28 See *United States v Omar Ahmed Khadr*, 4473.
29 See *United States v Omar Ahmed Khadr*, 4408.
30 In the Military Commission trial on 26 October 2010, forensic psychiatrist Dr Michael Welner testified that "there is no evidence from [Omar Khadr's] time in incarceration of acculturating." According to Welner, "he's been marinating in a radical jihadist community" and "the people that he is around are thoroughly devoted to that ideology; they are bitter and belligerent enemies of the United States." Suggesting that his faith was like a disease, Welner described Khadr's jihadism as a "tumor around his artery." This was further reinforced by his observation that "he is devoutly religious. And – devoutly religious is a particularly relevant risk factor in radical jihadists … [H]e does not internalize responsibility… [I]t – it is a – a clinical risk factor that is associated with a poor prognosis, people who just don't take responsibility for their own actions and blame everyone else and are chronically resentful and angry." Welner concluded that "if anyone believes that counselling is going to transform him from being a radical jihadist into somebody who is a devout Muslim but who is – is one who is not of a radicalist mindset, then that's foolish because it's a spiritual issue." "In my professional opinion, Omar Khadr is a high risk of dangerousness as a radical jihadist." See *United States v Omar Ahmed Khadr*, 4407, 4436, 4446, 4469–70, 4473, 4481.
31 See, for example, Welner, "Omar Khadr."
32 *United States v Omar Ahmed Khadr*, 4469.
33 See, for example, DiManno, 'Wrong Killer Shown Mercy." DiManno argues that Khadr was a "child of Al Qaeda privilege" and that he showed no remorse, unlike teen killer Beltway sniper Lee Boyd Malvo, trained by John Allen Mohammed to kill.
34 Walkom, "So-Called 'Secret Evidence.'"
35 *United States v Omar Ahmed Khadr*, 4396.
36 Minister of Public Safety, "In the Matter of Omar Ahmed Khadr."
37 Alsultany, *Arabs and Muslims in the Media*, 21.
38 See "Son of Al Qaeda," first aired on the CBC's *The Fifth Estate* in the winter of 2004 and again on PBS's *Frontline* on 22 April 2004.
39 It is interesting to speculate on the impact of such interviews on non-white groups, including Muslims. See, for example, Mahtani, "Representing Minorities"; Mahtani, "The Racialized Geographies."
40 See NWAC, *Report*.

41 "The Case of Omar Khadr," The National, CBC, 19 November 2008,
    http://www.cbc.ca/thenational/indepthanalysis/story/2009/11/13/
    national-thecaseofomarkhadr.html.

42 Alsultany, *Arabs and Muslims*, 7.

43 The government's position on Omar Khadr drew deeply on blood dis-
    courses. For example, Jim Judd, the CSIS director, appeared before the
    House of Commons Subcommittee on Public Safety and National Secu-
    rity, which was tasked with reviewing the Anti-Terrorism Act of 2001.
    This subcommittee began its work by hearing from Judd, who provided
    a security threat assessment. He reminded the committee that since the
    Anti-Terrorism Act was passed, the second generation of immigrant
    families in Europe, Canada, the United States, and Australia who came
    from middle-class backgrounds had become of particular concern. He
    then reiterated what could be found in the security certificate hearings:
    "extremists remain committed adversaries, ready to die for their causes."
    Noting particularly the five men held under security certificates as well
    as other suspected terrorists, and Omar Khadr's father Ahmed Khadr, he
    reminded the committee that "some of [the Khadr] children underwent
    weapons and explosive training at camps in Afghanistan." See Canada,
    House of Commons, Subcommittee on Public Safety and National Security
    of the Standing Committee on Justice, Human Rights, Public Safety, and
    Emergency Preparedness, *Evidence*, 38th Parl., 1st Sess., no. 6 (22 February
    2005) at 2, 3 (Jim Judd).

44 Canada, House of Commons, Subcommittee on International Human
    Rights of the Standing Committee on Foreign Affairs and International De-
    velopment, *Evidence*, 39th Parl, 2nd Sess, No. 10 (29 April 2008) at 1 (LCdr
    William Kuebler). Evidence both from this parliamentary subcommittee
    and from the legislative session is hereafter referred to as SDIR-EV.

45 In a largely fictitious story, first told by the Department of Defence in 2002,
    Omar was the lone survivor of a four-hour bombardment of an al-Qaeda
    compound near Khost, Afghanistan. The story was that he waited in the
    rubble and then rose up wielding a pistol and a hand grenade, taking a
    group of US soldiers by surprise and killing a medic before being shot
    in the chest. No part of this story is true, however, and the Omar Khadr
    it describes does not exist. "The real picture of Omar Khadr, which has
    been revealed in the last few months as the contents of U.S. government
    documents have been disclosed for the first time, is that of a frightened,
    wounded 15-year-old boy – a boy, like other children wrongfully involved
    in armed conflict, who had no business being there, who sat slumped

against a bush while a battle raged around him. Omar was then shot in the back, at least twice, by a U.S. soldier and was then about to be executed when another soldier intervened. Conveniently blamed for the unfortunate death of Sergeant Christopher Speer, official records were retroactively altered so that Omar could be held responsible. The real Omar Khadr has thus languished, almost forgotten, in Guantanamo bay, exploited as a source of information about his father and family for nearly six years." Ibid. at 2 (Kuebler).

46 Ibid. at 6 (Hon Jason Kenney).
47 SDIR-EV, No. 13 (12 May 2008) 8 at 1300 (David Sweet).
48 Mokhtari, *After Abu Ghraib*, 49.
49 SDIR-EV, No. 14 (13 May 2008) at 8 (Hon Roméo Dallaire).
50 Brooks, "US: Bombers Didn't Have Down Syndrome." Cross-posted at MSNBC, 20 February 2008, http://www.msnbc.msn.com/id/23261370/#. T0JP7oemh8E.
51 "Jason Kenney Uses Fake Down's Syndrome Suicide Bombers Story to Try to Discredit Dallaire,' *Rusty Idols*, 13 May 2008, http://rustyidols.blogspot. ca/2008/05/jason-kenney-uses-fake-downs-syndrome.html.
52 Debrix, 'The Hegemony of Tabloid Geopolitics," 8.
53 Coronil, cited in Silverblatt, *Modern Inquisitions*, 16.
54 Velshi and Anglin, "Who's Really Ignoring the Geneva Conventions?"
55 SDIR-EV, No. 16 (27 May 2008) at 3 (Howard Anglin).
56 Ibid., at 4 (Anglin).
57 Snyder, *Bloodlands*, 180.
58 SDIR-EV, No. 16 (27 May 2008) at 6 (Anglin).
59 Ibid. at 8 (Anglin). Translation: "[The] Law [may be] harsh, but [it is still the] law."
60 Ibid. at 5 (Anglin).
61 Ibid. at 15 (Kenney).
62 This contempt was infinitely more disturbing than the rare moments when Conservative ministers reminded the House that Omar had been video-taped making land mines (an image from the program Sixty Minutes), that his family was an al-Qaeda family, and that he was no "cherubic innocent" (Peter Kent, 12 March 2009, 1640). There was sustained discussion on Khadr only in March 2009, when the Standing Committee's report was retabled following the prime minister's proroguing of Parliament in the fall of 2008. NDP MP Wayne Marston reminded the House that "Canada appears to have been complicit in torture by proxy" according to the Supreme Court of Canada (12 March 2009, 1636.) The government remained

impervious to the child soldier argument, arguing that unlike the child
soldiers of Burundi, who had been recruited into the army because they
were desperately poor, Omar Khadr faced no such difficulty, and that he
had killed an American medic (12 March 2009, 1647). The Minister of External Affairs, when asked about Canada's obligations under international
law to children and to child soldiers, simply maintained that "children are
capable of horrendous acts that deserve prosecution in adult courts"
(p. 1640). As Opposition MPs point out (and as the government agrees),
this approach is nothing if not consistent with the government's response
to young offenders.

63 Optional Protocol to the Convention on the Rights of the Child on the
Involvement of Children in Armed Conflict, GA Res 54/263, UNGAOR,
54th Sess, *Treaty Series* 2173, No. 27531 (2000), 236.

64 Chikwanine has become a motivational speaker for the organization Me
to We, for which he makes the rounds of Canadian schools. Of course,
Chikwanine's and Khadr's cases are different. Chikwanine was abducted
without the knowledge of his family at age five, whereas Khadr was taken
to Afghanistan by his own family at twelve, and his father, Ahmed Khadr,
became notorious for his association with Bin Laden. Chikwanine killed
his friend, whereas Khadr was alleged to have killed an American soldier.
As Butler writes, not all deaths have been grievable. There is, too, an obvious geopolitical difference that is deeply significant: Chikwanine was rescued from Africa, whereas Khadr remains in an indistinct space between
Afghanistan and Canada, the country of his birth. Others have discussed
the difference between Khadr and Beah, speculating on why they have
been treated so differently. Jennifer Hyndman, for example, speculates that
it is felt "that Khadr, born in Toronto's 'global North' and with living parents at the time of the fighting – should have 'known better' than Beah, the
boy who lost his parents and then seemingly himself to civil war in Sierra
Leone" (251). I believe there is much more to Khadr's eviction from the
national (and from humanity) than meets the eye. The obvious asymmetries in his and Beach's stories do not account for our refusal to see Khadr
as a child soldier, given that he has never been understood to be securely
of the global North and that his family has never been understood to be a
normal family capable of protecting him. What seems so obvious warrants
close attention, especially given that these differences have enabled us to
condone torture. Butler, *Precarious Life*; Hyndman, "The Question of 'the
Political.'"

65 Winton, "Ismael Beah on Child Soldiers."

66 Jefferess, "Neither Seen nor Heard," 78.

67 Kielburger, "Omar Khadr." See also Kielburger, "Omar Khadr, Jean Chretien, and Me."
68 DiManno, "Wrong Killer Shown Mercy."
69 Steffler, "The Production and Use of the Globalized Child."
70 Walkom, "Tortured Logic on Security Threats."
71 Razack, "The Afghan Detainee Scandal."

5 Surveillance Effects: South Asian, Arab, and Afghan American Youth in the War on Terror

SUNAINA MAIRA

Introduction

The US-led War on Terror has been fought on battlefields in Iraq and killing fields in Afghanistan, in counter-terrorism operations in Pakistan and through drone warfare in Yemen, and it has been accompanied by a war at home. While dramatic military assaults overseas have increasingly been replaced by secret drone warfare *over there*, the counter-terrorism apparatus has shifted its focus to the "terrorists" and "terrorist sympathizers" (so-called terror symps) *here*. This domestic War on Terror is often invisible, for it is conducted covertly through a surveillance regime that targets, and also produces, gendered and racial bodies. The War on Terror also has a cultural front – a culture war in which Islam, gender, sexuality, and religion are central to debates about the meaning of national culture and Western secular democracy.

Muslim youth in the United States, in particular, are profiled as terrorists-in-the-making, as always susceptible to indoctrination by fundamentalist movements and recruitment by militant networks. The War on Terror is a technology of nation making that produces youth as subjects that must be preserved and protected, as well as monitored, contained, repressed, or removed, if necessary through violence.

The domestic War on Terror is conducted through undercover intelligence and policing operations that supposedly pre-empt terrorist attacks by "radicalized" Muslim youth in the United States. It involves surveilling and infiltrating targeted communities with the help of informants from those same communities. As a consequence of these tactics, the politics of resistance to this secret war have become more complex, more difficult, and more divisive. Furthermore, this internal war is one from which most American citizens and residents feel removed, even though it is happening in their midst and with their implicit or explicit consent. It is also a covert means of terrorizing specific populations. I want to emphasize that the backlash against Muslim and Arab Americans after 9/11 is not exceptional, but part of a longer history of state regulation and repression of groups defined as "enemy aliens" or "anti-American." Empire always works on two fronts – the domestic and the global; the "state of exception" in the War on Terror is constitutive of an imperial governmentality that rests on the exclusion of certain groups from citizenship at different historical moments.[1]

The politics of gender and sexuality infuse the culture wars. Orientalist imaginaries of enemy populations and (non-Western) "others" drive the politics of imperial feminism and homonationalism.[2] The notion of rescuing racialized "others," particularly women and queers, shapes a central political logic in the War on Terror, that of humanitarianism,[3] as I explore in the larger project on which this chapter is based. This concept disguises imperial interventions for neoliberal democracy through the language of human rights; it also regulates dissenting politics through the binary of "radical" and "moderate" Muslims, Arabs, Afghans, and Iranians. Radical Muslim or Middle Eastern youth – particularly males, who are presumably always prone to violence, but also females in some cases – must be contained by surveillance. For Muslim, Arab, South Asian, and Afghan American youth, each of these sites of the culture/class/racial wars – humanitarianism, homonationalism, and surveillance – is a site for the production and also the self-regulation of political subjecthood. Surveillance shapes the affective and strategic registers of political culture in the War on Terror – something that has not received sufficient scholarly attention.

This chapter is drawn from an ethnographic project that focuses on what it means for South Asian, Arab, and Afghan American youth to engage with the "political" at a moment when their politics are under constant scrutiny and often surveillance. I discuss how youth from targeted communities grapple with the knowledge that they are permanently under surveillance as a consequence of the state of permanent war, and how they reframe and resist that surveillance through tactics of counter-surveillance or "sousveillance." I examine the meaning of political subjecthood for young people targeted in the domestic War on Terror as well as the participation of youth in "counter-public" spheres. It has become increasingly difficult for young people who are objects of surveillance and profiling to constitute what might look like a "public" in the post-9/11 era, let alone a "counter-public." It is important to investigate how the surveillance state constitutes a nation's racial and gendered subjects and the American "way of life" in a time of permanent war.

The Study

This chapter is based on an ethnographic study that explored post-9/11 political mobilization and coalition building among university-age youth in northern California between 2007 and 2011. It is situated in Silicon Valley and Fremont/Hayward, where there are large concentrations of South Asian, Arab, and Afghan Americans and where a new generation of activists has increasingly engaged in antiwar and civil rights movements and progressive alliances.[4] The ethnography examines how young people are mobilizing around the notion of "rights" – civil, women's, gay, human – in response to technologies of racialized warfare and surveillance. At a time of political repression and moral panics about the "radicalization" of Muslim and Arab American youth, I explore these questions: What forms of politics are possible or permissible? And under a counter-terrorism regime, what does it mean to produce knowledge about communities that are the objects of hyper-surveillance and for whom political engagement, as defined by counter-terrorism regimes, is the threshold of who can be prosecuted, deported, incarcerated, or tortured? These are deeply fraught questions about the biopolitics of doing research when it can become a form of intelligence gathering, and when knowledge production itself can be terrorizing.

Silicon Valley is an interesting site for this research because it has an increasingly visible and organized Muslim American community, including Arab and South Asian immigrant families as well as Afghan refugees, in San Jose and its affluent suburbs as well as in the towns of Fremont and Hayward in the hinterland. These communities have established important Muslim institutions, such as the MCA (Muslim Community Association) mosque in Santa Clara, which draws a large and ethnically diverse (Sunni) Muslim population from the region, as well as a Shia mosque. There is a sizeable South Asian and Arab American community in the larger San Jose area and an Afghan American one in the Fremont/Hayward area (in fact, those two cities host the largest Afghan community outside Afghanistan); all are under-researched. The Arab American community is a diverse one that includes Egyptians,

Palestinians, Lebanese, Iraqis, and Yemenis, some of whom have lived in northern California for three generations. The South Asian community is largely comprised of Pakistani and Indian immigrants. South Asian and Arab Americans in this area tend to be upwardly mobile professionals, but there are also middle-class and some lower-middle-class families. The Afghan American community consists largely of refugees, who are less affluent. They came in two waves: the first after the Soviet invasion of Afghanistan in 1979, the second after the rise of the Taliban in the 1990s. The college-age youth whom I interviewed in Silicon Valley were generally the children of Arab, Indian, and Pakistani immigrants who had come to the United States in the 1960s and 1970s, most of them as graduate students or technical workers, or of Afghan refugees from Afghanistan or Pakistan. These middle- to upper-middle-class youth were students at private and public universities, including community colleges, and were engaged in politics both on and off campus, sometimes through organized groups (both faith-based and secular) as well as in informal ways.

South Asian, Afghan, and Arab American youth in this area grow up in racially and ethnically diverse communities and socialize and organize with other youth of colour, including Latinos, Asian Americans, and, to a lesser extent, African Americans. Young South Asian, Afghan, and Arab Americans attend the same high schools, and in some cases the same Islamic schools, so the politics of cross-ethnic coalition building are interesting to examine in a region where liberal multiculturalism is constantly invoked as a celebratory, and sometimes self-congratulatory, image. The intensified (re)codification of the racialization of Muslim-ness, and Arab-ness, has also generated new forms of solidarity. Coalitional categories such as Arab, Muslim, and South Asian (AMSA), Middle Eastern, Arab, Muslim, and South Asian (MASA), or Arab, Middle Eastern, Muslim, and South Asian (AMEMSA), and other unwieldy acronyms have been coined by activists to link communities that have all experienced intensified processes of disciplining, exclusion, and violence in the aftermath of 9/11. The contradictions between idealized narratives of liberal "tolerance" and self-reinvention in Silicon Valley and the realities of the conservative political culture in this hyper-capitalist region need to be situated in the history of the production of "Silicon Valley" as a space emblematic of technological "progress" and cultural heterogeneity. Furthermore, college campuses provide a particular context for activism, for they shape the alliances and movements with which these middle- and upper-middle-class youth engage as well as the forms of repression and disciplining they encounter in a climate of liberal multiculturalism.

Surveillance Effects

Technologies of regulating and repressing radical or "extremist" Muslim American youth and enemy subjects, within and outside the US, are used by the national and global security apparatus as part of an emerging and expanding culture of surveillance. While liberal/progressive critics have challenged post-9/11 surveillance in the War on Terror as repressive tactics of a new McCarthyism, I think it is important to consider the work of surveillance in reshaping political subjectivity as well as political mobilization. Surveillance has infused and sometimes transformed the everyday political culture of the post-9/11 national security state, as it has evolved since the Cold War and in the context of a "new Cold War," not to mention the many hot wars waged by the United States around the world, from Iraq to Afghanistan. Surveillance is fundamentally a technology of disciplining and managing racialized populations within neoliberal capitalism; it is a racialized mode of governmentality for the imperial state. As the national security state has developed since the 1950s, the "protracted afterlife of the Cold War" has shaped what Jodi Kim calls the Cold War as a "structure of feeling," and what I have described as "imperial feelings" or the affective dimensions of American empire as a way of life – sentiments variously of fear, anxiety, ambivalence, hatred, and desire.[5] I argue here that the culture of surveillance is related to the exceptionalist discourse of democracy and sovereignty, on the one hand, and to neoliberal governmentality, on the other, as well as to the resulting tensions that have emerged in the War on Terror between the police state's repression and notions of American "freedom." For those who experience the brunt of policing and the contradictions of "democracy" acutely in their daily lives, this tension is negotiated through sentiments of fear and anxiety but also through strategies of cooperating with, resisting, or renarrating surveillance.

Nearly all the young people I spoke to talked about the climate of surveillance and the chilling effect it had on the possibilities of dissent and on their understandings of what it means to be "political." These are what I describe as *surveillance effects*, by which I mean the social and cultural registers through which surveillance is negotiated in daily life.

In the post-9/11 state, surveillance often becomes normalized by those targeted in the War on Terror even as they or others resist it. Surveillance effects shape political culture and ideas of selfhood, producing objects and subjects of surveillance as well as self-surveillance, and are part of the bridge between the psychic and political affects of the War on Terror. Surveillance effects are related to the disciplinary technologies of "state effects": the state attempts to secure an image of itself as unitary, discrete, and all-powerful, despite contradictions to these "state effects" in everyday encounters with the state.[6] Technologies of control, containment, and regulation operate in the surveillance-security state in part through policies and representations of surveillance as "an all-encompassing, impenetrable, and infallible surveillance structure."[7] The effects of this surveillance, through knowledge of surveillance policies as well as of stories *about* surveillance, together produce the image of a powerful security state apparatus that is feared and thus repressive; yet surveillance regimes also produce the opposite effect – they provoke challenges to this apparatus. They also produce subjects who are aware that they are the potential targets of surveillance, because they fit a racial, religious, political or national profile, and so in some cases engage in self-surveillance or aid in the surveillance state of others – all the while hoping to exit this profiled category through disciplinary inclusion or through collusion with agents of surveillance.

For example, Laila, a young Pakistani American woman, had attended an Islamic school in Fremont that had received threats after 9/11. The teachers there were mostly Arabs and Afghans. She recalled that when students were discussing the war in Iraq, "the teacher yelled at us and said, 'Don't discuss it! Especially in school because it's not safe' ... Like, they really prevented us from discussing it. I don't know if this is true but we've made jokes that it's because our mosque was taped." In this case, the mere fear of surveillance, whether or not the school was actually surveilled or the mosque was infiltrated by FBI informants, produces the effect of repressing open discussion about the state's War on Terror and the military intervention in Iraq, regulating permissible political speech for Muslim American youth. But it must also be noted that the FBI has indeed targeted mosques and that in mosqued communities, this has heightened anxieties about political speech – indeed, any kind of speech. In 2012, an Associated Press investigation into the NYPD's surveillance program reported that "mosque crawlers" and undercover informants (referred to as "rakers," generally Muslim or Arab themselves) were being deployed to ferret out suspicious Muslim and Arab Americans, including students.[8] Azma, a Pakistani American who had attended protests in San Jose against the Israeli war on Gaza in 2008–9, said that her mother would talk to her on the way to school or back about critiques of the official narrative of 9/11: "My mom, actually when it [attacks of 9/11] first happened, she started researching online conspiracy theories ... And my dad got really angry at her because he told her that the FBI could be tracking your computer, so don't do that. And so she said that if you don't want me to do it at home, I'll do it at the library but he's, like, no, that's even worse!"

The fear of surveillance becomes internalized by those who are targeted so that it produces a regulatory apparatus through auto-censorship, without the need for direct state repression. Those who understand themselves to be the objects of this repressive regime are generally the ones to censor themselves, *also* an intended effect. Foucault's model of the panopticon is a system of surveillance which targets people in plain sight; it produces for surveilled bodies – or bodies that *may* be surveilled – the "principles of [their] own subjection" to technologies for managing and regulating them, without the need for physical coercion.[9] This then produces a blurring of the line between "who is watching and who is being watched," through diffuse mechanisms of control and the "affective resonance" of surveillance effects – fear, anxiety, vigilance, frustration, outrage, or bravado.[10] I would add here that fears of surveillance among those targeted in the War on Terror are well founded in the realities of surveillance practices, which resort to the Internet, undercover informants, and wiretapping. For example, it must be noted that electronic surveillance does, indeed, exist and has been authorized, including by Barack Obama, as evident in the (passing) controversy over the FISA act and electronic wiretapping, not to mention the Associated Press reports revealing the NYPD's surveillance of Muslim communities, including student groups, with the help of the CIA in New York and across the Northeast.[11] The NYPD "trawled daily through student websites run by Muslim student groups at Yale, the University of Pennsylvania, Rutgers and 13 other colleges in the Northeast. They talked with local authorities about professors in Buffalo and even sent an undercover agent on a whitewater rafting trip, where he recorded students' names and noted in police intelligence files how many times they prayed."[12] The point is that such surveillance stories *also help* do the work of surveillance in deepening these anxieties and producing self-regulation in those who are the objects of surveillance, by virtue of their race, religion, or nationality. So the student who worries that her e-mail is being surveilled or the immigrant father who fears that his wife is being monitored while she researches 9/11 on her computer or at the library cannot be dismissed as "paranoid," for this is an expression of the political subjecthood of life in a surveillance state, and of knowledge of the racialized technologies of panopticism.

Furthermore, "conspiracy theories," as Jodi Dean argues, can rupture this circuit of racialized surveillance and violence to the extent that they challenge the mythology of the liberal democratic state and suggest – however fictively or creatively – the possibility that national security is only a cover for the state's violence and strategic interests. This encourages publics to view secrecy as constitutive of the "warfare state."[13] Unofficial narratives about the "truth" of 9/11 suggest that truth is indeed often stranger than fiction, as are stories of surveillance. Conspiracy theories that go against the grain of official narratives, however, are evaluated through an ideological and racialized discourse, generally dismissed by the intellectual left and pinned onto "fringe" radicals and onto regions of the global South whose denizens presumably generate a profusion of wild accounts in repressive societies. Yet truth is indeed often hard to ascertain in the metropole, and power works in mysterious ways and generally always at the expense of ordinary lives. How then do cultures of surveillance, or cultures of conspiracy and secrecy, shape the politics and daily lives of those who are produced as objects of surveillance regimes?

My Friend "Joe" and Me

One way that political imaginaries, and imaginings of self, are shaped by surveillance effects is through normalization. It is striking, and troubling, to note the extent to which encounters with the FBI have become part of the everyday lives South Asian, Arab, and Afghan Americans since 9/11 and the degree to which knowledge of surveillance has become part of social life. FBI agents are now just another set of state officials whom Arab, South Asian, and Afghan Americans, and Muslim Americans more generally, must expect to encountering as part of a normalized routine. This ought to be considered highly "abnormal" in a liberal democratic state that claims to be a beacon of democracy and civil rights. Community activists I spoke to talked about FBI agents who regularly, and often overtly, attended Muslim American events and trolled the area's mosques. Some of these reports and anecdotes about surveillance were made by older members of the community and about other localities. The FBI's actions, as described to me, have only intensified the climate of permanent surveillance and deepened knowledge of the tactics and technologies of surveillance, especially among youth.

An example of one of several surveillance stories I heard was narrated by an Afghan woman, Zahida, who works as a realtor in Fremont and who was involved with Afghan relief programs in the Bay Area. She talked about her "friend Joe," an FBI agent who had been contacting Afghan Americans in the local community:

> He talks to everyone, people kept telling me, Joe called me, and I said, "Who's this Joe?" And he was going to the mosque, he was coming to every event and then he wanted to know about my charity. So I got his number and called him up and said, "What is this? Are you following me?" So we met and we talked and he said, "You are the most outspoken woman, so I wanted to talk to you." And one time, he came with his gun and I said, "I don't want you sitting here with a gun, you need to leave that behind!"

Zahida told me this story as we sipped tea in her living room in a Fremont apartment complex, while one of her young daughters watched TV and the other served me snacks. Neither daughter flinched or batted an eyelid while she laughingly recounted her surveillance by "Joe." She added, "He is Filipino, but I know his real name is not Joe! And now he's following the Somalis." Zahida was by turns witty and outraged while recounting stories of surveillance, of the Afghan community in Fremont/Hayward, and of the impact of the US occupation on Afghanistan.

Zahida narrated this story with emphasis on her boldness and lack of fear, which had registered with the intelligence agents, flipping the experience of questioning/questioned around by contacting the FBI agent herself. She explicitly challenged the production of objects of surveillance – Afghans, Iraqis, Iranians, Somalis – from communities linked to US overseas wars, occupations, and (proxy) interventions. If FBI agents (or increasingly, even law enforcement) can engage in pre-emptive surveillance, then the objects of that surveillance can try to pre-empt the encounter. The disciplining effects of surveillance regimes can be countered through attempts to take partial control of the process and its narration and through claiming the intimacy of surveillance effects as one's own ("my friend" the FBI agent). Yet this is *still* a process of normalization, of regulating one's political subjectivity in relation to the "superpanopticon's" regularization – not just disciplining – of populations through classification, data collection, and simulation.[14] For Foucault, "surveillance is permanent in its effects," but how exactly do these effects take shape in the post-9/11 moment of permanent surveillance for those who are constructed as the racialized and gendered objects of that surveillance?

In the face of increasing FBI scrutiny of Muslim Americans, and surveillance of Somalis, Afghans, Arabs, Pakistanis, and others in northern California, various campaigns have been launched to challenge panopticism and superpanopticism and its chilling regulatory effects on surveillable subjects. A Pakistani American professional, Farrukh Shah Khan, who founded the Pakistani American Cultural Center (PACC) in Silicon Valley, reflected on what it means to live with the panopticon or superpanopticon, through an allegory about the affective dimension of surveillance effects. I met Khan in the office where the PACC was first housed, a small, simple two-room suite in an office building in Milpitas. He reflected on how "scared" the Pakistani and Muslim American community was after 9/11 and on how they became "afraid to go to masjids," for they knew that mosques were being surveilled and infiltrated by FBI informants. This had the effect of transforming – in many cases undermining and shredding – social life and social networks. Khan said he began thinking about the film *The Matrix*, where the hero "escapes capture by 'the system'" with the help of "renegade, or 'good' people," and how the security apparatus after 9/11 was a "system trying to track connections with other Muslims":

> After 9/11, I was sitting in my cubicle and hearing a security guard walking outside, and I would think, they're coming to get me, and I have no one coming to help me. Others were also in this *Matrix*-type situation of targeting by the system … I would lie awake at night thinking, what if I'm … stopped by the FBI at the airport. I felt so cornered that I decided to fight back. Anything they said, don't do, I did! I went public, I started a TV show, I started a business. I felt if I was silent and I disappeared, no one would know. *The Matrix* image really stuck with me.

Khan here paints a moving picture of the anxiety and loneliness of Muslim Americans, sitting alone in their cubicles and feeling powerless in the face of surveillance regimes. He argues that there is no escape from the system except to stand in full view of the panopticon – that is, to engage in self-surveillance. Turning the spotlight on himself, inserting himself into the media by producing his own show, and organizing public events for the local Pakistani American community are tactics of counter-surveillance or sousveillance. Khan suggests that these tactics work on two levels: first, they create a network of support and solidarity if he were, one day, to be disappeared, having been surveilled all along; and second, he is recording himself before or at the same time as he assumes he is being recorded or surveilled by the state. Self-surveillance thus becomes a strategy for resisting surveillance and policing by resisting the disappearance of the object of surveillance.

This strategy has also been used by civil rights campaigns and by young people who are the objects of surveillance: they make surveillance itself the object. For example, the CLEAR (Creating Law Enforcement Accountability and Responsibility) Project, based at the City University of New York School of Law, offers legal representation and consultation to Muslims, Arabs, and South Asians targeted by national security and counter-terrorism authorities and who face searches by law enforcement, FBI requests for interviews, and border profiling while travelling overseas.[15] Ramzi Kassem, a civil and immigrant rights lawyer who supervises the project, observed that in some cases, clients from communities targeted by law enforcement videotape the FBI agents knocking on their doors and asking for interviews, recording and documenting acts of state surveillance. Other instances of counter-surveillance have dramatically highlighted the often Kafkaesque irony and painful absurdity of the reaches of the surveillance regime.

One of the most bizarre cases, this one from Silicon Valley in 2010, involved a twenty-year-old Egyptian American college student from Santa Clara, Yasser Afifi, who became the centre of a storm of controversy, and outrage, over the surveillance he was subjected to. While a student at Mission College in Silicon Valley, Afifi, whose father was a Muslim American community leader, took his car for an oil change at a local garage. To his surprise, he found a wire sticking out of the back of his car. The garage owner, Mazher Khan, pulled it out, and they found themselves looking at a device connected to a battery pack and transmitter that had been attached to the car's under chassis.[16] Afifi went home and showed the strange contraption to his friend, Khaled, who photographed it and posted the pictures online.[17] Khaled later remarked with wry humour: "My plan was to just put the device on another car or in a lake, but when you come home to two stoned-off-their-asses people who are hearing things in the device and convinced it's a bomb you just gotta be sure."[18] A reader quickly identified the device as an Orion Guardian ST820 tracking device. Afifi contemplated putting the device for sale online on Craigslist, but forty-eight hours later, the FBI came to his house and interrogated him, asking if he'd ever been to Yemen for "training."[19] They then demanded the device back: "It's federal property. It's an expensive piece, and we need it right now."[20] Video reports of this story that circulated online – some of them produced by white American youth – featured incredulous and shocked commentaries that this surveillance could be directed at a US citizen "just because he was half Egyptian." This underscored the racial, religious, and national dimensions of the production of citizens and subjects fit for surveillance.[21] Here, in the presumably postracial Obama era, liberal outrage over breaches of civil liberties had erupted, unsettling the rhetoric of colour blindness and multicultural democracy.

The Afifi incident came on the heels of a ruling by the 9th US Circuit Court of Appeal that it was legal for law enforcement to place tracking devices on cars without a warrant, even if the vehicle was in a private driveway.[22] The Fred Korematsu National Civil Rights Project at the Asian Law Caucus in San Francisco, which works with Arab, Muslim, and South Asian communities, has had clients who reported tracking devices under their cars. One case, involving a Yemeni immigrant man in the Bay Area, came to light just before the US proxy war in Yemen. I recount Afifi's case in some detail here not simply to illustrate the intrusion of surveillance technologies and new technologies of surveillance into the lives of Muslim and Arab American youth, demonstrating the intimacy of surveillance and its regularization, but because of the production of various affective responses. Afifi's case generated many news reports and videos: there was the tongue-in-cheek, Harold-and-Kumar-style bravado and sauciness of Afifi's friend, there was the outrage of white American youth that other young people could be racially profiled in the United States, and, finally, there was Afifi's calm but determined recounting of the story for media outlets during which he re-enacted the life of a surveilled subject. These are all surveillance effects, in a sense, and they mediate the production of selfhood at a time of permanent surveillance, where the self is constantly performed in public view.

Once Afifi realized that he had been tracked for several months, he filed a Freedom of Information (FOIA) request with the government to try to learn why, but the file provided to him revealed nothing. In 2011, the Council on American Islamic Relations (CAIR) filed a lawsuit against the FBI on Afifi's behalf. A video announcing the lawsuit, produced by CAIR-TV, featured several young civil rights lawyers and activists talking about the significance of the case. One of them is a well-known female lawyer, Zahra Billoo from the CAIR–Bay Area office, who remarked that the case was a fight for the civil rights not just of Muslim Americans but of all Americans.[23] In this video, Afifi looks confident but slightly more tense than in his earlier media appearances. He comments that he knows he must fit some sort of intelligence profile, given that he had sent money and made phone calls to Egypt, where he had traveled and where his younger brothers live.

In the larger project, I address more fully the contradictions of mobilizing against the War on Terror on the terrain of civil rights. Here I want to note that the language of liberal democracy is often invoked by those who are countering surveillance even as they acknowledge the ways in which profiling is a technology of global, imperial war. In some cases the professional, Muslim or Arab American civil rights activist may conform to the figure of the "moderate" Muslim who is "fit" for neoliberal democracy through a project of liberal reform. For example, Muslim and Middle Eastern American civil rights activists have been viewed as redeeming "American law and tradition" after 9/11 and as challenging the un-American and undemocratic excesses of the Bush administration. Surveillance effects, and their affective registers, reveal what is a stake here: the livelihood, and lives, of young people and their families, who could find themselves in danger if they fit "the profile"; the belief that surveillance must be resisted and can be through the law; and the counter-campaigns that test citizens' rights and civil rights on behalf of all Americans by confronting the national security/surveillance state.

A gendered politics is also at stake here, given the state's investment in policing and profiling Muslim and Arab males. The focus on the radicalization of young Muslim and Middle Eastern men in the homeland-based War on Terror means that expressions of bravado, anxiety, courage, and subversive humour are often filtered through a self-consciousness about what it means to embody the "terror threat" in the United States today. In the same vein, young Muslim American women lawyers working on civil rights perform a femininity that – perhaps sometimes self-consciously – challenges or responds to Orientalist notions of Muslim femininities, as some of these activists themselves observe. One way that youth who are in the bull's eye of the surveillance state respond to the perceived stigma of profiling or surveillance as suspect bodies is to turn their experience of surveillance into an achievement, a badge of honour rather than stigma. Jamil, an Indian Muslim American from San Jose, whose mother is Indian South African, recalled:

> It's definitely crazy at times, like okay, one crazy story – after 9/11, our house was bugged and there was a van outside of our house forever. They rigged the phone lines. Because my dad was involved with CAIR and the family was tied with CAIR because he's a Muslim leader or whatever. And I know a couple of other kids I hung out with, their parents were also really active, and they were like, "Yeah, we also heard it too" … So there's this weird van sitting in front of our house and … we could hear this weird clicking noise in the phone, like, we knew they were listening. After about a year or so they kind of … went away, I don't know why.

Jamil's narrative is important because it illustrates the attempt to find meaning in "crazy" times and the ever present possibility of surveillance at your doorstep. Even if electronic wiretapping today no longer always produces the proverbial "clicks" on the telephone line, reports have revealed that FBI agents have indeed been stationed in neighbourhoods with concentrations of Muslim Americans and that they have targeted community leaders.[24] It is crucial to read this empirical account not just as knowledge of technologies of surveillance but also as knowledge of the *intimacy* of the state's intrusions into everyday life. Those being surveilled may well be drawing on their past awareness of what it means to be surveilled. Surveillance effects involve attempts to understand and narrate surveillance by applying sedimented knowledge of stories that have circulated since the McCarthy era, films about repressive regimes, and personal experiences of surveillance in other countries. Jamil's story of intimacy with the surveillance state also illustrates an awareness of the experience of surveillability, an awareness that Muslim American community leaders – including his father, an activist in civil rights organizations such as CAIR – were indeed likely to be surveilled. This narrative might be read by some as post-9/11 paranoid hyperbole, but at a moment when young people were finding GPS devices on their cars, it is apparent that the stranger-than-fiction quality of life in the surveillance state demands meaning-making accounts, searches for explanations in the face of absurdist experiences of profiling and stories of surveillance.[25] Jamil went on to recall:

> Especially at MCA, when I drove down, on the right pole there was a huge beige box with three or four antennas, and they used to be listening into

> MCA through that box. My brother used to do rounds at security and he was like, "What is that box?" ... And apparently there was FBI listening across the street. It was actually a good thing because we got a lot of bomb threats, and so we had officers across the street. In a way they were kind of watching our back even though they were listening in on us! I wasn't there [at MCA] that day but my brother was and they had a bomb scare and had to evacuate the entire building. After 9/11, we got all the threatening phone calls and hate messages or whatever. I just heard they brought in the bomb squad. It was just crazy ... And it wasn't like a badge of shame, it was like, "Yeah, the FBI is listening into *my* house."

Jamil offers a doubly ironic twist on the state's logic of surveillance of Muslim Americans in the War on Terror. First, the FBI's presence, even if covert, might actually provide security in the face of the Islamophobic bomb threats directed at the MCA and other masjids in northern California and across the United States. This, of course, suggests that law enforcement officials would indeed spring into action and protect Muslim American communities. However, the lightness of Jamil's tone also suggests that this is an attempt to reframe and subvert the dominant discourse of counter-terrorism – to hint, with some humour, that it is Islamophobic and xenophobic racists who threaten security, not Muslim or Arab Americans.

The twist in his narrative expresses a subversive logic in which surveillance becomes not a "badge of shame" but a badge of honour, a sign of achievement. So, for Jamil, his family warrants surveillance because his father is a leader in the community, and other youth may also be objects of surveillance because their families are politically "active." Surveillability thus becomes an index of the political significance of the object of surveillance – an interesting example of the implications of surveillance effects for post-9/11 political culture and political subjecthood. This inversion of stigmatization is perhaps also an affective or psychic strategy for dealing with the anxiety of imagining oneself as an object of surveillance, by reclaiming the political agency of surveillance and to reassert the need to continue to engage in dissenting politics, despite and in some cases *because* of the climate of repression after 9/11. Notions of "moderate" and "extremist" Muslim American politics regulate acceptable political subjecthood – that is, which Muslim subjects are safe, acceptable, and assimilable.[26] But Jamil and others are renarrating their surveillability as "radical" political subjects, acknowledging the need for public politics but also normalizing the surveillance regime.

The young Arab, South Asian, and Afghan Americans I spoke to for this study were well aware of the direct *and* indirect impacts of surveillance on their own political organizing. For example, Aisha, a Palestinian American from Union City, which adjoins Fremont/Hayward, recalled the campus surveillance of student-labour organizing in which she had been involved: "Campus police were out with cameras when we were holding rallies and sit-ins. You wondered how much of it was going back to the administration? SOC [Students Organizing for Change] provided a space to assert ourselves politically but it also revealed repression." She astutely observed that awareness of repression that was in fact a key element in her politicization, and that oppositional movements reveal the repressiveness of the state, which in turn helps expose the repressiveness of liberal democracy. Alain Badiou argues that this exposure of repression is crucial for resistance to state power, which must be defined if it is to be resisted:

> Whenever there is a genuinely political event, the State reveals itself. It reveals its excess of power, its repressive dimension. But it also reveals a measure for this invisible excess. For it is essential to the normal functioning of the State that its power remains measureless, errant, unassignable. The political event puts an end to all this by assigning a visible measure to the excessive power of the State.[27]

This is a twist on Foucault's axiom about power and repression, for it suggests that the "genuinely political events" produced by the Palestine solidarity or antiwar movement interrupt state power by revealing the extent of its errancy and the depth of its repression.

While Badiou's argument is important when we consider the role of repression in "free" liberal democracy, Aisha and other youth also worried about the impact that exposing this repression would have on their lives and education, and about the impact of the invisible excesses of the surveillance state on their political organizing. For example, regarding the surveillance of campus protests, Aisha wondered:

> Was it going back to the FBI? We were getting arrested – would it limit our prospects for getting a job? I know petitions are part of the information age, which means you put signatures and also photos on the Web.

> We were part of the radical left but we were also trying to be part of the system, we wanted jobs for our economic livelihood. So we had to be strategic about how to assert our political views, we started signing petitions as organizations rather than as individuals. We were worried about going to graduate school.

This reflection speaks to the ways in which students worried about the implications of reprisals for their careers – a concern not to be taken lightly – and also about the implications of surveillance for their organizing strategies. Clearly, awareness of surveillance has shaped the political culture of student organizing in the post-9/11 era. There is a cautiousness in this generation, supposedly the pioneers of Facebook activism, when it comes to organizing through new media, which are vulnerable to electronic surveillance.[28] Abed, an Egyptian American, told me that his peers were well aware that their Internet postings could be taken out of context and used against them. The Internet is a double-edged sword that slices through debates about the potential and pitfalls of new media activism. Many Muslim, South Asian, and Arab American activists explicitly acknowledged, and often jokingly commented on, the possible surveillance of their e-mails, listservs, and Facebook pages, and some had begun resorting to face-to-face conversations when planning campaigns or discussing sensitive issues. One young Palestinian American woman who is a youth activist in the Bay Area said that she decided not to use a cellphone or Facebook for six months, because she strongly suspected that she was being surveilled. So in fact technology and social media have become sites of danger, of *excessive* knowledge production by and about young people who are targets in the War on Terror.

Yet in online discussions among community activists to which I was privy, I sensed that most activists of the Facebook generation simply took their surveillability for granted and that this was integral to their political subjecthood, not something to be denied, deflected, or deferred. For Jawad Rasul, a student in New York City who spoke publicly about this surveillance by the NYPD, the "experiences of being trailed by two different informants has changed how he acts in the day to day. To get ahead of those watching him, Rasul says he's tried to be as transparent as he can about his life. 'What I do is constantly update my facebook profile because someone told me that the anti-terror and other law enforcement agencies don't like surprises. So to keep the pressure off me I update everything on my wall with anything I am doing because I know they are most likely watching me.'"[29]

Social networking and social life have to be renarrated in the encounter with everyday surveillance. It is apparent that social selves are, in a sense, co-produced with the surveillance state. The Bangladeshi American artist Hasan Elahi has produced a digital installation that wryly and poignantly critiques this co-production of the self through surveillance. After he was detained in 2002 and learned he was on a terrorist watch list, he produced an installation that recorded all of his daily activities and whereabouts, titled "Hiding in Plain Sight." Commenting on this work of sousveillance, he noted that the visitors to his site included the CIA and the Pentagon: "So I'm looking at who's looking at me looking at me."[30]

Objects of surveillance have sometimes reported on agents of surveillance: in Irvine, California, members of the mosque told the FBI about an undercover nformant who had made provocative statements about jihad.[31] Youth and students from UC Irvine were also subject to surveillance – an issue that gained attention with the Irvine 11 case, in which eleven University of California students were prosecuted by the district attorney's office for protesting at a talk by the Israeli ambassador at UC Irvine after the massacre in Gaza in 2009. In the wake of this case, students began conducting silent protests nationwide at events related to Palestine in order to highlight the repression of critiques of US-backed Israeli state terror.

This has been a quick education in the methods of the surveillance state, which produces new repertoires of strategies and tactics – another important dimension of state power for oppositional movements to heed. The surveillance state and regimes of terror are globalized, and the United States and its allies are part of a global apparatus of surveillance, policing, and repression that is being resisted by transnational solidarity movements and youth networks, from Santa Clara to Cairo and from Fremont to Ramallah.

Conclusion

Technologies of surveillance attempt to regulate, control, and contain Muslim American subjects and Arab, South Asian, and Afghan American politics and youth activism, but they are also technologies that produce objects for surveillance: the terrorist, the activist, the "good" Muslim.[32] While American democracy presumably saves Muslims, Arabs, or Afghans from themselves, some believe that a new category of (Muslim or Arab American) activists is saving those excluded from American democracy, in the process saving liberal democracy itself.

Neoliberalism, democracy, and modernity are contested tropes in the civilizational clash of the War on Terror.

I argue that surveillance produces the language of democracy just as neoliberal democracy produces and requires surveillance. Civil rights becomes the terrain for staging a battle for democracy, which is viewed as the core of Western civilization; however, forms of civil disobedience that were acceptable for some in an earlier civil rights movement, and even celebrated in sanitized national mythologies, suddenly become unacceptable, even illegal, for certain movements that challenge overseas occupation and colonial regimes backed by the US state. These "uncivil" protests, such as those by Palestinian, Arab, and Muslim American students, are policed and criminalized by a surveillance apparatus that includes state agents and anti-Arab and/or anti-Muslim organizations, which invoke a discourse of civility, democracy, and modernity that is deeply racialized and gendered.

Furthermore, the politics of humanitarianism are increasingly paramount in late empire because they resolve the tension between the policing, global and domestic, of the security state and its self-image as a liberal democracy. That is, domestic surveillance and repression and US overseas interventions in the War on Terror are justified through the discourse of saving others for neoliberal democracy. These others, who must be rescued, regulated, and re-engineered to enter Western modernity, are racial others; a racialized logic of surveillance and containment fundamentally defines the post-9/11 culture wars, which are also racial and class wars.

Some resist surveillance and repression by calling for the rehabilitation of liberal democracy; others attempt to surveil technologies and agents of surveillance, turning their lens to the surveillance apparatus and the state itself. Counter-surveillance or sousveillance culture also, in some cases, generates a rethinking of political organizing, strategies, and frameworks, beyond the parameters prescribed by liberal democracy. Surveillance effects are complex, and there is much more work to be done here on the ways in which they are reshaping political subjectivity and strategies for different groups and movements. It is also apparent that surveillance relies on knowledge production by the state and the academy, which provides cultural and political expertise about populations and regions targeted in the War on Terror. So surveillance effects cannot be considered outside of scholarship. The question is this: Can we use our research and critique as a form of counter-surveillance?

NOTES

1 Agamben, *State of Exception*; Ganguly, *States of Exception*; Kaplan and Pease, *Cultures of United States Imperialism*.

2 See Puar, *Terrorist Assemblages*; Razack, *Casting Out*.

3 Williams, *The Divided World*.

4 Given Afghanistan's liminal location between South and Central/West Asia, it is often not included in South Asia, partly as a result of Cold War cartographies that continue to divide and partition regions in Asia. While Afghan American youth I spoke to generally consumed Indian popular culture, such as Bollywood, and often had family members who had lived as refugees in Pakistan (or had themselves done so), their identification with "South Asia" was at best ambivalent; some felt a connection with Indians or Pakistanis but also with Iranians. Also, Pakistani and Indian American youth did not always identify Afghans as South Asian, so I have not subsumed Afghan Americans in the category of "South Asian American." In the larger project, I dwell on the (re)suturing of Afghanistan to Pakistan/South Asia through the violently enforced label of "Af-Pak" in the US war and drone attacks on the border region, and also on the implications of viewing Arabs as West Asians.

5 Kim, *Ends of Empire*, 4; Maira, *Missing*; W. Williams, *Empire as a Way of Life*.

6 Mitchell, "Society, Economy, and the State Effect."

7 Puar, *Terrorist Assemblages*, 152.

8 See reports at "AP's Probe into NYPD Intelligence Operations," http://www.ap.org/Index/AP-In-The-News/NYPD (accessed 8 July 2012).

9 Cited in Puar, *Terrorist Assemblages*, 129.

10 Puar, *Terrorist Assemblages*, 129.

11 Hawley, "NYPD Monitored Muslim Students."

12 http://www.cbs3springfield.com/story/16970429/muslim-students-across-northeast-monitored-by-nypd.

13 J. Dean, *Democracy*.

14 Puar, *Terrorist Assemblages*, 115; Simon, "The Return of Panopiticism," 16.

15 http://www.law.cuny.edu/clinics/clinicalofferings/ImmigrantandRefugee/cunyclear.html

16 Zetter, "Caught Spying on Student."

17 http://www.msnbc.msn.com/id/3032619/ns/nightly_news/#43619156.

18 Zetter, "Caught Spying on Student."

19 "CA Man Finds FBI GPS Attached to His Car!", 16 October 2010. http://www.youtube.com/watch?v=6MwhMcfajDc.

20 Zetter, "Caught Spying on Student."

21 "FBI Caught Spying on Student," *The Daily Conversation*, accessed 15 November 2011 at http://www.youtube.com/watch?v=2pb1vf_i-VU.

22 In *United States v Jones*, the Supreme Court ruled in January 2012 that attaching a GPS device to a car without a warrant was a violation of the Fourth Amendment's protection against "unreasonable searches and seizures." The case, which involved the tracking of a narcotics dealer, simply restricted the use of GPS for surveillance by requiring a warrant. Barnes, "Supreme Court: Warrants Needed in GPS Tracking."

23 "Calif. Muslim Sues FBI," *YouTube*, http://www.youtube.com/watch?v=DgZsMsCdlHE.

24 Maira, "Deporting Radicals."

25 Žižek, *Welcome to the Desert of the Real*, 9–19.

26 Maira, "'Good' and 'Bad' Muslim Citizens."

27 Badiou, *Metapolitics*, 145.

28 For example, see the work of the Electronic Frontier Foundation on civil rights in a networked world and "surveillance self-defence."

29 Wessler, "Muslim Students Reeling."

30 "Looking at You Looking at Me: Surveillance Protest Art," Interview with Hana Baba, 4 April 2012 (originally appeared at KALWNews.org). Transcript accessed 8 July 2012 at http://blog.sfgate.com/kalw/2011/04/12/looking-at-you-looking-at-me-surveillance-protest-art.

31 Markon, "Tension Grows."

32 Maira, "'Good' and 'Bad' Muslim Citizens."

6 The Biopolitics of Christian Persecution

ANDREA SMITH

Islam is a religion in which God requires you to send your son to die for him. Christianity is a faith in which God sends his son to die for you.[1]

Evangelicals like to skip the cross and go right to the resurrection.

Soong Chan-Rah (evangelical scholar)

Why in this period of so-called liberal democracy are so many wars of genocide committed, yet these wars are *not* seen as contradicting democracy? While we often articulate racism as an aberration of democracy or as a result of scapegoating in times of social crisis, Foucault argues that racism is endemic and permanent in the modern state. He contends that the rise of the carceral system entailed a shift from punishment to normalization. This shift was effected through a policing of the body through the technology of the soul. That is, the person who failed to follow the norms of society became less a criminal and more a "deviant" who needed to undergo processes of normalization.

However, society simultaneously polices collective bodies and manages them as populations. In the service of life, others are allowed to die. "One might say that the ancient right to take life or let live was replaced by a power to foster life or disallow it to the point of death ... One had the right to kill those who represent a kind of biological danger to others."[2] Consequently, entire populations get marked as expendable because they are viewed as threats to the colonial world order: "Wars are no longer waged in the name of a sovereign who must be defended; they are waged on behalf of the existence of everyone; entire populations are mobilized for the purpose of wholesale slaughter in the name of life necessity; massacres have become vital. It is as managers of life and survival, of bodies and the race, that so many regimes have been able to wage so many wars, causing so many men to be killed."[3]

In a society based on normalization, racism marks certain people for death. Death need not mean direct physical extermination; it can include creating social conditions that mark communities of colour as suitable for death. Racial logics manifest themselves through population politics that essentially normalize racism. The "life" of society then requires the deaths of those populations that threaten it. "In a normalizing society, race or racism is the precondition that makes killing acceptable."[4]

As the above makes clear, evangelical Christianity has been shaped by a logic of biopower – the doctrine of substitutory atonement tells us that Jesus (or other populations put in his place) must die so that Christians can live. Rita Nakashima Brock and Rebecca Parker tell us that the cross in Christian theology coincides with Christian conquest and imperialism.[5] As Christianity embarked on the Crusades, its spread became increasingly tied to the deaths of others. The "life" of Christendom thrived through the extermination of Indigenous peoples, crusades against Muslim peoples, and the enslavement of Africans. While the rise of biopolitics is often linked to the rise of the modern biopolitical state, Brock and Parker suggest a different temporality – that biopolitics was central to the Christian conquest of the Americas. Thus, the resurrection of Christ symbolized the life of European Christianity at the expense of religious/racial others.

An ironic consequence of European Christian expansion has been that most of the world's Christians are now Third World people of colour. Biopolitics now structures not only the relationship between "saved" Christians and an "unsaved" world but also relationships *within* Christianity. Racial others who become incorporated into Christendom do not come down from the cross. In his analysis of Lamentations, Soong-Chan Rah notes that while evangelicalism is in some ways structured around the centrality of the cross, Jesus's suffering and death on the cross amount to only a brief "layover" on his journey towards his triumph, the resurrection. Building on Rah's analysis, it would seem that it is not that evangelicalism avoids the cross, but that it racially differentiates who gets the cross versus who gets the resurrection. This biopolitical relationship between peoples of colour and the cross has led William Jones to ask his famous question: "Is God a white racist?"[6]

Christian evangelicalism has always been involved in US imperialistic ventures around the world, yet it disavows this involvement by claiming to be championing "persecuted" Christians. Accordingly, no longer are Christians complicit in imperialism; rather, it is they who are most likely to suffer religious persecution. In this way, both in the United States and around the world, religion itself has become racialized. On the global stage, the notion that Christians are being persecuted aligns (white) American evangelical Christians with oppressed Third World Christians; this in turn allows white evangelicalism to evade its complicity in the oppression brought about by the spread of American capitalist exceptionalism. Theologically, the Christian persecution movement also aligns the fortunes of white evangelicalism with those of Third World Christians, whose sufferings and deaths strengthen and "purify" the faith. At the same time, however, this movement has sown seeds of its own destruction. By promoting the Christian persecution movement, many evangelical activists have found themselves compelled to engage with the broader international human rights movement. This engagement in turn has compelled many evangelicals to question some of the foundations of their organizing, including their investment in the American and Christian exceptionalism on which their movement is founded.

History of the Christian Persecution Movement

Allen Hertzke's *Freeing God's Children* documents the rise of the Christian persecution movement. He traces it back to the Russian Revolution in 1917, when missionary groups began to support Christians they felt were being persecuted by communists. One such organization was formed by Pastor Richard Wurmbrand, who spent four years in a Romanian prison for conducting an underground ministry. He left Romania in 1956 and founded Voice of the Martyrs.[7] Its goals were as follows:

1) Give Christian Bibles, literature and broadcasts in their own language in Communist countries and other restricted areas of the world.
2) Give relief to families of Christian martyrs.
3) Undertake projects of encouragement to help believers rebuild their lives where there is "Communist oppression."
4) Win to Christ those opposed to the gospel.
5) Inform the world about atrocities committed against Christians.[8]

Another prominent organization, Brother Andrew's Open Doors, was founded in 1955 to smuggle Christian materials into Eastern Europe and the Soviet Union. It now has offices in seventeen countries.[9] Open Doors USA organizes an International Day of Prayer for the persecuted church every 14 November.[10] It also sponsors Compass Direct News, which disseminates monthly reports on incidents of Christian persecution. These are routinely published in *Christianity Today*, a mainstream evangelical magazine, and *Charisma*, a charismatic Christian magazine. Other such groups include Christian Solidarity International, which engages in religious liberty advocacy and disaster relief,[11] and Christian Solidarity Worldwide (Baroness Caroline Cox), which focuses on Sudan, Burma, and Armenia.[12] A former human rights lawyer, Nina Shea[13] of Freedom House, has written *In the Lion's Den*, which documents human rights violations committed against Christians around the world. Paul Marshall, a political theorist and former Chair of Religious Studies at the University of Toronto, has documented the persecution of Christians in his book *Their Blood Cries Out*. These books have sold more than 100,000 copies and have helped generate interest in Christian persecution among evangelicals.[14] Nina Shea collaborated with Michael Horowitz (a Jewish advocate on the issue of Christian persecution) to organize a conference for Christian leaders on Christian persecution in 1996.[15]

As a result of the political pressure generated by these groups and individuals, in 1998 the US Congress passed the International Religious Freedom Act (IRFA). Horowitz drafted the first version of this bill in 1997; it called for denunciations and automatic sanctions.[16] It was criticized for making it too easy for victims of religious persecution to receive asylum.[17] The IRFA, which focused on diplomacy, was introduced to replace it. On 9 October 1998, the US Senate passed this second bill after removing its provision for mandatory economic sanctions; Republican supporters of free trade had argued that that provision would have harmed US business interests. The bill as passed provides the president with a broad menu of options, including public condemnation, withdrawal of aid, and various sanctions.[18] It has established the Commission on International Religious Freedom; appointed an ambassador-at-large, who works with the Democracy, Human Rights, and Labor Bureau but reports directly to the Secretary of State; and requires the commission to publish an annual report on religious freedom in 194 countries (the United States is not included on this list, although it has a long history of infringing on the religious freedom of Native peoples).[19] The bill was passed with bipartisan support, including from the Anti-Defamation League, Joseph Lieberman (the senior Democratic senator from Connecticut), the National Jewish Coalition,

Michael Horowitz of the Hudson Foundation, and *New York Times* columnist A.M. Rosenthal.[20]

In 1996, the US State Department Advisory Committee on Religious Freedom was formed, with representation from the National Association of Evangelicals (NAE) and the Southern Baptist Convention (SBC). The United States announced its first sanctions under this act in 2005, against Eritrea; they included the denial of export permits for defence articles and services.[21] In 2007, on the recommendation of Hillary Clinton, Don Argue, who had spearheaded the NAE's efforts in race reconciliation, was appointed to serve on the US Commission on International Religious Freedom.[22] While the IRFA was widely celebrated, evangelicals complained that it was "too ideologically diverse," for the commission included Muslim, Baha'i, Jewish, and Mormon representatives.[23] Today, many, including the editors at *Christianity Today*, complain that the IRFA has not been successful at either advocacy or reform. Countries are doing the minimum to meet its terms and are no longer being scrutinized.[24]

Whatever IRFA's actual shortcomings, the issue of Christian persecution has come to dominate evangelical thinking: *Christianity Today*, *Charisma*, and *World* (a politically right-wing evangelical magazine) feature articles on Christian persecution in almost every issue.[25] In 1996, *Christianity Today* listed the global persecution of Christians as the top religion story of the year; in 2000, the top story of the decade.[26]

The Logics of Christian Persecution – Christian and US Exceptionalism

The Christian persecution movement is premised on American and Christian exceptionalism. It holds that Christians are being systematically persecuted throughout the world simply because they are Christians. It is they, not people of colour, poor people, or Third World people, who have been targeted for "premature death." Richard Land of the Southern Baptist Convention notes: "Too often people in the West, peering through the selective prism of Christian history in the West, reflexively think of Christians as persecutors, rather than the persecuted."[27] The NAE's statement on religious persecution maintains that there are "reigns of terror now being plotted and waged against Christians."[28] Elizabeth Castelli notes that the myth of Christian martyrdom has a long history in Christianity. In *Martyrdom and Memory*, she contends that Christians have shaped their collective identity around martyrdom; they remember the history of early Christianity as marked by persecution and martyrdom even when the historical record suggests that persecution was not in fact prevalent. She argues that early Christian writers "did not simply *preserve* the story of persecution and martyrdom but, in fact, *created* it."[29] Historically accurate or not, this framing of early Christianity as martyrdom provides the lens through which evangelical Christians view themselves as persecuted today.[30] *Charisma* even maintains that persecution plays an important role in encouraging church growth among non-persecuted Christians: "In the West our blessings have let us be content without revival. If a man can live without revival, then he will be content without it. But when he is desperate for a touch from heaven, then God will bring brokenness – and he will no longer trust in the arm of the flesh."[31] In one of its publications, Open Doors contends that "Suffering Christians Can Help Your Church Grow" (2001). Voice of Martyrs says:

> Every day Christians in Bangladesh deal with the poverty that comes from the natural disasters and political hardships but endure even more than the average Bangladeshi: persecution by those opposed to the gospel. Materially, they have nothing. But spiritually, they have everything – Jesus Christ. And Christians in Bangladesh are doing more than dealing with, or surviving, the poverty and oppression. They are turning them into opportunities to witness of the eternal riches of Christ.[32]

Voice of the Martyrs literature follows the narrative of the persecuted Third World Christian who overcomes adversity to witness to God. Applying the logic of substitutionary atonement, the Third World Christian is brave on behalf of more privileged Christians, so that they do not have to be. The dynamics of biopower (which we will see again in terms of how Jews are situated in Christian Zionist narratives) are such that the Third World Christian must die so that First World Christians can live. This presumes that Third World Christianity is not "real" Christianity – otherwise, those Christians' deaths would be seen as killing Christianity rather than allowing it to thrive. The fate of persecuted Third World Christians is not seen as harming Christianity as a whole, for "real" Christianity is white Christianity, which benefits from this persecution. This logic of Christian persecution thus serves a purifying function for white evangelicalism. In *Faith Today*, for instance, persecution is used to critique liberalizing tendencies within the church.

Accordingly, persecution arises when stories of gay practices being sanctioned in Christian US churches reach overseas. "When Muslims hear about the liberal attitudes of North American Christians, it confirms their suspicion ... that all Christians are immoral."[33]

This logic bears a striking similarity to many colonialist narratives about Indigenous peoples that developed when the "New World" became the place where corrupted European society would be able to remake itself. As many historians have noted, the colonizers expected to find "Eden" in the Americas, "a place of simplicity, innocence, harmony, love, and happiness, where the climate is balmy and fruits of nature's bounty are found on the trees year round."[34] The uncorrupted "New World" and its innocent indigenes would offer an enfeebled European society the opportunity to reinvigorate itself. However, as Kirkpatrick Sale argues, the colonizers viewed this "paradise" through their colonial and patriarchal lens. Consequently, they approached the land and the Indigenous peoples they encountered on it as things to be used for their own purposes; the colonizers could not respect the integrity of either the land or its Indigenous peoples:

> The resulting tensions, then could be resolved ... only by being played out against ... the natural world and natural peoples ... The only way the people of Christian Europe ultimately could live with the reality of the Noble Savage in the Golden World was to transform it progressively in to the Savage Beast in the Hideous Wilderness.[35]

In this colonial imaginary, the Native represents an empty signifier that provides the means for Europeans to remake their corrupt civilization. And as Europeans remake themselves, Native peoples are rendered permanently infantile – or, as mostly commonly understood, as innocent savages. Genocide against Native people thus comes to be merely a stepping stone to Christian triumphalism. For instance, evangelical "historian" John Eidsmoe admits that Columbus converted the Natives by force, but he then asserts that "millions of people are in heaven today as a result."[36] Kay Brigham concedes that Columbus may have had "a dark [sic] side" in that he decimated the tribes he "discovered"; nevertheless, she "admire[s] his devotion and faith to God":[37] "I believe God raised up this man to extend the gospel to those religions that had never heard."[38] (For the record, Brigham also approves of the expulsion of Jews from Spain.) And David Neff of *Christianity Today* believes that Columbus "was motivated by a love for God" and so must be excused for his slaveholding, his rape of Indian women, and his role in attempted genocide.[39] And Pat Robertson contends:

> These tribes are ... in an arrested state of social development. They are not less valuable as human beings because of that, but they offer scant wisdom or learning or philosophical vision that can be instructive to a society that can feed the entire population of the earth in a single harvest and send spacecraft to the moon ... Except for our crimes, our wars and our frantic pace of life, what we have is superior to the ways of primitive peoples ... Which life do you think people would prefer: freedom in an enlightened Christian civilization or the suffering of subsistence living and superstition in a jungle? You choose.[40]

Similarly, narratives of Christian persecution often situate persecuted Third World Christians as empty signifiers who will reinvigorate (white) evangelicalism. These narratives often rest on the simplistic notion that "forces of darkness" are out to destroy Christianity simply because it is a beacon of light in a fallen world. As *Charisma*'s J. Lee Grady states: "Christians in other countries are displaying apostolic courage in the face of resistance. Risking jail, torture and martyrdom, they are proclaiming Christ, planting churches, and overthrowing demonic powers."[41] Carl Moeller of Open Doors USA contends that Christian persecution is the means by which God spreads His word: "At the same time, we shouldn't fear this in God's plan, because throughout history God has used persecution as a means of spreading his church throughout the world."[42] *World* combines persecution with a masculinist analysis: "We American Christians have become so prosperous, so successful, so optimistic that we have become spiritually soft and thus ineffective. The Chinese churchman sees that we could use the bitter medicine of persecution."[43]

To maintain this narrative, evangelical discourse often ignores the broader context in which "persecution" takes place – which is, that the conflict between Christians and other groups is often rooted in larger political, social, and economic forces, not simply religious intolerance. This narrative also minimizes the fact that other religious groups are persecuted along with Christians. And finally, it erases evangelicalism's complicity in supporting Western economic and political interests that may contribute to other countries not desiring an evangelical presence in their lands. Christians often face persecution, not as a special category of people, but as part of a broader policy of religious intolerance that affects other religions at least as much as Christianity. To acknowledge the persecution of other religions, however, would be to contradict the evangelical narrative that Christianity is being especially targeted for persecution by "demonic" forces because of its salvific power. Consequently, articles on Christian persecution often suggest misleadingly that *only* Christians are the victims of significant persecution and do not mention, or barely mention, other religious minorities that are also facing persecution.[44]

Also, by framing persecution as purely religious, evangelical discourse often ignores broader regional or political differences that provide its context.[45] For instance, *Christianity Today* has asserted that in Nigeria, "Muslim leaders are deliberately using fanatics in the name of Islam to engage in periodic attacks on Christians with the sole aim to intimidate, terrorize, and force Christians into submission and into renouncing their faith."[46] Similarly, *Charisma* asserts that Nigeria is leading a "Muslim-led holy war" against Christians.[47] Yet as evangelicals in Nigeria note, this persecution is often the result of conflicts that are mainly regional rather than religious, and the Nigerian state often violates the human rights of *everyone* in Nigeria, not just Christians.[48] Similarly, India, particularly when governed by right-wing Hindus, has often been often presented as persecuting only or primarily Christians.[49] According to these reports, the massacres in Gujarat mainly affected Christians, when in fact the principal targets of the Hindu right were Muslims.

This Christian exceptionalism depends in turn on US exceptionalism, which assumes that the United States should be the guarantor of religious liberty around the world. Evangelicals are not often called to account for their complicity in Western imperial interests that might spark anti-evangelical sentiment. When even the Institute on Religion and Democracy admits that the CIA is using missionaries as intelligence sources, Christian persecution becomes easier to comprehend.[50] For example, the CIA lied to the US Congress about a tragic incident in which Baptist missionary Veronica Bowers died along with her seven-month-old daughter. A Peruvian Air Force plane shot down the Bowers's plane after receiving a CIA tip that it could be carrying narcotics. The downed plane was owned by the Association of Baptists for World Evangelicalism. The ensuing scandal led to the suspension of the CIA-aided drug interdiction program, even though the CIA said that shooting down the plane had been an isolated error in an otherwise good program.[51] The NAE testified before the US Congress about "the need to keep pastors, missionaries and Christian workers free from recruitment by the

Central Intelligence Agency."[52] Yet when critics of the Christian right point to missionaries' complicity in US military interests, their criticism is dismissed as "scapegoating."[53] *Christianity Today* called it the "CIA Myth," adding that there was no basis to think the Summer Institute for Linguistics was ever involved in promoting US interests.[54]

Furthermore, the Christian right pays little attention to progressive Christians who are being persecuted by US-supported right-wing regimes;[55] it focuses instead on Muslim or communist groups and socialist or communist countries.[56] In one op-ed piece, Charles Colson and Pearcey discusses how the famous photograph of a nine-year-old South Vietnamese girl running down the street after being napalmed during a bomb attack made him question his support for the policies that supported her agony. Later, however, she became a Christian. While giving a talk at the Vietnam War Memorial, she said, "I thought I could not live, but God saved my life and gave me faith and hope." Colson concludes, "The world will always be full of wars and rumors of war, but Christ's resurrection brings peace – supernatural peace – to those who give their lives to him."[57] In a 2005 article, Nina Shea contended that the left did not want to address persecution in leftist countries.[58] As an example, she cited Hugo Chavez, the president of Venezuela, whom she described as persecuting Christians.[59] She called him a "terrorist supporting president" who needed to be combated by sending a million bibles to Venezuela.[60] His sins included expelling from his country the New Tribes Mission,[61] which he had called a "true imperialist infiltration that makes me ashamed."[62] He was accusing the NTM of working with the CIA, spying on his country, exploiting indigenous peoples, building luxurious compounds, and flying private aircraft in order to avoid customs. Pat Robertson had called for his assassination, claiming that Chavez was negotiating with Iran to procure nuclear material and that he had funded Osama Bin Laden after 9/11. The NTM disputed Chavez's charges but also criticized Robertson for providing cover for Chavez to continue the expulsion. Robertson's statements may well have lent credence to Chavez's accusation that his country was being targeted by right-wing evangelicals.[63] Chavez has since died. Another article does note that evangelicals in Venezuela supported Chavez and that Chavez was a Christian; even so, it concluded that under Chavez, "ensuing economic uncertainty, spiraling crime rates and political turmoil have driven Venezuelans to seek God as never before."[64] Since Christianity equals capitalism, Chavez must have been un-Christian by definition.

US exceptionalism is alive and well among those who believe that Christians around the world are being persecuted. For them, most of the world's problems are always another country's fault, even those that are the result of US policies.[65] Consequently, they support US allies but not US non-allies, regardless of their actual treatment of Christians. Voice of the Martyrs has over the years criticized the following countries: China, Iran, Pakistan, Indonesia, Sudan, the Comoro Islands, Equatorial Guinea, Nigeria, Somalia, Cuba, Cyprus, Nepal, Bhutan, Burma, Sri Lanka, Laos, North Korea, Vietnam, Afghanistan, Bangladesh, Brunei, Malaysia, the Maldives, Algeria, Egypt, Libya, Mauritania, Morocco, Sudan, Turkey, Tunisia, Iraq, Saudi Arabia, Kuwait, Oman, Qatar, Syria, Yemen, the United Arab Emirates, Azerbaijan, Tajikistan, Turkmenistan, Uzbekistan, and India. Add to these Tibet (annexed by China), Chechnya (part of Russia), and Chiapas (part of Mexico). According to Voice of the Martyrs, "radical Catholics" in Chiapas and Chechnya are persecuting Christians (the violence being perpetrated against Chechnyans and the indigenous peoples of Chiapas goes unremarked).[66] *Rutherford* accuses the Mexican government of persecuting Chiapans but adds that Indigenous peoples are being oppressed, not because they are Indigenous, but because they are Christian.[67] *World* accuses the Zapatistas of mindlessly massacring evangelicals.[68]

From the Christian right perspective, anti-Western equals anti-Christian. Or, as *World* puts it, US imperialist policies are "God's redemptive work" and those forces that oppose US imperialism, such as Cuba, are "Satan's response."[69] Kim Lawton echoes: "Whenever communism, Islam, or nationalism is struggling for dominance [i.e., any force that opposes Westernization or U.S. imperialism], there is a new surge of anti-Christian violence and repression."[70] Dean Curry goes so far as to argue that imperialism and colonialism have had *no* negative impact on Third World countries. Rather, Third World poverty is the result of "indigenous tyranny." In fact, had it not been for colonialism, Third World countries would be much worse off than they are today. He dismisses any complaints from the Third World as simply part of an "Anti-Western and socialistic" agenda.[71] But Curry does not answer this question: If colonialism is so benevolent, then why would anyone in the Third World want to embrace an "anti-Western and socialistic agenda?" This disavowal of Christian imperialism is particularly apparent in *World*'s analysis of Christianity versus Islam: "Christianity grew by the blood of its martyrs, but Islam grew by killing those who opposed it."[72] This history is obviously incomplete: the Crusades, the

Inquisition, and the genocide of Indigenous peoples certainly expanded Christendom. However, Marvin Olasky of *World* either disavows these actions or views them as aberrations.

Similarly, Olasky opines that the cause of poverty and other social ills in India is not "capitalism" but Hinduism. He contends that racism has virtually disappeared in the United States but continues unabated in India: "Why does such bigotry remain in India at a time when it is largely gone from the United States? One reason may be the difference between the biblical sense of equality and a common Hindu theology of inequality."[73] Similarly, analyses of Christian persecution in India conflate Dalits with Christians. That is, when Dalits face discrimination, it is because they are Christians facing religious discrimination, not because they are Dalits facing caste discrimination.[74] This appears to have undermined evangelistic efforts in India. *Christianity Today* reports that Indian Christians involved themselves in a mass Dalit rally to oppose the caste system. Overseas Christian mission organizations hyped this as an event where millions of Dalits would convert to Christianity; as a result, local groups in India accused the event of being a "Christian conspiracy."[75] In a more nuanced article, *Christianity Today* noted that anti-Christian sentiment is tied to a history of Western imperialism and criticized Indian Christians for not making common cause with Muslims: "'Please don't rape a nun, or murder a pastor, but please feel free to murder a Muslim.' The church is very naïve … The church cannot seek its own protection, but rather must pursue a just and free society."[76] It also noted that Christians make themselves vulnerable to persecution by displaying cultural insensitivity. Because of this, 50,000 Dalits converted to Buddhism instead.[77]

Similarly, articles on North Korea and other countries negatively affected by Western imperialism avoid any analysis of empire in their assessments of Christian persecution.[78] One article, for instance, contends that North Korea is kidnapping Japanese to teach spies their language, without any discussion of Japan's long history of colonization of Korea or its abduction of Korean women to serve as comfort women during the Second World War.[79] North Korea is so demonized that Franklin Graham's visit there was described as "partnering with the Devil … This isn't a misguided, misinformed regime that needs to be introduced to the salvation of Jesus Christ. This is a regime that is totally against Jesus Christ."[80]

Some articles note that evangelicals are also victimized by the Colombian army (Colombia a US ally), neglecting to add, however, that this victimization is aligned with US interests.[81] Or they insist that

"Marxist"[82] groups or "satanists"[83] are Colombia's only problem. Another article talks about FARC's interactions with Christian groups (FARC is a Colombian guerrilla movement), pointing out that it does not attack those who "genuinely serve the people without taking a political stance" or FARC's concern that churches "discourage their members from being involved in communal work."[84] Similarly, during President Fujimori's tenure in Peru, *Indian Life* complained that Maoist guerrillas were persecuting Incan Christians, conveniently forgetting the Peruvian government's repression of Indigenous peoples, which included sterilization campaigns. The brutal repression of Christian liberation theologians and their communities by US-backed regimes has been justified because they do not offer "genuine biblical teaching."[85] One article described how "Pablo" escaped assassination to serve God while working under Allende, but without attempting to explain why Allende was under attack (he was just "unpopular").[86]

The equating of anti-Western with anti-Christian contributes to a kind of foreign policy schizophrenia. Philip Yancey wrote an article on how Christians ministered to political prisoners in Chile. He asked, "Can the hope of the gospel survive those conditions?" Yet the article did not mention the Christian right's support of the Pinochet coup that led to these prisons being established. Nor did he acknowledge the role of the gospel in creating "those conditions."[87] And while many evangelical groups support immigration restrictions, they call for exceptions to be made for those who are persecuted for being Christian.[88] Ironically, at the height of the sanctuary movement, Christians defended themselves against prosecution by the US government by claiming that their actions were expressions of religious freedom. Yet the NAE rejected such claims when they were made by the religious left.[89]

Some writers argue that global instability is good because it opens people to hear the gospel.[90] Similarly, globalization and the forced migration it generates benefit missionary work because immigrants are more receptive to the gospel. "There are vastly more winnable people in the world now than ever before."[91] According to Donald McGavran, in *Charisma*, "immigrants represent the greatest missionary opportunity America has ever had."[92] Richard Pease talks about these migration patterns as providing great opportunities for Christians, for when people are uprooted from their countries and their traditions, when "they have lost everything," they are more likely to "come to faith in Christ." In other words, this forced dislocation is not a tragedy but a cause for celebration. He asks: "Is it possible that the sovereign Lord of history is at work in a special way in this situation?"[93] Raymond Bakke of International Urban Associates claims that "since God owns the whole world, he's bringing the whole world to the U.S. for a wonderful purpose – evangelism."[94] Some articles talk about exploiting global economic instability by providing "humanitarian" aid in conjunction with evangelistic efforts.[95] These destabilization trends are no longer viewed as caused by governmental and economic institutions (which are often supported by the Christian right); rather, God brings them about in order to create circumstances conducive to evangelism. From this perspective, the Indonesian tsunami of 2004 was an opportunity to advance mission work in Muslim communities.[96]

In these ways, the rhetoric of Christian persecution is linked tightly to Christian empire building. Because it is Christians who are "oppressed" and "persecuted," evangelists are justified in supporting genocidal policies in Latin America and elsewhere, as well as destructive economic policies and right-wing repressive regimes throughout the world – indeed, they are justified in supporting anything that makes the world "safe" for Christianity (right-wing Christianity, that is). The relationship between evangelicalism and US empire is clear when one notes how evangelicals often uphold a "civil gospel" that supports Christian America, but then trace Christian persecution to the fact that other religions, such as Islam and Hinduism, do not separate religion from the state.[97] Apparently, only Christianity can be legitimately tied to state power.

Evangelical Critiques of the Christian Persecution Movement

As the "global persecution" movement has developed, so have internal critiques of some of its presuppositions. Mark Galli of *Christianity Today* questions the romanticized notion that martyrdom strengthens and purifies the church, arguing that it sometimes contributes to the destruction of Christian presence in an area.[98] Jim Reapsome in *Evangelical Missions Quarterly* notes that "Western cultural imperialism – our movies, books, music, TV shows, fashions – is a horrendous obstacle for world evangelization."[99] Gustavo Parajon in *Christianity Today* challenges the anti-Sandinista efforts of the Christian right: "I find it very hard to understand how Christians in the U.S. who believe in the Almighty God ... would be so concerned about some supposed threat [i.e. the 'Communist' threat] that they would allow their tax dollars to support violence that devastates so many people, many of them believers."[100]

These alternative voices were few and far between in evangelical literature as the Christian persecution movement first gained popularity.

However, as that movement has developed, so have splits and tensions within it. These were evident in a debate published in *Christianity Today* between Michael Horowitz of the Hudson Institute's Project for International Liberty and Jeremy Gunn, Senior Fellow for Religion and Human Rights at Emory University. Horowitz's views represent the more simplistic analysis, which emphasizes punitive sanctions in efforts to destabilize countries seen as persecuting Christians. Horowitz tends to separate Christian persecution from its political and economic context: "The reality is this: the well-being of Christian communities in the developing world now increasingly signals and determines whether entire populations and cultures remain in the dark ages or enter a world of modernity [and] tolerance ... a particular contribution of Judeo-Christian culture-democracy."[101] He further argues that Christians are the "worst victims" because American elites have often been blind to the contributions that Christianity has made to Western art, music, and culture and to what it has meant to freedom, democracy, and economic growth.[102] He contends that State Department–centred diplomacy has largely failed, and he advocates a sanction-driven approach to addressing Christian persecution.[103]

Gunn, by contrast, argues that while it is important for the United States to intervene in cases of religious persecution, the United States is not in a position to hold itself as the guarantor of human rights globally. It cannot hold other countries accountable when it is not accountable for its own human rights violations:

We should candidly acknowledge that American governments have often supported regimes that have brutally suppressed a wide range of human rights, including religious freedom. The United States was one of the strongest supporters of many of the world's worst regimes after World War II, including those of Augusto Pinochet, Efrain Rios Montt, Ferdinand Marcos, the apartheid regime in South Africa, and others. Just as we wish others to recognize what they have done, we also must be willing to acknowledge what we have done. We will be more convincing and effective when we speak the truth about others' failings when we are known for speaking the truth about our own.[104]

Gunn further contends that the punitive approach is excessively narrow. Sometimes sanctions work and sometimes they do not. Particularly with increased anti-US sentiment, punitive sanctions may only increase persecution and resistance: "Americans sometimes believe that foreigners and their governments will naturally trust American criticism of their countries and believe that our motivations are good. Anyone who has traveled abroad and spoken to others will quickly learn that others do not see us as we see ourselves."[105] He also takes issue with the traditional framing that Christian persecution is the result of countries targeting people simply because they are Christian. In actuality, Christians are persecuted in countries where *all* human rights are suppressed. So to say, for example, that Uzbekistan – a country highlighted in the Christian persecution lists – persecutes Christians solely because they are Christian disregards that fact that Uzbekistan has also incarcerated thousands of Muslims. He concludes: "I also believe, however, that the United States will be most effective when it speaks clearly not only about religious persecution, but clearly, consistently, and accurately about all major human-rights abuses committed by friends and foes alike."[106]

One sees Gunn's more sophisticated analysis of Christian persecution reflected in some sectors of evangelicalism.[107] For instance, in a letter to the editor of *Christianity Today*, a writer working in Laos complains that

> a hard-line stance and threats/sanctions only evoke the response, "Go to hell." The people here have seen enough of poverty and hardship, and those in positions of authority are not the ones who suffer from sanctions. It is always the common man, usually quite far away from these issues, who will suffer. The response of Western Christendom should be very sensitive and careful, because it is the local people of the Way who will bear the fallout of militant and hardline reactions in the West.[108]

Some articles now note that while Christians may be persecuted in a country, the persecution may be the result of political factors other than a simple desire to stomp out Christianity.[109] *World* and *Christianity Today* have run articles contending that Vietnam is often targeted as engaging in religious persecution even though its policies are actually directed at political dissidents more generally.[110] The China Aid Association sent out a notice that it had supported Pastor Gong Shengliang, founder of the underground South China Church, after he was arrested in 2001 and sentenced to death for "organizing and utilizing a cult organization to undermine law enforcement, to intentionally cause bodily injury and to commit rape." The association at first assumed he was innocent, but then conducted an independent investigation and concluded he was guilty of sexually molesting women in his church.

Gong himself admitted to being guilty of some of the charges for which he was convicted.[111] An article in *Christianity Today* on the murder of SBC missionaries in Iraq noted that they were not attacked specifically for being Christians: "Another car full of Westerners would have met the same fate."[112] An article on Christian persecution in Turkey frames the issue in political rather than religious terms. That is, Christianity is associated with the interests of Western imperialism. This article goes on to say that this association applies to "evangelical and charismatic churches in particular because of their Western-style worship and close ties with (and often financial dependence on) U.S. and western European churches and missionaries."[113] However, the article stops short of validating the analysis that evangelicalism supports the interests of Western imperialism.

Another article in *Charisma* admits that colonialism has helped foster anti-Christian sentiment. It goes so far as to implicitly criticize the "War on Terror" as an imperial venture (which is surprising, since *Charisma* generally supported the war in Iraq). "Colonialism proved to be a great deterrent to the cause of Christian missions, even as the war on terrorism is proving to be today. The Christian message becomes blurred by association with Western politics and military objectives, raising a formidable psychological barrier for the Saudi Muslims to eventually want to consider who Jesus really is."[114]

Christianity Today reported that in Harare, Zimbabwe, three gunrunners posing as missionaries – John Dixon, Gary Blanchard, and Joseph Petty John of Indianapolis – were caught with a cache of sophisticated weapons.[115] It also reported that in Gambia, Davis and Fiona Fulton, who were sentenced to hard labour ostensibly because of their missionary work, were actually engaged in anti-government activities.[116]

In its newsletter, Open Doors ran an article that asked this question: "When do Christians deserve persecution?"[117] It noted that when conflict arises between Christians and other groups, Christians are not always blameless. According to Open Doors, real persecution happens "if opposition comes *after* Christians have tried every way to be friends."[118] Open Doors calls on its supporters to be sophisticated in their understanding of persecution: "Defining persecution is increasingly more complicated. It can be bound up in politics, sensationalized, or denied because it is not a welcome message. Regardless, we must learn to live with these complications so we can serve persecuted Christians."[119]

Mark Noll noted in his review of a book series, *Evangelical Christianity and Democracy in the Global South*, that "persecuted" evangelicals in the Third World often do not see themselves in political solidarity with American evangelicals because of US support for right-wing regimes. "To say that some group is 'evangelical' tells us almost nothing about its approach to politics."[120]

David Neff in *Christianity Today* argues that State Department reports "on human-rights violations have tended to minimize the seriousness of violations by America's historical allies and key trading partners."[121] Charles Taber notes in *Transformation* that "in exchange for relatively minor privileges, some Protestant bodies have given despotic governments fulsome praise and expressions of total support, and have become apologists for those governments among bodies related to them in the United States."[122] A powerful counter-example of evangelical discourse critiquing the notion that Christians are always victims is Jeanette Hardage's review of the video *Precarious Peace: God and Guatemala,* which documents the CIA-backed overthrow of a democratically elected government and the suppression (including massacres) of Indigenous people.[123] She notes that evangelicals either supported these massacres or refused to take a stand against them.[124] *Christianity Today* critiqued its own support for Efrain Ríos Montt's 1982 military coup in Guatemala that gained him the presidency. Noting that Luis Palau, Jerry Falwell, and Pat Robertson also supported him, *Christianity Today* now reflects that his rule was "probably the most violent period of the 36 year internal conflict, resulting in about 200,000 deaths of mostly unarmed indigenous civilians."[125] *Christianity Today* also ran an article criticizing the evangelical support in the 1990s for Peru's dictator, Alberto Fujimori.[126] *World* pointed out that under Fujimori, Christians were facing persecution after being falsely accused of membership of a guerrilla group, the Shining Path.[127] It also noted that the genocide in Rwanda had taken place in a largely Christian country.[128] *Christianity Today* reported that the Orthodox Church in Ethiopia was calling the British to account for plundering hundreds of sacred items in 1868 and was demanding the return of a four-hundred-year-old *tabor,* a sacred replica of the Ark of the Covenant. The replica was returned, and it was hoped this would lead to the return of other sacred objects (many of which are not even on display), over the objections of the British Museum.[129] And an article in *Christianity Today* noted that evangelicals had been instrumental in bringing leftist President Luiz Inácio Lula da Silva to power in Brazil as well as supporting left-wing movements in El Salvador.[130]

Christianity Today has published several articles calling on Christians to recognize and organize around the persecution of *all* religious minorities. An article on persecution in Pakistan asserted that "it is also important to convey concern not just for Christians, but for all religious minorities, as well as advocate human rights for Muslims. Diffusing the perception of evangelicals as just another narrow special interest group helps to disarm anti-West, anti-Christian bias."[131] *Christianity Today* has also published several articles and debates highlighting the need for a more sophisticated approach to addressing religious persecution.[132] One such article was by Robert Seiple, who served as ambassador-at-large for the Commission on International Religious Freedom. He called for Christians to address the persecution of *all* religious minorities, not just Christians. He contended that evangelicals must look at religious freedom in a larger context of illiteracy, poverty, and border wars. He then criticized the United States for not including itself in a report on religious freedom and for arrogantly attempting to impose five-year plans on other countries to eliminate religious persecution. He concluded that the United States needed to take a comprehensive approach to religious freedom in the context of human rights as a whole.[133] Garry Haugen of the International Justice Mission says that evangelicals must "address the suffering of the poor that comes from violence – the epidemics of slavery, police abuse, sexual violence, land seizures, illegal detention, and other forms of violent abuse and oppression."[134]

Evangelicals are sometimes critical of US policies when it appears to them that the United States is ignoring Christian persecution in countries where it has vested political interests.[135] Examples of this include the US alliance with Saudi Arabia, marked as a great persecutor of Christians,[136] and US reluctance to sanction Sudan, which has large oil reserves.[137] In addition, free-trade Republicans opposed the IRFA, with Republican senators Rod Grams of Minnesota and Chuck Hagel of Nebraska blocking a vote on the Nickles bill (which addressed religious persecution).[138] Some sectors of the Christian persecution movement have no problem with these compromises: "If politics is the art of compromise, international relations is the art of getting along with thugs ... Our prophetic calling – to seek real liberty for the oppressed – is sometimes best advanced by dealing with unsavory oppressive states ... And when this chapter of the war on terrorism is over, we should strongly lobby our government to make another repressive state tomorrow's target in the fight for liberty and justice for all."[139]

Interestingly, many on the Christian right favour a US-centric foreign policy and argue that the United States should not be involved in the UN. Yet the rhetoric of "persecuted Christians" is often couched in language that is rooted in the UN's human rights standards.[140] This rhetoric has sometimes contributed to Christians having to recognize international legal standards beyond those of the United States, even as some Christians worry that those standards represent a threat to US sovereignty. In addition, human rights rhetoric has brought some sectors into contact with other human rights advocates who are not Christian-centred. This dialogue has encouraged Christians to think about human rights on a broader scale. *Christianity Today* has opined that Christians need to show concern for all who are persecuted, whatever their faith.[141] "Care should extend to aiding persecuted Jews and Muslims, Hindus and animists, not just our own Christian brothers and sisters."[142]

As an example, evangelical Christians were involved in a campaign to stop the persecution of Sudanese Christians.[143] A Voice of the Martyrs ad in *Christianity Today* (12 June 2000) showed a photograph of a young Sudanese boy, with this text: "They killed his entire family. They threw him on a burning fire, and they left him to die. Why would a young boy be subjected to such cruelty? ... He is a Christian." Yet when the focus shifted to ethnic cleansing in Darfur, where most of the victims were Muslims, evangelical groups did not respond, because this narrative did not easily play into the narrative of Muslims persecuting Christians. Wilfred Mlay of World Vision complained that while evangelicals were focusing on tensions in southern Sudan, which is primarily Christian, almost no Christian groups were providing relief in Darfur.[144] Articles on Darfur often framed the conflict in terms of Christian persecution, even though those being attacked were Muslim.[145] Eventually, though, the NAE, the International Pentecostal Holiness Church, and the Assemblies of God signed a letter to President Bush on 1 August 2004 in which they called for action against the genocide in Darfur. "We view this as an opportunity to reach out to Muslims in the name of Jesus," stated NAE president Ted Haggard.[146] Articles in the evangelical press on Darfur finally began to acknowledge that Muslims, rather than Christians, were under attack.[147] Yet this crisis is still often (although not always) framed as an example of the evils of Arab governments.[148] For example, *World's* analysis put it that "the Khartoum regime's motive in Darfur soon became clear. Its leaders are not only Islamists but Arabists, who believe blacks – even Muslims – are 'slaves.' Witnesses say it is why Arabs rape women; to impregnate them and so water down the African races."[149]

Persecuted Christians and the "War on Terror"

Interestingly, the rhetoric of "persecuted Christians" translated into complicated positions on George W. Bush's "War on Terror." According to some in this area of activism, "there are times when you see such evil and such terror that there's no nice and easy way of finding solutions."[150] But at the same time, evangelical missions often see global unrest as an opportunity for mission work because missions can provide food, hospital care, and other needs to people in war zones. Thus, Voice of the Martyrs said in one of its pamphlets: "With the recent war in Iraq, a tremendous opportunity exists. No one knows for sure how the new government will take shape and how much 'freedom' Christians will have to be a witness. But we do know that the current upheaval has opened a tremendous door of opportunity."[151] Countries are more likely to accept Christian missions under these conditions, and this provides more opportunity to share the gospel. Some missionaries are now saying that the Muslim world has become more responsive to the gospel since 9/11 as a result of the War on Terror.[152]

But for others, US militarism places Christians in greater danger of persecution. Before 9/11, *Christianity Today* ran articles strongly criticizing US sanctions for their devastating impact on Iraqi Christians, particularly children.[153] It contended that "when broadly and harshly imposed, sanctions are 'weapons of mass destruction.'"[154] Ajith Fernando of Youth for Christ in Sri Lanka examined the impact of Western militarism on evangelists' efforts in the Third World after the Gulf War: "The bombings of Iraq and Yugoslavia remind many here of the attempts of Western nations to dominate poorer nations during the colonial era. Our concerted efforts to get people to separate Western political powers from the Christian enterprise do not have much success ... Christians are associated with the West and with colonialism."[155] Some of the biggest critics of the war in Iraq were foreign missionaries, who contended that Hussein generally allowed Christians to practise their faith in relative peace and that instability in the country might contribute to a backlash against Christians. Their predictions proved to be correct.[156] *Christianity Today* also contended that Christians in the Middle East are often safer under autocracies, which generally protect Christians and intervene if radical Islamists start persecuting them.

Moreover, in a democracy, countries may elect Islamist regimes that make things worse. Iraqi Christians are more vulnerable to political and criminal violence now that Hussein has been deposed.[157] They are accused of holding Western values even though "many Arab Christians oppose U.S. intervention in Iraq as well as the East's decadent values."[158] One Christian was forced to leave Iraq because "although I aided my Muslim colleagues, they identified me as a crusader because of the American presence."[159]

Missionaries often find that aggressive anti-Arab US foreign policies make their work more difficult.[160] For instance, Sat-7, a Christian satellite TV service, is broadcasting shows in Arabic and will soon be on the Internet. Its shows do Christian witnessing but are not openly critical of Islam. They also do not make political statements or say anything to embarrass governments. Sat-7 argues that the aggressive evangelism popular in Western countries is counterproductive in non-Western countries.[161] This strategy runs counter to the more virulently anti-Arab and anti-Muslim rhetoric of evangelical leaders who are not engaged in mission work.[162] Another article noted that there is increased persecution because "the current U.S. involvement in Iraq is adding to the anti-Western and anti-Christian sentiments."[163] Nearly one hundred retired SBC missionaries signed a plea in June 2003 asking Christian leaders to refrain from making inflammatory public statements about Muslims. They said it was harming missionary work to Muslim lands.

Fuller Seminary has received a $1 million grant from the US Department of Justice for a project to calm relations between Christians and Muslims. It proposes a code of ethics that rejects offensive statements about other faiths; affirms a mutual belief in one God; and pledges not to proselytize. Some evangelical leaders say this goes against the grain of the church's mission to evangelize the world.[164] An article in *Charisma* about Brother Andrew, an evangelical who smuggles Bibles into "closed" countries, says that "he doesn't think it's smart to fight fire with fire ... The more you fight [radical Muslims] militarily, the more they will fight. Almost all the actions the West takes are creating more fundamentalists and terrorists ... Bibles are better than bombs."[165] Similarly, Philip Yancey has asserted that "most of the Westerners who come here [to the Middle East] represent something other than Jesus. Some bring in military equipment. Some come to exploit the resources and invest their dollars. But you have a different calling: to make known the spirit of Jesus and to join the stream of liberation that broke free, 2000 years ago."[166]

Unsettling Christian Persecution

Evangelicals are engaged in strategic alliances with others to promote the Christian persecution movement. Ironically, this has destabilized the Christian and US exceptionalism that is the very foundation of that movement. *Christianity Today* ran an op-ed that resorted to persecution rhetoric when complaining about how evangelicals claim to be oppressed in the United States: "How soft we in the West have become. How could we possibly tell a fellow Christian hanging from a cross in Sudan that the American Civil Liberties Union is 'persecuting' us? How would the story of our church's zoning woes sound to a Christian sister in Pakistan who has been raped and forcibly married to a Muslim neighbor?"[167] The rhetoric of the global persecution movement rests on the assumption that evangelical faith itself is a marker of oppression, yet this article's engagement with global persecution undermines that assumption as it applies to white evangelicals in the United States (who often claim themselves to be victims of religious discrimination).

As these assumptions come to be questioned, so too does the efficacy of Christian persecution. *Christianity Today* ran an article criticizing how Christian persecution was being glamorized as a means to revitalize the Western church. In that article, Philip Jenkins contended that persecution was not just a "seed of the church"; actually, it could kill the church. For instance, Christianity would probably die in Iraq within the next generation. Implicitly employing Mbembe's necropolitics, this analysis turns our attention to the deaths that are the foundation of Christian life. According to the article, the deaths of Christians are just that – deaths.[168] Churches in South Korea were strongly criticized for sending missionaries to Afghanistan in 2007, who were then kidnapped. These churches' actions were not heralded, nor were they framed as signs of Christian persecution; instead, these churches were accused of being "self-centred" for not considering social and political issues.[169] Critics of the necropolitics embedded in Christian persecution requiring Third World Christians to die so that white Christianity can live suggest that the fate of Third World Christianity should not be separated from the fate of Christianity as a whole. When Third World Christianity dies, Christianity as a whole also dies. These critics question the racialization of religion that is embedded in the Christian persecution movement, which would sacrifice some Christians for the benefit of others.

Some evangelicals have gone so far as to call for a complete disengagement with this movement. In *Evangelical Missions Quarterly* (from the Billy Graham Center), one missionary argued that "I see no biblical precedent for using political means to fight persecution on others' behalf."[170] He contended that as long as the church is faithful, believers will be persecuted. This fact should be addressed through prayer and should not blur distinctions between the church and any government. Again we see emerging the contradictions between seeking state power that favours select populations and desiring to share the gospel with all peoples. On the one hand, evangelicalism's relationship with state power is what enables it to spread its message so forcefully. On the other, missionaries who want to share the gospel find that evangelical complicity in US imperialism dampens their ability to gain a receptive audience. These experiences then create a space for evangelicals to hear the other side of "Christian persecution." Ironically, many evangelicals have found that the best way to protect Third World Christians who face persecution is to challenge the US and Christian exceptionalist assumptions behind the Christian persecution movement itself.

NOTES

 1 McAdam, *Lessons from 9/11*, 418.
 2 Foucault, *History of Sexuality*, 138.
 3 Foucault, *History of Sexuality*, 137.
 4 Foucault, *"Society Must Be Defended,"* 256.
 5 Brock and Parker, *Saving Paradise*.
 6 Jones, *Is God a White Racist?*
 7 Voice of the Martyrs, *Faces of Persecution*.
 8 Voice of the Martyrs, *Faces of Persecution*.
 9 Hertzke, *Freeing God's Children*, 111.
10 Guthrie, "Q & A."
11 Hertzke, *Freeing God's Children*, 111.
12 Hertzke, *Freeing God's Children*, 113–14.
13 Shea contends that she was a liberal democrat until she started documenting so-called human rights violations committed by the Sandinistas in Nicaragua. Hertzke notes that many of these reports are dubious and even completely incorrect and that Human Rights Watch condemned Shea's reports as being politically suspicious as she was married at the time to Adam Meyerson, editor and later vice president of the very conservative Heritage Foundation. Hertzke, *Freeing God's Children*, 121.
14 Hertzke, *Freeing God's Children*, 120–6

15 Hertzke, *Freeing God's Children*, 125.

16 Carnes, *Religious Persecution Bill.*

17 Cagney, "Senators Champion Rival Bill."

18 Gardner, "Congress Approves."

19 Seiple, "Religious Liberty."

20 Aikman, "Persecutors, Beware." This Jewish support is noted by *Charisma* which frequently stresses that since Jewish individuals and organizations are supporting persecuted Christians, Christians should thus support the state of Israel. This will be discussed more in the next chapter.

21 Strichers, "Better Late than Never."

22 He eventually left to become president of Northwest University. Newsbriefs, *Charisma* 32; Passages, *Christianity Today.*

23 *Christianity Today*, "Persecution Panel Appointed."

24 *Christianity Today*, "See No Evil."

25 In addition to articles cited throughout this book, see also the following: Abraham, "Remember the Persecuted"; Abraham, "Uncovering Deeds"; Aikman, "Religious Freedom Matters"; Belz, "Count Your Blessings"; Belz, "Taking on the Thugs"; Carnes, "The Torture Victim Next Door"; *Christianity Today*, "Faith Perfected"; Donnally, "Actor Dean Jones"; Guthrie, "Kidnapped Missionaries"; Hulsman, "Bad Cops"; King, "Global March for Jesis"; Lombardo, "Christians in Sri Lanka"; Meral, "Bearing the Silence"; Newman, "Egyptian Christian"; Price, "Just Call Her Saint Caroline"; "Rearing Its Ugly Head," *World*; Religious News Service, "Three Killed"; Singh, "Radicals Attack"; Singh, "Anti-Conversion Conspiracy"; Stamp, "The Church Braves"; Taylor, "Under Suspicion"; 2000; and Wolf, "Inexcusable Silence." See also the bibliographical items listed under "Persecution Watch." Despite this prevalence, those in the movement complain that Christians are apathetic to this issue; see Cagney, "Evangelicals Warned."

26 *Christianity Today*, "Top Religion Stories of 1996"; *Christianity Today*, "Top Ten Religion Stories of the Decade."

27 Steinfeld, "Evangelicals Lobby."

28 Freedom House, *In the Lion's Den*, 11.

29 Castelli, *Martyrdom and Memory*, 25.

30 Castelli, *Martyrdom and Memory.*

31 Turner, "Why Isn't the American Church Growing?", 59.

32 Nettleton, "Having Nothing," 3.

33 Fieguth, "Persecuted," 20.

34 Stannard, *American Holocaust*, 166.

35 Sale, *The Conquest of Paradise*, 203.

36 Eidsmoe, *Columbus and Cortez*, 140. This sentiment is implicit in Janette Oke's 1996 novel *Drums of Change.* In this novel, a young Blackfoot woman, Running Fawn, is finally "saved" by those good Christian missionaries who were responsible for the near destruction of her tribe.

37 Brigham, *The Columbus Nobody Knows*, 27. She is quick to falsely assert, however, that these tribes were cannibalistic.

38 Brigham, *The Columbus Nobody Knows*, 28.

39 Neff, "The Politics of Remembering," 29.

40 Robertson, *The Turning Tide.*

41 Grady, "Invading the Darkness."

42 Guthrie, "Q & A."

43 Veith, "Praying for Persecution."

44 Christian Coalition, "Action Alert"; Flinchbaugh, "Pakistani Christians"; P. Johnson, "How One Woman."

45 Doyle, "Faces of Persecution"; Ecumenical News International and Religious News Service, "Will Shari'a Law"; Minchakpu, "Moving Toward War?"; Minchakpu, "Orphaned and Widowed"; Minchakpu, "Chroonic Violence"; Minchakpu, "Back to the Basics"; Minchakpu, "Religious Riots"; News Service Briefs, *Charisma* (June 2002); "Persecution Watch," *Charisma* (April 2004); Singh, "Harassed Kashmir Christians." By contrast, some *Christianity Today* articles on Nigeria have contended that framing conflict on religious grounds ignores the larger context of political and ethnic strife in the area. See Chambers, "Can Christianity and Islam Coexist"; *Christianity Today*, "Cartoon Chaos"; and Keene, "Mutual Mayhem." For a similar treatment of anti-Hmong repression being equated with anti-Christian repression in Vietnam, see Littleton, "Hmong Believers."

46 Minchakpu, "Eye for an Eye for an Eye."

47 Mundy, "Muslim–Christian Conflict."

48 Gbonigi, "Christians Facing Muslin Authorities"; Kure and Idowu-Fearon, "Evangelism among Muslims."

49 Abraham, "Deparation"; Abraham, "Crisis Averted"; Fischer, "The Fiery Rise"; Newton, "Fending Off Hindutva"; Newton, "She Chose to Forgive"; Religious News Service, "Priest Killed"; Singh, "Christians Scorn"; Singh, "Militant Hindus"; Singh, "Relief Abuses Rampant"; Singh, "Power in Punjab"; Singh, "Shock and Awesome"; Singh "Hindu Radical Redux." Some exceptions that did highlight the fact that it was Muslims under attack in Gujarat include Ankara, "Hindus Continue"; *Christianity Today*, "Hindu Radical"; David, "Critics Assail"; Sellers, "Hounded."

50 "CIA and Missionairies," *Faith and Freedom.*

51 Vincent, "Shoot First."

52 "Safety of Christian Workers Cannot Be Compromised," *NAE Leadership Alert.*

53 Freedom House, *In the Lion's Den*, 43.

54 Alford, "The CIA Myth," 58.

55 Belz, "Micromanaging Micronesia." One book review does make a brief (one sentence) mention that Christians are sometimes persecuted by other Christians, such as in Latin America; see Knippers, "A Global Scandal." Another article critiques Zambia for declaring itself a "Christian" nation despite its political and economic problems and widespread corruption. Of course, it may be that anti-black racism in this discourse precludes evangelicalism from seeing African countries as Christian; see Ecumenical News International, "'Christian Nation.'" For instance, a *Christianity Today* article focuses on the Congo, describing it as primarily Christian, but then the title of the article is "Heart of Darkness"; see Phiri, "Hope in the Heart of Darkness."

56 Bjelajack, "Evangelical Churches"; "Hall of Shame," *World*; Carnes, "China's New Legal Eagles"; "Tomorrow," *Link*; Flinchbaugh, "Pastor Champions Plight"; "Persecution Watch," *Charisma* 32; Lane, "Walking with Christ"; Voice of the Martyrs, "No Time to Lose"; Cleary, "Over the Wall"; Sellers, "Crushing House Churches"; Compass Direct, "House-Church Christian Dies"; Carnes, "The Torture Victim Next Door"; Hickey, "A Journey Underground"; Nickles, "A Precarious Step Forward"; Mathewes-Green, "Could We Survive Persecution?"; Compass Direct, "Authorities Crack Down"; Carnes, "Arrests of Pastor"; CT Staff, "House-Church Leader Arrested"; Aikman, "China's Crackdown"; White, "Dare to Be Faithful"; Buchan, "Khmu Christians Arrested"; Compass Direct, "Highlands Christians Targeted"; Frame, "Free China's Church"; Sellers, "Empty Legal Rights"; Nettleton, "My Grace Is Sufficient"; Carnes, "A Look of Love"; Mundy, "Chinese Christian Describes Torture"; Carnes, "New China"; Carnes," The Unlikely Activist"; Kennedy, "Cuba's Next Revolution"; Brookes, "China's Emerging Church"; Abraham, "Evil Teachings"; Belz, "Open and Shut"; Alford, "Abducted Pastor"; Callahan, "'Appalling' Persecution"; Compass Direct, "7 Christian Executions Suspected"; Olasky, "No es facil"; Sellers, "Dumped into Drums"; Abraham, "Freedom to Conform"; Cleary, "Dare to Speak"; Veith, "To: Our Chinese Monitor"; Abraham, "Justice Denied"; Fischer, "Enemies of the State"; Wood, "Vietnamese Churches"; Mundy, "Secret Government Report"; Gaines, "China Launches New Crackdown"; Belz, "A Complete Lie"; Belz, "Laying Down the Law"; Brown, "Christian Lawyer"; Bruce, "Sharing Jesus"; Belz, "Finding Their Voices"; Abraham, "Devotion Quotient"; P. Johnson, "Foreign Workers Flock"; Olasky, "The Panda in Winter"; "Newsbriefs," *Charisma* 32; Bruce, "Cuban Churches"; Mei, "The Price of Protest"; F. Brown, "Pentecostals"; Tennant, "The God Who Lives"; Belz, "Plane Truth." Anti-communism also intersects with pro-Zionist rhetoric in stories that feature

Russian persecution of Jews and messianic Jews; see Brown, "Opposition Is Mounting"; Brown, "Messianic Jews"; King, "The Exodus Continues." For a more complex rendering of the position of Christians in China, see Christianity Today, "Should Christians Continue"; Cook, "Behind China's Closed Doors"; and Galli, "The Chinese Church's." For Cuba, see Landers, "Cuban Catholics." A letter to *Christianity Today* further complains: "Why is it that CT can only paint China's incredibly complicated religious landscape in black and white? My Christian Chinese friends, most of them evangelicals, would be stunned and hurt to see so many one-sided portrayals of the religious situation in China ... The religious trends here are largely positive"; Letters, *Christianity Today* 26, 8. Also, *Christianity Today* notes tensions with many evangelicals in China who have severed ties with the Southern Baptist Convention because of its support for clandestine missionary activity; see Walker, "China's Leaders." Interestingly, Gao Zhan, who was a Christian human rights activist, was imprisoned in the United States for selling illegally more than $539,000 worth of militarily sensitive semiconductors to an institute in Nanching that was connected with the country's military. It is not clear if she is an agent or a double agent, or for which government. She had been sentenced in China, but Bush had her released and returned to the United States; however, she had also been under investigation in the United States at the time, so it is not clear why Bush had her released. She claims her motivations were to finance a women's research centre in China; see Plowman, "Motivated by Money."
57 Colson and Pearcey, "Victory over Napalm."
58 Shea, "The Daniel of Religious Rites."
59 Alford, "Character Assassination."
60 Alford, "Ministry at the Centre."
61 "Persecution Watch," *Charisma* (December 2005); "The Buzz," *World.*
62 Alford, "Character Assassination."
63 Belz, "Public Disaster"; Olasky, "The Panda in Winter."
64 Miller, "Prophet to a Nation," 40. See also "Persecution Watch," *Charisma* (December 2005).
65 Coffin, "A Different Kind"; Loconte, "The United Nations' Disarray"; Olasky, "No es facil."
66 Voice of the Martyrs, "Faces of Persecution." For the perspective that Indigenous peoples are oppressing Christians in Mexico, see also Isais, "Mexico"; and MacHarg, "Healing the Violence." *Christianity Today* has run somewhat more balanced articles on the Indigenous uprising in Chiapas; it is critical of the movement but also suggests that some of their claims would benefit Indigenous peoples; see Alford, "Words against Weapons"

and Alford, "A Peacemaker in Power." Freedom House's *In the Lion's Den*, a primer on Christian persecution, mentions only China, Sudan, Pakistan, North Korea, Saudi Arabia, Vietnam, Egypt, and Nigeria as sites of Christian persecution. The US Commission on International Religious Freedom's 2004 Report lists eleven countries: Eritrea, India, Pakistan, Saudi Arabia, Turkmenistan, Vietnam, Burma, China, North Korea, Iran, and Sudan. Seven other countries are on the list for lesser violations: Egypt, Indonesia, Nigeria, Uzbekistan, Belarus, Cuba, and Georgia. See Morgan, "Black Eye for Freedom"; see also Belz, "Faces in the Crowd."

67 "Mexico," *Rutherford*. *Indian Life* ran an article that briefly mentioned that the "fundamental motivation" behind this persecution is "economic, political, and agrarian" rather than religious; see Rasmussen, "Caciques Rule."

68 Alford, "Massacre Post-Mortem."

69 Belz, "Faces in the Crowd."

70 Lawton, Persecuted Church."

71 Curry, *A World without Tyranny*.

72 Olasky, "Beyond Wishful Thinking."

73 Olasky, "Touching, Teaching."

74 Arora, "Premeditated Mobs"; Belz, "Opening the Safety Valve"; Christianity Today, "Top Ten News Stories, 2003"; Dean, "Castes Vote"; Grady, "They Burn Bibles"; Lindner, "Reaching Hidden People"; Lindner, "Christians Face New Wave"; Nelson, "Under Siege"; "Newsbriefs," *Charisma* (February 1999); Newton, "Blockbuster Evangelism"; Newton, "Machete Attack"; Newton, "Hindu Extremes"; Singh, "Harassed Kashmir Christians"; Singh, "Under Siege"; Wunderink, "Case by Case." An exception is Abraham, "Left Behind." Another article does not conflate Dalits with Christians but does suggest that Christianity saves Dalits from caste discrimination; see David, "Caught on Tape"; Grady, "God's Moment for India"; Singh, "Quitting Hinduism"; and Sreeprasad, "Dalits Join Church. A *Charisma* article frames the oppression of Dalit Christians as religious persecution, but the Dalit Christian interviewed frames it as caste persecution; see Newton, "Dalit Christians Fight." Philip Yancey does completely distinguish the two and focuses on caste discrimination specifically, likening it to contemporary race discrimination in the United States rather than religious discrimination; see Yancey, "A Dream That Won't Die."

75 Singh, "Dalits Renounce Hinduism," 26.

76 Stafford, "India Undaunted," 33.

77 Stafford, "India Undaunted," 33.

78 Carnes, "Termites to National Security"; Chenoweth, "The Heartless Homeland"; *Christianity Today*, "Nichtmares and Miracles"; Compass Direct, "Highlands Christians Targeted"; Guthrie, "Deconstructing Gulags";

Hyeok, "The Nightmare"; Miller, "Rebels Kill"; Morgan and Neff, "The Vulnerable"; Morse "View from the Axis"; Sellers, "Forgotten Gulag"; Sellers, "The Vioent Face"; Sellers, "Criminal Faith"; Sellers, "Lip Service."

79 Yancey, "The Japanese Joseph."

80 Moon, "World's Worst Persecutor," 20. Similar critiques were made when Rick Warren accepted an invitation to preach in North Korea; see "Open Doors," *Charisma* 32.

81 Alford, "Caught in the Conflict"; Alford "Death Threats Denied"; Alford, "New Life"; Belz,"Let My People Go"; MacHarg, "Twenty-Five Pastors Killed"; Miller, "Up from the Ashes?" *World* did briefly mention that some groups say that "human rights violations are more common among Colombian soldiers than the guerrilla fronts. They oppose increased US military aid to Colombia's military, given its past history of abuse"; Belz, "To the Front Lines," 16. *World's* stance, however, was to support increased funding for Colombia to stop rebel forces.

82 Fidler, "Infiltrating the Darkness."

83 Flinchbaugh, "Christians in the Line of Fire."

84 MacHarg, "Death in the Night," 31.

85 Carter, "Faith Defeats Communism."

86 Matthews, "Pablo's Prayer."

87 Yancey, "Holy Subversion," 14.

88 Freedom House, *In the Lion's Den*, 13; Lawton, "Evangelicals and Catholics." NAES has been generally unsupportive of the claims of persecuted refugees in Latin America, although it supports relaxing the borders for "Christians" who are being persecuted (those in Latin America apparently do not qualify).

89 Frame, "Sanctuary Workers Indicted."

90 Foreman, "World Relief."

91 Donald McGavran, in Mumper, "Where in the World," 21; see also Divino, "Why Don't They Look Like Us."

92 Farrell, "Mosques on Main Street," 56.

93 Pease, "The Mission Field," 22. See also Bailey, "The Muslims Are Coming Here!", 7; and Lotte, "How to Meet the Needs."

94 In Guthrie, "A Crescent for a Cross," 40. See also Bjork, "Foreign Missions"; Carnes, "'The Peoples Are Here'"; P. Johnson, "The Latinos Are Coming"; Lu, "Drawn by Grace."

95 Guthrie, "Muslim Mission Breakthrough," 25. For articles suggesting that poverty, the War on Terror, and natural disasters have been helpful in bringing more Muslims to Christ, see Lukins, "Behind the Black Wall"; Lukins, "When a Nation Is Shaken"; and Price, "It's God's Hour."

 96 Carnes, "Walking the Talk."
 97 Abraham, "Deparation"; Mitri, "Who Are the Christians?"
 98 Galli, "Sometimes Persecution Purifies."
 99 Reapsome "What's Holding Up World Evangelism?", 22.
100 Parajon, "One Nicaraguan Christian."
101 Horowitz and Gunn, "Breaking Chains," 49.
102 Cromartie, "The Jew," 53.
103 Horowitz and Gunn, "Breaking Chains II."
104 Horowitz and Gunn, "Breaking Chains," 54.
105 Horowitz and Gunn, "Breaking Chains," 53.
106 Horowitz and Gunn, "Breaking Chains," 81. In the following *Christianity Today* issue, Gunn and Horowitz responded to each other's analyses. Horowitz did not actually address Gunn's substantive arguments, for which Gunn took him to task. Horowitz and Gunn, "Breaking Chains II."
107 For additional discussion on the need for evangelicals to have a more sophisticated understanding of geopolitics, see Galli, "Our Geopolitical Moment."
108 "Letters," *Christianity Today*, December 2001, 12–13.
109 Fawzy, "Christian–Muslim Dialogue"; John, "Christians and the Blaspheme Laws"; Marshall, "Correcting the Secular Vision"; Mombo and Mwaluda "Relationship and Challenge"; Mugyenzi, "Seeking Understanding in Uganda"; Nyberg, "Missionaries in Congo Flee"; Ponniah, "The Situation in Malaysia"; Rogers, "Burma's Almost Forgotten"; Sellers, "The Violent Face of Jihad"; Sellers, "Religious Cleansing."
110 Abraham, "Layered Over"; Galli, "A New Day in Vietnam."
111 Imprisoned Chinese House-Church Leader, *Charisma*.
112 Moll, "Four Missionaries Murdered."
113 Dixon, "In the Shadow of the Mosque," 58.
114 Baker, "Unlocking the Heart of Islam," 92.
115 Okite, "Missionaries or Mercenaries."
116 Wunderink, "You've Got Jail."
117 "What Defines 'Real' Persecution?", *Open Doors Newsbrief.*
118 "What Defines 'Real' Persecution?", *Open Doors Newsbrief.*
119 "What Defines 'Real' Persecution?", *Open Doors Newsbrief.*
120 Noll, "Early Returns Are Mixed," 54.
121 Neff, "Progress for the Persecuted."
122 Parajon, "One Nicaraguan Christian," 2.
123 While problematically criticizing evangelical theology, one article does critique evangelicals for not addressing social problems in Guatemala. "Some believe the evangelical community has purposely avoided public

criticism or action because it witnessed what happened when Roman Catholics and mainline Protestants fell into liberation theology. That doctrine provided the theoretical basis for a so-called "preferential option for the poor," but class warfare is not biblical, and in practice the government viewed the Catholic church as joined with leftist guerrilla groups; Dabel, "Bulldogs, Bodyguards." An interview with Ruth Padilla Dborst ,who works with the International Fellowship of Evangelical Students, quotes her saying that evangelicals should be "biblically conservative yet socially active" (32). She also calls for trade agreements that address political power between Guatemala and First World countries. See Crouch, "Liberate My People."

124 Hardage, "Witnesses amid War."

125 Alford, "The Truth Is Somewhere," 20–1.

126 Miller, "Divorcing a Dictator." Another article mentioned that evangelicals were also persecuted under this regime; see Alford, "Imprisoned Evangelicals"; Miller, "Christians to Help Investigate."

127 Alford, "Maximum Security."

128 Lawton, "Faith without Borders."

129 Okite, "Returning a Tabot."

130 Alford, "Values Voters"; Guilherme, "Evangelicals Grow."

131 Sellers, "Ordinary Terrorists."

132 Horowitz and Gunn, "Breaking Chains"; Horowitz and Gunn, "Breaking Chains II"; Neff, "Operation Human Rights"; Seiple, "Religious Liberty."

133 Seiple, "Religious Liberty."

134 Tennant, "Long Road."

135 Belz, "A Milestone"; Christianity Today, "Commission Urges Economic Sanctions"; Johnson, "Deliver Us from Kony"; Sellers, "Crushed by a Soviet Relic."

136 Abraham, "Soft on Saudis"; Abraham, "'Wrist Slap'"; Moore, "US Ally"; Sellers, "Flogged and Deported"; Sellers, "To Confront a Theocracy."

137 Moore, "Justice Delayed." See also Institute for Religion and Democracy, Information Packet on Church Alliance for a New Sudan, Washington, 20 August 2001.

138 Carnes, "Religious Persecution Bill."

139 Christianity Today, "Persecution Is a Holy Word," 30, 31. For similar sentiments, see Blunt, "Justice before Peace?"

140 Baker, "Christians Cleared of Blaspheme"; Doyle, "Faces of Persecution"; P. Johnson, "How One Woman Challenged Oppression"; Price, "Persecuted Church Takes Spotlight."

141 There are some limitations on this concern. Christian groups are opposed to attempts to elevate non-binding religious defamation resolutions at the

UN to international treaty status. While these resolutions are intended to speak to xenophobia and racism, some think they would be used to crack down on Christian converts and evangelists. See Walker, "Christians Oppose."

142 *Christianity Today*, "Persecution Is Persecution Is Persecution."

143 Aikman, "A Campaign against Cruelty"; Carnes, "Mixing Oil and Blood"; *Christianity Today*, "Confronting Sudan's Evils"; Cox, "The Price of a Slave"; Gardner, "Slave Redemption"; Kisuke, "Sudanese Christians Bloody"; Sellers, "No Greater Tragedy"; Stewart, "Christians Still Being Enslaved"; Zurowski, "Camel Boy 'Crucified.'"

144 Guthrie, "A False Cry of Peace."

145 Abraham, "Out of the Shadows"; Aikman, "The Crisis in Darfur"; Nyberg, "Ethic Cleansing."

146 "News Briefs," *Charisma* 30.

147 Abraham, "Deadline on Darfur"; Alford, "Fragile Accord"; Anderson, "Giving Hope a Chance"; Belz, "Baroness for Battle"; Belz, "Plane Truth"; *Christianity Today*, "Never Again?"; Johnson, "Gridlock on Genocide."

148 Abraham, "Spectator to Genocide"; Belz, "Improbable Cause"; Belz, "Name Change"; Belz, "Too Little, Too Late"; *Christianity Today*, "Hotel Sudan"; Dean, "Looming Storms"; Dean, "No Way Out"). An alternative framing was offered in *Christianity Today*: "Like most genocide and mass murder, the crimes in Sudan have been driven mostly by powerful people trying to stay in power"; Phiri, "Building a Peace," 61.

149 Abraham, "Slave-to-Slave," 25.

150 Price, "Persecuted Church."

151 Voice of the Martyrs, "Ministering in Iraq," pamphlet, n.d.

152 Guthrie, "Door to Islam."

153 Lehman, "Death by Sanctions"; Veenker, "Sanctions Missing the Mark."

154 *Christianity Today*, "A Silent Holocaust."

155 Fernando, "Bombs Away," 77.

156 Guthrie, "Keeping Their Heads Low"; White, "Dampening the Fuse in Iraq."

157 Belz, "Kidnapped."

158 Hoffman, "The Risks of Regime Change," 86.

159 Gaviak, "Longing to Be Heard," 88.

160 Sellers, "Big, Soft Targets."

161 Smith, "Deconstructing Islam." At the same time, fear of Christian persecution is used to justify continuing US presence in Iraq. See Belz, "First Guns, Then Ballots."

162 "Arabs Outside Middle East to Hear Webcasts," *Christianity Today*.

163 Dixon, "Three Christians Martyred."

164 "News of the Year," *World*.
165 Grady, "Secret Agent Man."
166 Yancey, "A Living Stream," 35.
167 *Christianity Today*, "Persecution Is a Holy Word."
168 Guthrie, "The Other Side of Church Growth."
169 Abraham, "Zeal for the Lost"; Pulliam, "Costly Commitment."
170 Ramstad, "Persecution," 474.

Violence in a Far Country:
Other Women's Lives

7 Introduction to Section Two

ROSHAN JAHANGEER AND SHAIRA VADASARIA

over there is over here.

there is life here. anyone reading this is breathing, maybe hurting but breathing for sure.

Suheir Hammad, "first writing since"[1]

This collection of essays explores the inner mechanics of the "War on Terror" and the epistemic frameworks through which we come to know and respond to histories of violence. The authors of this section persuasively and relentlessly write against racial and sexual violence, daily misogyny of multiple kinds, imperial wars of terror and the vectors of power that bind these seemingly dispersed trajectories together as intimately connected allies of empire. Their commentaries force us to confront the intricate continuities between politically powerful binaries: "local versus global," "private versus public," "traditional versus modern," and "religious versus secular." These binaries not only provide ideological currency for the "War on Terror" but the discursive logics imbued within them organize violence against women of colour in discrete but deliberate ways.

We open our introduction to this section by asking, What is at stake in engaging with the question of violence against women at this particular historical conjuncture? How might we do so without contributing to an imperialist feminist legacy that seeks to "save brown women from brown men" within an infantilizing rescue narrative?[2] What does it mean to think through the question of violence against women against the backdrop of the "War on Terror"?

This collection of work opens up an analytical space to interrogate these questions by mobilizing the discussion in a different direction. Instead of asking how and why violence against women of colour takes place, the authors anchor their critiques in anti-racist and anti-imperialist transnational feminist analyses and ask, What do responses to the question of "violence against women" seek to do in the geopolitical spatial and temporal ordering of the "War on Terror"? What forms of racial logic do they rest upon and consolidate? How might we track the circuits of their production? What kinds of discourses do they speak through? And perhaps most significantly, how are they heard and by whom? These questions offer important interventions that force us to think about empire's methodology – that is, the methods through which practices of empire building organize racial, gendered, and heterosexist patriarchal violence, as well as shape our capacities to imagine and mobilize alternative responses to the "War on Terror."

Although the responses to violence against women vary, a closer look at these modes of contestation reveals structures of power animated by practices of empire building. In Nadine Naber's essay, for instance, we see how activist organizing carried out through a "logic of emergency" and within a "diaspora of empire" responds to imperial and colonial violence in Iraq and Palestine as urgencies "over there" at the expense of responding to heterosexist patriarchal encounters between "organizers" in the United States "over here."[3] By contrast, Inderpal Grewal's essay highlights how the "local" versus "global" binary at times mimics the logic imbued within liberal accounts of "pathological" versus "cultural" violence. Taking "honour crimes" as an example, racial constructs of cultural difference are already embedded in a spatial–temporal grid that demarcates "traditional" (read: "backward," "primitive," "static," "fixed") from "modern" (read: "rational," "forward," "dynamic").[4] Culture and patriarchy stand in as interpretive frameworks from which to explain violence. Accordingly, if "traditional" equals "violent" and "modern" represents "non-violent," then patriarchal violence done by white men can only be explained through individual pathologies. This invites an important question: What prevents us from considering the killing of white Canadian or American women by their significant others as "honour killings"? When we attribute the cause of crimes to values such as "honour" in the context of non-Western cultures, violence committed against white women in Western cultures is made thinkable only in the context of individualized "crimes of passion." Conversely, when those from non-Western cultures (i.e., "Muslims") commit similar crimes, it is the whole culture and/or religion that needs to be reformed, and if not reformed, then eradicated.[5] Given the prevalence and pervasiveness of these unequal representations in the media, how can we conceive of "honour killings," "collateral damage," or even "domestic violence" as a necessity of empire building, which takes place within the broader geopolitical project of the War on Terror?

The authors respond to these questions in a number of ways. First, they consider what violence against women in the form of honour killings, rape, and domestic violence/intimate partner abuse has to do with torture, terror, imprisonment, and execution. In doing so, they vehemently disrupt the "private versus public" and "domestic violence versus state violence" binaries, thereby revealing that the personal is *not* just political. Rather, the personal and the political co-constitute each other in ways that deeply structure how one inhabits the space between life and death. Second, they theorize against the hierarchization of violence – a classical model within mainstream political theory that legitimizes state violence while delegitimizing substate violence along with its associated groups. What becomes evident in their writings is that violence operates in a continuum such that one state's "War on Terror" works in concert with substate "terrorist" movements; there is no eternal position of terrorist or of victim in this continuum. Likewise, violence is also seen to circulate transnationally, such that one country's understanding of "honour crimes" becomes used, post hoc, to name domestic violence against women elsewhere. As both Indepal Grewal and Amina Jamal show us in their chapters, some women's lives are more vulnerable than others to such violence.[6] In light of the "collateral vulnerability" of some women's lives over others, we take seriously Meyda Yeğenoğlu's provocative question and echo it here alongside some of our own: What would it mean for states to pronounce a "war on domestic violence"? How would a "war on domestic violence" compare to the seemingly endless "War on Terror"?[7] What would the scope of such a war be? Which bodies and communities would be targeted? Who would the "casualties" of this war be? What forms of violence would be executed? And finally, what would the "terrorist" look like in this equation?

Jasbir Puar's insights into the framing of the "terrorist" as both a monster and a sexual deviant[8] reminds us that the terrorist is already constructed as being outside of humanity, not part of the fraternity of brothers needed to enact a Derridean "politics of friendship"[9] that is at the core of the communicative ethic deemed necessary for democracy. When he enacts violence, it is not only against individuals but also against culture, community, and humanity. In short, in acting against humanity or life itself, he is acting against the Sovereign – this is what allows state violence to be directed towards him with impunity. However, the problem with this theoretical framework is that the very idea of sovereignty is already imbued in patriarchy. The Sovereign as protector of life itself resists the inclusion of women as anything other than victims who need to be protected and/or saved from the external threat of the monster-terrorist. This framework forecloses a space to critically address violence against women in general and violence against women of colour in particular; it also affirms a structure of state power and politics that organizes conditions of racist and patriarchal violence.

As the authors of this section demonstrate, violence is contextually specific: we can name it in its different guises. We can trace the scars it leaves on those who are the most vulnerable to its effects. The aftermath of violence might reverberate in complex ways, but in the project of empire, violence is specific. Whether it is the violence of "collateral damage," which affects those whose social positioning is the most precarious, or "honour killings," which travel transnationally as a performative discourse, or the silencing of sexist and homophobic violence that takes place in activist communities – each form reflects transnational variations of a conception of politics that leaves women's everyday experiences of war's effects out of its equation. Only when they are caricatured as "Third World" victims by powerful states do such women's lives become a convenient excuse for invading another country. Indeed, the lessons of 9/11 have taught us to be wary of where, how, and why states take an interest in "other women's lives."

These chapters show how the legacies of colonial and imperial heteropatriarchal violence have been inherited and internalized by various communities, outsourced, refurbished, and sold back to aid in the project of empire. By examining the multiple fields of power that unite the "local and the global," the "modern and traditional," the "religious and secular," the "private and public," the heteropatriarchal sexism "over here" and imperial/colonial bombing of "over there" within a larger project of empire, these chapters uncover the messy but precise terror of empire's war.

NOTES

1 Hammad, *Zaatar Diva*, 98–102.
2 Mani, "Contentious Traditions"; Spivak, "Can the Subaltern Speak?"
3 See Nadine Naber in this volume.
4 See Inderpal Grewal in this volume.
5 Mahmood, "Feminism, Democracy, and Empire: Islam and the War of Terror."
6 See Amina Jamal in this volume.
7 See Meyda Yeğenoğlu in this volume.
8 Puar, *Terrorist Assemblages*.
9 Derrida, *The Politics of Friendship*.

8 "Collateral Violence": Women's Rights and National Security in Pakistan's War on Terror[1]

AMINA JAMAL

Pakistan's ambivalent positioning in the War on Terror – as the United States' least reliable but much desired ally – has not only amplified its present-day militarism, violence, and terrorism but also intensified long-standing cultural-political struggles that are affecting all aspects of Pakistani life, including gender relations, human rights, and violence against women. Even before 11 September 2001, Pakistani society was frayed by violence related to ongoing rivalries among a variety of sectarian and religious militant groups and the lasting effects of the US-Soviet proxy war in Afghanistan.[2] Soon after the 9/11 attacks, former President General Pervez Musharraf pledged support for US-led counter-terrorism efforts, thereby signalling a withdrawal of Pakistan's traditional support for militant Muslim groups. However, the army and intelligence agencies continue to nurture these groups as militant proxies for perceived strategic ends in a foreign policy calculated in terms of relations with India.[3] The negative effects of this indeterminacy have been economically and politically considerable and socially immeasurable.[4]

Feminist scholarship and human rights reports emphasize that, besides being faced with the incalculable violence of displacement, terrorist suicidal bombings, and counter-terrorism strategies of the US-led coalition forces and the Pakistani state, women are affected by an increase in militancy, religious extremism, and intolerance. Indeed, this literature suggests that the state's indecisive policy of engaging in counter-terrorism while also tolerating religious militancy resonates in its ambivalent stance towards gender issues: the state tends to waver between representing itself as an enlightened Muslim nation committed to international human rights and placating religious extremists by undermining important areas of women's rights.[5] Indeed, the ongoing securitization and militarization of the Pakistani nation-state has been experienced by many Pakistanis as an overall diminishing of human rights and women's security.

In this chapter I explore some of the effects of the War on Terror on Pakistani women – effects that are proliferating beyond the actual field of military conflict. I bring under scholarly consideration what one may call "collateral violence" against Pakistani women – that is, violence against women that is heavily inflected by contestations over the state's enlistment in the global militaristic and counter-terrorism project.

The term "collateral violence" has its roots in a similar term, "collateral damage," which has often been used in the US-led wars in Iraq and Afghanistan, during which the coalition forces have determined the enemy to be unidentifiable, amorphous, and dispersed instead of a nation, a people, an individual, or specific body of land or water. Collateral damage is deemed to be an apt term for damage and violence whose effects cannot be controlled or predicted by either the targets or the perpetrators. The US Air Force defines it as "unintentional damage or incidental damage affecting facilities, equipment or personnel occurring as a result of military actions directed against targeted enemy forces or facilities. Such damage can occur to friendly, neutral, and even enemy forces."[6]

Besides underscoring the devastating impact on human lives and property, the notion of "collateral violence" enables me to deepen and complicate the space carved by critical postcolonial feminists to examine the important, albeit amorphous, linkages between cultural-political constructions of Muslim women as victims/subjects of human rights and the conflicting security interests of nation-states in the War on Terror.[7] Worth repeating here are Kapur's comments on the US military invasion of Afghanistan:

> First, the current interest in the issues of women in Afghanistan has been largely framed within the parameters of religion and the rhetoric of civilization. Second, culture is being invoked not only to justify military and some feminist interventions, but also in ways that are universalizing and unreflective of the complexity and diversity of the traditions and practices that operate in the region.[8]

An important part of Kapur's argument is that women's rights are not easily divisible through geographical or ontological framings, nor is it possible to reduce the world to a rhetoric of good versus evil. In addition, I contend that serious attention to women's rights requires a sober and even painful engagement with the complexities that arise from the interactions of culture, history, politics, and faith as well as the avoidance of exaggerated polarizations and paternalisms. These are important considerations for engaging with women's human rights in Pakistan at this juncture, for the War on Terror has highlighted and intensified cleavages along ethnic, sectarian, religious, and social identities in addition to those of class, gender, and sexuality. In the interest of enhancing feminist theory and feminist political strategy across transnational sites, I focus on an episode in the War on Terror between January and May 2011 during which two women who may be termed victim-subjects of human rights were discursively pitted against each other as opposing symbols of secular versus religious violence and as oppositional victim-subjects of human rights. These women were Aasia Bibi, also named Asia Noreen, a forty-five-year-old Christian Pakistani woman, who was sentenced to death on 9 November 2010 for making derogatory remarks about the Prophet Mohammed, and Aafia Siddiqui, a US-based scientist of Pakistani origin who at that time had been arrested for allegedly shooting a US Marine in Afghanistan. Due to a number of events related to Pakistan's involvement in counter-terrorism, but deeply rooted in long-standing class, cultural, and religious differences within Pakistani society, sympathy for Aasia came to be interpreted as antipathy towards Aafia, and vice versa. While these extreme positions were not the only responses to the plight of the two women, they became discursively constructed as the only (mutually exclusive) possibilities for ethical and unethical action.

War, Collateral Violence, and Transnational Feminist Practices

In examining such an emotionally congested nation-space where the binaries of Islamic versus secular, pious versus sinner, citizen versus other, are frequently invoked and reworked in gendered ways, it is pertinent to ask what kind of feminist strategy might further the interests of what Spivak has referred to as transcultural literacy.[9] I propose that answering this question may require many of us, who are scholars of colour theorizing secular versus religious struggles in postcolonial societies of our originary affiliation, to re-examine some of our own assumptions about power, state, community, and self-formation that have become ineluctable in postcolonial and post-structuralist analyses of gender, agency, and power since Michel Foucault's interventions into social-political thought. Drawing upon Foucault's ideas about disciplinary practices of the modern state in Euro-American societies, postcolonial feminists trace the circulation of geopolitical power in the discourses of postcolonial states and deplore the tendency of civil activists, especially feminist movements, to seek state-led social transformation instead of local- and community-based alternatives.[10] To complicate the discursive reaches of Western geopolitical power, transnational feminist scholars consider the multiple ways in which modernist secular ideas encounter local reworkings of religion, culture, tradition, and identities in postcolonial contexts. We engage the ways in which different forms of state and non-state power shape women's subjectivities and then reconsider the possibilities of inhabiting feminist spaces in specifically configured postcolonial locales. Recalling Zygmunt Bauman's observations about the state of contemporary capitalism and the increasing irrelevance of state communism (but *not* socialist objectives), one may remark that feminist politics cannot remain local now that power has become global. As Bauman has emphasized in another context, the social-political inequality in our contemporary period cannot be adequately explained by sole reference to local, immediate, and direct causes or to malevolent acts of individuals. In addition, Bauman rightly points out, contemporary inequality cannot be addressed solely through the resources and capabilities of local agencies.[11] Transnationally dispersed notions of power lead Bauman to bemoan the "pitifully local" nature of politics in Western societies in an era when the state is enmeshed in globalized forms of power.

Bauman dismisses the assumptions about randomness and neutrality that uphold the concept of "collateral damage," arguing instead that the chances of becoming a victim of collateral damage are tied to one's social position and therefore predictable.[12] His linking of inequality – which he considers to be fundamentally a social problem and not an economic one – with collateral vulnerability is important for speaking about women, violence, and the state in Pakistan. This is worthy of consideration by postcolonial feminist critics in the global North who are dismayed by Muslim women's feminist movements that seem to ignore global imperialism, Western Islamophobia, and Eurocentric histories of the discourses of rights and freedoms in their struggles for women's human rights against local community and state power. In the case of Pakistan, where all women, be they feminist or fundamentalist, Muslim or otherwise, elite or poor, are invariably caught up in ideological battles currently raging among local, state, and global political forces, it is appropriate to state that, rephrasing Bauman, now that power is global, feminist politics becomes disempowered when it remains local. The need for feminists in the global North to develop critical insights into transnational politics in an era of increasing imperialism, neoliberal restructuring, and Islamophobia has been ably theorized by feminist scholars, particularly those who study critical race theory and postcolonial feminism.[13] While their insights are immensely useful for feminists everywhere, their arguments may be complicated when we turn our scrutiny towards the particular circumstances of feminist politics in many contemporary Muslim societies, such as Pakistan, where feminists must confront not only imperialism, racism, and sexism but also misogynist and repressive forces enabled by the unfortunate intersecting of puritanical Islam and Western modernity – a brand of Islamism that is historically entwined with the birth and local-global politics of the modern nationalistic Saudi kingdom on the Arabian Peninsula. We may comprehend the limitations and possibilities of feminist politics and women's lives in such a context by paying attention to the hegemonic discourses that compress all discussions related to women, gender, religious minorities, and citizenship to an immutable choice between Islam and secularism. We may then notice the myriad ways in which, battered by both religious militancy and secular militarism, the secular and religious may implicate each other in unpredictable ways, connect variously with the powers of the nation-state, and bring into play subject-agents imbued with the potential to transmute themselves beyond the boundaries of religious/secular, community/state, ethical/political, and local/global. It may be worthwhile for postcolonial critics to ask whether it is tenable or even possible for feminist politics in the South to remain clear of ideas that seem to resonate with social-philosophical universalism, and even transnational power networks, in their traffic with local politics, when all other forces have become globalized.

Secular and Religious Violence in Pakistan, 2010–2011

A series of seemingly unrelated events implicated in local, national, societal, and transnational practices of power became a topic of public interest in Pakistan from January 2010 to June 2011; together, those events opened a discursive space in which dichotomous notions of secular and Islamic worked to locate differently situated women as deserving or unworthy victims of violence.

Aasia Bibi

The conviction of Aasia Bibi in November 2010 brought Pakistan's controversial blasphemy laws to the attention of many international human rights groups, who believe the law is often used to oppress religious minorities. A resident of the village of Ittawali in Nankana district, Aasia pleaded that she had been framed. Her own account was as follows: She was working in a field on 14 June 2010 along with some other women. An argument started between her and two women when they refused to drink water fetched by her because she was a Christian.[14] A false case under the blasphemy laws was registered against her with the help of a local Imam. According to a petition submitted by Aasia to the provincial governor, Salman Taseer, a district court in Nankana sentenced her to death and ordered her to pay a fine of Rs100,000. In the petition that was handed to Taseer, who met with her in the Sheikhupura district jail, Aasia contended that the judge who had ruled for her to be punished had ignored the law and the facts under "pressure of some religious extremists."

An investigation by the National Commission on the Status of Women found that the case had been filed under pressure from influential local people for the purpose of settling personal scores.[15] When the case received international media attention, Pakistani President Zardari asked the Ministry for Minority Affairs to investigate it and submit a report within three days.[16] Leading clerics of the Deobandi and Barelvi schools of Islam, leaders of the main politico-religious party and Islamic movement Jamaat-e-Islami (JI), and members of the JI Women's Wing protested vehemently against a pardon for Bibi. Islamist politico-religious parties organized massive rallies in Pakistani cities to pressure the government to sentence Bibi to death. This campaign against Bibi culminated in Taseer's assassination on 4 January 2011.[17] In a related event, Pakistan's only Christian minister, Shahbaz Bhatti, Minister for Minorities, was shot dead on 2 March 2011 after pushing for the reform of blasphemy laws. Several other women's rights activists and female politicians were threatened with the same fate if they continued to speak out for any reform to the blasphemy laws.

Aafia Siddiqui

Aafia Siddiqui, an American citizen of Pakistani origin, is serving a life sentence in a US prison after being sentenced on 23 September 2010 to eighty-six years in prison for firing on US soldiers and FBI agents in

Afghanistan. Siddiqui, a thirty-eight-year-old divorced mother, holds a bachelor's degree in biology from MIT and a doctorate from Brandeis University.

The US government has stated that Siddiqui was taken into custody in Ghazni, Afghanistan, in July 2008; her family and supporters contradict this, contending that she was kidnapped by unknown military agencies in Pakistan and handed over to US authorities in 2003.[18]

Siddiqui's story came to public attention in Pakistan in late March 2003 when the Pakistani media began reporting that she had been arrested and turned over to representatives of the United States. By 2008, many believed that five years after disappearing, she and her three children were most likely dead. The information that she was alive and in US custody emerged in July 2008, from the accounts of released hostages and detainees in Afghanistan. Yvonne Ridley, a former Taliban hostage turned Taliban supporter, and Moazzem Begg, another Bagram jail detainee, began speaking to media about a woman in Bagram prison who had been heard screaming at night, a woman whom they called the "Grey Lady of Bagram."[19] A petition for habeas corpus was filed with the Pakistani High Court in Islamabad requesting that the Pakistani government free Siddiqui or provide information about her detention.

Aafia's sister, Fauzia Siddiqui, with support mostly from politico-religious parties, started a campaign to pressure the Pakistani state for Siddiqui's repatriation to Pakistan, using the state's position as a front-line ally of the United States in its War on Terror. This campaign developed frenzied proportions in February 2011, involving sit-ins, rallies, protests, and public speeches and statements, all of which were heavily covered on major Urdu television channels and in the local and national Urdu press.

The International Justice Network (IJNetwork), which represents the family of Aafia Siddiqui in the United States, monitored her trial in the US Federal Court of the Southern District of New York; it began on 19 January and ended with a guilty verdict in September 2010. IJNetwork contends that forensic and scientific evidence presented during the trial in New York was insufficient to prove Siddiqui's guilt and argues that she did not receive a fair trial.[20]

Community/Society/State and "the World"

The juxtaposing of Aasia and Aafia began in late 2010 when several parliamentarians of the ruling Pakistan People's Party (PPP) responded to

Aasia's conviction by calling for modification in the punishment specified under the controversial blasphemy laws.[21] Those laws make it a capital offence for anyone to make "derogatory remarks, etc., in respect of the Holy Prophet."[22] The laws have their origins in the Indian Penal Code under British colonial rule. They had been introduced to prevent communal conflicts and protect places of worship for all religions. Under General Zia ul Haq's military dictatorship in the 1980s, the laws were amended to focus on derogatory comments against the Prophet Mohammed and the death penalty was introduced for those found guilty. Since then, feminist and human rights groups in Pakistan have engaged in a nationwide campaign for the total repeal of the blasphemy laws. Since the 1980s, an estimated six hundred people have been accused of blasphemy, and many have been jailed, although no one has yet been executed.[23] The campaign for the repeal or reform of the blasphemy laws gained momentum in 2012 due to the presence of some women-friendly parliamentarians and politicians in the ruling PPP, which was elected in 2008.[24] Pakistani liberals, while critical of US actions in Iraq, Afghanistan, and Pakistan, pointed out that politico-religious parties were displaying a double standard in that they were playing up the violence suffered by Aafia at the hands of US authorities while ignoring the widespread violence against women in their own society. In their view, those who claimed to speak "for Islam" were insincere and politically motivated. For example, on a blog managed by members of the PPP, a well-known English-language journalist, Anas Abbas, pointed to the complicity of Pakistan's right-wing parties and politicians with the country's powerful military establishment and argued that the anti-US rhetoric deployed by those forces should be scrutinized for its deeper significance beyond simply Islamic cultural nationalism. He suggested that the highly orchestrated campaign for the release of Aafia was an attempt by politico-religious groups to deflect public attention from the role played in her kidnapping and rendition by Pakistan's powerful military and its security agencies, Inter-Services Intelligence (ISI), Military Intelligence (MI), and the Intelligence Bureau (IB).

A counter-campaign led by Pakistan's politico-religious parties and anti-state militants vowed to subvert any attempt to debate the blasphemy law. Prominent leaders of Jamaat-e-Islami declared that any attempt to modify the blasphemy laws – and the consequent release of Aasia Bibi – would itself be construed as an act of blasphemy against the Prophet Mohammed.[25]

Supporters of Jamaat-e-Islami, including thousands of women, marched through the streets of major cities with placards warning the state not to repeal or amend the blasphemy laws and demanding that the sentence against Bibi be carried out.[26] Their efforts were supported by the more politically radical Urdu press, whose members tend to position themselves as culturally and religiously more authentic than their English-language counterparts. Indeed, a well-known journalist called for Aasia to be deemed a sinner who had contravened a divine injunction; compared to that, Aafia's lesser offence against (US) man-made laws had been minor.[27] It was this frenzy that culminated in the assassination of Salman Taseer, the governor of Punjab – Pakistan's largest and most powerful province – by a member of his own security detail. Taseer's killer, Mumtaz Qadri, said that he had acted in response to the governor's secular views and support for Bibi. Pakistan's liberal-secular and progressive groups and human rights supporters were particularly dismayed by the widespread praise for the killing, praise that was orchestrated by the politico-religious parties. In a grotesque display of religiosity, a group of lawyers showered rose petals on Mumtaz Qadri as he arrived in court.[28] The Pakistani Taliban and clerics associated with the politico-religious parties declared that it would be considered a sin to participate in the funeral prayers for Taseer.[29] Both opponents and proponents of liberalism and secular politics attributed Taseer's killing to his secular views and lifestyle, neither of which he had hidden. His opponents, exemplified by leaders of the main politico-Islamic parties, prominent journalists in Urdu and local-language newspapers, and hosts on Urdu television programs, observed that Taseer had displayed a flagrant disregard for Islamic culture and tradition when he described the blasphemy law as a "black" law. All of this made him a blasphemer in the eyes of many.

These developments were somewhat disrupted by the intervention, rare in Pakistan's recent history, of some *ulema* (Islamic scholars), who shifted – albeit slightly – the terms of the debate from its hardened oppositions. In Pakistan, these *ulema* are to be differentiated from the leaders of politically engaged religious parties. Javed Ahmed Ghamdi and Khalid Hassan, Islamic scholars, who maintain a strict distance from religio-politics in Pakistan, used the media's widespread reach to challenge the politico-religious parties' contentions about the sanctity and integrity of the blasphemy laws by offering their own interpretations based on the Quran and Hadith. They questioned the legality and religious basis of the blasphemy laws and openly accused politico-religious leaders of misleading the nation.[30]

A few weeks later, Pakistan's only religious-minority parliamentary representative, Shahbaz Bhatti, a Christian, was assassinated after he supported the victims of the blasphemy laws. Eventually, Prime Minister Syed Yousuf Raza Gilani made a public announcement in which he denied that the government had any intention of changing the blasphemy law: "If we [i.e., the State] don't honor blasphemy law then who will do it. We will not introduce any amendment in the constitution or law nor have we constituted any committee. We are sincere in blasphemy law. We will neither amend any constitution nor bring any change in this law. We have never ever thought to do so."[31] Pakistani Interior Minister Rahman Malik was widely quoted by the local and national media that he would personally shoot anyone who was proven guilty of committing blasphemy against the Prophet Muhammad. (He later recanted that statement in an interview with an international news agency.)[32]

Such pronouncements from a mistrusted and unpopular government would have done little to alleviate the tensions around Aasia Bibi were it not for another event more directly linked to the War on Terror, one that further convoluted the violent protests in Pakistan. On 26 January 2011, Raymond Davis, an American employed by the US Consulate in Lahore, shot dead two Pakistani men in what he said was self-defence. Another Pakistani man was killed accidentally by a US embassy vehicle that responded to Davis's call for help. Davis's arrest and subsequent indictment for murder sparked intense public debate within Pakistan and internationally over diplomatic status and the likelihood of immunity for the American, whom Pakistanis widely believed to be an intelligence agent. If found guilty as charged, Davis could have faced the death penalty.[33] Many Pakistanis, especially leaders of pro-Taliban and anti-US opposition political parties and some prominent media hosts and columnists, began to call for the release of Aafia Siddiqui in exchange for Davis.

The impasse over Davis ended two months later when he was released through recourse to the Shariah-based law of *diyat* (or monetary retribution), which was paid to the heirs of the two victims. Davis was quickly flown out of Pakistan.[34] A police official told *Dawn*, a national English-language daily newspaper, that the heirs of the two men killed had each been given Rs100 million in compensation.[35] Protests erupted in several cities as many Pakistanis took the settlement to be more a sign of the state's further capitulation to US dominance than of the expansion of Shariah laws.[36] For some, Davis's repatriation to the United States was particularly reprehensible considering the ongoing captivity of Aafia Siddiqui in a US jail.

The turmoil over Aasia versus Aafia began to subside in April 2011 after US commandos launched a night-time raid on a compound in Abbottabad, a major military town north of Islamabad, and killed Osama Bin Laden.

Violent Associations: War, Community, and Gender, January 2011 to May 2011

The two women's variable positioning as victims/subjects/agents supports some of the critiques of universal human rights discourses among postcolonial and transnational feminist scholars who warn against the power of such universalism to colonize Muslim women's experiences through culturalist understandings of violence against Third World women.[37] Conversely, the appropriation of "Islamic" as a bulwark against Western universal power is frequently deployed by politico-religious forces in Pakistan as much to undermine feminism and women's citizenship rights as to challenge Western global dominance.[38] I contend that the critical insights of postcolonial feminism regarding the relationships among Muslim women, secularism, Islam, and the War on Terror may be productively annotated by situating them in the locally inflected contradictory experiences of contemporary globalizing militarism and neoliberalism.

In her essay "The State and the Limits of Counter-Terrorism in Pakistan and Sri Lanka," Pakistan feminist scholar Rubina Saigol warns us against analytically isolating different forms of terrorism along the lines of state and non-state acts, national and global, privatized and public. She contends that "analyses based on singular visions, either from the perspective of global hegemony or from the peripheries of subjugation and oppression, miss the deeply intertwined nature of the different forms of terrorism."[39] Reflecting Pakistani citizens' experiences of terrorism in its multifarious and deeply intertwined forms, Saigol deplores singularly focused understandings of terrorism that result when "*either* states *or* non-state actors are terrorist, *either* the government *or* a sub-national group is terrorist, *either* the imperial powers *or* transnational movements challenging them are terrorist."[40] For Saigol, terrorism and counter-terrorism may be fully understood when terrorism is viewed on a continuum of levels from global to state to substate in such a way as to dispense with the idea that some may be "permanently terrorist" and others permanent victims whether they be a movement, a state, a group, or an imperial power.[41]

Saigol's multifaceted analysis can be applied to the conflict of Aasia versus Aafia through a nuanced reading of discursively constructed political positions. These became most amplified in Pakistan from January to May 2011. Opposing subjects constructing themselves as feminist/liberal/progressive on one side and Islamic/nationalistic on the other implicated the violence suffered by these women in larger national questions related to the War on Terror, US operations in Afghanistan and Pakistan, the Pakistani state's military operations against "Islamic" militants and "terrorists," loyalty to "Islam" versus loyalty to "the West," and other local, national, and global issues. Through the operations of globally, nationally, and locally dispersed networks of power and multiply related fields of violence, the two women became discursively conjoined despite incommensurable divides of class, nationality, ethnicity, and religion.

The above discussion, while amorphous and partial, may nevertheless offer some insights into the treacherous terrain constructed when repressive politico-religious politics are mounted under the banner of Islam. Some attempts have been made to disrupt that terrain by those for whom feminist politics finds natural allies in Pakistan. They include liberal, secular, progressive forces and individual progressive-minded Islamic scholars and religious leaders.

Aasia and Aafia each experienced different forms of violence emanating from the convoluted interconnections of state–society–community. And they were tied together forcibly so that they constituted the battleground for political struggle between an ineffectual and dependent state and its multiply situated critics. They were appropriated as potent symbols of the nation's honour against the military and political might of the United States by politico-religious groups such as Jamaat-e-Islami and Tehrik-e-Insaf, which interpret all local and global events through a dichotomy of Islam versus the West. For liberal feminists and human rights groups, such as the Women's Action Forum and the Human Rights Commission of Pakistan, they signified the underside of a particularistic vision of community enshrined as the Islamic Republic of Pakistan that has been unable to inculcate the civilizing force of a unifying universalism embodied in the ideas of nation-state and global community. For traditional mainstream Muslims who had managed to survive decades of the copiously funded and highly politicized doctrine of "Islamization," the two women represented the nation-state's failure to infuse itself with the true spirit of Islam.[42] These different discourses coalesced and clashed so that support for Aasia Bibi was deemed to be a mark of secularism, implying a move against Islam in support of Western militarism; in contrast, the release from a US prison of Aafia Siddiqui came to be represented as a religious obligation and a matter of national honour. Aafia Siddiqui, a middle-class Pakistani scientist with superior American credentials, was unequivocally embraced as a "daughter of the nation" and a victim-subject of human rights, while Aasia Bibi, a poor rural Pakistani woman belonging to a threatened religious minority, was thrust into the undeserved status of a mala fide outsider bent on destroying the national social fabric.[43] Women, religious and ethnic minorities, the sexually other, and the impoverished have long been faced with the state's ineptitude and violence, both intended and unintended. There is no question, however, that for these groups the experience of precariousness and violence has intensified and become more complicated because of the accelerated militarization of society that began in the 1980s with the entanglement of the Pakistani military and hence the state in the US–Saudi–Soviet–Afghan ideological and armed conflict. Setting aside the stories of Aasia and Aafia, there is a plethora of literature published by the Human Rights Commission of Pakistan, feminist scholars, women's groups, human rights groups, and other concerned writers documenting the vulnerability of the rights, status, and security of women, religious minorities, and the rural and urban poor.[44]

Conclusion

An engagement with the collateral violence of the War on Terror is instructive for a wider understanding of feminist struggles over the nature of the state, the notion of community, and the state–citizen relationship in Pakistan. Such an engagement helps illuminate that so-called secular struggles, with which mainstream Pakistani feminism is closely affiliated, usually involve much more than simply opposition to Islam or a rejection of its authority. As well, the religiously motivated campaigns of political Islamic groups and "religious" extremists in Pakistan directed against both the language of universal human rights and the issues encompassed by international human rights protocols need to be understood as more than a disavowal of secularism and a rejection of Western dominance. They implicate much deeper and wider classed and gendered processes of subject formation as well as long-standing matters related to struggles over how authority is to be constructed in the region. We have yet to see, either in Pakistan or in Bangladesh, serious studies of the type undertaken by various Indian scholars who have attempted to re-engage the concept of secularism and its relationship to emancipatory politics in South Asia. Nor have Muslim women sufficiently engaged the cultural and political implications of the insertion of colonial secularity into ongoing religious debates and dissensions within Muslim South Asia. It is easy to agree with scholars such as Needham, Sunder Rajan, and Shabnam Tejani that secularism – including its espousal by mainstream feminism – may reflect a variety of concerns, including gender, class, caste, and communal anxieties, which are often subsumed when the secular is simply engaged as the opposite of "the religious."[45] Feminist politics in Pakistan must traverse a dense terrain in which the distinctions between the West and its Others, powerful globality and powerless locality, modern and premodern, and religious violence and secular violence are neither unambiguous nor permanently settled.

NOTES

1 The research for this paper was enabled by funds from the Social Sciences and Humanities Research Council of Canada (SSHRC).
2 This conflict ended in 1989 with the fall of the Soviet Union, the withdrawal of the United States from Afghanistan, and the beginning of a bloody war among Afghan groups for dominance in the country. Pakistan along with the UAE and Saudi Arabia gave diplomatic recognition to the repressive Taliban regime, which set up the Islamic Emirate of Afghanistan between 1966 and 2001.
3 Rahman, "Can Pakistan End Terrorism?"; Rashid, *Taliban*.
4 Rahman, "Can Pakistan End Terrorism?"; Nangiana, "Militancy Has Cost Pakistan 9,000 Lives."
5 For a good discussion of Pakistan's counter-terrorism policies, see Rahman, "Can Pakistan End Terrorism?" See also HRCP, "Govt–Taliban Deal Worries HRCP."
6 USAF, "Intelligence Targeting Guide," 1998.
7 I use the term victim-subject as used by postcolonial feminist scholars such as Kapur, "Un-Veiling Women's Rights"; See also Abu-Lughod, *The Muslim Woman*; and Razack, "Geopolitics."
8 Kapur, "Un-Veiling Women's Rights."
9 Spivak, "Use and Abuse of Human Rights," 134.

10 Grewal, "On the New Global Feminism"; Spivak, "Diasporas Old and New"; Grewal, *Transnational America*; Spivak, "Use and Abuse of Human Rights"; Mahmood, "Feminism, Democracy, and Empire."
11 Bauman, *Collateral Damage*, 4.
12 Bauman, *Collateral Damage*, 5.
13 Grewal, "On the New Global Feminism"; Spivak, "Diasporas Old and New"; Grewal, *Transnational America*; Razack, "Geopolitics"; Spivak, "Use and Abuse of Human Rights"; Mahmood, "Feminism, Democracy, and Empire."
14 "Religious Parties Threaten Protest in Blasphemy Case," *Dawn* (Lahore).
15 "Christian Woman Sentenced to Death," 2010; Jinnah Institute, "Research Brief: Aasia Bibi's case."
16 "Christian Woman Sentenced to Death," 2010; Jinnah Institute, "Research Brief."
17 I discuss these murders in further detail later in this chapter.
18 Siddiqui, "Three Women One Story."
19 Siddiqui, "Three Women One Story."
20 IJN, "Statement by Family."
21 Esposti, "Pakistan's Blasphemy Law."
22 Pakistan Penal Code 295-C: "Use of derogatory remarks, etc; in respect of the Holy Prophet. Whoever by words, either spoken or written or by visible representation, or by any imputation, innuendo, or insinuation, directly or indirectly, defiles the sacred name of the Holy Prophet Mohammed (PBUH) shall be punished with death, or imprisonment for life, and shall also be liable to fine."
23 Jinnah Institute, "Research Brief."
24 Pakistani feminist scholars have clearly demonstrated how international – mainly US and Saudi – support for Zia's government, in return for his acting as intermediary between the United States and the Afghan Mujahedeen against the Soviet Union, did much to further the so-called Islamization project in Pakistan. This Islamization program overhauled Pakistan's legal system and introduced a series of laws that have violated the human rights of many citizens, especially women and religious minorities.
25 "Religious Parties Threaten Protest."
26 "Religious Parties Threaten Protest."
27 Barq, "Two Women, Two Stories, Two Points of View."
28 Shah, "Mainstream Pakistan Religious Organisations."
29 Shah, "Mainstream Pakistan Religious Organisations."
30 Ghamdi, "The Penal Law." Ghamdi has been living in Malaysia since being threatened with death by militants opposed to his progressive and humanist understanding of Islam.

31 "No Change to Be Made," *The Nation*.

32 "Rehman Malik Sees Accord," *Dawn*.

33 "Court Indicts Raymond Davis," *Dawn* (Lahore).

34 The Law of *Qisas* (retribution) and *Diyat* (blood money), passed in 1990, covers all aspects of intentional and unintentional murders, bodily injuries, and abortion. According to this law, the compensation for a victim of murder – or bodily injury, if it is a woman or non-Muslim – will be half that for a Muslim male. See "Blood Money Option"; Weiss, "Implications of the Islamization Program for Women."

35 Sheikh and Chaudhry, "Davis Buys His Flight to Freedom."

36 Yusuf, "Fallout of the Davis Case."

37 Grewal "Women's Rights as Human Rights"; Kapur, "Un-Veiling Women's Rights"; Razack, "To Essentialize or ot to Essentialize"; Mahmood, "Feminism, Democracy, and Empire"; Spivak, "Use and Abuse of Human Rights."

38 For analysis of the power of the military in shaping and controlling "the state" and manipulating national political, economic, social, and cultural life, see Siddiqa, "Military Inc."; Rouse, *Shifting Body Politics*; Rashid, *Taliban*; Said Khan, "The Impact of the Global Women's Movement"; and Devji, "Red Mosque."

39 Saigol, "The State and the Limits," 1.

40 Saigol, "The State and the Limits," 10.

41 Saigol, "The State and the Limits," 10.

42 Supporters of universalized notions of fundamental rights and the human rights of women, sexual minorities, and religious minorities tend to refer to themselves as liberal progressives. Muslim women's feminist groups in Pakistan who ascribe to these objectives call for a secular state in which religious identity and political status are separated. Their projects are in opposition to those groups of men and women who reject secular or universalized notions of rights and who seek the Islamization of state and society by taking over the state through democratic means. These politico-religious groups, such as the Jamaat-e-Islami, are not to be confused with Muslim extremists, militants, and terrorists, who operate outside the sphere of electoral politics.

43 When I visited Karachi in June–July 2011, posters of Aafia Siddqui wearing an American graduation cap and gown, with the slogan "Daughter of the Nation," were plastered on walls, lampposts, shop windows, and so on.

44 See, for example, Haqqani, *Pakistan*; Siddiqa, *Military Inc.*; HRCP, "Militancy Intensifies Threats to Rights"; Jahangir, *Protecting Women*.

45 Needham and Sunder Rajan, The Crisis of Secularism"; Tejani, *Indian Secularism*.

9 Outsourcing Patriarchy: Feminist Encounters, Transnational Mediations, and the Crime of "Honour Killings"

INDERPAL GREWAL

"I'm so angry. These incidents are no longer restricted to remote villages or city fringes," said Advaita Rajvanshi, a New Friends Colony resident. "The honor killing menace has now reached the capital's posh localities."[1]

In this chapter I examine how media representations of "honour killings" become part of emergent cultures in different parts of the world. I suggest this occurs because such concepts circulate among multiple media, scholarly, and NGO circuits even when the approaches, struggles, and agendas differ. Rather than suggest how to define or eradicate such violence, I examine how this concept produces meaning, culture, and identity in linked and divergent ways.

I take it as a given that many forms of violence occur in order to control the sexuality of women (and men and others) and that women are subordinated and constrained in multiple ways specific to widely different notions of gender and sexuality that exist as these articulate with other social factors. Moreover, women have always tried to escape violence and many have paid dearly for that struggle. But the issue at hand is at what point and where that violence gets named as a specific crime called "honour" killing, with honour as a stable and unchanging term, and under what circumstances that naming occurs. I am thus interested in the process through which powerful circuits of knowledges produce hegemonic meanings as a consequence of which other possibilities, struggles, and violence remain submerged.

A second issue this project raises is that of feminist scholarship that engages with empire, race, and postcoloniality. In postcolonial and critical race scholarship, much has been said about the essentialist understanding of the woman subject. The "global feminist" project and an essential understanding of patriarchy as the same either globally or structurally has given way to understandings of gender as uneven, unstable, and contingent. Research on the patriarchy of the state has now shifted to examining what Wendy Brown calls the "masculinity" of the state. Feminist research, though, as Mrinalini Sinha has pointed out, has also become wary of "a potential evasion of the central feminist problematic: the gendered evasion of power." Sinha suggests that masculinity research does not necessarily evade these questions, though it may help us understand how "the pursuit of an always-elusive ideal of masculinity has animated some of the central events of history."[2]

Yet for analysing some regions and cultures, patriarchy continues to be the preferred analytic even if it is considered inadequate for understanding other regions. There seems to be geopolitics of colonialism and race in which some cultures are understood solely through patriarchy while others are seen to have outgrown it. My chapter investigates the phenomenon that the research on patriarchy continues to describe some parts of the world but not others. For some scholars, modernity involves disguising patriarchy as fraternity; Juliet Mac Cannell, for instance, has suggested that modernity claims the "alibi of fraternal love."[3] Tuija Pulkinnen argues that both Carole Pateman and Jacques Derrida share the belief that modernity involves a move from "undemocratic patriarchy to democratic brotherhood."[4]

I argue that the concept of patriarchy has been "outsourced" from the United States and Europe to do its messy work elsewhere. Such outsourcing requires many Americans to believe that patriarchy no longer exists in their country, or that, if it does, it is limited to zones believed to be anachronistic to the rest of the country. In this process, outsourcing as metaphor indexes the participation of corporate and transnational media and the value and profits that are extracted from such narratives of difference of a "patriarchy elsewhere." The profits are material in a number of ways, including fiscal gain, the production of media narratives that circulate transnationally, and the wars fought ostensibly to "save brown women from brown men," as Gayatri Spivak brilliantly argued.[5]

"Honour Killings": The Patriarchy of "Honour"

Feminist debates over "honour killings" are ongoing and vexed, as the use of the analytic of patriarchy continues to inform research on violence against women.[6] Having examined the circulation of "honour killings" as a concept in media coverage in India and in the "West," I conclude that feminist research is better served by examining how millennial modern subjects are being made by disavowing the existence of patriarchies even as gendered subordination and violence continues. In divergent yet linked ways, patriarchies and fraternities remain the locus of desire, struggle, nostalgia, and contradiction for gendered and sexualized subjects everywhere. Feminist research in this new century cannot disavow the project of examining and challenging gendered subordination, violence, and inequality, and it can argue for complex subjectivities that incorporate race, class, sexuality, religion, nationalism, colonialism, and neoliberalism.

Within feminist cultural studies, popular culture and the media industries have been subjects of analysis, pushing against the valorization of "high culture" or "exotic cultures" as the only subjects worthy of academic interest.[7] Media productions, in their relations with powerful culture industries, can reveal multiple and complex masculine power formations that are heterogeneous, as well as contradictory and conflicted (sometimes) and collaborative (at other times). The example of "honour killings" as they are made visible through multiple media platforms reveals both the crude mappings that I critique, but also the collaborations and struggles of feminists to make violence visible in ways that can become "voiced" and public.[8] Feminist debates on "honour killings" have yet to engage with the fact that the circulation of that topic in the popular media is important for understanding the term and its rapid circulation in many parts of the world. The term "honour killing" has circulated because it has the power to diagnose both the nature of a crime and its solution as being linked and confined to some particular societies following a racial logic. It proposes an analysis of power, its exercise, and the cause of the crime as this reified "culture" – there is little examination here of the history of the media in which such cultures and crimes are produced, defined, read, and understood. The identification of violence as "honour killing" may even foreclose a more mediated, historicized, multifaceted, or conflictual analytic.

Thus I understand "honour killings" as a media-ted concept that circulates as a transnational and national symbol of particular cultures; called a "crime" of "culture," its depiction and spectacularization moves us some distance but without separating us completely from the notion of "honour" societies as an anthropological concept. As media project, it is indeed different from culture as ongoing understanding of the social; yet the mediated notion works because of its presumed connection to an anthropological "real" as the foundation on which the "culture" of distant others can be produced as knowledge. At the same time, its visibility across media cultures in various genres of visual and print media as well in the discourse of NGOs and feminist advocacy networks (in Keck and Sikkink's terms) means it is a product of that anthropological culture as translated across transnational media and its technologies.[9]

What becomes of anthropological culture in its mediations? To add to Lila Abu-Lughod's recent analysis, I bring together some very divergent knowledge projects across different histories and technologies: anthropology of "honour" societies, feminist knowledges about patriarchies, the spectacle of violence on women in national and transnational media, and representations of violence in journalism. All of these focus on violence on female bodies, but they are also linked through shared and divergent assumptions about culture, gender, and social hierarchies created through media that build on other and prior knowledges. Yet in these days of transnational media corporations, such assumptions are not simply nationally bound. Rather, they become linked to geopolitical and national projects and to ideologies and "information" that circulate through and by means of media technologies.

The use of the term "honour killings" suggests notions of cultural difference that have been based on academic social science research in North America and Europe as well as in the Middle East and Asia. At this point, the term exists in a field of transnational overdeterminations. In this research, anthropological concepts such as "honour societies" are believed to signal "traditional" societies very different from "modern" ones. The complex of "honour" has been understood in anthropological research as a feature of particular societies, mostly located in the Mediterranean, the "Middle East," and South Asia. Pitt-Rivers defined it this way:[10] "The notion of honor ... is a sentiment, a manifestation of the sentiment in conduct, and the evaluation of this conduct by others, that is to say, reputation. It is both internal to the individual and external to him – a matter of his feelings, his behavior, and the treatment that he receives." Note that Pitt-Rivers refers to the object of analysis as a "him" – this is certainly a male subject, and a form of masculine power based on reputation and sentiment rather than a notion of violence (as patriarchy). Lila Abu-Lughod sees "honour" as part of the stratification and hierarchy in Mediterranean societies, and this approach, along with the wide range of behaviours associated with honour, has been influential in anthropology.[11] In a monograph on the topic, Frank Stewart sees "honour" as a right to respect or recognition within a particular society rather than as a sentiment.[12]

This notion of "honour cultures" has not, however, died out with a critique of those anthropological knowledge traditions that produced non-Western societies as "backward" or "primitive." It continues to have explanatory value for some researchers. In Bourdieu, the concept moves from a cultural relativist idea within anthropology to understanding it through an adjudication of rights. He sees the concept of "honour" through the conflict between particulars and universals (1990), and he suggests that the "ethos of honour" is to be opposed to a "universal and formal morality, which affirms that equality in dignity of all men and consequently the equality of their rights and dignities."[13]

Already for Bourdieu, cultural difference between modern and non-modern cultures is signalled by the term, and this move continues in other work. Mark Moritz considers honour cultures to be "those cultures that have what Stewart calls a code of reflexive honor: that is, a culture that demands a counterattack on the part of a man whose honor has been impugned and in which a failure to do so results in the loss of honour." In a crucial shift from describing culture to describing violence, Moritz continues:

> A feature of many honor cultures is that men are prepared to use violence and even die to defend their reputation as honorable men. Moreover, aggression in these specific contexts is institutionalized, regarded as legitimate and necessary by the society at large. Other features associated with many, but not all, honor cultures include a concern with the chastity of women, extreme vigilance about one's reputation and a sensitivity to insults, male autonomy, patrilineal kin groups, and assertive and often violent relations outside of the kin groups.[14]

It is clear that much of this anthropological literature, which earlier had not been linked to gendered subordination or the control of women, has shifted to the supposedly feminist approach that we have found since the 1990s and into this new century. Some scholars saw "honour" in terms of personal or individual differentiation from society – indeed, this is the case in some of the social stratification literature. But even among those who might critique such a literature, there are many who use the term "honour crime" to make a political point about violence against women. The use of "honour" in relation to culture and society has moved from a description of social differentiation within cultures to one of pathology of culture: from a cultural ideology existing across a society to a crime. Michael Herzfelt, among others, has critiqued the use of the term for referring to what he sees as quite divergent and broad practices.[15] His thinking also marks a move from structural functionalist analysis towards a more fluid view of social life within anthropology as well as a critique of colonial ideas about culture and modernity.[16]

Yet the struggle over the term has come to focus on whether culture becomes fixed; on whether the media have the power to change it; and on whether transnational mobility entrenches "tradition."[17] In one set of arguments, cultures are unchanging or ahistorical; even mobility or diaspora contexts cannot alter them. This line is taken especially in some research on the Middle East. Yotam Feldner writes that "today, honor killings are prevalent mostly among Muslim populations" and that the "notion of honor" exists in "traditional Arab Society," in which there are two kinds of honour, that of the family or tribe and that of the individual. One, "sharaf," translates as "dignity"; the other, "ird," as "chastity" or "purity" and is related only to the honour of women.[18]

For scholars who struggle against ahistorical formulations but who wish to retain the notion of honour as pathology, the term describes the effects on particular communities of a racist Western context. In this view, immigrant communities in Europe are in *conflict* with their host cultures; furthermore, the process of immigrating to a racist host culture is what makes immigrant cultures more "traditional."[19] Unni Wikan, in a book examining the "honour killing" of a young immigrant woman in Sweden, suggests that honour takes on a different meaning in immigrant communities in hostile states. She argues that racism in the West encourages men to turn to "honour" in order to claim cultural difference; but even in her argument, culture remains the explanation for violence. "Honour," then, refers to the respect and reputation that are necessary for immigrants to survive. She does not link this effect to Islam, instead arguing that it is part of patriarchal and "tribal" social structures,[20] although her research does not explain how it is that the term sticks only to Muslim bodies and communities. In the Swedish case mentioned here, Shahrzad Mojab and Amir Hassanpour argue that it is not culture that is at fault but a racist Swedish culture that views Kurds as unassimilable and that ignores a Kurdish history of feminism.[21]

These anthropological descriptions still posit some cultures as distant from the "West," as unchanging and ahistorical, or becoming as violent and pathological as they are mobile or displaced. Yet they do not explain why the term "honour killing" has come to be applied mainly to family violence in Muslim communities, be they in Europe or the Middle East, and why the anthropological use of the term as descriptive of a broader concept of "Mediterranean" society seems to have fallen out. Much of this research, even from feminists, relies on Weberian divisions between traditional and modern societies to implicitly suggest that "modern" societies are not "honour" societies. When "honour" is related to "diasporic" and mobile societies, it is in order to demarcate "immigrant" from "host" cultures. Thus for instance, in the United States, when a man murders his wife for trying to leave him, no one calls this an "honour killing" (unless, of course, the killer is a Muslim or South Asian). And when a Muslim father or brother murders a daughter or sister, it is called an "honour killing" because it is assumed that modern, non-Muslim men do not kill their daughters or sisters. In the United States, when entire families are killed by their fathers, brothers, or relatives, these are not called "honour killings," and neither are those murder-suicides, all too common, where the man kills his wife and family and then himself. Thus "modern man" is not motivated by something called "honour," so patriarchal violence and control of women by families exist elsewhere in time and place, reflecting that allochronic discourse that Johannes Fabian identified in his classic critique.[22]

The history of this concept in anthropology as it relates to the Middle East, and especially to feminist anthropology, is similarly long and vexed. Much of it is based on foundational work by Nawal Al Sadaawi, Fatima Mernissi,[23] and Kitty Warnock.[24] Yet even in their works, the emphasis on patriarchy and masculinity as the sources of violence remains within the frame suggested by Moritz. With regard to feminist research that critiques notions of "honour killings," much of it is concerned with understanding how patriarchy has continued into the present day and with arguing against colonial representations. Lama Abu-Odeh contends that honour society is organized around the notion of purity and that in such contexts, violence is seen as protection."[25] In the most perceptive of these analyses, Diane King suggests that patrilineage and reproductive sovereignty explain "honour killings" in Kurdistan.[26] She seeks to embed the practice in frameworks of money and power rather than in an ahistorical "tradition." Even in anthropology, the term "honour" seems to have become sutured to a crime rather than to behaviour or even to masculinity – to a crime, moreover, that is understood through narratives and images, overlaid from European colonialism onto twentieth- and twenty-first-century cinema and television.

The "crime of culture" has taken on a new life in journalism and the media. Honour is used solely to explain a crime – more specifically, the *cause* of the crime. In other words, "honour killing" refers not simply to a cause of death but also to that cause being the work of a patriarchy. This patriarchy of "honour killings" is understood to be sometimes unchangeable and sometimes recuperable by localized factors. The term "honour killing" enables the articulation of this patriarchy in some sites and locations and communities but not in others – it sticks to a crime by certain bodies against other bodies, and it can move to some new bodies but not to others. It seems to have little explanatory value for societies seen as "Western," yet a great deal when the concept is yoked to Middle Eastern or South Asian bodies and groups.

Patriarchy as a Concept in Feminist Analysis

If "patriarchy" is not seen as having explanatory value in some sites, it is also because academic knowledges have understood patriarchy as an essentialist notion that is yoked to that of the "essential woman." Heidi Hartmann has defined patriarchy as "a set of social relations between men, which have a material base, and which, though hierarchical, establish or create interdependence or solidarity among men that enable them to dominate women."[27] For some, such as Juliet Mitchell, patriarchy is a universal ideology that predates capitalism; for others, it is linked to the emergence of capitalism.[28] Critiquing some of these approaches, Chantal Mouffe suggests that patriarchy is as essentializing a concept as "woman" or "man"; following Gayle Rubin, she argues that a "sex/gender system" would be a better tool for studying how "women's subordination is constructed in different practices, discourse and institutions."[29] Theories of patriarchy have been critiqued for being too structuralist, too static, and too totalizing and for being unable to address subordination outside the family or changing institutions and diverse histories. Going beyond structuralist notions of society and beyond binary gender, many scholars have begun to think of power and gender as more fluid, dynamic, and mutable. The turn to masculinity studies and queer theory has been an important reason for not producing totalizing understandings – "men" as a category has become complicated by articulations of a variety of sexualities and masculinities, including female, and transgender studies have further articulated the malleability and performativity of gender as well as its complex relation to bodies, sexualities, biology, desire, and so on.[30]

Yet patriarchy has not always been yoked to universalizing or essentialist analyses; in the work of Michelle Rosaldo, Jane Collier, and Sylvia Yanagasako, for instance, the term refers to inequalities not only between women and men but also between different groups of men.[31] Wary of stereotypes and colonial histories within their discipline of anthropology, they pushed for a more dynamic and divergent theorization of the term. That term could be useful if it were unyoked from the critique of the essential "woman" and if it were connected to a networked and dynamic notion of power and sovereignty (as Diane King suggests) or even treated as an imaginary produced by desire and nostalgia – an imaginary that can have material effects that make it responsible for so much gendered violence.

If the term "patriarchy" was coined by feminist and women's movements and academic knowledge production, it has come to be naturalized in relation to the global South as well as among communities that have migrated from the global South to the West – and today especially to Muslim communities, which seem to be understood through patriarchy. How are we to explain the erasure of patriarchy as a concept for the "West," especially since there is considerable evidence that inequalities (not to mention many forms of violence, often fatal) persist in that "West" across gender and that gender and sexuality remain critical aspects of identities and political subordinations and mobilizations? One answer is that patriarchies are now consolidated – in the United States, for instance – in many localized social and political formations. Religious groups, right-wing conservatives, homophobes, and white supremacists – all of these may nurture patriarchy both as a networked form of power and as a heteropatriarchical imaginary. Fraternities – male-identified collectives or networks – may not need to control women to gain legitimacy, but they still create networks of power and support, be it racial, sexual, financial, social, or political. These networks may distinguish themselves from patriarchies but still work through forms of masculinity that exist to suture relationships between men.[32] In particular, societies that see themselves as liberal may retain male power as hegemonic while enabling some groups of women to gain power. But in order to consolidate the West as modern, liberal Western cultures have both disavowed patriarchy and "outsourced" it. Thus, in the case of white males, violence against women is blamed on individual criminality rather than cultural factors, and in the case of minority groups, it is linked to pathological cultures. And this is where the media step in to circulate the outsourcing of patriarchy though the workings and ideologies of technologized capital.

"Honour Killings" in English-Language Transnational Media

In the United States and throughout the transnational print media (a search of LexisNexis pulled up more than nine hundred entries from the United States, Britain, Australia, Pakistan, the Middle East, and India), "honour killings" are represented as the work of "Muslim culture," which nurtures an intractable patriarchy. Often, though, the terms "Muslim" and "South Asian" are collapsed – an indication that religion and culture are being confused during the process of constructing racial difference. In the West's English-language press – specifically the United States and Britain – all references to the term "honour killing" involve the killings of young women of Muslim, South Asian, or Middle Eastern descent. These accounts are all quite similar: the young woman was marrying, in love with, or eloping with a young man of a different race, religion, caste, or subcaste and was refusing an "arranged marriage"; for this, she was murdered by her parents or brothers. In the United States, legal scholar Leti Volpp sees evidence of a cultural bias against Muslim communities, for the cause is always assumed to be the exercise of patriarchal power in the name of "honour."[33] In her powerful critique, Sherene Razack has identified the racist project at work in such representations in Canada.[34] A patriarchy, Indian, Muslim, is described as "traditional," and the young woman is always understood as "modern" and thus in conflict with the patriarchal traditional family that does not want to change after it joins the diaspora.

In the more than nine hundred entries on the topic from the United States, Britain, and Australia, the pattern was as follows: "Honour killings" were understood to be the workings of a primordial, unchanging, and ahistorical Muslim patriarchy. Of those news items *not* about Muslim-majority countries, most concerned Muslim or South Asian diasporas in the Britain or the United States, and it was presumed that the female victim had been killed by family members. In a handful of articles – perhaps two or three out of nine hundred – some community members protested the use of the term "honour killing," asking that the crime be seen as domestic violence instead. But these few voices were drowned out by the relentless circulation of culturalist narratives blaming Muslim societies for crimes against women. The notion of "honour" as an attribute of immigrant males from the Middle East or South Asia retained its power. It was presumed that the patriarchy had travelled to the West without change or alteration.[35]

News reports about "honour killings" – in Britain, for instance – have led to the mobilization of a broad apparatus of governance and anti-immigrant discourse that claims itself as concerned about multiculturalism. When honour killings serve to index the patriarchy of racial others who have immigrated to Europe, denunciations of those cultures can be framed in terms of protecting women. In response to the discourse of "honour killings," immigration tests require young women to testify that they did not undergo a forced marriage, welfare agencies have made it their task to shelter young South Asian women, and the police keep close watch on Asian males and families.[36] For conservative commentators in Britain, "honour killings" are indicators of a too-tolerant multiculturalism and a flawed immigration policy. In 2011, while Europe was in the middle of a financial crisis, British Prime Minister David Cameron, French President Nicolas Sarkozy, and German Chancellor Angela Merkel stated that multiculturalism was against Western values of gender equality.[37]

Scholars and activists have denounced this conservative and often racist media coverage even as some of them suggest that "honour killings" are a form of crime that should be addressed and prevented. Caught in the web of debates about human rights, multiculturalism, racism, and feminism, there seems to be little opportunity to problematize the articulation of these crimes outside of genealogies of racial, colonial, and postcolonial law and order. Thus Meetoo and Mirza ask why it is that "only in relation to religious and ethnic communities is the concept of 'honour' invoked as a motivation for domestic violence."[38] Dustin and Phillips write that the "discourses over culture tending to misrepresent minority cultural groups as monolithic entities, and initiatives to protect women become entangled with anti-immigration agendas."[39] I would suggest that pervasive anti-Muslim racism, hypertrophic since 9/11, also has much to do with this representation and governance.

"Honour Killings" in Indian Print Media

But what about outside the "West"? In the summers of 2009, 2010, and 2011, the English newspapers in Delhi were full of stories about "honour killings." The newspapers stated that "khap panchayats" – informal village- and upper-caste-based organizations – were enabling and abetting these murders. It seemed that the victims were young couples or women who had crossed caste lines to marry into a different caste or who had run off with cousins or partners from castes or groups deemed off limits for marriage. The papers reported that the fathers, mothers, and brothers of these young people – most of whom were girls or women – were killing their daughters or sisters as well as their lovers or husbands. The Lok Sabha is considering legislation that would criminalize families involved in such "honour killings." Also, the Supreme Court is seeking ways to codify "honour killings" as a separate crime punishable by death, and the Home Ministry is planning changes to criminal penalties in the Indian Penal Code.

A database search of one newspaper, the *Hindustan Times*, indicates that it has dramatically increased its representation of this crime over the past decade. In 2004, *HT* published six articles: one on *khap panchayats*, "Gotra Khaps Losing Out to Times, Awareness," in 26 October 2004; one on general issues of violence against women and girls; one on a man killing his sister's lover (but not the sister); one on a British conference reporting that in London, "117 deaths and disappearances of Asian women are being re-investigated" (7 December 2004); and one on Pakistan reporting that these crimes exist because of the lack of democracy and human rights in Pakistan: "Establishing Democracy First Step towards Human Rights in Pak: Experts" (10 December 2004).

In 2005, there were eighteen articles. Most of these focused on Pakistan because of coverage of the Mukhtaran Mai case; several others concerned a couple in the South Asian diaspora in Britain. In 2006, *HT* published fifteen articles, fourteen of them on Pakistan and one on German Muslim migrants. In 2007, there were again fifteen articles, nine of them on Pakistan (one reporting that the Pakistan Supreme Court had declared "honour killing" to be "culpable murder for which, in law, death or life sentence was prescribed") and two on Pakistani-origin girls in Britain. In 2008 and 2009, these articles trebled: forty-one in 2008, thirteen of these about Pakistan, as well as a few about Muslims in Europe and Britain, and the rest about India.

In the academic literature on women and media in India, very few feminist publications before 2005 refer to "honour killings" when discussing media coverage of violence against women. In a book titled *New Woman and Mass Media* (2001), Uma Singh tracks how crimes against women are reported. Crimes against women include dowry deaths, sex-selective abortions, rape, sexual harassment, murder, trafficking, and the "exploitation of minor girls" (66), but there is no mention of

"honour killings."[40] According to Sameera Khan, the women's movement, as it agitated for more attention to women's issues, "helped
bring the increasing rates of violence against women – particularly
rape, molestation, dowry deaths, and domestic abuse – to the media's
notice." Yet Khan does not mention "honour killings" as a distinct issue in the category of "crimes against women."[41] Most of the academic
publications relating to women prior to the new century do not list
"honour killings" when discussing either violence or crimes against
women or the media coverage of women's issues.[42] In their anthology
about the topic, Lynn Welchman and Sara Hossain write that indeed,
"in the last few years there has been a spurt in discussions on and serious academic interest in the question of honour killings," but they do
not examine how and why this has emerged over the past six or seven
years.[43]

In 2006, there is one citation of "honour" as a sociological issue for
women. It is found in a scholarly book about gender in Indian cinema
by Indubala Singh. In her introduction, she discusses gender ideologies: "Consistent with the cultural norms pertaining to the status of
women in India is the honour of the family, which is closely linked to
the female behavior. The need to preserve honour is expressed through
elaborate codified behavior patterns that require the women to be dependent."[44] In this 2006 work, there appears a growing use of the term
among feminist researchers.

Singh does not suggest that an honour culture exists only in rural
India. For their part, the news media blame most of these killings on
khap panchayats, the Hindu, North Indian, upper-caste-based, village-
level groups that police the boundaries of caste through gender and
sexuality. Any discussion of "honour killings" in India links the *khap
panchayats* to these murders,[45] even though newspapers also report on
such incidents in southern India as well as in cities. Some groups – such
as the Sarv Khap Mahapanchayat in Haryana – are seeking changes
to the Hindu Marriage Act that would disallow marriage within particular caste groups as "incest," even though there are very few laws
specific to incest. India's Supreme Court has stated that these murders
are "barbaric" and evidence of a "feudal mindset" and is seeking to
increase the penalties for such crimes.

Prem Chowdhry has examined "honour killings" in the state of Haryana in the colonial and postcolonial periods and argues that the present
day has seen the development of a new notion of honour among rural
elites – mainly of the Jat caste – who feel threatened by the changes

being brought about by globalization. Her work helps us understand how honour is being used to control women's sexuality in both cities and villages.[46] Her focus on the Hindu Succession Act of 1955, which allowed women (mothers and widows) to inherit ancestral property, and its amendment in 2005, which extended daughters the same rights as sons, brings to light that honour is not simply about culture or tradition – it is just as much about economic transactions and how these are controlled through women's sexuality. When we merge the economic issue of property and inheritance with the "crisis of masculinity" argument, the notion of honour exposes itself as both an alibi and an economic ruse. At the same time, the focus on Haryana's Jats does not accord with the many cases of "honour killings" mentioned in the media that do not concern Haryana. It is debatable, though, whether all of these factors – property, sexual control, the crisis of masculinity, the rise in elopements, the emergence of individuality and of "choice" in marriage, class interests that may clash with caste interests, globalization, increased media coverage, and NGO interest – can be understood through the notion of honour. One can add to this list the struggles around quotas for Dalits and OBCs, rising property costs, the crisis in agriculture, and the emergence of new jobs for women.

Pratiksha Bakshi and her colleagues argue that the greater participation in governance extended to *gram panchayats* (elected village councils), which overlap considerably with upper-caste *panchayats*, has exacerbated the rift between tradition and modernity and thus led to "honour killings." They suggest that the rift between tradition and modernity develops parallel to the one between the governance of polities and the governance of communities, as well as among the various local sovereignties.[47] In identifying rural, caste patriarchy's nexus with political power, and the conflict of these with the new economies that seem to threaten these power formations, Bakshi and her colleagues use the term "honour killings" to describe what they see as a coherent phenomenon. For them as well, the conflicts between sovereignties – local and central – lead to something called "honour," which is understood as empirically real as expressed by the media, the *panchayats*, the international press, and the victims as well.

Although all of these changes heighten struggles over gender and sexuality, the use of honour has other genealogies when we examine how the media have become globalized. Feminist and other scholars working on the topic have argued that the increase in "honour killings" has been the result of economic liberalization, but they have paid little attention to how the term is used transnationally and they have not examined the media's role in circulating the concept. In the globalized media, law and order is a spectacle; the news presents "honour killings" through narratives that describe the violence, the mode of death, the condition of the body, and the escape, pursuit, and capture of the criminal. The same dynamic is also visible in media accounts of village *panchayats*, which describe gatherings of rural upper-caste men (mostly of the Jat caste, especially in Haryana), or describe parents and families whose pathologies are most clearly understood in terms of "honour." This news reporting is buttressed in the opinion pages by writers who create a distinction, first, between an India of human rights and empowered women and a Pakistan that lacks these, and second, between urban and rural, between the "India shining" of NGOs and cosmopolitan and global subjects and the India of rural patriarchy and poverty. The problem of ongoing inequalities in India across gender, sexuality, caste, and religion is ignored when it is contained within one region or caste, or when it is seen as a rural problem in which the "national-modern," as Tejaswini Niranjana calls it, in its new mode as "global modern," is absolved of its participation in such violence. Even those who disagree that "honour killings" are the result of notions of honour, still believe they arise from an "old order" that is determined to maintain sexual control by repressing "individual freedom." Niranjana has argued that in South Indian cinema, "romantic love" is refigured in "national-modern" terms in which caste and community are replaced by the individual and in which women's agency is expressed in the service of a cultural nationalism that is in the "vocabulary of the multinational market economy."[48] This "moral panic" discourse is also being used by Hindu nationalist groups to foment anti-Muslim hatred by accusing Muslims of luring Hindu girls to elope with them.[49]

This distinction between rural or urban is clear to newspaper readers. For instance, in a *Times of India* blog in response to an article on "honour killings," posted in June 2010, one commentator stated: "Like the scourges of dowry and female foeticide, a generation ago, honour killings seem to be spreading to newer areas … Not very long ago, we thought that such barbarism belonged to remote tribal reaches of Pakistan … Most of us are baffled by the phenomenon. This is so much at odds with the new India we hope and dream about." A *Times of India* article on the same topic on 31 March 2010 began by describing a *khap panchayat* as a "Taliban-style caste panchayat." The term's stickiness to Muslim bodies circulated by transnational media is visible in such narratives.

The *Deccan Herald*, another daily newspaper in Delhi, published an opinion piece in its magazine section titled "Feudal Mindset: In the Heart of Darkness."[50] Its author, D.R. Choudhry, argued that such killings were occurring not because of an ahistorical "culture" but because "traditional rural structure is fast cracking up under the impact of modernization. Change has come home because of improved means of transport, evolved interpersonal communication, an elaborate network of educational institutions, exposure to the world beyond the village borders and more through the media." These changes, he continued, had led to the *khaps* passing "barbaric edicts." As a consequence, "Haryana has become a killing field for the youths who dare to opt for a matrimonial alliance of their choice." In this writer's view, law and criminal penalties were required; otherwise, "we will lapse into the dark zone of barbarity and depravity." Law-and-order measures, court directives, and police protection were the solutions. This author approved of the death penalty for five people involved in one case of "honour killing," as well as life imprisonment for the leader of the local *khap*.

Although news dailies diverge politically, they all seem to use the term "honour killings," which suggests that print journalism's culture is connected, powerful, and transnational. It is striking that even the Hindi-language newspapers, which have far more readers than the English dailies, also use the English term "honour killings," suggesting both its Western provenance and its power to circulate.

Clearly, this discourse is proliferating – the reports all provide a sense that this violence is increasing in India in the era of economic globalization. These reports suggest that in contemporary culture, changes are occurring that are unlike anything in the past. News reports from Punjab tell us that many young women who have "disappeared" are actually the victims of "honour killings" and that the courts are full of young couples seeking protection from their families. Surprisingly, protection has been granted to lesbian as well as heterosexual couples. Newspapers are ending their decades of ignoring violence against women – violence that pervades all aspects of urban/rural, new/old India – and beginning to focus on rape and on presenting "honour killings" as a singular crime whose cause, being identifiable, can be addressed.[51] That said, the news media are more accustomed to following trends, and they publish stories and ideas that already hold the public's interest. Consequently, only a few types of crimes receive attention, and even when they do, the analysis is reductive and sensationalized and often contradictory. Newspaper coverage of "honour killings" suggests that women are more constrained in rural than in urban India; but that same coverage also reveals that rape is a common occurrence in urban areas such as Delhi. Although the local news covers rape extensively, policing against rape remains a challenge and the laws regarding sexual assault are often murky. For instance, Section 377 (the anti-sodomy statute) was initially "read down" rather than removed from the Indian Penal Code in 2009 because it was used to prosecute sexual assaults against minors owing to the lack of specific laws against these crimes.[52] Many criminal and harmful acts seem not to be addressed by specific laws, enabling activists to seek special penalties for "honour killings."[53]

I ascribe the use of terms such as "honour killings" to the pervasive circulation of the concept in international media in relation to Islamophobia in the aftermath of 9/11 as well as to the expansion and globalization of the media now that India is emerging as a modern-day global power. Note that anti-Muslim sentiment is nothing new in India, as evidenced by the widespread discrimination and poverty besetting Indian Muslim communities. In the past two decades, right-wing Hindu parties have encouraged anti-Muslim sentiments and launched pogroms against Muslims. Setting aside the anti-Muslim genealogy of the term, media productions of "honour killings" serve to distinguish the middle-class metropolitans who see themselves as modern from the "barbaric" rural patriarchy that enables these crimes – and not just in "remote regions" of Pakistan. This is an example of modernity attempting to expel patriarchy, and Islamophobia, to rural areas. Such "outsourcing" is visible in the opinion pages of newspapers. The *Times of India*, a more conservative paper than the *Hindustan Times*, posted an opinion piece on its blog by Nandita Sengupta, regarding her visit a village where a murder had occurred:

> This is in Kinanagar, near Meerut. In two hours, one can travel 200 years back. Or perhaps not. The reality is that honour killing is as contemporary and happening as it always was ...
>
> Kinanagar is a huge village, more than 10,000 heads. Signages proudly proclaim it is a PM *sadak yojna lab* ... The roads are great, the houses neat. Kinanagar may proudly feature as a feather in some ministerial cap. It's doing well. The kids are in school, and the inter-college admissions are full. More colleges are required. The elders are happy.
>
> But as governments carry progress on silk-smooth roads into these villages, who is responsible for nurturing their hearts and souls? ... It's all very well to decry in cities the horror of it all, but what is being done about it beyond the omigosh anguish?"[54]

Even if there *is* material progress, Sengupta writes, these village folks have a patriarchal culture; caste and religious divisions are embedded in their lives, and progress cannot change this. At the same time, both the story she tells and the language she uses ("omigosh anguish") produce her as a transnational, cosmopolitan subject. She goes on to write that "the real story is really in the decay that sets in as a direct result of the police-pradhan-politician's indirect endorsement of honour killings," and she calls for government intervention in naming the crimes for what they are and punishing villages where they occur.

Again, the idea is that cultural change has come to the cities but not to the villages and that this unchanged culture is hidden inside people. So when a young urban woman is murdered in the city, or a couple is, this is treated as a scandal and blamed on the encroachment of the old rural India into the new global metropolitan India.[55]

The spatial divide between rural and urban India has become a temporal one. In most accounts, the cities are where these eloping couples – in the news stories, generally from rural areas – find refuge until, as often happens, they are brought back to their village by force. In an India where the economy is unsettled, where social and cultural divisions are changing as a result of new media outlets, where girls and women enjoy new employment opportunities, where corporate entrepreneurship has become a force, and where gender and sexuality are now being used to sell goods to a burgeoning consumer culture, whatever falls outside this liberalized global economy and its circulation has become tradition, archaic, rural, and "barbaric." In this new modernity, Islamophobia can be articulated as characteristic of some other nation and state rather than as endemic in India.[56]

India's Metropolitan Media Culture

The concepts of "honour" and "tradition" are being recuperated in these stories even though they are increasingly being seen as signifiers of backwardness, akin to caste identity, which must be disavowed. The media – print, television, cinema, the Internet – become vehicles for this progress and thus view themselves as outside tradition. In particular, as the newspapers post online editions that are read in South Asian diasporas all over the world, the separation between the "rural" India and this transnational "global India" circulates widely.

The increased use of the term "honour killings" signals the rise of media that are transnationally connected (some to transnational corporations) and that are expanding their reach and clout. In this regard, it is important to consider the history of print newspapers in India, especially the English-language ones. The Indian English-language press was founded largely by nationalist and reformist movements during the struggle for independence, and its anti-state ideologies became pro-state after independence.[57] In 1971, after Indira Gandhi declared a state of emergency, the press became much more independent from the state and new media outlets came into existence. For instance, *Indian Express*, a more right-wing Hindu English-language daily, began publication, and its stance has been somewhat more anti-Muslim than that of other newspapers. Joseph and Sharma have remarked on its anti-Muslim coverage of Shah Bano controversy.[58] Since then, many dailies have become less regional and more pan-Indian, with offices in several cities. The vernacular press has also developed a large public; by 1978, the Hindi press had many more readers than the English one. The vernacular press also has greater reach and more stringers across smaller cities.[59]

With the emergence of new media and powerful diasporas, English-language dailies have developed transnational publics. Arvind Rajagopal points out that English-language dailies have become more powerful because the language of the global India is English and is dominated by upper castes, whose members are "not always well-informed on historical or domestic issues." The Report of the Joshi Committee noted in 1985 that there is a class and gender bias on Indian television that erases the struggles of women and their achievements.[60] Robin Jeffrey has argued that Indian news media are controlled largely by those who were educated in Europe or North America, "so that the 'package" is international, though the content is sensitively local."[61] Almost all editors and reporters are of higher caste; very few are Dalits.[62]

Rajagopal's concept of "international audiences" signals the complexities that arise when news dailies publish print editions for transnational audiences. He does, though, suggest importantly that the "state and its failures" remain the focus of news reporting and that the media have not shifted as much to scrutiny of the private sector. Hence much of the coverage of "honour killings" and related crimes focuses on law and order or government corruption rather than interrogating how urban and rural cultures are infused with gendered inequities that remain unaddressed.[63]

The expansion of the media (TV, multiple twenty-four-hour news channels, the Internet) since the end of state controls has become a sign of progress. "India shining" is now the media industry's ideology, and this is linked to the new global urban elites and their projects. Thus the members of that industry are seeking new law-and-order mechanisms for "women's issues." So it is possible for *India Today*'s online edition to conclude an article on "honour killings" with this summary: "A complete overhaul of the Special Marriage Act is needed to aid marriage across caste and religion."[64]

Kalpana Sharma has pointed out that with the new and expanded media, there has emerged as a frenzy of crime coverage both in newspapers and on television.[65] She points out that crimes committed against middle and upper classes receive much greater attention than crimes against working-class or Dalit women. Maxine Lloyd argues that on the television news, caste is viewed as "backward and uncivilized," even though that particular medium operates with a normative upper-caste and Hindu bias: "many news articles and commentaries treat caste politics and parties as harmful to India and detrimental to modernity." Thus when communities that have been discriminated against, such as Dalits or Muslims, organize by caste or religion, the TV news tends to portray them as a problem: "Organizing politics around caste is seen as a threat to an idea of Indianness where differences should be minimized."[66]

Reports of rape have increased dramatically in Indian cities, so even more reporters are covering this topic. The recent horrific gang rape in Delhi and the protests that followed testify to the ongoing coverage, to police inaction, and to a tolerance for violence against women that continues in urban areas despite the pervasive sense that urban India is less patriarchal than rural India. Yet even in this case, which made headlines globally and created huge street protests, the rapists were identified as migrants to the city and thus as outsiders destroying the city. While it is commonly believed that the issue of rape is not covered adequately in the news, rape has been a staple of cinema and journalism; furthermore, when these crimes are covered, that coverage is often sensationalized, with multiple and complex effects that cannot be controlled by feminists' views of such crimes.

The ambiguity of visual representations of rape in Hollywood cinema has been well documented.[67] The spectacle of the rape of women is also not new in Indian media, and Hindi cinema's focus on it has long been a problem because it naturalizes violence and provides, as Karen Gabriel argues, both "pleasurable spectacle" and a "male fantasy of control."[68] News coverage of rape may be the result of feminist organizing, but it also recuperates narratives of male control and protection. Indian programming, both TV and Web, relies heavily on Hindi feature films. Commercial Hindi cinema relies on nationalist and patriarchal ideologies, with the result that such narratives pervade televisual and cinema culture.

Crimes such as rape and "honour killings" are well reported in the news, but that coverage often simply replicates "police handouts" and can be sensationalized and biased as well as "poorly researched."[69] A term such as "honour killing" becomes very convenient when police are investigating a murder, since such a crime may not require a great deal of investigation. Reduced coverage of socio-economic issues[70] may actually discourage police from investigating whether the murder had a motive related to, say, money or property. In rural areas, this lack of attention to the economic issues is a major lacuna in narratives of "honour killing." Prem Chowdhry has suggested that with regard to inheritance and property, legal and cultural biases mean that control of property remains in the hands of men. As a consequence, violence may be applied to help ensure that women marry appropriate partners.[71] Property laws may have changed, but the practices of inheritance and property remain with men, and women are often forced to sign away their rights, as Chowdhry also reveals. Given that so many women have no access to the courts or the time or power to seek legal remedies, and given the multiple ways in which men control property within existing marriage and inheritance laws, there is little to ensure that women can escape their constraints, wherever they live and whatever their class or caste.[72] Neither legislatures nor courts are anxious to deal with these questions of property and rights. "Honour killings" and the media outrage against them have increased the power of the media and the law-and-order apparatus in ways that do not address the multiple forms that violence takes. In these ways, "honour killings" as crimes of culture confound some key issues facing modern India, relegating the problem of gendered violence to particular regions, religions, and castes. Flavia Agnes has written that "unless property is situated at the centre of the discourse on women and legal reform," economic rights will not be available to Indian women.[73] What we find, then, is that pervasive social and economic issues remain unrecognized even while the courts in India seem on the verge of creating special laws around "honour killings."

Finally, "honour killings" work well in cinema and on television. Nicole Rafter has argued that crime movies allow audiences to identify with the restoration of order; they are asked to assent to violence done in the name of restoring order.[74] Feminist media and literary scholars recognize that the crime and its detection reflect forms of power that shore up patriarchy. Detection, which provides the satisfaction of closure, is the product of powerful ideas about colonial science, policy, and race as well as a long history of print and now visual culture. The media spectacle is important here: the crime and its graphic details link up to the pervasiveness of the cinema of crime and revenge in India, as well as the television crime shows circulating transnationally from the West.

"Honour killings" produce an easy upper-caste and class and racial and developmental answer to the crime. The viewer becomes the detective in the Western crime show – or the police, in the Bollywood tradition – and particular cultures are criminalized in order to bring closure to the crime. Law and order are the coordinates through which it can be decoded, and the crime can be outsourced to places and times that are distant from the global, modern subject. The viewer joins with the state, thereby utilizing its sovereign powers to "solve" the crime. No further investigation is required then – no knowledge, as Prem Chowdhry has argued, of the multiple economic arrangements in which errant young people can be disposed of lest they claim their rights.

NOTES

Many colleagues, friends, and audiences have helped me think through this project. In particular, I want to thank colleagues and audiences at Utrecht University, the University of Waterloo, Harvard University, Brown University, the University of Connecticut, and the University of Toronto, as well as the organizers of the first annual conference of the *International Feminist Journal of Politics* and the audiences at the University of Free State in Bloemfontein, and the University of Witwatersrand WISER group and Centre for Indian Studies in Africa. A shorter version of this paper was published in as "Outsourcing Patriarchy: 'Honor Killings' and Transnational Mediations" in *International Feminist Journal of Politics* 15(1) (2013): 1–19.

1 http://blogs.wsj.com/indiarealtime/2010/07/13/posh-delhi-enclave-confronts-honor-killing. This is the *Wall Street Journal* blog "IndiaRealTime"; however, it was launched in 2010 by Indian and Western journalists. For its personnel, see http://blogs.wsj.com/indiarealtime/bios.

2 Sinha, "Giving Masculinity a History."

3 McCannell, *The Regime of the Brother*.

4 Pulkkinen, "Tradition, Gender and Democracy to Come."

5 Spivak, "Can the Subaltern Speak?", in *Colonial Discourse and Postcolonial Theory*.

6 See, for instance, the use of the notion of "honour" in Menon and Bhasin, "Abducted Women, the State, and Questions of Honour." What is curious about this essay is that "honour" is mentioned when referring to an "abducted" woman returned to India years after the Partition, who then finds a life of *izzat*, which is translated as "honourable" or "respectable" life. This use of the term is quite different from that in "honour killings," which I discuss in this paper precisely because the contemporary term is used in reference to a patriarchal sentiment.

7 The Birmingham School of Cultural Studies was important in treating popular culture and communication as critical for understanding the "social." Feminists such as Hazel Carby and Angela McRobbie were central to these endeavours.

8 The difficulty of trying to change the meanings of the term is apparent in feminist filmmaker Kim Longinetto's attempt to create a more complex narrative. In an interview in *Feminist Review*, Longinetto discusses her film *Pink Saris*, a documentary featuring an Indian girl named Rekha who gets pregnant and wants to commit suicide because she fears her family will kill her. "I had a very strong sense of jeopardy because all these girls are at risk," says Longinetto, who then adds that she had to explain to Western audiences aspects that Indian audiences would have understood: "So I had to put a title at the front of the film: 'Rekha has to get married because if they are pregnant, unmarried girls are sometimes killed by their family' … So you have to give audiences guidelines but I try to keep it to a minimum. But even that makes me cringe slightly because I feel like I'm saying something definitive about a culture."

   Longinetto is aware that she may be reductive; even so, she uses explanations that do not broaden any explanations of the practice. In explaining the mother's words as a threat, Longinetto tells us that "unmarried girls who get pregnant are sometimes killed by their families." Yet the "sometimes" becomes a *fact* of culture rather than something that is contested within India precisely because the audience is assumed to be Westerners who don't know India, and we really don't know how and where Longinetto gets this "cultural" knowledge. What might have been useful would be to see how the documentary is a genre with particular protocols and narratives and how documentary cinema is a genre that has a "reality effect" that overdetermines what Longinetto may wish to nuance. Longinetto's problem is that the concept of "honour killings" is already embedded in a powerful history of knowledge production. Consequently, it is difficult to evade the conventions of the feminist documentary genre, which have long relied on colonial representations as indexing the real. But it is not only a "Western" audience that consumes this concept; in different locations, it can link up to different hegemonic meanings produced through multiple, interconnected, and divergent histories and media circulations. Thyne nad Al-Ali, "An Interview with Kim Longinetto."

9 Keck and Sikkink, *Activists beyond Borders.*

10 Pitt-Rivers, "Honor."

11 Abu-Lughod, *Veiled Sentiments.*

12 Stewart, *Honor.*

13 Bourdieu, "The Sentiment of Honor."

14 Moritz, "A Critical Examination."

15 Herzfeld, "Honor and Shame."

16 An interesting use of the term "honour" to describe Western societies is unusual and an exception in this literature. Orit Kamir uses it in this way to work against the kinds of usages that I critique in this paper. See Kamir, "Law, Society, and Film."

17 Ilkkaracan, "Women, Sexuality, and Social Change."

18 Feldner, "Honor Murders."

19 For a critique of this discourse, see my *Transnational America;* see also Lowe, *Immigrant Acts.*

20 Wikan, *In Honor of Fadime.*

21 Mojab and Hassanpour, "The Politics and Culture."

22 Fabian, *Time and the Other.*

23 Mernissi, "Virginity and Patriarchy."

24 Warnock, *Land before Honour.*

25 Abu-Odeh, "Crimes of Honor."

26 King, "The Personal Is Patrilineal."

27 Hartmann, "The Unhappy Marriage," 14–15.

28 Mitchell, *Psychoanalysis and Feminism.*

29 Mouffe, "Feminism, Citizenship." See also Scott, *Gender and the Politics of History.*

30 Butler, *Gender Trouble;* Halberstam, *Female Masculinity.* Both have been especially influential in this regard.

31 Rosaldo, "The Use and Abuse of Anthropology"; Yanagisako and Collier, "Toward a Unified Analysis."

32 In cinema today, the Judd Apatow oeuvre is a good example of this fraternal power. Important theorizations of homosociality were produced

by Eve Sedgewick in her influential *Between Men*, and also by Nelson in *National Manhood* and Fuchs in "The Buddy Politic."

33 Volpp, "(Mis)Identifying Culture." See also Volpp, "Feminism versus Multiculturalism." Rupa Reddy's analysis of "honour crimes" in the Great Britain suggests that legal responses need to emphasize patriarchy rather than culture. See Reddy, "Gender, Culture, and the Law."

34 Razack, "Imperiled Muslim Women."

35 However, Fox News commentator Phyllis Chesler has suggested that the American "liberal media" recognize only honour killings by Hindus or Sikhs, not by Muslims. According to her, it is important to recognize that it is mainly a Muslim problem. That is a factually incorrect claim, as my search of news media in Lexis-Nexis databases has revealed.

36 See the report by Southall Black Sisters and Women Against Fundamentalism that critiques the terms under which notions of "integration" are framed: "Joint Submission to the Commission on Integration and Cohesion," 2007; accessed 21 August 2012 at http://waf.gn.ape.org/docu ments/WAF_SBS_report.doc.

37 See for instance, David Cameron's 2011 speech in which he declared that the "doctrine of state multiculturalism" had failed; accessed 21 August 2012 at http://www.newstatesman.com/blogs/the-staggers/2011/02/ terrorism-islam-ideology.

38 Meetoo and Mirza, "There Is Nothing 'Honourable' about Honour Killings."

39 Dustin and Phillips, "Whose Agenda Is It?"

40 Singh, *New Woman and Mass Media*.

41 Khan, "When Survivors Become Victims."

42 See, for example, Prasad, *A Pressing Matter*. Also see Bathla, *Women, Democracy, and the Media*. Bathla uses generic categories such as "crimes against women," or "violence against women," and the one particular crime she discusses extensively is rape, including its frequency and representation. Under the topic of violence, Sharada J. Schaffter mentions dowry murders, rape, domestic violence, torture, sexual harassment, and incest. Schaffer, *Privileging the Privileged*, 43–5.

43 Welchman and Hossain, "Introduction," in *Honour*.

44 Singh, *Gender Relations and Cultural Ideology in Indian Cinema*, 21.

45 See, for instance, three articles in the journal *Mainstream*: Ray, "Khap Panchayats"; Dahiya, "Khap Panchayats"; and Vakil, "No Honour in 'Honour' Killings."

46 Chowdhry, *Contentious Marriages*.

47 Pratiksha Bakshi; Baxi, Rai, and Ali, "Legacies of Common Law."

48 Niranjana, "Nationalism Refigured."

49 Gupta offers a fine analysis of this anti-Muslim strategy in "Hindu Women, Muslim Men."

50 Choudhry, "Feudal Mindset," 1.

51 Menon, "Embodying the Self."

52 Jyoti Puri, forthcoming monograph, Duke University Press.

53 Moreover, it is doubtful that "law and order" solutions can change social attitudes or an "honour culture" if that culture is indeed the problem. In some cases, addressing cultural problems through law and order solutions has led to increased incarcerations that do little to change underlying attitudes. Indeed, often these incarcerations generate even more opposition to change. For instance, the crime of "dowry murder" has led to the incarceration of entire families, and what has been accomplished by doing so is unclear. In many instances, the court system and the state have failed in bringing accountability even where culpability is clear.

54 Sengupta, "Death of Two Lovers."

55 For instance, after the murder of Vimal and Hari Lal in the New Friends Colony in Delhi, one resident of the colony, Advaita Rajvanshi, told a reporter: "I'm so angry. These incidents are no longer restricted to remote villages or city fringes. The honor killing menace has now reached the capital's posh localities."

Vaibhav Batra, a thirty-three-year-old local resident, said: "This has brought bad name to our colony, considered one of the posh localities of south Delhi. People, though literate, are indulging in such a dastardly act. It is very shameful for a country, which is claiming to be developed. With the Commonwealth Games on our doorstep, such incidents will mar the image of the country." Accessed 14 January 2014 at http://blogs.wsj.com/indiarealtime/2010/07/13/posh-delhi-enclave-confronts-honor-killing.

56 This pervasive bias against Muslims sometimes reveals itself in honour killings. Thus one article in *The Times of India* mentions the film *Azaadi Live*, starring Sara Khan and Angad Hasija, in which these two actors depicted an honour killing after having "studied the heart wrenching stories of numerous victims in India." The news item mentions that the two actors had not been able to find an apartment to purchase in Mumbai because no one would rent to a Muslim. They described this as "their fear of selling it [an apartment] to a Muslim." "No Freedom for Love: Sara Khan," *The Times of India*, 10 August 2010, accessed 14 January 2014 at http://timesofindia.indiatimes.com/entertainment/tv-/No-freedom-for-love-Sara-Khan/articleshow/6287886.cms#ixzz100zpZnM6.

57 Joseph and Sharma, "Introduction," in *Whose News?*

58 Joseph and Sharma, "Introduction," in *Whose News?*
59 Rajagopal, "The Public Sphere."
60 Report of the Working Group on Software for Doordarshan, *An Indian Personality for Television*, New Delhi: Ministry of Information and Broadcasting, 1985.
61 Jeffrey, *Media and Modernity*, 191.
62 Jeffrey, *Media and Modernity*, 200.
63 Agnes, "Women, Marriage." Agnes points out that economic rights remain inaccessible to many women.
64 Shah and Kallury, "Statutory Warnings."
65 Sharma, "When Survivors Become Victims."
66 Lloyd, "Politics without Television," 72.
67 Haskell, *From Reverence to Rape.*
68 Gabriel, *Melodrama and the Nation*, 320.
69 Sharma, "When Survivors Become Victims."
70 Joseph, *Women in Journalism*, 280.
71 Chowdhry, *Contentious Marriages, Eloping Couples.*
72 Agnes, "Women, Marriage, and the Subordination of Rights."
73 Agnes, "Women, Marriage, and the Subordination of Rights."
74 Rafter, *A Shot in the Mirror.* The literature on television police dramas is vast, but see, for instance, the following: Clarke, "Holding the Blue Lamp"; Landrum, "Instrumental Texts and Stereotyping"; Sparks, *Television and the Drama of Crime*; Sumser, *Morality and Social Order*; Cavender and Bond-Maupin, "Fear and Loathing"; Christensen, Schmidt, and Henderson, "The Selling of the Police"; Gunter, *Television and the Fear of Crime*; Hall et al., *Policing the Crisis*; and Lichter and Lichter, *Prime Time Crime.*

10 Diasporas of Empire: Arab Americans and the Reverberations of War

NADINE NABER

In the classroom, the Muslim student is transformed into a terrorist. It comes straight from teachers. Every day, students ask me, "What should I tell my teachers?" Teachers say racist things in class like, "Muslim men aren't afraid to die because when they die they believe they will be given seventy-five virgins in heaven."

> Hatem, Palestinian community-based scholar, Berkeley, 2000

It was hard to make interventions about what sexism [in our community] because we were always responding to attacks against our communities. To be "a good Arab activist" you have to respond to violence, to racism.

> Camelia, Egyptian political activist, San Francisco, 2001

It's the most terrifying thing that a person can deal with, knowing that their loved ones are stuck in a situation that they can do little to nothing about. Half of who I am was [in Lebanon]. The greatest fear was that I could risk losing [them].

> Roulah, Lebanese resident of Dearborn, 2006

These quotes are taken from ethnographic research among Arab diasporas in California and Michigan between 1999 and 2006, a period of massive US imperial expansion in the Arab region.[1] During this period, the effects of US war in the Middle East reverberated within the geographic boundaries of the United States, impacting the lives of Arab and Muslim diasporas in distinct ways. Hatem's quote reflects how the Islamophobic discourse that has justified the War on Terror permeates the lives of Muslim students in Berkeley, California. Camelia refers to how communal engagements with the crises of war and racism can foreclose opportunities for addressing intra-communal experiences of sexism. Roulah's quote points to the ways the Israeli invasion of Lebanon in 2006 connected people living in the United States to their counterparts in Lebanon. In this chapter, I explore how *US-led military violence* (bombing, support for Israeli colonization, and sanctions, for instance) constitutes the experiences of the Arab diasporas I have been working with and compounds their engagements with US *gendered-racial violence*.

Bringing feminist empire and diaspora studies together, this chapter centres upon engagements with US imperialist war from the location of the diaspora. My aim is to intervene in the ways critical scholarship tends to frame the War on Terror in terms of two distinct contexts (here, in the United States, and there, in the countries the United States is invading).[2] Consider, for instance, that a great deal of research and advocacy frames US-led militarism and war as taking place "over there" (in Muslim-majority countries) and locates racism, discrimination, and hate crimes as *impacts* of the War on Terror experienced "over here" (in North America).[3]

As we will see, the Arab Americans with whom I worked may not experience military violence in the same ways or to the same degrees as those in the countries targeted directly by the bombs or bulldozers. Yet their lives are constituted by military violence all the same. For my interlocutors, military violence (bombs, bulldozers, etc.) and gendered and racial violence in the United States magnify each other. They are moving parts of the same imperial present and take place in the same spatial-temporal context. Imperial violence extends into my interlocutors' lives in profound ways – through simultaneous engagements with military and racial violence, through fear, through a sense of belonging to communities in crisis, and by altering concepts of gender and sexuality as well as relations and solidarities within and beyond Arab communities.

Since 1999, I have been working as an ethnographer-activist with Arab immigrant communities on a range of issues, including race, gender, and sexuality, generational tensions, feminist and religious-based activisms, and transnational alliances. Between 1999 and 2002, I worked primarily in the San Francisco Bay Area, and between 2004 and 2006, primarily in Dearborn, Michigan.[4] Here, I look back and take stock of the ways the theme of imperial violence has underpinned these research projects. I focus on stories in which imperial violence became a central theme. These stories tended to come primarily from community-based political activists, people who directly experienced the violence of war and racism, and people with loved ones living in the Arab region. I also take a look forward by considering the kinds of political concerns and commitments that open up when we look at the violence of the War on Terror through the lens of "diasporas of empire."

Diasporas of Empire

Generally, scholars have theorized imperial diasporas in terms of people who reside in the countries that formerly colonized them – Algerians in France, South Asians in England, and so on. Kobena Mercer theorizes the diaspora of empire as a "reminder and a remainder of the nation's historical past."[5] Yet as this chapter will show, Arab diasporas cannot be understood as postcolonial diasporas wherein the diaspora has moved into the seat of the former empire. Rather, the stories of Arabs in the United States becoming a diaspora of empire point to a moment in which the empire and its subjects exist in a transnational and contemporaneous frame. The subjects of the current empire "over there" also reside "over here" within the empire itself.

Of course, to a certain extent, my interlocutors' stories constitute what James Clifford theorizes as a diasporic "connection (elsewhere) that made a difference (here)."[6] Yet my interlocutors' stories also depict the historically specific and subjective conditions that emerge among diasporas residing in a nation (the United States) at war with their homelands. My interlocutors live their lives between the United States and other places, through travel, transnational relationships, and political affiliations; they live in a "home away from home" or "here and there,"[7] criss-crossing regional and national borders[8] or "dwelling here with solidarity and connection there."[9]

Their stories call for a theorization of diaspora as a state of consciousness that emerges out of the relationship between Arab Americans, the movement of diverse Arabs to the United States, and US imperial and racial determinations. Conventional US diaspora studies reveal diasporic immigration as tracing a route *back to* the *formerly* imperial metropole, whereas what I refer to as "diasporas of empire" emerge against the highly invasive and shifting relations of power that are central to *contemporary* US neocolonialism and imperial formations. This formulation requires us to expand feminist diaspora studies beyond the focus on gendered experiences of migration, displacement, and racism (or how gender takes on new forms from the homeland to the diaspora) towards an analysis of how gender and diaspora are constituted by relations between diaspora and varying forms of empire (settler colonialism, imperial war, etc.) and the ways empire shapes diasporic connections and relations to real or imagined homelands.

Furthermore, until now, most critical scholarship on the War on Terror has used the framework of imperialism primarily for analysing the Middle East and South Asia. Research focused on the impact of the War on Terror on US-based diaspora communities relies primarily on nation-based concepts of immigrant rights, civil rights, racism, and discrimination. By conceptualizing diaspora through the lens of imperialism and empire, we can expand the kinds of questions we ask about how the War on Terror takes on local form in the United States. Primarily, this chapter articulates diaspora not only as related to an originary homeland through travel, imagination, and displacement but also as linked to the violence of war "over there." Drawing on Inderpal Grewal and Caren Kaplan's theorization of transnationalism, I use the term "linked" to call attention to diverse, unequal, and uneven transnational relations. Here, Arab diasporic life is constituted by linked violences that are not necessarily the same (i.e., the violence Arab Americans experience in the United States and the violence people in the Arab world experience). Yet the violence of imperial war constitutes them as subjects and profoundly constitutes their lives, beckoning them into the violence of war and racism simultaneously. Here, the homeland and diaspora or "war over there" and "gendered racism over here" are interconnected, within a similar spatial-temporal location. In other words, "over there" *is* "over here." Gendered racism shapes the grammar of war and violence, and similarly, war produces and enables particular forms of gendered racism. As the experiences and reflections of Arab Americans shared in this chapter will demonstrate, these are not distinct phenomena.

Three moments of military violence were particularly disruptive in the lives of my interlocutors between 1999 and 2006. The stories of activists involved in a leftist Arab movement in the San Francisco Bay Area in 1999 and 2000 elucidate the first moment. The stories of Arab Americans who encountered the post-9/11 racist backlash in San Francisco and of community leaders who advocated on their behalf illustrate the second moment, from 2001 to 2003. The stories of Lebanese living in Dearborn, Michigan, whose loved ones faced the Israeli invasion of Lebanon in 2006 reflect the third moment.

The Late 1990s and the Leftist Arab Movement
in the San Francisco Bay Area

The first moment took place between 1999 and 2001. This was the period of the beginning of the second Palestinian *intifada* (uprising) and massive Israeli state attacks against Palestinians. It was also the height of US-led sanctions on Iraq and a period of ongoing US bombing in Iraq coupled with devastating economic crises across the region.

The events that transpired in the late 1990s in Palestine developed in continuity with the history of Israeli colonization. The period often referred to as the "peace process" (between 1993 and 1999) entailed a doubling of the Israeli settler population in occupied Palestine.[10] This was an extension of policies whereby Israel gained control over 78 per cent of Palestinian land.[11] Also during this period, new Israeli policies divided Palestinian territory into non-contiguous areas and strengthened physical separation through road closures and the establishment of checkpoints and Israeli-only bypass roads. These measures, and the expansion of Israel's border control and military occupation in the mid-1990s, challenged Palestinian political leaders as the territories lost physical and political sovereignty; at the same time, US mediators were adopting less ambitious objectives for peace. By 2000, with an increase in Israeli military violence against Palestinians, including a growing number of children killed by Israeli forces, it had become clear that negotiations would not deliver a Palestinian state.

No moment better captures the urgent tenor of this period, which mobilized activists in the San Francisco Bay Area along with social justice advocates all over the world, than an event that took place on 30 September 2000, one week before the start of the second Palestinian *intifada*. Twelve-year-old Mohammad al-Durrah and his father (filmed by Talal Abu Rahma, a Palestinian cameraman freelancing for France 2) sought cover from Israeli gunfire behind a concrete pillar. The footage, which lasts just over a minute, shows the pair holding on to each other, the boy crying and the father waving, then a burst of gunfire and dust, after which the boy is seen slumped across his father's legs. This incident confirmed my interlocutors' view of Israel's apparently limitless brutality towards Palestinians. The dominant US and Israeli narratives of this period sadly distorted the US role in the crisis. My interlocutors, activists in a leftist Arab movement in the San Francisco Bay Area, were deeply outraged and expressed dissonance not only with US actions but also with US narratives.

Around the same time, international human rights reports were documenting the rising number of deaths caused by US-led sanctions on Iraq. The Red Crescent, the Red Cross, and various UN agencies repeatedly and graphically reported that tens of thousands were dying every year from those sanctions. Meanwhile, the US government continued to defend the measures, with Madeleine Albright declaring during a *60 Minutes* TV interview in 1995 that the deaths of more than 500,000 Iraqi children as a result of US-forced sanctions were "worth it."[12]

The devastation caused by the war on Iraq and the colonization of Palestine heightened the sense of political urgency among the Arab activists with whom I worked, and the Islamophobia and anti-Arab racism that fuelled US empire in their own lives compounded their outrage and frustration. Scholarly and community-based publications documented a massive rise in hate crimes against Arabs in the United States in the five years that followed the first Gulf War.[13] Samia and Raydah, who entered high school and college in the 1990s, discussed their encounters with anti-Arab racism of that period:

> Samia: When people hear I am Arab they associate it with war. All you hear in the media is when Arabs kill people, so they assume that I am a radical or terrorist.
>
> Raydah: I always felt that either I didn't know enough to defend myself or it didn't matter how much I knew – people already labelled me. Oh, Palestinians are terrorists, or Saddam Hussein is the worst. You feel like they see all Arabs as terrorists.

In most of my interlocutors' stories, an understanding of how others in the United States perceived them shaped a shared sense that dominant US discourses associated them with potential "enemies of the nation." As young adults, their attempts to articulate Arabness entailed negotiating with dominant US discourses and totalizing debates about their communities. Perhaps most importantly, they realized they would need to grapple with the ways in which Arabness is conceived in the United States. Interlocutors often shared feelings of alienation over the way Arabness was viewed in US public spaces. They described having to constantly explain their positions on Palestine while they were active in political organizations across the Bay Area. Dahlia, an Iraqi refugee, recalled a neighbour seeing her family as potential terrorists. Several interlocutors' stories reveal the ways in which gender permeates anti-Arab racism, almost literally rendering Arab American women unintelligible beyond dominant US discourses about them. Yara, a Lebanese interlocutor, described people's shock and curiosity when she spoke, as if they had never before heard an Arab woman speak. Another woman, Tala, told me, "I was standing at the Muslim Student Association's table on my college campus. A student approached the table and asked me if women cover their faces from the bruises they get after their husbands beat them."

Activists in the leftist Arab movement shared a collective analysis that finds parallels with Arab and Muslim feminist scholarship that has argued (a) that US corporate media representations of Arabs and Muslims as backward and uncivilized rely heavily on images of gender and sexuality, and (b) that these gendered and sexualized media images work to support and legitimize US-led imperialist ambitions in the Middle East. Dominant European and US discourses have represented Arab, Muslim, and Middle Eastern women as highly sexual, exotic victims of patriarchy and misogyny as a way of legitimizing colonial and imperial domination. These same discourses have portrayed the Arab and Muslim worlds as both exceptionally homosexual and manifestly homophobic.[14]

Daily exposure to racist and Islamophobic discourses, coupled with outrage over military violence and imperial expansion, helped strengthen the bonds among Arab Americans and inspired the revival of the leftist Arab movement in the San Francisco Bay Area, a movement that had been dormant since the early 1990s. The movement developed a "divest from Israel" campaign and another that called for an end to the sanctions on Iraq.[15] I spoke to activists in this movement over a ten-year period, between 1999 and 2009. Nearly every activist I spoke with over the years shared the sense that the late 1990s, when they revived the leftist Arab movement, were the most momentous years of their lives. Activists remember this period as one that "institutionalized a new Arab discourse" and "moved the streets." Experiencing this period together, with all of its intensity and with little sleep, contributed to a profound sense of connection and alliance with one another.

But while the violence of war and racism mobilized my interlocutors and brought them together, it also put into play a series of silences and exclusions that had profound effects on peoples' daily lives. These silences and exclusions were a response to the barrage of news and information about the violence, bodily harm, and death in Palestine and Iraq, as well as the general sense of non-belonging in the United States and the political outrage that activists shared. My interlocutors responded to these events, mobilized by a logic of emergency. The women I worked with found it difficult to find a language to address anything other than the brutal violence taking place in Palestine and Iraq. The result was an official movement discourse that resembled the narrow, one-dimensional focus of conventional nationalisms and that foreclosed the possibilities for addressing sexism and homophobia among activists. The adrenaline was always running high, and leftist Arab activists threw intense energy into mobilizing people and sparking resistance to the United States and Israel. The urgency of this mobilization complicated interpersonal relations in the group. As Camelia explained, "It was as though ... once we dealt with all the immediate problems of death, starvation, bombing, political prisoners, then we can look at women's rights."

In addition, while the racial discourses that justified imperial war in Palestine and Iraq were the target of my interlocutors' activism, the need to combat Orientalism – and a particular understanding of how this could best be accomplished – came to dominate their work. Reactions to Orientalism foreclosed the possibilities of addressing internal movement hierarchies, particularly as they related to gender and sexuality. Women and men, to different extents, were similarly invested in a "common culture" that emerged in what I refer to here as the Leftist Arab Movement (LAM). This "common culture" assumed that publicly discussing Arab communities' sexism and homophobia could endanger the goals for which activists were fighting. Members shared the view that US Orientalist representations of Arabs and Muslims – specifically, images of hyper-oppressed Arab and Muslim women and Arab Muslim sexual savagery – were among the most common images Americans saw, especially in the news media and in Hollywood productions. In their analyses, Orientalist representations were a key reason why so many Americans supported US military interventions in the Middle East, and why many Americans, particularly liberals, expressed profound empathy for Arab and Muslim women – perceived to be victims of their culture and religion – but little concern about the impact of US policies on Arab and Muslim communities.[16] In response to all of this, my interlocutors tended to operate under the tacit understanding that discussing sexism and compulsory heterosexuality within Arab communities might only reinforce Orientalism. Women discussed with me the ways in which the movement had mobilized an exclusively externally focused form of anti-imperialism/anti-Orientalism and had foreclosed the possibility of tackling intra-communal matters of sexism and homophobia. At times, this resulted in the movement engendering its own forms of coercion and repression. Aisha explained:

> We were operating with the mindset that we are always under attack – by feminists, soft leftists, racists … If I was going to come out and say this person was sexist, I would be giving fuel to the fire, or legitimizing the attacks against our communities … How can I bring up sexism when Zionists are waiting for any moment that we would falter to dismantle our work? I felt like I had to shut up and deal with the sexism.

Dahlia echoed these concerns:

> If I were to come out publicly and say this person is sexist … I can hear it now – even from other progressive activists … "Even progressive Arab women are oppressed by progressive Arab men!" That would just legitimize further violence, colonization, and oppression against us. If we were to talk about homophobia … people would say, "Oh my God! The leftist Arab movement is homophobic!" So there was never a place to talk about what was going on in our organizations or internally.

In Camelia's view:

> I would see myself as a traitor if I said [LAM] was sexist publicly. Our countries are under attack and anything that can be used against us will be. Some people were sexist but a lot of us were not politically mature enough to deal with it. It wasn't just when it came to sexism … We also had a hard time discussing whether or how to critique Saddam Hussein in public. Some people felt strongly that we should not hold back and others were more hesitant. Many of us internalized this idea that we could only criticize what the US does. Our internal stuff was not for the public – untouchable. It was kind of naïve.

Underneath the tacit agreement to mute feminist critiques within the Arab Left was a visceral fear of betraying one's home community.[17]

The suppression of discussions of sexism was deployed as a tactic to avoid the reification of Orientalist/racist assumptions. This was seen as a necessary component of resisting empire *from within empire* – or, as one LAM activist put it, "living among our oppressors." The tacit fear that at any moment non-activists would use any articulations of sexism against the activist collective and its goals reflects the ways in which the violence of military war compounded with the violence of racism required my interlocutors to make heart-wrenching choices, choices that often led to the disappearance of sexism among activists. This fear was constituted by profound sense of belonging to a "diaspora of empire." Here, empire inscribes itself on the diasporic subject within the domestic (national) borders of empire, thereby generating a movement logic in which the urgency of responding to colonization and military war overdetermines and suppresses possibilities for addressing multiple power struggles taking place within the diaspora. Such dynamics are, of course, similar to those that women of colour feminists have described as having plagued various progressive civil rights and social justice movements in the United States in the 1960s and 1970s, which required women, for example, to choose between fighting sexism *or* racism.[18] The historical and spatial dynamics of transnationalism, diaspora, and empire that circumscribed my interlocutors' lives produced problems that were similar to but also distinct from that ones that faced these earlier US-based movements. While the patriarchal logic of nationalism and national liberation structured the patriarchy underlying US people-of-colour-based movements of the 1960s and 1970s, a diasporic anti-imperialist politics fuelled the patriarchy underlying the leftist Arab American movements of the early twenty-first century. Diasporic anti-imperialism dismissed patriarchy as less important than community-based engagements with both domestic US racism and the experience of enduring war from the distance of diaspora. As I have elaborated elsewhere, in this diasporic space, multiple homeland nationalisms (Iraqi, Palestinian, etc.) conjoined and were remade through US racial politics, producing complex gender structures that cannot be explained through feminist analyses of the national liberation movements of the 1960s and 1970s. For this imperial diaspora, it was not only a struggle over prioritizing sexism *or* national liberation, but also a struggle over multiple competing political agendas (such as whether on not to condemn Arab dictators like Saddam Hussein, and whether to focus on ending domestic racism rather than foreign wars). All of this exacerbated the problem that anti-imperialism had been prioritized over sexism.[19]

**Arab Americans in the San Francisco Bay Area
after the 9/11 Attacks**

The 9/11 attacks justified war on Afghanistan and Iraq, support for the Israeli occupation of Palestine, Israel's war on Lebanon, and the transfer to the Philippines of US troops who had carried out human rights violations against local people under the guise of "saving innocent people from terrorism," among other variations of US imperial expansion. The repeated US-led framing of 9/11's aftermath as an endless, fluid war facilitated the Bush administration's conflation of diverse individuals, movements, and historical contexts such as Bin Laden, Saddam Hussein, any and all forms of Palestinian resistance to Israeli occupation, Hizballah, Hamas, and al-Qaeda under the rubric "Islamic fundamentalists/Muslim terrorists."[20] These military interventions and the racial discourses that drove them expanded anti-immigrant practices beyond the "illegal criminal" to encompass the "evil terrorist enemy within." Resorting to FBI investigations and spying, INS police raids, detentions, deportations, and interrogations of community organizations and activists, immigration policies related to 9/11 have targeted immigrants who fit amorphous characterizations of a "terrorist profile." The INS has targeted non-citizens from Muslim-majority countries as well as some individuals from Muslim-majority countries who are naturalized. These tactics are part of the federal government's "wide range of domestic, legislative, administrative, and judicial measures in the name of national security and the war on terrorism."[21] Louise Cainkar notes that "these measures have included mass arrests, secret and indefinite detentions, prolonged detention of 'material witnesses,' closed hearings and use of secret evidence ... FBI home and work visits, seizures of property, removals of aliens with technical visa violations and mandatory special registration."[22]

Among Arab diasporas in the San Francisco Bay Area, 9/11-related hate crimes and other forms of public harassment disproportionately targeted persons who displayed what dominant government and corporate media discourses often constructed as a "Arab/Middle Eastern/Muslim" identity. One's name, appearance, or nation of origin could signify an association with the enemy of the nation. These identity markers drew many people into joining the "War on Terror" through hate crimes and various forms of violence, harassment, and intimidation in the public sphere – at school, on the bus, at work, at home, and on the streets.[23] Teachers and youth group leaders reported that boys with names like Mohammed or Osama were disproportionately harassed at school. Nayla, a Muslim American youth group leader, recalled that schoolchildren would often shout, "Look, Mohammed the terrorist is coming!" when a young boy named Mohammed entered the playground. Amira, a college student, recalled reading the words, "I hate Mohammed. All Mohammeds should die," on a wall outside the

Recreation and Sports Facilities Building at the University of California, Berkeley.

Names signifying an "Arab/Middle Eastern/Muslim" identity marked particular men and boys as alien to the nation and connected them to "the terrorists." Also, imperial racism articulated "Arab/Middle Eastern/Muslim" masculinity as inherently violent towards women. One cab driver discussed his passengers' reactions to him when they read that his name was Mohammed: "Once, a woman got in my car. She looked at me, then read my name, then asked me if I was Muslim. When I said 'yes' she replied, 'how many girls have you killed today?'" Here, the passenger reified the Islamophobic discourse that intrinsically links Muslim masculinity to misogynist savagery.

Women who wear a headscarf disproportionately encountered Islamophobic attacks. Lamia, a community activist, summarized what she had witnessed through her work with Arab Muslim youth in San Francisco's Tenderloin District: "After September 11, girls who wear *hijab* received lots of harassment on the bus, at school, and on the street. People would try and pull their *hijab* off." Salma, an Iraqi youth, elucidated Lamia's point:

> At school, kids take off their shirts and put them on their heads and say, "We look like Osama's daughter now. We look like you now." Some kids would come up to us and say, "Why don't you take it off? Are you still representing Osama?"

In this narrative, young Arab Muslim girls are constructed as if patriarchal kinship ties are the sole determinants of their identity. Reduced to "daughters of Osama," they are transformed into the "property," "the harmonious extension"[24] of the nation's enemy within, or into symbols connected to the "real actors" or "terrorists" who do not, however, stand on their own (and lack agency). The "daughter of a terrorist" metaphor also amounts to a condemnation of Muslim women for veiling.[25] Here, the "veil" serves as a boundary marker between "us" and "them"; thus, as long as women remain "veiled," they remain intrinsically connected to "potential terrorists."

In the diaspora, military violence produced disciplinary effects on the level of the emotive and the psyche. Racial violence induced among my interlocutors a state of consciousness I refer to as "internment of the psyche" or a sense of internal incarceration. This manifested itself in the fear that at any moment one could be harassed, beaten up, picked up, locked up, or "disappeared."[26] Several community leaders recalled how women would debate whether they should remove their scarves. As Amal, another university student put it, "I knew I had to prepare for at least some kind of backlash because I was visually identifiable. My mother, who doesn't cover, specifically told me, 'Don't go outside for a month or two. Wait till things die down.' I was like, 'I shouldn't hide. I shouldn't be scared or restrain my lifestyle because of ignorance.'" In this sense, considerations of whether to remove a headscarf and when to go out in public generated an "internment of the psyche" – that is, an awareness that one must become habitually concerned about hegemonic misinterpretations and mistranslations and that one might be under scrutiny – by strangers, hidden cameras, wiretaps, and other surveillance mechanisms of the security state, as well as by invisible arbiters of behaviour. All of this rendered them vulnerable to the "truths" the state had contrived, even if they were engaging in lawful activity.

The internment of the psyche operates much like Foucault's "panopticon,"[27] the disciplinary mechanism of generalized surveillance that injects power's effects into the psyche. As a form of discipline, it "induces within individuals a state of consciousness that assures the automatic functioning of power."[28] In covert and unspoken ways, this internment links sociopolitical institutions to the individual psyche, "making it possible to bring the effects of power to the most minute and distant elements" of daily life.[29] Several interlocutors reflected on this sense of collective fear, a fear of being monitored by the state or simply mistrusted. They told of how they changed their names, avoided signing forms or petitions, and considered whether to shave their beards or avoid wearing the *hijab*. And this sense of being spied on was intensified even *within* Arab American communities – something that played out in particularly gendered ways. Because of this intense politicization of the personal, quotidian, and intimate, many of my interlocutors felt a heavy burden to "represent" themselves and their communities in particular symbolic ways, not only when interacting with non-Arabs, but also among themselves. From beards to veils to names, nothing was "just" a personal practice anymore; everything was now deeply meaningful within and beyond community boundaries.

Engagement with the military and racial violence of the War on Terror brought political activists into new alliances. The War on Terror's reverberations in the San Francisco Bay Area altered relations both within and among the various South Asian, Arab, and Muslim communities, inspiring new coalitions and polarizations.[30] These reverberations also brought about new conceptualizations of military violence. Consider the experiences of Arab activists who participated in a rally held in Snowpark in Oakland, California, in 2002. A broad, people-of-colour-based coalition crafted slogans and speeches linking US imperialism abroad to internally focused US colonization and racism. After this rally, the organization United Communities against War and Racism (UCAWAR) was formed to mobilize grassroots communities of colour against war and racism simultaneously. During this period, several Arab feminists were working with women of colour organizations such as the Women of Color Resource Center and INCITE! Women of Color against Violence. These organizations framed the "War on Terror" in terms of its global *and* local impacts. INCITE! developed an anti-militarism campaign that cast military violence in transnational terms, focusing on how the War on Terror was affecting women both in countries the United States was invading and in the United States itself. One of their fliers read in part: "Invading armies have never liberated women. Only we can liberate ourselves ... The police and militaries have been attacking our communities for centuries. Resist the war of terror in our communities!" This excerpt was part of a broader campaign that INCITE! had developed that conceptualized US imperialism in terms of interconnected components, which included the wars on Afghanistan and Iraq, the gendered and racist discourse that had justified those wars, and the racist violence against communities of colour in the United States.

Southern Lebanese Diasporas in Michigan, July 2006

The Israeli invasion of Lebanon began on 12 July 2006 when Hizballah militia attacked an Israeli army convoy and captured two soldiers. Hizballah said it had captured these soldiers in order to bargain for the release of three Lebanese detained in Israel without due process and to reduce Israeli pressure on Gaza.[31] Israel responded with a naval blockade, a ground invasion of southern Lebanon, and massive air strikes targeting civilians and Lebanon's civil infrastructure. The invasion killed 1,200 Lebanese, wounded 4,000, and displaced one million more; it also destroyed tens of thousands of homes as well as hospitals, schools, factories, roads, airports, power stations, fuel depots, warehouses, and most of the country's bridges.[32] Lara Deeb explains that as the invasion continued, "Israel's initially stated goal of securing the release of the two captured soldiers ... faded from Israeli discourse and gave way to two additional stated goals: the disarmament or at least 'degrading' of Hizballah's militia, as well as its removal from south Lebanon."[33] Throughout the invasion, Hizballah launched rockets into northern Israel, killing forty-three Israeli civilians and wounding dozens more.[34] International human rights organizations criticized both Israel and Hizballah for attacking civilians and criticized Israel's indiscriminate attacks against civil infrastructure and villages and its use of cluster bombs and white phosphorus shells. The Bush administration backed Israel, resorting to rhetoric that justified the invasion, and failed to support international calls for a ceasefire.[35]

In interviews, members of the Lebanese diaspora from the predominantly Shi'i Muslim south of Lebanon living in Dearborn, Michigan, reflected on how they experienced the invasion. "The military approach was beyond normal rules of war," Mohammed told me. "The main target was civilians. Anyone could be a target. If the bombardment got heavy around them, there were no safe areas to go. This is why there was so much anxiety and fear." Hussein reflected on how most Lebanese families in Dearborn had family living in Lebanon: "The same family has one leg here and one leg there literally."

The racial discourses that reinforced US support for the invasion compounded my interlocutors' sense of outrage and their desire for connections with one another. The Lebanese with whom I worked all realized that dominant US government and media images were portraying Lebanese, Arabs, and Muslims as terrorists and devaluing their casualties in the invasion. People told me how they flipped back and forth between contradictory images on Arabic and American TV stations. Arabic Satellite TV showed horrifying images of death and destruction in Lebanon as a consequence of Israel's disproportionate use of force. Meanwhile, the US corporate media tended to portray the Israelis as defending themselves against Lebanese terrorists and to suggest that the sufferings of the Israelis and Lebanese were more or less equivalent. Many interlocutors accused the news media of supporting terrorism when they gave space to community leaders who criticized the Israeli army's actions. Several community leaders said that the media and pro-Israeli pressure groups "did not leave the community to freely express its views." Mohammed, director of a leading Arab American civil rights organization in Michigan, explained:

There was tremendous pressure to intimidate the community to suppress their views. This wave of labeling and general condemnation took the community's reaction out of context and made it look like support for

Hizballah. People were crying, saying, "It's my family, it's my father, my sister my mother, my cousin, my nieces, my nephews." But they projected it as terrorism. There was a well-orchestrated effort to make you feel like you were committing a crime for calling for ceasefire. The minute you become critical, you're anti-Semitic, and pro-terrorist. They didn't want us to speak about the war.

Most interlocutors said that the invasion had brought Lebanese together in Dearborn and had strengthened community bonds. Roulah told me that familial relations became stronger: "They [family] understand exactly what you are going through, because that person who may be over there [in Lebanon] is just as important to them as they are to you." Suleiman likewise noted: "We spent days and nights together. It made us closer to each other. The war showed us how much we love each other – how much we care – how much we get scared for each other."

People turned to one another to cope with the death and destruction wrought by the military invasion. Sara's extended family in Dearborn includes five hundred people. During the war, she spent her time with relatives there as they waited for news about their loved ones in Lebanon: "We turned to each other here. You couldn't be there to save your grandmother, to save your grandfather, aunt or uncle. Having each other kind of helped keep us stay afloat until it ended."

Sara's quote illustrates that transnational social fields and connections were intensified during the invasion of Lebanon. Because Sara was in Dearborn during that time, she could not physically help her loved ones in Lebanon. She turned to her counterparts "over here" (in the United States) to cope with the news about family "over there" (in Lebanon), whom she could not physically protect, save, or secure. Turning to one another for comfort, security, and care helped them deal with the massive death, destruction, and loss taking place in Lebanon. One interlocutor, remembering the political protests that were held in Dearborn during the invasion, told me:

I recall daily, all you would have to do is to stand and stop on a sidewalk on Warren Avenue and in seconds, in minutes, in hours you see the two sides are full and packed. That is what was happening. My God, this participation, it had everyone. Even senior citizens who barely walked, who barely can stand, made a point to show up. They made a point to come and cry out. To come and show their anger, their call to end this madness.

> I tell you, the heat index was so high or sometimes it rained, and people didn't care. Everyone responded. Everyone came.

In Dearborn during the war, the Bint Jubeil Cultural Center served as a meeting place for Lebanese and their allies. There, people came together to hold memorial services for persons killed in Lebanon, to raise relief funds, and to carry out media and letter-writing campaigns. The centre's director asked me, "Which story do you want me to pick? Everybody had relatives in Lebanon." Eyad, a prominent newspaper editor in the community, told me that "anyone you grab on the street will tell you a story that happened to one of their family." Some stories were more tragic than others. Local newspapers reported that one woman in the community had six hundred family members directly targeted by the Israeli bombardment. One man lost twelve family members; another lost more than forty. Ali is a musician and a recent immigrant who came to the United States in his early twenties. His immediate family and most of his closest friends live in Lebanon:

> The friends who taught music to me growing up were now dead. After this, every friend I had before, every person in my family, is two times more that friend and two times more my family. Every enemy that I had before is two times more my enemy. When you're killing our children, the Christians and the Muslims, and the Sunnis and the Shias, they're going to build stronger bonds.

Roulah's statement that "everyone who wasn't your family became your family" reveals how intensified concepts of belonging took form on Dearborn's streets. Zain told me: "If one family lost someone, everyone lost that person. Family came together and community came together as a family." Every community leader I spoke to shared the view that the massive destruction was serving as a catalyst, bringing people together and producing a collective experience in which "you would make a call and everybody would show up."

Configured as "family," Lebanese transmigrants idealized connection and support as responsibilities they owed to one another. As one interlocutor put it, "We became one another's backbones." In the face of war, the concept of "family" offered such a powerful sense of comfort that my interlocutors rarely referenced the power imbalances and exclusions that underlie the very same (heteropatriarchal) family structure to which they turned. Zain, referring to Dearborn, told me that "you looked at every person and knew exactly what they were feeling because you were feeling the same thing. People I don't even know. Everyone found a kinship in their frustration, anger and sadness."

All of the massive funerals, mourning ceremonies, and house visits in Dearborn reinforced the dynamic in which the concept of "heteropatriarchal family" linked Lebanese diasporas together. Typically, southern Lebanese families organized memorial services to mark the passing of an individual family member. In the summer of 2006, several memorials were held that marked the passing of more than one individual. Nasser recalled:

> When my mother died, I had a memorial for her. At least 3,000 people attended. I announced it in the local newspapers and said, "Sunday at the Islamic Center." Three or four other families contacted me and said, "We lost our loved ones too. Can you include us?" That's how we comforted each other.

Firyal's aunt and grandmother were casualties of this war. She recalled:

> It was an amazing outpouring of people caring and wanting to be there and cry with us, to make sure we ate, drank, and were feeling okay. Over 3,000 people went through this house. We put an obituary in a local paper for my aunts and my grandmothers and people we didn't know sent flowers, breakfast, lunch, dinners. It took three hours to shake every hand. In Dearborn, the two main halls where Arab weddings are held cancelled all the weddings, engagements, baby showers, bridal showers. They opened their doors to mourners.

Memorials that previously would have involved one extended family expanded to include multiple families or even the (long-distance) nation as an imagined family. Responsibilities typically associated with extended kin were now shared among Lebanese who had faced similar losses and tragedies.

Relocating Violence, War, and Resistance

In these stories, we have seen how the violent realities of military war constituted the lives of Arab Americans at different moments and in different geographic locations. In the late 1990s in the San Francisco Bay Area, leftist Arab activists grappled with multiple forms of violence – the realities of military-based bodily harm, death, and killing and the linked realities of gendered racism and intra-communal sexism.

Their stories show how different forms of life and death are relational and interconnected – the urgency of Palestine and Iraq, dominant US racial logics that work to quell critiques of Israel, and the silencing of feminist critiques within the diaspora. This does not mean that activists attributed the same urgency to every issue, but rather that military violence, racial violence, and heteropatriarchy interacted with and intensified one another. The violence of war and racism in Palestine and Iraq produced a logic of emergency that led the leftist Arab movement to operate on a continuum with war on one end and sexism and homophobia in the diaspora on the other. Women activists in particular struggled with this formulation.

In the San Francisco Bay Area in the aftermath of 9/11, intensified US military invasions, anti-immigrant policies, and gendered racism augmented one another. We saw the internalization of the War on Terror in terms of the internment of the psyche, a form of internal incarceration. Then in 2006, a wave of panic and worry washed over Dearborn, Michigan, as Lebanese diasporas waited to learn whether their loved ones in Lebanon were alive or dead. We saw their outrage heightened by their engagements with gendered racist discourses that supported the invasion. We also saw how these experiences strengthened intra-communal relations and intensified relationships within the diaspora. Of course, concepts of family and kinship, when extended and fortified beyond the extended family, reify heteronormative kinship ideals and come with their own sets of exclusions. Yet interlocutors focused primarily on how the invasion inspired a sense of rights and responsibilities among the Lebanese diaspora, which people tended to conceptualize through an affective language of comfort and security.

These stories tell us something about Arab diasporas; they also tell us something about the US empire itself – namely, that the empire and the logics through which it works are transnational (in the context of the War on Terror). But at the same time, this point is familiar. US empire studies and anti-imperialist and transnational feminisms have already established that the empire is transnational.[36] Yet even these frameworks have tended to focus on how US-led imperialism (abroad) *impacts* US-based structures of power (racism, classism, heteropatriarchy). There remains a strong tendency to spatially and geographically separate US-led empire abroad from the realities of US-led racism within the United States and to define US imperialism primarily in terms of invasions overseas (Panama, Nicaragua, and so on), with US-based racism as an effect, impact, or result of imperialism.

Consider, for instance, these arguments: that white supremacist racial ideologies (against African Americans, for instance) *reinforce* US imperialist interventions in the global South;[37] that US imperialist interventions shape domestic US structures of race and racism; and that US imperialism impacts Third World women and US women of colour differently. There has been less research on how US imperialist interventions extend directly into US state structures and everyday lives (e.g., on how the global war on drugs and the US-based criminalization of people of colour are part of the same war).[38] In addition, while US ethnic studies have developed a framework for examining "internal colonization" or "the colonized within," it tends to focus on people targeted by histories of US settler colonialism within the geographic boundaries of the United States – such as Native Americans, Hawaiians, and Puerto Ricans. Within the framework of empire studies, Arabs, Muslims, and South Asians are primarily considered targets of imperial wars "abroad."

The framework diasporas of empire requires us to consider the War on Terror not in terms of *the* war and its "backlash" or *the* war and its "impacts" or "effects," but in terms of multiple violences with interconnected consequences that extend transnationally in similar spatio-temporal contexts. Taking the lead from my interlocutors and framing Arab diasporas as diasporas of empire opens up new possibilities for anti-imperialist feminist theory and activism to commit to ending both military violence "abroad" and the multiple, interconnected reverberations of empire within (heteropatriarchy and settler colonialism, gendered and sexualized racism, the criminalization of communities of colour, and so on). Many of the activists I work with understand these connections intimately, often experiencing their consequences in their daily lives because of how they dress as well as through their efforts not just to survive crises but to create conditions in which *all* members of their communities can thrive. Overall, interpreting Arab American experiences through the framework of diaspora of empire shows the transnational, deeply intimate violence of empire – but doing so also allows us to turn the moments in which transnational histories rub up against one another into moments of cross-border alliance and movement building. Moreover, the stories Arab American activists tell shed light on the transnational underpinnings of empire and on how imperial war "over there" reverberates "over here." Bringing this analysis together with what transnational anti-imperialist feminists have been arguing for decades, it is now clearer than ever that the War on Terror has entailed a restructuring of US domestic *and* foreign policy, which in turn has entailed an expansion of the conjoined heteropatriarchal, racist, and classist structures of the prison-industrial complex (PIC) *and* the military-industrial complex (MIC), both of these driven by the economic neoliberalism of the late twentieth and early twenty-first centuries and both disproportionately impacting women of colour, poor women, queers and transgender people, sex workers, immigrant women, women with disabilities, and other marginalized women in the United States and in the countries it is invading.[39] Researching and teaching beyond one-directional feminist analyses that focus on *either* the devastation resulting from US imperialism and war in the MENA region *or* racial–classist–heteropatriarchal violence in the United States means taking seriously how US "domestic" politics and US "foreign" politics exist within a similar historical and political frame. The points where the US "domestic" and "foreign" conjoin – and are made and remade through each other – are crucial axes for alliance building and accountability across disciplines and borders. Yet while framing the domestic and foreign structures of US imperialism as relational and mutually constitutive, I want to avoid assuming shared experiences, or that people drawn into US imperialism (and its racial and heteropatriarchal foundations) from varying locations share *equal* struggles. Rather, we might ask how the histories of people from different political locations within the United States and the MENA region (and beyond) rub up against one another when they are drawn into similar imperialist structures in different ways and to different degrees. For instance, how are we to approach alliance building and power asymmetries when it comes to Arab women living in the United States and Arab women living in countries targeted by US-led war? Or between the US military recruitment of working-class US women of colour (who will face high risks of sexual assault) through false promises about employment and education *and* US-led bombing, killing, and sexual assault of women in the Arab region and their communities? Future research might also address the flow of implications and feelings of identification and disidentification in the opposite direction, so to speak. We might consider what the people living in Lebanon during the Israeli invasion made of the outpouring of support from Arab Americans in Dearborn and the ways that diasporic (dis)identifications with empire resonate across borders, so that the flow is never simply one way or another, but back and forth.

NOTES

1 US imperialism in the Middle East has entailed neoliberal economic expansion and domination. See Mitchell, *Colonizing Egypt*; Elyachar, *Mountains of Dispossession*. See also Incite!, *The Revolution*; and Abdo, "Imperialism, the State, and NGOs," regarding support for the NGO-ization or professionalization of revolutionary social movements; support of puppet governments through the threat of military or economic domination (e.g., Jordan and Egypt); wars on countries that do not comply with imperial interests; the economic and military backing of Israeli-settler colonialism and expansion; and the circulation of media and government discourses on terrorism and Islamic fundamentalism.
2 There are indeed exceptions to this trend, such as Razack, *Casting Out*; Moallem, "Whose Fundamentalism?"; and Maira, *Missing*.
3 See Human Rights Watch, "We Are Not the Enemy."
4 See the following, all by Naber, for more details on each of these studies: "So Our History"; "The Rules of Forced Engagement"; "Transnational Families"; and *Arab America*.
5 See Mercer, *Welcome to the Jungle*.
6 See Clifford, *Routes*, 269.
7 See Gilroy, *The Black Atlantic*.
8 See Shohat, *Area Studies*, 206.
9 See Clifford, *Routes*, 255.
10 See Farsoun and Aruri, *Palestine and the Palestinians*, 292.
11 See Johnson and Kuttab, "Where Have All the Women."
12 See Clark, "Fire and Ice"; Gordon, *Invisible War*.
13 See ADC, *1991 Report*; Wingfield and Karaman, "Arab Stereotypes"; Sabbagh, *Sex, Lies, and Stereotypes*; Hatem, "How the Gulf War."
14 See Puar, *Terrorist Assemblages*; Al-Sayyad, "You're What?"; Razack, *Casting Out*; Massad, *Desiring Arabs*; Hayes, "Queer Resistance."
15 See Naber, *Arab America*.
16 See Jarmakani, *Imagining Arab Womanwood*; Abu-Lughod, "Do Muslim Women"; Razack, "Geopolitics."
17 Several scholars of US immigrant communities and communities of colour document similar scenarios in which racism produces the flip side of discrimination's distancing role. Gutierrez, *Walls and Mirrors*; Moghissi, "Away from Home."
18 Robnett, *How Long?*
19 See Naber, *Arab America*.

20 The differences between Hizballah and al-Qaeda alone affirm this point. Hizballah is "a political party" and "a powerful actor in Lebanese politics" as well as "a provider of important social services." See Deeb, *An Enchanted Modern*. According to Deeb, Hizballah's militia arose to battle Israel's occupation of southern Lebanon in 1982 and 2000 and to advocate for Lebanon's disenfranchised Shi'i Muslim community. Al-Qaeda is an international alliance of militant Islamist organizations, a fringe group, and a diffuse movement comprising individual non-state actors or small cells operating independently.

21 See Cainkar, "Islamic Revival," 1.

22 See Cainkar, "Islamic Revival," 1.

23 See Naber, "The Rules."

24 Shohat and Stam, *Unthinking Eurocentrism.*

25 See Ella Shohat and Robert Stam for an analysis of colonialist discourses on "veiling." In their critique of colonialist Hollywood films, they write that "The orient is … sexualized through the recurrent figure of the veiled woman, whose mysterious inaccessibility, mirroring that of the orient itself, requires Western unveiling to be understood." *Unthinking Eurocentrism*, 149.

26 See Naber, "The Rules."

27 See Foucault, *Discipline and Punish*, 209.

28 See Foucault, *Discipline and Punish*, 209.

29 See Foucault, *Discipline and Punish*.

30 See Naber, "So Our History."

31 See Khalidi, "Foreword." See also Deeb, *An Enchanted Modern*, for an overview of Hizballah.

32 Sayed and Tzannatos, "The Economic and Human Costs."

33 Deeb, "Hizballah."

34 Amnesty International reports, using numbers from the Israeli Ministry of Foreign Affairs, that 101 civilians were either moderately or seriously injured, with many more "lightly" injured; MDE 02/025/2006, 8. AI also states that only twelve Israeli soldiers were killed during the war, all as they entered southern Lebanon.

35 Amidst numerous calls for a ceasefire and condemnations of the violence from political and religious organizations, such as the European Union and the Catholic Church, the official US position was that "Israel had a right to defend itself." Although the UN was dismayed by the violence from its onset, the UN Security Council did not call for a full cessation of hostilities until 11 August, when it issued Resolution 1701, mostly because the United

States continually blocked any votes on a ceasefire Zunes, "Washington's Proxy War," 108–12.

36 Kaplan, *The Anarchy of Empire*; Harvey, *The New Imperialism*.

37 See Love, *Race over Empire*.

38 I have drawn upon the following studies as examples of rthnic studies scholarship that theorizes US imperialism "abroad" and "domestic" US racism as extensions of each other: Kim, *Ends of Empire*; Diaz and Kauanui, *Native Pacific Cultural Studies*; Diaz and Kauanui. "Native Pacific Cultural Studies."

39 See Mohanty, Pratt, and Riley, "Introduction"; Razack, "Geopolitics, Culture Clash"; Bacchetta et al., "Transnational Feminist Practices"; and Shohat, "Introduction."

11 Sovereignty, War on Terror, and Violence against Women

MEYDA YEĞENOĞLU

Violence against women is a global phenomenon. It cuts across the boundaries of social and economic class positions. The most pervasive violation of human rights that we know of today is violence against women: it is on our streets and in our homes, schools, prisons, workplaces, and institutions. Under-reporting makes it difficult to estimate its prevalence, but the available statistics show that at least one of out every three women around the world has been beaten, coerced into sex, or otherwise abused in her lifetime and that the abuser is usually someone known to her. In a survey of about 24,000 women in ten countries, the World Health Organization found that between 10 and 69 per cent of women reported having been physically assaulted at some point in their lives. In the United States, the National Coalition Against Domestic Violence reports the following: one in every four women will experience domestic violence in her lifetime; every year, an estimated 1.3 million women are victims of physical assault by an intimate partner; according to police, almost one-third of female homicide victims are killed by an intimate partner; in 70 to 80 per cent of intimate partner homicides, no matter which partner was killed, the man physically abused the woman before the murder; 7.8 million women have been raped by an intimate partner at some point in their lives; and each year there are nearly 16,800 homicides and 2.2 million injuries resulting from intimate partner violence. And most cases of domestic violence are never reported to the police.

Although it has been emphasized time and again that people all over the world should fear and prepared for the next terrorist attack at any moment, on US soil there have been 0 attacks since 9/11. In 2011, the Worldwide Incidents Tracking System reported that France had suffered 2 attacks the previous year resulting in 16 wounded and 0 deaths. In Germany there had been 3 attacks resulting in 2 wounded and 2 deaths. In the United Kingdom there had been 15 attacks resulting in 5 wounded and 1 death.

I begin by asking a simple question: Considering the alarming statistics from all over the world, why does violence by men against women not arouse a reaction as strong as the one against terrorist violence? What prevents us from imagining a "war on domestic violence" comparable in scope to the "War on Terror"? Why don't states declare a "state of exception" in the face of the alarming numbers of women harmed and killed as a result of domestic violence? Given that the kernel of the issue is *violence*, why is the public's reaction, and the state's, so much less weaker when women are injured, tortured, or killed as a result of domestic violence?[1]

These questions can be addressed in a number of ways. One can examine the international context and how the discourse on the "War on Terror" is intermingled with the "feminist" project of "saving oppressed Muslim women from their oppressing states and nations." Or one can examine the discourses that culturalize racism[2] when the women being subjected to violence are immigrants to Western nation-states. In this chapter, as my reference point, I will be taking the social and cultural context in Turkey, which is not reducible to either of the above two contexts. I aim to offer a comparative analysis of how the state, as the proprietor of legitimate authority and power, responds to the *transgression of law through the exercise of violence*. The two instances I analyse are the *transgression of law by terrorist violence* and the *transgression of law by men's exercise of violence against women*, so-called domestic violence. Understanding the different nature of the state's response to these two forms of violence will illuminate a number of issues. To unpack them, first, we need to consider the relationship between the legal system and sovereignty; second, we need to understand the prevailing and canonical model of politics on which sovereignty is based and how this model is an androcentric one that places the fraternal or the brother at the centre of the hegemonic model of politics; and third, we need to explore the kind of message the sovereign state perceives as being transmitted to its power and authority when violence is exercised by terrorists *versus* when it is exercised by men.

This chapter is not based on a specific case analysis; generally, though, my reference point is Turkey, where Kurdish guerrillas (the PKK) and the Turkish state have been at war for almost thirty years. Throughout those years, Turkey's governments (starting with the military coup in 1980) have adopted the discourse of terrorist violence when dealing not only with the PKK but also with the Kurdish people's social and political rights. A variety of culturally fashioned racial discourses have arisen and have been placed in the service of the war against PKK "terrorists."

In Turkey, we have also seen an enormous increase in domestic violence. The official figures tell us that 953 women were murdered by their husbands in 2009. According to Fatma Şahin, Turkey's Minister of Family and Social Affairs, 666 women died as a result of domestic violence between 2009 and 2012. Based on information from the Interior Ministry, 171 women died as a result of domestic violence in 2009; 177 in 2010; 163 in 2011; and 163 in 2012.

It is now almost commonplace in Turkey to come across headlines reporting a woman's violent murder by her ex-husband, fiancé, or a male relative. Earlier this year, the Turkish Interior Ministry issued its latest figures for the number of women murdered, which showed a 1,400 per cent increase between 2002 and 2009. There is widespread agreement that the problem is getting worse. As it turned out, most of the murdered women had applied to the authorities for help or requested some kind of restraining order. It has been reported that while rates of violence are higher among poor and rural women, one-third of women in relatively high economic brackets have also been subjected to domestic violence. It is this alarming new development that I will be addressing in this chapter. To prevent any misunderstanding, I underline that women who are murdered come from a variety of social, cultural, ethnic, and religious backgrounds. Most of them are poor, lower-middle-class, or middle-class. Some have jobs, some are housewives, and some are professionals. In other words, women who are murdered do not belong to a single cultural, ethnic, religious, or class background. I must add that owing to deeply entrenched Eurocentric and racist biases, most of the domestic violence in Turkey might be easily assumed to be happening within the Kurdish community. As the above data demonstrate, this is not the case. "Honour" is often assumed to be the most prominent motive behind domestic violence in Turkey. Indeed, this is the pervasive discourse among white Turks, who assume that "backward" Kurdish traditions are the sole cause of the violence these women are subjected to. In this chapter I do not focus on the racialized discourse directed towards "honour killings." Rather, when I refer to domestic violence in Turkey, it is specifically to the recent increase in violence that has led to the murder of "white Turkish" women. If

I opened this chapter to discourses about the Kurdish community, I would have to address other issues, such as how discourses on violence against Kurdish women perpetuate racial divisions, and how mainstream feminist assumptions about a universal and transcendent womanhood reinscribe a duality between "backward Kurdish Others" and "civilized Turks." And I would also have to discuss – as Sherene Razack's work teaches us – how notions of culture are put in the service of discussing violence against women, thus pre-empting racism in a process she calls the "culturalization of sexism."[3] All of this would have required attention to the complex intermingling of racism with sexism, which Razack captures with the powerful phrase "patriarchal violence eclips(ing) racial domination."[4] However, "culturalization of the race question" is not a relevant framework for this chapter. Instead, I narrow my focus to the issue of violence against women by taking it as a *primary issue* (because the women who are subjected to it are predominantly "white Turks"), emphasizing the role of familial, fraternal, and androcentric political friendships established among brothers that result in the failure of the state to act forcefully to safeguard women from violence in the private and public domains. I will be using the generic term "domestic violence" to compare the state's response to the terrorist (i.e., by the racialized male Kurdish other) to its response to men of the same race.

Legal System and Sovereignty

In recent decades and especially since 9/11, people have been encouraged to fear terrorist attacks. Right after 9/11, on 26 October 2001, the US Senate passed the Patriot Act, which suppressed freedoms by broadening the powers of law enforcement and immigration authorities to detain and deport immigrants suspected of terrorist-violence-related activities; in effect, this act eradicated the legal status of the individual. Giorgio Agamben writes that this has led to the production of a legally unnamable and unclassifiable being, for the detention of detainees has become "indefinite not only in a temporal sense but in its very nature as well, since it is entirely removed from the law and from the judicial oversight."[5] He suggests that this could be compared to the "situation of the Jews in the Nazi *Lager* [camps] who, along with their citizenship, had lost every legal identity.[6]

The distinction between legal and illegal violence cannot help us comprehend the reasons why terrorist violence has been assigned the status of exceptional and the zealous reactions against it. The world-wide entrenchment of the "War on Terror" discourse has led many critics to examine the problem of sovereignty and how a state of exception has been declared as a means to control terrorist violence.

It would be a mistake to think that the state of exception on which the "War on Terror" has been erected has led to the nullification or collapse of law. On the contrary, when a state of exception is declared, the law proliferates so excessively that sovereignty and violence blend together. Thus, the state of exception marks an instance where *law and lawlessness amalgamate* and the border between legality and violence disappears. As Agamben puts it, the state of exception "is the legal form of what cannot have legal form."[7]

For Agamben, it is sovereignty that can explain the paradoxical and ambiguous condition created between law and lawlessness. Indeed, sovereignty by definition is the capacity to declare exception to established norms of civil liberties, human rights, rule of law, and so on. For him, the sovereign is the one to whom the law has conceded the power to declare the state of exception, which entails the suspension of law itself and enables the sovereign to reside simultaneously inside and outside law. Agamben formulates this paradox as follows: "'the law is outside itself,' or: 'I, the sovereign, who am outside the law, declare that there is nothing outside the law.'"[8] The sovereign's ability to suspend law and stand outside law eliminates the distinction between violence and law and creates the "threshold in which violence passes over into law, and law passes over into violence."[9] Moreover, he suggests that in contemporary politics, the state of exception has become the dominant paradigm of governance.[10] Saul Newman and Michael Levine note that the distinction between authoritarian and liberal democratic regimes is becoming irrelevant now that modern democratic states are becoming increasingly authoritarian.[11] As they put it, this condition, which results in a permanent state of exception, leads to the partial or complete erosion of the space of politics. In liberal democratic societies, when the state of exception is no longer an exception but the rule, the discourse of war and violence becomes the primary condition of society. Sovereignty then comes to represent another form of violent domination, with the legal system functioning as a systematized and codified form of violence. That the state of exception has become the central paradigm of many governments today, be they democratic or totalitarian, attests to the fact that states are now permeated by violence.[12] Furthermore, once violent domination becomes a defining characteristic of sovereign states, the distinction between war and politics disappears. When the logic of war sets the security paradigm, politics becomes inconceivable without war. This results in the total disappearance of the space of politics, or at best the incorporation of politics into war. Newman and Levine also suggest that Michel Foucault, who traced the historical emergence of a discourse on war, is a useful source for supplementing this analysis of war to expose how *racism* serves as the nexus between war and politics.[13]

The close links among war, violence, and politics were examined by Foucault in *Society Must Be Defended*,[14] in which he sets out to liberate our understanding of power from the grip of classical political theory, which confines power to a central sovereign and a juridical model. This model limits power through various laws, codes, and institutions as embodied in the king or the modern state. Foucault's framework shows us the limitations of seeing power through the lenses of law and sovereignty and suggests that we must assess sovereignty from the perspective of violence, since violence and war are not exterior to civil society but constitutive of it. When violence is posited as an ontological condition of sovereign power, how are we to understand the relationship between the violence posed by the terrorist and the violence involved in the sovereign state's declaration of war on terror? What, explains why terrorist violence triggers state violence?

When states go beyond the parameters of law in the name of enforcing it, the distinction between *law-making* and *law-preserving* violence is suspended.[15] When examining sovereignty from the perspective of violence, law, and authority, it is vital to consider whether the distinction between legitimate and illegitimate violence is a valid one. Only then can we make sense of the violence that is operating today through the declaration of "War on Terror." Walter Benjamin's analysis might help us explore the roots of the opposition between legitimate and illegitimate violence and its significance for understanding how the state, the legal system, and violence are linked.

In "Critique of Violence," Benjamin focuses on the complicity of what appear to be two different forms of violence.[16] He asks what enables us to distinguish between *legitimate* and *illegitimate violence*. This distinction is based on the licence granted by the state and the legal system. States exercise a monopoly on violence and forbid others to commit it, for if they did so, they would be undermining the legal system and hence the authority of the sovereign state. In other words, violence that is outside the law is a fundamental threat to sovereignty. This is one reason why the violence posed by terrorism is unacceptable to the sovereign authority: the terrorist challenges the absolute control and possession of violence by the state and its legal system. As Newman's reading of Benjamin suggests, "the state, according to this analysis, sees in the terrorist a rival to its monopolistic exercise of violence." Benjamin here discusses the "great criminal" and the admiration he arouses because of the "unsanctioned" violence his deeds invoke. Do we not see this "great criminal" in the figure of the Osama Bin Laden, who, while not arousing our admiration, at least aroused our fascination? Bin Laden was a highly transgressive figure, one who was outside the law and who embodied an excessive violence that threatened it."[17] Marc Redfield suggests that when the state perceives a threat to its monopoly on violence, the terrorist "becomes the abject double of the 'sovereign' – he is above the law in his putative power to declare war."[18]

Aided by Benjamin's analysis, Newman in "Terror, Sovereignty and Law"[19] explains why the state perceives a threat to its monopolistic control of violence. Benjamin's distinction between law-making violence and law-preserving violence is important here. Law-making violence is directed against existing laws and conditions. It has the effect of establishing new laws. It breaks existing laws and threatens to replace them. Law-preserving violence, by contrast, maintains and preserves the authority of the existing legal system. Law-making violence functions outside the law. The crux of the matter about law-making violence is not that it is beyond the law, but that it is connected to the principle of sovereignty. Law-preserving violence, in aiming either to change particular laws or to enforce them, maintains the authority of the legal system and the state. Law-making violence, by contrast, sets out to overthrow existing laws and replace them with new ones. *Alternative* law-making violence, represented by terrorist violence, presents a supreme challenge to the state's authority. Illegal (terrorist) and state (legal) violence share an analytical structure and logic.[20] Both are excessive, arbitrary, and outside the domain of law. But because terrorist violence is outside the state's control, it comes to represent an alternative law-making violence, and that is why the state perceives a fundamental threat to its monopolistic control over violence. Law-making violence is different from law-preserving violence; both, however, preserve the law and thereby maintain the legal system's power and authority. In doing so, they sanction power and sovereignty.

Law-making violence has a paradoxical structure: it aims to establish a new system of law and to end violence, but it also reasserts and ratifies violence at the moment the law is established. This attests to the irreducible violence that inheres in the foundation of law. For Benjamin, then, law originates in violence and the idea that *justice* is attained through the exercise of law is no more than a concealment or disavowal of the violence that underpins the legal system. This foundational violence is disavowed in the lawmaking process. Violence thus inhabits the very core of political and legal authority. There exists an ambiguous and paradoxical relationship between law and violence: law reaffirms violence and violence reaffirms law. The irreducible link between violence and law attests to the existence of power. This is why violence against the law always ends up restoring the law. No lawmaking process is independent of the institution of power.

Jacques Derrida, in "Force of Law,"[21] when analysing Benjamin's *Critique of Violence*, considers how the law's inaugurating or founding moment is rooted in something pre-existing. This pre-existing thing is the foundation of law and as such is extralegal and violent (because it is not legal). Thus, the founding moment of law is a disavowed act of violence or crime. That founding crime or originary violence is hidden. Derrida explicates this founding or inaugurating violence in terms of what Montaigne and Pascal called the "mystical foundation of authority."[22] This originating moment has its roots in violence that is itself not grounded. As Derrida puts it, "since the origin of authority, the founding or grounding [*la foundation ou le fondement*], the positing of law [*loi*] cannot by definition rest on anything but themselves, they are themselves a violence without ground [*sans fondement*]. This is not to say that they are in themselves unjust, in the sense of 'illegal' or 'illegitimate.' They are neither legal nor illegal in their founding moments. They exceed the opposition between founded or unfounded, or between any foundationalism or anti-foundationalism."[23]

This foundational and mystically hidden violence is what sovereign power is about. This close link between law and violence helps us explain why the state responds so furiously to terrorist violence; it is because the violence of terrorism exposes the violence hidden in the foundation of legal authority.

Role of Historical and Existing Cultural Contexts, Agendas, and Traditions

Foucault's analysis, like Benjamin's, underscores how war, violence, and politics intermingle. As such, it is a useful framework for examining how the realm of power and politics is infused with violence. Foucault's analysis unshackles power from law and sovereignty and uses war as a tool for analysing power relations. Calling for a new analysis of power that goes beyond questions of law and sovereignty, he suggests that we examine society's power relations from the perspective of war. In *Society Must Be Defended*, he asks, "Can we find in bellicose relations, in the model of war, in the schema of struggle or struggles, a principle that can help us understand and analyze political power, to interpret political power in terms of war, struggles, and confrontations?"[24] In his analysis, sovereignty is to be understood as based not on rights but on violence. Violence is intimately connected to power and war; therefore, power relations must be understood as a particular encoding of violence. In their reading of Foucault, Newman and Levine suggest that "instead of society being founded on the idea of the contract, it is based on a violence, both metaphorical and real, which continues to haunt it. Political sovereignty itself is merely a form of conquest that has fallen silent and now tries to disavow the violence of its own origins through the discourse of law, contract and rational agreement."[25] Like Benjamin and Derrida, Foucault reveals how war, politics, legality, and violence are indissoluble and how law is no more than codified violence and is therefore foundational to social relations, which are woven into power relations. In this way, "law itself comes to reflect its violent origins once again, being mobilized as a tactic of war, a vector for sovereign violence."[26]

Foucault's analysis is important in another sense. His emphasis on the need to recognize the importance of historically conditioned social and cultural forces, and on the ideological frames that shape war and political violence, is useful when we examine the racist and religious ideologies of today's sanctioned War on Terror. Andrew Neal in "Cutting Off the King's Head" suggests that "Foucault has exposed the discursive and historical dimensions of modern nation-state sovereignty, charting a genealogy of how political authority became entwined with powerful ideas of collective identity and how the nation-state thus went on to become the dominant subject of universal history itself."[27] Therefore, the political will of the sovereign is always circumscribed by cultural contexts, agendas, and traditions. If we remain within the sterile juridical model of sovereignty, we will never grasp the nature of the specific exclusions that are managed by the nation-states. Only by attending to the historical and discursive dimensions of modern nation-state sovereignty can we come to understand how notions of collective identity and universal values come to be represented by the modern political authority.

A fundamental discursive ingredient in the discourse of "war on terror" is the construction of the enemy or the dangerous other, who is represented as foreign, backward, racialized, barbaric, an outsider. "War on terror' is thus shaped by a stubborn determination to find, designate, name, and identify the enemy. This outsider poses a threat not only to our way of life but also to the liberal and universalistic ideals represented by the national culture. Today's geopolitics of terror cannot be understood simply as governance exercised by rational sovereign authority; it is also a politics based on the construction of enmity and on the threat that spreading enmity poses to the entire machinery of the nation-state. What is new and terrifying, Neal suggests, is that the "enemy of the state" and the "enemy of the nation/society/people" are now one thing. The state's suspension of law, mobilization of the state of exception, and implementation of violence through heightened security measures, all of these justified by the language of war, are in the name of a national ideal.[28]

The enemy is defined by the social and cultural context. The opposition between enemy and friend never exists unarticulated in terms of pre-existing national, economic, racial, religious, and other distinctions. Thus, the political designation of "enemy" is always based on already available definitions of the national collective's way of life. Newman and Levine supplement their analysis of sovereignty based on the convergence of war and politics with an analysis of racism as underpinning the war/politics nexus.[29] Foucault's following suggestion is absolutely crucial for understanding how racism is what today supports the language of the War on Terror:

> The war that is going on beneath order and peace, the war that undermines our society and divides it in a binary mode is, basically, a race war. At a very early stage, we find the basic elements that make the war possible, and then ensure its continuation, pursuit, and development: ethnic differences, differences between languages, different degrees of force, vigor, energy, and violence; the differences between savagery and barbarism; the conquest and subjugation of one race by another. The social body is basically articulated around two races. It is this idea that this clash between two races runs through society from top to bottom which we see being formulated as early as seventeenth century.[30]

The discourse in response to terrorist violence is based on the construction of an enemy mainly in terms of race, religion, and ethnicity. The "national ideal" that is being protected from the enemy's violence is shaped and conditioned by knowledge about otherness. The terrorist is threatening our way of life, our cultural and political space, our national collective. National identity and common values are believed to be represented by nation-states. In the mechanism of the state, racism comes to dominate politics. Racism no longer belongs to the twisted ideas of extremist groups; on the contrary, it has come to dominate mainstream politics and public opinion. Foucault in his 1976 lectures came close to predicting the racism and nationalism that characterize today's language of the War on Terror: "At this point, the racist thematic is no longer a moment in the struggle between one social group and another; it will promote the global strategy of social conservatism."[31]

Racism and nationalism sustain one aspect of the ideology and logic of the "War on Terror"; the other is sustained by the phallocentric nature of politics. These two foundational principles help explain the zeal with which both the sovereign power and the public react to the violence wrought by terrorism. The same principles explain the lack of response to violence against women among both states and the public. To understand the dynamics here, we need to identify the characteristics of the canonical model of politics as well as what that politics entails.

Politics of Friendship

In this section, I incorporate the analysis Derrida offers in *Politics of Friendship*.[32] Derrida approaches the question of friendship through an analogy with politics and describes friendship in terms of relations between brothers. This brotherly relationship also describes how politics is configured, which is based on familial, fraternalistic, and androcentric relations.[33]

Derrida suggests that the canonical model of politics in Roman, Jewish, Christian, and Islamic cultures has been based on this prevailing model of friendship.[34] Politics, especially republican democracy, is conducted in terms of congeneric doubles (congeneric: belonging to the same genus, of related origin or nature).[35] In this model, friendship refers to a relationship between men, who have a contract according to which one will survive and succeed the other. Central to this contract is that they agree politically. According to Derrida, this model is based on the exclusion of women: friendship between a man and a woman is impossible, and so is friendship between women. Women, then, are excluded from friendship. At work here is the neutralization of sexual difference.[36] The brother, literally or figuratively, has been placed at the centre of the model. When the brotherhood is made central to politics, we have a phallocentric model in which there is no possibility to acknowledge woman as a friend. In canonical politics, sexual difference is neutralized and remains unimaginable. Brotherhood is about filiation, but not *any* filiation: a woman cannot appear in this fraternity. Filiation with brothers rather than sisters forms the basis of fraternity. Sexual difference must be kept outside the borders of fraternity.[37]

For Derrida, politics – be it of the nation-state or of sovereignty – shares this phallocentric concept of friendship bonds based on brotherhood.[38] The key concepts of politics, such as sovereignty, power, and representation, are all marked directly or indirectly by this model. Fraternity establishes equality and shared origins among men. Brothers share the same origin and thus are equal to one another and can have reciprocity. Of course, fraternity is not always limited to biological brotherhood.[39] It surpasses biological, national, and other empirical formulations of brotherhood. Symbolically, conventionally, and through authorized engagement, fraternization produces a determined politics that regulates fraternity through the symbolic projection of real or natural fraternity.[40] The Greek *polis* is an arena of like-minded men related to one another in citizenship by the bonds of friendship, who "agree about their interests, adopt the same policy and put their common resolves into effect." Derrida calls for us to examine the understanding that this configuration of politics brings to the fore. Such a politics is fraternal, familial, and androcentric. Therefore, friendship that is private and friendship that is public and political imply each other. The concept of fraternity overlaps the private and the public. Public and political friendship illustrates that our relationship to the other passes through the universality of law. The law demands that friends who are in agreement show mutual respect for the law.

Risks of Friendship and by Way of Conclusion

But friendship also entails risks; the relationship is vulnerable. The security and comfort based on filial love and sameness can be undermined because of the brother's *difference* from us. The political realm is also vulnerable to this threat. The brother can be a friend but can also be turned into an enemy in the process of fraternization. The brother's difference or distance from us might bring potential conflict or grievance. This fragility must be recognized.[41]

In light of Derrida's analysis of friendship, I ask what the violence posed by terrorists does to this friendship. It does two things:

1 Terrorist violence challenges the state's monopoly on violence. The law's transgression by the terrorist is directed at the legal system as such. It does not challenge a particular law; rather, it directly challenges the authority and foundation of sovereign states. Hence, the terrorist, in exercising violence, launches a rivalry at the sovereign state's "ownership" of violence. Most important, the irreducible violence, which inheres in the foundation of law but has been disavowed in the lawmaking process, is unconcealed as the sovereign makes violence its modus operandi through the state of exception and suspension of law.

2 Perhaps more importantly, by challenging the foundations of the sovereign's authority, terrorist violence disrupts the pact between brothers by disrupting the familial and fraternal political friendship. The terrorist does not respect the universality of law, which requires that both sides show mutual respect. Thus, the "war on terror" may be one brother's infuriated response to the disturbance the other brother has posed to the pact on which the two had once agreed.

Terrorist violence implies a confrontation directed at the very source and foundation of law. What the terrorist does – unlike the *criminal* who exercises violence on women – is disturb and unsettle the politics of friendship. It is because state sovereignty, which is based on a patriarchal pact, is perceived to be threatened, weakened, and waning that the threat of terrorist violence is responded to so strongly.

The violence against women that is exercised in the domestic space does not constitute an unsettling of the terms of brotherly friendship. In response to violence in the domestic space, the sovereign simply invokes the discourse of legality in the name of protecting of individual woman. The discourse of war renders the violence of terrorism unacceptable by countering it with another form of violence; by contrast, the violence of sexism is relegated to the status of mere legal unacceptability and is dealt with through various legal and institutional mechanisms. The existence of the phallocentric pact and the brotherly filiation ends up feminizing the victim of sexual violence. With terrorist violence, national integrity is perceived to be at stake, because the sovereign has come to represent the national and universal values of the collective; whereas with male violence, the unity, harmony, and well-being of the family unit or an individual woman is thought to be at stake. Domestic violence, that is, poses no threat to established fraternity among brothers. This disparity in the values is the reason why not all violence is regarded as having equal standing. The violence of sexism is relegated to simple legal and criminal unacceptability; the violence of terrorism is perceived as being directed at the very foundation of authority and hence as undermining the fraternal contract.

Domestic violence, rather than challenging and threatening the authority, power, and sovereignty of the state, invites the state to maintain and exercise its sovereign lawmaking capacity. Domestic violence is codified as a criminal act against which police action, criminal sanctions, and juridical procedures must be mobilized. It is not war measures but legal procedures that are called on to be marshalled. As such, domestic violence, no matter how unacceptable and objectionable, is sanctioned violence because it results in the preservation and safeguarding of the existing legal system and perpetuates the sovereign state's authority and the legal system even as it transgresses the law and occupies the space of criminality. The criminal act of domestic violence, rather than challenging the foundation of the legal system, breaches only particular aspects of it. It therefore has the status of being a particular type of violence, one that reaffirms the place and authority of sovereign power. In this respect, domestic violence attests to the double erasure of women from the bonds established by men. The woman is erased, first by the fraternization of politics and then through the reinstantiation of the patriarchal pact.

NOTES

1 Of course, if one addresses the international context, one has to attend to
   the fact that some Western states, such as the United States, Canada, and
   Britain, have declared what amounts to a war on violence against Muslim
   women in Afghanistan and Aborginal women in Canada. This discourse of
   "saving Muslim women from oppressive Muslim men" has been a powerful instrument for justifying the invasion of Afghanistan. When women
   who are subjected to sexual and domestic violence are immigrants living in
   Western states, the discourses mobilized usually serve as an important

excuse to intervene in Muslim/immigrant communities so as to limit their rights. I thank Sherene Razack for pointing to the intermingling of race with issues of sexual violence in these contexts, which has helped me attend to the specificities of the different contexts in which the issue of domestic violence is framed. See Razack, "Domestic Violence as Gender Persecution" and "What Is to Be Gained?"

2 Razack, "What Is to Be Gained?"

3 Razack, "What Is to Be Gained?", 898.

4 Razack, "Domestic Violence," 47.

5 Agamben, *State of Exception*, 3.

6 Agamben, *State of Exception*, 4.

7 Agamben, *State of Exception*, 1.

8 Agamben, *Homo Sacer*, 15.

9 Agamben, *Homo Sacer*, 32.

10 Agamben, *State of Exception*, 2.

11 Newman and Levine, "War, Politics and Race," 25.

12 Newman and Levine, "War, Politics and Race," 23–4.

13 Newman and Levine, "War, Politics and Race," 24.

14 Foucault, *Society Must Be Defended*.

15 Newman, "Terror, Sovereignty, and Law," 574.

16 Benjamin, "Critique of Violence."

17 Newman, "Terror, Sovereignty, and Law," 572.

18 Redfield, *The Rhetoric of Terror*, 5.

19 Newman, "Terror, Sovereignty, and Law."

20 Newman, "Terror, Sovereignty, and Law," 574.

21 Derrida, "Force of Law."

22 Derrida, "Force of Law," 242.

23 Derrida, "Force of Law," 242.

24 Foucault, *Society Must Be Defended*, 23.

25 Newman and Levine, "War, Politics, and Race," 34.

26 Newman and Levine, "War, Politics and Race," 36.

27 Neal, "Cutting Off the King's Head," 395.

28 Neal, "Cutting off the King's Head," 394.

29 Newman and Levine, "War, Politics and Race," 24.

30 Foucault, *Society Must Be Defended*, 59–60.

31 Foucault, *Society Must Be Defended*, 62.

32 Derrida, *The Politics of Friendship*.

33 Lynch, "Aristotle and Derrida," 98.

34 Derrida, "Politics and Friendship."

35 Lynch, "Aristotle and Derrida on Friendship," 99.

36 W. Young, "God and Derrida's Politics."
37 Lynch, "Aristotle and Derrida," 101; Derrida, "Politics and Friendship."
38 Derrida, "Politics and Friendship."
39 W. Young, "God and Derrida's Politics."
40 W. Young, "God and Derrida's Politics."
41 Lynch, "Aristotle and Derrida," 105–6.

Terror and the Limits of Remembering

12 Introduction to Section Three

KENDRA-ANN PITT

During a trip home to Barbados in December 2011, I was visited by one of my "fictive" uncles. He, like my mother, is Guyanese, and we sat around the table "old talking" about family, politics, and life. As we eased later into the evening, I asked him to share his reflections on race and politics in Guyana. It was then that he told us of his experiences as a journalist during the racialized violence in Guyana in the 1960s,[1] of his friends who had been displaced as a result of that violence, and of the atmosphere of fear produced during this period. As I listened in awe to this story that I had never heard before, I was struck by the tributaries of silence that had always seemed to course through the intimate spaces of my family life; by how meanings of gender, class, race, disability, and sexuality reverberate as themes defining the bodies embedded in these silences; and by how these silences are related to a politics of memory forged in communities coming to terms with violent pasts, and living in a present during which violence is continuously reinvented. The chapters in this section attend to such complexities as they variably engage with questions of memory, violence, and power.

Memory is imbued with movement through the bodies that are mobilized in its production. These bodies construct memory in its various expressions; they give it form through their presence and absence; they engage with and transmit it. They tell us about flows of power, and they represent a fluidity that offers up possibilities for their repositioning, allowing memories of violence to be reshaped. Memorializing violence, then, is a political act, and the writings in this section tell us of the divergent practices and sites associated with such acts, while grounding the work of the body within them.

In her chapter, Merlinda Bobis demonstrates the possibilities associated with repositioning, redefining, and remembering bodies as she reckons with the events of the Total War, which took place in the Philippines between 1987 and 1989. She engages in a self-reflexive exploration of the creation of her novel *Fish-Hair Woman* and the performance play *River, River*. In doing so, she illustrates how it is possible to interrupt linear and blockaded understandings of the sites of struggle, pain, and power associated with violence. The use of bodies in the re/presentation of narratives of violence is what allows this to occur – her body, fictional ones from various social locations, and those involved in sharing and receiving these stories.

Honor Ford-Smith also takes up the work of the body as she examines the performance of memorials of violence in working-class urban communities in Jamaica. She considers the absence and presence of various bodies in these memorials and how they are related to power and hierarchy, while accounting for the complex contradictions they hold within them. Like Bobis, Ford-Smith establishes points of connection between the violence in the communities under discussion and the historical and contemporary geopolitical networks of power that contribute to its production. She demonstrates how rearranging bodies through memorialization and acknowledging their position in spaces of memory where they often remain absent, crucially gives form to the "absent referent"[2] in narratives of violence.

Alissa Trotz's chapter illustrates how, in the wake of recent violence in Guyana, images of bodies have been mobilized through the activation of memories of racialized violence. She shows how dominant, deeply embedded, and widely travelled notions about gendered, classed, sexualized, and racialized bodies are used to incite divisive party politics and ignite memories of public terror in order to discipline the body politic in the contemporary moment. The rehearsal of narratives of violence animates hegemonic social relations and speaks to the significance of memory in producing discursive possibilities for subjects.

Sara Ahmed, referencing the work of Judith Butler, has noted that it is through sensations of pain that bodies find form, producing the effect of boundary.[3] Trotz reminds us to consider how collective bodies are produced as boundaries of racialized difference are re/inscribed through memory. The scripts of racial terror – along with the pain and fear experienced when those scripts are mobilized – can become part of how racialized collectives come to know themselves and one another, further entrenching boundaries of difference and the multiple inequities they reproduce.

In this section's final chapter, Teresa Macias addresses the work of the Chilean National Commission on Political Imprisonment and Torture, exploring the commission's acknowledgment of state-sanctioned torture in the wake of Chile's authoritarian regime. She concerns herself with the parallels between the state interventions that regulated the intricate operations of the body through acts of torture, and the documentation of this torture in the production of a legitimized national narrative. Highlighting a mirroring of biopolitical technologies, of systematized and bureaucratized articulations of power that work on the body, Macias reminds us to be vigilant of the "non-spectacular" and of the ways that systems of domination persist in spite of our attempts at liberatory projects. She ultimately asks us to consider how bodies, power, and voices might coalesce and perhaps produce ethical narratives.

Memories are visceral. They access our senses while integrating and constituting our affective experiences. Grief, pain, sadness, anger, and fear are often integral to how we create records of experiences of violence. They are both productive *elements* of memory and *products* of memory. In a recent conversation with an activist from the Caribbean, we discussed the challenge of working across racialized boundaries in anti-violence work. She explained that one group she worked with had attempted to address issues of racialized difference within the group and the wider community. She told me, "We had to stop. The women felt it was too painful to go there."

In the bid to produce ethical approaches to memorializing violence, these points of pain, anger, and fear are central. When I remember my uncle's retelling of his story and how I could hear and see fear as he spoke, and when I think of how these women halted their workshops because it was too painful, it reinforces that while memories of violence hold social, cultural, and political histories, they also encapsulate affective ones. This knowledge is significant to an ethical praxis of memorializing violence. As Fellows and Razack note, the truths we *feel* can impede the dismantling of hierarchy in our political work.[4] It is necessary to bear witness to, to be accountable to, and to engage with one another's affective "truths" in spite of the contradictions this may present – and all while attending to the relations of power that are active during such encounters.

Activist Selma James makes the argument that equitable collective action is rooted in understandings of the individual. This, however, is not the untethered individual of neoliberalism; rather, the individual as she conceives it is always defined through its relationships to various collectives: "You begin with yourself and with everybody else at the same time … It is a false choice that you have to choose between 'all of us' and 'me.'"[5] Her perspective is instructive here. It points to the need to engage with our multiple narratives, to reimagine and redefine the boundaries of difference through which we so intimately and easily know ourselves – to seek out new possibilities. As they wrestle with ethics, memory, violence, and the operation of power in their writings here, all four authors illustrate how critical it is to reimagine the limits and boundaries of individual and collective bodies, along with the pain held within and producing them. In so doing it is possible to critically engage with the bodies of knowledge that have been gifted to us, to begin to recover those that have been hidden away in the spaces between us, and to create new intimate and political spaces for "old talk" that are rooted in the considerations and complexities of equitable social action.

NOTES

1 This violence is discussed in Alissa Trotz's chapter in this section.
2 Adams cited in A. Smith, *Conquest*, 22.
3 Ahmed, *The Cultural Politics*, 24.
4 Fellows and Razack, "The Race to Innocence."
5 James, "Sex, Race, and Class."

13 "Weeping Is Singing": After the War, a Transnational Lament

MERLINDA BOBIS

Paghaya. Deep weeping. *Pag-haaaa-ya.* The wail is in the middle syllable. For some, a stifled exhalation; for others, a near-scream, but always the breath travels the full distance from the groin to the gut, welling up to the throat. It is a weeping that is not about this or that moment. It has a history as long as the distance covered by that breath.

[The gravedigger] Pay Inyo told me not to forget this lesson of weeping: "You have to weep not from the throat but from lower down, just as in singing, so you don't grow hoarse, because it takes forever to get to the last note. Remember, weeping is like singing ..."[1]

Lambat na itom na itom
pero sa dugo natumtom
samong babaying parasira
buhok pangsalbar-pangsira
kang samong mga padaba
hale sa salog, hale sa salog
Very black net
but blood soaked
our fisherwoman
hair to save-fish
all our beloved
from the river, from the river[2]

Water–body–story–song. After a war, lament is fluid in these scenes from my novel *Fish-Hair Woman* and its stage adaptation, *River, River,* excerpts of which are deployed with Philippine Indigenous beliefs as "a localised theoretical framework" of this chapter. It argues through stories about bodies: it argues towards the water.

In my home region, Bikol, the term *iraya* refers to where water originates. In *Fish-Hair Woman*, Iraya is the setting of the war, a mythical village that is the wellspring of water and stories. So in this chapter, I return to this wellspring in a *grassroots storytelling-theorizing*,[3] a discursive style in which storytelling argues about and for the lived life from the ground up. It is a local philosophizing that I intentionally privilege over Western and now-globalized epistemology – for how can I tell the story about my home region Bikol in the Philippines, its war, its bodies, through Western thought? Yet Western epistemology has always done so from the safe distance of the academy. Could it be that the violence in a far country grows even farther away and stranger as it is abstracted and reduced into "a knowledge"?

In an earlier essay, I wrote that postcolonial epistemology can be "sometimes reductive and prescriptive"[4] and "can also turn paradoxically neo-colonial" in reading and framing culturally specific experiences, phenomena, literature, and art, and thus must also be decolonized.[5] As Walter Mignolo proposes with his *decoloniality*, as an alternative to postcolonial epistemology, one must act at "the fundamental level of thought" and "delink from the logic of coloniality." Moreover, "the epistemic has to have a material dimension," which is "not that of the structures of political economy but of the corporeal experiences of those who have been excluded from the production of knowledge by modernity," including the *damnés*, the wretched of the earth.[6]

This chapter is my attempt at decoloniality, but without erasing the input of the West in the formation of my transnational imaginary. I do not (and perhaps cannot) delink from Western thought, but I can displace it from its normative centrality. In its stead, I restore the wretched body: the body (in weeping as in singing) making its own arguments about terror, about love, and about bodies. I begin with the hair, my trope for memory: the 12-metre hair of the Fish-Hair Woman keeps growing into a net for trawling corpses from the river. Disappeared bodies and their histories are retrieved and re-membered in story and song, in a radical weeping. And the remembering body must sustain this weeping. Because it takes forever to get to the last note.

These propositions align with *Loss: The Politics of Mourning*, which asserts that the politics and ethics of mourning lie in how remains (of what is lost) are "produced, read, and sustained."[7] In their introduction to that collection of essays, David L. Eng and David Kazanjian reference Walter Benjamin's "historical materialism," which is "a creative process, animating history for future significations as well as alternate empathies ... [It] establishes a continuing dialogue with loss and its remains – a flash of emergence, an instant of emergency, and most important a moment of production."[8]

The moment of critical production and emergence (of this chapter) must evoke the moment of creative production (of the novel and the play), which must return to the instant of emergency: that war. In choosing my particular discursive style, ambitiously I hope to close the distance between the reader/audience of these remains (essay, novel, play) and the lived losses in that far country. I must avert the "indolence [and safety] of the heart,"[9] especially my own. So in this chapter, I tell stories that examine my politics, ethics, and aesthetics of mourning: how I attempt to sustain "a continuing dialogue between loss and its remains" through a long and fraught story-making about the 1987–89 Total War in the Bikol region, Philippines. How while crossing borders between cultures and story forms, this "creative process [is] animating [a specific] history [and evoking other histories] for future significations as well as alternate empathies." So the story is not merely "that violence in a far country." Through seventeen years of researching–writing–performing about Bikol's Total War, what began as a short story became a radio play, a novel, and a one-woman stage play that I once hoped to develop into a local–global community play. The singing is taking forever to get to the last note. Because there is too much history of terror, love, and bodies to be retrieved – too much weeping to be heard.

The Philippines' history of conflict[10] covers nearly four hundred years of Spanish colonization (1521–1893), forty years of American rule (1901–41), and three years of Japanese occupation (1941–45) and all the attendant bloody wars. Then in the 1950s, the country's dispossessed launched a guerrilla war against the feudal system controlled by a few landed families. This movement grew into the New People's Army (NPA), the armed wing of then outlawed Communist Party of the Philippines. It expanded its aim to include "liberat[ing] the Philippines from the forces of [US] imperialism and feudalism"[11] and the nearly twenty-year dictatorship of Ferdinand Marcos. Counter-insurgency operations were assisted by the United States, which to this day has clout in Philippine politics. Marcos was deposed in February 1986 through "People Power," and Corazon Aquino, the widow of the assassinated political reformist Benigno ("Ninoy"), became president. Hopes for a new political era were short-lived; between 1987 and 1989, the Aquino government launched an all-out military purge of the NPA. Total war was declared against the countryside:

Following the collapse of the peace talk and ceasefire on February 1987, Madame Aquino "unsheathed the sword of war" and declared a "total war against insurgency at the grassroots level." ... "To our soldiers let me say: go out and fight. Fight with every assurance that I will stand by you through thick and thin, to share the blame, defend your actions, mourn your losses and enjoy with you the final victory that I am certain will be ours. You and I will see this through together."[12]

My region Bikol, the fourth-poorest region in the country and a hotbed of insurgency,[13] was militarized, including my grandmother's village. In 1991, when Bikol was still dealing with the tail-end of the war, I went to Australia to study for a doctorate, for which I wrote an epic poem about war.[14] In 1994 I began writing the short story "Fish-Hair Woman."[15] In 1997 I returned to my grandmother's village to hear the stories of the war first-hand and to grow the short story into a novel, which I could not finish and was rejected multiple times by Australian publishers in 2002 and later by American ones. I wondered: Is this writing not good enough? Or is this aesthetics so alien that it cannot find a home in the West? Or is my far country so far indeed that its story of violence and loss is unwelcome in the West, or if welcomed at all, only within the framework of an "other suffering"? It was not enough to ask questions. For this story to be heard in the public space, I would have to creatively strategize. So I offered what is most private: my own body. I would have to perform the story, and the weeping would have to become a singing: a militant dirge.

A dirge is a lament for the dead, an incantation of grief. But it is also a story for the living responding to war and terror – a dirge is militant. It restores breath, kickstarts the lungs, slaps ears into attention and (other?) sensibilities into empathy as it connects different notes (and different lives?) together at the moment of voice/song/story production. These parenthetical queries are "covert notes" that push the militancy to an uneasy ambition: to implicate the West in a mourning that is not only about the Philippines. For are we not all already implicated in a geopolitics that constantly inspires–produces terror? In this moment of emergency, can we keep responding with an indolence of the heart or with a terror of the other's terror that drives us to lock our borders and quarantine the nation? Yet continue to send troops, armaments, and foreign policies that fight a war in a far country?

Is it possible to respond with an alternative *creative-critical empathy*?

Empathy has been defined in philosophy, psychology, and neuroscience. Most definitions focus on the self's identification with another's emotion – without, it seems, much room for critical intellection. However, in "Ethics and Cognitive Science," Alvin Goldman proposes that empathy is "the ability to put oneself into the *mental shoes* of another person to understand her emotions and feelings."[16] Even better is Frans de Waal's definition: "The capacity to (a) be affected by and share the emotional state of another, (b) assess the reasons for the other's state, and (c) identify with the other, adopting his or her perspective."[17] Empathy develops from an emotional response to "a thinking through" about the other, thus facilitating identification. More specific to my topic is Kathleen Barry's *critical empathy,* which "engages our objective knowledge that questions, challenges, and sets right the distortion and disinformation that we receive through presidents and their generals with our subjective knowing that we receive from feeling, emotional awareness, and intelligence. Critical empathy, further, refuses selective empathy, that identification with the suffering of some, refusing to acknowledge it in others."[18] Critical empathy offers an alternative psychological space to terror. It is not afraid of emotion or critique; it is intellectually rigorous, challenging master narratives. I argue that this challenge needs to start at home: empathy must critique itself. But is critique enough? What is one to do after understanding that one's empathy is compromised?

Tell an alternative story that engenders a *creative-critical empathy,* one that constantly interrogates itself and its production to facilitate new modes of relating with suffering in storying loss and its remains. This strategy underpins my creative re-visions, which I interrogate in this chapter. How can this militant weeping–singing create a self-reflexive transnational empathy? Interrogation must begin at the grassroots: at the critical moment of emergence, of creative production. No, even earlier: at the moment of emergency. It must begin with the finding of remains. It must begin with the body.

But Whose Body? *Kapwa*

Dios mabalos, bako mi iyan –
Pero, kay-isay iyan –
Dae mi aram –
Siguro, hale sa kataid ming baryo –
Pero, bako rebelde iyan –
Ay, sadit-sadit, akion pa iyan!
Thank God, it's not ours –
But whose is it? –

We don't know –
Perhaps it's from the next village –
But it's too tiny, too young!

After I trawled a boy's body, which nobody claimed, the cracks began to show. Ay, so many bodies before him, for nearly a year. Nightly I felt the seams of my scalp, it hurt, and hurt even more after the boy. I kept seeing the small head thrown too far back, flopping behind him. Around his throat was a necklace of weeds and the fattest prawns.[19]

Pero kay isay iyan – but whose is it? The question is posed in my first-language Bikol,[20] then in English, and in a Philippine village, then in Australia. *Whose* is this found body? Such is the pivotal ethical question. On the one hand, we query the *ownership* of the remains of a war, the found bodies and stories, and rightly argue that the body can only be storied and mourned for by its kin, those of its race, gender, culture, and history – because otherwise the body could be co-opted into or could disappear in another's self-serving narrative. On the other hand, if we declare, "[The body is] not ours / We don't know," then we can push it away. It is not my story. It is not about me. So it is not grievable.[21]

So whose is the body?

I respond to this vexing ethical question with *kapwa*, an alternative belief that engenders an alternative empathy. *Kapwa* is a kinship principle from my first home.[22] Throughout this chapter, I raise key methodological questions about my creative process and respond with Philippine Indigenous beliefs to frame my arguments. As stated in the opening of this chapter, its theoretical framework is localized: this evokes *Pantayong Pananaw* ("From Us for Us"), "an indigenising imperative"[23] that directs a Filipino to approach Philippine studies through Filipino discourses, in the Pilipino language.[24] However, while this chapter and the creative works may be "From Us," they argue not only "For Us." In the spirit of alternative empathy and the Indigenous belief of *kapwa*, I include Australia, the West. I am a transnational wary of essentializing "a Filipino creative process" or of dismissing the other home of my imaginary. Moreover, it is only while interrogating my story-making now that I realize how these Indigenous beliefs have driven my creative production in Australia. Mine is an uneasy recognition engendering an ethically fraught return to Iraya, the wellspring. It seems the writer herself is a "found body" retrieved from the West by her grassroots memory, this hair that refuses to stop growing. Retrieved, interrogated, and critiqued, as much as the foreign story-makers (creative writers, journalists, scholars, policy makers) who "colonize" the story of a distant war to serve their own occupations: "have you studied the history of colonisation? Empires take land, water, air, bodies. In this devastating dispossession, just maybe, a people might survive. But when you take their story, their memory – this is the irrevocable devastation."[25]

Philippine professor Inez Carillo interrogates the intent of story-makers from the West. She excoriates an Australian ex-diplomat searching for the writer Tony McIntyre, who disappeared in the conflict: *You are interested solely in finding a white body, that writer who came to take our story ten years ago.* Her accusation extends to the expatriate writer:

> I don't like those who take because they can, because they don't have to answer for the taking, or for whatever they've taken. Because they're able to leave the source. The foreign writers who come to dirty their fingers for a while can go afterwards and publish to the world – but you know what, Mr Baker? The worst are our own expatriate writers, those migratory birds. First they abandon us to fly to a greener pasture, then return as vultures to feed on our despair. Then they take off again. Take, then take off. Just like that. A simple equation.[26]

The novel's transnational intent – the reading, production, and sustaining of remains (of bodies and their stories) between the Philippines and Australia – is itself critiqued in a self-reflexive text.

So who is the body?

My response is a deceptively simple equation: *Kapwa* = Self + Other = SelfOther.

Kapwa is a Pilipino word that is "widely used when addressing another with the intention of establishing a connection."[27] In the Western concept of *alterity*, Self and Other are separate entities (and words) that can interconnect; in *kapwa*, they are organically bound. Virgilio Enriquez, the Father of *Sikolohiyang Pilipino* (Filipino Psychology), defines *kapwa* as "shared identity":

> The *ako* (ego) and the *iba-sa-akin* (others) are one and the same in *kapwa* psychology: *Hindi ako iba sa aking kapwa* (I am no different from others). Once *ako* starts thinking of himself as separate from *kapwa*, the Filipino "self" gets to be individuated in the Western sense and, in effect, denies the status of *kapwa* to the other. By the same token, the status of *kapwa* is also denied to the self.[28]

Supporting this concept, Filipino Indigenization scholar Felipe de Leon writes that in Philippine culture, there is an

> underlying belief in the shared identity of human beings. Individual experience is only apparent and relative for we all exist within a cosmic matrix of being at the deepest center of which is a creative living principle of energic process. This implies a unity of creation – oneness of inner and outer reality, of noumena and phenomena – that is essentially an Asian concept yet distinctly Filipino in its recognition of the vital principle, especially in people.[29]

Distinctly Filipino but expansive, *kapwa* can cross transnational borders to include an Australian body and sensibility in the mourning of a Philippine war. This is a proposition in *Fish-Hair Woman*, which is conceived as "a shared mourning" through the shared production of remains, of stories. As metafiction, the novel tells a story while it interrogates the construction of story "written" by two main protagonist-storytellers: (1) the Filipina Stella Alvarado, whose family and village have been devastated by the Total War and who writes about it from her exile in America, and (2) the Australian Luke McIntyre, who goes to the Philippines to search for his disappeared father Tony and who eventually writes about this search. Like the mythical Fish-Hair Woman retrieving the dead, Stella and Luke attempt to retrieve their *own* lost bodies. But as they read, produce, and sustain these losses through writing, their texts grow from and into each other and become one story. This produced body of story becomes the body of *kapwa*. An organic transnational kinship is proposed.

As a kinship principle, *kapwa* is a priori to empathy. The empathic urge, which begins with the premise of separateness (self and other interconnecting), is spurred by the recognition of a prior shared identity in suffering. But how can the West recognize (and care for) *kapwa*? By implicating its body at the moment of emergency. In the militarized village of Iraya, Tony "suffers" the violence initially as a self-serving other. Stella, who becomes his lover, critiques his "literary caring" for the war: "how you loved us too for our stories so magical and terrible. As much as you loved our war."[30] Then he falls in love with people, with bodies, and his own body is violated and dumped in the river. He too is lost, a kin in suffering, and retrieved in a story running between the Philippines and Australia. Kinship is further creatively produced as Stella and Luke "co-write" this transnational story through the metafictive design of the novel. The social belief of *kapwa* is politicized and then aestheticized. Moreover, it can be ethically harnessed prior to mourning.

The ethics of *kapwa* entail more than kinship in suffering after a war. They also entail kinship in agency *before* a war. If the body of the self is one with the other's body, then each is inevitably hurt by the loss and anguish that the other experiences. Thus, each takes extreme care to keep the other safe. Other-preservation is self-preservation: kinship is inherently self-interested even prior to the violation. Thus, *kapwa* can be not only the ethical underpinning in mourning with others after a war, but also in stopping a war. The private (and local) urge can become a public (and global) cause.

But in the journey from private mourning to public story-making, whose bodies are negotiated, and how?

In 1997, during field research in my grandmother's village, to flesh out my own narrative, I took note of how bodies told their stories. In one instance, a woman recounted:[31] "*Tinorture su sakong tugang – pano ki cigarette burns su lawas – tapos binadil sa ngimot*" – my brother was tortured – the body was full of cigarette burns – then he was shot in the mouth." I felt deeply for her. Yet a day later, she became the writer's "found body" in my notebook: "face painfully thin, white hair, deep-set eyes with only three teeth, endless talker." Beside her was another woman with a kerchief that covered her mouth throughout the interview. Again I wrote: "Shutting out the smell of the dead or shutting up a scream." As I picked up the image of kerchief on mouth, I revised–transformed it into a literary detail (which I never used in the novel because of an ethical "niggle"). I instinctively fictionalized as I listened to the others' tragedy. In effect, I "took" the bodies of the women and the body they were mourning for.

T.S. Eliot, in "Preludes," evokes the writer moved by suffering:

> I am moved by fancies that are curled
> Around these images, and cling:
> The notion of some infinitely gentle
> Infinitely suffering thing.[32]

The creative products I conjure around real lives are the writer's "fancies," her "notion[s]" about suffering. Do they move me more than the story of torture? I wrote to a friend in Australia:

> Times like this, I feel like an intruder ... now that I'm consciously doing
> research ... everything could be material, even people's hearts! The more

I see of life here, the more I feel strange. I'm the alien appraising violence and grief from the outside. This is and is no longer my country ... I wonder whether the misting of eyes that remember the dead moves me as narrative detail or as a human twitch of my own heart.[33]

So Who's/Whose Weeping? *Paghaya*

I am flat footed
I am honestly splayed
No airs about my toes
My nails are rimmed with earth
Packed in for sixteen years
My nails are black and broken
Long dead before I died

[Tony] wept on my wet, salty hair that had wrapped the naked body of a female guerrilla. Perhaps barely sixteen and with hardly any face left, she could have been anyone's daughter. Dark blotches, the size of a fist, covered her pelvis and breasts that had lost their nipples.[34]

In "Song of the Feet," "I" is a dead girl. In life, she had been a farmer who turned guerrilla during the war after her land was stolen by the Spanish *mestizo* whose family had controlled most of the land in her village for centuries. She sings of her body inscribed with her sixteen-year history of working the land, and of the land's history of colonization. As Rebecca Mabanglo Mayor asserts: "the body remembers, the body of the earth, the body of the blood, the body of the genetics, the body of social thought and social structure, and so there is no erasure, no sure erasure, only the bending of perspective, the revision of history."[35]

The girl's weeping is a remembering of the layers of losses in her history. Remembering historical violence is an organic continuum from the past to the present, the private to the public space, the material to the conceptual. Thus, inevitably the weeping spills into the other's space. Witnessing the retrieval of the girl's mutilated body, Tony weeps. Mourning flows from the dead to the living, from the female to the male body, from a Filipino to an Australian. Because it takes forever to get to the last note, given the history of and continuing global wars.

So who's weeping? Multiple bodies. But who owns this or that particular lament? And if and when we map out these territories and find the definitive border between self and other, will we discover the demarcation line between tears? If we are to find an alternative empathy, interrogation must extend beyond the specificities of *who* and *whose*, which rightly so examine contexts of mourning. As with *kapwa* that offers latitude,[36] the open-endedness of *how* is as crucial. How to sustain this long weeping across bodies, landscapes, histories, cultures, languages?

> Mamay Dulce's face sags into a query forever unanswerable, as she drops to the floor, legs and arms pushing out, lips stretched into a grotesque wound. Where it comes from, Miguelito will never know. The breast or deeper down, from the little toe perhaps or the soles that catch the sing-song wail of the earth that might even wake the dead.[37]

This is *paghaya*, an infinite keening that is uncontained and thus sustained: "Where it comes from [and perhaps where it will end, we] will never know." With such latitude, it is unafraid to accommodate the other, or maybe it is afraid. *Paghaya* is often attributed to women. True, when we say that *"nagparahaya siya"* – *siya* has been weeping so much and so loudly – *siya* is a non-gendered pronoun. Even so, *paghaya* evokes this image: women wail, and tear at their hair, unlike men, who do not (must not) perform their grief. How terrifying it is to petrify in one's unwept weep.

During the twenty-year insurgency in Bikol and the eventual Total War that purged it, men and women were both combatants and victims. One such combatant was Nanette Vytiaco, whose body was found by her father:

> Hindi umiyak si Antonio Vytiaco, nang kalungin niya ang gutay-gutay na bangkay ng panganay niyang anak na si Nanette. Hindi siya umiyak, bagkus lihim niyang nausal na, "Sana'y lumaban si Nanette, totoo sana ang balitang siya'y lumaban bago napatay." At nang kalagin niya ito mula sa pagkakatali at pagkakabitin na parang baboy sa isang tulos ng kawayan, hindi pa rin siya umiyak, walang luhang pumatak.
>
> [Antonio Vytiaco *did not cry* when he cradled the mangled body of his eldest daughter Nanette. He *did not cry*, instead he silently said, "I hope Nanette fought, that the news that she fought before she was killed is true." And when he freed her from being bound and hung like a pig from a piece of bamboo, still he *did not cry*, no tear fell.][38]

In this account by journalist Ella Gajo Jamoralin, in contrast to *paghaya*, Antonio Vytiaco "did not cry." This containment of grief can be read as protest: I will not be broken, just as I hope my daughter's spirit was un-broken. But why the repetition of "did not cry"? Did this stoicism move Jamoralin ("the human twitch of her own heart"), or did she want to move the reader with these reiterations? This is creative empathy: her-self empathic, perhaps she styles her writing (as I do in the novel and the play, and even in this chapter) to inspire the same response in oth-ers. But is her style not her own containment of grief, her "bending of perspective" as the private mourning moves to the public space? In order to also evoke the cultural image of the heroic male who does not cry? But is this critique not my own "revision" of Jamoralin's story? And is it not that even in the father's initial "interpreting" of the body, perspective is already somehow "bent" and history revised? Realisti-cally we mourn according to what moves us and how we are moved. So perhaps we can only hope that the kinship continuum in "being moved" is balanced by a continuous and critical acknowledgment of where one's grief sits in this mourning:

> I lived with her stories for years before I began to write. I tuned in to her voice, hoping my own telling could be imbued by it. How I listened. Even so, I know I can never capture the currents of her river, her village, her history, and most especially not her grief. True, I have been undone by it, and in finishing this mesh of our lives, I'm simply making sense of that undoing. In my own grief. I am and will always be an outsider.[39]

Such is critical empathy: "I am your kin in mourning" in perpetual tension with "I am and will always be an outsider." Like Luke, I address my first home as other, an expatriate telling about its war. Covertly I ad-dress Australia, because this war and its mourning (that its public will read/not read) are outsiders. In the publishing industry, migrant litera-ture is not quite equal to the host nation's literature.[40] So I strategize, couching the novel as "the longest love letter in the world"[41] to the white man and Australia, to implicate them in desire, then in empathy. "The bridge in a love affair argues the case of the lover to the beloved, spans the river of desire,"[42] the Fish-Hair Woman observes. Love be-comes an aesthetic and political strategy. And some Australian readers have responded to this strategy and met these bodies and stories at the bridge in empathic recognition if not comprehension. But often the engagement by the Australian imaginary is a reality check each time: these "strange bodies and stories" are from a far country after all, still supplicants to the nation.

Paghaya is strange, it makes people feel strange. *Paghaya* is alien, so it is not a good weeping. A review in an Australian newspaper dismisses the novel as confusing. It sums up the book as an invitation "to recognise the love and suffering in her country's past."[43] True, literary taste is paramount in reviews, but reading the novel as only a suffering from a far country, despite half of it being about Australian lives, confirms how the West sometimes responds to a war over there. It is not about us, so it is not grievable. Does aesthetics get in the way of empathy? Is empathy, in fact, culturally entrenched and not as fluid as I have been arguing? Or is literary critique an excuse to withhold empathy, because "that war" is strange, confusing, messy like *paghaya*? Is the weeping style of the other so alien and unsettling that it stops the self's own tears in its tracks? Perhaps grief must be familiar and safe: quiet, tidy, civilized behind dark glasses, those signifiers of mourning that identify the bereaved. Even in mourning, let us demarcate between self and other. Or let us emulate the neat and artful grief of a book. *Paghaya* is uncouth, like having a choleric in public.

So keep your grief private? And keep your war as private as your grief?

No. I hold fast to the runny, messy (even unwelcome) continuum of *paghaya* to the public space, implicating the white man in this "weeping style" through the character of Luke. The son is my alternative to the father Tony, who came "all the way from the base of the earth to gather our grief into print, so he could purge his own."[44] This self-serving containment of grief is "purged" indeed, in Luke:

> The howling bounces around the trees used for coffins. It climbs to a mournful pitch, slopes down and tapers to a whimper. Then it starts again, the same distressing ascent and decline. Sometimes it simply keels over.[45]

As visceral and messy, Luke's howling resonates with *paghaya*. Characteristically fluid, *paghaya* spills into a white body. Just as fluid is the continuum of trauma between the Philippines and Australia: the dead are found in a river in Iraya, and Luke found his mother in the bathtub in Sydney:

> First attempt: razor, wrist. The cleaner found both of them just in time. She had passed out; he was catatonic. Sitting on his haunches and hands limp on the edge of the red bathtub. He was seven.[46]

Afterwards Luke howled in his childhood nightmares, which return when he reads Stella's story of the retrieval of the dead from a river lined with *dita* trees used for making coffins. Different traumas resonate with one another in *kapwa*, and mournings commingle in *paghaya*. The white man grieves for himself and for a far country. But can the far country grieve for the white man? Should I be asking this, if indeed alternative empathy is not selective? Some Filipinos are doubtful about the love story between Tony and a Filipina guerrilla and the fact that the disappeared white body is loved and missed, when many Filipino bodies have disappeared and are more deserving of attention. I myself query whether the love affair with Tony is colonial love. But is love only "From Us for Us?"

"Who shall miss the likes of us when we disappear? ... Will you also search for me?"[47] Asked by a Filipino soldier who committed atrocities, these questions could be raised by the white corpse. In response, the novel also "retrieves" their lives, which are humanized even as they are critiqued. So I enjoin the reader, in *kapwa* with the writer, to imagine with me and make room also for the unloved, the uncertain, the unknown:

> How much can the heart accommodate? Death and love, an enemy and a sweetheart, war and an impassioned serenade, and more. Only four chambers, but with infinite space like memory, where there is room even for those whom we do not love. Even sight is as expansive. So dear reader, when your eyes pass over these stories, consider your capacity to gather all of them, even the gaps in between, those that I dare not tell or do not know of yet or perhaps would never even imagine, but which might be utterly clear to you.[48]

In principle, *kapwa* and *paghaya* have infinite room. But in practice, which losses and remains are allowed in? Once inside, can different (and conflicting) bodies and stories continue to critically and creatively negotiate with one another? Or are they reconciled and reconstituted under a single ownership on publication?[49] Creative–critical empathy is not only about critically understanding one's context and vested interest in this or that mourning, or about creatively strategizing to inspire kinship among those whom we'd rather leave at the door. It is also about making room for differences and tensions that will never be reconciled by kinship.[50]

How to Make Room? *Nagtawo*

<table>
<tr><td>Here, here, my brow unkissed</td><td></td></tr>
<tr><td>*Angog ... hadoka*</td><td>(Brow ... kiss it</td></tr>
<tr><td>*Mata ... piyunga*</td><td>Eyes ... close them</td></tr>
<tr><td>Here, here, my eyes unclosing</td><td></td></tr>
<tr><td>Here, here, my cheeks too pale</td><td></td></tr>
<tr><td>Hear my lips bewail</td><td></td></tr>
<tr><td>*Pisngi ... kolora*</td><td>Cheeks...color them</td></tr>
<tr><td>*Ngabil ... kiputa*</td><td>Lips ... close them)</td></tr>
<tr><td>Ay, Iraya![51]</td><td></td></tr>
</table>

This is the "Song of the Face" of a corpse: lay my body by listening to my cry, by witnessing what I have suffered, and by loving my face into being. Then my eyes and lips can close, and my cheeks will be restored to life. The dead sings to the beloved, as I sing to the audience in my performances in the West: Let us be tender with the dead, even those that are not ours. This militant dirge unfolds in militant love: watchful, active, and urgent, love accommodates the strangers in the theatre and their own dead, as they view and hear the dead in a far country and in another tongue. All are "captured" in the weeping–singing that cannot be set aside like a book. Moreover, this publishing in space[52] cannot be reconstituted into a single ownership of bodies, because space and story keep extending and morphing. Different bodies (your and my remains) become stories that become ritual that becomes our different bodies breathing together in the theatre. Breaths collide–collaborate[53] in re-membering a face with a kiss, this negotiation in touch, in articulation. Bodies and languages touch: brow–*angog*, eyes–*mata*, cheeks–*pisngi*, lips–*ngabil*. In corporeal continuum from the private to the public space, bodies come into being. The dead come to life!

This development resonates with the uncanny phenomenon of *nagtawo*, meaning "became a person" or "became a body." In Bikol, we believe that the dead or the dying can translocate anywhere in order to appear to the beloved. The person comes into being corporeally to tell the story of one's passing. The body is in two places at once: in its place of death and in the presence of the loved one. *Nagtawo* crosses borders between the living and the dead, for love. And the beloved who sees the apparition may avert death if s/he cloaks the body in this moment of emergency in a gesture of salvation, also for love. It is not enough to witness; the spectator must touch, in fact embrace the apparition so that it can fully become a body, a person.

I now invoke a relevant point of view about love and Western theatre. In *Mourning Sex: Performing Public Memories*, Peggy Phelan meditates on Caravaggio's painting "The Incredulity of Saint Thomas," in which the doubting apostle Thomas puts his finger in the wound of the resurrected Christ. Phelan argues that "the question of love is the question of the painting":[54] "Do you love me?"[55]

> "Do you love me?" is a social question, a question of relation. It is fundamentally a question of perspective, of where one is in relation to the other ... a question that can come into being only if the other is cast as witness, an auditor, who will testify to the authenticity of the interrogation as pure form, as that which is forever the question. "Do you love me?" is an elaboration of the questions "Do you see me?" and "Do you hear me?" and these three questions constitute the trinity of Western theatre, a set of technologies designed to ask what it means to be, and to make, embodied form from that which is not Present.[56]

For me, encountering this quote from Phelan in relation to Caravaggio's painting is as uncanny as *nagtawo*. Phelan's arguments resonate with my own, and Thomas touching the wound of Christ (after he invites the apostle to "touch me") eerily evokes the "Song of the Face" of the corpse in *River, River*: touch my mutilated body to make it real with your own body. Phelan adds:

> Western theatre is itself predicated on the belief that there is an audience, an other willing to be cast in the role of auditor. The "act" at the heart of theater making is the leap of faith that someone (that ideal spectator some call "God") will indeed see, hear, and love those brave enough to admit that this is the movement that keeps us from our deaths (or at least from permanently dark houses).[57]

This recognition, "the loving" of one another, averts death: it is the principle of *nagtawo*. The bodies of war in the Philippines *nagtawo* (come into being, I hope) in all the far countries where I perform the play. Singing the song of the corpse's face in an Australian theatre, I too raise the question: Do you love me? Can you love me?

Me, your cultural other. Me, your "absolute other": the dead.[58]

In performance, the dead are translocated from my first home so that they can appear in my new home, Australia and the West. The dead are in two places at once, like my performing body weeping–singing in Bikol and in English, in a musical style that shuttles transnationally: between the chanting style of the *pasyon*, the Philippine tradition of chanting the "Passion of Christ" on Good Friday, and the music written by Australian composer Sarah de Jong.

The *pasyon* is inherently a transnational form: the Spanish colonial story of Christ Indigenized with Philippine chanting. Historian Reynaldo Ileto cites a "particular style called *tagulaylay* [a native dirge that] … hark[s] back to pre-Spanish modes of singing."[59] He argues that the *pasyon* was used by the masses to subvert Spanish colonialism; it has always been a militant dirge. So, as I sing *River, River*, I come into being in distant places, translocating between past and present militancy. I *nagtawo*: I become multiple, conflicting, and connecting bodies: the dead, the gravedigger, the village, the Fish-Hair Woman, the soldiers, the Australian. Shuttling between kinship and contestation across plural borders, the performing body keeps expanding space:

As it desires – "… my tapis wrap betrayed me, reweaving flowers into fishes, which grew as luminous as the moon on the river then swam to my breasts, biting behind the nipples."[60]

As it grieves – "I wanted to pull out every strand that heard my heart break."[61]

As it critiques – "… how dare you wrap it around that white body?"[62]

As it re-members – "And the river in my pelvis and his lemon grass fish swimming from the belly of a dead girl now growing her face and nipples back."[63]

As it accommodates – "We sing them all to sleep."[64]

But does one hour in the theatre inspire in the audience "a conversion to something close to love"[65] for the losses and remains of a far country? How successful is this aesthetic choice of putting one's own body on the line[66] to foster creative–critical empathy? *Nagtawo* is most effective if the seer of the dead and the dying acknowledges and cloaks the apparition in reciprocal kinship.

My creative relationship with the Australian Broadcasting Corporation (ABC), which produced *River, River* as a transnational radio play in 2005, has always been of reciprocal kinship. I have worked with ABC artists through six radio plays about war and conflict. Contributing their own aesthetics, they have brought to national radio the creative and political intent of these plays. Perhaps they hear acutely the weeping–singing from a far country, because their medium is sound: voice, breath, bodies. ABC Radio produced *River, River* with a cast of transnational voices: a family of chanters originally from Bikol, a Tongan-Australian opera singer, Australian and Filipino artists, and myself as performer. In 2008 this transnational collaboration was repeated: *River, River* was developed for the stage, with a community choir of Filipino Australian women and collaborating Australian artists.

But the arts centre where the play was to be performed wanted to revise it, because "it is not contemporary and cutting-edge" and the audience might perceive it as "simply folklore."[67] The Total War is folklore? The producers never engaged with the history and politics of the story. I grasped this when they wanted to Australianize the play and thus Australianize a Philippine war, its remains, its bodies – which, it seems, cannot be loved in their "original selves." Jane Ulman, who produced the ABC radio version, lamented: "It seems that the source of a culture is not as interesting or as legitimate as the Australianization of that culture."[68] So, empathy is only possible after creative colonization? But can we empathize if we refuse to cross over to the aesthetic other?

How to Cross? *Maki-agi tabi* – Please-May-We-Pass

> They will utter the usual greeting of a stranger to the homes of the seen and unseen. "Please, may we pass" [*Maki-agi tabi*]. We called this out not only to the homes of the living, but also to the haunts of the spirits: a mound of earth, a wooded spot, a river. Or a distant land?
>
> Please, dear reader, may we pass – let my memories pass through this page, through your eyes that have seen safer coffee groves.[69]

In Bikol, we are cautioned by the village elders: before you cross a river for the first time, you must respectfully call out "Maki-agi tabi" (Please may I pass). If you don't, you could hurt the unseen spirits and they could make you sick. In *Fish-Hair Woman*, Luke is told that his father Tony disappeared because he ventured into the river without calling out his respect. Meanwhile, in her manuscript about the war, Stella calls out to all her readers: "Please, let my stories pass." There must be reciprocal respect before reciprocal kinship in crossing the story border from whatever side: the ethics of *tabi* (please) must attend the aesthetic crossing, and the politics of the story must not be left on the other bank. This was my strategic response to the falling out with the arts centre. This was meant to drive the latest revision of *River, River*.

With no arts funding, I went solo with small performances of the play, translocating the Total War in Spain, USA, Australia, Canada, and Singapore and returning it to the Philippines. In this transnational continuum, I received generous empathic responses from audiences. Perhaps with individuals, kinship is easier; at the structural level, it seems harder to be kindred. In our creative development at the arts centre, individual artists achieved a crucial aspect of creative empathy: various aesthetics crossed towards one another and created a new, shared mode of storytelling. But the institution was perhaps snagged by the national imaginary – and thus could not cross to the other side?

So is "trans*nation*al empathy" inherently problematic? When national politics, aesthetics, and culture are deemed at stake, does the river become unnavigable? Was I not also holding fast to my own national imaginary as Filipino? Can we leave the nation behind in storying a war driven by national politics? Should we locate ourselves first in relation to the nation, to understand where we are, before we translocate to the other side? Can we de-structure, de-territorialize the nation, and render it fluid (trans-nation/nation-in-transit) to ease our navigation away from it? And finally, a niggling query: Can too much self-reflexivity "scare" empathy and snag a fluid crossing?

Please-may-we-pass: we call this out to the homes of the seen and unseen.

I hoped (and still do) to touch base with the yet unseen: the answers to the above questions. Thus, I planned to reinvent *River, River* as a local–global play in my new home, multicultural Wollongong in the Illawarra region. I invited storytellers from different cultures to revision the play with me on-site at a border: an ecologically compromised waterway where salt and fresh water meet. The individual storytellers were open to the project and enthusiastic about this meeting of plural cultures.

"Please-may-we-pass." Perhaps our respective stories and histories of losses and remains could pass through this water and its own history of mourning, and pass through our eyes in the spirit of witnessing.

"Please-may-we-pass." Perhaps in the continuum of *paghaya, kapwa,* and *nagtawo,* our different waters and stories of disappearance could flow with the disappeared flora and fauna of the local water.

In *Forgetting Aborigines*, Aaron Corn proposes:

The same-moiety meeting of fresh and salt waters at this site [*guana*] and the yellow foam [*djinkungun*] that they produce represent the fruitful interaction of two similar and equal socio-political entities that do not assimilate each other and produce something entirely new through their co-operation.[70]

This is a fitting metaphor for a new attempt at kinship: the focus is on *similarity* and *equality of entities* rather than on difference or on domination of the other. The hope is for a fluid and "fruitful interaction" of different waters, underpinned by the ethics of *tabi*, the ethics of please. Unfortunately, I could not get the necessary traction for this re-vision. It was deemed too ambitious by a local theatre company, which advised that I return to developing the one-woman play instead. But when I pitched the solo performance to them, again we were snagged by our differences in aesthetics. The verdict: they wanted to be moved because I was so moved in my storytelling, but they were not moved. After nearly twenty years of engaging in transnational dialogue between loss and its remains in order to develop alternative empathies, I am still doubting the efficacy of such a dialogue in Australia.

Please-may-we-pass. If these losses and remains are to gain passage, perhaps my aesthetics has to become like Australia's local water. Or I should work with this water and leave Iraya behind. Or I should follow "a hegemonizing course" for the water, where it is allowed to flow.

According to Eng and Kazanjian, loss can be counter-intuitive: it is "productive rather than pathological, abundant rather than lacking, social rather than solipsistic, militant rather than reactionary ... The politics and ethics of mourning lie in the interpretation of what remains – how remains are produced and animated, how they are read and sustained."[71] But the storyteller cannot control the politics and ethics of her mourning once it is out there, manifested as remains, because she is not the sole interpreter/reader of those remains. Moreover, sustaining remains must be a social act: it must be a co-production, a co-animation with her audience that may or may not wish to listen. I am now pursuing this social act, but with a new water project: "Re-thinking River Responses: What Is Lost/What Is Found."[72] This practice-led research is currently investigating creative-critical empathy as a methodology in narrating and rethinking loss around rivers in terms of ecology, culture, and social interaction. Community participants with diverse histories are collaboratively storying loss in relation to their respective rivers and memories of waters. Remembering loss is a form of mourning; rethinking loss as a community methodology to animate remains *towards something newly found* moves on from mourning: perhaps towards an alternative empathy?

I wish to preserve faith, like the old gravedigger in the novel enjoining us to accommodate all bodies in the pool of grief – while recognizing the human tendency to delineate, to own and disown:

> *Magdara ki balde sa danaw nin sakit*
> *Siguraduhang ruluho ini*
> *Magdara ki balde sa hararumon na danaw*
> *Iwalat mo duman ini*
> Take a pail to the pool of grief
> Make sure it has holes
> Take a pail to the deepest pool
> And leave it there

> This is the wake of the world: each of us standing around a pool that we have collected for centuries. We are looking in with our little pails. We try to fathom the depth of the pool until our eyes are sore. We try to find only what is ours. We wring our hands. Ay, how to go home with only my own undiluted pail of grief? To wash my rice with or my babies, to drink? But the water is my dead kin, an enemy, a beloved, a stranger, a friend, someone who loved me or broke my heart. How to tell them apart? How to cleave water from water?[73]

This little parable rekindles hope: our wish to contain mourning is futile. The hegemonic pail has holes. And we cannot cleave water from water.

NOTES

1 Bobis, *Fish-Hair Woman*, 137–8.
2 Bobis, *River, River*, 2009. Performed but unpublished, so pagination indefinite. Citations are mostly songs adapted from the novel. Singing style harmonizes Bikol and English languages. Video of play's creative development available at http://www.merlindabobis.com.au/dramatic.htm.

3 See Bobis's essay "Confounding Light: Subversion and Transnational Sympathy," which discusses "grassroots theorising" (now reworded as "grassroots storytelling-theorising"): "In the literary academy, there is an established hierarchy of knowledge and knowledge production: scholarship at the top feeding on the next in line, published literature that, in turn, feeds on the lived life and its local storytelling. All these levels of knowledge production are about story-making, yet the story product that is privileged as 'knowledge' is theory that is several times removed from the original premise of the argument: the body doing or being done to; the body living-telling its story. So is it possible to re-orient the hierarchy of the academy? Can it recognise the currency of grassroots theorising as an equal and potent player in knowledge production? This is a theorising grounded in the immediate and lived experience. You hear it in the 'philosophising' about local and world events at the corner store, in the political debate at the barbershop, or in the storytelling about a wedding or a war in the kitchen." Merlinda Bobis, "Confounding Light," 153–4.

4 In *The Politics of Storytelling*, Michael Jackson critiques epistemology, asserting that it is "inevitably reductive" and "seeks to convert subjects of experience into objects of knowledge," when, in fact, "the empirical reality of human life" is constituted by "the phenomenal interplay ... between the confusion and flux of immediate experience on the one hand, and finite forms and fixed ideas on the other." Jackson, *The Politics of Storytelling*, 125.

5 Also in "Confounding Light," Bobis argues that postcolonial epistemology "sometimes prescribes that in their story-making, colonised peoples *must decolonise* in a fashion aligned with globally established postcolonial scholarship" and that "postcolonial epistemology can also turn paradoxically neo-colonial. Thus, it needs to be decolonised by relocating its attention from the globalised theoretical discourse of the academy to the particular lived experience and its own storytelling. This local storytelling is an embodied 'grassroots theorising,'" 145, 147.

6 See Bobis for Peng Cheah's discussion on Walter Mignolo's *decoloniality*, which he explains thus: "It involves generalizing the experiences of decolonization and anticolonial struggles in Asia, Africa, and Latin America as well as the experiences of the *damnés*, the wretched of the earth, into a new epistemic frame. The project of decoloniality therefore involves a double gesture: first, the re-embodiment and relocation of thought in order to unmask the limited situation of modern knowledges and their link to coloniality, and second, an other-thinking that calls for plurality and intercultural dialogue." In Bobis, "Confounding Light," 149.

7 Eng and Kazanjian, *Loss*, Preface.

8 Eng and Kazanjian, *Loss*, 1.

9 Walter Benjamin writes: "To historians who wish to relive an era, Fustel de Coulanges recommends that they blot out everything they know about the later course of history. There is no better way of characterizing the method with which historical materialism has broken. That method is a process of empathy whose origin is the indolence of the heart, *acedia*, which despairs of grasping and holding the genuine historical image as it flares up briefly. Among Medieval theologians, it was regarded as the root cause of sadness … The nature of this sadness stands out more clearly if one asks with whom the adherents of historicism actually empathize. The answer is inevitable: with the victor." In Eng and Kazanjian, *Loss*, 1.

10 Bobis discusses Philippine history in relation to the narrative of war in her essay, '"Storying."

11 Jones, *Red Revolution*, 5–6.

12 Craige and de Guzman, *Counterinsurgency War*, 40.

13 Paz Verdades M. Santos writes that poverty has made Bikol "one of the most fertile grounds for Communist insurgency since the 1960s." Santos, "Center of Gravity," 43.

14 This epic poem (in English and Pilipino) about war was published as *Cantata of the Warrior Woman / Kantada ng Babaing Mandirigma Daragang Magayon*, 1993, 1997, and 1998 (in Bobis's poetry collection, *Summer Was a Fast Train without Terminals*, 67–200). Bobis performed the epic as a one-woman play in Australia, the Philippines, France, and China between 1992 and 2006.

15 "Fish-Hair Woman," published in Bobis's short story collection *White Turtle*, 10–23.

16 Goldman, "Ethics and Cognitive Science"; italics mine.

17 De Waal, *The Age of Empathy*.

18 Barry, *Unmaking War Remaking Men*, 191.

19 "Child Chant" and text about child's body, in *River, River*.

20 Bikol/Bicol, the language of the Bikol region, has multiple variants across different provinces. *River, River* uses the variant from Albay.

21 Judith Butler problematizes grievability: "Some lives are grievable and others are not; the differential allocation of grievability that decides what kind of subject is and must be grieved, and which kind of subject must not, operates to produce and maintain certain exclusionary conceptions of who is normatively human: what counts as a liveable life and a grievable death?" Butler, *Precarious Life*, xi–xv.

22 See the extensive discussion of *kapwa* in "Confounding Light" in relation to "transnational sympathy," which in this essay is reframed as "transnational creative-critical empathy."

23 Ramon Guillermo examines *Pantayong Pananaw*, March 2003. See also Salazar, *Pantayong Pananaw*, 1997.

24 Pilipino: The Philippines' national language in a country with over a hundred languages.

25 Bobis, *Fish-Hair Woman*, 228.

26 Bobis, *Fish-Hair Woman*, 226.

27 De Guia, "An Ancient Reed," 90.

28 Enriquez, "*Kapwa*," 43.

29 De Leon, quoted in Strobel, *Filipinos*, 34.

30 Bobis, *Fish-Hair Woman*, 203.

31 The account of this interview is discussed in Bobis's *A Novel-in-Waiting*, 14–15.

32 Eliot, *Selected Poems*, 24.

33 Bobis's correspondence, November 1997.

34 "Song of the Feet" and text, *River, River*.

35 Rebecca Mabanglo-Mayor on Filipina comfort women, quoted in Strobel, *Filipinos*, 8. The entire essay is available at Mabanglo-Mayor's blog, http://wordbinder.blogspot.com/2007/07/eros-as-living-in-body.html.

36 Bobis attributes latitude to the transnational imaginary that is "a liminal space of agency which can serve a decolonising function as it facilitates the creative collision-collaboration of diverse cultural identities – and consequently the infinite imagining of cultural products and culture itself." In Bobis and Herrero, "Sensing and Sensibility," 231.

37 Bobis, *Fish-Hair Woman*, 90.

38 Jamoralin, "Bayani ng Kababaihang Bikolnon," 121; my translation and italics.

39 Bobis, *Fish-Hair Woman*, 302.

40 Literary gatekeeping by the host nation is discussed in Bobis's "The Asian Conspiracy": "Getting into the literary gate is its own story of migration. When we migrate the body, we migrate its voice, its stories, its particular style of story-making. So this 'Australianisation', this process of legitimation of the story or the story-maker, is like stamping our immigration papers at the gate? And we get through – if we 'sound Australian'?" (3).

41 Half of the novel is Stella's manuscript about the Total War and her family. This "longest love letter in the world" is addressed obviously to Tony, and covertly to Australia, Philippines, and the novel's readers.

42 Bobis, *Fish-Hair Woman*, 139.

43 Dempsey, "Review."

44 Bobis, *Fish-Hair Woman*, 6.

45 Bobis, *Fish-Hair Woman*, 1.

46 Bobis, *Fish-Hair Woman*, 127.

47 Bobis, *Fish-Hair Woman*, 231.

48 Bobis, *Fish-Hair Woman*, 142.

49 *Fish-Hair Woman*'s ending raises the issue of reconstituting ownership of story on publication.

50 See the discussion on the tension between differentiation and collectivization/reconciliation, and storying as "a return to the water," in Bobis, "Passion to Pasyon."

51 "Song of the Face," in *River, River*.

52 See Bobis, "Border Lover," 2003.

53 Bobis, "Border Lover," 118: "Between the body and the word, between different cultures, languages, or diverse art forms, there is a problematic borderline. When these unlike elements come together, some kind of 'collision-collaboration' happens. Imagine two cars colliding. After the collision, the eye perceives the point of impact as an obvious gap, a fault-line, a negative space. But from my experience, I have found that this space between the two colliding elements actually emerges as a third element: hybrid, ambivalent, constantly interrogating itself."

54 Phelan, *Mourning Sex*, 30–1.

55 Phelan references Irigaray: "Luce Irigaray, our great interpreter of surfaces and cavities, has suggested that 'The typical sentence produced by a woman is: "Do you love me?"' (Irigiray, "An Ethics," 134). Such a question must go beyond the surface: it must be a question forever welling up within one's own body, and a question infinitely more difficult for the subject to recognize within the body of the other." Phelan, *Mourning Sex*, 31.

56 Phelan, *Mourning Sex*, 30–1.

57 Phelan, *Mourning Sex*, 30–1.

58 Zygmunt Bauman writes: "Death is the absolute *other* of being, an *unimaginable* other, hovering beyond the reach of communication; whenever being speaks of that other, it finds itself speaking, through a negative metaphor, of itself … Death is not like other 'others' – those others which the ego is free to fill with meaning, and in the course of this meaning-bestowing act to constitute and to subordinate." Bauman, "Mortality," 2.

59 Ileto, *Pasyon and Revolution*, 16.

60 Bobis, *River, River*, excerpts adapted from *Fish-Hair Woman* with revisions for performance.

61 Bobis, *River, River*.

62 Bobis, *River, River*.

63 Bobis, *River, River*.

64 Bobis, *River, River*.

65 Bobis, *Fish-Hair Woman*, 4.

66 Putting one's body on the line is discussed in Bobis, "The Asian Conspiracy."

67 Bobis, "The Asian Conspiracy." See also Bobis, "Passion to *Pasyon*."

68 Bobis, "The Asian Conspiracy." See also Bobis, "Passion to *Pasyon*."

69 Bobis, *Fish-Hair Woman*, 56.

70 Aaron Corn in Healy, *Forgetting Aborigines*, 202.

71 Eng and Kazanjian, *Loss*, x.

72 This water project was originally conceptualized as a river project on loss and empathy, with the story of *River, River* in conversation with the stories of specific water sites and communities in three countries: Philippines (Naga and Lupi rivers: Bikol), Canada (Fraser River: Vancouver), Australia (Allens Creek: Illawarra). But given the difficult hurdles in negotiation, the writer-performer decided to exclude the Australian process. The Canada and Philippine processes are currently in progress.

73 Bobis, *Fish-Hair Woman*, 276.

14 Gone but Not Forgotten: Memorial Murals, Vigils, and the Politics of Popular Commemoration in Jamaica

HONOR FORD-SMITH

Kingston, Jamaica, 8 June 2012

I am at a sunset Vigil for Kavorn Shew, dead at 25 from a police bullet. Neighbours and family say police murdered Shew in his bed. His brother says he heard the police planning how they would report on their mission after they killed Kavorn.

It is sunset when the crowd makes its way slowly up the main road and turns off into the Mountain View neighbourhood. Youth, community members, representatives of activist organizations and even some members of the business community are all walking together – wearing white shirts as a gesture of solidarity and mourning. The crowd stretches across several slopes winding its way through the dusk in silence. Then it comes to a halt outside Kavorn's home. Candles are burning in the darkness as singing erupts and folks sway to popular spirituals like "Satan gimme pass."

Kavorn Shew was active in several youth organizations including the police youth club. He had played a role in the peace movement in Mountain View, where the murder rate was lowered significantly between 2007 and 2012. He was active in anti-violence organizing throughout the city and had been accepted to join the police force. Youth all across Kingston knew and respected him.

In their own defense the police regurgitated the hollow but familiar script that nearly every Jamaican knows by heart: Police on patrol entered a community and encountered men acting suspiciously. Gunmen opened fire on them. The police were forced to return fire resulting in persons losing their lives.

Immediately after the shooting, community members demonstrated. They held a meeting with the police demanding accountability and planned a march. When Jamaicans for Justice, a human rights organization fighting police executions like this, condemned the killing, expressed solidarity with

Figure 14.1. Vigil in protest of the murder of Kavorn Shew at Mountain View, Kingston, 2012 (photo courtesy of Jamaicans for Justice)

Kavorn's family and linked them with families of other victims of police shootings, the police claimed the march was a demonstration that could not take place without the required permit.

All day the event has been on again, off again. At 6 PM, we gather outside the police station anyway and begin to walk in single file along the sidewalk of the main road. The vigil cannot be stopped as long as it does not obstruct traffic. It is seen as a religious act that draws on wake traditions in which community members keep watch, pray and sing over the body of the departed. Such acts are outside the domain of the state. For a couple of hours the candles flicker in the wind as voices ring out. A preacher offers words of comfort and appeal for calm. For a few moments it seems that we are strong in numbers and will not give in to the power of violence.

It is commonplace to see, hear, and read about Jamaican violence and to encounter spectacular images of the "criminal Jamaican" in the mainstream media and popular culture around the world. But acts of mourning such as the vigil described above demonstrate that far from being pathologically and inherently violent, Jamaicans actively resist violence in ways that are rarely reported. Acts of public memorialization have proliferated in Jamaica, where one consequence of the geopolitics of neoliberalism has been a dramatic rise in violent deaths since the late 1990s. Caught between extrajudicial killings by the state on the one hand and militarized strongmen on the other, community members attempt to reclaim the dignity of their dead in acts of memorialization that protest the unbearable human pain and environmental costs of violence.

Moving away from arguments that moralize, pathologize, and culturalize the roots of violence in racialized working-class communities, I argue that popular commemorative acts are haunted by interlocking local and global tensions that produce both state violence and violence that is simplistically labelled "criminal." I analyse two examples of popular working-class commemorations – vigils and street murals – mapping the ways these responses dramatize the hopes, desires, and survival strategies of local residents at the same time as they are haunted by invisible geopolitical presences. The proliferating memorials make vivid the many messy layers of violence that Jamaicans must negotiate and the violent losses on which the installation of the neoliberal order depends. More than this, they also dramatize how human subjects, caught in the web of hierarchical power relations, struggle to resist terror and elude death in the everyday. Grasping the meanings embedded in mourning practices can, I propose, complicate how we think of violence and criminality and nudge us towards reimagining transnational cultural and political possibility in the contemporary geopolitical moment.

I begin by discussing what attending to commemorative performance in the current context might help us understand. Then, showing how performances invoke older spiritual traditions of memorialization forged in transnational formations of racialized citizenship, I propose that taken together these performances reveal ambivalence about the effectiveness of challenging state violence in purely secular ways. Turning to the popular commemorative murals that appear on the walls of every neighbourhood in working-class Kingston (in spite of the police, who smother them with their signature blue paint), I show how these extend the work of mourning into the built environment, resurrecting heroes of Cold War struggles, "outlaws" who operate trafficking networks locally and in the north, and unwilling victims of violence. The faces and bodies on the walls complicate easy narratives of Jamaican criminality by dramatizing the other side of that story – the thwarted humanity of those who have been criminalized, the deep desire for respectability and recognition, and the grief that materializes on walls and even cars to publicly transform the fragmented cityscape into a mosaic of mourning. Conversely, community members interpret these murals in conflicting ways that reveal painful disillusionment with formal politics and the state. These murals show how violence generates "useful" and respectable occupations in the legal, penal, and security systems and encourages a constant search for and cleansing of the enemy within while exploiting the caring labour of women. The last section of this chapter connects the work of commemoration to the broader geopolitical imperial agenda and draws out some of the ways in which the issues raised by memorialization might contribute to discussions about alternatives beyond the liberal focus on individual rights and freedoms.

Memory, the Body, and Neoliberal Violence

Diana Taylor has famously argued that "performances function as vital acts of transfer transmitting social knowledge, memory and a sense of identity through reiterated, or what Richard Schechner has called 'twice behaved' behavior."[1] The implications of her argument are that if we want to understand how biopolitics circulate over time and across space and how this informs effective resistance, we need to explore precisely those areas that dominant knowledge-producing practices have excluded. Studying performance is important, Taylor argues, because embodied performances offer insights different from what the archive offers. Social meanings given to embodied repertoires are historically specific in terms of their enactment and their viewing and reception. They are also affective, enabling us to care – a word Connerton tells us originally meant "to mourn." So through the act of mourning, caring can be linked to remembering.[2]

Mourning is also a way to care because it *re-members* the dead, that is, it invokes the spirit, experiences, and wisdom of the person who has passed, as many Caribbean religious traditions assert. It is a way of mobilizing and sharing stories that incite acts of humour and love that re-create collective bonds. Mourning practices everywhere attempt to account for loss in productive ways. All societies do this, for in all societies death gives meaning to life and is the source of rebirth. Memorialization is the place out of which we re-create the meanings and relationships that are being threatened by death. The elegiac impulse is perhaps the original site of creativity in religion and art. But in societies like Jamaica where genocide, uprooting and forced transportation, racial slavery, and indentureship structured social formation, mourning practices and orality were sites where knowledge that was suppressed and excluded from the formal colonial archives broke through both sonically and visually to elaborate community-making memory.

Embodied practices in *nine nights* (wakes) in particular became sites for enacting and performing repertoires of memory because they allowed for a remembering of past community in affective ways. Kinesthetic commemoration of the ancestral past in Kumina, Pukkumina, and all the other African Caribbean religions enabled the reproduction of memory while bringing about ruptures with the enduring colonial narratives. These ruptures were not always discrete or pure. They overlapped with dominant forms of power because they borrowed and restructured repertoires of signs from European, Taino, and Asian cultures with predominant West African cultures. Nettleford describes the significance of Jamaican dead yard dances such as Kumina, Pukkumina, and Revival Zion, arguing that the dance that was performed in popular spiritual practices acted as a site of cultural maronage for resistance to colonization.[3] In kinetic acts of transfer, the dance stored embodied knowledge and performed difference. These acts of living memory produced social spaces in which opposition to the dominant order could be tested.

Paul Connerton discusses the birth of histories from the spirit of mourning in the late twentieth century and argues that the memorialization of horrific forms of social and political violence was imagined as a virtue and that forgetting was seen as a failure.[4] At highly publicized memorialization commissions, victims and perpetrators told stories of their experiences in dramatic revelations. At a time when emancipatory narratives were being discredited, this unleashed a culture of trauma and regret and the collective past became imagined as a repository for unfulfilled claims and subjugated identities. Challenging the notion that remembrance is necessarily positive, he proposes that memorialization can be a mode of state legitimization and is not necessarily an opportunity to repair injustice. Acts of memory can, he suggests, be reframed as ways of forgetting, and forgetting can be an important requirement for constituting new identities. While the conceptual workings of power always mediate specific scenarios of rememberance, Connerton suggests that new forms of historical narrative are generated when conventional forms of mourning are not adequate to express the "sheer accumulation of pain entailed in the process of historical transformation and enlightenment."[5] He later adds: "It is a distinctive feature of such historical catastrophes and traumas that they precipitate cultural bereavement for which mourning customs are often difficult to find or invent, or which are widely felt to be scarcely adequate to the immensity of the bereavement, and where the emotional responses of the bereaved lack the formalised channels which might, to some extent, ritualise and contain those responses of loss and grief."[6]

Connerton does not theorize commemoration in relation to the violence that neoliberalism has unleashed against materially impoverished racialized populations around the world. In the case of Jamaica, new forms of popular memorialization such as vigils and street murals may have emerged as responses to the high body count, injury, and disability that affect impoverished urban communities. The links to neoliberalism are obvious. The retreat and reorganization of the bankrupt state as a result of structural adjustment and free trade has been well documented.[7] After forty years of debt servicing combined with lingering colonial legacies, Cold War conflicts, political clientelism, corruption, widespread unemployment, and state bankruptcy, urban spaces have fragmented into fortified neighbourhoods.[8] Some scholars refer to these as garrison communities because they are protected by groups of armed men. These groups, which formed after independence in support of political parties and then mobilized in opposition to socialism, were supported by some elites. Later, capitalizing on informal economies, they became linked to trafficking and violence. Leaders of the most powerful of these groups, often referred to as "Dons," control significant resources and space and dispense favours to their communities in return for loyalty, protection, and support.

Jamaica's high murder rate is generally assumed to be linked to high levels of crime. That rate has fluctuated between 58 and 64 per 100,000 (in a population of 2.5 million) since 2005 in spite of increased policing, surveillance, and investment in violence prevention programs by NGOs and bilateral agencies. The problem with these figures is that they are themselves forgetful. That is, they "forget" those murders that are a result of state violence, and they do not explain that most of the violence occurs in urban spaces where impoverished black people live. Nor do the statistics include those who are executed extrajudicially or wounded and disabled by police. For example, in 2012 between January and March, the police killed fifty-six people, yet at the end of 2012 they reported a *reduced* murder rate of 1,087, a figure that excluded the numbers they themselves had murdered.

"In time the slave surrendered to amnesia. That amnesia is the true history of the new world. It is our true inheritance." Walcott wrote this in his much-cited essay "The Muse of History" in the 1970s.[9] But perhaps Walcott was wrong. Is it possible to obliterate memory of violent acts like the Middle Passage or the destruction of iconographies of memory? Do memories of violence vanish? Do they form an invisible ecology in the same way that the eating of air by plants results in a release of carbon monoxide into the air at the end of a day of making oxygen for us to breathe?

I propose that in moments of incalculable social violence, the pain of loss re-emerges in new forms of commemoration that are haunted by traces of older struggles. Avery Gordon describes haunting not as an example of the occult but as a social phenomenon that performs "an animated state in which a repressed or unresolved social violence is making itself known sometimes very directly, sometimes more obliquely."[10] She proposes that the term haunting refers to moments in which something suddenly reminds us that the trouble we thought had been resolved is clearly still around. Haunting is a term that "describes those singular, yet repetitive instances when home becomes unfamiliar, when you lose your bearing on the world, lose direction, when what's over and done with comes alive and what's been in your blind spot comes into view."[11] Artefacts such as memorial T-shirts, posters, colourful funeral programs, elaborately decorated coffins, buttons, long obituaries, dance hall funerals, new modes of funeral dress, and memorial concerts are responses to the rise in the deaths, but they are also more than this. As the examples discussed below show, they haunt us with the unresolved social contradictions that produced the epidemic of death in the first place. They remind us covertly and overtly of the shadowy genealogies of violent death in Jamaican society. They spring up where the high body count contradicts the stories that justify it and bring into view the sides of the story that dominant narratives cannot represent – the desires and longings of the communities that bear the brunt of the legacies of violence. They transform urban spaces into living deathscapes and confront us with the ways these acts of commemoration implicate us.

Vigils: Secular Politics and the Sacred

Vigils like Kavorn Shew's mobilize sacred languages and rituals that bypass the state, which is largely secular in character. The state routinely engages in rituals of violence against those constructed as threatening – the proverbial enemy within. In their own commemorative rituals, communities turn the state's definition of itself as secular and reasonable on its head, appealing instead to transcendent or divine forms of justice that might protect them from state violence.

One example of a long-standing commemorative performance that appeals to divine justice and that protests state violence is the Rastafarian "Bad Friday" commemoration of the Coral Gardens Massacre, which took place on Good Friday in 1963. This recalls one of the landmark acts of the newly independent Jamaican state against its citizens. In 1963, less than a year after the British flag was lowered, the state, headed by Alexander Bustamante, let loose on the Rastafari community of Coral Gardens in northwestern Jamaica in retaliation for the actions of five people involved in a land dispute. More than 150 people were arrested, tortured, and jailed, and an unknown number of Rastafari were killed. At the annual vigil, elders testify and there is drumming and poetry. In 2007, on the anniversary of the abolition of the trade in African bodies, the community used these performed memories to call on the state to formally apologize and offer reparations to the families scarred by the event. The Coral Gardens commemorations keep alive the memory of colonial and state repression and the story of the event. The community's claims have become better known as a result of the performance of counter-memories of the violent acts of the post-independence state.

In her discussion of this vigil and of violence in Jamaica, Deborah A. Thomas writes that the claims for reparations mobilized in Coral Gardens remind us that citizenship is not a static notion; rather, it is something that has developed over time in relation to transnational processes of violent racialization.[12] Contemporary state violence has to be seen as part of a project of class formation that implicates the local state and the geopolitical circuits to which it is connected. The counter-narratives enacted at vigils enable participants to envision alternative narratives of justice and belonging that bypass this problematic formation and to claim cultural authority over their history. They also enable communities to draw on this authority in negotiations with a government eager to incorporate all such narratives into "brand Jamaica" for consumption in the global market.[13]

Performances like the vigil for Kavorn Shew mount claims to forms of citizenship forged within transnational processes while also appealing to divine justice. They covertly demand accountability, and to that end, they overtly depend on popular Christian frameworks such as singing, candle-lit processions, dance, sermonizing, and prayer. In so doing they are haunted by the ghost of the struggle for emancipation during which Christianity became a vehicle for opposition to slavery. By invoking this reference, vigils like the one held for Shew appeal to the state; they also avoid being shut down by the state since they appear to transcend its domain. Without the cover afforded by religion and the support of the entire community, secular acts might be seen as a challenge to the state and be shut down or lead to recriminations.

One story dramatizes this clearly. Jason Smith was shot and killed by police in the market near his house. He was fifteen years old. Some time after, his mother Monica Williams commissioned two memorial murals in his memory by a local artist. A third portrait adorned the bonnet of her car and travelled with her all around the city. At the bottom of the murals were the words "Police Brutality."

Meanwhile, Monica pursued her quest for justice in the courts, eventually winning a civil suit against the police. She spoke out against police violence and declared her son's innocence in the media, at public discussions, and at vigils. She discussed her case in a film about police violence made for the website of Jamaicans for Justice, a local human rights organization. Every year she applied to the police for permission to hold a secular memorial vigil for her son. This included a march to the place near the market where he was shot followed by a meal with all who attended, a viewing of the video of his funeral, and music. Sometimes the police refused permission for the participants to march to the market.

In May 2012, police shot another family member five times in the back right outside the family compound. Terrified, Monica painted out the words "police brutality" on the murals. But the family and sympathizers continued to protest his death, denouncing police violence in a small demonstration outside the police station. Immediately after this, police painted out the memorial murals covering the wall of the compound in their signature colour, blue. Jason's face disappeared from the walls of his mother's compound. Monica's family has reported

Figure 14.2. Memorial for Jason Smith by Vermon Grant, Spanish Town, Jamaica, 2009 (author's photo)

repeated intimidation by police and soldiers, who arrive at their compound heavily armed at unpredictable times and occupy their yard for no stated reason. I witnessed one such incident in 2012. Monica became afraid to speak out. Demoralized, she wanted to leave the country. Human rights organizations have denounced this intimidation and vigilantly support the family, but those groups lack the resources to constantly physically protect them or any other family, so the threat of murder and the atmosphere of police impunity act as effective silencers.

The blue patch on the compound wall that has covered Jason's portrait is haunted by this terror. The ghost of his image can be seen

Figure 14.3. The wall outside the family compound after police painted out the mural by Vermon Grant in memory of Jason Williams. The square of blue paint corresponds to Figure 14.2 (author's photo)

through the police paint, bringing into view lingering questions about the relationship between contemporary state violence and its origins in a transnational world structured by colonial legacies. Vigils animate his memory and extend his presence from the wall to the street, but at the same time, the obliteration of his image demonstrates that protests framed entirely in terms of individual human rights and legal redress may lack impact. Unlike the demand for reparations mounted by the Coral Garden community, the court case that Monica Williams brought against the police was an individual legal challenge made by a singular subject that depended on the authority of the secular state. The court challenges made by women who have lost their children to police bullets address extrajudicial killings as violations of individual rights and freedoms; if their challenges succeed, they are compensated with money. Mounting a legal challenge, however, takes considerable courage; some, like Monica Williams, find that courage with the support of civil organizations. But it has to be said that this strategy does not address the ways in which state violence affects marginalized urban communities as a whole. Nor does it address the fact that violence has been normalized as an ordinary part of social relations. Nor does it address the desires and aspirations of those who have had to learn to live with death. For all of this, we have to turn to the popular street murals.

Desire and Masculine Respectability in Kingston's Popular Memorial Murals

Commemorative murals, much like vigils, reframe stories of violence from the perspective of family and friends and appeal to both the sacred and the secular to mobilize affect. These are not the only street murals one finds in Kingston, but they were probably the predominant kind up until 2012. Since 2010, the police have been actively suppressing the murals in a number of communities, claiming that they are illegal and that they glamorize criminality. As new memorialization practices, the murals reframe media representations of criminal Jamaicans and challenge the state's marking of some citizens' bodies as disposable. Commemorative murals map violence onto the built environment of the city, thereby extending the presence of loss into the everyday world of passers-by. They assert that all those who have been killed deserve respect, not because of who they were or what they did, but "because you remember how valuable life is," as the Jamaican poet Mbala put it. "It is part of a process of remembering that we the living, we have value as well. Our lives mean something."[14]

The layered historical contempt with which inner-city residents are regarded by the state and the middle class was vividly demonstrated during the Tivoli uprising of 2010. At that time, the army and police shelled and shot their way into a barricaded residential community with little thought to the deaths, destruction, trauma, and disability that would result. Ostensibly, their goal was to capture and extradite a powerful community "don" who was wanted by the Americans on charges of trafficking and murder. The army assault and occupation did not result in his capture. An American surveillance plane, a Lockheed P-3 Orion, was flying above Kingston on 24 May 2010, the date of the army assault, and the tape shot from the plane was released as a result of pressure

Figure 14.4. Memorial for fallen members of the Rich and Famous, by Anthony Brown, Hannah Town, 2009 (author's photo)

from a *New Yorker* journalist. According to him, the tape in its present form raises more questions than it answers.[15] In an eerie echo of the drone attacks in Pakistan, there is evidence that those who were killed in Kingston were not armed insurgents but residents unable to leave their homes in the space marked for attack. Three years after this violent and unnecessary incursion, the official death toll of those who were killed in Tivoli Gardens in the name of the state remains contested, as are the implications of this armed operation for other neighbourhoods in Jamaica. In communities where the residents are caught between intermittent attacks by police and armed strongmen, murals frame the dead as fallen warriors in a war on the poor. Memory is projected onto places that exist as a mnemonic for the body;[16] the dead become a haunting presence among the living as they go about their business.

Figure 14.5. Zico, by Anthony Brown in Hannah Town, Kingston, Jamaica (photo courtesy of Kara Springer)

The work of the artist Anthony Brown at one time mapped the bodies of the fallen onto the walls of the Hannah Town community, literally linking place to embodied memories of violence. In the fall of 2013, all of his work was painted over by the police. Brown's murals of the Upsetters and the Rich and Famous marked the corners still controlled by these crews. Larger-than-life full figures looked out at passers-by, their power and authority greater in death. These images gave the community character, joining the private world of the home to the more public world of the street.

Brown worked a number of citations into these images. The first of these was spiritual but could also be read as political. Zico was depicted with a strong aura rising from behind him as if he were a saint or apostle. He appeared with a dove on his shoulder, a citational reference to Jesus after his baptism, or Bertrand Aristide making a triumphant speech on his return to Haiti after his first exile, or Fidel Castro on the day of his famous speech just after coming to power. The dove was a symbol of peace and a signifier of the Holy Spirit, which can manifest itself in the body of the believer. In much the same way, the spirits of these dead men became present in the lives of those who passed by their murals. Psalm 35, which appeared beside Zico's image, served notice on the living by appealing to an avenging divinity. "Plead my cause O Lord with those who strive with me. Fight against those who fight against me." Brown said this was a very popular psalm for memorials. Archaic calligraphy gave the inscription a formal weight and invoked the written textual authority of the Bible.

The black star over the head of Touchy was the artist's gesture to Pan-Africanism and the transnational struggles of black folks. It also cited the Black Star Steamship Line of Marcus Garvey, Brown's hero, whose memorials he said he would much rather be painting. The star also doubled as a symbol of the Rich and Famous. Between each panel of murals Brown had painted a large yellow star with the word SUPER; this combined elements of American popular culture with elements of African nationalism.

Down the street was Brown's detailed portrait of Dada (an alias), the former leader of the Upsetters, who had been executed by the police. Relaxed and confident, Dada dominated the urban landscape, appearing against the zinc fence that framed his domain. Dark glasses hid his eyes and reflected the community as if to say, "Look at me to see who you are." Psalm 35 appeared as a caption below this mural, and the words "Gone but not forgotten" appeared on a banner beside his alias.

Figure 14.6. Dada on the Upsetters corner, by Anthony Brown, 2009 (photo courtesy of Judith Salmon)

Beside him were portraits of his comrades who had been either executed or imprisoned by a special police squad. The Upsetters still held their corner and defended their turf, although police routinely shot their members and took others into custody. Both revered and feared, loved and criticized, Dada had become mythologized in community lore as someone who tackled both rival gangs and corrupt police.

In contrast, the mural portraits of Kimarley and Mollo depicted young men who embodied the desire for respectability and educated civility. Commissioned by their families, they depicted the bodies of youth who had been shot and killed because they were in the wrong place at the wrong time.

Kimarley had been shot because he had witnessed the murder of his friend. Until then, he had done well at high school in spite of the odds against him and "never mix up inna notten." Brown's portrait of him recalled Marcus Garvey attired in his scholarly robes, embodying images of the modern African diasporic subject as responsible, respectable, educated, and ready to rule. Kimarley's mural, then, expressed thwarted desire for educational attainment.

The image of Mollo standing outside his mother's house as he once stood in life held together the extraordinary and the unthinkable with a reminder of what could have been. Portrayed in a magical garden, Mollo's body haunted his mother's wall. The geometric green-and-white pattern around him drew the viewer to his image in the same way a Haitian *vévé* might appeal to the energy of a divinity.

Brown worked from domestic photographs and funeral programs, transposing the personal and private archival practice of the family photograph onto the public archive of the local community. In his hands, the bodies of the dead moved from inside to outside and from private to public. Loss was projected from the family onto community space through these images. Brown's work largely conformed to the tropes of domestic photography – a man posing beside a car, a youth in a graduating gown, images taken from passports or visa applications, and so on. He remained faithful to the photograph but added his own ideas. In a context in which attacks on communities by gangs and state forces had become normalized, and where people often found themselves caught between the two, the murals challenged the normalization of violence, turning spaces of terror into places of memory. They reminded us that those celebrated as community heroes were also physically and materially marginalized as worthless lives within the narratives of the neocolonial nation.

Geopolitical Ghosts and Contested Memories

Geopolitics haunted these murals both in terms of what they showed and in terms of the violence of what was not shown. In 2010, during the occupation of Tivoli Gardens, police painted out the murals, destroying

Figure 14.7. Commemorative mural of Kimarley, by Tony Brown (photo courtesy of Kara Springer)

Figure 14.8. Mural for Mollo, by Tony Brown (photo courtesy of Kara Springer)

a visual genealogy of powerful "dons" and local leaders. They attacked the walls as well as the community, painting out murals of outlaw leaders like Claudie Massop and Christopher Coke and Jim Brown, Coke's father. These men were militant activists for the conservative Jamaica Labour Party at the height of the Cold War. On the ground, they led the violent campaign against the elected socialist government for control of the state, helping the JLP take power in 1980. The illegal trafficking networks of men like Massop and Coke procured the arms that undermined the anti-colonial socialist project in the 1970s.

The murals commemorating these men forced us to complicate easy notions of innocence and crime. Criminals, it seems, are seekers of justice when their work is in harmony with imperial agendas. Illegal networks of violence organized by these men in collaboration with the United States and conservative forces helped install the global order we now call neoliberalism. Painting out murals induces amnesia, but when troubled this veiling of the past creates an echo chamber for the invisible but ghostly spectres of history: the formation of the Caribbean by a criminal act that dispossessed Aboriginal people and illegally commodified land; piracy as a foundational moment in the birth of capitalism; the illegal capture and bloody transportation of Africans; the violent suppression of an agenda of redistribution; and the installation of new class and racial formations in harmony with neoliberal agendas. The outlines under the police paint call attention to the unrealized desires that are in part the result of the defeat of a struggle for redistribution. All of this has complicated our understanding of the links between global power relations and local crime.

The meanings of the murals shifted depending on who looked at them. For the police, the murals were threats, performances by dissenting subjects who celebrate criminals. Community members, though, had their own interpretations. Marley, a student and community AIDS activist who grew up after the Cold War ended, saw the figures on the walls as an incitement for new kinds of masculinity. While some named the figures on the walls as soldiers, protectors, and warriors, he saw them as something against which to differentiate himself: "I am so glad these murals are here. I need them. I don't want to be another face on the wall. They are a reminder of the path I do not want to go down. Every day when I see them, it helps me make up my mind not to get involved in that. They help me remember what I want for my life. They help me set my goals."[17]

CG, a woman activist, proposes a gendered reading. For her, the murals were best understood in terms of all they did *not* represent, which was women and children. The murals ignored the contributions of women and the ways they had been affected by violence. She reminds us that gun violence is not the only form of violence that deforms. So do rape, domestic violence, and other forms of abuse. It is always the women of the inner city who must manage the everyday consequences of violence, the retreat of the state, and the economic forces that produce unemployment, marginalization, and hunger. Women bear the burden of caring for the wounded, the survivors who are left behind. "Rather than remember 'pure bad man' they [the commemorations] should encourage us to remember those who contribute to the life of the community, who work so hard to build up the community. We the members of this community should decide this together."[18] Anxieties about masculinity that occlude the caring work of women risk reinscribing a global order in which violence is gendered in terms of where, how, and whom it claims. Those who care for life, she asserts, should be recognized, remembered, and memorialized by the communities they serve with their labour.

The murals enacted a cynical commentary on the politics of the nation-state – a commentary that echoed the disillusionment of community members. Few national politicians were portrayed on murals. Again and again, residents expressed deep anger that their trust had been betrayed and described the huge personal and collective cost of a formal political system that had failed. In discussions, community members who were over fifty traced the trajectory of this disillusion from independence in the 1960s to the present day. They offered a litany of examples of innocent people dying violently for popular struggles that failed. As one woman put it: "Long time now politician give the youth them gun and make the youth do their wrongs for them. Then when the youth get strong, them same one turn round and make the police come kill them. Long time now that is going on and it have to stop. It can't work because we tired of it now."[19] This view – that politics was just "polytricks" or "folly tricks" – was repeated countless times. Politics here means partisan bickering for control of the state or the cynical use of ordinary people for the gain of individual political elites and not the broader organization of power for the equitable sharing of resources.

The idea that a just nation-state might be possible was never mentioned in any of the community discussions or interviews I conducted. In fact, some community members suggested that NGOs had replaced the state in terms of providing services and that these groups were just as unreliable and exploitative as the state. According to CG, "they should be glad we down here a kill we one another or they wouldn't get nothing to eat, for is we them live off."[20]

Yet this sense of mistrust, which went hand in hand with the desire to "make it" as an individual, was contradicted by the bonds of solidarity that were so evident at community events as well as by a sense of connection to similar communities overseas. Perhaps the mural of Papa Smurph represented a vision of possibility that straddled the tension between the global and the local. Papa Smurph, aka Murphy, painted by an anonymous muralist, was a masked man in white suspended over the illuminated skyscrapers, sitting on top of the world in the realms of the heavens. Murphy, in death, was mobile, a man and a supernatural spirit, a masked gangster and a godlike figure who embraced his apotheosis while maintaining his outlaw status, as the words "gangster for life" suggest. His image was rooted in the local, on the corner in Kingston where he once hung out, but it was also a visual bridge connecting his neighbourhood in Kingston to the hubs of earthly global power imagined to exist in metropolitan cities like New York, Chicago, Los Angeles, and Detroit. The mural's self-parodic style appropriated elements of an American TV series, *The Smurfs*, in which Papa Smurf, a wise elder and counsellor, protected a village of creatures called Smurfs from evil. So Murphy was imagined watching over the welfare of his neighbourhoods at home and in diaspora from the safety of the heavens, his white attire symbolizing spiritual purity and/or perhaps social whiteness. With humour and defiance, the mural mixed displacement and rootedness, stubbornly insisting on the sacred and the secular and linking the local to the transnational. It also connoted the ways in which the fragmentation of local urban communities into tightly guarded neighbourhoods had been the result of local violence, whose cause lay in global structures.

Scholars such as Richard Drayton point out that the violence brought to bear on Jamaicans is part of a global pattern of aggression, one that raises questions about the relationship between global geopolitics and the violence of nation-states. He asks whether the attack on Tivoli Gardens in Kingston was driven by "the need of the interlocked global security establishment to justify its existence? What are the long-term consequences for democracy of treating the urban poor as an enemy population to be beaten into submission, the militarisation of policing, the expansion of intrusive surveillance of society?" He links the Jamaican crisis with security networks in the United States, Britain, and Canada and with the "War on Terror." He argues that the approach used in Jamaica in Tivoli Gardens was similar to the one followed for street fighting in Iraq, citing a 2009 manual on counter-insurgency operations compiled for the US Joint Chiefs of Staff that equated police actions against "criminal organizations" with counter-insurgency operations and that discussed key tactics, which included aerial and electronic intelligence and targeting, the use of "passes" to restrict movement, and information management. In this vein, for two years the Canadian Special Operations Regiment (CSOR) combined operations in Afghanistan with the training of the Jamaican special forces, the Ninjas. In March 2010, Jamaican newspapers reported that a joint US–UK–Canada intelligence operation was being run from Kingston. Advisers from all three NATO powers are active in Jamaica. The Jamaican army has been tightly integrated with the US military since the early 1980s; in a striking parallel, those whom the army is now fighting in Jamaica were in large part *created* by the United States and the JLP in the 1970s and 1980s. The extent to which the state and regional states are acting in accordance with US and other Western agendas has clear implications for how Jamaicans and others similarly positioned at home and in diaspora deal with questions of security and of the state's dememorializing strategies.[21]

The human cost of global security operations raises questions about the form states will take in this new arena of global politics. This security agenda, which has been felt around the world from Iraq to Somalia to Colombia, points to a shift in global governance and transnational interconnectedness. The casual and impersonal brutality of new technologies of violence and the penetration of new forms of surveillance are driving a shift towards global government, a shift that entails invasive scrutiny and observation on the one hand and the expansion of criminal justice systems on the other. Both security interests in the US and US security policy in the Caribbean and Latin America are driven less by the need to maintain state sovereignty than by drug control, immigration control, and other matters related to policing the borders of the North. In much of this hemisphere, military apparatus is being used more and more for policing operations rather than for war. In other words, one of the critical things that has shifted in the geopolitical reality is the role played by transnational surveillance and military technology on the one hand and by expanding criminal justice systems in the United States and other Western powers on the other. The commemorative murals and the vigils both perform and represent the everyday lived reality of this experience.

Conclusion

New forms of commemorative performances of vigils and murals have emerged as responses to the violence that has marked the installation of the neoliberal order in the Caribbean. The examples I have discussed mobilize community agency, create counter-narratives, inscribe living memories of loss on place, and speak back to the criminalization of the Jamaican. Questions of geopolitical interconnectedness are largely ignored in the local and mainstream media, which tend to focus on state corruption, economic crises, and pathological criminality. By contrast, local, place-based commemorative murals and vigils move the discussion away from pathologies of criminality and individual corruption and instead refer us to the layered, lived reality of geopolitical power in the inner city. They attend to the thwarted desires of youth whose lives are being wasted, and the interpretations they generate call attention to the labour of women like Monica Williams and CG, who care for communities and families by attending to the injured, recording their pain of loss, and remembering what should have been. These new vigils and murals link appeals to divine justice with Pan-Africanist politics. They mix global forms of popular culture with sacred iconographies, and they make claims to forms of citizenship forged by centuries of transnational racial formation while expressing people's desire to maintain ownership of their own cultural subjectivity.

Nevertheless, while vigils and murals protest covertly and overtly and contest the state's unpredictable violence, they are also expressions of ambivalence regarding how to challenge and transcend that violence. Local people call on divine justice for retribution, but they also take material action at the local level or at the level of individual legal redress. Commemorative murals resurrect the bodies of area leaders while grieving victims of violence. They challenge the police but stop short of revealing the identities of police executioners. They display the unrealized hopes and ambitions of human subjects in ways that demonstrate how the politics of the local and the global have overtaken the politics of the nation-state. This can only be understood by connecting the work they do to the broader geopolitical imperial agenda.

The murals and vigils offer a partial picture that in some ways resists the power exercised by the media, the state, and official narratives, but they cannot on their own materialize struggles that can fully address these tensions. For this, other forms of mobilization will be needed across the borders of place and time. Under the present geopolitical order, the state and those who elect it have to "wheel and come again," as the deejays say. But conditions also suggest a new role for popular local collectivities in relation to the transnational and trans-imperial workings of power. One thing that emerged alongside the organization of communities in their own defence was an immediate style of local governance, along with a sense of community identity, confidence, and autonomy that brought results in ways that the formal state sector has been unable to do. There are perhaps important lessons about alternatives here. Developing a better understanding of how local groups make meaning from their own difficult circumstances might be one way to begin developing ways of building opposition to the inequity and violence that surrounds us. When we listen to the music and the talk, and when we walk around town looking at the popular media that adorn community walls, we can see the contradictory ways in which folks stubbornly assert the desire for a form of visibility that serves them locally and that also joins them to a wider world alongside others who struggle in different ways to confront the new imperialism.

But no listening or looking can happen where people are afraid to speak. People from all levels of the society expressed fear of speaking out publicly about state and other forms of violence. Terror prevents a full discussion of the possibilities and pain of the new moment and allows the police to kill with impunity. This silence enables violence to become a form of government through security.[22] "Power and violence are opposites; where the one rules absolutely, the other is absent," Hannah Arendt wrote long ago. Power, she proposed, is the concerted exercise of collective will. This, she contends, can be an antidote to violence. While many propose that violence is the ultimate demonstration of power, she proposes that loss of power or fears of weakness can be an incitement to substitute violence for power. Reversing this requires new forms of transnational dialogue and organization that will create bonds of solidarity able to inspire the exercise of collective will. This is one way to speak back to fear and isolation. And speak back we will, from local sites to national, regional, diasporic places and beyond.

NOTES

I would like to thank the following for their comments on this essay: Horace Levy, Suvendrini Perera, Sherene Razack, Alissa Trotz, Jacqui Alexander, and Joan French. I am also grateful to the women of Hannah Town, Lana Finikin, the animators of the Sistren Collective, the Williams family, Jamaicans for Justice, Owen Ellis, and Hilary Nicholson. I would also like to thank my research assistants: Anique Jordan, Danielle Smith, Kara Springer, Tanisha Sri Bhaggiyadatta, Camille Turner, and others. This paper would not exist without the work of Tony Brown and Vermon Grant. I thank them for that and for the generous amounts of time they spent with me.

1 Taylor, *The Archive*, 2–3.
2 Connerton, *The Spirit of Mourning*, 4.
3 Nettleford, *Dance Jamaica*.
4 Connerton, *The Spirit of Mourning*.
5 Connerton, *The Spirit of Mourning*, 12.
6 Connerton, *The Spirit of Mourning*, 17.
7 Klak, *Globalization and Neoliberalism*; Mullings, "Neoliberalization."

  8 Gunst, *Born fi' Dead*; Gray, *Demeaned but Empowered*; Tafari Ama, *Blood, Bullets, and Bodies*; Levy, *They Cry "Respect"!*; Harriott, *Understanding Crime in Jamaica*.
  9 Walcott, "The Muse of History."
10 Gordon, *Ghostly Matters*.
11 Gordon, *Ghostly Matters*, xvi.
12 Thomas, *Exceptional Violence*.
13 Thomas, *Exceptional Violence*, 174–6.
14 Mbala, personal communication, 28 May 2009.
15 Schwartz, "Traces of a Massacre," accessed 14 January 2014 at http://www.newyorker.com/online/blogs/newsdesk/2013/05/video-massacre-in-jamaica.html.
16 Connerton, *The Spirit of Mourning*, 85.
17 MT, personal communication, 23 May 2012.
18 CG, personal communication, 6 May 2009.
19 BF, personal communication, 6 May 2009.
20 CG, personal communication, 3 May 2012.
21 Drayton, "From Kabul to Kingston."
22 Arendt, "On Violence," in Schleger-Hughes and Bourgeois, *Violence in War and Peace*, 236–43 (Oxford: Blackwell, 2004).

15 "Lest We Forget": Terror and the Politics of Commemoration in Guyana

D. ALISSA TROTZ

Dust don't disappear when you sweep it behind bed
People stay quiet but all the questions in their head
Is true time could heal and bad times could change
people mind
But we have to figure out how to talk, leave the hurt behind
And if you bright and reading plenty book
You must realize how the silence must look …[1]

These fragmentary notes encounter an out-of-the-way space – the Caribbean. Unusual because – except perhaps for Haiti or the holding pens of Guantanamo Bay – the region has been peripheral to contemporary discussions of terror. Unexpected because this requires us to engage not just neo-imperial but also neocolonial state violence. Unanticipated because until the 1980s, the anglophone Caribbean was described in several quarters as one of the world's largest groupings of "stable democracies." Only recently have we have heard calls to reckon publicly with the legacies of what anthropologist Veena Das has described as "critical events."[2]

But for those who have lived the violence, like the subjects of the poem by Grenadian Merle Collins that frames this chapter, the Caribbean is not such a surprising place. What is strange is not violence, but conversation, and ways of publicly reckoning with the trauma and incoherence that terror leaves in its wake across the archipelago, imposing limits on what can be said, offering the illusion of safety in silence. The internecine violence leading up to the 1980 Jamaica elections. The December 1982 Suriname murders. The 1983 implosion of the Grenadian revolution and the US invasion that followed.

And in what was then British Guiana, the racialized terror that convulsed the country's coast in the 1960s, at the height of the anti-colonial period and on the eve of independence.[3] The British and US imperialist aggressors were intent on removing the threat of communism represented by the 1953 Guyanese elections. The first under adult suffrage, they had been overwhelmingly won by the People's Progressive Party (PPP) under Premier Cheddi Jagan, who thus led the first democratically elected self-professed Marxist government in the Western Hemisphere.[4] After just 133 days in office, Jagan's government suspended the constitution, which helped set in motion external and internal forces that led to the tragic collapse of a movement that had begun to galvanize the country under a multiracial, anti-colonial, nationalist banner. In the competition for state power, the two major political parties splintered along racialized lines, representing primarily African and Indian Guyanese (the former the descendants of enslaved peoples, the latter of indentured labourers and the majority of the population).[5] In the early 1960s, violence erupted along the country's coast. By July 1964, hundreds had lost their lives, innumerable properties had been destroyed, and thousands had been forced to seek permanent refuge and attempt to rebuild their shattered lives in villages alongside others whom they often did not know but were presumed to know simply because they "looked like them." Political independence, coming in 1966 on the heels of racial terror, has with few exceptions entrenched a climate of distrust and suspicion and produced a bitterly divided political landscape that continues to stalk the country nearly half a century after independence.

How might we "figure out how to talk, leave the hurt behind?" What I offer are provisional reflections, a brief impression of my attendance at one of the few public annual ceremonies that explicitly addresses the 1964 violence in Guyana,[6] and an account of an ongoing search for a way to tell a partial story (and a recent, tragic event that reminds us how urgent and necessary a task this is), in which ethical witnessing is as much about futures dreamed of as it is about pasts remembered.

An Early Morning Boat Ride

I have come to Linden to attend the forty-third anniversary commemoration of the explosion of 6 July that sank the Sun Chapman *launch during the 1964 disturbances in what was then British Guiana. "Linden" is of relatively recent provenance; it is the name given to a town that prior to 1970 consisted of three communities: Wismar, Mackenzie, and Christianburg. It is also the name of*

Figure 15.1. Approaching Hurudaia, Demerara River (author's photo)

the then prime minister, Linden Forbes Sampson Burnham, two years after the first fraudulent national elections that would maintain his party in power for twenty-eight years.

Reaching Hurudaia, the site of the tragedy, means a one-and-a-half hour boat ride from Linden up the Demerara River, on one of the two river taxis specially commissioned for the day.

I am trying to imagine the Demerara River four decades ago, before the highway was built connecting Linden to Georgetown. It is still early enough to see the fog on the road ahead of us before the rising sun burns it away, and to wind our windows up against the cold breeze on this early tropical morning. Then, the river was the only access route to the capital city of Georgetown, sixty-five miles away. The passenger launch was returning to Linden from Georgetown and was just moving off from Hurudaia, one of the stops along the way, when it exploded.

On one bank of the river sit the rusting structures of the bauxite industry, a lonely monument to another time, when at its peak, Guyana was producing some 90 per cent of the world's calcined bauxite. Over the past decades, this community's labour force has fallen from more than five thousand to some six hundred. Originally owned by the Canadian multinational Alcan/Demba, the bauxite industry was nationalized in 1971 as part of the government's cooperative socialist strategy. The move back to privatization began in the late 1980s after the government adopted an Economic Recovery Program (which the Guyanese dubbed the "Empty Rice Pot" program) and signed an arrangement with the International Monetary Fund. Today, China's Bosai Minerals Group has a 70 per cent stake in Linden's bauxite and the industry employs less than 5 per cent of the local workforce. It is no longer a company town, but in transition to what? In 2002, the Government of Guyana partnered with the European Union, which provided funding, on a seven-year project to promote small business development and economic diversification. This was the Linden Economic Advancement Program (LEAP). Today, the acronym sounds prematurely ambitious, perhaps overly optimistic, perhaps someone's idea of a bad joke. Linden is strategically located on the only overland route connecting the country's coast to a hinterland region that has a bridge to Brazil and its own version of the El Dorado promise (one that has precipitated a hasty scramble for gold, diamonds, lumber, and ecotourism, all on Indigenous people's lands). Yet it seems as if everything passes through, nothing stays. Linden was once a destination for migrants, principally men, from other parts of the country in search of work; today it is the conduit, as well as a space that people leave. One report I have been able to get my hands on – statistics are hard to come by in Guyana – names Linden as the highest per capita recipient of remittances from family members living abroad.

The launch that is taking us to the commemorative event at Hurudaia is retracing the path taken by the first rescue boats that responded to the news of the explosion. It strikes me that we are going towards where the Sun Chapman *was headed from. Will we meet halfway? I am thinking of the interviews we have done, the accounts we have been given of dismembered bodies tied together and trailing in the water behind returning vessels. On the river at day-clean (local parlance for sunrise or daybreak), keenly aware of the fragrance of the morning dew, I suddenly remember the words of one woman I interviewed: "I will never forget how the river smelled, it smelled of death." People speak of how smells trigger memories, but here it is as if memory has its own suffocating smell, one this woman seemed unable to escape. We pass a churchyard on the river's west bank, in which a mass grave had been hastily dug over forty years ago. For many bereaved families, memorial would have to follow burial.*

As we continue upriver there are fewer signs of human settlement until we approach a sudden opening, dramatic because all around and on the opposite

Figure 15.2. Sun Chapman commemorative site, Hurudaia (author's photo)

bank has been, with the occasional interruption, an unending meeting of tree, bush, water. We have arrived at Hurudaia landing. The entire area has been cleared and prepared by the Sun Chapman Memorial Committee.
A painting on canvas (created in the Guyanese diaspora by a one-time resident now living in the United States), shades of red, shades of brown, recreates the scene of the tragedy. Its evocation of Africans packed on slave ships makes me think of the temporal layering, the multireferentiality of representations, and the kind of work they do in structuring how we remember.
A concrete wall stands in the middle of the clearing, commanding attention. Carefully printed in black letters are the names of the women, men, and children who perished in the explosion. Six months earlier we had interviewed an elderly man, who told us that his twin brother had gone down with the Sun Chapman. It was on him that the task of identification fell, and he described to us the chain and the scar that allowed him to say with certainty that the body

Figure 15.3. Sun Chapman memorial wall (author's photo)

laid out in front of him was his birth companion. As I move closer to the wall, there is a sudden jolt of recognition as I see his brother's name and realize I can at least partly locate him in a dense web of connections.

There is a line acknowledging eleven still unidentified victims, symbolizing a tragic mystery, a festering wound still unresolved that speaks to the disturbances of that period that tore the country apart. The board says this brings the total dead to forty-three, but there are thirty-four listed names, not thirty-two, which makes for forty-five. Even the numbers, it seems, cannot add up to finite closure. Some may see this as requiring clarification, but I think there is a lesson here. We can read the concrete edifice as possessing a certain unanticipated vulnerability, a confession of unknowing at the heart of the tragic events of 1964. Perhaps, then, it is better to read it as a cautionary note about the tragic consequences of certainty and about the humility that undecidability (not indecision) substitutes for arrogant knowing.[7] What happens at the limit of explanation – do we then begin to feel? These unclaimed bodies raise so many questions. Are two of the listed names persons who never returned but whose earthly remains were among those "unidentified"? And what of the others? Were they women, men, or children? Was an unexplained absence never registered, did no one get worried when the end of month came and no money was sent home? Did they have no friends or family on board? Does unidentified mean that no loved ones came forward to give them a name, an identity, or that the bodies were made unrecognizable by the explosion? In the absence of family, what would it mean to claim them as belonging to all of us? Is it too late?

An industrial and multiracial bauxite mining town at the time of the disturbances, Linden was the only space outside the main coastal belt that was directly affected by the terror of the early 1960s, and one of the few communities in which *both* Africans and Indians were reported as targets of violence. At the height of the euphemistically titled "civil disturbances" and following news reports of attacks along the coast, the homes and businesses of Indian residents were burned and looted on 25 May 1964. The official inquiry into that violence, *The Report of the Wismar, Christianburg and Mackenzie Commission,* describes the emergency evacuation of most of the town's Indian community (some three thousand people, roughly 17 per cent of the population at the time) following brutal assaults on Indian residents (including sexual violence against women in full public view).[8] On 6 July, the *Sun Chapman,* a launch owned by an African Guyanese businessman, sank on its return trip from the city, triggering retaliatory violence that targeted Indians who had remained in or returned to Linden.[9] In all, between fifty-five and sixty people perished in Linden in the May-to-July violence.

Linden is deeply symbolic for both African and Indian Guyanese today, a bifurcated marker of what "each side" did to "the other." For African Guyanese, the tragedy revolves around the launch and the explosion is attributed to a bomb planted on board by agents of the PPP, which was in power at the time; what happened to the Indian community is downplayed or ignored. For Indian Guyanese, the explosion was an accident caused by PNC agents who were smuggling explosives. The violent expulsion of Indian Guyanese from the area (words like genocide, pogrom, massacre, and ethnic cleansing are regularly invoked), including and especially the sexual violence against women, is viewed to this day as an unforgivable assault on the Indian community.[10]

There is, then, no mutually agreed account. In narratives now almost fifty years in the making, the past is reordered and reworked, resulting in sharply drawn and incommensurable renderings in which aggressor and victim are not only racially marked and clearly separate but also locked into roles through which the sequence of events, past and present, is understood. Mostly though, an uncomfortable silence hovers at the edges of conversation, of our imagined lives and relations to one another.[11]

Academic productions are no less implicated in these representations.[12] Really just another mode of storytelling (although it carries the weight of institutional legitimacy), much of the existing scholarship fails to engage the violence of the 1960s in any detail. It privileges the role of destabilizing external factors, or it emphasizes political parties, labour movements, and other internal actors. People appear as collateral damage, as numbers on a page. Once the various human costs are downplayed (and, more difficult to face, when human participation in the violence is sidelined),[13] there is a tendency to treat the violence as an inevitable effect of and testimony to the *fact* of difference. Colonial scripts are rehearsed; support is lent to static portrayals of irrevocably racialized difference; questions are avoided, like these: What is the purpose of these apparently self-evident truths? And whose interests do such narratives serve?[14]

> *The coolie ... and ... [the] negro ... are totally*
> *different people; they do not intermix. That is, of*
> *course, one of our great safeties in the colony*
> *when there has been any rioting.*[15]

In her moving account of ghosts and haunting, Avery Gordon urges us to imaginatively reinvent social analysis so that it can become more attuned to what lies beneath the surface of things, to look for what we cannot see (in fact, to train ourselves to first be aware that the unseen exists). For Gordon, the "seemingly not there" is a presence with "living effects, seething and lingering, of what seems over and done with, the endings that are not over."[16]

In March 2012, in his national budget presentation to parliament, the Minister of Finance announced that the long-established subsidized electricity rates to Lindeners – part of an arrangement worked out decades ago with the bauxite industry – could no longer be afforded and would be gradually phased out starting on July 1st. Asking how they could pay in the midst of economic stagnation, and demanding proper consultation, the entire community immediately began to mobilize. Several marches and public meetings between April and July culminated in a planned five-day community wide strike. On the evening of the first day of the strike, armed police amassed near a bridge which women, men and children had occupied all day, and teargas, rubber bullets and live rounds were fired into the panicking crowd. Three men were killed, and twenty others were shot and injured. Lindeners shut down all access through their community, refusing to back down until a negotiated agreement was reached with the government, the terms of which had now widened well beyond the original remit of the protest. The government – since 1992, the PPP has been in office, and is widely seen as deriving the majority of its support from Indian-Guyanese – accused the opposition of inciting the protestors, and charged various sections of the media with inflaming racial tensions. This charge did not, it seems, extend to the state media (which from the start characterized the grievances of the community as baseless), and the way in which the disturbances of 1964 were all too easily supplying the conceptual frame through which the contemporary crisis in Linden was being represented. On the day of the scheduled rate increase, Lindeners had planned and publicized a "Day of Protest and Prayer." That morning, an editorial (of all things!) appeared in the state-controlled newspaper defending the decision, warning that "… hatred of Indians is ingrained into their [African-Guyanese] psyche. Many Indian persons, who grew up in the arms of black people in rural communities have today become fearful anytime a black youth gets too close to them."[17] More explicitly and incredibly, three days after the fatal shootings, in the same newspaper, a well-known journalist would write the following partial and interested account of what happened to Indian-Guyanese (and only Indian-Guyanese) in 1964, as if to warn that Linden 2012 would go this way too, leaving no space for engagement with the state violence that left three dead and scores injured, except perhaps as a legitimate response to rioters plucked from a script nearly 50 years prior: "Like the government and the parliamentary opposition, the foreign diplomatic missions, would be conscious of the haunting human tragedies of murder, rapes, destruction to properties and mind-boggling dislocation of at least 3,000 individuals, including children, compelled into an exodus from the mining region with the spectre of raw racism looming large in that horrific tragedy of 1964 often despairingly recalled as the 'Wismar massacre.'"[18]

But here we see that an active summoning of ghosts will not necessarily lead to resolution; instead, it keeps alive the "living effects," which will return again and again to remind us that we mark time in the same place and that it is not "over and done with."

This cannot be the answer …
but
there is a way in which the tape keeps looping.

How can we name, remember, and respond to terror without reproducing the terms of engagement that enabled it in the first place? Clearly, reconciliation is not to be found via a search for a singular, sovereign account of what actually happened. Instead, we might ask how the events of 1964 are remembered and what meaning is given to them from the space of the present. How are the boundaries of difference partly enacted through the stories we tell about the past?[19] One cannot begin with the assumption that efforts to democratize the archive (by seeking out oral histories, for example) will produce a transparent gateway to the "facts" of the past. Ann Laura Stoler and Karen Strassler distinguish this recuperative position, which they refer to as the "hydraulic/storage model of memory," from an approach that recognizes experience as a contested category and that sees oral histories, in addition to being multiple and unfinished, as productive rather than simply reflective of a given reality.[20] Underlining the double-sidedness of historicity – "the distinction between what happened and that which is said to have happened" – anthropologist Michel-Rolph Trouillot directs our attention to the operations of power in the production of historical narratives.[21] We must examine how power infuses both popular and official memories of past terror, conditioning the structures of remembering and forgetting.[22] This raises crucial questions for us about who tells (or gets to tell) the story and about the silences this entails. In short, what difference might it make to think of "difference" as the effect of violence, not the other way around?

Choreographing Memory: Preliminary Notes on a Method

In her superb study of cultural memory in the Americas, *The Archive and the Repertoire*, Diana Taylor urges us to see performance as epistemological. Embodied practices that are meaning-making, performances are a key site of transmitting social identity and traumatic memory. They constitute a repertoire that entails "gestures, orality, movement, dance, singing – in short, all those acts usually thought of as ephemeral, nonreproducible knowledge."[23] Focusing not just on what is said but on how it is enacted and accomplished is a useful way of moving below the surface of the annual ceremony at Hurudaia, a ritualized performance about a "critical event" that is simultaneously archival (in the traditional sense of the word) and extratextual. It enables us to approach it as a production participating in the construction of forms of affinity.

Here I share a work in progress, drawing mainly on *The Archive and the Repertoire* as a methodological guide, in which I sketch a few directions that I find helpful in my efforts to disentangle how the annual *Sun Chapman* pilgrimage at Hurudaia produces an interested account of the 1964 terror. First, Taylor makes a compelling case for challenging the hierarchical boundaries between performance as "[expressive] embodied praxis and episteme," what she refers to as repertoire, and the official archive of memory.[24] For Taylor, the repertoire becomes important in its own right as a system for storing and transmitting knowledge and history that interacts with the archive. This is a particularly compelling approach, one that begins with an inventory of the different kinds of evidence on display: magnified media reports and inquest findings temporarily attached to trees; poetic, musical, singing, and spoken-word tributes; prayers; the laying of wreaths; the giving of lengthy political speeches; and eyewitness testimonies from survivors and others who lived through the shock when the news first reached the town that the launch had gone down. But more than a list is at stake here, for we must think about how the pieces are put together. What is the status of the various kinds of – oral, written, embodied – evidence? How do the archive and the repertoire relate to each other – that is, how does an account by someone who was there and can tell the audience "what really happened" relate to a speech that draws heavily on the inquest to underline the irrefutability of the scientific evidence? Do the performances bring the archive to life while also exceeding it?

An emphasis on the repertoire reveals embodiment to be central to the generation of this accounting.[25] This requires a careful tracing of how the ceremony produces African Guyanese subjectivities, both in terms of the participant-spectators and in the identification of the *Sun Chapman* explosion as metonymic of the political violence of 1964. A further line of inquiry encompasses the ways in which "African Guyaneseness" is sutured to the major opposition political party, the PNC, and how this assumed connection is produced through the organization and careful choreography of the ceremony as well as through the ways in which a younger generation of Lindeners is actively conscripted into remembering what they have not directly experienced.

I have attended the ceremony for a number of years, observing shifts in what is emphasized and noting what seems rarely to change.[26] A diachronic approach to these ritualized performances suggests that besides investigating the ways in which we remember, one must also account for the times in which the remembrance occurs. What does the invocation of the past address in the present? In her study of how the labour movement enlists history (slavery) as a crucial dimension of its organizational and educational work in contemporary Guadeloupe, Yarimar Bonilla takes her cue from Stephan Palmié's suggestion that we think of the historical imagination not as a "mere deposit of past social experience, but as a repository of ways of engaging the present." In other words, how are "narratives of … [the] past … reworked in the service of contemporary political action[?]"[27] Approaching the commemoration in this way, as a form of work whose terms and objectives we must investigate, prompts a serious consideration of how connections are articulated and secured between a more distant past – whether represented by speeches, or by images such as the one illustrated earlier of the sinking launch, which seems to be a direct reference to the slave ships of the Middle Passage, or by the more recent past of 1964 – and the situation facing the vast majority of Lindeners today. This means investigating the political and economic developments that have resulted in Linden having one of the highest unemployment rates in the country and becoming a space of exodus with a high dependency on remittances, as well as exploring whether and how these conditions manifest themselves in relation to the July commemoration. How is marginalization articulated, where does it intersect with the public act of memorialization at Hurudaia, and what kinds of nostalgia for the past does this produce?[28] What claims about the present are uttered at the site, and how are Lindeners' grievances recast in relation to a government that is perceived to be acting in favour of Indian Guyanese? How might Lindeners also be nourished by the racialized affinities that are the effect of the ruling party's own ongoing performance of Indian victimhood as the sole story of Linden?

Finally, if time is one dimension, place is another. Instead of thinking of Linden as a place where terror was experienced, the methodological injunction here is to explore the processes – including the violence of dislocation – through which places are constituted.[29] In attending carefully to how practices of memorialization are spatialized and the ways in which Linden has come to matter today as a particular kind of place, Michel-Rolph Trouillot reminds us to listen carefully for the sounds of silence in the story.[30] This requires us to move beyond what is said and what appears to be visible at the ceremony and train ourselves to see what is absent yet always there.[31] The text on the monument – "If we forget the past we do so at our own peril" – asks us to contemplate just who is the "we" that is being interpellated here. How are the 25 May and 6 July assaults on the Indian Guyanese who called Linden home in 1964 made to disappear, and what kind of historical archive results from the effacement of that violence? What emerges is not just a relationship to a past experience of terror, but the active creation – through who is remembered and, importantly, who must be forgotten – of racialized space and affiliation. Tracking the modalities through which this erasure is accomplished, and the histories it animates, is therefore key.[32] But it is not, and cannot be, enough.

Hopeful Interruptions

The workshop that inspired this collection asked participants to reflect on a number of questions: "How do we name, remember, and respond to atrocity and terror?" "How might we transform these responses into a collective politics for social and political action?" The stakes are dangerously high.

With respect to the various investments in stuck and separate narratives of the past that we have seen here in relation to contemporary events that engage violence in colonial Guyana, we might add another question: "How might we name terror without reproducing the terms of engagement that enabled it in the first place?" Notwithstanding some unofficial and popular mutterings in the local press over the past few years in support of such an idea, a Truth and Reconciliation Commission will not get to the bottom of this matter. One person's facts are another person's rumour. Opposed facts are the terms through which each "side" emerges, each as victim of the other. Truth is nowhere to be found. How might one move beyond this cul-de-sac of memory so as to reach towards a more tentative politics of affinity? Diana Taylor's engagement with performances that contest state-sponsored terror in Latin America traces how, instead of congealing an asymmetrical difference, grief might be transformed into public mourning/affirmation and action for change.[33]

With this in mind, let me end for now with an incipient beginning, sharing two examples that will be my guides as I continue to try to tell this story, searching again for possible cues and clues that point to an *otherwise* that the initial search was unable to see. The first makes clear the role the labour movement played during the anti-dictatorial struggle in Guyana from the early 1970s through the mid-1980s. At the height of what has often been referred to as the civil rebellion of the late

1970s, political activist Rupert Roopnaraine described unforgettable moments between sugar workers (a predominantly Indian Guyanese workforce, and fiercely supportive of the PPP, then in opposition) and bauxite workers from Linden (predominantly African Guyanese):

> One of my enduring memories of the period was one such encounter in a bottom-house ... where a strapping African brother from Linden was grounding with an Indian family that had joined in the exodus from Wismar in the wake of the atrocities in the 1960s. I have always thought of that encounter as an exemplary moment of healing. It was a feel of where united working class action could lead.[34]

Solidarity between sugar and bauxite workers was again evident in May 1983, during the food rebellions, when bauxite workers were invited to meet sugar workers in the sugar belt. This event led to the founding of the Sugar and Bauxite Worker's Unity Committee (SBWUC). The SBWUC decided on a one-day-a-week strike for essential foods, a move that brought out Indian and African villagers in marches to demonstrate their support. One unity committee from villages on the coast sent Indian Guyanese delegates to Linden.[35] Six years later, Roopnaraine, speaking at the end of what some came to call the April Worker Rebellion, which saw sugar and bauxite workers in a solidarity strike, would again make this point: "The unity between sugar and bauxite workers is important ... given the conditions of Guyana and given Guyana's history ... because it forges, at the level of the working people, a racial unity without which we cannot proceed in this country ... The only way we can consolidate the necessary unity in this country is for the grass-roots people, the rank and file to build the unity."[36]

The focus on organized labour, while critical, is incomplete, perhaps most obviously because since Linden's emergence as a bauxite town, the vast majority of its women can be found in the informal and domestic economy. This brings us to the second moment, a march and public meeting in 2002 organized by Red Thread, a grassroots women's organization that draws on women's caring work to ground an activist agenda that contests divisions of race and place across the country.[37]

The handbill distributed by the participants that day referred explicitly to the traumatic events of 1964. It challenged participants and onlookers alike to engage in difficult but necessary memory work and reach for a shared vocabulary, one that rejected the simple binary of victim and oppressor that could be mapped neatly onto Indian and

Figure 15.4. International Women's Day March, Linden, 2002 (photo courtesy of Frank Fyffe)

African bodies: "[Ours] is a struggle of women of all races for women of all races. Because Wismar was a symbol of the terrible racial violence of the 1960s, we, the women, send out this call – Let us make Linden a symbol of how women can cross race divides and fight for a world which values all women's work and all women's lives!"[38] Using megaphones, some of the women explicitly addressed the violence facing the Indian Guyanese community and particularly its women. As far as I have been able to discern, this was the first time that the terror and grief experienced by *all* who considered themselves Lindeners in 1964 had been publicly acknowledged in this way.

Moreover, staging the march as part of International Women's Day and in solidarity with the Global Women's Strike Network (of which Red Thread is an active node) shifted the focus from parochialized understandings of the local. It foregrounded the historical and transnational dimensions of contemporary structural violence, urging us to look for overlapping experiences of exclusion that haunt our present and that are obscured by existing narratives.[39] The march uncompromisingly linked the resolution of a painful past to regenerative practices that would build on the everyday caring work that falls to women, offering this as the foundation for a differently imagined political horizon. Along similar lines, and drawing on her research with one community in downtown Kingston, Jamaica, anthropologist Faye Harrison suggests that even as political terror was deepening in the 1970s, one could find efforts by local women and men to draw on practices that would create safe zones of yard and community, challenge representations of militarized masculinity valorized in gunman culture, and foreground the transnationally mediated structural violence of poverty and marginalization that framed the lives of inner-city Kingstonians.[40]

Reflecting on the difficult task of confronting the horrors of partition, a task that includes finding ways to tell stories that seem not to be for the telling, Urvashi Butalia argues that "the exploration of memory can never be separated from the ethics of such an exploration" and that "in any such exploration of the past, the aspects we choose to illuminate are determined not only by the present we live in, but the future we wish to work towards."[41] And Merle Collins brings us face to face with the limits of our academic projects in addressing this, with the lines "If you bright and reading plenty book / You must realize how the silence must look," not only because there is an implied responsibility – "We have to figure out how to talk, leave the hurt behind" – but also because accountability is no easy matter; the "brightness" that comes from reading *plenty book* is no guarantee of illumination. What kinds of public intellectual work might enable us to raise critical questions about historical and contemporary processes of violence, nationalism, and state formation in the Caribbean and elsewhere, reading across superficially separate spaces in the region and beyond for the resonances that exist? How might we tell more complete, more complex stories? And is the standard academic format – the book, the journal, the conference presentation or workshop paper – really up to this multidimensional past? I have few answers. For now, the two examples offer a glimpse of alternative scripts that might perform the necessary work of interruption, by severing or rendering conjunctural the ties between political and racialized identities. Might a fragile connectedness exist elsewhere, inside and even beyond these public performances? I think again of those numbers that stubbornly refuse to add up on the commemorative monument at Hurudaia – a concrete wall that calls for eternal peace for those lost to violence – as a necessary slippage that is, when you think of it, not really a mathematical error. I prefer to think that it beckons us to reclaim and mourn all those lost to the violence of 1964 as belonging to all of us. And this is where I will begin.

Last words…
It is late afternoon by the time the launch brings us back to where we began. We stop for gas before heading out of Linden. On the hour-and-a-half drive back to the capital city, exhausted, we carefully avoid the topic of how we spent our day. But we somehow find ourselves talking about the river. We vie to see who can name all of the water spirits that we have learned through childhood folklore: Fairmaid, Massacuraman, Watermooma. We discuss how the glass-like calm at the surface hides the eddies and undercurrents that make the waters so dangerous and unpredictable, even for those who can swim. As we enter and reach the limits of the city, abutting the Atlantic Ocean into which the Demerara river ritually empties herself, one body of water into another, I find myself thinking about the secrets of these waters, what they witnessed and who they claimed, and all the souls that traverse the murky brown depths, surely to protect and not harm us.

NOTES

An early version of this essay was presented at the Caribbean Studies Association, Jamaica, 2009. I would like to thank participants at the Workshop on Women of Colour and the War on Terror (Toronto, 2012) as well as the editors for discussion and feedback, and Terry Roopnaraine for a compassionate read. This work owes everything to the women of Red Thread, Guyana, whose vision for another world inspired it and to whom it is dedicated.
1 Excerpt from Collins, "Shame Bush."
2 Das, *Critical Events*. On Grenada, see Collins, 'Tout Moun ka Pléwé"; on Jamaica, see Meeks, *Envisioning Caribbean Futures*.
3 As a continuing legacy of colonial settlement patterns, the vast majority of Guyanese (close to 90 per cent) inhabit about 10 per cent of the land, consisting of a narrow coastal strip that is six feet below sea level. The indigenous/Amerindian populations, currently accounting for some 10 per cent of the population, live primarily in the hinterland and interior.
4 The election, and the immediate move to imperialist destabilization, occurred six years before the Cuban Revolution, one year before the

CIA-sponsored coup against Guatemala's Jacobo Árbenz Guzmán, and twenty years before the overthrow of Salvador Allende in Chile. In a fascinating essay, historian Richard Drayton directs us to consider other transnational circuits, arguing that the US–British alliance against the anti-colonial movement in British Guyana set an early stage for the Blair–Bush joint offensive against the Middle East in the post 9/11 period. See Drayton, "British Guiana."

5 The People's Progressive Party (PPP) split into two factions in 1955, led by Cheddi Jagan and Forbes Burnham (in 1957, the party led by Burnham would be named the People's National Congress, PNC). Initially split along ideological lines, increasingly both parties came to depend on racialized support from African and Indian Guyanese. After two elections won by the PPP, in December 1964 the PNC was able to form a coalition government following a deeply contested change in electoral arrangements (from first-past-the-post to proportional representation). The PNC would hold on to power for the next twenty-eight years through a combination of electoral fraud and state intimidation and violence.

6 There are two others. One commemorates the death of Kowsilla, a female sugar worker in March 1964; the other, the May 1964 bombing of a bookstore at the Freedom House Headquarters of Cheddi Jagan's party, which killed a young man, Michael Forde, after whom the store is now named. The ceremony I introduce here comes from a larger research project on the constitutive and transnational relations between terror, place, history, and memory, as well as work with a women's organization, Red Thread, that involved oral histories of the 1960s disturbances.

7 I take this necessary injunction to know one thing for certain, and that is that we do not know, from Maria Lugones's discussion of arrogant perception and the undecidability that comes from an awareness that we inhabit several worlds, complexly, never fully, and always in relation to others. Lugones, "Playfulness."

8 According to the commission, the only government-ordered inquiry into the disturbances, it was "given the task to investigate the causes of the racial violence on 25 May 1964 by Africans against the minority East Indian population residing in Wismar, Christianburg and Mackenzie, the bauxite mining communities in the upper Demerara River, 65 miles south of Georgetown." In such a racially charged environment, it is no surprise that the commission was criticized for restricting its remit. One African activist staged a hunger strike to protest the failure to call for similar inquiries into violence erupting elsewhere on the coast.

9 While eleven bodies were unidentified, it tends to be taken for granted in all of the newspaper and other reports that all of those who perished were African Guyanese.

10 One can occasionally track these parallel narratives in the daily newspapers. In the 26 May 2011 Independence supplement of the state-owned *Guyana Chronicle*, for instance, it is striking that the only references to 1964 are an article ("Who Sank the Sun Chapman, Really?") and the reproduction of a letter (Letter on the Sun Chapman Demise), both of which reiterate the explosives-smuggling theory and refute the position taken by a leading member of the opposition (published as a letter to the press in 2003!) that violence against Indian Guyanese in Wismar was a retaliatory response to the launch's sinking.

11 These silences are not just public; they are equally likely to occur in intimate domains. I have been repeatedly struck by interviews during which younger family members have been exposed to the events of 1964 for the first time. I also have paternal and maternal relatives on both sides who at one time or another settled in Linden. It was only two years ago, after starting this research project, that I learned that one of my maternal uncles, a child at the time, had to be rushed to town for fear he would be targeted during some of the violence.

12 For a rare scholarly attempt to consider moments of unity and coalition, see Abraham, *Labour and the Multracial Project*.

13 Mamdani, *When Victims Become Killers*.

14 I discuss this racial inevitability thesis in terms of its consequences for women in Trotz, "Between Despair and Hope."

15 P.P. 1898, L (C. 8656), Royal Commission, Appendix C, vol. I, evidence of M.J.E. Tinne, 4 January 1897, q. 1082. For the way this quotation, which I stumbled across in the archives years ago and have never forgotten, seems to haunt my own reflections on Guyana, see Trotz, "Behind the Banner of Culture?" See also Trotz, "Resurrecting Conversation Tree: Legacies of Walter Rodney for Our Times," plenary talk, Walter Rodney Commemorative Symposium, 12 June 2010, WBAI/Pacifica Radio (99.5 FM) and York College, CUNY.

16 Gordon, *Ghostly Matters*, 195.

17 Editorial, *Guyana Chronicle*, 2 July 2012.

18 Singh, "Guyana's Political Trauma." This remarkable opinion piece – submitted as objective journalism – was reproduced in the *Guyana Chronicle*, the *Trinidad and Tobago Express*, and the *Jamaica Observer*.

19 Sarkar, "Difference in Memory"; Scott, "Experience."

20 Stoler and Strassler, "Castings for the Colonial"; Portelli, "What Makes Oral History Different."
21 Trouillot, *Silencing the Past*, ch. 1 and p. 3.
22 Alonso, "The Effects of Truth."
23 Taylor, *The Archive*, 20.
24 Taylor, *The Archive*, 17.
25 A crucial point that is the subject of Connerton, *How Societies Remember*.
26 Taylor notes that this dynamism is an essential feature of the repertoire, although it does not necessarily follow that meanings can therefore shift arbitrarily. Taylor, *The Archive*, 20.
27 Bonilla, "A Striking Past," 17, 18.
28 Such nostalgia must necessarily be selective and a partial forgetting, since the decline of the bauxite industry – which is indisputably linked to the current crisis in the community – began in the 1970s, under the PNC dictatorship.
29 See, for instance, Hyndman and de Alwis, "Bodies, Shrines, and Roads."
30 Trouillot, *Silencing the Past*.
31 This is what I understand by Gordon's description of a "seething presence."
32 For a discussion of how these colonial traces shape violence in present-day Jamaica, see Thomas, *Exceptional Violence*. Thanks to Terrence Roopnaraine for emphasizing, in relation to this point, that "acts of ethnic hegemony relentlessly work the tension between presencing as a process of making subjective beings into objects where power is enacted, and erasure as a way of depopulating discourse. This has always been the way of the Americas, whether we're talking of slavery, indenture or indigenous peoples." Correspondence with Roopnaraine, August 2012.
33 For a recent, highly charged, and deeply significant Caribbean iteration, see Ford-Smith, "Local and Transnational Dialogues."
34 Roopnaraine, "Race and Rebellion."
35 Andaiye, "Making Grassroots Women."
36 Roopnaraine, speech to workers at Wismar Boat Landing, Linden, 1989.
37 Trotz, "Red Thread."
38 Andaiye, "Notes on Women and Ethnic Conflict, Part 1," presentation made during a panel discussion at the National Library, Georgetown, 15 August 2002.
39 For an elaboration of palimpsestic time, see Shohat, "Area Studies"; Alexander, "Transnationalism"; and Gordon, *Ghostly Matters*.
40 Harrison, "The Gendered Politics."
41 Butalia, *The Other Side of Silence*, 289, 278.

16 "Tortured Bodies": The Biopolitics of Torture and Truth in Chile

TERESA MACIAS

Introduction

"For torture to be effective," they'd tell us, "it has to be limitless."[1]

In Chile during the 2004 congressional debates over compensation for victims of political imprisonment and torture by the authoritarian regime, a member of the National Congress stated that while "it would be inappropriate" to describe "the atrocious methods of torture used" by the regime, everybody should be aware "that in this room, at this very moment, there is a [female] colleague … whose sister's nipples were cut during torture."[2] This sensational statement is hardly unique or isolated. In the months that followed the release of the Report of the Chilean National Commission on Political Imprisonment and Torture (henceforth the Torture Commission and the Torture Report), detailed descriptions of torture and its physical effects (particularly on the bodies of women) became a common fixture of media reports, documentaries, public debates, and even commercial advertisements.[3] Images of raped, mutilated, electrocuted, and half-drowned bodies regularly appeared in public discussions of torture. These images were evoked not only to support and justify monetary compensation but also – and most importantly – to mediate a celebratory catharsis of the nation's capacity to overcome the dictatorship's violent legacy. They became part of the script and vocabulary that mediated the nation's reconciliation.

How have we come by these images and stories of torture? How have we come to know these mutilated and ravaged bodies in so much detail? What processes mediate our use of these images and stories?

How are we to explain the power that torture exerts on the body, and what happens to that power when the nation takes it upon itself to document torture? This chapter uses the Foucauldian concept of biopower to trace how power has worked both in the practising of torture and in the investigations conducted by the Torture Commission. I pay particular attention to the ways in which power imprinted itself on the bodies of torture victims, first through torture and later as a consequence of the investigations that produced a national truth about torture.

Biopower, Michel Foucault tells us, is a form of power that captures, regulates, and disciplines human life in order to advance a specific social order.[4] Biopower is a fundamental condition of modernity, one that marks a shift in how power operates in Western societies, from sovereign power concerned (as Foucault argues) with control over a territory with an undifferentiated population[5] – a population that must at times be subjected to death in the defence of the sovereign – to a conception of power as preoccupied with administering the life not only of the whole population but also of each and every one of its members.[6] This transition manifests itself through power–knowledge techniques and institutional practices that authorize both an *"anatomo-politics of the human body,"* understood as the preoccupation with the body, its anatomy, birth, health, criminality, sexuality, sanity, and mortality, and a *"biopolitics of the population"* that sees the body in the context of the population as a whole.[7] Thus, Giorgio Agamben tells us, biopower is concerned with life as the target of regulation and discipline and, it follows, with the "growing inclusion of [human] life in the mechanisms and calculations of power."[8]

In the first part of this chapter, I argue that the centralization of life and body manifests itself in the anatomo-politics of torture – its intense preoccupation with the body, its functions, endurance, limits, and so on.[9] This calculated exercise of force so as to extend life and prolong death is a concrete example of biopolitics. Foucault traces in the centralization of the body a preoccupation with both "submission and use" and "functioning and explanation."[10] Torture encompasses these same preoccupations by harnessing a profound knowledge of the body's functioning – knowledge that allows the body to be captured through the calculated infliction of pain. In this way, the body is made the surface on which the larger social project is inscribed. Torture, then, mediates the insertion of life into the realm of state power, making possible the realization of insidious power relations that, because they have positive *and* negative effects, produce *and* destroy. We have here a biopolitics that is deeply concerned with the most minute and intimate calculations of the body, calculations that are meant not to kill but rather to postpone death even while they maintain death as a permanent figure on the horizon. Although many prisoners die as a result of torture, the goal of torture is rarely to kill; rather, it is to inflict power on life. Torture, as Sherene Razack argues, is about the inscription or staking of a specific social order on bodies; that is why it is never solely about completely eliminating the body.[11] Torture is ultimately productive: it produces nation, social order, and the subject-citizen.

The analysis later in this chapter of the Torture Commission and its report will demonstrate that documenting torture *also* requires biopolitical corporeal technologies that render the tortured body minutely and intimately known; but now it is for the purpose of producing a national truth about torture. Biopower offers a framework that facilitates the uncovering of an ongoing preoccupation with life and the body; this uncovering is evident in the processes of documenting torture. Producing a national story of torture requires the careful regulation of torture accounts, and Chile's TRC ensured this regulation through its truth-gathering and reporting practices. Those practices required, first, the measurement and calculation of tortured bodies; after this, torture stories were carefully organized into a national truth. Thus, the processes of documenting torture disrupted the power of torture yet also reimprinted biopolitical power on the tortured bodies that the commission had been tasked with representing.

The Torture Commission was the latest episode in a fifteen-year history of truth and reconciliation commissions (TRCs) in Chile that began in 1990 with the Rettig TRC, which investigated Chileans who had been executed or who had disappeared.[12] Chile's experience with TRCs is part of a long transnational history of them. Since the 1970s, post-conflict societies in the global South have convened TRCs in order to document violence and negotiate transitions to liberal democracy.[13] Located rather unremarkably in a long, transnational history of TRCs, the Chilean Torture Commission nevertheless offers a unique opportunity to examine the ways in which TRCs organize how torture will be known as a national truth. As I will demonstrate, the collection, organization, and reporting of torture accounts in Chile required the systematic exertion of state power on the bodies of torture survivors in ways that revealed the biopolitical function of the Torture Commission and that closely resembled the original acts of torture. In other words, documenting torture in Chile helped perpetuate the biopolitical regime that required torture in the first place. The torturers inscribed a political project on bodies; then those who investigated torture used the same bodies to sustain national reconciliation through specific torture accounts and images.

While TRCs have specific value for victims and survivors, who are able to seek justice by demanding recognition, and while the act of testifying before a TRC may be liberating, an analysis of Chile's Torture Commission uncovers more sinister effects. This chapter acknowledges the suffering of survivors and activists, but its focus is on the insidious ways in which power works.

The Biopolitics of Torture

Torture in Chile followed highly regulated and disciplined procedures. The torturers required intensive training, and the intimate encounter between torturer and prisoner was never left to chance. Torture, Richard Rubenstein observes, was characterized by "routinization, rationalization, and bureaucratization"; it became an ordinary and organized practice and an intrinsic element of the repressive state.[14] Its practice was supported by other actions that were organic to the work of ruling. Torture took place in torture centres. Those centres were assigned budgets and personnel; they were embedded in institutional hierarchies; they were regulated, and their procedures were documented; they kept careful records, reflecting the intelligence-gathering purpose of torture. Torture machines were built and tested, manuals of torture were written, and torturers were properly trained in national and international training centres.[15] Employment files were kept for torture personnel, who collected salaries and commendations. The pay for torture fed families and stimulated the economy.

In torture centres, prisoners were subjected to carefully calculated forms of torture that included electric shock, rape (often by animals or instruments), waterboarding, full or partial submersion in sewage or excrement, prolonged hanging or standing, asphyxiation, mock execution, the witnessing of the torture of other prisoners or family members, confinement in overcrowded cells or prolonged isolation, calculated beatings, and drugging. Pregnant women were subjected to electric shocks, which were sometimes applied directly to the fetus through the uterus. Many of these pregnant women suffered miscarriages, and some were forced to give birth to children conceived through torture.[16] Doctors and other health professionals were employed to monitor and regulate the intensity and duration of torture, often providing "aftercare" such as pain medication and the regulation of water intake so as to ensure the prisoner's survival and, thus, the prolongation and efficiency of the torture.[17]

Tomas Moulian argues that Chile's transformation to neoliberalism was strengthened by the terror practices of the dictatorship, the objectives of which were not only to repress internal enemies but also to bring about a new social order.[18] Central to Moulian's argument is that without torture, the neoliberal authoritarian regime could not have arisen, for both revolution and torture were part of a regime that extended from the level of the state to the most minute practices of power on the surfaces of bodies. According to Marnia Lazreg, torture is a practice with "layered meanings" – that is, meanings that can be traced through complex social relations extending from the most intimate encounters between torturer and prisoner to larger social reordering projects in which torture becomes part of "techniques of population screening and social engineering" as well as a catalyst for "identity formation and crystallization."[19]

That torture is bureaucratic in nature does not mean that, as Moulian suggests, the "cruelty of the regime was impersonal and cannot be explained in terms of the psychopathic actions of individuals with sadistic tendencies" who simply "carried out their ordered tasks and followed the rules of the trade to which they were assigned."[20] Rather, the actions and complicity of torturers were part of a larger system that linked torture to the larger social project in ways that made torture the torturer's doing but not exclusively so. If we follow the work of torture through its layered meanings, we find that besides sustaining the overthrow of a particular political system, torture mediates the establishment and preservation of social hierarchies through which subjects and nations come to understand themselves as part of specific political and social projects and which ultimately give birth to a New World Order.

Razack argues that torture is intrinsic to nation-building projects. It enables those who participate in them to "mark the boundary between self and other."[21] In other words, besides advancing specific political and social enterprises, torture helps constitute hegemonic subjects who, as they carry out torture, understand themselves to be part of a complex process in which discourses of difference and (in the case of Chile) communist subversion are deployed so as to produce an image of the Other that justifies torture. Thus, by inflicting intimate violence, individuals turn themselves into citizen-subjects by inscribing the hegemonic project on the victim's body. "Torture links the body to the state," argues Razack, suggesting that the practice of torture submits bodies, the prisoner, and the torturer to the biopolitics of a new social order.[22] Torture, Razack continues, is not designed simply to obtain information; it is also meant to "stake" identity on bodies of victims and torturers, imprinting on them the power of the state.

The permanent erasure of the body is not intrinsic to the work of torture. What *is* intrinsic is the body's permanent inscription within a power regime that requires not the death of the victim, but rather that victim's continuous presence as both cautionary tale and as terrain for the ongoing work of power. Building on Foucault's concept of biopower, Agamben argues that totalitarian terror and by extension torture reflect a heightened preoccupation with the role of human life and the body[23] – which Agamben calls *bare life* – in the constitution of modern conceptions of power, their connection to the construction of the modern nation-state, and their inseparable relation to citizenship. Modernity, continues Agamben, requires power to capture bare life in order to place it within knowledge–power regimes that ultimately render life knowable as well as classifiable into citizen and *homo sacer* – the latter referring to life that while excluded from society is fundamental to the constitution of citizen and nation. To be clear, *homo sacer*, which the tortured victim comes to embody, is the life not excluded from but rather *captured* by the grip of power, which authorizes the constitution of the nation, the subjectification of the citizen, and the design and implementation of those institutional procedures and practices that render the state's power over life thinkable and practicable. The location of *homo sacer* is one of *exclusive inclusion*, continues Agamben, in which "human life is included in the political order" insofar as it is subject to systematic relegation to spaces (the camp, the asylum, the prison) in which its subjugation, elimination, and extermination are not just authorized but necessary.[24]

In her work on pain and the body, Elaine Scarry argues that torture inscribes power on bodies by, simultaneously and in mutually sustaining ways, giving voice to the torturer and rendering the tortured victim silent.[25] In other words, torture mediates the torturer's claim to be the voice of the state through the violent silencing of the prisoner. Torture, continues Scarry, transforms the "body [of the torturer] into voice": a voice that she associates with a sense of self that allows subjects to use language to project themselves onto the world.[26] "Through this ability to project words and sounds into his environment," continues Scarry, "a human being inhabits, humanizes and makes his own space much larger than that occupied by his body alone."[27] Torture grants the torturer the capacity to transform himself into voice, to brutally project himself onto his environment, inscribing and inflicting himself on the prisoner. He becomes a voice that demands the submission and destruction of the prisoner for "the question, whatever its content, is an act of wounding."[28] The state invests the torturer with its voice, for let us not forget that it is the state that grants the power to systematically torture; this is not a common crime. The state provides the torturer with a repertoire of words, symbols, expressions, and truths that through repetition and internalization, as Razack suggests, allow the torturer to know himself as part of a national project, to be part of the moral universe provided by totalitarianism.[29] In this sense, while the body of the torturer becomes voice through torture, it is only voice as long as it embodies the power of a voiceless entity – totalitarianism, or God in Scarry's case.[30] This is not to say that torturers are powerless cogs in the machine of torture. Torturers are the voice of the state because they embody the state; they use it to make themselves subjects, and they understand their role in torturing prisoners as part of a great project of which they are a part.

The transformation of body into voice is predicated, continues Scarry, on the inverted effect of torture on the prisoner. Torture returns the prisoner to the state that preceded language, transforming him into a voiceless body that betrays and hurts the prisoner. The tortured body makes sounds, but his voice has become "a weapon against him, made to betray him on behalf of the enemy, made to be the enemy."[31] This accomplishes the ultimate destruction of the self, its transformation into an entity without identity or voice. Thus, torture cannot simply be explained as a process for obtaining a confession, for confession rarely ends the torture and the content of confession only has value if the torturer assigns it value. As Nelly Richard argues, giving up names ultimately deprives the prisoner of voice; voice becomes "unusable" sounds and screams that only the torturer can convert into "usable signification."[32] Torture is thus an identity-making practice that requires the destruction of the tortured self: the transformation through the act of forced confession into a voiceless body that only speaks what the torturer demands. When torture achieves this transformation, argues Idelver Avelar, the torturer becomes subject through the "brutal act of de-subjectification" of the prisoner.[33]

The overwhelming presence of the body in torture is further sustained by the calculated rendering of the body so that it is minutely observable through the "fragmenting action" of the torture machine and through the merciless eye of the torturer, who examines, fragments, positions, probes, and penetrates in order to anatomically uncover the body's secret information and turn it into usable information or a tool for terrorization. Torture, in this way, is a corporeal technology that reduces the body to object. Yet as object, the body does not disappear or become discarded; it remains the terrain on which can be accomplished the subjectification of the torturer, the nation-building project, and the New World Order (in the context of the politics of the Cold War and its globalized socio-economic and political implications for the global South). It is critical to reiterate here that besides giving birth to new subjects, torture helps consolidate a political, economic, and social order that constitutes the perfect habitat for the subject who claims citizenship and subjecthood through torture.[34] In the context of the knowledge–power relations that produce enemies of the state and mediate their torture, a specific concept of nation becomes naturalized: a nation in which communism is the enemy and capitalism the salvation. In this way, Macarena Gomez-Barris argues, torture "cannot be separated from the neo-liberal turn of the nation: It was, after all, through severe punishment of the social and individual body that the military state imposed its multifold project of 'fiscal discipline,' free trade, flexibilization of labor, the privatization of state enterprises, and the reentrance of the nation into global capitalist economic structures."[35]

Torture, then, cannot be separated from the other phases of the authoritarian regime, for without torture, authoritarianism could not have achieved such a thorough social reordering. Nor could the negotiated transition to liberal democracy have been possible without torture, in the sense that the investigation of torture served as a tool for neutralizing alternative ideologies and political differences, and this ultimately created the environment for a negotiated transition based on a politics of consensus that rendered innocuous and irrelevant the conflicts of the past.[36] The authoritarian regime, then, would not have had the same impact had it not expressed its power on the surface of bodies. Yet the success of the transition cannot be separated from torture either, for its existence has been cemented first by torture and later by the investigation of torture.

Accounting for Torture

On 12 August 2003, President Ricardo Lagos announced the creation of the Torture Commission to investigate cases of political imprisonment and torture committed during the authoritarian regime. The commission's members included eight representatives of the country's political, social, and religious sectors; excluded were representatives of human rights organizations and members of the Association of Ex-Political Prisoners. It was given six months to collect and organize testimonies of torture and political imprisonment and to prepare a report. That report, released on 29 November 2004, was based on testimony given by 35,868 people, of whom 27,255 were regarded as legitimate cases of torture and political imprisonment.[37] Michelle Bachelet, Lagos's successor, reconvened the commission in 2010, and 32,000 new cases were reviewed. Of these, 9,795 were officially recognized as cases of torture in the commission's August 2011 report.

The Torture Commission had as its mandate to end the "conspiracy of silence about torture that had slowly extended throughout the country." This mandate challenged the commission to "truthfully *prov[e]* torture thirty years later" with "more than *30,000 people… parad[ing]*" in front of the commission's offices.[38] To address this challenge, the commission developed methods for collecting and verifying massive numbers of claims and then organizing and presenting them in a coherent manner as a generalized truth about torture. Thus, the production of a national truth about torture was regulated by two key processes: a gathering and verification process, the objective of which was to collect individual testimonies and render them legitimate in order to prove that torture was practised; and a process for organizing those verified testimonies into a generalized truth in the form of a report. The power of the commission over the bodies of torture survivors was observable both during the gathering and verification process and during the process of organizing torture stories into a report. During the gathering and verification of torture testimonies, tortured survivors were required to exhibit the wounds of torture, to make their bodies visible and the object of observation and evaluation by the commission's staff. During the report-writing process, torture stories were subjected to fragmentation and calculation as well as organizing practices that allowed the commission to fashion a report that accounted, in a summarized manner, for the large number of torture testimonies heard by the commission. In this way, the commission's power to hear, verify, and organize resembled the biopolitical effects of torture.

The carefully bureaucratic process of gathering torture claims entails gathering massive amounts of data; more disturbing, this process resembles the intimate encounter between the voice of the state embodied in the state worker and the body of the torture victim that accomplished the biopolitical function of torture in the first place. Unlike the public trials of army generals in Argentina and the public hearings of the South African TRC, Chile's TRCs have bureaucratized their collection of testimony so that it centres on documentation and administration. During the Torture Commission, those who claimed that they had been tortured were required to fill out an application for a one-hour interview with one of the TRC's fifty staff. Most of those staff were lawyers, psychologists, or social workers, who met individually with applicants, collected their testimonies in an "impartial and objective manner," and assembled a file for later evaluation and verification.[39] The application collected demographic information as well as information about the "conditions of the arrest," including a detailed description of the torture and of the place where it was conducted.[40] Applicants were required to provide supporting documentation, such as copies of applications for habeas corpus and certificates provided by the police or military institution that carried out the arrest. They were also required to describe torture centres in detail so that their descriptions could be compared with those of other victims. In this way, they would be able to "prove that they in fact were in the torture centre they claimed to be."[41] The application form functioned as a cap on the information collected so as to simplify the investigators' work: "In order not to create false expectations about information that was not pertinent, the applicant had to fill out a form that collected solely the information we were interested in. The form also reduced the amount of information in order to allow us to do the work in the limited amount of time we had."[42]

The application was the starting point for the interview between the applicant and a member of the TRC team. In those interviews, applicants were again required to "describe incidents of torture in a summarized and brief manner" so that the torture could again be entered into the questionnaire.[43] After they had narrated the events "without interruption on the part of the professionals ... necessary questions could be asked so as to obtain precise details to facilitate the later investigation and verification process."[44] After the interview, the TRC employee was required to "review the information and supporting documentation and consign the information to an electronic file" that constituted the official "entry point into the Commission's database."[45]

These procedures describe a bureaucratic, calculated, and uniform process of data collection that transforms individual stories of torture into data that can later be subjected to analysis, investigation, and verification. The process is driven by individual forms and by individual stories of torture – stories that victims are required to narrate in detail – but does not focus on the particularities of these stories. The ultimate objective is to produce units of forensic information. While relying on careful examination of the individual victims' wounds, the data gathering is meant to produce undifferentiated units of analysis.[46] Just as with the torture itself, the body and its multiple wounds are made temporarily emphatically present by the state worker's examining eye within a regulated face-to-face encounter; the tortured body must exhibit its wounds for the state worker to see, measure, legitimize, and produce as a torture case. The tortured body is rendered here as a unit of analysis that is subjected to observation, comparison, and measurement in order to render a "pass" or "fail"; this erases the survivor's voice and turns testimonies into information, files, and data. The data become a stand-in for the tortured body, for use in producing a national truth that forces the tortured body to speak what the state demands. Meanwhile, the body itself is forced back into silence, again becoming a voiceless entity on which both torture and the extraction of torture testimonies have been inflicted.

Cornejo, Rojas, and Mendoza have observed that the professionals who gather the testimonies pay a high personal and emotional cost. They must maintain an impartial and detached stance as they gather data about horrendous tortures. What is vital to remember here is the impact of this intimate encounter between the "state listeners" and the torture victim.[47] It is, after all, during this encounter that the data-gathering procedure is inflicted on the torture victim and that processes of subject formation are repeated. In many important ways, these intimate encounters resemble the torture itself. On the one hand, they are encounters between a torture victim and a professional state listener; once again, the tortured body is being captured in the technology of data gathering so that those data can be transformed into the *materia prima* for constructing a national truth: a truth that imposes the state's voice on torture accounts. On the other hand, in the intimacy of the interview, the listening professional, as Razack suggests, building on Sarah Ahmed's work on encounters, "is able to 'become without becoming': to become the vicariously traumatized subject that witnesses and claims the trauma of torture without actually being tortured."[48] Through the decentralization and desubjectification of the torture victim, the state worker becomes the subject; as Razack observes, the encounter allows the subject – the state worker in the torture case – to transform himself while the victim remains simply "the mechanism for his transformation."[49]

The listening professional becomes the subject also through the agency and pleasure associated with listening. As Cornejo, Rojas, and Mendoza's research indicates, listening to torture testimonies transforms state workers into keepers of a secret that is often felt as a burden but that also marks them as keepers of a sacred knowledge that ultimately transforms the worker into a subject.[50] This process is mediated through the act of transforming the secret of torture into a national truth – an act that allows the listener to both "collect testimonies, corroborate them [and finally] use them to remake history."[51] The trauma of the torture survivor becomes secondary: it is simply the mediator of the subjectification process undergone by the state listener and later by the nation, which can experience itself as compassionate and humanitarian as it reads the torture report and accepts its truth.

The second moment in which the biopolitical function of the Torture Commission becomes evident is located in the highly regulated process for analysing torture stories and organizing them into a generalized narrative of torture for presentation to the nation in the form of a TRC report. Two biopolitical technologies are evident here: the methodical statistical organization of torture stories, and the heavily regulated inclusion of testimonies in the report's narrative. Together these technologies contribute to the discursive dispersion as well as the specific production of an entity that becomes known as the torture victim.

Once the commission had collected testimonies of torture and subjected them to a "rigorous process of analysis and validation," those cases that were deemed legitimate became units of statistical analysis and management. Confusion was reduced by grouping stories of torture into measurable categories.[52] The methodology guiding the "quantitative analysis" of cases involved "the definition of variables and categorization of the available data according to those variables."[53] Individual experiences of torture were captured within generalized quantifiable instruments of data management that produced a population of tortured bodies with specific demographic characteristics. The resulting report is an example of positivist and reductionist methods of data management. Its language is painstakingly statistical; the victims have been turned into graphs and tables. They have been compared, ranked, and generalized in ways that serve to fragment and decontextualize torture. The report groups victims into graphs so that they can be compared and classified according to categories such as gender, age, occupation, political affiliation, and organizational involvement.

This statistical language extends to the analysis of torture practices. Methods of torture are described in minute detail, using percentage figures to support classifications. We see here the entrance of disciplinary technologies that capture, minutely and individually manage, and fragment tortured bodies in ways that have allowed the report to organize a sort of massive autopsy. The experience of torture has been dissected, examined, and inspected in great detail in order to produce, with the support of statistics, a "complete truth" about torture. The report perpetuates the permanent exposure of torture wounds by discursively materializing the act of torture in countless details that multiply and atomize the torture experience. Statistical language continues to dominate; categories of torture such as "repeated beating," "mutilations," "hangings," "electric shock," "mocked executions," and "rape" are supported with figures on how many victims said they had experienced one or more of these forms of torture.[54] Methods of torture become systematized and classified. Torture experiences are forced to find their meaning within these systems and classifications and are subjected to statistical variables.

Woven into the statistical language are carefully chosen excerpts from personal testimonies, but once again, these testimonies are fragmented as well as fixed at a specific moment of terror. The report subjects these testimonies to discipline and surveillance and makes them speak to the statistical language; the testimonies are being used strategically to buttress the statistical data. Testimonies are carefully controlled so that they never disrupt the report's positivist narrative and statistical organization. They are allowed into the report only in relation to the classification instruments determined by the statistics. For instance, after providing a short definition of torture by electric shock and offering a statistical figure of how many victims experienced this form of torture, the report includes excerpts of testimonies. In the following example, the testimony is used to confirm the definition of torture and indicate its statistical significance: "they positioned me naked on the grill and they applied electricity to my hands, ankles, head and testicles. I lost consciousness and they woke me by throwing icy water on me."[55]

When the report turns to the issue of sexual torture, images of raped bodies of women, sodomized bodies of men, and bodies penetrated by animals or by instruments make their appearance. Once again, statistics serve as the organizing instrument. We learn, for example, that approximately 3,400 women experienced some form of sexual torture and that 316 were actually raped; that 229 were subjected to torture while pregnant; and that 20 suffered abortions and 15 gave birth while in prison.[56] Excerpts from testimonies again sustain the classifying method. Most of these testimonies are quite graphic and disconcerting and are meant to confirm the report's classifications and claims. They amount to an endless chain of torture moments that sustain and confirm the report's organized and systematic truth; they become windows into histories of terror that illuminate the violent encounter.

Data management technologies, supported by carefully introduced testimonies, have the effect of constructing a social category: the tortured body reduced to classifications such as age, gender, method of torture, and so on. The positivist and reductionist process of presenting the information reduces complex personal experiences to manageable information that can be included in the national narrative in a non-threatening manner. The process is intrinsically violent not only in its reductionism but also in its temporal paralysing effect. The reduction of torture to statistics not only empties the experience of torture of any complexity, agency, or historical context but also pins the tortured body to the moment of horror: the tortured body is always portrayed only in his/her moment of violence, it is allowed to speak only of the horror, the rape, the electric shock. The statistical classification of bodies by data management systems generates undistinguished stories of pain that are valid only in their capacity to fit within the imposed categories; the testimonial irruptions then individualize the pain, making it possible for the reader to see the tortured body in its totality and specificity. This dual portrayal of the pain, imposed as described here, functions as a repetition of the violence, which highlights again how the report imposes its biopolitical function on the life it is charged with describing.

Conclusion

The Torture Commission is an example of what Agamben calls a "double-sided political event": its report has granted recognition to stories of torture even while submitting life to new and ongoing forms of biopolitical regulation.[57] Survivors may experience the act of speaking about torture as liberating and as a precondition for inclusion in the post-authoritarian nation; yet that same act carries within it the possibility, indeed the certainty, of further submission to the biopolitical power of the state, which is now exercised through politics of recognition and reconciliation. In this way, speaking of torture does not disrupt but in fact *reinscribes* the biopolitical work that torture originally accomplished, even granting that such biopolitics are now being deployed for the purpose of acknowledgment.

This presents concrete challenges for any attempt to imagine fairer governmental processes for documenting torture. Michalinos Zembylas, building on Levinasian ethics, argues that processes of mourning and documentation should resist the historicist temptation to reduce experiences of suffering to generalized narratives.[58] Sergio Villalobos-Ruminott proposes a materially and historically grounded approach that would examine the power relations that determine "the hand with which history is written."[59] Approaches such as Zembylas's would resist universalizing and generalizing experiences of suffering, but they would also lead to rather existential forms of remembrance and mourning. Thus, they would risk removing practices of remembrance from power relations and political projects centred on torture and perpetuated through practices of remembrance. Villalobos-Ruminott opens up the possibility for a political and critical approach that would interrogate the conditions under which remembrance took place, highlighting and materializing the power relations and practices of exclusion that determine how torture is remembered. More inclusive processes of nation building, he suggests, require that we take into account who is telling stories of torture and who is deciding what is done with them.

Perhaps if different hands were to write stories of torture, they would capture not only the countless moments of terror in which victims became voiceless bodies but also the minute moments and the at times (by comparison) minor instances in which solidarity, mutual comforting, embracing, and beholding gave survivors the strength to resist one more day. Perhaps we would find in these stories the vestiges of dreams, of memories, of the friendly eye that Jacobo Timerman affectionately remembers looking at him through the open peephole of the cell across the hall.[60] Perhaps we would be able to read in those stories about more than terror; perhaps we would find in them a different expression of human life captured through the power of discourse. Perhaps these stories would also shed light on the political projects accomplished through torture and consolidated through national reconciliation discourse. Avelar suggests that a truth-telling process controlled by survivors might result in "more pluralistic processes of subject formation" in which the "voice of the tortured subjects" could exist, coexist, and resist in spite of and beyond the practice of torture.[61]

As long as the telling of histories of torture is organized primarily from the centralized location of the state and within power relations that were established and cemented through torture, the documentation of torture will continue to exclude torture victims and give precedence to the hegemonic hand that writes history. As Razack suggests, when a national history of innocence is at the centre of collectivist accounts of violence, we run the risk of purposely avoiding seeing the power relations and the histories of domination that continue to rely on torture and in which we are embedded.[62] Within these narratives, torture cannot be rendered critically and politically intelligible, for the history of innocence prevents us from granting victims the status of subjects. More transformative and just processes of telling the truth require that we find ways to upset, as Diana Taylor suggests, these unequal power relations by aligning ourselves with strategies that open up spaces for victims and survivors to exercise truth-telling power.[63] The victims that the TRC reports allow us to see might be allowed to look back at us from their own truth narrative and tell us something more about ourselves. Taylor argues that a reciprocal and political practice of gazing – and, I argue, truth telling – can catch the spectator, those for whom the story is told, "off balance in the spectorial gaze, suddenly aware that the object of the gaze is also the subject who looks back, who challenges and objectifies us," making visible "the specificities of our position, and the ensuing limits to our perspective."[64]

Such truth telling may force us to locate ourselves politically, economically, and historically in the story of torture, thereby forcing us to accept more fully the "heavy weight of sorrow" that goes with the political act of witnessing.[65] This reciprocal relationship may push us to critically and politically think about terror and our complicity in it, avoiding what Razack argues is the unproblematic humanitarian contemplation of terror that allows us to consume terror stories without having to think about our role in them.[66] If we are to be more fully accountable for the past, we need to ask ourselves what we gain from processes of truth telling and what the implications are of granting survivors the power to gaze back at us through their own truth-telling processes. Finally, a critical approach to accounting for torture requires that we disrupt the systems of domination that sustained violence to begin with and their continuation in contemporary politics.

NOTES

The research on which this essay is built was partly funded by the Doctoral Fellowship of the Canadian International Development Research Centre. I would also like to acknowledge the research assistance of Leanne Gislason and the editorial work of Catherine van Mossel.

1 Martin Grass cited in Feitlowitz, *A Lexicon of Terror*, 8.
2 Cámara de Diputados / Chamber of Deputies, Minutes of Proceedings / Diario de Sesiones, 31st Sess., 352nd Congress, *Ley No 19.992: Establece*

pensión de reparación y otorga otros beneficios a favor de las personas que indica, 15 December 2004, 30.

3 A poignant example of the use of torture in advertisements is the now infamous campaign by a major department store in Chile in which images of torture were used to advertise a new brand of jeans.

4 Foucault, *The History of Sexuality*; Foucault, *Power/Knowledge.*

5 Foucault, *The History of Sexuality*, 136–9.

6 C. Gordon, "Governmental Rationality."

7 Foucault, *The History of Sexuality*, 139; italics in the original.

8 Agamben, *Homo Sacer*, 119.

9 Foucault, *Discipline and Punish*, 136.

10 Foucault, *Discipline and Punish*, 136.

11 Razack, "Racism, Empire, and Torture," para. 4.

12 In addition to these two commissions, Chile instituted in 1999 a Human Rights Discussion Table or *Mesa de Dialogo* with the mandate to promote dialogue between representatives of different sectors of society and the Armed Forces in order to find the whereabouts of detained and disappeared people. This panel, however, does not qualify as a Truth Commission, for it did not produce a report.

13 In the last few years, TRCs have also begun to appear in white settler societies such as Canada as strategies to account for colonial histories and their impact on indigenous peoples.

14 Rubenstein, "The Bureaucratization of Torture," 33.

15 Reszczynski, Rojas, and Barceló, *Torture et Résistance au Chili*; Stanley, "Torture, Silence, and Recognition"; and Stover, *The Open Secret*. See these works for examples of research on the organization of torture and its routine character in Chile.

16 Comisión Etica Contra la Tortura, *Informe de la Comisión Etica*; Arce, *The Inferno*; Rojas, *Tejas Verdes*. In addition to the Torture Report, reports by human rights activist organizations such as the Ethical Commission Against Torture and the testimonial work of survivors such as Arce and Rojas constitute important sources for mapping the detailed and consistent practice of torture in Chile.

17 Lira, "Psicología."

18 Moulian, *Chile Actual*, 25.

19 Lazreg, *Torture and the Twilight of Empire*, 6.

20 Moulian, *Chile Actual*, 174, 175.

21 Razack, *Casting Out*, 79.

22 Razack, "Racism, Empire and Torture," para. 7.

23 Agamben, *Homo Sacer*, 83.

24 Agamben, *Homo Sacer*, 85.

25 Scarry, *The Body in Pain*.

26 Scarry, *The Body in Pain*, 45.

27 Scarry, *The Body in Pain*, 49.

28 Scarry, *The Body in Pain*, 46.

29 Razack, *Dark Threats and White Nights*, 160.

30 Scarry, *The Body in Pain*, 200. Scarry writes in her study of the Bible: "As God in the sense of hurt is a bodiless voice, so men and women are voiceless bodies. God is their voice; they have none separate from him."

31 Scarry, *The Body in Pain*, 48.

32 Richard, *Residuos y Metaforas*, 65.

33 Avelar, "La Práctica de la Tortura," 168.

34 Grandmaison, "Violencias Extremas," 135–56.

35 Gomez-Barris, "Torture Sees and Speaks," 87.

36 Richard, *Residuos y Metaforas*, 27.

37 CNPP, *Informe de la Comisión Nacional sobre Prisión Política y Tortura*, 34.

38 CNPP, *Informe*, 18; italics added.

39 CNPP, *Informe*, 33–4.

40 CNPP, *Informe*, 41–2.

41 Maria Luisa Sepulveda, General Secretary of the National Commission on Political Imprisonment and Torture, in discussion with the author, Santiago, April 2005.

42 Sepulveda, discussion with author, April 2005.

43 CNPP, *Informe*, 41.

44 CNPP, *Informe*, 42.

45 CNPP, *Informe*, 42.

46 Wilson, *The Politics of Truth and Reconciliation*, 19. Even though he does not adhere to a biopolitical analysis, the concept of "forensic information" is used here in a manner analogous to what Wilson identifies as the forensic model that took over after the public hearings of the South African TRC and that regulated the management of the information collected in the hearings.

47 Cornejo, Rojas, and Mendoza, "From Testimony to Life Story."

48 Razack, "Stealing the Pain of Others," 379.

49 Razack, "Stealing the Pain of Others," 379.

50 Cornejo, Rojas, and Mendoza, "From Testimony to Life Story," 126–7.

51 Sepulveda, discussion with author, April 2005.

52 CNPP, *Informe*, 74; Neu, "Accounting and Accountability Relations"; Poovey, *A History of the Modern Fact*. Neu and Poovey provide valuable analysis of the governmental role of statistics.

53 CNPP, *Informe*, 469–76.

54 CNPP, *Informe*, 226–42.
55 CNPP, *Informe*, 234. The *parrilla* or grill is a contraption made out of a bed frame to which electric cables have been connected. Prisoners are made to lie down on that frame; they are tied down while electrodes are attached to different parts of their body. This quote is included in the text of the report and is attributed to a survivor of torture.
56 CNPP, *Informe*, 242, 252.
57 Agamben, *Homo Sacer*, 121.
58 Zembylas, "Bearing Witness," 223.
59 Villabos-Ruminott, "Fin de la Dictadura y Destrabajo del Pensar," 73.
60 Timerman, *Prisoner without and Name, Cell without a Number*.
61 Avelar, "La Práctica de la Tortura," 183.
62 Razack, "Stealing the Pain of Others," 391.
63 Taylor, *Disappearing Acts*.
64 Taylor, *Disappearing Acts*, 261.
65 Taylor, *Disappearing Acts*, 265
66 Razack, "Stealing the Pain of Others," 387.

SECTION FOUR

Thinking Humanitarianism /
Thinking Terror

17 Introduction to Section Four

GULZAR R. CHARANIA

I am presently reading Sarah Schulman's *Israel/Palestine and the Queer International*.[1] I was drawn to it partly because I am curious about people's political investments, how we learn to care about certain things, people, and places. As Schulman maps out in her "long, subtle, slow, stubborn journey"[2] regarding Israel and Palestine, we need to account for our carings and not carings. I bring up Schulman in the context of these remarkable chapters because they too ask us to account for what it means to respond to suffering, oppression, and terror and the ways in which our caring comes to be articulated through messy humanitarian interventions. They point to the uneasy entanglements of caring with practices of state surveillance, regulation, and militarization. While the chapters provide no easy answers, they open up a productive set of disparate but related questions about the histories, current mobilizations, and expanding nature of terror and humanitarian regimes. They also insist that we think critically and collectively about other ways to care.

As the authors track terror and the humanitarian impulse in places that might be more or less familiar, they ask us to consider how we, as Westerners or as Southern elites, are often placed in and place ourselves in the role of what Inderpal Grewal refers to as the "adjudicating subject," that is, the subject who determines who and what is deserving of our care. These adjudications advance a particular global order and accompanying constellations of power, but there is often little transparency about the specific locations and histories from which they are enunciated. To put it simply, the places and priorities from which we judge are obfuscated. These scholars lay bare these inclinations. And of course, far-off places can sometimes be comforting because distance allows lack of implication. These authors insist that we read across distances and categories of here and there, North and South, majority and minority, human and non-human, settler and citizen, in all of their complexities and unevenness. This leads us back to the fundamental problem of how and what to care about as well as to questions of ethics, accountability, and political life.

The authors of the following chapters provide many compelling entry points for thinking about terror historically, relationally, and with all its gendered and racialized complexities, but it is to the issue of time that I first turn. What is terror's time? Or perhaps more accurately, what does terror *do* to time? How does terror mobilize time, recast it, stop it, suspend it, speed it up, compress it, and demarcate it? At the heart of these questions is a preoccupation with the past: its uses, its selective containment, and how it can be harnessed not only to national and imperial futures but also to futures denied and rendered unimaginable. In other words, these chapters specify the geopolitics of terror, time, space, and memory. They attend to its instrumentality in consolidating the interrelated logics of settler colonialism, imperial expansion, and national innocence. Read across and against one another, the chapters track how "terror" travels and the work it does as it travels. Terror shows itself through brute force but also through the stories it tells and how it organizes life for people in material and incredibly devastating ways. Yet terror is also terrifyingly productive. It turns out to be a practice – both spectacular and ordinary, a legal apparatus, a cultural signifier, a bureaucratic system, a flight manifest, a job, an opportunity, a market, and a pedagogical tool. Terror's lesson is its ability to be many things, to authorize an endless number of wars and interventions. Reading through this set of chapters makes clear that terror's capaciousness can be conveniently and disturbingly harnessed.

Second and perhaps most importantly, the authors in this section ask us to put terror and humanitarianism in conversation and to consider their proximity to each other. They are not as strange to each other as we might suspect. These scholars disturb humanitarianism's presumed innocence so that it becomes less an antidote to terror and at times the mechanism of its expansion. The state-driven workings of truth and reconciliation commissions, the intensification of security and military interventions, concerns about protecting women, children, and even animals, variably rely on and produce the Western or imperial humanitarian subject alongside the passive recipient of such supposed benevolence. The shifting categories of deserving or not, victim or threat, among others, are complicated by proximity and distance, by relations of power and what is at stake. The scholars here insist that we take stock of the racialized and racially inflected gendered hierarchies produced by such a "bifurcated international system"[3] with its deepening divide of "sovereignty and citizenship" on the one hand and "trusteeship and wardship" on the other.[4] In their own ways, each points out that such ahistoricized relationships and gestures do not get us closer to thinking about a responsive politics that centres justice and political agency. The question of justice also requires a re-engagement with time that is outside of the "temporal present" of the humanitarian crisis.[5] For it turns out that, like terror, humanitarianism turns on a perpetual present that quickens the arrival of particular futures while foreclosing others.

The chapters assembled in this section, either centrally or at their edges, gesture to the risks of engaging narratives of violence and terror. Knowledge production in places such as the academy is fraught with difficult and complicitous histories, institutional constraints, and its own regulatory mechanisms. Stories, lives, and experiences cut short, irreparably harmed, and struggled for and through can be and often are recuperated into various state, international, and power–knowledge regimes that purport to recognize or address the legacies of terror while simultaneously advancing and authorizing it. It turns out that colonial and imperial terror have quite a lot to do with organizing systems of knowledge, with specific knowings and forgettings, with the turning of socially produced desperation into pathologized people and populations who require more policing and management, more healing and instruction. There is no talk of justice; instead there are selective recollections of history, and conveniently little attention is paid to land and resources that, like the people, seem to be in need of increased oversight and control. But narrating terror from the position of less circulated "subaltern histories"[6] can also instruct us in its contested genealogies, with corresponding attempts to prioritize or disappear certain bodies, struggles, and relations of power. Doing so makes clear the circulation of "new forms of state racism,"[7] which are often recycled from and reliant on much older technologies of racial governance, with revived and shifting targets of intervention. Taking stock of anti-colonial and anti-racist struggles reveals terror's imperfect efforts to discipline and silence[8] and further suggests forms of intervention, response, and political imagination that are desperately required.

While I certainly read this set of extraordinary chapters through the lens of my own intellectual preoccupations, I am left wondering if a different orientation to terror and humanitarianism might do something else to and with time, to our mobilizations of the past, to the creation of more livable presents and possible futures. To end, I return to Schulman, because her narrative, like the chapters here, clears some analytic, affective, and political space to consider how the struggle for solidarity and justice and the refusal of our own "willful ignorance[s]"[9] provide some alternative ways of imagining how else we might care.

NOTES

The author thanks Ruthann Lee, R. Cassandra Lord, and Carmela Murdocca for their comments.

1 Schulman, *Israel/Palestine*.
2 Schulman, *Israel/Palestine*, 1.
3 See Arat-Koç in this volume, referencing Mamdani.
4 See Arat-Koç in this volume, referencing Mamdani.
5 See Ticktin in this volume.
6 See Smith in this volume.
7 See Smith in this volume.
8 See Smith in this volume.
9 Schulman, *Israel/Palestine*, 1.

18 From the Northern Territory Emergency Response to Stronger Futures: Where Is the Evidence That Australian Aboriginal Women Are Leading Self-Determining Lives?

NICOLE WATSON

Introduction

It is now six years since the Northern Territory Emergency Response (NTER), otherwise known as the Intervention, was imposed on thousands of Aboriginal people living in townships throughout the Northern Territory of Australia. The NTER was the Commonwealth's response to allegations that Aboriginal children in remote communities were being subjected to sexual abuse. The measures that fell under the umbrella of the NTER included child health checks, prohibitions on alcohol and pornography, the auditing of computers, the compulsory acquisition of Aboriginal lands, and the quarantining of social security payments.

There was no prior consultation with those who would be forced to live under the measures. Sue Gordon, the former head of the Northern Territory Intervention Taskforce, justified the absence of consultation by reference to the nature of the crisis:

> I have pointed out very clearly that this was an emergency, and if you have an emergency like a tsunami or a cyclone, you don't have time to consult people in the initial phases.
>
> Every day that there's a delay, that means another child is at risk, one way or another. That can be health wise, it can be abuse, something like that. I've been on bodies appointed by four separate Labor governments, looking at abuse and welfare issues. I don't know why we need to delay any further.[1]

The former Minister for Indigenous Affairs, Mal Brough, similarly painted a picture of communities in the throes of a catastrophe. He claimed that "each and every day, children are being abused. We need strong powers so that we are not weighed down by unnecessary red tape and talkfests, and can focus on doing what needs to be done and doing it now."[2]

Six years later, Aboriginal communities are no longer compared to natural disasters, but the Commonwealth's power over Aboriginal lives remains undiminished. In June 2012, the Commonwealth Parliament passed a suite of legislation that effectively extended some of the NTER measures for another ten years.[3] Although the government claimed that the legislation was informed by widespread community consultation, independent analysis suggests that the process was fundamentally flawed.[4] Bipartisan support among the major parties effectively denied the Australian people any meaningful debate over the legislation's provisions. Its passing attracted minimal media coverage, and with the exception of a small number of bodies,[5] criticism within the Australian human rights community has been relatively muted.

To some extent this lack of engagement can be explained by the government's position that the measures are widely supported by Aboriginal women.[6] Also, a small number of high-profile Aboriginal women have publicly expressed their approval of the measures.[7] This chapter takes the position that although the opinions of such individuals should be respected, they are not a stand-alone justification for imposing racially discriminatory measures. A mature public debate would be informed by an analysis of the ways in which NTER measures can affect Aboriginal women, engagement with evidence-based research, and consideration of Aboriginal women's historical experiences of state interventions.

This chapter will argue that earlier state interventions in the name of protecting Aboriginal women invariably resulted in a binary that rendered their rights invisible while simultaneously subjecting them to excessive regulation. This binary finds resonance in key NTER measures. There is little evidence that Aboriginal women are any safer as a result of those measures. Yet they have been deprived of myriad rights, so that the state's long-standing imperative to control Aboriginal women is fulfilled. This chapter has three parts. Part One discusses the history of the binary of invisibility and control. Part Two provides a background to the NTER, and Part Three argues that the binary of invisibility and control finds resonance in key NTER measures.

Part One: The Binary of Invisibility and Control

For over two centuries, racism and patriarchy have shaped the lives of Aboriginal women. As stated by Behrendt:

> The bodies of black women are contested terrain, the spoils of colonial conquest. Aboriginal women, who enjoyed power and respect within their traditional communities, fell to the lowest rung on the socio-economic ladder in colonial society because of the double taint of a subordinated race and a subordinated gender. Through this transferred misogyny many black men have been quick to learn that exploitation of black women was acceptable and quick to forget the status Aboriginal women held in their own communities.[8]

Racism and patriarchy have served to make Aboriginal women's rights invisible. At the same time, their bodies have been subject to excessive regulation. This binary of invisibility and excessive regulation has enabled seemingly contradictory stereotypes of Aboriginal women to coexist. On the one hand, they have been cast as morally permissive women who deviously captivated white men. Alternatively, they have been portrayed as the wretched victims of barbarous Aboriginal men, whose salvation lay in assimilation.

This binary saw the theft of Aboriginal women's land and rampant sexual violence on the frontier. Colonial police forces overlooked the abuse of Aboriginal women and were often complicit in it. Aboriginal women were denied the protection of the rule of law, but at the same time they were subject to a form of wardship under protectionist legislation, which existed in most parts of Australia during the earlier part of the twentieth century.[9]

An enduring feature of protectionism was the regulation of Aboriginal women's sexuality. Robert has argued that Foucault's theory of "biopower," which designates reproduction and population as mediums through which power operates, finds resonance in the discourses of miscegenation.[10] Aboriginal women's bodies were disciplined at the point of sexual contact with white men and, later, in the implementation of child removal policies. Although Robert's focus was on literary constructions of interracial sex, there were multiple dimensions of this biopower, such as labour arrangements in the pastoral industry that rendered Aboriginal women vulnerable to sexual exploitation. In some jurisdictions, such as Darwin in the earlier part of the twentieth century, biopower operated on the Aboriginal population through compulsory medical checks, forms of identification known as "dog tags," and nightly curfews.[11]

The protectionist system made Aboriginal people vulnerable to indefinite incarceration on remote reserves. Foucault's work revolving around the panopticon finds resonance in the reserve system, under which Aboriginal inmates were subject to various forms of surveillance, such as inspections of wards' homes and the removal of Aboriginal children to dormitories. Many Aboriginal women showed considerable bravery in their attempts to keep their families together in spite of the protectionist regimes. Of one Victorian mother who resisted separation from her young daughter, a frustrated mission superintendent wrote:

> Emily keeps the whole station in a state of ferment & while she remains here there will be no peace. She is clever in a criminal way & has a most insidious and plausible manner ... which generally impresses and imposes upon anyone who does not know her thoroughly – that is what education has done for her.[12]

While Aboriginal women's lives were subject to excessive regulation, their rights – in particular, their labour rights – were invisible. The most common employment for Aboriginal women during the protectionist era was domestic service in white households. Many were denied the ability to manage the paltry wages they were paid, for such wages were usually given to the protector on the ward's behalf.

One of the most humiliating aspects of this system was the need to ask the protector for permission to spend one's own wages. During its inquiry into the treatment of former Aboriginal wards, the Senate Standing Committee on Legal and Constitutional Affairs received evidence from one former ward that she preferred to run away rather than face the continuing degradation of having to ask permission to spend her own money:

> I ran away ... in 1967, just two days after my father's funeral. I borrowed $12 from my married sister rather than go to the police station and be interrogated about what I wanted my money for. Growing up, that is all you saw – our people, my parents, my sisters and other family members being questioned: "What do you want your money for? You don't have any money." It was humiliating and degrading. So I left, a 16½-year-old, and started a new life in Townsville. That $12 was the best investment I have ever made. I educated myself.[13]

Drawing from the English tradition of apprenticing young wards, the New South Wales Aborigines Protection Board adopted a form of compulsory apprenticeships for Aboriginal girls. More than five hundred Aboriginal girls were apprenticed to affluent Sydney households in the earlier part of the twentieth century.[14] The conditions endured by some teenage apprentices could have provided the background for a Dickensian novel. Many worked seven days per week, were underfed, and were denied access to wages, which were managed by the Protection Board.[15]

Welfare payments – in particular, maternity payments – were also liable to be controlled by government institutions. Even when Aboriginal women were allowed some discretion in spending those payments, they were still subject to surveillance. In New South Wales, the Protection Board issued a list of items acceptable for purchase that included food, clothing, and medical treatment. A woman's spending might be scrutinized over several years before she was considered trustworthy.[16]

Like their ancestors, Aboriginal women today continue to grapple with invisibility while at the same time being prone to excessive regulation. In the early 1990s, researchers such as Bolger powerfully elucidated the invisibility of female victims of Aboriginal family violence.[17] Although invisible as victims, Aboriginal women are subject to excessive regulation by the criminal justice system. The first survey of the needs of Aboriginal women in custody was undertaken by the New South Wales Aboriginal Justice Advisory Council in 2003. The result was the ground-breaking report *Speak Out Speak Strong*.[18] At the time of the study, Aboriginal women constituted 31 per cent of the female prison population in New South Wales, which made them the fastest-growing prison population in the country.[19]

Like their ancestors, the participants in *Speak Out Speak Strong* had long experience of the law's regulation but had been denied protection. The results were devastating for them. The report offered disturbing revelations linking childhood sexual abuse to addiction and incarceration. Seventy per cent of the participants had been sexually assaulted as children, and almost all of those women reported having a drug problem.[20] Few of the women had ever had access to a professional counsellor. In light of this history, it beggars belief that anyone would rationally argue that perpetuating the binary of invisibility and control is an answer to the multiple levels of disadvantage endured by Aboriginal women. Yet this is precisely what the NTER has delivered.

Part Two: The NTER

In the two decades that preceded the NTER, numerous reports had attested to the suffering of Aboriginal victims of sexual abuse.[21] Perhaps what was different in 2007 was its public airing. In the lead-up to Prime Minister John Howard's announcement of the NTER on 21 June, the ABC television program *Lateline* publicized shocking allegations of pedophile rings operating in the Northern Territory.[22]

Those allegations were followed by the public release of a report by the Northern Territory Board of Inquiry into the Protection of Aboriginal Children from Sexual Abuse, *Ampe Akelyernemane Meke Mekarle, "Little Children Are Sacred."*[23] The report painted a horrific picture of communities in the throes of addiction and dysfunction. The report was unequivocal in its demand that governments abandon imposed solutions in favour of working in partnership with communities. The need for a new approach was all the more pressing given the "sufficient evidence to show that well-resourced programs that are owned and run by the community are more successful than generic, short term, and sometimes inflexible programs imposed on communities."[24] The inquiry's ninety-seven recommendations advocated a holistic response, emphasizing the need for community consultation, family support services, education, employment, and housing.

Sackett has argued that special inquiries are another means of disciplining Aboriginal people in the Foucauldian sense.[25] Inquiries build the state's information reservoir on Aboriginal people, which is then used for the purpose of further intervention into Aboriginal lives. Although Sackett was referring to the Royal Commission into Aboriginal Deaths in Custody, his argument finds resonance in the Commonwealth's response to *Little Children Are Sacred*.

Howard and his Minister for Indigenous Affairs, Mal Brough, both described remote Aboriginal communities as disaster areas where the rule of law had either broken down entirely or was on the verge of collapse. Howard went so far as to describe the crisis as Australia's Hurricane Katrina.[26] But rather than implement the inquiry's recommendations, the Commonwealth imposed a five-year intervention to "stabilize" Aboriginal people.[27]

In August the Commonwealth Parliament passed the voluminous legislative package that would authorize this dramatic stabilization of Aboriginal people.[28] In his second reading of the Northern Territory National Emergency Response Bill, Brough again conjured imagery of a people who had lost their moral compass: "When confronted with a failed society where basic standards of law and order and behaviour have broken down and where women and children are unsafe, how should we respond? Do we respond with more of what we have done in the past? Or do we radically change direction with an intervention strategy matched to the magnitude of the problem?"[29]

The legislation's stated goal was to protect women and children, yet its specifics were not targeted to either group. Rather, well-being was to be improved through a series of disciplinary measures, such as an income management regime. Under that regime, varying amounts of income support payments would be quarantined for expenditure on priority needs.[30] The quarantined funds would be held in individual accounts that would commonly be accessed by way of a debit card. Those quarantined funds could not be spent on alcohol, pornographic materials, or gambling.

If Foucault's theory of biopower can be understood as the exercise of power over the bodies of certain populations, we find it reflected in the income management regime. That regime was initially applied on the basis of physical presence in a "relevant Northern Territory area," defined by reference to different forms of Aboriginal land tenure.[31] It was subsequently reformed with the aim of achieving consistency with the Racial Discrimination Act 1975 (Cth).[32] The modified regime was applied throughout the Northern Territory to individuals who fell within certain categories contained in Part 3B of the Social Security (Administration) Act 1999 (Cth).[33] Those categories covered individuals required to be managed for the purpose of child protection, individuals who were classified as vulnerable, disengaged youth, long-term welfare recipients, and those whose children were not meeting school enrolment and attendance requirements.[34]

Foucault's concept of panopticism comes to mind when one considers the various means of surveillance imposed under the rubric of the NTER, such as the auditing of publicly funded computers.[35] The brief of the Australian Crime Commission, a body ordinarily associated with investigating large-scale and organized crime, was expanded to include "Indigenous violence or child abuse."[36] To coordinate implementation of the NTER measures, government business managers (GBMs) were sent into communities. The GBMs exercised broad powers over bodies integral to community life, on behalf of the minister.

Aboriginal populations were to have even greater contact with the criminal justice system as a result of blanket prohibitions on alcohol[37] and changes to the administration of the Northern Territory's criminal justice system. In determining bail and sentencing applications, courts would no longer be able to consider customary law or cultural practices that might mitigate the seriousness of the behaviour in question.[38]

As part of the NTER reforms, the Howard government moved to abolish the largest and most enduring Indigenous employment program, the Community Development Employment Projects Program (CDEP). At the time the legislation was passed, Brough claimed that CDEP would be replaced with "real jobs."[39] Also, moving CDEP workers onto work-for-dole programs would allow for "a single system of income management to apply to welfare payments."[40] This issue is discussed further below.

The Commonwealth's grip on community life extended to land, which is the most substantial asset owned by many communities as well as the lynchpin of culture and identity. The Commonwealth's acquisition of interests in Aboriginal lands was governed by Part Four of the Northern Territory National Emergency Response Act 2007 (Cth). The objectives of Part Four were to improve the delivery of services and promote economic and social development.[41] Five-year leases over certain Aboriginal lands were granted to the Commonwealth,[42] which was entitled to use the subject land for any purpose it considered to be consistent with the objectives of Part Four.[43]

Although protecting children from sexual abuse was supposedly the point of the NTER, the Commonwealth failed to invest in strategies to address the underlying causes of abuse. Programs to develop parenting skills were overlooked, and so was community education to break the cycle of intergenerational abuse.[44] Likewise, the Commonwealth failed to invest in mechanisms to measure child well-being in the Northern Territory.

In June 2008, the Commonwealth appointed a Review Board to assess the NTER. When it reported in October, it identified some positive outcomes, such as an increased police presence in areas that had previously been neglected by law enforcement. However, the board also described a "strong sense of injustice" on the part of many Aboriginal people, who had been painted unfairly as the authors of their own poverty.[45]

This frustration was reflected in the submission of the Australian Indigenous Doctors Association, which revealed that the measures had "created a feeling of 'collective existential despair' ... characterized by a widespread sense of helplessness, hopelessness and worthlessness, and experienced throughout entire community(s)."[46] Those sentiments resounded in a 2010 health impact assessment of the NTER measures, which stated that their intended health outcomes were unlikely to be achieved because of negative impacts on psychological and social well-being.[47]

The NTER Review Board made three overarching recommendations:

- The Australian and Northern Territory Governments recognize as a matter of urgent national significance the continuing need to address the unacceptably high level of disadvantage and social dislocation being experienced by Aboriginal Australians living in remote communities throughout the Northern Territory;
- In addressing these needs both governments acknowledge the requirement to reset their relationship with Aboriginal people based on genuine consultation, engagement and partnership; and
- Government actions affecting the Aboriginal communities respect Australia's human rights obligations and conform with the Racial Discrimination Act 1975 (Cth).[48]

Aboriginal people in the Northern Territory continue to suffer unacceptably high levels of disadvantage, and arguably, those who suffer the most are children. In its submission to the UN Committee on the Rights of the Child, Concerned Australians observed:

> The majority of children growing up in the Northern Territory are most likely to live in unacceptably poor accommodation. There are no guarantees that they will have access to a safe water supply or to a functioning sanitation system. In the majority of cases, despite a recent Government building programme, children will live in overcrowded conditions, and some in situations where the overcrowding and allied problems are extreme.[49]

Recent Developments

In the latter half of 2011, spurred by the looming expiry of some of the NTER measures, the Commonwealth engaged in widespread community consultations. The process began on 22 June of that year with the launch of a discussion paper, *Stronger Futures in the Northern Territory*.[50] That document listed eight areas for future action, with an emphasis on school attendance, employment, and alcohol abuse. The paper's tone suggested that the NTER had improved the lives of Aboriginal people in the Northern Territory.

Five days after the launch of the discussion paper, Aboriginal leaders and other prominent Australians sent a strongly worded letter to the minister in which they expressed their concerns about the poor accessibility of the discussion paper:

> This document of 28 pages including the questions, is provided to Aboriginal communities in the English language.
>
> For these consultations to mark the beginning of a new era of co-operation, it seems to us that these critical questions, through which Government hopes to determine the views of the people, should be provided in languages common to the five Regions of consultation and in hard copy for the purpose of circulation to those living in homelands and without computer access ...
>
> It is understood from the Department that the itinerary for these consultations is not yet available. However it is our understanding that it is intended that they will commence within a matter of days. We consider it essential to provide a minimum of one month before commencing such consultations in order to enable community leaders to hold discussions with their people, some of whom will be required to travel considerable distances.[51]

These concerns were ignored. Just six days after the launch of the discussion paper, the first consultation meeting was held in Tennant Creek.[52] Between what remained of June and August, consultation meetings were convened in more than one hundred Aboriginal communities in the Northern Territory. All meetings were facilitated by staff of the Department of Families, Housing, Community Services and Indigenous Affairs, who controlled the agenda and recorded the conversations.[53] The Commonwealth has yet to make those records publicly available. However, a representative sample of transcripts suggests that specific proposals being considered by the government were not revealed.[54]

On 23 November 2011, the government tabled three bills under the umbrella of "Stronger Futures in the Northern Territory."[55] The package effectively continued many of the NTER measures discussed above. Together with their explanatory memoranda, the three bills ran to over three hundred pages. Even for lawyers, unravelling the legislation was an onerous task because it required reference to earlier legislation. It beggars belief that the general consultations conducted between June and August could have provided the foundations for such an intricate result. Nonetheless, the legislation was passed by the Australian Senate in the early hours of Friday, 29 June, after a debate that had only begun on Thursday evening.

The Public Debate over the NTER

Debate over the NTER measures has to some extent been overshadowed by the diversity of opinion among a handful of high-profile Aboriginal women. This has been represented in the media as reflecting a division between Aboriginal people in the remote north and those in cities on the eastern seaboard.[56] In reality however, Aboriginal women's opinions are not defined by geography. Both supporters and opponents of the NTER can be found throughout Australia.

This diversity of opinion should be expected. An individual's opinion is shaped by an unknowable number of conscious and subconscious factors, such as family history, education, religion, and professional associations. These factors will inevitably come to the fore in any discussion about an issue as complex as child abuse. What I find startling is the often unarticulated but strongly held view that Aboriginal women should not disagree with one another. In particular, debate among Aboriginal women scholars is a logical outcome not only of our vocation but also of our diverse backgrounds and expertise.

Arguably, the most prominent Aboriginal woman scholar who has written in support of the NTER is Marcia Langton. She has written two papers on the NTER, both of which were published in the *Griffith Review*. The title of the first, "Trapped in the Aboriginal Reality Show,"[57] is a reference to the voyeuristic imagery of violence in Aboriginal communities, imagery that has become a macabre form of entertainment in Australian public life.

Many critics of the NTER would agree with Langton when she argues that the crises in remote communities are rooted in twenty-five years of neglect by successive Northern Territory governments. Likewise, the violence against women and children that Langton so powerfully describes is not denied by most critics of the NTER measures. Langton argues that by the time that the NTER was announced, the crises had reached the point when prior consultation would have been an "indulgent fantasy."[58] Once again, few critics would claim that decisive and urgent action was not required; most, though, have deferred to the recommendations in *Little Children Are Sacred*.

Langton appears to defend the NTER on the basis that it is precisely what many have sought for decades – "protective interventions to prevent the abuse, rape and assault of Aboriginal women and children, and decisive action against the perpetrators."[59] But neither in "Trapped in the Aboriginal Reality Show" nor her subsequent essay, "The End of Big Men Politics,"[60] does she explain how the measures described above actually protect women and children. Where is the evidence that coercive measures like income management are effective in transforming the dysfunctional behaviours that Langton so vividly describes?

Langton argues that Aboriginal opinion is divided into "two camps":

> There are, as some journalists are delighted to report, two camps on these matters, one concerned with symbolic outcomes and the other with the practical. In reality, the two camps are divided by historical issues: those who have lived through the many tragedies and their aftermath in remote Australia committed to preventing the destruction of their societies in a haze of alcohol and drug abuse; and those with cosmopolitan urban experience who have allowed libertarian leanings, and deep political disappointment, to confuse their logic.[61]

This argument overlooks the Aboriginal women who are at the forefront of the grassroots movement against the NTER, such as Rosalie Kunoth-Monks, a community leader from Utopia in central Australia. In a report by Concerned Australians, Kunoth-Monks strongly objected to the NTER's top-down approach: "The biggest thing that we have an argument with the government is, we're not white people. We have our own language. We have our own ceremonies. We have our own land. What we want from government is real help and real funding rather than putting law on top of our Law."[62]

Other Aboriginal women from the Northern Territory have voiced similar concerns about the loss of autonomy and cultural authority. Among them is Barbara Shaw of the Mount Nancy Town Camp near Alice Springs. Shaw has been a passionate opponent of the NTER who has spoken in domestic and international forums and was an applicant in litigation in 2009 that attempted to prevent the Commonwealth's takeover of the Alice Springs Town Camps.[63] Other Aboriginal women have expressed concern that community self-esteem has suffered because the NTER measures were imposed arbitrarily and in the absence of prior consultation. For example, the founder of the Central Australian Strong Women's Alliance, Elaine Peckham, said that

> what the Intervention has done in the past and will continue to do to us is stop us believing in ourselves. Most of us have done nothing wrong

and we have always been accountable people all our lives so far as I can remember. But we're feeling like we've done something really wrong, like we are bad people, and we are being put down. And now we are feeling it emotionally in ourselves and are hurting and are suffering from what the Intervention has done to us.[64]

As would be expected in relation to any important public policy, there are also Aboriginal women in the Northern Territory who have spoken in favour of the measures. Among them is the parliamentarian Bess Nungarrayi Price, whose community of Yuendumu is subject to the NTER. In a speech to the conservative think tank the Bennelong Society, Price said she had embraced the NTER because "it meant at last somebody was acknowledging that there was a crisis and that it needed to be addressed."[65] Price's personal story is compelling, and when she discusses the human costs of addiction,[66] it is impossible not to be moved. But like Langton, she does not base her support of the NTER on evidence of improved outcomes for women and children.

Aboriginal women scholars such as Larissa Behrendt and Irene Watson have offered alternative perspectives to those of Langton and Price. Behrendt has drawn attention to research indicating that effective programs are invariably developed in partnership with Aboriginal communities.[67] Watson has argued powerfully that a dialogue about violence in isolation of a broader debate about colonization is simplistic. Rather than seeking solutions from a society that also suffers from patriarchal violence, Aboriginal women should be empowered through the strengthening of women's law.[68]

The debate thus far has been at times personal and has failed to address some core questions. The most important of which is, how do the various components of the NTER actually impact Aboriginal women? This analysis can be contextualized by Aboriginal women's historical experience of state interventions, which, at least ostensibly, have been meant to protect them. In reality, however, those measures have perpetuated the binary of invisibility and control.

Part Three: Key NTER Measures and the Binary of Invisibility and Control

Income Management

As stated above, the income management regime was initially applied on the basis of physical presence on certain Aboriginal lands, irrespective of personal circumstances. This attracted the criticisms that the regime was racially discriminatory and that it unfairly punished individuals who were already spending their income support payments on necessities for their children and themselves. However, Minister Brough insisted that a blanket approach was necessary in order to protect vulnerable women and children. In his second reading of the Social Security and Other Legislation (Welfare Payment Reform) Bill 2007, Brough said:

> The welfare reforms outlined in this bill will help to stem the flow of cash going towards substance abuse and gambling and ensure that funds meant to be for children's welfare are used for that purpose ...
>
> This broad-based approach is needed to address a breakdown in social norms that characterises many of our remote Northern Territory communities.
>
> In particular, this approach is essential to minimise the practice known as "humbugging" in the Northern Territory, where people are intimidated into handing over their money to others for inappropriate needs, often for alcohol, drugs and gambling.
>
> If certain groups, such as the young and old, are excluded from this measure, it could leave them potentially even more vulnerable.[69]

Brough's successor, Jenny Macklin, has similarly defended the income management regime. In interviews she has referred to conversations with Aboriginal women, whom she does not name:

> We've had plenty of Aboriginal women say that they feel that they've got much better control over their money now, they're not being harassed or humbugged for money in the same way that they were before, more money is being spent on food, more money is being spent on clothing for children, less on alcohol, I would have thought that's exactly what we should be doing, making sure that the welfare money that's made available for people, is spent in the interests of children.[70]

But where is the research that proves there is a nexus between the blunt instrument of income management and Aboriginal women's self-determination? In a recent report on women's experiences of income management, prepared by Equality Rights Alliance, 70 per cent of respondents considered that the BasicsCard had not improved their personal safety,[71] and some even believed that the new scarcity in cash had led to an increase in crime.[72] Rather than offering protection from "humbugging" by relatives, 91 per cent of the women surveyed believed that income management had made no difference to their family relationships.[73] The study was confined to Alice Springs and Darwin. Consequently, the study may not reflect the views of Aboriginal women in remote communities.

Proponents may argue that even in the absence of proof of enhanced personal safety, income management should still be defended because it is a valuable tool for ensuring that children are properly fed and clothed. Once again, however, research on the impacts of the income management regime suggests otherwise. In a paper published in *Medical Journal of Australia*, researchers from the Menzies School of Health Research examined purchases made at stores in ten communities over a three-year period.[74] The study revealed that income management had no apparent nexus with healthier food purchases.[75]

The indignities described by former wards during the protectionist era find resonance in the shame felt by some women in relation to the debit card, or "BasicsCard." Seventy-four per cent of the women in the Equality Rights Alliance study said they felt that others "aren't as nice to me when they see that I use BasicsCard."[76] One woman argued that "it was just enforced over everybody and I don't see why it should happen to people who are doing the right thing. I would have been embarrassed to go to Woolworths with BasicsCard. I have no history of mismanagement or social problems."[77] These women's difficulties were compounded by a lack of trust in Centrelink staff. Particularly concerning was the suggestion that some women had been deterred from seeking a crisis payment in order to escape an abusive relationship, for fear of triggering a referral to income management.[78]

Like earlier interventions, the income management regime appears to have curtailed women's freedoms. The above-mentioned report by the Equality Rights Alliance suggests that compulsory income management has restricted women's choices as consumers. Women who prefer to buy their children's clothing from second-hand stores or small chains are now being compelled to shop at larger department stores that have facilities for the BasicsCard.[79] Others encounter difficulties buying prescription medicines, for not all drugstores accept the BasicsCard.[80]

The Loss of Labour Rights

I am unaware of any research that has elucidated the NTER's impacts on Aboriginal women's labour rights. However, it is possible that as a result of reforms to CDEP, some Aboriginal women in the Northern

Territory may enjoy fewer labour rights than before. Since its introduction in 1997, in the Northern Territory community of Bamyili,[81] CDEP has expanded to become the most important Indigenous employment program in the country. Although complex, CDEP has enabled Aboriginal people to earn the equivalent of their income support payments, and it is possible for them to perform additional work for "top-up" wages.

Aboriginal women employed as CDEP workers have performed a variety of functions important to their communities. Some of these have involved highly skilled work in fields such as eldercare and education.[82] In an unpublished report, the Northern Territory Working Women's Centre identified a number of disadvantages faced by Aboriginal women CDEP workers, including a lack of recognition for the skills they bring to their positions, uncertainty over award coverage, and neglect of workplace health and safety.[83] In spite of these shortcomings, CDEP has become the largest employer of Aboriginal women in remote communities; for many, CDEP is their only source of employment.[84]

The abolition of CDEP was one of the original NTER measures introduced by the Howard government. The Rudd government that followed placed a temporary freeze on the dismantling of CDEP; soon after, though, it announced significant reforms that will lead to the program's gradual demise. In July 2009, CDEP ceased to operate outside of remote areas. It continues to operate in remote areas, but in two streams. The "new" CDEP is akin to a work-for-dole scheme and catches individuals who commenced the program after 1 July 2009. The "old" CDEP is being gradually phased out.

For Aboriginal women, the consequences of these reforms could be profound. Instead of being paid wages, some will now receive income support payments. Furthermore, entitlements to superannuation will not be enjoyed by individuals compelled to work as part of their mutual obligation requirements. The irony is that in some cases, women will be performing the same work as before the reforms.[85] The possibility of a loss of rights by Aboriginal women workers is a concern not only for individuals but also for their families, and more research into this issue is required.

The Compulsory Acquisition of Aboriginal Lands

One of the most controversial aspects of the NTER was the compulsory acquisition of Aboriginal lands. In his second reading of the Northern

Territory National Emergency Response Bill, Minister Brough justified the Commonwealth's acquisition of Aboriginal lands on the basis that it would "give the government the unconditional access to land and assets required to facilitate the early repair of buildings and infrastructure."[86] For many communities, however, the timely or even untimely repair of buildings and infrastructure has yet to occur.

Few commentators have considered how the compulsory acquisition of Aboriginal lands has affected women's law, identity, and health. But it is crucial that Aboriginal women be able to fulfil their custodial obligations. Rosalie Kunoth-Monks has spoken of the importance of land to health: "Health is about being emotionally sound, mentally sound, and knowing who you are, as well as being physically fit. You know who you are when you are on your land, doing what generations of Aboriginal people have done, taking care of that land, singing the songs that the mythology brought forward, right up to today."[87]

Her statement found resonance in the health impact assessment of the NTER measures carried out by the Australian Indigenous Doctors Association in 2010: "Ownership and control of land and housing have a positive influence on psychological and physical health. Aboriginal identity is tied to land, cultural practices, systems of authority and social control, intellectual traditions, concepts of spirituality, systems of resource ownership and exchange. Loss of control over land, a lack of engagement with non-Aboriginal Australia and resulting powerlessness has had ongoing, serious negative impacts on health."[88]

The compulsory acquisition of Aboriginal lands is yet another example of the binary of invisibility and control. In common with income management and the dismantling of CDEP, the rights of Aboriginal women have again become invisible. The state's control over Aboriginal women has been consolidated just as their ability to assert ownership over their lands has been curtailed.

Conclusion

The tragic allegations contained in *Little Children Are Sacred* demanded an urgent and considered response by Australian governments. Although the NTER was a timely response, its measures were at odds with the tenor of *Little Children Are Sacred*, which emphasized empowering Aboriginal communities to own the solutions. Aboriginal people were subjected to a raft of extraordinary measures that included the compulsory acquisition of their lands and the imposition of the income management regime. All the more galling was the absence of prior consultation. Many of the key NTER measures were later repackaged under the benign guise of "Stronger Futures" and effectively extended for a further decade.

In spite of their profound consequences for Aboriginal people, the public debate over the measures has been minimal, and perhaps overshadowed by the publicized narratives of a small number of Aboriginal women. This chapter takes the position that a mature public debate would not only critically engage with such narratives but also consider research on the impacts of key NTER measures. A mature public debate would also allow for consideration of Aboriginal women's historical experience of state interventions, which have rendered their rights invisible even while subjecting them to further regulation.

NOTES

1 Australian Broadcasting Corporation (ABC), "Intervention Bills to Pass, Despite Inquiry," *PM Monday to Friday*, 10 August 2007 (Sue Gordon).
2 Commonwealth, *Parliamentary Debates*, House of Representatives, 7 August 2007, 17 (Mal Brough, Minister for Families, Community Services and Indigenous Affairs and Minister Assisting the Prime Minister for Indigenous Affairs).
3 *Stronger Futures in the Northern Territory Act 2012* (Cth); *Social Security Legislation Amendment Act 2012* (Cth); *Stronger Futures in the Northern Territory (Consequential and Transitional Provisions) Act 2012* (Cth).
4 Nicholson, Watson, and Vivian, *Listening but Not Hearing*.
5 Australian Lawyers Alliance, "The Stronger Futures Legislative Package: Assessment of Non-Compliance with Human Rights," 29 June 2012.
6 Rintoul, "Jenny Macklin Defends Northern Territory Intervention."
7 Rintoul, "Bess Price Takes On Her Critics over NT Intervention."
8 Behrendt, "Consent in a (Neo)Colonial Society," 353, 364.
9 For a history of protectionist legislation, see Kidd, *The Way We Civilise*.
10 Robert, "Disciplining the Female Aboriginal Body," 69.
11 Paisley, "Race Hysteria, Darwin 1938," 43, 44.
12 Grimshaw and Nelson, "Empire, 'the Civilising Mission,'" 295, 296 (footnotes omitted).
13 Legal and Constitutional Affairs Committee, Senate, *Unfinished Business: Indigenous Stolen Wages* (2006) [5.27].
14 Walden, "That Was Slavery Days," 196.
15 Walden, "That Was Slavery Days," 205.

16 Greer, "'In the Interests of the Children,'" 166.

17 Audrey Bolger, *Aboriginal Women and Violence: A Report for the Criminology Research Council and the Northern Territory Commissioner of Police* (1991).

18 Lawrie, *Speak Out Speak Strong*.

19 Lawrie, *Speak Out Speak Strong*, 7.

20 Lawrie, *Speak Out Speak Strong*, 5.

21 Bolger, *Aboriginal Women and Violence*; Boni Robertson, *The Aboriginal and Torres Strait Islander Women's Taskforce on Violence Report* (1999); Aboriginal Child Sexual Assault Taskforce, *Breaking the Silence: Creating the Future: Addressing Child Sexual Assault in Aboriginal Communities in NSW* (2006).

22 ABC, "Crown Prosecutor Speaks Out about Abuse in Central Australia," *Lateline*, 15 May 2006; ABC, "Paedophile Rings Operating in Remote Communities: Brough," *Lateline*, 16 May 2006.

23 Anderson and Wild, *Little Children Are Sacred*.

24 Anderson and Wild, *Little Children Are Sacred*, 53.

25 Sackett, "A Post-Modern Panopticon," 229.

26 "Abuse Crisis Like 'Hurricane Katrina,'" *Sydney Morning Herald*, 25 June 2007.

27 Commonwealth, *Parliamentary Debates*, House of Representatives, 7 August 2007, 18 (Mal Brough).

28 *Northern Territory National Emergency Response Act 2007* (Cth); *Families, Community Services and Indigenous Affairs and other Legislation Amendment (Northern Territory National Emergency Response and Other Measures) Act 2007* (Cth); *Social Security and Other Legislation Amendment (Welfare Payment Reform) Act 2007* (Cth).

29 Commonwealth, *Parliamentary Debates*, House of Representatives, 7 August 2007, 10 (Mal Brough).

30 *Social Security (Administration) Act 1999* (Cth) 123TH.

31 *Social Security (Administration) Act 1999* (Cth) 123UB.

32 *Social Security and Other Legislation Amendment (Welfare Reform and Reinstatement of Racial Discrimination Act) Act 2010* (Cth).

33 This is a result of the Northern Territory becoming a "Declared Income Management Area." See *Social Security (Administration) (Declared income management areas) Determination 2010*.

34 *Social Security (Administration) Act 1999* (Cth) s. 123TA.

35 *Northern Territory National Emergency Response Act 2007* (Cth) Part 3.

36 *Families, Community Services and Indigenous Affairs and Other Legislation Amendment (Northern Territory National Emergency Response and Other Measures) Act 2007* (Cth) Schedule 2.

37 *Northern Territory National Emergency Response Act 2007* (Cth) Part 2.

38 *Northern Territory National Emergency Response Act 2007* (Cth) ss. 90–1.

39 Commonwealth, *Parliamentary Debates*, House of Representatives, 7 August 2007, 7 (Mal Brough).

40 Commonwealth, *Parliamentary Debates*, House of Representatives, 7 August 2007, 7 (Mal Brough).

41 *Northern Territory National Emergency Response Act 2007* (Cth) s. 30A.

42 *Northern Territory National Emergency Response Act 2007* (Cth) s. 31.

43 *Northern Territory National Emergency Response Act 2007* (Cth) s. 35(2A).

44 Arnie, McGuiness, and Robinson, "In the Best Interests of the Child?", 42.

45 Peter Yu, Marcia Ella Duncan, and Bill Gray, *Report of the NTER Review Board* (2008), 9.

46 Australian Indigenous Doctors Association, *Submission to the Northern Territory Emergency Response Review Board* (2008), 17.

47 Australian Indigenous Doctors' Association and the Centre for Health Equity Training, Research, and Evaluation, University of New South Wales, *Health Impact Assessment of the Northern Territory Emergency Response* (2010), ix.

48 Yu, Duncan, and Gray, *Report*, 12.

49 Michele Harris and Georgina Gartland, *Children of the Intervention: A Submission to the UN Committee on the Rights of the Child* (2011), 6.

50 Government of Australia, *Stronger Futures in the Northern Territory: Discussion Paper* (2011).

51 Letter from Professor Jon Altman and colleagues to the Hon. Jenny Macklin MP, Minister for Families, Housing, Community Services, and Indigenous Affairs, 27 June 2011, accessed 8 January 2014 at http://www.concernedaustralians.com.au/media/Let-A-Nicholson-Stronger-Futures-27-6-11.pdf.

52 Alastair Nicholson, Nicole Watson, and Alison Vivian, *Listening but Not Hearing: A Response to the NTER Stronger Futures Consultations, June to August 2011*, Jumbunna Indigenous House of Learning, 2012, 72.

53 Nicholson, Watson, and Vivian, *Listening but Not Hearing*, 96.

54 Nicholson, Watson, and Vivian, *Listening but Not Hearing*, 101.

55 Social Security Legislation Amendment, Bill 2011; Stronger Futures in the Northern Territory, Bill 2011; Stronger Futures in the Northern Territory (Consequential and Transitional Provisions), Bill 2011.

56 Langton, "Aboriginal Sophisticates Betray Bush Sisters."

57 Langton, "Trapped in the Aboriginal Reality Show," 143.

58 Langton, "Trapped in the Aboriginal Reality Show."

59 Langton, "Trapped in the Aboriginal Reality Show."

60 Langton, "The End of 'Big Men' Politics," 13.

61 Langton, "Aboriginal Sophisticates Betray Bush Sisters," 158.

62 Concerned Australians, *This Is What We Said*, 21.

63 *Shaw v Minister for Families, Housing, Community Services and Indigenous Affairs* [2009] FCA 1397.

64 Peckham, "Speech on Income Management."

65 Price, "Inaugural Peter Howson Lecture."

66 Price, "Inaugural Peter Howson Lecture."

67 Behrendt, 'The Emergency We Had to Have," 15.

68 Watson, "Aboriginal Women's Laws and Lives," 95.

69 Commonwealth, *Parliamentary Debates*, House of Representatives, 7 August 2007, 6 (Mal Brough).

70 ABC, *ABC National Radio*, 16 June 2010 (Fran Kelly and Jenny Macklin), accessed on 8 January 2014 at http://www.jennymacklin.fahcsia.gov.au/transcripts/2010/Pages/cdep_16jun10.aspx.

71 Equality Rights Alliance, *Women's Experience of Income Management in the Northern Territory* (2011), 33.

72 Equality Rights Alliance, *Women's Experience*.

73 Equality Rights Alliance, *Women's Experience*, 19.

74 Brimblecombe et al., "Impact of Income Management," 549.

75 Brimblecombe et al., "Impact of Income Management," 553.

76 Equality Rights Alliance, *Women's Experience*, 31.

77 Equality Rights Alliance, *Women's Experience*, 32.

78 Equality Rights Alliance, *Women's Experience*, 35.

79 Equality Rights Alliance, *Women's Experience*, 23.

80 Equality Rights Alliance, *Women's Experience*, 25.

81 Race Discrimination Commissioner, *The CDEP Scheme and Racial Discrimination* (1997), 7.

82 Rachel Uebergang, Kerriann Dear, and Sandra Dann, *Increasing Indigenous Economic Opportunity: The Future of the CDEP and Indigenous Employment Programs*, accessed 8 January at http://www.wwc.org.au/uploads/pdfs/NWWC%20Increasing%20Indigenous%20Economic%20Opportunity%20Submission.pdf.

83 Sue Murdoch, *ATSI Women on the CDEP Scheme: Workplace Issues Identified by the Project Officer on Behalf of the NT Working Women Centre, Darwin, NT* (2002).

84 Commonwealth of Australia, *Australia's Combined Sixth and Seventh Report on the Implementation of the Convention on the Elimination of All Forms of Discrimination against Women* (2008), 9.45.

85 Gibson, "Working for the BasicsCard."

86 Commonwealth, *Parliamentary Debates*, House of Representatives, 7 August 2007, 14 (Mal Brough).

87 Concerned Australians, *Loss of Rights*, 50.

88 Australian Indigenous Doctors Association, *Submission*, 28.

19 Power in/through Speaking of Terror: The Geopolitics and Anti-Politics of Discourses on Violence in Other Places

SEDEF ARAT-KOÇ

This chapter underlines the challenges of speaking of violence and terror in other places in ways that would inform and enable effective approaches to ending the violence and formulating just, democratic, and peaceful solutions. Empirically focusing on the Kurdish issue in Turkey and the ways it has been framed as an issue of terrorist violence, this chapter raises questions about whether, when, and how violence gets talked about in national and international discourses, and about the implications of these ways of talking or remaining silent about violence. After reviewing the "Kurdish question" in Turkey, I analyse two dominant contemporary discourses on violence and terror. These discourses not only overlook, dismiss, and distort civilians' myriad experiences of violence but also constitute new and powerful systems of governmentality in the ways they address and manage violence. The first discourse, "the War on Terror," has empowered the Turkish state to expand its definition and interpretation of "terrorist violence" to quell dissent while strengthening its legitimacy to conduct state terrorist violence. The second discourse is an international one – potentially applicable but not yet hegemonically applied by Western powers to the Kurds in Turkey – and speaks of violence in other lands. This discourse, "humanitarian intervention," claims to address different forms of violence, including state terrorist violence in some contexts. It does so, however, by replacing nation-state sovereignty with imperial sovereignty and by stripping those who receive humanitarian aid of their political subjectivity, reducing them to bare life. In effect, both discourses work as anti-politics, thus eliminating the space for political agency and democracy.

The "Kurdish Question" in Turkey

Kurds are dispersed over several neighbouring countries in the Middle East: Turkey, Iraq, Syria, and Iran. The majority of Kurds, about 55 per cent, live in Turkey. It would be rather simplistic to reduce the "Kurdish question" in Turkey to a straightforward case of ethnic discrimination and to equate it with minority issues elsewhere. The "Kurdish question" in Turkey has a number of contradictions and complexities. People with Kurdish background make up more than an insignificant percentage of the economic and political elite in the country – including several cabinet ministers, prime ministers, and presidents. And despite more than two decades of armed conflict between the Turkish military and the Kurdistan Workers' Party (PKK), and incitements by ethnic-nationalist groups and leaders, ethnic conflict has yet to develop in Turkey.

Complex and multidimensional, the "Kurdish question" weaves together cultural, social, economic, political, and ideological as well as international and transnational dimensions, with one or more of these dimensions acquiring weight at different historical conjunctures. Despite this complexity, it is possible to relate the modern politics of the "Kurdish question" in Turkey to conceptions of the nation under the Turkish Republic – specifically, the crude assimilationism the Turkish state adopted in relation to ethnic minorities. Founded on the remains of the multiethnic Ottoman Empire, and receiving huge numbers of Muslims fleeing persecution or civil strife in the Balkans and the Caucasus, the Turkish Republic acquired a large population of people of non-Turkic ethnic backgrounds. In addition to Kurds, they have included Bosnians, Crimean Tatars, Albanians, Circassians, Abkhazes, Georgians, and Arabs, as well as Muslims originally from Macedonia, Serbia, Bulgaria, and Greece, among others. Rejecting the Ottoman Empire's political and administrative structures, including its "multicultural" model of organizing and governing minorities, the new Turkish state claimed to be developing a civic notion of Turkishness that would apply to anyone who lived within the boundaries of the Turkish state and who had Turkish citizenship. This civic notion of citizenship was ostensibly universalistic and inclusionary, but it also suppressed ethnic identities. The concept of Turkishness was adopted by most ethnic groups and functioned as a "melting pot"; but it did not necessarily succeed among Kurds.[1] Having developed a uniform notion of Turkey as "one people, one state, one flag," Turkish nationalism has denied the existence of the Kurds as a distinct ethnic group. Until recently, the position of Turkish political leaders has been to reject even that the Kurds have a separate language, by defining Kurdish as a "mountain dialect of Turkish." The Turkish Republic has managed Kurdish nationalism for most of its history by winning over large Kurdish landowners and has always denied there is a Kurdish problem. And when it is acknowledged, the Kurdish question has been identified at most as a socio-economic problem of underdevelopment in southeastern Turkey, a predominantly Kurdish area. In most modern state and media discourses, however, the Kurdish question is simply presented in a securitization discourse, as a problem of terrorist vioence.

The identification of the Kurdish issue as a problem of terrorist violence began in the 1980s. That was when the PKK, founded in Turkey in the 1970s, transformed itself into a paramilitary group following the military coup of 1980. After many of its members had been exiled, tortured, imprisoned, or executed, it launched a series of armed attacks against the Turkish military. Founded as an organization articulating Kurdish nationalism in Marxist-Leninist terms, the PKK identified Kurdish tribal leaders, large landowners, and comprador bourgeoisie to be as much a problem as the Turkish state in the exploitation and oppression of the lower classes. The PKK has been identified by the Turkish state as a secessionist organization and a terrorist one.[2] Since the 1980s, the Turkish state has identified it as one of its most serious domestic problems.

As the Turkish state responded to PKK attacks with militaristic measures, the 1980s and 1990s witnessed an escalation of conflict. The conflict reached its highest level in the mid-1990s. In addition to the more than 30,000 dead, the toll of the conflict included thousands of villages evacuated, illegal detentions, torture, and extrajudicial killings; millions were forced to migrate to nearby major centres or the western part of the country.

After the capture of Abdullah Öcalan, the PKK leader, in 1998, relative peace came to Turkey's southeast. Precipitated partly by Turkey's candidacy for European Union membership, the militaristic approach to the Kurdish issue gave way to cultural and linguistic reforms. AKP, the "moderate Islamist" party, in power since 2002, has made some gestures to demonstrate that it is moving away from the crude assimilationism that has long prevailed. Adapting a "neo-Ottoman" approach to Turkish identity, the AKP has taken steps to recognize the cultural distinctness of the Kurds. Some of these steps in the early years of AKP rule involved "decriminalizing Kurdish culture,"[3] including in the publishing and broadcasting sectors. In 2008, one channel of TRT, the state-owned radio and television system, began broadcasting in Kurdish.

In 2009, the Turkish government announced a policy of "Kurdish opening" and more generally a "democratic opening," raising hopes that it was changing its approach to the Kurdish issue by offering political dialogue and conciliation and broadening Kurdish cultural rights. The "opening" soon closed again, however, as a result of pressure from far-right ethnic-nationalist (Turkish) parties, incidents of attacks on Kurds in different parts of the country, and a shift towards nationalism within the governing party. The "opening" had hinted at a new approach to the Kurdish issue; some observers, however, suggest that the closing that followed should not have been a surprise. Saraçoğlu argues that AKP's conservative ideology, while critical of Kemalist assimilationist nationalism, has always viewed the Turkish nation as a traditional "family," emphasizing unity, order, and harmony. According to Saraçoğlu, AKP has taken a three-pronged approach towards the Kurds: service, respect, and elimination. "Service" here refers to development and charity projects in the region to integrate Kurds into the AKP's hegemonic project. "Respect" is about a politics of recognition that respects some of the folkloric elements of Kurdish culture, but sees Kurds as a Sunni-Muslim group rather than an ethnic-national one. "Elimination" is the flip side of service and respect. To the degree that these latter approaches fail to establish AKP hegemony among the Kurds, and cannot quash an independent Kurdish identity and movement, elimination entails neutralizing the Kurds politically and in terms of ideology.[4] Nuray Mert's view of the "Kurdish opening" is similar. She argues that while the prime minister sincerely wanted to solve the Kurdish problem, his approach was not negotiations with an independent movement, but rather the imposition of the government's own terms on the Kurds: "He simply wanted Kurds to give up their political demands and accommodate the policies of the government. Otherwise, they would prove to be 'terrorists,' 'friends of terrorists' and above all, 'enemies of the country.'"[5]

In 2009, within months of the Kurdish opening, the government started targeting the *Koma Civakên Kurdistan* (the Union of Communities in Kurdistan; KCK), a transnational Kurdish organization with affiliates in Turkey, Iran, Iraq, Syria, and the diaspora. The KCK, which was based largely in urban areas, had been founded in 2005 to carry out Öcalan's vision of "democratic confederalism." There have been multiple waves of arrests since 2009; under the Anti-Terror Law, more than 8,000 people have been detained on the accusation of working for a wing of the PKK, and more than 3,500 alleged members of the KCK have been arrested. The detainees have included academics, mayors, and parliamentarians of the Kurdish Peace and Democracy Party, the BDP (the Kurdish party currently in parliament), as well as trade union organizers, human rights activists, lawyers, journalists, publishers, and university students.

Several obstacles have been raised against the political expression of Kurdish issues and demands. Since the early 1990s, over time, a number of political parties representing Kurds and the Kurdish cause in Turkey (HEP, ÖZDEP, DEP, DDP, DKP, HADEP, DTP) have been disbanded by the Constitutional Court based on allegations that they are linked to the PKK. Many Kurdish mayors and other politicians have been harassed, arrested, tried, and imprisoned. Another obstacle has been an electoral system that now places a high threshold on parties seeking representation in Parliament. To hold any seats in Parliament, a party needs to win at least 10 per cent of the national vote. This rule, though, was circumvented in the 2007 and 2011 elections when a number of independent Members of Parliament were elected who, following the elections, joined a solidarity bloc with the Kurdish party. Some of those independent members were ethnic Turks.

From the time it launched its campaign for the 2011 elections until March 2013, AKP's stance on the Kurdish issue became increasingly hard-line and militaristic. Many saw this as a return to the policies of the 1990s. Since the elections, AKP has also pursued an aggressive policy towards the BDP, the Kurdish party in Parliament. The result has been a steady shrinking of political space for articulating, debating, and negotiating the democratic demands of Turkey's Kurdish minority. There has been a new "opening" in the relationship of the ruling AKP towards the Kurds since March 2013, but the process has been managed in a secretive way and strictly controlled by the government. The outcome is rather uncertain.

Politicians and human rights groups in Europe and (less often) the United States have urged the Turkish government to change its approach to the Kurdish issue. Yet I will argue here that whatever the West says, the discourse, politics, and the institutions of the "War on Terror" have for many years in effect authorized the Turkish government (a "friendly regime") to label Kurdish political voices as "terrorist" and take steps to silence those voices, including by escalating state terrorist violence. Also, the discourse of humanitarian intervention that the West resorts to when speaking of violence "everywhere else" serves as a mechanism for controlling rather than protecting and empowering the Kurdish people. I argue that these two discourses – one empowering the national government, the other empowering Western powers that have geopolitical interests in intervention – have together produced an *anti-politics machine(ry)*[6] that has contained and manipulated the political agency of the Kurds and muzzled their voices.

Ever-Expanding Notions of Terrorist Violence and Invisibilizing State Terrorism: The "War on Terrorism" and Opportunities to Silence Dissent

The "War on Terror" has allowed states around the world to label acts of minority dissent as "terrorism." Once certain movements and activities, and even affiliations and thoughts, have been framed as "terrorist," the state is able to dismiss minority grievances. The reduction of issues to ones of violence versus security, and the militarization of the state's response, create an *anti-politics* in which a *political* settlement of issues becomes impossible.

Another prominent result of the global "War on Terror" has been to justify, in the name of anti-terrorism, state policies and activities that would otherwise be illegitimate. Yet another has been to render state terrorism both natural and invisible. In addition to the wars and security practices of Western states, state terrorism has been commonly used and easily legitimized – as it has gone largely unquestioned – by states in friendly relations with the United States and European governments.

Anti-terrorism legislation in Turkey dates back to 1991. It was formulated specifically to address the PKK's activities. While not new and unique to the post-9/11 period, the anti-terrorism law received support and justification through discourses and practices of the global "War on Terror," which has provided a context in which the Turkish government has few incentives to address the Kurdish question except through militarization and securitization. The anti-terrorism law was amended in 2006 – ironically, during a period associated by national and international actors with "democratization" in Turkey – in a context of heightened security measures taken by countries around the world. Turkey's 2006 amendments were draconian. The new legislation defines terrorism in very broad and vague terms that criminalize many non-violent activities. In 2008, a higher court interpreted the amendments to mean that anyone who acted in a "PKK-inspired manner" could be convicted of belonging to a terrorist organization.[7]

Turkey's broadened definition of terrorism includes "terrorist propaganda," which prosecutors have interpreted to include criticism of the state and politicians. That interpretation has been used to close newspapers and has cast a chilling shadow over freedom of expression in Turkey. Activities such as wearing or carrying emblems, signs, banners, or leaflets of terrorist organizations, and shouting or broadcasting their slogans, also count as terrorism. The amendments have also increased the discretion of security forces while limiting the rights of those detained and convicted.[8] Another key amendment allows the courts to charge children between fifteen and eighteen as adults. In the first few years after the amendments came into effect, more than 1,500 children were prosecuted under the law.[9]

In Turkey, as elsewhere, membership in an "armed terrorist organization" is a criminal offence. The problem is that Turkish courts have tended to apply a very loose definition of "membership" so that it includes not only armed militants but also those on the margins of organizations or who merely sympathize with a general political cause, regardless of whether they are in any way involved in the planning or execution of acts of violence. In the KCK investigations in recent years, this principle appears to have been taken one step further: the definition of "membership in a terrorist organization" has been extended to those who share the PKK's stated goal of greater rights and freedoms for Turkey's Kurds.

Precisely at a time when Turkey was being touted as a "model democracy" for the Middle East,[10] it has convicted more people of terrorism than any other country. As of late 2011, Turkey had convicted close to 13,000 people of terrorism, which was roughly one-third of the world's total and far more than any other country – even China, with its 7,000 convictions in a population of 1.3 billion people.[11] And in Turkey, many of these people have been detained or convicted because of their presumed association with the Kurdish movement. It is estimated that by the end of the summer of 2012, more than 2,100 people connected to the BDP, including 274 elected officials – Members of Parliament, mayors, and municipal councillors – were in detention on charges of belonging to a terrorist organization. Another 5,000 may face charges of spreading the ideas of a terrorist organization or attending a meeting.[12] Many of those arrested under terrorism charges are (Kurdish) children who have thrown stones at the police. Also heavily represented among those facing lengthy jail sentences on terrorism charges are about 100 Kurdish journalists,[13] as well as lawyers representing those who have been accused of terrorism!

As a result of the amendments to the law, politicians, the media, and the security forces have further expanded the public discourse of "terrorism." As this discourse expands, there are absurd references to seven-year-old child terrorists[14] – or, in the case of the KCK, to an "unarmed terror organization." In a speech in December 2011, the Minister of the Interior, Idris Naim Şahin, suggested that the activities of the PKK (the terrorist organization), the KCK (which conducts non-violent struggles in urban areas), and the BDP (the Kurdish party in Parliament) were all intertwined and that works by writers, poets, and artists were now also suspect:

> The activities of the terror organization are not just confined to brutally attacking security forces in rural and urban areas and back alleys. There is a backyard that feeds terrorism. It involves efforts to present it as innocent, reasonable and legitimate, through painting, writing poems or daily columns. They try to demoralize army and police personnel fighting terrorism by making them the subject of their art and writing. The backyard of terrorism is Istanbul, Izmir, Bursa, Vienna, London and Washington. It is university posts and civil society organizations. They have infiltrated into all these spaces. It is sometimes a cultural, educational association, sometimes a "think-tank." It is easy to fight terrorism in the mountains. In the backyard, however, quick grass and watercress are mixed together.[15]

The discourse of terrorism feeds the practices of security forces, continuously supporting, legitimizing, and normalizing state terrorism. Within days of Şahin's speech, in late December 2011, a drone attack in Uludere/Roboski, a rural area in southeastern Turkey, killed thirty-five civilians, all peasants, nineteen of whom were children between twelve and fifteen. Here, young Kurdish smugglers travelling in the mountains at night were judged to be PKK militants. Smuggling is widespread in impoverished Kurdish villages near the border, where most peasants are landless. Human rights groups described this attack as a massacre, as "execution without trial." However, the TRT blamed it on the PKK, stating that its activities had made drone attacks necessary.[16] The Turkish prime minister told journalists: "This is not a region where people live. It is a terror region."[17]

As the definition of terrorism expands, political expression by Kurdish groups and their allies becomes criminalized. In Newroz in the spring of 2012, a festival became a site of state violence when the government insisted that the event would only be allowed on 21 March.

When Kurds attempted to extend the celebrations into the week – especially into the weekend, when more people could attend – they faced barricades, tear gas, and attacks by the police. By the end of the week, 659 people had been detained around the country, 71 arrested, and many wounded, including elders of the BDP and the Kurdish movement.[18] Another example of the criminalization of dissent was the response to a rally organized by the BDP in July 2012 to call for the release of jailed PKK leader Öcalan and to celebrate the first anniversary of the declaration of the BDP's vision of "democratic autonomy." When the provincial governor of Diyarbakır refused to permit the rally,[19] Kurds went out anyway. The police resorted to water canon, tear gas, and beatings of protesters – the leg of a female BDP deputy was broken – and arrested large numbers of Kurds.

The securitization of the Kurdish issue has choked off political debate and resolution. After the government's harsh response to the "illegal" rally of July 2012, BDP co-leader Selahattin Demirtaş pointed out that every single application for a political demonstration made by the BDP in the past year had been rejected. Vahap Coşkun argues that the so-called KCK operation is actually an operation to suppress the BDP. According to Coşkun, what is happening is that at a time when the outright banning of political parties would reflect badly on Turkey, whose government wants to project an image of democracy, a "postmodern process of party closing" has developed whereby a party is permitted to remain open but is effectively disabled through the arrest and imprisonment of its elected officials and supporters, the banning of demonstrations, and constant harassment and threats of closure. One aim of this "postmodern" process, according to Coşkun, has been to criminalize the BDP. The government expects there to be a reaction when it bans a demonstration. Then people violate the ban and clash with security forces, and the BDP is blamed. In this way, the government's anti-democratic practices are legitimized and normalized.[20]

Whether/How (State) Violence Elsewhere Gets Heard in the West Today: Selective Attention, (Geo)Political Mediations, and "Humanitarian Interventions"

The West's "adoption" of minority causes, wherever they develop, has always been selective, often based on the amenability to Western (more specifically, US) interests of whichever government is ruling over the minority. A blatant example of the West's selective attention to the plight of Kurds has been the West's complicity in the massacre of Iraqi Kurds. The 1988 massacre of Kurds in Halabja by poison gas received almost no attention when Saddam Hussein was on friendly terms with the United States during the Iran–Iraq War. But that massacre was suddenly "remembered" and instrumentalized after US relations with Hussein changed following the Iraqi invasion of Kuwait, which led to the first Iraq War in 1990–1.

Two factors have contributed to the West's relative lack of attention to the Kurds of Turkey. First, the left-wing tendencies of Turkey's Kurdish movement, while they have weakened over the years, have never been in harmony with US interests. (By contrast, northern Iraq's Kurds *have* been in harmony.) The second factor has to do with relations between Western governments and the Turkish government. From the beginning of the "War on Terrorism" until the Gezi Movement in the summer of 2013 (when the repressive politics of the AKP became finally visible to foreign observers), Western governments have promoted Turkey in the Middle East and Muslim-majority countries elsewhere as a "good Muslim" model for "moderate Islam" and as a "model democracy." More recently, from the beginning of so-called Arab Spring until early 2013, especially in the context of NATO's intervention in Libya and pressure on Syria's Assad regime, Turkey's foreign policy has pleased the United States and Western European governments. In this climate, Western governments and media seem to be engaging in wilful ignorance with regard to Turkey's remilitarization of the Kurdish issue and its creeping political repression.[21] The West's condoning of these developments will likely continue as long as the Turkish policies in the Middle East continue to align with those of the Western states and their dominant interests.

How can Kurds in diaspora and their allies, as well as independent human rights groups in the West, express their solidarity with the Kurds in Turkey? What discourses are available for them to talk about this violence and repression? Beyond geopolitics, what language can Westerners use when talking about human rights in other countries? Instead of providing a formulaic and detailed answer to these questions, I offer a serious caution regarding which language and discourse *not* to use. Even though the geopolitics of the region has so far ruled against the adoption of humanitarian discourse in relation to Kurds in Turkey, instability of the region and volatility of its politics mean that there is a great deal of uncertainty around the nature of Western interests and interventions in the future.[22] I will be focusing here on humanitarian intervention as the dominant discourse – if not the only one – in the early twenty-first century for talking about violence, including state violence. I will be discussing the ways in which, instead of providing a real voice to oppressed minorities and supporting popular sovereignty, the discourse of humanitarian intervention serves as yet another mechanism of anti-politics, one that shifts sovereignty from nation-states to imperial powers and that robs subjects of political agency.

Wendy Brown warns eloquently against assuming that any outside discourse for addressing violence can *merely* help stop violence. Discourse is never neutral or non-political:

> There is no such thing as *mere* reduction of suffering or protection from abuse – the nature of the reduction or protection is itself productive of political subjects and political possibilities. Just as abuse itself is never generic but always has particular social and subjective content, so the matter of *how* it is relieved is consequential. Yes, the abuse must be stopped, but by whom, with what techniques, with what unintended effects, and above all, unfolding what possible futures? The pragmatist, moral and anti-political mantle of human rights discourse tends to eschew, even repel, rather than invite or address these questions.[23]

Frustration with the difficulties of ending violence leads some political actors to call for international intervention to end the violent suppression of minorities. This strategy has gained popularity since the Cold War ended, now that a single super power has replaced binary geopolitics. The frustrations generated by the Westphalian model of nation-states have led, in this new era, to calls from the political right *and* left to envision a "global civil society," global democracy, or "cosmopolitical democracy."[24] This would enable people to be heard in the global community irrespective of the power of their voices within nation-states. It is understandable that this would appeal to human rights activists, but serious questions must be raised as to whether it is possible given the present power relations in international politics. Whatever we might think of cosmopolitical democracy, we need to debate *who* would be shaping and enforcing it: "*which* authority may use force to violate state sovereignty, *who* such force should be used against or *which* human rights have to be protected."[25]

Humanitarian intervention promises justice in a post-Westphalian order. In various NATO and US interventions in the post-Cold War era – in Somalia, Iraq, Yugoslavia, and Afghanistan – that term has been used rhetorically. More recently, it has been embedded in international law through the doctrine of the "Responsibility to Protect." That doctrine was put into effect to justify the 2011 NATO intervention in Libya. Expressed in terms of humanitarian intervention and responsibility to protect, international humanitarian discourse treats Third World peoples as wards of the West. This has introduced an unequal notion of humanity for Third World peoples by denying them political power, citizenship rights, and the right to self-determination. In this sense, international humanitarian discourse is inherently anti-political and anti-democratic.

A blatant contradiction of humanitarian intervention has to do with the inherent militarism and violence of the intervention it advocates. Fassin and Pandolfi argue that humanitarianism has become the "justification for extralegal action" and that the logic of humanitarian interventions amounts to a "form of naturalization – or depoliticization – of war."[26] They suggest that humanitarian crises are approached as states of exception and that they form the basis for a "government that is at once military and humanitarian, resting on a logic of security and a logic of protection, on a law external to and superior to law, rooted as it is in the legitimacy of actions aimed at protecting life."[27]

Humanitarian interventions set out to end the violence of the state actors in the country of intervention, yet they are blind to their own violence. Interventionists see themselves as simply adding a "few more dead bodies" to the equation. Especially when those bodies are "bare life," it does not seem to matter what the costs of the intervention might be; indeed, the killing of the extra "few" through war is viewed as productive.[28] Speaking of the second Iraq War in 2004, Tony Blair has said:

> Let me say once again, I do not disrespect anybody who took a different point of view, but what I always had in mind was the nature of this regime. When you read the details of the torture chambers, the prisons, the thousands upon thousands of people that Saddam killed, *far more than any coalition action could ever do*, then I think, even if people have disagreed with us going to war, they can at least see that the Iraqi people have greater freedom and greater hope today than they had in the days under Saddam.[29]

Mamdani asks why the current discourses of international justice focus solely on what is labelled as genocide and not on mass violence in forms such as counter-insurgency. He asks why international justice would not be applied to, for example, the Iraq War, and he suggests that the main difference relates to the labels attached to different forms of mass violence rather than to their impact on people: "Labeling performs a vital function. It isolates and demonizes the perpetrators of one kind of mass violence and at the same time confers impunity on the perpetrators of other forms of mass violence."[30] He grants that there is nothing new about powerful nations using and manipulating legal concepts to suit their interests. What *is* new, he argues, is that in the War on Terror, "the action against violence is simultaneously being moralized and legally regulated."[31]

Several recent studies have raised alarm by documenting and analysing recent changes in humanitarian activism, even as practised by non-state NGOs. These studies bring to light trends towards professionalization and institutionalization in humanitarian organizations, which are abandoning their principles of neutrality and peacefulness in favour of militarization as well as cooperation with Western foreign policy.[32]

Observers are also alarmed that some institutions of the "post-Westphalian" world order, such as the International Criminal Court (ICC), are focusing exclusively on African countries. Mahmood Mamdani warns that "its name [not]withstanding, the ICC is rapidly turning into a Western court to try African crimes against humanity." In these circumstances, the ICC may achieve no more than "politicized justice."[33] Through the selective application of universal principles and international law, national sovereignty is being replaced by imperial sovereignty. Under the present conditions, the United States can simultaneously define the universal and opt out of its application and force. The United States leads humanitarian interventions and has been an outspoken advocate for war crimes tribunals in Yugoslavia and Rwanda, yet it opposes the ICC's jurisdiction to try US leaders and soldiers.

The contradictions of international justice today suggest that rather than a post-Westphalian transition, we are experiencing a transition to imperial sovereignty. Mamdani argues that this so-called transition from the old system of sovereignty to a new humanitarian order is "not a global but a partial transition ... confined to those states defined as 'failed' or 'rogue' states." The result, he adds, is a bifurcated international system very much like that of the colonial era, when state sovereignty existed in some parts of the world but was absent in most of Asia, Africa, and the Middle East. One part of the bifurcated international system is defined by sovereignty and citizenship, the other by trusteeship and wardship.[34]

What makes the bifurcation particularly racist is that its logic applies not just to states but also to peoples. Costas Douzinas argues that for cosmopolitan humanitarianism there is not one type of humanity; rather, there are three: the victim, the evil-doer, and the rescuer.[35] The first two are elsewhere. The "rescuer" is the white Western subject. For Douzinas, "the premise and appeal of humanitarianism is distance and alienation."[36] What humanitarians feel towards the victim is not sympathy arising from shared humanity and experience, but pity and a sense of superiority.[37] A key characteristic of humanitarian discourse is precisely its attempt to erase the interconnectedness of histories and experiences: "We shed tears … out of a sense of superiority and charity rather than out of shared history, community or humanity. If we have a shared history, humanitarianism in its celebration of our goodness erases it … The horrors visited by the West on its 'others' are conveniently forgotten and displaced. Horrible atrocious acts are only committed by the evil inhuman other."[38]

What is striking about some of the discourses advocating humanitarian intervention is that what sounds like a form of xenophilia expressed for the dependent other may actually be an expression of contempt for Third World political subjects who act independently of or in contradiction to Western interests. Miriam Ticktin argues that humanitarianism emerged as a reaction to "Third-Worldism." Third-Worldism recognizes Third World peoples as political agents who are able to shape their future. Ticktin counters that articulations of humanitarianism – for example, by French intellectuals – have depicted the Third World as a place of misery and barbarism and its peoples as victims.[39]

A third major problem with recent discourses and practices of cosmopolitanism has been that they invoke forms of politics that are inherently anti-political and anti-democratic. This renders invisible the connectedness of the histories and present relationships of the fortunate and the unfortunate; it also presents Western governments and corporations as saviours, even when they are directly implicated in the poverty and suffering of the recipients of humanitarianism. There is also the fact that humanitarianism is conditional on the absence of political agency on the part of the recipient. Politics, it seems, is the prerogative of the imperial power and its (consenting) citizens.

Cosmopolitan discourse tends to see sovereignty as intrinsically in tension with human rights, if not always contradictory to those rights. It does not acknowledge that the very enjoyment of human rights may be contingent on sovereignty.[40] It also overlooks the differences between human rights and the political and substantive rights of citizenship. Reminding us that without citizenship, the "human" is reduced to "bare life," Slavoj Žižek questions the value and integrity of the human in the humanitarian perspective:

> Paradoxically, I am deprived of human rights at the very moment at which I am reduced to a human being "in general" … What, then, happens to human rights when they are the rights of *homo sacer*, of those excluded from the political community; that is, when they are of no use, since they are the rights of those who, precisely, have no rights, and are treated as inhuman? Jacques Rancière proposes a salient dialectical reversal: "When they are of no use, one does the same as charitable persons do with their old clothes. One gives them to the poor."[41]

Mamdani argues that in celebrating human rights, the international humanitarian order does not acknowledge citizenship. Instead,

> it turns citizens into wards … To the extent that the global humanitarian order claims to stand for rights, these are the residual rights of the human and not the full range of rights of the citizen. If the rights of the citizen are pointedly political, the rights of the human pertain to sheer survival; they are summed up in one word: protection. The new language refers to its subject not as bearers of rights – and thus active agents in their emancipation – but as passive beneficiaries of an external "responsibility to protect" … Humanitarianism does not claim to reinforce agency, only to sustain bare life.[42]

The language of cosmopolitan humanitarianism defines the targets of humanitarian intervention not as fully human, as having political agency, but rather as pitifully dependent. Douzinas writes that in the eyes of the West, recipients of humanitarianism are:

> an amorphous mass of people … The victims are paraded exhausted, tortured and starving, but always nameless, a crowd, a mob that inhabits the exotic parts of the world. As a former president of the Medecins sans Frontiers put it, "he to whom humanitarian actions are addressed is not defined by his skills or potential, but above all, by his deficiencies and disempowerment. It is his fundamental vulnerability and dependency, rather than his agency and ability to surmount difficulty that is foregrounded by humanitarianism."[43]

Cosmopolitan humanitarianism attempts to shape and restrict the subjectivity of the recipients of interventions through an *anti-politics*.[44] Žižek argues that "today's 'new reign of ethics' … relies on a violent gesture of depoliticization, depriving the victimized other of any political subjectivization."[45] Finkielkraut captures the irony in the kind of xenophilia expressed in humanitarianism: "The humanitarian generation does not like men – they are too disconcerting – but enjoys taking care of them. Free men scare it. Eager to express tenderness fully while making sure that men do not get away, it prefers handicapped people."[46]

Focusing on occupied Gaza, Hagar Kotef articulates how humanitarian logic is similar to security logic and also corroborates it. "In reducing the subject to its corporeal needs," she writes, "humanitarianism produces the surface on which and through which security operates."[47] Stripping the subjects it "protects" of their citizenship, humanitarianism makes them vulnerable to security discourses and practices. In this way, humanitarianism perpetuates the regimes it purportedly opposes:

> Humanitarianism declares itself to be outside of politics, to address all human beings beyond the paradigm of citizenship. It thereby produces a subject-configuration for the security discourse, a surface on which security forces operate (but which is also the product of these forces). The subject at the focus of humanitarian discourse – but surprisingly enough, also of security – are neither the citizens nor the citizens-to-be and are hence never to be included or fully excluded. This is what allows humanitarianism to be fully universal and security not to reduce its subjects to enmity and yet not to protect them as citizens. The subject that emerges by this solidarity of security and humanitarianism is a thin subject, which is but its own survival.[48]

Alana Lentin also articulates how discourses of terrorism and humanitarian intervention may complement each other in producing subjects who are denied political agency:

> All Arab-looking people are potentially subject to investigation under anti-terrorism legislation, while a war is waged to bring democracy to Arabs whose human rights have been violated. In neither case can it be said that Arabs are being seen in a truly humanistic light. They constitute either threats or victims, and as such are stripped of autonomy. In either case, they are dehumanised (cf. Fanon, 1967), seen either as incapable of action or as the architects of actions so monstrous as to not qualify as human.[49]

Heriberto Cairo suggests that, given the bare humanity of the kinds of subjects that humanitarian discourse produces, the forms of domination prevailing in the post–Cold War era are not simply based on geopolitical relations among states; they are "also constructed around a biopolitical sense of duty to relieve 'suffering' on the part of 'brutalized' people."[50] This sense of duty, he argues, is very similar to the claims about "uncivilized" and "unchristianized" peoples under colonialism. In this world context, nation-state sovereignty is giving way to a form of suzerainty.[51]

The recolonization enabled by humanitarian intervention may involve a complete restructuring of the social, economic, and political order through the interests and visions of the imperial patron. Brown warns that the politics of cosmopolitan humanitarianism may monopolize political space altogether.[52] Žižek argues that rather than being neutral, "humanitarian interventions" are politically constitutive and may even stand in direct opposition to collective justice projects. According to him, the US invasion of Iraq

> was not only motivated by hard-headed politico-economic interests but also relied on a determinate idea of the political and economic conditions under which "freedom" was to be delivered to the Iraqi people: liberal-democratic capitalism, insertion into the global economy, etc. The purely humanitarian anti-political politics of merely preventing suffering thus amounts to an implicit prohibition on elaborating a positive collective project of socio-political transformation.[53]

Conclusion: Can the Subaltern Speak?

This chapter has underlined the difficulties inherent in speaking about violence and terror. The two dominant contemporary discourses on violence and terror discussed in this chapter not only overlook, dismiss, and distort the variety of experiences of violence encountered by civilians, but also constitute new powerful systems of governmentality in the ways violence is defined and addressed. One of these discourses, the "War on Terror," has empowered state actors – especially those who have good relations with imperial powers – to simultaneously legitimize state terrorism and render it invisible; it has also criminalized many forms of political dissent. The other, "humanitarian intervention," claims to address state terrorism and abuses of power at the nation-state level, but it does so by replacing nation-state sovereignty with imperial sovereignty and by stripping the recipients of humanitarianism of their political subjectivity, reducing them to bare life. In this way, people are defined either as "terrorist" subjects, defined by their violence rather than by the nature of their issues and demands, or as helpless victims who need the West's protection. Both discourses work as *anti-politics*, eliminating the space for political agency, political will, self-determination, and democracy.

What are the implications of this in terms of Kurdish politics, and more generally in terms of repressed and brutalized minorities? Some civil society and human rights groups, frustrated with the obstacles they face to having their voices heard and issues addressed, have become overly optimistic in the post-Cold War era about the possibility of leapfrogging politics at the national level. The discourses, institutions, and real-life examples of humanitarian intervention suggest there is no solution to violence and repression outside *politics*. They also suggest that leapfrogging local, national, and regional politics may not offer long-term peace and democracy for peoples. Instead of empowering recipients of humanitarianism by addressing abuses of nation-state sovereignty, the *anti-politics* of humanitarian intervention result in a humanity further stripped of political agency and the possibility of self-determination and popular sovereignty.

A "politics of place" as defined by Arif Dirlik[54] might provide peaceful and democratic alternatives to the anti-politics of state repression on the one hand and imperial humanitarianism on the other. Dirlik offers *politics of place* as an alternative to what he sees as the two dominant and competing political logics at present: identity politics and ethnic nationalism, on the one hand, and neoliberal imperial cosmopolitanism represented by globalism, on the other. Advocating a new form of politics informed by places, Dirlik clearly distinguishes "place-*based* politics" from essentialist "place-*bound*" nativism or ethnicist politics. The concept of *place* allows for a political imagination based on a contextualized and historicized understanding of the relations between different peoples who have interacted and coexisted in places over time, as well as for relations among the local, the regional, and the global. It allows for ways to remember, acknowledge, and address historical tensions and injustices among peoples while also allowing us to imagine peaceful coexistence.

Turkish and Kurdish intellectuals and political activists have made several gestures indicating that they want to achieve peace through negotiation. In a press conference in June 2012, MP Ahmet Türk, a prominent Kurdish politician, criticized the government for making deals with Iraqi Kurdish leaders such as Barzani and Talabani while refusing to negotiate with the Kurds in Turkey:

> For 30 years, there is a people,[55] its demands, its politics and leaders. There is a political party represented in parliament and engaged in the issues of this country. The involvement among Kurdish intellectuals and opinion leaders in peace is obvious to all. You cannot succeed if you dismiss Kurds in Turkey and only seek solutions abroad. We do not mind the initiatives of Barzani and Talabani. However, you cannot solve the problem by excluding us, the people. You cannot solve it by excluding the PKK."[56]

The current moment in Turkey is especially challenging. Violence by the state and the PKK escalated significantly between 2011 and 2013, and the fuelling of nationalist sentiments – by politicians and the media – threatens to heighten anti-Kurdish feeling in Turkish civil society. As anti-terrorism discourses and practices expand, it is difficult to see how Kurds in Turkey may not be seduced by the possibility that imperial humanitarian intervention would favour them. The points of caution regarding humanitarian intervention suggest, however, that as seductive as that possibility might be, it is not a realistic formula for freedom, democracy, and peace for Kurds. National and regional politics in Turkey is difficult, messy, and frustrating, but there may be no good political alternatives to talking to one's neighbours.

Postscript

In late December 2012, Turkey's Prime Minister Erdoğan announced that the government was negotiating a peace process with the jailed PKK leader Öcalan. After several delays, in March 2013, a letter by Öcalan was read during Newroz celebrations in Diyarbakir. It called for an end to armed struggle and declared that PKK guerrillas would disarm and withdraw from Turkey. A second phase of the peace process is expected to involve constitutional and legal changes in Turkey that would recognize Kurdish rights.

As of this writing, it is too early to know how the peace process will proceed and how successful it might be. Several months of ceasefire have been a great relief to Kurds and Turks alike who have suffered nearly three decades of civil war. Still, significant numbers of Turks remain to be convinced that peace will benefit all, after decades of nationalist propaganda that any concessions to Kurds would threaten Turkish sovereignty and unity. Also, there are signs that the peace process may not represent a significant change in the government's approach and discourse. The government has not entirely abandoned the logic and language of the "War on Terror."[57] Since the peace talks began, new waves of KCK arrests have taken place, and the courts have taken a hard line in KCK trials. The official inquiry into the Uludere/Roboski massacre has failed to criticize state policies and decisions, specifically as they relate to drone warfare. Also, the approach to peace has the characteristics of an *anti-politics*. There is no open and inclusionary dialogue among different sectors of society; instead, negotiations are being held in secret among a small group of politicians. Critics are concerned that within this framework, "peace" will be defined, not necessarily in ways that involve the popular interests, demands, and aspirations of most Kurds, but rather in such a way that the Kurdish issue will be resolved in terms of the ruling party's vision of a "neo-Ottoman" Turkey gaining further power, influence, and resources in the Middle East.

NOTES

This is a revised and expanded version of a paper presented at the "Violence in a Far Country: Women Scholars of Colour Theorize Terror" workshop at OISE, University of Toronto, 18–19 May 2012. I would like to thank the organizers of the workshop, Sherene Razack and Suvendrini Perera, for their intellectual leadership; and participants of the workshop, especially Miriam Ticktin, for very useful and valuable feedback on my presentation.

1 Among the factors contributing to this has been the significant size of the Kurdish population, as well as their geographic concentration (until the forced migration of the 1990s) in one region of the country.

2 Since the 1990s, there have been compromises in the politics of the PKK from the Marxist-Leninist ideology to which it originally subscribed.

3 Tuğal, "Democratic Janissaries?", 10.

4 Saraçoğlu, "Islami Muhafazakar Milliyetçiliğin Millet Tasarımı."

5 Mert, "The Kurds and the Conservatives."

6 I have borrowed the term "anti-politics machine" from James Ferguson, who has used it to critique the ways some development discourses and projects have served to expand and strengthen state power in Lesotho by presenting development strategies issues as technical rather than political ones. Ferguson, *The Anti-Politics Machine.*

7 Human Rights Watch, *Protesting as a Terrorist Offense.*
8 KHRP, "Turkey's Anti-Terror Laws."
9 American Bar Association, "Turkey's Anti-Terrorism Law."
10 It is only with the Gezi Park demonstrations across Turkey in June 2013 that this image, otherwise popular internationally, started to be shattered.
11 Buğlalılar, "The Epidemic of Terrorism." Beyond the specifically "terrorism-related" charges, there has been a very rapid increase overall in rates of detentions, arrests, and imprisonment in Turkey in recent years. In September 2012, in response to a question from the opposition party in Parliament, the Minister of the Interior stated that between 2009 and May 2012, 795,613 people had been detained. Of these, 3,049 were students who had participated in demonstrations. See *Haberler.com,* "4 Yılda 795 Bin Kişi Gözaltına Alındı."
12 International Crisis Group, *Turkey: The PKK and a Kurdish Settlement.*
13 Hawramy, "Turkey Would Rather Jail Journalists." In a recent televised message to representatives of media corporations and editors, Prime Minister Erdoğan demanded that they discipline and expel reporters and columnists who were critical of government policy on the Kurdish issue. He also instructed journalists to stop covering the conflict between the Turkish Armed Forces and the PKK, as he thought such reporting might serve PKK propaganda: "This [news about the conflict] must be ignored; there is no other way." "The most important target of terrorism is propaganda. [Terrorism] gets it done for free here. On whose side will the media be?" See Öğret and Ognianova, "Erdoğan Tells Media."
14 The reference, by Prime Minister Erdoğan, is to children participating in protests, who are seen by the prime minister as being used by the PKK. "Erdoğan," *CNN Türk.*
15 Arısoy, "PKK, KCK, BDP İç İçe." Author's translation.
16 "Bir Tek AKP Suçsuz," *Sendika.Org.*
17 "Halkın Oturduğu Bir Bölge Değil, Terör Bölgesi," *IMC-TV.*
18 *Sol Portal,* "Newroz Bilançosu."
19 The language used by some of the politicians and the media in relation to these events raises the question of whether Kurds in opposition are regarded as citizens of the city or of Turkey. In his explanation for not granting permission for the demonstration, Governor Toprak stated he banned it in order to "protect citizens"; *Sol Portal,* "Diyarbakir Valisi Mustafa Toprak." The daily *Zaman* reported on the tensions by stating that "the illegal demonstration disturbed peace in Diyarbakır"; *Zaman,* "Yasaklı miting Diyarbakır'ın huzurunu kaçırdı."
20 Coşkun, "Kürt Meselesini Derinleştirmek."

21 In July and August 2012, the Turkish army conducted a major operation in the southeast to counter PKK forces entrenched near Şemdinli township. In an article in the Turkish daily *Hürriyet*, columnist Ahmet Hakan asked why the uprising in this region had not been treated as another site of the "Arab Spring," why "Şemdinli cannot be Aleppo." His answer was that a major factor was the absence of interest by Western politicians and the media in the Kurdish cause in Turkey. Hakan, "Şemdinli Neden Halep Olmaz?"

22 In the summer of 2012, Syrian President Bashar al-Assad extended relative autonomy to Kurds in northern Syria. As there is already a Kurdish autonomous region in northern Iraq, the Turkish government has been alarmed that this development could foster collaboration between the PKK and Kurdish groups in neighbouring countries and that in the long term it could pave the way for a Kurdish state in the region. In early October 2012, after Syria shelled a Turkish border town, killing civilians, the Turkish Parliament authorized the government to launch military action for one year. This open-ended authorization has been interpreted by many as not just for a war on Syria, but also as approving any cross-border operations by Turkey into northern Iraq and northern Syria to attack PKK bases. In response to the possibility that Turkey could use the authorization to invade the autonomous Kurdish region in northern Syria, the BDP's co-leader, Gültan Kışanak, has said that they would stand in front of Turkish tanks to prevent that from happening ("Kışanak," *T24.Com*).

23 Brown, "The Most We Can Hope For," 460.

24 Archibugi, "Cosmopolitical Democracy."

25 Archibugi, "Cosmopolitical Democracy," 147.

26 Fassin and Pandolfi, "Introduction," 13.

27 Fassin and Pandolfi, "Introduction," 15–16. Anne Orford discusses the decision by the European Court of Human Rights to dismiss a human rights case relating to how certain states conducted the Kosovo intervention on the UN's behalf – specifically, regarding use of cluster bombs. She argues that when the court decided that "it was not competent to review the acts carried out on behalf of the U.N.," it "identified the UN and the states and personnel acting its authority, with the Universal. The representatives of universalism should not be asked to take responsibility for the effects of their actions ... Those acting under the authority of the UN represent human rights and the rule of law merely by heir presence." See Orford, "The Passions of Protection."

28 Cairo, "The Duty of the Benevolent Master," 298.

29 Cited in Cairo, "The Duty of the Benevolent Master," 297.

30 Mamdani, *Saviors and Survivors*, 281.
31 Mamdani, *Saviors and Survivors*, 281.
32 See Chandler, *From Kosovo to Kabul (and Beyond)*; Foley, *The Thin Blue Line*; and Rieff, *A Bed for the Night*.
33 Mamdani, "The New Humanitarian Order."
34 Mamdani, "The New Humanitarian Order."
35 Douzinas, "The Many Faces of Humanitarianism."
36 Douzinas, "The Many Faces of Humanitarianism," 16.
37 Douzinas, "The Many Faces of Humanitarianism," 16.
38 Douzinas, "The Many Faces of Humanitarianism," 15.
39 Ticktin, *Casualties of Care*, 21–2.
40 For a different perspective on the relationship between sovereignty and human rights, see Conlon, "Sovereignty vs. Human Rights."
41 Žižek, "Against Human Rights," 127.
42 Mamdani, *Saviors and Survivors*, 274–5.
43 Douzinas, "The Many Faces of Humanitarianism," 13.
44 An interview on CBC radio's *The Current* on Wednesday, 7 January, may help demonstrate the irony of the humanitarian position. During the Israeli attack on Gaza, a Canadian humanitarian worker volunteering with the International Solidarity Movement – sympathetic to the plight of Palestinians, in this case – protested the attacks on civilians. The argument she used to defend the innocence of civilians in Gaza was rather shocking. She said that most of the people who had been killed or wounded were "not political at all." She did not say they were "not armed militants," nor did she say they were "not terrorists"; she said they were "not political at all." She was no doubt speaking in good faith, to argue the innocence of those hurt and to appeal to the sympathy of the Canadian radio audience; even so, her choice of words needs to be questioned. Perhaps unintentionally, she was implying that Palestinians can only be considered "innocent" if they present themselves as, and effectively accept, a state of pitiful, naked humanity, a child-like innocence and helplessness, a non-politico-human status, and as completely dependent on the pity and charity of outsiders. There was also the implication – again, perhaps unintentional – that resistance, the struggle for dignity and justice, and a desire for self-determination are inherently illegitimate and suspect – as really or potentially "terrorist" – if they are exercised by Palestinians who disagree with Western mainstream solutions to the Palestinian question. If, to deserve Western recognition and protection of their human rights, Palestinians need to strip themselves of politico-human status, what is left of the "human" in humanitarian discourse? Arat-Koç, "Human Rights Discourse."

45 Žižek, "Against Human Rights," 128.
46 Cited in Douzinas, "The Many Faces of Humanitarianism," 20–1.
47 Kotef, "Objects of Security," 182.
48 Kotef, "Objects of Security," 186–7.
49 Lentin, "Racism and Human Rights."
50 Cairo, "The Duty of the Benevolent Master," 289.
51 Cairo, "The Duty of the Benevolent Master," 289.
52 Brown, "The Most We Can Hope For."
53 Žižek, "Against Human Rights," 126.
54 Dirlik, "Place-Based Imagination."
55 By this, Türk is referring specifically to the development of an ethnic/national identity among Kurds in Turkey.
56 "Ahmet Türk." Author's translation.
57 In fact, after the Gezi Park protests in Taksim, Istanbul, were repressed by brutal police action. Erdoğan has reverted to a discourse of terrorism in his references to PKK leader Öcalan. In several speeches in June 2013, as in previous periods, Erdoğan called Öcalan "the chief terrorist."

20 Africa, 9/11, and the Temporality and Spatiality of Race and Terror

MALINDA S. SMITH

Introduction

There are some moments we remember for a lifetime, such as the end of foreign subjugation that marked colonial rule in one's home country; the assassination of civil rights leaders Malcolm X and Martin Luther King, Jr; and the release of anti-apartheid leader Nelson Mandela from prison after he had served twenty-seven years for terrorism and treason. The 9/11 terrorist attacks are another such moment. Like many others, I recall where I was when I learned of them: I was in Johannesburg, South Africa, having just left a highly contentious UN World Conference against Racism, Racial Discrimination, Xenophobia, and Related Intolerances (UN WCAR) that had been held in Durban. It would be intellectual conceit to say that at the time, I grasped the full significance of either event. Unlike witnessing the end of the colonial order or the release of Mandela from apartheid's tyranny, there was no ready script or frame of reference to help make 9/11 intelligible. This was the witnessing of uncertainty in real time; I was caught up in the violence of reality television from the relative safety of a friend's living room. For many Americans, Canadians, and Australians, terrorism was no longer a theoretical abstraction or something that happened to abstract strangers in distant lands.

At the time of 9/11, some Western media speculated about whether the terrorist attacks were related to the anti-racism conference that had ended in Durban two days earlier. Despite the resistance of former colonial and current occupying powers, the anti-racism conference had enabled historic human rights debates and resolutions to unfold around many contested issues, including reparations for slavery and the designation of the transatlantic slave trade and apartheid as crimes against humanity. The Durban anti-racism conference had also addressed perennially contentious issues concerning race and religious intolerance, as well as the politically taboo question of whether Israel's continued occupation of Palestinian lands represented a new form of apartheid.[1] The events of 9/11 displaced these debates from the headlines. However, the issues that had threatened to derail the Durban conference have continued to reverberate in post-9/11 politics and policies as well as in the racial, legal, and military tactics, strategies, and technologies mobilized and deployed in the "War on Terror." Since 9/11, there has been a systematic rolling back on a planetary scale of historic postwar legislative achievements and international treaties whose aim had been to combat racism and xenophobia and to advance racial justice and religious accommodation. The post-9/11 technologies of power have rendered the postwar anti-racism regime dispensable and non-performative, reproduced colonial and apartheid practices of legislated racial and religious profiling and surveillance, and normalized legally sanctioned discrimination on the basis of race, skin colour, religion, and national origin. As Sara Ahmed puts it, when "speech acts do not do what they say: they do not, as it were, commit a person, organization, or state to an action ... they are nonperformatives."[2]

This chapter revisits the events of 9/11 and the ensuing "War on Terror" from an African-centred perspective. It uses 9/11 as a point of departure for thinking through the temporality, spatiality, and coloniality of Africa's experience with racism, political violence, and terror. How do we, as scholars of Africa and the diaspora, make sense of the claim that for the United States, 9/11 was an unthinkable and world-altering event? And how do the discourses on political violence and terrorism developed in its aftermath objectify, form, and perform Africa, particularly in the moments we have come to know as "post-9/11"? My answers to these questions draw on knowledge that is local and subaltern; that is discontinuous as well as disruptive to progressive notions of history that treat events in metropolitan centres as normative; and that may even be characterized as "illegitimate"[3] from the standpoint of conventional terrorism studies.

This chapter unfolds as follows. The first section, on "performative myths," examines the claim that "9/11 changed everything" and demonstrates how silences on subaltern histories are, in fact, determining silences.[4] The second section, on "productive myths," engages in a deconstructive analysis of the claim that "9/11 changed everything."

It unsettles three foundational myths of 9/11's state of exception by systematically juxtaposing them with subaltern histories and counter-narratives from Africa. The third section, on "disciplining myths," explores how 9/11 myth making constitutes Africa as a new frontier in the "War on Terror." It examines the repressive legal, extrajudicial, and security order that emerged in East Africa after 9/11. The performative and productive aspects of 9/11 myth making have given rise to new forms of state racism that are implicated in the reproduction of repressive and disciplinary forms of imperial and colonial violence. The fourth section recentres African subaltern histories and the place of race, terror, and torture in colonial and apartheid regimes. The chapter concludes with a call for a new anti-colonial and anti-racism order.

The Performativity of 9/11 Myth Making

The al-Qaeda attacks on the World Trade Center and the Pentagon, the iconic institutions of US economic and military power, have been characterized as unprecedented and even as unimaginable. Captured on television and in real-time, this event was no simulacrum, no Hollywood-style *Zero Dark Thirty*, no hyper-paranoid television episode of *Homeland*. Susanne Karstedt claimed at the time that "not even the world's leading factory of fiction had come up with such imagination and images, which made the event in a way unthinkable."[5] These claims about 9/11's historical significance require us to think through the spatiality and temporality as well as the performative, productive, and disciplinary aspects of the moment that has come to be known simply by its date, "September 11," or by the numbers "9/11." The weight this event exerted on the collective imaginary and the ways in which it has exposed our lack of mental preparedness is evident, Richard Falk suggests, in the "mere fact that we can find no better descriptive language for their occurrence than the date."[6] Despite all efforts to resist it, the moment and mobilizations seem to have created a vexed epochal chasm, and much scholarly literature and popular discourse now refers to "before 9/11" and "after 9/11."[7] This before-and-after demarcation has become the means by which diverse theorists have come to mark and name international as well as domestic security policies in the aftermath of the attacks on the World Trade Center and the Pentagon.

The epochal claim that "9/11 changed everything"[8] was, perhaps, a necessary overstatement of solidarity in a moment of utter bewilderment. Even if in that initial moment no one could find a specific example of how "9/11 changed everything," was it possible to perform this change, to bring it into being, rhetorically and discursively, over time? Discourses, Michel Foucault reasoned, are "practices that systematically form the object of which they speak."[9] The repetition – "before 9/11," "9/11," "post-9/11," "9/11 changed everything" – functioned to form, perform, and reconstitute the world and to bring into being the perception of a radical historical discontinuity, a watershed moment between a known past and an unknown and perilous future. The statement "9/11 changed everything" has been repeated so often that it has become part of the prevailing common sense, a fixture in everyday discourse that is etched on the popular imaginary as a self-evident truth-claim. Taken literally, this truth-claim reflects a cultural–ideological bias in conventional scholarship on terrorism, which too readily treats political violence experienced by Western states as novel, unprecedented, and exceptional. It is as if this one event on US soil had forever transformed our perspectives on the imaginable future, including how we speak, think, and narrate the world, political violence, and resistance.

Once 9/11 had been framed in terms of a war, initially a "War on Terror" and later a "War against Terrorism," there was only one possible response – a war without limits, including institutional limits, and without a foreseeable end.[10] To launch an endless war on *terror* was to articulate a space and perpetual moment and mobilization outside of the constitutional legal order, a state of exception, and a radically new conceptual imaginary. Georgio Agamben maintains that this declaration of a state of exception to law is not a temporary pragmatic accommodation.[11] Rather, it needs to be understood as an indefinite technique of government, beyond what historically has been understood as a temporary state of emergency during times of conflict, revolution, and war. The twentieth-century wars against fascism and communism were understood as ideological. By contrast, to declare a war on *terror* was to declare a war on ontology itself, to make an assessment about a state of being. And it was to launch a war on a perceived threat against a state of being rather than against an ideology or a nation-state. The naming of the war was a speech-act that brought into being a state of exception in terms of both its ambiguousness and its ubiquity. This speech-act required a kind of "magical thinking,"[12] a conceptual sorcery capable of conjuring up "a finite group of evil people who can be physically eliminated."[13] It required us to accept that there was a discrete population *out there*, an irreducible enemy that could be identified, classified, profiled, targeted, and destroyed. The all-too-familiar spectral character in this script of good and evil is the racialized other and the figure of Muslim as the "barbarian."

Historical thinking and understanding, at least that which fell outside the official orthodoxy of 9/11 as unprecedented and of the US as exceptional, became criminal, subversive, unpatriotic, and even a betrayal Western civilization.[14] For intellectuals and artists, the post-9/11 world, Peter McLaren noted, has been "transformed into pure intensity where to seek refuge in the sanctuary of reflection … [is] to engage in an act of unpardonable treason, where previously silenced realities are now guaranteed never to be heard."[15] In the aftermath of the attacks and to this day, there has been very little about 9/11 that is *"safe* to say"[16] without being labelled as naive or traitorous or being accused of giving aid and comfort to the enemy. Post-9/11, we "entered a new, Orwellian world." Similarly, John Le Carré has added that this world is one "where our personal reliability as comrades in the struggle [against terrorism] is measured by the degree to which we invoke the past to explain the present."[17] Any claim that we needed to be attentive to the historical context for the 9/11 atrocities was "by implication to make excuses for them. Anyone who is with us doesn't do that. Anyone who does is against us."[18] In the moment after 9/11, it became politically dangerous and intellectually unsafe to try to assess the broader historical and political meaning, however shape-shifting, of the 9/11 terrorist attacks.

Productive Myths: Deconstructing "9/11 Changed Everything"

Juxtaposed against the rhetorical permissiveness – that "9/11 changed everything" – and the accusatory indictment – of naively engaging in intellectually traitorous thinking – this chapter shifts to a closer exploration of the temporality and spatiality of the 9/11 terrorists attacks in relation to Africa. One way to disrupt the performative myth making of "9/11 changed everything" is to closely interrogate the statement's claim that the moment was unprecedented by juxtaposing its constitutive aspects with subaltern, discontinuous, and disruptive African counter-narratives. Rethinking 9/11 and terrorism from Africa and the geopolitical, epistemological, and cultural peripheries allows us to see the ways in which the hegemonic 9/11 narratives were produced. And it enables an exploration of the cultural and normative elements of the production of hegemonic voice and stories about political violence and terrorism. A counter-narrative method of thinking about 9/11 and the "War on Terrorism" can be both "politically tactical and epistemologically significant."[19] To facilitate my analysis, I pose three simple questions.

A first and critical intervention is to ask this simple question: Was 9/11 a novel, unprecedented event? The dominant narrative of 9/11 displaced from historical memory onto 9/11 other attacks on the Twin Towers and other epochal events. Clarifying what was not novel draws into stark relief not so much the exceptionalism of the event but rather its opposite: the hyper-exceptionalism of the response in the form of a global "War on Terrorism." The simultaneous terrorist attacks on the World Trade Center and the Pentagon on 9/11 struck, by North American metrics, an unprecedented number of victims. Among the casualties were nearly 3,000 people from the United States and at least 500 nationals from 91 other countries, including a dozen African countries.[20] In an essay on black victims of 9/11, Leslie Goffe found that at least one-third of all victims were from overseas – that is, immigrants and possibly undocumented workers.[21] Assensoh and Alex-Assensoh have found that, despite the plethora of media stories, photographs, and memorials dealing with the victims, families, and first responders, "missing from much of the discussions ... [was] a thorough examination of how African immigrants and African Americans were affected by the attacks." Even in tragedy, Africans and American Americans were rendered invisible. "Such an exclusion is no surprise, as scholars have indicated that American media typically fail to include blacks in both the daily and important representations of mainstream American life and culture."[22] As well, many scholars of Africa and the diaspora predicted, correctly, that the 9/11 tragedy would serve as a pretext "to reinforce an old agenda, tightening immigration into the US, restrictions on human rights and increased racial profiling, or using race to decide whether to stop and search a suspect."[23] Post-9/11, people of African descent were invisible as victims and survivors of it, yet alongside Arabs and South Asians, they soon became hyper-visible in post-9/11 surveillance and profiling.

What was also different about 9/11 was that unlike most other terrorist activities, this simultaneous event in New York and Washington was captured on television and in real-time. People the world over witnessed the second airplane flying into the Twin Towers and saw the human and infrastructural devastation of its explosion at the time of impact. In fact, this image has been repeated again and again – for over a decade. Yet, when compared to the simultaneous car bombings in two East African countries a few years earlier, this difference – captured on television and real-time – seems woefully inadequate for establishing an epochal shift that would warrant the launch of a global "War on Terrorism." Pre-9/11, two of al-Qaeda's most audacious terrorist attacks had been the 7 August 1998 simultaneous car bombings of the US embassies in Nairobi, Kenya, and Dar es Salaam, Tanzania. These simultaneous acts caused untold human and infrastructural devastation. The bombing in Nairobi killed 247 Kenyans and 12 Americans and injured some 5,436 people, while the one in Dar es Salaam killed 10 and injured 70 others. At the time, few in the US government or among conventional terrorism experts believed that the twin attacks in East Africa constituted a threat to the US or to the West, let alone Western civilization.

When the bombings in East Africa are compared to the bombings in the United States, it is clear how the attacks were framed differently and which lives seemed to matter to the global media. As Omofolabo Ajayi-Soyinka has written, Kenyans "were particularly bitter" that, while 12 Americans lost their lives, so did more than 200 Kenyans, yet "the U.S. government behaved as if Kenyan (or Tanzanian) lives did not matter."[24] Many across East Africa wondered how the global media determined whose lives were "grievable"[25] and worthy of memoralization. Even when the US Agency for International Development allocated $37 million for Kenya, $29 of it was for the reconstruction of buildings. This prompted Peter Anyang Nyong'o, a Kenyan parliamentarian, to ask, "If the U.S. government can give prompt attention to inanimate objects like buildings, why can't even more attention be paid to human beings?"[26]

If our critical thinking about 9/11 shifts to the specificity of that date, a subaltern excavation reveals "other 9/11s." There is a history of epochal moments of political violence in other geopolitical spaces on that date. Those moments include 9/11, 1973, when the United States supported a coup d'état against the democratically elected government of Salvador Allende in Chile and set in place the brutal dictatorship of General Augusto Pinochet. The same date is associated with *non-violent* political actions, including the events leading up to 9/11, 1906, that gave rise to Gandhi's *Satyagraha* in South Africa.[27] This South Africa case is instructive for thinking about alternative responses to political violence.

When Mohandas Gandhi arrived from India to work as a lawyer in South Africa, he was rudely confronted by the strictures of legislated racism. He purchased a first-class ticket and boarded the train, and took a seat, only to be summarily thrown off the train. The front of the train was designated first-class and was reserved for whites. Under apartheid laws, black Africans and Indians were required to sit at the back, signifying their racially unequal status. For Gandhi this racist and dehumanizing experience led to a long night of humiliation and reflection that he would remember as one of the most creative nights of his life. It was the spark that ignited his movement for non-violent social change.

Gandhi's response to the violence of apartheid and racial injustice helped foster various institutions of civil society and democracy, including the Natal Indian Congress to fight for greater social justice, as well as newspapers such as the *Indian Opinion*. It also led to legal petitions advocating for more racially just laws.[28] The non-violent movement gained momentum after 22 August 1906, when the Transvaal passed new British imperial legislation that created a state of exception for people of colour. The Asiatic Law Amendment Act (the "Black Act") required the registration of all Indians, Arabs, and Turks and the fingerprinting and stamping with an identity mark of all persons over the age of eight; it also required people of colour to obtain and carry a racial identity card, which had to be produced on demand for the state police and security officials. The new law permitted the police to enter, at their discretion, the home of any Indian, Arab, or Turk and to treat persons without an identity card as suspicious and subject to a fine, imprisonment, or deportation. These imperial practices of racism and technologies of biopower have been reproduced across time and space, including during the "War on Terror."

On 9/11, 1906, 3,000 mostly Indians demonstrated non-violently at the Johannesburg Empire Theatre. Gandhi argued that the Asiatic Law was unjust and degrading and that it reflected a state-legislated "hatred of Indians." He drafted a resolution that encouraged non-compliance. What was born in South Africa on this "other 9/11" was *Satyagraha*, what Gandhi called "the force which is born of truth and love or non-violence." Born in anti-colonial and anti-racism struggle, this countervailing "force" of love and non-violence was a powerful response to state-legislated racism. This response was world-transformative and has continued to shape anti-colonial and social justice movements. What has persisted over time, from South Africa in 1906 to the United States in 2001, is the state's resort to racial classification, racial profiling, fingerprinting, and indefinite detention; all of these signify states of exception that allow police and security forces to act with impunity.

This intersection of imperial power and racism was evident in apartheid South Africa in 1906, as it is today in the United States post-9/11.

A second simple but important question is this: Was the attack on US soil unique? The US homeland was attacked on 7 December 1941, when Japan bombed the Hawaiian island of Oahu. And in the two decades before 9/11, American nationals had carried out a number of racially and religiously motivated terrorist attacks on US soil. In April 1995, Gulf War veteran Timothy McVeigh exploded a truck bomb in front of the Alfred P. Murrah Federal Building in Oklahoma City, killing 168 people and injuring another 450. At the time, this was the deadliest terrorist attack ever carried out on US soil. One year later, a US army veteran named Eric Robert Rudolph bombed Olympic Park in Atlanta, Georgia, killing one spectator and injuring 111 others, while that city was hosting the Olympic Games. The Federal Bureau of Investigation (FBI) had labelled Rudolph, a member of the white supremacist Christian Identity Movement, a terrorist, and had placed him on its Ten Most Wanted list.[29] Rudolph later called his act a protest against the "abortion holocaust" and the "homosexual agenda." These hate-motivated domestic terrorist attacks by Americans have garnered less scholarly attention than attacks by "enemy aliens" and have never led to calls for the surveillance, racial profiling, or the fingerprinting of white American men.

This brings me to a third question: Was the method deployed by 9/11 terrorists – the use of everyday modes of transportation as weapons of mass destruction – a novel one? It was not, either in the United States or in Africa. The 1993 attack on the World Trade Center had some similarities to the 2001 attacks in terms of both space and method. For al-Qaeda, the target of the attack – the most potent symbol of America's global economic power – remained constant. In 1993, the terrorists had intended to toppled the North Tower so that it fell onto the South Tower, causing mass destruction and death. That effort did not succeed, although it killed 6 people and injured more than 1,042. What had changed by 9/11, 2001, was the use of airplanes rather than car bombs, which achieved the devastation that had eluded the terrorists eight years earlier. And unlike in 1993 or in the 1998 car bombings in Nairobi and Dar es Salaam, much of the world witnessed the devastation of 2001 on their TV and computer screens.

In the decades prior to 9/11, a significant number of terrorist attacks involving airplanes were carried out across Africa and various global spaces, claiming victims from dozens of countries but never giving rise to a global war. Twice, the African state of Libya was declared responsible. In December 1988, Pan Am Flight 103 en route from London to New York exploded over Lockerbie, Scotland, killing 243 passengers and 16 crew from 29 countries, as well as 11 people in Lockerbie.[30] And on 19 September 1989, UTA Flight 772 from Paris to Brazzaville exploded over the city of Ténéré, Niger, killing all 156 passengers and 14 crew from 18 countries, including the wife of the US Ambassador to Chad. Libyan government officials were convicted of both these bombings. In October 2008, Libyan leader Muammar Qadhafi agreed to pay compensation to the victims. This acknowledgment of responsibility paved the way for US president George W. Bush to sign an executive order granting the Libyan government immunity from any further US prosecution for the terror attacks.

Disciplinary Myths and the Post-9/11 Racial Order

The previous sections were about how we name and remember events like 9/11 in the United States as well as in South Africa and Chile. This section is about how we respond to those events and how the responses perform, produce, and consolidate naming and remembering. A few years after 9/11, much had already changed, as Ajayi-Soyinka writes: "Nothing is the same anymore; the material aspects of the American way of life and the democratic process have indeed changed. It is precisely this shift in the democratic process that has the most negative impact on Africa."[31] In the United States, the Patriot Act and other new laws, as well as the introduction of the Terrorist Information and Prevention System (TIPS), have sought to limit civil rights and liberties in the name of national security. These changes are performed daily, from "airport checks to colour-coded terror alerts to antiterrorist measures that profile specific ethnic/national groups and organizations."[32] These new laws have cleared the way for unprecedented surveillance, profiling, wiretapping, telephone eavesdropping, and e-mail snooping.

After the Bush administration declared the events of 9/11 as exceptional and unprecedented, as "an act of war," an overwhelming military response, a "War on Terrorism," was presented as both appropriate and unavoidable. But the war metaphor was not perfect: the front line was transnational and dispersed. The theatre of this war shifted from Afghanistan in 2001 to Iraq in 2003 and then to a "new front" on the African continent, which included the 2006 proxy intervention by Ethiopia into neighbouring Somalia and the constitution of Ethiopia as "Africa's

Guantanamo Bay." Under the administration of Barack Obama, the United States' first African American president, the technologies of war have expanded to include an unprecedented degree of surveillance at home and around the world as well as drone warfare abroad,[33] and the theatres of conflict have become more diffused, an example being the 2011 intervention in Libya that deposed Colonel Qadhafi.[34] Some African scholars[35] have cautioned that groups that engage in terrorist acts have primarily local grievances, such as Boko Haram in northern Nigeria and al-Shabab in Somalia. These groups too often are conflated with al-Qaeda, both by the United States and by African governments wishing to discredit their opponents. Too often, anti-terrorism strategies have drawn few distinctions between groups like these and have undermined regional peace talks.

In the hegemonic post-9/11 anti-terrorism narratives, "Africa" has been reduced to a stereotype. "Reductive repetition motif," Stefan Andreasson argues, "reduces the diversity of African historical experiences and trajectories, sociocultural contexts and political situations into a set of core deficiencies for which externally generated 'solutions' must be devised."[36] In her testimony before the US Congress two months after 9/11, Susan Rice, who had been the Clinton administration's Assistant Secretary of State for Africa, characterized the continent as the world's "soft underbelly for global terrorism."[37] She testified that the continent posed a threat to US national security because "much of Africa has become a veritable incubator for the foot soldiers of terrorism" and because the continent's "poor, young, disaffected, unhealthy, undereducated populations often have no stake in government." She added that these disaffected youth saw few prospects for a better future and thus were easily exploited by terrorist networks. She concluded: "These are the swamps we must drain … [or] we are going to place our national security at further and more permanent risk."[38] At the launch of the African Union's Centre for the Study and Research on Terrorism, Algeria's President Abdelaziz Bouteflika reproduced this rhetoric, stating that African counter-terrorism initiatives were necessary "so that the continent does not become a breeding ground for terrorism and a base for terrorist groups which could then indiscriminately attack African countries and other regions of the world from our continent."[39]

Post-9/11, Africa's fifty-four diverse countries were being discussed as a single undifferentiated security threat, as a "swamp" that needed to be drained, a dangerous "sleeping giant,"[40] a "breeding ground for terrorists,"[41] and an ungoverned space in which al-Qaeda could relocate, reassemble, and re-create "another Afghanistan."[42] The heterogeneity of Nigeria, Africa's most populous state, was reduced to a "potent" mix of ethnic and communal tensions, radical Islam, and anti-Americanism, all of which were fuelling militancy and political violence.[43] West and Central Africa were "fertile breeding grounds" where terrorism could germinate and "where disorder and poverty harbour extremism."[44] States like Sudan and Somalia were "anarchic zones" where "rogue" leaders roamed and where "lawless bazaars" run by unholy alliances of criminal and illicit networks were trading "blood diamonds" and laundering money to help al-Qaeda hide its ill-gotten gains.[45] This stereotypical description of Africa – as outlaw, rogue, swamp of ungovernable disorder– buttressed the case for externally generated solutions and even for the return of the United States to Africa as a "reluctant imperialist."[46]

Repressive legislation emerged in post-9/11 East Africa, strengthening authoritarian regimes and undermining efforts to advance a postcolonial constitutional order. Across Africa, many states introduced counterterrorism laws that mimicked the US Patriot Act of 2001. States granted themselves sweeping powers to monitor personal telephone calls and e-mails and to violate press freedoms, including by intercepting communications and forcing journalists to divulge their informants.[47] According to Amnesty International, these "draconian measures … threaten[ed] the human rights of their own citizens, immigrants and refugees."[48] Post-9/11 legal tactics to combat terrorism have included weakening domestic and international human rights protections. Counter-terrorism laws such as Tanzania's Prevention of Terrorism Act (PTA; 2002) and Kenya's Suppression of Terrorism Bill (2003) run counter to national constitutions as well as to the commitments these states once made as signatories to the UN Declaration of Human Rights (UNDHR). Under Tanzania's counter-terrorism law, for example, law enforcement has been granted sweeping powers to transgress basic human rights and civil liberties. Overriding constitutional guarantees, Tanzania's PTA has empowered the police to arrest and detain a suspect without a warrant, charge, or trial. This directly contravenes Article 9 of the UNDHR, which guarantees a person protection from arbitrary arrest and detention. Furthermore, while the constitution includes protections against statesanctioned violence, Section 29(6) of the PTA exempts law enforcement from liability in a criminal or civil trial even when a suspect dies from excessive use of force. Law enforcement's ability to violate the constitution with impunity extends to invasions of privacy, search and seizure, how evidence is obtained, and whether that evidence can be used against an accused. Although it violates the right to privacy under Section 16(1) of Tanzania's Constitution as well as Article 12 of the UNDHR, the PTA's Section 31(3) grants law enforcement the authority to plant surveillance technology without a warrant and to use the resulting evidence in court. Gus Hosein, a Senior Fellow at Privacy International, has found that "almost every country that changed its laws to reflect the environment following September 2001 increased the ability of law enforcement and national security agencies to perform interception of communications, and transformed the powers of search and seizure, and an increase in the type of data that can be accessed."[49]

In post-9/11 East Africa, security laws, policies, and practices rival and often surpass those of the colonial state in their degree of repression. "Common features of the new anti-terror laws," Lumina writes, "are broad and vague definitions of new offences, wide powers of detention without trial, prolonged incommunicado detention (which is known to facilitate torture), intrusions of privacy,"[50] as well as new measures designed to inhibit the mobility of refugees and asylum seekers and to enable their easy deportation. In a scathing review of the anti-terrorism laws, Issa G. Shiva similarly writes that "the definitions of terrorism are so wide that these laws are worse than some of the draconian statutes during the period of one-party authoritarian rule"; moreover, those laws enable the state's repressive apparatus to "ruthlessly suppress"[51] civil dissent.

Domestic security forces in Djibouti, Ethiopia, Kenya, Tanzania, and Uganda have strengthened their international partnerships with the FBI, the CIA,[52] and other intelligence agencies. US intelligence agencies have been authorized to operate in East African countries, including to arrest, interrogate, and to indefinitely detain suspects without charge and without access to legal counsel. Law enforcement can now use evidence obtained from wiretapping and hearsay. Gone are the presumption of innocence, the guarantee of a fair trial, and due process of law. Civil libertarians have criticized the post-9/11 secret trials conducted by military tribunals under rules intended to limit the rights of the accused and circumvent due process. Ali A. Mazrui writes: "Even the leaders of Nazi Germany were given a public trial at Nuremberg after World War II with access to counsel and proper representation. Some of those tried at Nuremberg had been responsible for the death of millions of people."[53]

Furthermore, East Africa and the Horn of Africa have joined a global rendition network. Renditions are not new – in fact, they can be traced back to the 1960s, when the Israeli government justified abducting Nazi war criminal Adolf Eichmann from Argentina so that he could be "rendered to justice."[54] Renditions have been a part of US security practice since the Reagan administration; however, most instances of rendition have occurred since then, especially under the post-9/11 Bush administration. The Clinton administration required receiving countries to issue a warrant or indictment for a rendition; the Bush administration dispensed with this legal requirement.[55]

Post-9/11, the Bush administration and its "coalition of the willing" established a global extralegal practice of "renditions to torture"[56] rather than renditions to justice. Condoleezza Rice, Bush's Secretary of State, defended the practice, insisting that "rendition is a vital tool in combating transnational terrorism. Its use is not unique to the United States."[57] Indeed, the Bush administration relied on the bilateral cooperation of European, African, and Asian countries. One EU report identified fourteen European countries that were part of a rendition network. Countries such as Cyprus, Germany, Spain, and Turkey served as "staging points" for renditions; others such as Greece, Ireland, Portugal, and Britain were "stop-off points"; and Bosnia, Italy, Macedonia, and Sweden allowed residents of their countries to be abducted by the CIA.[58] Many of the people subjected to rendition were shipped to Guantanamo Bay Detention Camp in Cuba. Others were sent to sites in Iraq such as Abu Ghraib Prison, Camp Nama at Baghdad International Airport, and Balad Special Forces Base north of Baghdad; to the Bagram Theater Internment Facility in Afghanistan; or to lesser-known sites such as Camp Justice on Diego Garcia, a small British territory in the Indian Ocean used as a high-security based by the US Army and Navy.[59]

Two reports for the Council of Europe have mapped a global system of extraordinary renditions to "black sites" and what Swiss politician Dick Marty has called the emergence of an international "legal apartheid."[60] "Black sites" here refers to secret military prisons funded and operated by the CIA where detainees are interrogated and tortured. The reports confirm that some detainees have been held for days, some for weeks, and others for years, without formal charges or access to a lawyer; these detainees have been routinely subjected to "gross violations of human rights."[61] Marty points out that "such actions would no doubt have been ruled unlawful and unconstitutional" in the US and the EU. Since 9/11, an international system of "legal apartheid" has emerged in which citizens of African and Middle Eastern states are legally subjected to different and unequal treatment than Americans and Europeans.[62]

The post-9/11 international system of legal apartheid is evident in two types of "rendition to torture." According to Amnesty International, the first type of rendition relies on "partners in crime."[63] In these cases, the CIA, British intelligence (M15), and Canadian intelligence (CSIS), among others, cooperate to render suspects to third countries. Or the "partners in crime" have suspects arrested in other countries, with a wink and a nudge that the detainees will face interrogation and torture in the quest for intelligence.[64] In one example, two British residents, Bisher Al-Rawi and Jamil El-Banna, while on a business trip to The Gambia in West Africa, were picked up by that country's National Intelligence Agency. Both men were interrogated, threatened with beating and rape, then transferred to Bagram and from there to Guantanamo Bay, where they faced more harsh interrogation. This chain of events was possible after M15 provided the Gambians with false information enabling the men's arrest.[65] Although the two men were technically in Gambian custody, the CIA was in charge of their detention, and they were interrogated by US intelligence agents in The Gambia.[66] The second type of rendition is to "black sites" in Eastern Europe, initially in Poland and later Romania. These secret prisons were operated "directly and exclusively by the CIA."[67] They held "high-level detainees" (HVDs), who were subjected to the most brutal forms of torture, including waterboarding, as was the case with suspected 9/11 mastermind Khalid Sheikh Mohammed and suspected al-Qaeda operative Abu Zubaydah.

Across East Africa, as in Eastern Europe, the CIA has exploited a loophole in aviation regulations that allows private planes to land without the same scrutiny as faced by commercial airliners. Leasing contracts and flight manifests from airports in Szymany, Poland, and in Nairobi, Dar es Salaam, and Mogadishu reveal that a significant number of individuals have been moved across national borders with minimal documentation.[68] Secret flight manifests[69] also show that many suspected terrorists have been apprehended in Somalia and Kenya and rendered to Addis Ababa, where they have been questioned and subjected to "massive and systematic violations of human rights."[70] Human rights organizations have also documented the disappearances of Kenyans, Tanzanians, and Somalis from third countries such as Pakistan and their rendition to other countries in East Africa, including to the US military base at Camp Lemonier in Ville de Djibouti, to black sites in Somalia, and to Jamida Prison in Ethiopia. The Kenyan Muslim Human Rights Forum's 2007 report "Horn of Terror"[71] details more than 150 detentions as well as 117 renditions from Kenya to Ethiopia; some of these detainees have been Muslims carrying Kenyan national identity documents.

The existence of "Africa's Guantanamo," as Ethiopia is now known, became more visible after the United States supported Ethiopia's July 2006 intervention in Somalia. Ethiopia claimed that this intervention was to prevent extremism in East Africa; however, it was working with the United States to prop up the Somali Transitional Government (STG) against the Islamic Court Union (ICU).[72] US Special Forces took part in the intervention and were deployed throughout Somalia alongside Ethiopians and STG forces.[73] During this intervention, internally displaced persons and fleeing civilians and fighters were indiscriminately rounded up and rendered to black sites in Ethiopia. Human Rights Watch has documented that detainees were brutally interrogated by Ethiopian security officials in Addis Ababa. According to John Sifton, an HRW expert on counter-terrorism, the United States acted in Ethiopia as "ringleader" in a "decentralized, outsourced Guantanamo."[74] While the detainees were technically in Ethiopian custody, Ethiopian security officials were junior partners in a process overseen by some two hundred CIA and FBI officials based in Ethiopia.[75] Interrogations were conducted by both Ethiopian and US intelligence officials in at least three different sites, including the capital, the Ethiopian air base at Debre Zeyit some thirty-seven miles from Addis Ababa, and an eastern desert site near the Somali border.[76]

A unique feature of Africa's black sites – and a striking difference from Afghanistan and Iraq, where the rationale for the "War on Terrorism" included saving Muslim women – is that in East Africa, Muslim women and their children are also subjected to rendition and inhumane prison conditions. According to a 2007 report by the Kenyan Muslim Human Rights Forum, known detainees have included nineteen women, several of whom were pregnant, fifteen children, and at least one infant.[77] The detainees were held for weeks without charge in Nairobi; then, without any notice to families or their lawyers, they were subjected to extraordinary rendition to Ethiopia. In Addis Ababa, some of the detainees, including several of the pregnant women, were interrogated by US intelligence agents based at a villa.[78] Some of these women were detained because their husbands or brothers were of interest to intelligence agents; in other words, they were bait in a fishing expedition. Other women were reportedly tortured in the belief that because of family ties, they had information on the Islamic Court Union.

Few women have spoken publicly about their experiences with rendition and detention in East Africa. One who has confirms that both the Kenyan government and US intelligence agents took part in her interrogation in Addis Ababa. Kamilya Mohammedi Tuweni, an Arab–Swahili translator and mother of three originally from the United Arab Emirates,[79] recounted how she was arrested in Kenya while on a business trip, beaten in detention, then relocated to Somalia,[80] where she was again interrogated and forced to sleep on a cold cement floor with more than twenty-two other women and children. About ten days later, she was secretly flown to Addis, where she spent another two and a half months in prison and was interrogated by US officials at a villa. No charges were laid against her, but consistent with US counter-terrorism practice, she was photographed and fingerprinted and a DNA sample was extracted from her before she was freed.

Despite the evidence, including from released detainees, Ethiopian officials initially denied the existence of secret prisons. Similarly, US intelligence officials initially denied being involved in interrogations in Addis Ababa. An FBI spokesperson, Richard Kolko, claimed that the Ethiopian detainees never were in US custody. Instead, "while in custody of the foreign government, the FBI was granted limited access to interview certain individuals of interest."[81] Kolko added, "We do not support or participate in any system that illegally detains foreign fighters or terror suspects, including women and children."[82] Yet many of the people detained and eventually released by the Ethiopians after the intervention in Somalia were not terrorists. They were innocent civilians caught up in an indiscriminate sweep of people fleeing Somalia. Notwithstanding Kolko's claim of deniability, the CIA and FBI in East Africa, like M15 in The Gambia, were active partners with local law enforcement in the arrest, detention, rendition, interrogation, and torture of terrorism suspects.

Recentring Africa: The Coloniality of Race and Terror

The tactics and strategies of extremist groups such as al-Qaeda, like the actions of alienated youth influenced by them – who include the Nigerian "underwear bomber" Umar Farouk Abdulmutallab,[83] the Boston Marathon bombers Tamerlan and Dzhokhar Tsarnaev,[84] and disaffected youth movements like Somalia's al-Shabab[85] – deliberately aim to traumatize, to engender fear and insecurity, and to expose human vulnerability and fragility. The physical and psychic dangers of the post-9/11 moment have been shaped by spectacles of violence and by the palpable fear of terrorism. And for intellectuals there has been another kind of danger, this one less visible: it is now traitorous to think critically and historically about the root causes of terrorism in general and of the 9/11 attacks in particular – that is, to ponder the difficult and thorny *why* questions. The post-9/11 moment is a politically, rhetorically, and conceptually polarized one in which it is intellectually dangerous to historicize acts of terrorism, even in terms of the moment deemed "the past" – the moment "before 9/11."

The significance of 9/11 for Africa was debated at a conference I attended on Africa and global governance in Addis Ababa in December 2004. The question then, as now, was this: Was 9/11 a defining moment for Africa? Frene Ginwala, former Speaker of the National Assembly of South Africa, cautioned against using 9/11 as the principal lens through which to interpret African histories and experiences, including of political violence, and against prioritizing terrorism as a major item on Africa's global agenda. Ginwala was all too familiar with South Africa's own anti-colonial history in which the armed wings of national liberation groups such as the African National Congress – the Umkhonto we Sizwe (MK) founded by Nelson Mandela and led by Rashid Aboobaker Ismail – were labelled as terrorist organizations, banned by the apartheid regime, and placed on pre-9/11 international terrorism watch lists. Many African anti-colonial intellectuals argued that it was important to distinguish acts of terrorism committed in the context of a struggle for national liberation.

Historicizing the study of terrorism exposes the subjective and value-laden contours that have made a widely accepted definition of terrorism difficult to develop. To understand and combat terrorism, we must first define it. In a commentary on domestic terror and human rights in Africa, Cephas Lumina reminds us that the international community has been attempting to formulate a universally accepted definition of terrorism for more than eighty years – long before 9/11 and the "War on Terrorism."[86] This "definitional knot," as Lumina calls it, "is primarily attributable to the fact that terrorism is a controversial and elusive concept which evokes strong emotional and contradictory responses."[87] In the post-9/11 environment, African governments have been pressured to introduce legislation that often reflects a historical amnesia regarding political violence during their own national liberation and postcolonial struggles. When Tanzania enacted its PTA in 2002, for example, its justification was the 9/11 attacks in the United States, not the al-Qaeda attacks of 7 August 1998 in Dar es Salaam.

Political action, including violence and extremism, is often understood through hegemonic narratives: "what" gets labelled as terrorism and "who" gets branded a terrorist do not fall outside those narratives. National liberation movements across Africa resorted to political violence, including acts of terrorism, against the colonial regime. The subaltern histories of anti-colonial and anti-apartheid intellectuals and activists remind us that "someone else's terrorist is another person's freedom fighter."[88] Often, the "terrorist of yesterday is the hero of today, and the hero of yesterday becomes the terrorist of today."[89] Some of Africa's best-known organic intellectuals in the decolonization struggle advocated political violence against colonialism and apartheid. At the time, those who argued for leaving all options for resistance on the table were labelled as terrorists, as traitorous or treasonous. Amilcar Cabral, for example, called for a "people's war" against the fascist brutality of Portuguese rule in Guinea-Bissau and on the Cape Verde Islands. Cabral was eventually betrayed and assassinated by agents of the Portuguese colonial rulers.[90] Frantz Fanon, one of the best-known anti-colonial theoreticians, advocated political violence against the terror and torture practised by French colonialism. Fanon argued that political violence could psychologically emancipate those who practised it from the "systemized dehumanization"[91] of colonial rule. A psychiatrist by training, Fanon volunteered to train Algerian anti-colonial fighters in psychological techniques for resisting the torture that was being systematically practised by the French colonial regime in Algeria.[92] France responded by declaring him *persona non grata.*[93]

Internationally, it was the anti-apartheid movement – not the racist apartheid regime with its monopoly on legitimate force – that was labelled as terrorist. In June 1967, when the regime introduced its "Terrorism Bill," which became the Terrorism Act No. 83 (1967), it defined terrorism as any act that endangered the maintenance of law and order in the Republic of South Africa. To cast the net as wide as possible, the apartheid regime recast many ordinary criminal acts as terrorism and made terrorism equivalent to treason. Under the Terrorism Act, only the authority of a police officer was needed to indefinitely detain, without a right to trial, a black African suspect. Since the law included as terrorism the intent or conspiracy to endanger the prevailing apartheid order, any act by an organization that aimed to overthrow the apartheid regime was by definition terrorism and thus treason. In the United States, the Nixon administration and later the Reagan administration maintained friendly relations with the racist regime. Under Reagan, the ANC was branded a terrorist organization. Instead of distancing itself from the brutality of apartheid, the United States supported the imprisonment of Mandela; it also banned the ANC and placed both it and anti-apartheid leaders on its pre-9/11 terrorism watch list. Reagan insisted that it was in the United States' national security interest to support the apartheid regime because apartheid South Africa was "a country that has stood by us in every war we've ever fought, a country that, strategically, is essential to the free world in its production of minerals."[94]

The ANC remained on the US terrorism watch list throughout the administrations of George H. Bush and Bill Clinton. It was not until April 2008 that then Secretary of State Condoleezza Rice urged the US Senate to remove the ANC from the terrorism list because it had become a "rather embarrassing matter that I still have to waive in my own counterpart, the foreign minister of South Africa [Nkosazana Dlamini Zuma], not to mention the great leader Nelson Mandela."[95] On 1 July 2008, at the height of a new global "War on Terrorism" and the production of a new terrorism watch list now populated by Muslims, Bill H.R. 5690 was signed into US law. That bill "authorize[d] the Departments of State and Homeland Security to determine that provisions in the Immigration and Nationality Act that render aliens inadmissible due to terrorist or criminal activities would not apply with respect to activities undertaken in association with the African National Congress in opposition to apartheid rule in South Africa."[96] Until the bill's passage, even Mandela, as President of South Africa, had required special waivers by successive Secretaries of State in order to enter the United States. Mandela was ninety years old by the time his name was removed from the terrorism watch list.

What we see in the imprisonment of Mandela by a white supremacist regime in South Africa, in the assassination of Cabral by the colonial regime in Guinea-Bissau, in the coup d'état against Patrice Lumumba in the Republic of the Congo and his subsequent assassination,[97] and in the declaration of Fanon as *persona non grata* by the French colonial regime, is that no matter how racist, brutal, unjust – and terrorizing – the colonial regime, it had the right to use force under international law. Colonial violence, repression, disappearances, assassinations, and indefinite detentions were not understood as state-sanctioned terrorism; rather, they were "legitimate" national security practices by the state (including South Africa's apartheid state). In contrast, victims of the colonial or apartheid state's political violence were terrorists who could be imprisoned, tortured, assassinated, or expelled from the body politic.

Re-examining 9/11 and terrorism through the lens of African colonialism and apartheid reveals the selectivity as well as many of the historical uses and abuses of the concept of terrorism. An African-centred critical approach to terrorism acknowledges the contested contextual, methodological, epistemological, political, and normative dimensions of terrorism, which conventional approaches too often avoid.[98] Conventional terrorism studies tend to focus on non-state and transnational actors rather than, for example, the terror of slave-holding societies or the terror of colonial or apartheid states. A critical perspective also recognizes the interpretative dimensions of political violence and the need to explore the images and narratives of terrorism, how the story of an event is told, and from what standpoint.[99] Despite the democratizing influence of the Internet and new social media, the power to interpret events is significantly shaped by the modern state with its monopoly on the legitimate use of force, its power to influence access to information, and its disproportionate authority to tell stories and to generate a hegemonic narrative that can shape how a given act of political violence is understood and acted upon.

Conclusions

After almost a century of colonial and anti-colonial wars, the Cold War, and intrastate and interstate conflicts, since 9/11 the African continent has become a theatre in a new war.[100] Alfred G. Nhema and Tiyambe Zeleza of the Organization for Social Science Research in Eastern and South Africa summarize it best when they state that "the US-led 'war on terror' [was] a crusade that knows no spatial or temporal bounds, spares no expense, leaves a trail of wanton destruction."[101] The "War on Terrorism" buttressed the power of authoritarian leaders and strengthened the repressive arm of the state, including the police, military, security, and intelligence forces. From an African perspective, this was a familiar script: the new war was similar to the "savage wars of conquest" and was "reminiscent of the wars of colonization of a bygone era."[102]

This chapter began by reflecting on the paradoxical legacies of 9/11 and the 2001 Durban anti-racism conference. Durban was historic: it was the first UN anti-racism conference convened outside Europe; it was held in post-apartheid South Africa in the city where Gandhi launched his non-violent movement; and it tackled an unprecedented number of perennially thorny issues, including the transatlantic slave trade and apartheid as crimes against humanity. Despite these historic achievements, Durban was performed, formed, and produced as a failure. By contrast, despite representations of 9/11 as a global watershed, this chapter has suggested that 9/11, 2001, was not, at least in the initial moment, epochal. Yet through various performative, productive, and disciplinary myths, 9/11 has been consolidated as a watershed with a distinctive before and after. Paradoxically, the execution of 9/11's performativity has helped consolidate the postwar anti-racism regime as non-performative.

The production of the post-9/11 epochal shift relied on the mobilization and reproduction of familiar disciplinary constructs of colonial racism. On a planetary order, the post-9/11 epochal shift has inaugurated a return to state-legislated racism and a global apartheid legal order. The chapter's recentring of Africa's experience of imperial, colonial, and apartheid terror is a necessary disruption of claims that 9/11 was something new, at least when it comes to the technologies of racial orders such as colour-coded profiling, fingerprinting, photographing, DNA collection, separate lines in airports, and "black sites" of torture. The imperial state's reliance on racial logics is not novel, as this chapter has demonstrated with examples as diverse as Gandhi's resistance to the Asiatic Law Amendment (the "Black Act"); the apartheid state's legal apparatus, which produced the anti-apartheid movement as terrorist and treasonous; and 9/11's counter-terrorism laws, which have rendered nonperformative the UN anti-racism regime. These paradoxes and perverse developments highlight the need for a new anti-colonial and anti-racism order.

NOTES

This essay is dedicated to the great Madiba. It builds on and extends my effort to craft an African-centred critical terrorism studies in *Securing Africa: Post-9/11 Discourses on Terrorism* (Farnham: Ashgate 2010). Thanks are owed to Janet Phillips for her research assistance. Sections of this chapter have been excerpted by permission of the publishers from "Post-9/11: Thinking Critically, Thinking Dangerously" and "Terrorism Thinking: '9/11 Changed Everything'" in *Securing Africa*, ed. Malinda S. Smith (Farnham: Ashgate, 2010) © 2010.

1 Mann, *Dispatches from Durban*; Mu'id, "United Nations World Conference against Racism." In contrast, see Bayefsky, "Terrorism and Racism."

2 Ahmed, "The Nonperformativity, " 104.
3 Foucault, "Two Lectures," 83–8.
4 White, "Thinking Race," 408.
5 Karstedt, "Terror and 'New Wars,'" 138.
6 Falk, *The Great Terror War*.
7 James der Derian, "9.11: Before, After, and In Between," Social Science Research Council, New York, 18 January 2002, http://essays.ssrc.org/sept11/essays/der_derian_text_only.htm; der Derian, *Virtuous War*.
8 Websites that archive media research on 9/11 include "September 11 News.com – September 11, 2001 News Archives," http://www.september11news.com; and American Social History Project / Centre for Media and Learning, "September 11 Digital Archive," http://911digitalarchive.org.
9 Foucault, "Orders of Discourse"; see also Foucault, "Politics and the Study of Discourses."
10 Keen, "War without End?", 87, 93–7.
11 Agamben, *State of Exception*.
12 Keen, "War without End?", 87.
13 Keen, "War without End?", 87.
14 American Council of Trustees and Alumni (ACTA), "Defending Civilization: How Our Universities Are Failing America, and What Can Be Done About It"; Brown, *Regulating Aversion*.
15 McLaren, "The Dialectics of Terrorism," 170.
16 Der Derian, "9.11."
17 Le Carré, "A War We Cannot Win."
18 Le Carré, "A War We Cannot Win."
19 May, "Thinking from the Margins."
20 Some five hundred foreign nationals perished in the 9/11 attacks, including from a dozen African countries: Côte d'Ivoire, Egypt, Ethiopia, The Gambia, Ghana, Kenya, Liberia, Malawi, Nigeria, South Africa, Togo, and Zambia.
21 Goffe, "Black Victims of September 11."
22 Assensoh and Alex-Assensoh, "African Immigrants and the Aftermath of September 11," 611; Onyeani, "Africans and the 9/11 Deaths," 1.
23 New York University professor Manthia Diawara, quoted in Goffe, "Black Victims of September 11."
24 Ajayi-Soyinka, "The Fashion of Democracy," 604.
25 Butler, *Frames of War*; Butler, *Precarious Life*.
26 Professor Nyong'o, a Kenyan MP, quoted in Kamau, "Still Waiting for Compensation," 3.
27 Although space does not permit it here, in my edited book, *Securing Africa*, I discuss the US support for the 11 September 1973 Chilean coup d'état

that deposed the democratically elected government of Salvador Allende
and installed the brutal dictatorship of General Augusto Pinochet.

28 Loveland, *By Due Process of Law*, 86.

29 FBI, "Ten Most Wanted Fugitives."

30 A Libyan intelligence officer was convicted of this attack, and in 2004 Colonel
Muammar Qadhafi's government settled a lawsuit with the families of victims, allowing diplomatic relations with the United States to resume in 2006.

31 Ajayi-Soyinka, "The Fashion of Democracy," 603.

32 Ajayi-Soyinka, "The Fashion of Democracy," 603.

33 Theoharis, "Who Is the Target of NSA Surveillance?"; Mueller and Stewart,
"3 Questions About NSA Surveillance."

34 Campbell, *Global NATO and the Catastrophic Failure in Libya*.

35 Cilliers, "Africa, Root Causes, and the 'War on Terror"; Obi, "Terrorism in
West Africa"; Tynes, "US Counter-Terrorism Policies in Africa."

36 Andreasson, "Orientalism and African Development Studies."

37 Susan E. Rice, then Assistant Secretary of State for Africa in the Clinton
administration, in testimony before the US House Committee on International Relations, November 2001. In January 2009, Dr Rice became Barack
Obama's Ambassador to the United Nations, and in May 2013, she became
his National Security Advisor.

38 Testimony of Dr. Susan Rice, "Africa and the War on Global Terrorism" (15
November 2001), US House of Representatives, 107th Congress, Committee on International Relations, Hearing before the Subcommittee on Africa
of the Committee on International Relations (Washington: US GPO, 2001)
at 6 (Susan E. Rice), http://commdocs.house.gov/committees/intlrel/
hfa76191.000/hfa76191_0f.htm.

39 "Africa: The Breeding Ground for Terrorism," *African Terrorism Bulletin* 2
(March 2005), http://www.issafrica.org/Pubs/Newsletters/Terrorism/
0205.htm.

40 Lubold, "Africa Command?"; Roos, "Terrorism Is International."

41 Lyman and Morrison, "The Terrorist Threat in Africa."

42 Lubold, "Africa Command"; Malan, "The Post-9/11 Security Agenda and
Peacekeeping in Africa."

43 Lyman and Morrison, "The Terrorist Threat in Africa," 75–86.

44 Cenzer, "Specters of War."

45 BBC News [World], "Poverty 'Fuelling Terrorism.'"

46 Mallaby, "The Reluctant Imperialist."

47 Mitchell, "Police in Kenya," A12.

48 Amnesty International, 2001, quoted in Lumina, "Terror in the Backyard," 28.

49 Hosein, "Beyond September 11."

50 Lumina, "Terror in the Backyard," 128.

51 Shivji, quoted in Nader, "What the Rest Think of the West."
52 "Do CIA, FBI Operate Freely in EA?", *Horizon* (Dar es Salaam), 7–13 November 2007, 3.
53 Mazrui, "September 11, 2001 Consequences for Africa," 10.
54 Satterthwaite, "The Legal Regime."
55 Benjamin, "5 Myths about Rendition"; Byman, "Extraordinary Rendition, Extraterritorial Detention."
56 Amnesty International, "Below the Radar."
57 Rice, quoted in Rose, "I helped M15."
58 BBC News [Americas], "CIA Jail Allegations"; Amnesty International, "Below the Radar."
59 Smith, *Securing Africa*.
60 Marty, "Secret Detentions."
61 Marty, "Secret Detentions."
62 See Goetz, Rosenbach, and Stark, "Taking the 'War on Terror' to Africa."
63 Amnesty International, "Partners in Crime."
64 David Ignatius, "'Rendition' Realities," A21.
65 Norton-Taylor, Grey, and Vikram Dodd, "M15 Tip-Off to CIA."
66 Whitlock, "Courted as Spies," A1; Rose, "I Helped M15."
67 The fourteen countries are Austria, Belgium, Cyprus, Denmark, Germany, Greece, Ireland, Italy, Poland, Portugal, Romania, Spain, Sweden, and the United Kingdom. See BBC News, "CIA Jails in Europe 'Confirmed.'"
68 Smith, "Counterterrorism from George Bush to Barack Obama," in *Securing Africa*.
69 For example, African Express Airlines flight (flight number AXK527) rendered ninety people from Nairobi to Addis Ababa. See "The CIA's Tentacles," *Spiegel International Online*.
70 See Rosenbach and Goetz, "'Massive and Systematic Violations' of Human Rights."
71 "Kenya's Shame a Lesson to Tanzania," *Horizon* (Dar es Salaam), 8–14 August 2007, 2; "Kenya: Muslim Group Berates State over Fate of Terror Suspects," *AllAfrica.com*, 7 October 2008.
72 Sanders, "Ethiopia's Intervention."
73 Duhul, "Al-Qaida Suspects Still Alive in Somalia."
74 Conroy, "Feds Working in Secret African Prisons."
75 "US Interrogates Suspects in Ethiopian Jails," *Spiegel International Online*.
76 See also AP, "US Interrogating at Africa's Secret Prisons."
77 Conroy, "Feds Working in Secret African Prisons," 1 of 3.
78 See, "Ethiopia/Kenya: Account for Missing Rendition Victims," Human Rights Watch, http://www.hrw.org/en/news/2008/10/01/ethiopiakenya-account-missing-rendition-victims.

79 Conroy, "Feds Working in Secret African Prisons," 3.
80 This rendition is corroborated by a review of flight manifests, which show that more than thirty people were transferred to Somalia in a plane officially chartered by the Kenyan government. The unscheduled flight was African Express Airways flight 5Y AXF. The manifest indicates that she was taken to Mogadishu, Somalia.
81 Conroy, "Feds Working in Secret African Prisons," 3.
82 Conroy, "Feds Working in Secret African Prisons," 3.
83 Umar Farouk Abdulmutallab pled guilty to attempting to blow up Northwest Airlines Flight 253, which was en route from Amsterdam to Detroit with 289 passengers on 25 December 2009.
84 CNN Library, "Boston Marathon Terror Attack Fast Facts," 9 June 2013.
85 Al-Shabab is Arabic for "the youth." It was formed in 2005 by some three dozen young Somalis and had grown to about five thousand members by 2009. It is a self-proclaimed ally of al-Qaeda; however, most serious scholars of al-Shabab and Somalia suggest it is an interclan alliance concerned mainly with local grievances. See Fergusson, *The World's Most Dangerous Place*; and Hansen, *Al-Shabab in Somalia*.
86 Lumina, "Terror in the Backyard."
87 Lumina, "Counter-Terrorism Legislation."
88 Hübschle, "The T-Word."
89 Ahmad, *Terrorism*, 12–13.
90 Chabal, *Amilcar Cabral*; Dhada, "The Political Thought of Amilcar Cabral"; Bienen, "State and Revolution."
91 Fanon, "Letter to the Resident Minister"; Fanon, *The Wretched of the Earth*.
92 Bancel, Blanchard, and Lemaire, "False Memory"; Shatz, "The Torture of Algiers."
93 Gordon, Sharpley-Whiting, and White, *Fanon*.
94 Democracy Now, "Allied with Apartheid."
95 Rice, quoted in "US Takes Nelson Mandela Off the Terrorism Watch List," *The Australian*, 3 July 2008.
96 "Mandela Off U.S. Terrorism Watch List," *CNN.com*, 2 July 2008.
97 De Witte, *The Assassination of Lumumba*, 1–3; Zeilig, *Lumumba*, 117.
98 Gunning, "A Case for Critical Terrorism Studies"; Jackson, "The Core Commitments of Critical Terrorism Studies."
99 Jarvis, "The Space and Faces of Critical Terrorism Studies."
100 See Nhema and Zeleza, *The Roots of African Conflict*, 3.
101 Nhema and Zeleza, *The Roots of African Conflict*, 3.
102 Nhema and Zeleza, *The Roots of African Conflict*, 3.

21 Humanitarianism as Planetary Politics

MIRIAM TICKTIN

In January 2010, newspapers carried a series of stories about homeless Chihuahuas in California being rescued and flown to new homes around North America – from New York City to Houston to Edmonton. In one case, Virgin Airlines donated $12,000 in travel costs for the dogs and their human companions. These flights – termed "Chihuahua airlifts" – were organized by philanthropists in concert with the American Society for the Prevention of Cruelty to Animals (ASPCA); in one case, the *New York Times* wrote that "15 homeless dogs from the Bay Area were flown to Kennedy by the airline so they could be adopted by New Yorkers."[1] Another article stated that "animal lovers are determined to rescue those that they can from a sad and lonely life in a shelter in California."[2] Upon arrival, they were given behavioural and medical assessments to make sure they had adjusted and were fit for adoption. There were people lined up waiting for the arrival of these dogs, because as one of them said, many "may come from puppy mills or brokers where they often live in horrible conditions."[3]

Another story was carried in May 2010, about a two-year-old female pit bull who had been doused with gasoline and set on fire in Baltimore. A young policewoman happened to notice the smoke and put out the flames with her sweater, but the dog, subsequently named Phoenix, survived for only four days, having received burns over 95 per cent of her body. The story was picked up in a matter of hours and disseminated nationwide in newspapers, on radio and TV, and on websites. The intensity of the response was striking: people responded by offering a $26,000 reward for the culprits; others held a candlelight vigil.[4]

I begin with these stories foregrounding the suffering and rescue of animals because I want to think about whose lives are grievable today. This requires simultaneously asking whose suffering is narrated in the dominant media, what types of violence are rendered visible, and hence what compels action in terms of either care or struggles for justice. I write this in the context of the ongoing global War on Terror, which has structured the visibility of suffering, rendering the violence done to the gendered and racialized bodies targeted by war impossible to perceive as such. First among these are Muslim bodies. It has created a world where the divide between those who are considered human (as the Bush administration stated, those "who are with us") and those who are expulsed from that category (those "who are against us") is stark. As Puar and Rai have suggested, those who are excluded are not just lesser humans – they have become "monster";[5] these figures are both racial and sexual outcasts or "abnormals," half-human, half-animal. These monsters cannot suffer; their pain is unthinkable.

In thinking about the visibility of suffering in the context of the War on Terror, I want to take a closer look at the politics of humanity and inhumanity. Perhaps counter-intuitively, I will discuss what I see as an *expanding* politics of both humanity and humanitarianism (as the politics of humanity that focuses on care and rescue), which I will argue have grown in scale to include non-humans, to the ecological and even planetary level. I want to think about what this expansion means: Which lives does it newly recognize? And which lives does it cast aside? So far, the most productive analyses of the War on Terror have engaged theories of race, empire, gender, and sexuality to help explain its workings. Yet there is also a burgeoning literature on how the politics of nature and the human–nonhuman divide are central to the War on Terror.[6] For instance, cultural geographer Jake Kosek shows how bees' capacities for detection and intelligence gathering have been harnessed by the US Department of Homeland Security, to be used as detection devices. Indeed, they work alongside dogs that in turn work with soldiers to detect mines in the Middle East.[7]

I want to build on these frames of analysis that bring the language of ecology alongside those of race and empire. This chapter will suggest that we need to pay careful attention to new and expanding discourses and technologies of humanity, for they are changing the terms and sites of both war and politics. My underlying argument is that we need to understand more about these new, seemingly unrelated sites in order to know how to make room for those whose lives have thus far not been "apprehendable."[8] This chapter will first discuss the logic of an expanding politics of humanity and humanitarianism; then it will investigate one technology that I see as part of this expanding regime of care – veterinary forensic science – to think about the consequences and effects of such expansions. I will end by trying to understand the politics involved in this potentially planetary humanitarianism and what it means for lives touched by the War on Terror.

The Expanding Politics of Humanitarianism

First, before thinking of new technologies of humanity, I want to examine what I see as an expanding politics of humanitarianism. For this, let me return to the stories of animal rescue, which are becoming increasingly common in American media – indeed, the storyline is familiar. The victims being rescued here resemble those at the heart of humanitarian narratives: poor starving children, innocent women. These stories are powerful; as many scholars have shown, humanitarian narratives helped shape the subject of humanity that we now understand as "human," joining humanity with its cognate, humane. That is, as Thomas Laqueur has argued, in the late eighteenth century, the human began to be conceived not as a physiological fact, but as "ethical subject – the protagonist – of humanitarian narrative."[9] "Humanity" referred to this shared sentiment of sympathy or benevolence – which did not necessarily mean shared species or biological fact. As Lynn Festa writes in her discussion of humanitarian sensibility, also in the eighteenth century, "sentimentality is a literary form: a rhetorical structure designed both to incite feelings in readers and to direct those feelings towards their 'proper' objects."[10] Yet with the humanitarian narrative, this sentimental form rests on an unstable definition of humanity – it relies on its malleability. On the one hand, the lack of rigorous definition of the human allows for an expansion of the types of life it includes; on the other, because of the instability at the heart of the sentimental literary form, it can work on a case-by-case basis, providing a poor or inconsistent basis for ethics.[11]

If the content of this sentimental form is flexible, what precisely evokes this compassion today? What makes one type of content more compelling than another? The more recent histories and anthropologies of humanitarianism suggest that while humanitarianism is premised on the moral imperative to relieve suffering, whatever its cause, form, or context (at least in the form perhaps best embodied by Médecins sans Frontières), the innocent victim is often the most morally legitimate sufferer.[12] Children are perhaps the most exemplary humanitarian subjects today – the archetypal innocent victims. It is no accident that children are the face of humanitarianism in fund-raising and publicity campaigns; they serve as generic human subjects, outside time and place. Women, too, can more easily inhabit this position of innocent victim, although this gendered subject is also clearly a racialized one, in that (certain) women of the global south or "Third World" are perceived as the most innocent (read, passive) victims in need of rescue from their (barbaric) men or "cultures."[13]

The politics of humanitarianism has entailed both the search for and the production of innocent victims, since the "pure" victim is a placeholder, always just out of reach. There are child soldiers, for instance, as Liisa Malkki points out, which troubles the image of the child as innocent. Indeed, child soldiers are seen as an abomination, a category mistake that leads to them being labelled "youth" or "teens" as opposed to "children" whenever possible, to set aside and protect a time of innocence, when they are still unworldly and untainted.[14] Similarly, the recent focus on victims of human trafficking pictures young girls or women who have been kidnapped from their homes and locked away in brothels; yet this picture of innocence too is complicated when we realize that many of these girls or women who engage in sex work actually chose to leave home and generally knew what they would be doing, even if they did not know the exact conditions of their employment. Here, the victim is implicated in her own situation of exploitation, and her status quickly shifts from endangered to dangerous, innocent to delinquent. For women, innocence is still inextricably tied to sexual innocence.

Insofar as humanitarianism depends on the figure of the innocent victim as the highest moral good – the goal driving humanitarian action, in an attempt to steer clear of explicit political solutions or goals[15] – I suggest that it works through a logic of *expansion*, in which new territories of innocence must be discovered and incorporated. The innocent sufferer can never be isolated for long enough to keep it uncorrupted by history or context. In this sense, humanitarianism is constantly displacing politics to the limit of innocence, a border that must be drawn and redrawn.

While animals are selectively incorporated into this politics of humanity in these new ways – and of course the flip side and in the larger context for this is the overwhelming nature of institutions and practices like factory farming and animal experimentation, which touch billions of animals, leaving just a tiny few to be saved – I do not mean to suggest that they represent a novel terrain of innocence; they have been variously included in and excluded from this category of universal solidarity over time. In the eighteenth century, the sentimental mode that eventually turned into abolitionism was "notoriously indiscriminate in its choice of objects, embracing not only human beings but lapdogs, dying birds, and (as one eighteenth-century critic grumbled), 'efts, toads, bats, every thing that hath life.'"[16] Indeed, Joanna Bourke writes how in 1872, a woman known as "the Earnest Englishwoman" asked to let women "become animal" – that is, to be treated as animals – in order to reap the benefits they were denied because they were not part of "mankind."[17] So what is new here, how has this politics expanded?

Insofar as the content of humanity – its sentimental community – has always been unstable, alternately including and excluding subjects depending on the changing "distributions of sentiment,"[18] I turn to examine the new technologies that help produce humanity as a category and that help sustain this particular project of sentiment. Why technology? In his discussion of the relationship between terrorists and humanity, Faisal Devji,[19] following Hannah Arendt, suggests that "global humanity" was produced by the very technology that enabled its destruction – that is, the atom bomb. This technology helped "humanity" emerge as a global historical actor for the first time. In this sense, global humanity cannot be understood outside the technologies that helped produce it. Ecological, biological, and other threats have replaced the nuclear threat that initially gave meaning to this category, but they share and perpetuate the logic of a technologically interdependent humanity – a humanity that I want to suggest is being constructed on a planetary level now, in relation to emerging politics of war and security, ethics and technologies, and new forms of capital.

Veterinary Forensic Science

In this remainder of this chapter, I will focus on one emergent technology: veterinary forensic science. Forensic science – meaning the use of science to answer legal questions – has been expanding in scope and relevance in recent years; this has been accompanied by the development of new subfields (such as linguistic forensics), as well as an increased public focus, evinced by television shows such as *CSI* (*Crime Scene Investigation*). As part of this expansion, veterinary forensic science is a new subfield of scientific expertise, inaugurated in 2008 at the University of Florida with the support of the ASPCA. The goal in applying forensic sciences to veterinary medicine is to "aid in the understanding, prevention and prosecution of animal cruelty." This new set of experts is mobilized around identifying, measuring, and alleviating animal suffering and helping promote animal and human health and welfare. These veterinarians are some of the new players who are helping adjudicate and manage humanitarian interventions.

We may seem to be moving into a terrain that feels far from the War on Terror and our discussion of whose lives are grievable, but this is precisely the point: these emergent sciences and technologies are at the frontier of this war. They are part of new arsenals of technology such as those funded by DARPA, which researches robots modelled on insects, including cyborg insects ("cybugs") that see, hear, and potentially attack in remote battlefields.[20] These veterinary experts are part of new regimes of humanitarianism that decide whose lives are grievable and whose suffering is recognizable; and as part of new regimes of humanitarianism, they are implicated in regimes of security and violence. Much literature has shown that humanitarianism is inevitably accompanied by its seeming opposite, whether this is understood as policing, security, or militarism.[21] This link is exhibited in many ways: both humanitarianism and its flip side rely on and sustain the logic of crisis or emergency, with its focus on the temporal present and the state of exception; this idea of crisis is central to the War on Terror. Humanitarianism also often follows on the heels of and smooths over the damage wrought by military intervention.[22] But perhaps most importantly, humanitarian institutions increasingly work directly in concert with security forces, implicitly or explicitly, intentionally or not: they may hire private security forces – often former military personnel who participated in other conflicts – to protect their officers, or they may come together to form military–humanitarian interventions, for instance, as prompted by the "Responsibility to Protect" doctrine.[23] In what follows, we see this same complementarity of regimes of humanitarianism and security present in the new veterinary forensic science. First, we will look at how this and other technologies expand regimes of rescue; then we will turn to see how they simultaneously help develop new logics of criminality and security.

A. On Rescue

Veterinary forensic scientists work in new "humanitarian" teams: they join with disaster response teams, emergency animal services, and animal relief. For instance, veterinary forensic scientists work with the American Humane Association (AHA), which has a disaster response team. One of the AHA's most recent projects was an attempted large-scale animal rescue operation in Japan, in response to the earthquake and tsunami. Interestingly, illustrating my earlier point about the categories of innocence and their expansion, the AHA protects both animals and children, focusing on promoting their interconnected well-being. Veterinary forensic scientists also work with the National Animal Rescue and Response Team, formed in 2006, when disasters like Hurricane Katrina "impacted more people and their companion animals than in the history of the United States." Other veterinary forensic scientists have gone with humanitarian teams to Haiti. These groups and experts engage with the same emergency medical techniques and technologies as other (human) emergency response teams, working on a model of crisis and with the same structures and logics. This fulfils a moral purpose for the humanitarian, regardless of what it does for the animal. An innocent other is required to enact these humanitarian politics (insofar as it is a politics of suffering/politics of humanity) – that is, an innocent other provides the subject of sympathy or pity as well as the moral imperative to act. We must ask here what it means that the resources (financial, emotional, mediatic, and so on) dedicated to this moral purpose are now going increasingly to animal rescue – and what it means for other types of suffering and violence. Will they be rendered ever more marginal, less and less recognizable?

B. On Criminality

Veterinary forensic scientists collect medical evidence not just to document or help relieve suffering, but to be used in legal cases. When we look from the angle of the courtroom, we see a different impact of this expertise and a different interaction with humans and humanity. These veterinarians have played a role in the shift in focus towards animal cruelty. In the United States before 1990, only six states had felony provisions in their animal cruelty laws; now forty-six states do. While there are several reasons for this change in animal cruelty laws – including changing perceptions of animals as part of larger kinship structures, as innocent victims, and as rights-bearing subjects (most recently, dolphins were voted to have the right to legal personhood by the American Association for the Advancement of Science) – one reason that stands out is the belief that acts of animal cruelty are linked to other crimes more narrowly related to humans.[24]

In particular, the link between animal abuse and interpersonal violence has received a lot of recent attention,[25] and the links have been substantiated such that many US communities now cross-train social service and animal control agencies in how to recognize animal abuse as a possible indicator of other abusive behaviours. A 1997 study of forty-eight of the largest domestic violence and child abuse shelters in the United States found that 85 per cent of women who came also reported incidents of animal abuse;[26] and one quarter of battered women delayed going into shelters for fear of the well-being of family pets. Some shelters have adapted, offering refuge to abused pets as well as to people. As with pediatricians who must notify the police if they suspect child abuse, veterinarians must notify the police if they suspect abuse in the animals they treat. In fact, *animal* control officers are now on the list of those bound by law to report suspected *child* abuse; not only that, but several districts and states in the United States have created online registries that resemble those for sex offenders, tracking animal abusers across county and state lines, with the idea that this will serve as an early warning system for other crimes.[27]

We can see how this type of veterinary forensic expertise actually works as a new diagnostic of human cruelty or criminality. While the laws are in place to protect against animal cruelty or to protect endangered species, in many ways this has allowed for new ways to patrol and discipline humans and their relationships with one another; it also allows for new ways to configure who is exemplary of humanity and who falls on its outer edges – who newly becomes animal or monster. For instance, veterinary forensic science was instrumental in convicting NFL quarterback Michael Vick for running a dog-fighting ring. A forensic veterinarian found evidence in "mass graves" on his property where eight pit bulls were buried that corroborated statements by witnesses that the dogs had been killed by hanging, shooting, drowning, or slamming them to the ground. Vick was sentenced to twenty-three months in jail on a felony charge for his role in the ring, with the judge remarking that Vick had not accepted full responsibility for "promoting, funding and facilitating this cruel and *inhumane* sporting activity."

We should take the role of race seriously here, even though a full discussion of this is beyond the scope of this chapter. As one example of this, his punishment, as some have noted, exceeded that given to others for charges of rape. In other words, when Vick was convicted for animal cruelty, he was being charged by the same American courtrooms that send one in three black men to prison; yet this does not enter the frame of the conviction.

Similarly, there are those like former French actress Brigitte Bardot – who also draws on veterinary expertise to make her point, and who has used the treatment of animals to mark and exclude Muslims in France. Suggesting that the ritualistic sacrifice of sheep for Eid is "unspeakable" and "undignified," her discourse contributes to an already anti-immigrant discourse that uses terms such as inhumane, uncivilized, and barbaric to describe Muslims. Muslims, in this discourse, exemplify new forms of animality. In the latest round of French elections (in the spring of 2012), far-right candidate Marine Le Pen used halal meat and the killing of animals as a cornerstone of her campaign, which helped her attract the biggest vote for a far-right candidate in recent history: 18 per cent in the first round.

The War on Terror works by playing with the boundaries of the human, and working with the discourse of race; this is how certain bodies are made killable. This was already demonstrated in the colonial era, when in southern Africa, the treatment of people *like* animals became the treatment of people *as* animals – revealing an ontological shift. As historian Clapperton Mavhunga writes, the pesticides used to exterminate vermin in order to help agricultural development soon became the same technologies used to exterminate guerrillas fighting for independence, with the understanding that they, too, were subhuman "vermin beings" from which the white race needed to be protected.[28] As Kosek states, "What it is to be human is a product of the shifting cartography of what it is to be animal."[29]

C. On Security

There is yet another side of veterinary forensics: these new experts are concerned with biosecurity and bioterrorism that targets animals or agriculture, as well as with emerging diseases – in particular, zoonoses, which are diseases and infections transmitted naturally between vertebrate animals and humans. Forensic veterinarians investigate zoonoses that affect humans and animals; most recently, they have been concerned with emerging infections, from BSE (mad cow disease) to the Ebola and Marburg diseases. We can recognize here an expanded or altered version of what Andy Lakoff has called "global health governance,"[30] which combines humanitarian technologies with logics of biosecurity. Yet what we see here is that this field of global health has expanded to include a new ecological field and to produce new notions of what might constitute "health."

As I see it, this is where the humanity project changes scales. These various technologies and forms of expertise such as veterinary forensic science that expand the terrain of humanitarianism, meet in the emergent form of "One Health," which incorporates the health of humans, animals, and plants and treats them in relationship to one another. Still relatively amorphous, the "One Health" concept is being developed at the level of international multilateral organizations, governments, NGOs, private organizations, and individuals as well as educational institutions.[31]

"One Health" came into being primarily to counter zoonotic threats, which are on the rise – supposedly, three quarters of emerging infections originated in animals. SARS, avian flu, and the West Nile virus are just a few examples. But as one of the founders, Dr Laura Kahn, stated in an interview, it is not new that human and animal health are linked; rather, "it struck me how many of the bioterrorist agents and emerging infectious diseases are zoonotic … Yet in my research, I found that physicians and veterinarians rarely, if ever, communicated or collaborated with each other."[32] In other words, bioterrorism and concerns over preparedness are a driving force for this new collaboration, even if it may now claim other, more innocuous goals as well, such as improving the lives of all species – human, animal, and plant – by integrating human medicine, veterinary medicine, and environmental science.[33] Ultimately, One Health focuses on health at the individual, population, and ecosystem levels, moving both humanitarianism and health from the level of the population to the level of the planet.

Planetary Politics?

What kind of politics is this expanded, potentially planetary politics of humanitarianism, one that inflates the subject population while maintaining a focus on innocence and suffering? What technologies of power does it rely on? Is this a politics that promises to expand our vision of life, of who is recognized as well as apprehended?[34] Will it bring trans-species connections, new biosocial collectivities, or political solidarities? Does it have the potential to remake Otherness – to let in those erased by the War on Terror?

There are several possibilities. First, we might ask if this is simply a new form of biopolitics, one that expands the power over life. On the one hand, we could say that thinking in biopolitical terms is no longer appropriate here. Foucault's notion of biopower referred to the regulation of a national population, constituted and managed as "society." This expanded politics of humanitarianism is no longer about the nation-state; indeed, it is no longer just about the human – or perhaps it is more accurate to say that the terms by which one decides who belongs to humanity have shifted radically.

On the other hand, we could modify notions of biopower in order to think about this type of politics. New notions of biopolitics have been proposed that allow for such visions. For instance, in discussing the biodiversity census, political theorist Rafi Youatt suggests that it will help construct new ideas of a multilayered and multispecies global community.[35] He proposes an ecological view of biopower, one that gives non-human actors active roles.[36] Insofar as biopower moves into the subjective lives of biological species, their actions and transmutations in turn transform biopower. Youatt argues that through the global biodiversity census, different biosocial collectivities can be forged – rather than being grounded on radical human/non-human difference (difference in capacity), they could be based on difference in ecological function. This biopolitics could "reterritorialize the category of the human," grounding it relative to other species and to local ecosystems that make up the global ecosystem.

Italian philosopher Roberto Esposito also proposes an "affirmative biopolitics" more generally, which is a politics *of* life instead of a politics *over* life. In suggesting that we can move beyond the stalemate between immunity and community (*immunitas* and *communitas*) – a dyad that always creates an outside, an Other, against whom one must be protected or immunized – Esposito argues that through the continual deconstruction of any normative system (a community where there are certain norms to follow), one can defend the difference of life forms with their associated norms. This offers a critique of Otherness, which inevitably results in immunization from the implicit threat of contagion and death.[37] This focus on difference (and not Otherness) is the basis for change and for elaborating a radical tolerance towards the world, which is understood as a multiplicity of different living forms. An affirmative biopolitics "takes place when we recognize that harming one part of life or one life harms all lives"[38] – for Esposito, all lives are inscribed in *bios*.

Can we see the beginnings of an affirmative biopolitics or ecological biopower in the expanded technologies and politics of suffering just discussed? This is ultimately an empirical question, but from this brief look, it seems that One Health and other technologies such as veterinary forensic science are built on the idea of security, protection, and immunization, albeit at a different scale, one that has expanded in the types of subjects and populations it protects, disciplines, and controls. While they may respond to injury or suffering of innocent victims, in some senses, this recognition of what Butler might call the "social vulnerability of bodies"[39] is often simultaneously structured around the threats of bioterrorism, zoonoses, or disasters. If we return to Arendt's notion that global humanity was first produced as a substantive category by the threat of destruction, then we can argue that this expanded politics of humanity follows in the same footsteps.

Yet do these technologies offer possibilities for new types of collectives, new kinds of social formations? When animals are treated and protected as victims, they are (as with humans) largely perceived as passive; they are spoken for and responded to in the terms of the humanitarians. As with humans, this presumes and imposes a commonality that may or may not exist – it does not leave open the possibility for radical alterity. This was shown quite vividly with the story of a woman who adopted a chimp (subsequently named Travis) and treated him as a son.[40] Travis lived like a human for fourteen years – eating steak, drinking wine, even acting in commercials. Everyone around town knew him. One terrible day, however, he become hostile and attacked and mauled a family friend, biting and clawing off her face and hands. The police were called, and an officer fatally shot Travis. The police officer went into a crippling depression afterwards, related to the shooting of Travis, whom he had known for years, and whose devastating violence haunted him. The police officer was initially denied the worker's compensation claims he could have made had his depression been caused by shooting a human suspect. The Stamford police ended up covering his therapy costs when the police unions got involved; subsequently, State Senator Andrew J. MacDonald (from Stamford) introduced legislation that would cover an officer's compensation for mental or emotional impairment after killing an animal when under threat of deadly force.

What is difficult to think here in all the coverage of the tragic event is that Travis was not a human, but a chimpanzee – his difference was not acknowledged in his life or in his death. Here, there is no space for the non-innocent animal. This erasure of difference can be understood in some senses as a politics of displacement, where the push is to incorporate the extreme externalities (where the external still remains industrial/factory farming but now includes other subjects and objects as well). Of course, it can also be seen as a form of colonial expansion, not just in terms of the profits to be made from new subjects of crime, but also in terms of colonizing new landscapes to produce innocent victims, reproducing a certain sentimental political project of "protection" in the process – a "predatory compassion," one might say.

So where do we end? Whose lives are grievable, whose suffering is notable? Will this expanded form of humanitarianism eventually help disturb our own assumptions about our ontological status as humans, eventually producing a very different planetary set of relationships and individuals? While it might have seemed that narrating new forms of suffering could render visible many lives – especially those touched by terror – we can see that expanding the category of humanity is not an easy or straightforward answer; the desire to open up the category to let in the excluded is matched by similar neoliberal, neocolonial, and capitalist desires to expand and incorporate.[41] We need to find new ways to render visible violence and injustice that refuse a focus on innocence.

NOTES

1 Siebert, "The Animal-Cruelty Syndrome."
2 Bustamente, "Airlift Rescues Abandoned LA Chihuahuas."
3 Bustamente, "Airlift Rescues Abandoned LA Chihuahuas."
4 Siebert, "The Animal-Cruelty Syndrome."
5 Puar and Rai, "Monster, Terrorist, Fag."
6 Kosek, "Ecologies of Empire"; Devji, *The Terrorist in Search of Humanity*; Zerner, "Stealth Nature"; Asad, *On Suicide Bombing*; Butler, *Precarious Life* and *Frames of War*.
7 Kosek, "Ecologies of Empire."
8 Butler, *Frames of War*.
9 Laqueur, "Mourning, Pity, and the Work of Narrative," 38.
10 Festa, "Humanity without Feathers," 7.
11 Festa, "Humanity without Feathers," 5.

12 Ticktin, *Casualties of Care.*

13 Much feminist postcolonial theory has demonstrated this; see, for example, Mohanty, "Under Western Eyes"; Spivak, "Can the Subaltern Speak?"; Razack, "Domestic Violence as Gender Persecution"; and Kapur, "The Tragedy of Victimization Rhetoric."

14 Malkki, "Children, Humanity, and the Infantilization of Peace," 63–4.

15 Again, I'm referring to humanitarian action largely as a response to emergency in terms of basic human health, exemplified by MSF.

16 Festa, "Humanity without Feathers," 5.

17 Bourke, *What It Means to Be Human.*

18 Stoler, *Along the Archival Grain.*

19 Devji, *The Terrorist in Search of Humanity.*

20 Zerner, "Stealth Nature."

21 On humanitarianism and policing, see, for instance, Ticktin *Casualties of Care*; and Ticktin, "Policing and Humanitarianism in France." On compassion and its counterpart, repression, see Fassin, "Compassion and Repression." On humanitarianism as the left hand of empire, see Agier, "Humanity as an Identity and Its Political Effects." On the relationships between humanitarianism and militarism, see Fassin and Pandolfi, *Contemporary States of Emergency.*

22 Agier, "Humanity as an Identity."

23 Pandolfi, "Laboratory of Intervention."

24 Siebert, "The Animal-Cruelty Syndrome"; see also Cooper and Cooper, *Introduction to Veterinary and Comparative Forensic Medicine.*

25 See, for instance, Kurst-Swanger, "Animal Abuse." There are also many newspaper reports about this.

26 Siebert, "The Animal-Cruelty Syndrome."

27 Suffolk County on Long Island in New York was the first to create a registry, but California was the first state to bring such a bill to the legislature, in February 2010. The most recent is Arizona's House Bill 2310, which, again, would create a registry of "convicted animal abusers similar to the state's current sex offender one." Visit http://www.abc15.com/dpp/news/region_phoenix_metro/central_phoenix/az-bill-would-treat-animal-abusers-like-sex-offenders#ixzz23NDq5Zy9. See also "Lawmakers Consider an Animal Abuse Registry," *New York Times*, 21 February 2010; as well as Siebert, "The Animal-Cruelty Syndrome."

28 Mavhunga, "Vermin Beings."

29 Kosek, "Ecologies of Empire," 670.

30 Lakoff, "Two Regimes of Global Health."

31 Among many others, the following promote the One Health concept: the World Bank, the World Organization for Animal Health, WHO (World Health Organization), FAO (Food and Agricultural Organization), the US Centers for Disease Control and Prevention, the European Commission, the American Veterinary Association, The Bill and Melinda Gates Foundation, and the One Health Center at the University of California's Global Health Institute. http://www.onehealthinitiative.com

32 See International Innovation (Research Media Ltd), "One Health Initiative," 38–41. See also the Bulletin of the Atomic Scientists interview with Laura Kahn, 2012.

33 From One Health mission statement: http://www.onehealthinitiative.com

34 Butler, *Frames of War*.

35 Youatt, "Counting Species," 405.

36 As Dominic Pettman asks in *Human Error*, however, who is *giving* agency here? Non-humans play roles dictated by humans.

37 Esposito, *Bíos*; Campbell, "Bios, Immunity, Life," 16.

38 Esposito, *Bíos*; Campbell, "Bios, Immunity, Life," 16.

39 Butler, *Frames of War*.

40 See, for instance, Lee, "Travis the Menace." There were many reports about Travis.

41 See also Ahuja, "Abu Zubaydah and the Caterpillar," on how non-human life gets incorporated into the war on terror.

SECTION FIVE

Terror Circuits

22 Introduction to Section Five

HENA TYYEBI

Visuality has long been a key site mobilized in imperial projects and in the constitution of hegemonic ways of ordering social life. Attempting to unpack visuality necessarily involves examining its entanglements with histories of colonization and violence and the ways in which racial and colonial logics structure visual fields. In the contemporary digital age, where visual culture has appeared to largely displace the privileging of the textual, the chapters in this section attempt to theorize the ways in which visual images, cultural productions, and digital technologies are bound up with imperial projects such as the War on Terror and its attendant and ongoing violences. The chapters explore these increasingly pressing questions and further interrogate the subjectivities and new forms of responsibility that emergent visualities engender for spectators of violence.

Visuality of Empire

Edward Said's early theorizations of the constitutive role of cultural production in colonial projects provide a useful framework to begin thinking about themes of visual representation and empire. In *Orientalism*, Said examines the extent to which Western cultural meanings in the form of literature, scholarship, and folk wisdom are entangled in the subordination of colonized lands and subjects.[1] The production of cultural knowledges is seen as being intricately tied to empire, shaping colonial desires and constructing normative frameworks for imperial practices. Said's work emphasizes the significance of interrogating the epistemologies surrounding empire and examining cultural texts and meanings not as objects of study in and of themselves but in terms of the knowledge systems in operation to create these cultural products. Consequently, imperial knowledge production and the visual representation of the racialized, gendered, and colonized subject cannot be seen as representing true anterior reality but is instead seen as making these subjects the object of knowledge and power. The chapters in this section all examine the pivotal role that visual culture comes to play in this process as it aids in engendering colonial fantasy-desires and providing symbolic rationalizations for imperial practices.

In exploring the linkages between visual representation and empire, many theorists of visual culture draw on Frantz Fanon's insights in *Black Skin, White Masks*, where he attends to the racialized structure underlying and enabling the act of looking.[2] Fanon describes the centrality of cultural productions such as cinematic film in fixing colonial representations and knowledges of racialized subjects and of blackness. These visual representations automatically inhere in the encounter between black and white and allow the white gaze to fix this past in the present. Many of the chapters in this section similarly explore the crucial role of visuality in demarcating and solidifying the construction of boundaries between the barbaric Orient and the progressive West, wherein the visual representation of the racialized Other figures centrally in upholding the civilized order.

Counter-Visualities

Unpacking visuality carries the potential to generate new knowledges of racialized, gendered, and colonized subjects and in turn the ordering of social life. In her discussion of black female spectatorship of cinema, bell hooks locates the possibility of agency and resistance to racialized power relations in the oppositional gaze: "That all attempts to repress our/black peoples' right to gaze had produced in us an overwhelming longing to look, a rebellious desire, an oppositional gaze. By courageously looking, we defiantly declared: Not only will I stare. I want my look to change reality."[3] Nicholas Mirzoeff has similarly posited a counter-visuality that challenges the authority of visuality and its legitimization of Western hegemony through an assertion of the "right to look."[4] The chapters in this section attempt to lay bare the racial and colonial logics that underlie the structure of looking and in doing so locate potential spaces and sites for critical and alternative viewing strategies.

Emergent Visualities and Spectacles of Violence

In the contemporary context of the War on Terror, enactments of visuality continue to be intimately bound to the hegemonic social order and serve to obscure underlying power relations. As several of the contributions highlight, the digital era and the proliferation of mobile technologies have added a new dimension to the relationship between visual representation and empire. The enhanced circulation that digital and mobile technologies enable has resulted in the hyper-visibility of visual images from the War on Terror. From the visual images documenting the torture of detainees at Abu Ghraib to the widespread surveillance of Other/Muslim bodies, these chapters trace how emergent visualities appear to be rapidly transforming the forms that imperial violence and terror can take and, at the same time, implicating spectators of violence in a far country in novel ways.

NOTES

1 Said, *Orientalism*.
2 Fanon, *Black Skin, White Masks*.
3 hooks, *Black Looks*, 116.
4 Mirzoeff, *The Right to Look*, 25.

23 Visual Colonial Economies and Slave Death in Modernity: Bin Laden's Terror?

ANNA M. AGATHANGELOU

On the death of Muammar Qadhafi, Hillary Clinton said, "We came, we saw, he was killed." Her comment points to how visual technologies contribute to shaping the "global" as an American controversy. Speaking of the Byzantine Empire, an ostensibly different topic but following a similar path, Mondzain writes:

> In the most learned translations, the word economy is rendered by different terms such as incarnation, plan, design, administration, providence, responsibility, duties, compromise, lie, or guile, as is relevant, without the reader being warned of the return of the same Greek word – *oikonomia* – in each case. To attempt to rule over the whole world by organizing an empire that derived its power and authority by linking together the visual and the imaginal was Christianity's true genius.[1]

Interestingly, Clinton and Mondzain both link the founding of an iconocracy in the "empire of the gaze and vision,"[2] thus recognizing that visuality is a method of making connections about the structuring and ordering of the world. However, temporally and spatially, the "empire of the gaze and vision" is constantly shifting.

While I understand the image as a vehicle for making the world present to us, the visual also itself is a "heterogeneous ensemble consisting of concepts, institutions, procedures, regulatory decisions, and scientific knowledge"[3] that translates world views into political power. Figures like Bin Laden put into play a series of spatial operations that aid in the exercise of temporal, imperial authority.[4] Thus, the image is what I have chosen to call onto-politico-economic or incarnate in the *flesh*. Indeed, this image has an ontology of the visual entangled with race.

Instead of understanding race as a medium,[5] thereby making it possible for us to trace how and what image ontology brings to visibility, this dominant incarnation of flesh (i.e., the black body) sustains in a Manichean way (i.e., black and white) in place as a foundation for race. Mondzain argues that "incarnation, for the iconophile, is imaginary, it is the entry of the natural image into the flesh of the visible image (iconicity)."[6] Of course, onto-politico-economic visuality cannot proceed without the construction of that which is onto-politico-economically present, or that space within which tensions exist. If such a construction is characteristic of the creativity of art, as is suggested by visuality, more than one insight may be expressed through more than one mode of expression. In this context, then, we might well ask what insights the materiality of Osama Bin Laden offers us. In fact, the existence of Bin Laden and the disruptive practices of terror point to the limits of a universal political economy of power that claims to be universal but not truly global.[7] His marketed products, including his *eau de parfum*, have become visual signifiers of a channelling of desire that calls attention to abandoned radical projects. But what projects? Could their visual expressions disrupt foundational claims of the kind necessary for normative forms of world politics understandings and the political? Could the "passages of the image"[8] of Bin Laden articulate analogies (i.e., the power to imagine and represent)? What kinds?

In what follows, I argue that global empires and contemporary regimes of visuality are constitutive of each other, incarnating themselves in flesh, not just by mediating the economy but also by systematically drawing on the black body, on the fungibility of the slave, as the ground for a dominant ontology of the image. Indeed, the slave is the generative condition of possibility of geopolitical shifts and imperial relations, the expendable reserve for the constitution of inter-state, civil society, and subjects. I seek to articulate something radical, not to suspend momentarily the dominant epistemologies of visual economies but to permanently rupture them. Radical re-orientation channels desire in a new way; it short-circuits the current visual order by reinvesting affective energies into social relations and practices that disrupt enduring visualizations. The visual reports and documentations that issue from dominant and colonizing mechanisms still presuppose the gaze of a universal observer, a visual moment that serves as a mediation between the "object" of colonization and the assemblage of an archive about the object that is structurally prior to the images generated about it. To be considered radical, a transformation must disrupt, once and for all, such kinds of mediations as well as the fantasmatic world that grounds them, including the dialectic mediation through the existence and body of the slave that any kind of change, any process of movement, may require.

Corporeal Openings in the Time of the Present: Bin Laden

A few weeks after the 9/11 attacks on New York City and Washington, Mary Gordon wrote in the *New York Times* that "to have an enemy with no name and therefore no face, even worse, a name and face that can only be guessed at, is the stuff of nightmare."[9] Who was this faceless and nameless signifier of terror(ism) that was operating without any easily identifiable inter-state and structural framework? The US administration moved quickly to give a name and a face to this force. This type of move is not new: it is part of a Manichean visual matrix that multiple imperial projects depend upon to consolidate themselves.

Many theorists who engage with empire and visuality articulate how images are technologies of global power deployed to galvanize intense affect in international politics.[10] Others argue that this technology is in crisis, reassembling images to disrupt "the eruptions of collective aspiration."[11] Mirzoeff pushes the boundaries of the political when he states: "Simply, the right in the right to look acknowledges the patriarchal slave-owning genealogy of authority – and refuses it. Autonomy implies a working through of Enlightenment claims to right in the context of coloniality with an emphasis on the right to subjectivity and the contestation of poverty."[12] In his view, visuality is a set of mechanisms that organize the world, thereby naturalizing the underlying power structures. He calls for counter-visuality, a set of tactics to dismantle the visual strategies of the hegemonic system or "the attempt to reconfigure visuality as a whole"[13] and "the right to look."

With Mirzoeff, I argue that visuality is not merely about images; rather, it is a structuring method of making the world. If visuality and the social order are co-constituted, then exploring how such dominant readings/understandings emerge could highlight the tensions generated at the moment of the empire's erection and those at the shifts of geopolitical power. Even when dominant images organize us to subscribe and consent to certain dominant projects,[14] they also point to the arbitrariness that such images reveal by affirming the possibility of a force against any content as "stable," thereby summoning us to recognize that questions of justice and freedom cannot be easily resolved.[15]

Faces are never just faces. They become technologies for contesting the coloniality of global power as well as intertwined global divisions of labour, racial, and ethnic positionalities and Eurocentric world views. As I articulate it here, coloniality of power is an "onto-political structuring of racial and sexual relations, experiences and racial-sexual knowledge production articulating geopolitical positions and marginalized inscriptions."[16] This capital structuring, in the words of Beller, "targets not just territory but also consciousness, visual relations and the imagination itself in its struggle to organise production – which is to say, value-productive labour, and therefore corporeal performance."[17] Capital can no longer obfuscate its ground for an enduring terror and fungible violence or the racist ideas that come from a presumption that subjecthood originates either in force or in a social covenant that uses force. It is becoming more apparent that capital's infinite desire for expansion depends on slavery relations, even at the moment that different revolutions obfuscate its brutality by evading that "blacks are the remnants of an unhistorical, unethical substance, neither life nor being."[18] This enduring ontology of the visual and one that depends on a specific model of a "body" and visual matrix (i.e., blackness and whiteness) evades a pivotal question about the image ontology that is being invoked by such a Manichean visual matrix. Today, capital targets bodies as biomatter to generate subjects anew. This world order disciplines the colonial and failed political through surveillance and military complexes, forcing some into sovereign relations and others into slaughtering.

The actions of the United States against terrorists should be understood in the context of a "caricatured" world view supposedly articulated by Thomas Hobbes. In *Leviathan*, Nyquist tells us, Hobbes reformulates the opposition between "unbound and bound servant as one between servant and slave," preparing the ground for treating slavery in a way that allows also for the commodification of the enslaved. The slave is not a stand-in for the resistant royalist; rather, the "captives" become the "slaves," who are "bought and sold as Beasts."[19] Nyquist adds: "Unlike servanthood, slavery remains in the precivil condition of war."[20] This dominant presumption in world politics informs and shapes the visualization of the Hobbesian state. Brederkamp argues that Hobbes "pursued visual strategies as core political theory."[21] This strategy presents the figure of the Leviathan as "the icon emerging out of the juxtaposition/unity/homogeneity of the more than 300 people who form his body."[22]

This visualization can be found in other radical articulations. For instance, while Marx points to this economy, he allows for a space to think about slavery as a remnant of the past rather than as a constitutive relation that makes value possible: "The worker can create nothing without nature, without the sensuous external world. The more the worker by his labor appropriates the external world, sensuous nature, the more he deprives himself of means of life."[23] This fundamental gap between the producer/labourer and his material object is sutured through the slave, bound with an economy of blackness and slaughtering. Global capitalism's desire to constantly imagine and articulate a slave "body" that can slaughter by assuming him/her structurally dead and ontologically impossible, while also offering masculine and Orientalist fantasies through such expenditure, is no longer easily recuperated. Capital finds itself opening up forcefully and in new ways the safety nets that were promised through the creation of the sovereign boundaries of nation-states to appropriate bodies and their land for its renewal.

At the same time, this opening up exposes the slave as a material body and as a site upon which terror and violence can be committed with impunity to perpetuate transnational capital and whiteness. As Fanon articulates it: "It is a war in which blackness is understood as a source of historic failure in need of cathartic cure and/or annihilation. A war in which the death of blacks, as utter abjections, 'is a nothingness' without history and so indistinguishable from the unhistorical nothingness of a people without time."[24] For Fanon, this slaughtering of blacks embodies lawless violence and is the Eurocentric articulation of Hobbes's "state of nature." Fanon's approach exposes the myths of images of the "state of nature." In this state, the wild, disordered place full of species and flesh, the social contract's protection of the law does not apply, leading to slaughtering with impunity. Race is a corporeal and an abstraction agent of the visual, a form of power and economy, visual and otherwise, of civil society and institutions and lived experience.

These Eurocentric readings of Orientalism evade that colonialism transforms juridical law into a will to power based on antagonism between slaves and non-slaves. White bodies, and white but not quite, are positions that issue some form of legitimacy, mortgaged to black/slave flesh in their assemblage of humanity and a life for themselves. These tensions between slavery and colonization are crucial if white and white but not quite masculinities and femininities are not to be sutured out of the material exhaustion and slaughtering of the slave. Fanon writes: "Formal capital relations are both colonial and slave-based …

As constellations of worldviews [images are] abstracted from their contexts and reinserted in other spaces to participate in our onto-political structural contestations, they are not us but still vital to our struggle to either reanimate or kill life."[25] Paradoxically, this desire to both incorporate and slaughter the black challenges the rigid boundary of imagined coherence of the sovereign body. Faces could be border zones dividing inside from outside or, as Fanon argues, the "raw material for the coherency and the capacity of whiteness as a positionality of subjecthood."[26]

Tausig posits that normative readings of the face are "the figure of appearance, the appearance of appearance, the figure of figuration, the un-appearance, if you will, of secrecy itself as the primordial act of presencing. For the face itself is a contingency, at the magical crossroads of mask and window to the soul, one of the better-kept public secrets essential to everyday life."[27] Both mask and window facilitate the imagining of a subject: the mask hides the truth, while the windows or eyes access the soul, or so the race image story goes.

President George W. Bush articulated this division of the world on 10 October 2001 when he unveiled the "Most Wanted Terrorists" list at the FBI headquarters in Washington, employing the imagery of dark and light to illuminate the significance of the "War on Terror." On a well-circulated board with photos of the "terrorists" (see http://www. september11news.com/OsamaBinLaden.htm), a camera shines a light on the images, illuminating their faces. This supposedly ethnographic and visual documentation of masculine Arab faces attempts to capture and multiply the paradoxical and hyperbolic modes of visibility. Assembling all these photos together on a wall "maps the implementation of an archival form of power, a 'datapower' operating through the capture, storage, and retrieval of information"[28] about Arabs. Pointing the camera on their faces punctuates the frame and the environment "according to a schema of traceability which, under ideal circumstances, would be embedded within the material conditions of action itself";[29] in this case, a "terrorist" is exposed within the matrix of global power to generate a particular response.

If the photographs of the faces of the terrorists and the shapes of the words on the page are treated as the visual syntax of the formation of the empire, what does this visual syntax enable? The epistemological move to fetishize a subject structures our reading and the positionality of the Arab, a subject out of this historical time who disobeys the social contract of sovereignty. It makes the "War on Terror" both imaginable and possible. Such heterogeneous assemblages of images mobilize a specific sensorium of racial death, enabling a democratic agent to proceed by turning the remnants of Orientalism into elements of a new raw material for his/her projects.

Many images produced to control the anxiety triggered by the attacks on the Twin Towers turned the Arab masculine body into an emblem of the corruptibility of vision. To fashion a transnational figure of terrorism, various media present the "lure" of violence as a corporeal surface comprised of a racial and geopolitical conflation of signs (e.g., the Arab with a turban). This subject thus embodies a figure whose lack of interiority accompanies a malleable surface that shifts according to others' desires. His flexible corporeality makes him simultaneously a commodity and a technology whose value lies in being usable for others' purposes. The Arab body's expendability as a technology of capture, however, sometimes moves from primitive to forceful aggression, revealing the limits of a racially delineated and perversely sexualized visibility.

While postcolonial theorists argue for positive images in response to Oriental instrumental coding of Arab male bodies, this geopolitical moment demands that grasping the transmutation of the "new" being in the world account for technologies of capture and the ways in which those technologies refashion environments and subjects. Within these new matrices of power, bodies of Arabs and black flesh become experimental sites of newer technologies of violence. In an image circulating on the Internet, the Empire State Building is anally raping Osama. The inscription asks, "You like skyscrapers, huh, bitch?"[30] This fantastical hyper-feminized hyper-sexualization of Bin Laden is a consistent theme in normative discourses of the War on Terror; at the same time, it refashions the political environment and political imaginaries to right the capture and, above all, to see as viable the anal penetration of Bin Laden.

In different visual expressions, Bin Laden is presented as a figure that morphs between conspicuous visibility and the lure of vision and meaning beyond what is immediately legible. This objectified (and eroticized) portrayal, another technology of capture, refashions the environment to reimagine the US subject and the US sovereign "nation" as possible experimenters in practices of colonization carried out only on internal and external enemy "others." These images, and other ensembles, such as "concepts, institutions, procedures, regulatory decisions and scientific knowledges,"[31] geopolitical consciousness, nation, and ethnicity, are being put to use through a complex process of negotiation in the United States. Visual technologies are used as methods to capture the "other" (including blacks in the United States) in a bid to open up spaces with the potential for the creation of new value; in this way, the geopolitical boundaries of centres and margins are transformed and differences are forcefully transmuted into new raw material for experimentation for the consolidation of specific world-making projects. This articulation and focus on the "capture" is not to subsume the sideways open-ended and unruly engagements that disrupt strategies and methods of Manichean zonings as well as name strategies in such zoning-making; it is rather a way to highlight it and in so doing to reorient us in thinking otherwise the terms of knowledge production – itself a naturalized form of modern disciplinary formation – by focusing on multiple worlds.[32]

For example, Bin Laden's figure, reduced to a face and one hand, appears on toilet paper, with its Western connotations of cleanliness and civilization. His hand is raised as if he is admitting to his terrorist crimes, and his forehead is marked as a target. The reduction to a face occludes any attempt to illuminate Bin Laden's depth as a subject of politics. At the same time, his transformation from a close ally of the United States to a displaced global subject is made visible. Osama is told by the American user of the paper to "kiss my butt"; through this intimate and sexual subordination, terrorism will be "wiped" out.

Simply stated, the events of 9/11 mark an intensification of US policy. In October 2001, President Bush authorized the CIA to carry out missions to assassinate Osama Bin Laden and his supporters. He publicly declared that Bin Laden was "wanted, dead or alive." President Obama maintained this policy, and on 2 May 2011, CIA operatives and US forces killed him in a firefight in Abbottabad, Pakistan. Around the world, people celebrated his death; in the United States, especially in New York City, people took to the streets in celebration, waving flags and honking horns. An Associated Press photo shows American servicemen hanging from a lamppost, waving flags, and cheering. Indian sand artist Sudarshan Patnaik was recruited by Getty Images to capture the death of Bin Laden with sand on a beach in Puri, India. The design features an open book with the verso page showing Bin Laden's face (beige on white); on the recto, THE END is written in red sand, marking this event as the colour of blood. The sand "pages" are set on green (grass?), and we see an Indian subject carrying water on his shoulders looking away from the book, perhaps towards the unseen water beyond this space that had as its ground the corporeal slaughtering of Bin Laden.

The reactions to the death of this patriarch who defied the sovereign borders of the United States reveal an epochal anxiety and feed into a dominant narrative worldwide of the triumph of a neoliberal and war capitalist economy. The narratives circulating in newspapers relate the killing to cutting-edge military power and technology (especially DNA) while successfully excluding the notion that bruised sovereignty is not a form of "borrowed institutionality" and therefore does not require structural adjustment. While this technology of capture of the event indexes a much more complicated moment, the visualizing of the death of the enemy in a way that can circulate worldwide seems to establish this moment and this death as a "decipherable trace"[33] for reference about this violence. This image, like the sand itself, leaves a "trace" that the master now can extend his "life" in a new way in an imperial matrix of power, as the master's life is animated cognitively and literally by the value of Bin Laden's death. This and other images guard an archive that points to the "pre-emptive manhunt" that "founds the irrevocable death" of Bin Laden and many others.[34] However, "this merger of securitarian technologies of capture" that demands a priori the collating of "data" about the "terrorists" as well as the "brutality of predatory violence"[35] shifts and guards against the destruction of the system and intensifies its capture technologies to emerge anew.

The score in the "game" between Obama 1 and Osama 0, as expressed on an iPad carried by a US citizen who himself is posing for the photo with a smile on his face, mediates the dominant imaginary of power relations in the current geopolitical environment and attempts to sustain the idea that in the sphere of foreign policy, the United States remains dominant. Unresolved problems of economic and other social relations in the United States are uncritically and surreptitiously dismissed, and in this global match, Obama, a black man, can defeat a major enemy: "Official: Bin Laden Dead. We got him! Vengeance at last! US nails the bastard."[36]

This scoring makes invisible that the United States faces the demands of a late capitalist reorganization of the world economy while struggling to implement a regulatory system that sustains its role as the leader of the global economy. In the South Asian context in which Bin Laden is killed, the machination of this body remains a process of bioregulation in the global contestation of power. This loss and this death are signals to the masculine white value-producing function of global power and to the reserve of masculine neoliberal military ethics.

Even since his death, the being and practice of Bin Laden have value in the contestation and consolidation of imperial world-making projects. Even when this death could lead to the transmutation of this dead colonized body into the reanimated global body of the white subject, the series of visualizations reveals anxiety about that species (i.e., the black) whose roar could shake the dominant structures that are anchored on its flesh. This anxiety, even when displaced, is a mobilizing force of securitarian technologies of colonization, capture, and, above all, brutal predatory and gratuitous violence: the anxious subject trembles in fear that the fundamental source, the raw material, the flesh that constitutes it as coherent and powerful, may violently expose its cynegetic extermination. What if its death does not hold a place in this order and thus has no place in its economy?

Whither "My Own Appearance"? Could It Be Before, Now, and After?

Both Said[37] and Callahan[38] talk about visual geopolitical and biopolitical intertwinement in the form of images or maps, for such visualities participate in producing ideas, affects, and subject formations. However, both authors launch their critiques from the standpoint of the dissolution of the sovereign and current order. This limit to modern visualization registers a "tragic" inability to achieve the reconciliation/order that is its main inheritance. It intrudes into our visual productions through mediation by the flesh, through the slave who is always there without being there. In Fanon's words, the *sale negre* and all the images it gives rise to flow from the arresting and fetishistic stereotypes of the civil society:

> "Dirty nigger!" Or simply, "Look, a Negro!" … I came into the world imbued with the will to find a meaning in things, my spirit filled with the desire to attain to the source of the world, and then I found that I was an object in the midst of other objects. Sealed into that crushing objecthood, I turned beseechingly to others. Their attention was a liberation, running over my body suddenly abraded into nonbeing, endowing me once more with an agility that I had thought lost, and by taking me out of the world, restoring me to it. But just as I reached the other side, I stumbled, and the movements, the attitudes, the glances of the Other fixed me there, in the sense in which a chemical solution is fixed by a dye … Ontology, when we admit, once and for all, that it sets existence to one side, does not permit us to understand the being of the Black. For the Black [*le Noir*] no longer has to be black [*noir*], but must be it in the face of the White [*en face du*

Figure 23.1. Before/After Osama Bin Laden (photo courtesy of Bob August, bobaugust.com)

Blanc]. Some may take it in their heads to respond to us that the situation is reciprocal [*est á double sens*]. We respond that that is false. The Black has no ontological resistance in the eyes of the White.[39]

In conversation with Fanon, who argues that "the movements, the attitudes, the glances of the Other fixed me there, in the sense in which a chemical solution is fixed by a dye," I ask, "What kind of referentiality and what kind of affect does the Black deliver? Whither the slave in visuality?" Sexton argues: "Black life is not social life in the universe formed by the codes of state and civil society, of citizen and subject, of nation and culture, of people and place, of history and heritage, of all the things that colonial society has in common with the colonized, of all that capital has in common with labor – the modern world system."[40]

If this is the case, then the empirical existence of slavery is also contemporary, and the slave is everywhere as the reserve for the constitution of (white) life and its ordering of the world. And if the empirical existence of the slave is everywhere, what is the slave's immediate political relevance in this contestation between Bin Laden (terrorism) and the United States, as the fantastical expression of the leadership of whiteness?[41]

I take a different approach to the dominant critical visual dimension of circulating images. Instead of deconstructing the mere content of the images and, hence, their unwitting visual ideology, I argue that authors such as Mbembe, Sexton, Hartman, Wilderson, and Keeling expose the liberal idea of visuality that supposes (following Kant and Schiller) that the experience of the autonomous work of art gives rise to the free play of our faculties: the work of visuality involves a purposeful purposelessness – we could almost say a decisive indecisiveness – that mediates between the physical realm of nature, the chemical visual imaginary, and the moral realm of freedom.[42] Such critics expose that this idea of the visual is part of a liberal notion of culture, according to which individuals form themselves just as they artificially create the state.[43]

Attention to questions of the slave and slavery in the visual field forces us to problematize even the most radical Orientalist critiques and the ways these critiques have been picked up by those seen as terrorists and those who participate in shifting the locus of the empire in the name of collective or national resistance against foreign capitalist postcolonizers. The "war over the production of spatial visualities"[44] depends on a capacity to articulate the conflict between the United States and its subjects and others in the East (China and India). An assumed death, that of the slave, works to this conflict between East and West, the United States, India, China, and Bin Laden. This assumed nonexistence of blacks seems to emerge out of a desire to overcome all sorts of limits, including stagnation, loss of material value (geopolitical restructurings), and loss of dominant roles in an order and a modernity whose condition of possibility is the disavowal of black death.

The materiality of slavery and the disavowal of gratuitous violence on blacks depend on a set of global technological visual interventions that perform existential death, even when the transmutation of geopolitical capital and power maintains its *expenditure*. Gratuitous violence that makes and sustains slavery is and has been modernity's major process of movement and reanimation. Even when it is denied, the anxiety about turning into a slave mobilizes an image ontology that works to materialize gratuitous violence again and again.

Going beyond Mbembe,[45] who argues that imperial relations are colonial, but like Fanon and Sexton, I argue that this anxiety is slave-based, even at the moment when modernity invisibilizes the raw material it requires to consolidate anxiety[46] as its dominant affective expression. Fanon says: "Violence is the visibility, the shared evil that forces together the oppressor and the oppressed. Violence is the awareness of freedom's proximity of the fragility of survival."[47] Ultimately, this visuality makes this forcing together possible. For its possibility, modernity requires technologies of capture, that is, violence that is fungible and accumulative. This violence for Fanon is not mere conflict but also "a struggle to ... death."[48]

Drawing on Fanon, I articulate ontological-visual structuring technology as a slave-cratic capturing technology.[49] In addition to its "structuring [of] coherent subjectivities and incoherent species, experiences of exploitation and alienation, sexual and racial violences of accumulation," it structures fungible positionalities through terror.[50] In other words, if we presume the black body to be either structurally impossible (yet materially flesh) or already slaughtered, both the subject and the body politic can commit gratuitous terror on it. Of course, what is important here is that our reading has to also, in addition to noting this violence, challenge these affects and effects. In the image above, Bin Laden's face turns into O.J. Simpson's (a black man accused of killing his white wife), but Simpson is now a Muslim with a covered head. What is at stake in this epistemological capture and shifting indexing? Does racial purity (and read here the dominant desire, a black man is always a dead man) in the global environment accompany political and economic power through emancipation and reconstruction?

In another visual medium, a famous set of cards, the "Iraqi Most Wanted" deck, sets out to identify all the terrorists in the world in a further bid to connect faces and names, indexing the traces of violence in world politics. While these cards are ostensibly about Iraq, in the French version of the deck, Bin Laden is dressed in khaki, described as a CIA agent charged with combating the Soviets in Afghanistan and mediating between Arab nationalists and Islamicists. On the card, the provoker of the clash between the Arabo-Musulmanic and the Judeo-Christian world becomes the Joker,[51] thus articulating a cognitive capture. After all, he is just a joker, a fool!

Ferraris writes that *any* response to the ontological question of "What is there?" comes down to "a finger, generally the index [which] gives a sign towards something, and indicates it as *this*. [This] is *presence*, ontology in the simple and hyperbolic sense."[52] He engages with the "obstinate superstition" that "holds [children] incapable of abstraction." For him, children who "look at the finger ... instead of what the index is pointing to"[53] are "if anything *more* abstract [than adults], since they produce an inflation of presences."[54] What they are staring at is *"the agency which designates – the act of designation –* rather than that which is intended. Thus the over-attention of the naïve, captive, and attentive disciple inadvertently and unintentionally points to the fact that we are always guided, led, directed, pointed to something, by some guide or guiding act of designation."[55]

If we agree that "the presence of the index is no less problematic than everything it points to,"[56] we must consider the obsession with portraying Bin Laden as an event in the archive that is the terrorist (and not the panoptic effect of making him visible). Is this move an attempt to evade engaging with modernity's technologies of expenditure? That is, an ontology of potency that paradoxically draws on death specifically of the slave to constitute new life? And that generates a "thanatological dead end" even if blackness does not will its own death? Importantly, in Marriott's words, could blackness be the "image ... the multiple grave from which selves rise, vigorously, politically"?[57]

Interestingly, Bin Laden takes the idea of turning the non-Western subject into a child and pushes its logic to "children" as the zone of global power contestations:

> What has the West given the world? A lust for power and a license to loot and plunder the poorer countries ... We are against the American system but not the American people. Islam does not allow killing of innocent people, men, women and children even in the event of war ... Millions of innocent children are being killed as I speak ... I swear by God, who has elevated the skies without pillars, neither America nor the people who live in it will dream of security before we live it in Palestine, and not before all the infidel armies leave the land of Mohammed, peace be upon him.[58]

In his speech, Bin Laden brings to the fore the injustices that the West (read a Western modernity) has committed, but his entry point is the killing of the child and the looting of Palestine. Bin Laden's speech remains within the ethical grammar of modernity but disrupts this grammar by referring to Palestine. While epistemologically he looks to the West and articulates a global space that accounts for violence and violations beyond the borders of North America and Europe, he indexes a visual trace of the oppression of all Muslims by citing Palestine. Palestine points to other mnemotechnics of global power expressed in the worlding of the brutality and securitarian technologies of extermination of both people and land. Palestine is also a visual archive of an international anti-colonial struggle expressed in the worlding of anti-colonial anti-haunting low-tech projects of justice.

Palestine here is encoded in a triple manner: first, the West and America are looters and plunderers of poor countries; second, Islam serves the world better with a social imaginary that does not depend on killing innocent children; and third, Palestine is an archive of struggle and a social imaginary about the claiming and ordering of the world otherwise without the violence and (in)security that comes with oppression. Importantly, Bin Laden's "data" represent a form of power that refashions familiar narratives expressed in policies and practices of the United States and other Western powers, thus opening up spaces to direct critical challenges against such cognitive captures. This intervention presents a reading of power that interrupts the moment of agency and asks questions about the theft of land and the fungible terror that figures as the most troubling expression of modernity's power.

A well-trained disciple of the United States and its darling in the 1980s when it was fighting the former Soviet Union, Bin Laden is able to point to the problems of the West, enunciating them from a homogenous, albeit fetishized, locus in the East. Here, Ferraris's episteme can be expanded to include Bin Laden. The problem is not just Bin Laden (the pointing finger) but that to which Bin Laden points. It is as if he is asking, "What happens to my fist (noun-object) when I open my hand?"[59] The question suggests that ways of thinking determine what can be seen, understood, or expressed. Thus, what may seem like an *object* may be better construed as a *process* (i.e., finger as shifter, the finger that points simultaneously towards the fool and towards the body politic) *within an onto-politico-economic framework.*[60]

The expression of the acts and embodiments of Bin Laden cannot be reduced to a Euro-logocentric expression of meaning or even to the direct transmission of a "real" tradition. It is always the performative reiteration of "material" from heterogeneous realms or registers: myths, historical events, and entry positions organizing bodily practice. Such expressions or encounters can be placed in historical environments and accounted for in world politics, but processes like Bin Laden are equally *productive* of these historical genealogies. As technologies of articulations, they negotiate, invent, and transform institutions, discourses, ideas, regulatory decisions, procedures, fantasies, and bodies.

But what is the nature of this contestation? Drawing on Greek theory, Webb argues that "the visual impact is not an end in itself but has the further effect of producing an emotional impact, involving the listener in the events ... [and producing] sources of visual experience which transport the reader back to the events described, involving him both imaginatively and emotionally."[61] Under the French imperial moment, Fanon writes of the suture of language and the visual and of the entanglements of the visual and the affective. He theorizes the tensions in language by pointing to the tensions between slavery and colonization. Accounting for those encounters/struggles/voyeurisms that segregate the world into the zones of the colonized and those of the colonizer, he shows how the colonizer systematically pushes to transmute slavery and constitute the black body as an object, the reserve for the constitution of the structures of modernity,[62] of gratuitous violence.[63] For Orientalism to work, the logic behind any given appropriation, gaze, or visual expression need not be accurate; the less cohesive the logic, the more productive Orientalism becomes in the organization of a universal order that is not truly global – that is, imagining and making political claims whose principal goal is life rather than moribundity and dead ends.[64]

Postcolonial theorist Rey Chow emphasizes the encounter and argues that many key historical intellectual and cultural encounters with the forces of "modernity" are "specifically grounded in visuality."[65] In effect, visuality is an assemblage of concepts, institutions, procedures, set of knowledges, regulatory mechanisms, and decisions drawn upon by imperial leaders and subjects to order the world by appropriating the vital energies (i.e., structures that always depend on and maintain ontological expenditures) of those whose expression and political claims problematize and at times render impotent the suturing and mediations of modernity.

Bin Laden's depiction as the militant who brought terrorism to the United States presumes that the US was a safe haven in which Bin Laden intervened. A rhythmic motif accompanies the image of the United States as a still and sovereign site that exploded through Bin Laden's movement and then returned to stillness; this encapsulates the fundamentals of the terrorist *event* and the expression of Bin Laden's terrorism. Bin Laden thus expresses a global contestation of power by disrupting even momentarily what is articulated as a "normative" body's and body politic's dominance. His penetration into the sovereign's lands and the destruction of the masculine body gesture to the matrix of the negative economy. The loss of 3,300 lives marks the foreclosure of the dominant inscription on the US (always presumed to be white) body. This act of terrorism generates a negativity that disrupts the dominant structures' practices and questions dominant institutions and normative subjects and norms; it also *indexes an ongoing worlding anti-colonial and internationalist project that could unify the colonized and brutalized "rest" of the world*, not merely a moment in world politics.

Bin Laden's secret penetration into the United States to mobilize terrorists enables a profound transformation both in Orientalist *discourses* of flesh and the body and in Western *bodies*. His body signals a displacement in many registers and realms: the universal and its trajectory of a world that is not truly global, the international, the domestic, the public, the private discursive, and the corporeal. His penetration collapses two of the major fantasies of conquest: sovereignty and that capital and power cannot be accessed without a white and heterosexual human subject at the helm. As fantasies are dynamically linked with what Butler calls "social norms," values and practices that "are variously lived as psychic reality"[66] are no longer possible.

Postcolonial critiques feature ethical dilemmas, thus exposing that the colonial transmutes into a dominant matrix of a global whose fundament is fungibility and terror, and the colonial body transmutes itself in an uneven distribution of flesh into a global structure whose basic "law" and "dog" are white.[67] But they miss what Fanon problematizes in his work – ethical dilemmas for the black are impossible. Fanon brings to the fore the idea that "the Negro is a symbol that cannot enable the representation of meaning because it has no referent."[68] Fanon is clear that visual images are themselves engineered technologies that "simultaneously make visible and proclaim invisible the lawless privilege of whiteness."[69] The "gratuitousness of the violence that made the Negro"[70] triggers my claim that dominant and critical visual fields depend on a *structural adjustment, an ontological structure that anchors itself with economies of slave death, always maintaining expenditure with reserve*, one that presumes a black authentic and productive subjectivity.

However, such subjectivity is an oxymoron, as the black subject is not theoretically or politically accorded an "ontological integrity" that it can claim.[71] The flesh is the species that constitutes the raw material required by abundant matter to erect itself as performative identity. There is *no* essential "being" behind this doing and becoming that pushes us to ask: How does this visual expression consolidate a *normal process?*

What kinds of processes does it depend on? What does it presume about global relations and world-making projects, radical and otherwise?[72] One reading is the presumption that Bin Laden is a legitimate subject of politics, albeit in a territorial conflict with the United States. In Fanon's words, this is a fantasy, even when real.[73] It points to the identification of a hyper-masculine phallic and heteronormative terrorist in conflict with the United States.[74]

Norms are not just corporeal expressions; corporeality is also a mode of fashioning and interpretation that subjects normativity to an iterable temporality sustained by the idealizations furnished by fantasy.[75] However, this fantasy could very well be a *reassemblage* of dominant norms that do not simply *repeat* but rather transform and *disrupt* these norms, fantasies, and discourses.[76] And they do. The world cannot continue its business as usual. The economy of death that maintains structural adjustments and mediations as its ground and constitutive processes always in the name of freedom and democracy is an antagonistic moment that calls into question the political in its international iterations. Importantly, and more concretely, it calls into question whether freedom and democracy are resolved questions.

Bin Laden intervenes in this universal albeit fantastical life, entering the discourses and lived practices of international politics in a specific manner. His intervention gestures to the multiple connections among signification, identification, desires, bodily practices, and the epistemological shifts of history. Indeed, his "penetration" might be regarded as an emergence out of multiple projects whose trajectories converged as the event, reopening questions of global power and the US imperial role in the world. Importantly, this event manifests a sociogeny of fabulation about claims to life.

The psychosocial and economic harm to the colonized has endured well into the postcolonial era. The US project of global military supremacy narrates anew the global experiences of violence by orienting the world and US citizens towards an order whose ground structures and forms of political action depend on the value of the death of the slave and the theft and destruction of Aboriginal lands.[77] This project presumes an international spectrum where the relation of the sovereign universal subject towards another is consolidated and made possible through the value of the flesh and lands of those who are ontologically dead or non-existent.[78] This "matter," the life source that makes possible such "imperial sovereign adjustments,"[79] can render impotent the real/fantasy that this order depends on: conflict of territorialization. More so, and in the words of Lyndon Barrett, "the perplexity [of value is the] impossibility of determining whether value is understood primarily in regard to the dynamics of distinction or of exchange."[80] If the slave-cratic visuality includes a set of concepts, practices, and forestructures of inquiry, then I suggest that colonial imperial-sovereignty as well as capital's value be read as fabulations, more specifically, as fantasies summoning power as a technology that severs being from its existence, thereby rendering it flesh.

The assembled images of Bin Laden are radically indeterminable; that is, they cannot be easily mapped onto any teleological schema of identity and freedom, activating all the while "an onrush of sensations" that short-circuits imperial sovereignty and its contingent ensembles of slave-cratic-visuality, including the ways in which dominant image frames refashion modernity's claim to freedom and non-violence.[81]

American leaders have deliberately enlisted support from many Islamic states in the "War on Terror" to gain access to Central Asian and North African energy resources and to consolidate the military-industrial and security-industrial complexes.[82] This strategy has fanned the flames of hatred against the United States, especially given the US's heightened state of militarism to safeguard its long-term objectives in the region. Bin Laden expresses modernity's conflicting visual world-making projects' trajectories. A political Muslim and a militant, he notes the importance of revitalizing Islam by reclaiming the medieval era when Islam was "golden" and the political and the sacred first merged. This harkening, problematic in its expression of a supposedly outdated vision of the world, needs to be understood and explained:

> [Bin Laden] posit[s] a distinct identity for political Islam, one that is separate from the project of Western secular separation between church and state. In this context, Islamic revivalism is at best a late nineteenth century development, and the actions of political Islamists have formed in the period when Western modernity had its greatest influence in the colonies – that is, both are articulated in the spread of Western education, the propagation of the ideology of nationalism, and the emergence of anticolonial movements. As such, political Islam and its militant tendency should be seen as a contemporary political response to a "moral decline" that is perceived to have accompanied Western modernity ... The political Islamist position is as much a "modern" manifestation – albeit not within a Eurocentric notion of capitalist modernity.[83]

The encounter with the terrorist, then, is an encounter with a fantasy that challenges and disrupts a modernity that seeks to bring about equality and fraternity. Both the fantasy and the incitement call out to the *visual fashioning, and adjustment of "Eastern" and "Western" bodies through the mediation of flesh*. From a "Western" perspective, we need not distinguish the vast differences between, say, the many different kinds of Muslims and nationalists. What *matters* is a fantasy about the physicality of the terrorist. The fantasy connects elements hitherto geographically, culturally, politically, and otherwise distinct, but now captured as the property of the universal progenitor.

For that subject constituted as Eastern, always hiding in a cave (and therefore out of this world and out of this world's time), Bin Laden works within the framework of a modernity of a nationalistic-Muslim imaginary, calling for an identification with "traditional" Islamic values, including dress; at the same time, US foreign policy frames him as a modern, swift-moving, and seductive subject who knows the technologies of capture and unexpected attacks as mechanisms of universal power and techniques of terrorism.

In the following, Fandy refashions the world environment of terrorism in which Bin Laden's threat is less dangerous than that of politics and capital:

> Whilst Bin Laden justifies murder via video recordings, sometimes in the name of the poor and the weak and other times in the name of Palestine and resistance, "Bin Lehman" does not present any such recordings and does not need to justify the mass murders caused by its banks. It is a killing out of greed. For that reason I say that "Bin Lehman" is more dangerous to the US and the world than Bin Laden. Obama's battle, which will be the real test of the future of America's power, is not against Bin Laden abroad, but against "Bin Lehman" at home.[84]

Fandy's archive indexes "Bin Lehman" as a shifter of political power at home as the real test for Obama and the future anterior power of the United States. This conjunction of the "domestic" and the "international" that comes with Bin Lehman and Bin Laden allows us to read against the affects and effects of a foreign policy that continues to materialize the index as trace of terrorism. Importantly, this conjunction itself allows us to mobilize a visual index that points simultaneously toward the "domestic" and the "international." Bin Laden was a millionaire who made

Figure 23.2. A bottle of cologne with a picture of Osama Bin Laden is displayed at a cosmetics shop in Lahore (photo courtesy of *Daily Times*, Pakistan)

his money from his stake in the family construction business as well as other investments. A man of the market, as Bin Lehman he crossed borders with ease. In addition to his visual constitution as terrorist, he appears as the agent of the market, a man of stylish commodities: unisex products are produced in his name. One of these is the New Bin Laden *eau de parfum* found throughout West Asia and in bazaars across Afghanistan, Pakistan, Central Asia, and parts of India. Bin Laden is cited as providing the following evasive response to products cashing in on his name, such as T-shirts, thermoses, lighters, desktop air conditioners, and YBA art installations: "Everyone has his or her own unique tastes and body chemistry ... What works for me and my friends may not work for you."[85]

If this response comes directly from Bin Laden, then its nonchalance brings to the fore, it seems to me, the corporeality that a universal political economy must capture to continue and create anew an order whose major technology of capture is the generating of value. It turns its own criticism of terror into something for sale. Bin Laden's answer, while complicating the visibility of terror as a shifting index, points simultaneously to those who are terrorized and oppressed and the "global" body politic. He refashions power by arguing that what may work for one body may not work for others who are not of the Euro-North American world.

The discussion about the cologne and the affective emergences it mobilizes allows the reader of critical global politics to wonder about contemporary contestations in world politics. Could this product be gesturing to other social demands? Could the sensations that emerge from this visual encounter catalyse enough *raw energeia* (reserves that can be expended with impunity) to orient and make claims for another kind of world? While the dominant and popular reading points to the US audience's difficulty critiquing capitalism – that reading talks about the cologne as "urine" – I argue that the global flows of these images (i.e., data) challenge popular visual indexes.

If the product is communicating something about Bin Laden, this communication may well be about global politics and the formation and possibility of the survival of subjects, including himself. In fact, this product and its visibilization open up the space for a sustained account of world politics and their constitutive element: fungible and gratuitous terror. This dimension of visuality is compelling: it opens up the space for a critique of imperial terror. That is to say, if the cologne is circulating in the market, and if Bin Laden is being generated in that form, it follows that ridding world politics of this "terrorist" may be possible. However, the radical imaginary of the terrorist is more difficult to eradicate, as its circulation cannot be easily and linearly mapped.

This product also provides us with the data required to consider the geopolitical shifts that challenge a political whose assemblage is merely constitutive of state relations, a cognition of an East/West dichotomization that technologies of capture draw upon to make possible militant attacks and markets whose priority is profit. Not surprisingly, products sold in the name of a terrorist disrupt popular understandings. For the first time, the state gains consistency and coherence apart from the domination of the market. In the market, however, the terrorist is still a constituent element of decisions to produce commodities. Hence, even if we remain within the conservative heteronormative Orientalism of "us" and "them," as championed by Bush, the question remains: If Bin Laden is the personification of the ultimate male fantasy and practice of terrorist hyper-masculinity, what happens to that fantasy and practice when he is reanimated in the market and in conjunction with the Lehman brothers?

What happens politically when these visual technologies assemble Bin Laden as an enemy of masculinity, using techniques appropriated from the masters (in this case, US leaders)? In fact, the Bin Laden visual archive gestures to a fearless, powerful, empowering, lean, and muscular "terrorist" leader whose masculine power unfolds when he refuses the seductions of the sovereignty of the West, without necessarily avoiding fetishizing forms of production such as explosives, the ultimate expression of which is militant insurgency.

Does the visual archive created by Bin Laden in the various Bin Laden products point to activities proliferated by certain areas of ideological tension related to globalization and mediation and their results? Or is it merely a marketing strategy? Could what Bin Laden archives as data of the formation of the international point to other world-making projects and world views, albeit rife with tensions? In his engagement with Japanese identity vis-à-vis the West, Chan argues that the Japanese had to construct a stereotype of themselves *for* themselves. They had to colonize themselves to prevent too easy a colonization by others.[86] Chan notes that Asians "simultaneously orientalize *and* occidentalize [themselves] to *play with* borderlines."[87] This is suggested by the archive that is Bin Laden; it may be a peculiar kind of "resistance," an incitement to violence[88] akin (albeit only partly) to what Fanon says about decolonization – namely, that "decolonization itself is always a violent phenomenon"[89] and that the origin of violence is colonization.

Could the archive that Bin Laden constitutes point to the fact that terror can no longer be contained outside Euro-American landscapes (if it ever was contained)? Are these data a form of power that inquires into a radically indeterminable revolutionary moment, all the while indexing the theft and slaughter of the Enlightenment revolutionary imaginary of *liberté*, *égalité*, and *fraternité* that has been mapped onto the teleological schema of modernity? Could this inciting be contained in these archival constitutions of the terrorist? Or is there something else about modernity that is being opened up now? Chow writes:

> For those groups on the side of non-white cultures, the problem presented by multiculturalism remains one of tactical negotiation. Negotiating a point of entry into the multicultural scene means nothing less than posing the question of rights – the right to representation and the right to culture … To put it in very simple terms, a non-white culture, in order to "be" or to "speak," must (1) seek legitimacy/recognition from white culture, which has denied the reality of the "other" cultures all along; (2) use the language of white culture to produce itself; and yet (3) resist complete normativization by white culture.[90]

This complicated situation, born of the complexities of "looking at and being looked at, being placed and placing, decided and deciding,"[91] is always asymmetrical. While Chow's engagement with ethnic politics points to colonization, her argument still presumes the slave relation or antagonisms. Therefore, I argue along with Fanon and the Afro-pessimists that these racial politics are global; they have been part and parcel of modernity and play a significant role in asymmetrically locating the "other" of conflict in the market while fundamentally depending on antagonism – that is, on materializing an image ontology that indexes a trace of the black body and its fungibility as the ground and the constituent material of the political.

As a Way of Conclusion

The assembly of data in the form of a heterogeneous ensemble of images is a means of archiving data. By fashioning the fluidities of everyday expression as vital insights, visuality-as-bearing-witness provides a lens for viewing the fundamental antagonisms of the emergent global relations even as it indexes historical world-making projects and formations.

Rather than highlighting visuality's capacity to accurately represent a past or access the identity of a subject, I cite Fanon's notion of visuality-as-ontologico-contestation in which the "self, the peremptory sense of the self of the present disavows an image of itself as an originary past or an ideal future and confronts the paradox of its own making."[92]

This idea pushes us to navigate the tensions of the present, tensions that have been created not only by targeted acts of terror but also by the quotidian transformations of bodies' spatialities and temporality.

In an age marked by acts of terror and the massive proliferation of data, we need to rethink the notion of how visuality and optics can be assembled as technologies of capture in the emergence and shifting of world-making projects. Importantly, visuality-as-ontologico-contestation of a becoming global order that claims to safeguard law makes life possible and keeps peace while constantly materializing an image ontology of race that depends on expending blacks as its major reserve. It indexes itself as a data power that affirms radically indeterminable moments without rushing to resolve major questions of politics, such as freedom and democracy. This archive of terrorism indexes a notion, a set of practices, and concepts of visuality-as-an-open-ended-contestation of global power. Such a forestructure of inquiry – which is a "real leap" (Fanon 1967) – points to actors and their objects of desire as part of a mobile and transforming infrastructural landscape, not as static indicators to be rearranged through new infrastructural input. Visuality-as-politico-ontologic-structural-contestation, in other words, does not merely plot known historical transitions linearly.

By maintaining visuality as an ecology of mobile forms and processes, an ecology with a profound bearing on our understanding of the past and the present, we create a framework that affords readings that cannot be known in advance. Such an approach has practical pedagogical implications, particularly for the understanding of subjects and of those who are presumed to be socially dead and ontologically impossible but at the same time are harnessing creativity for the production of their present worlds. By providing a theoretical apparatus for a visuality of emergent relations rather than isolating certain forms as belonging to the past and others to the present, visuality as contestation of global power and a modernity whose claim to life is problematic creates a vision of life that does not leave the species and the flesh of the slave as the reserve for constant experimentation.

Bodies and visuality play a central role in constituting our understanding of global power. A different understanding of visuality moves away from an identity-based sense of bodies and bears witness to the social death of bodies and lands by being willing to render impotent its claims. Corporeal understandings of terror and its disruption that underpin normative international relations theory are inadequate to describe the complexities of global politics. These understandings underwrite non-Western corporealities as nothing more than zones of terror and violence displacing the terror that comes with ordering the world of social death.

Visuality as an onto-epistemological approach acts as a forestructure to guide our inquiry of terror and enables us to think in the interregnum, that unequal world where asymmetries of violence and terror seem to always want to rule. In that space, the "shadow that the light of [the slave] has not been able to illumine,"[93] we need to think anew visuality, its onto-epistemologies and methods.

NOTES

The author thanks Sherene Razack and Suvendrini Perera for organizing the workshop "Violence in a Far Country" in May 2012. Special thanks to all the participants for the great conversations and solidarity. Thanks also to the reviewers of the chapter at the University of Toronto. Their comments were very helpful. Also special thanks go to Elizabeth Thompson and Kole Kilibarda for reading closely the manuscript and providing me with insightful feedback. A shorter version of this chapter engaging with the epistemology of terrorism appeared in Andreas Behnke and Christina Hellmich, eds., *Knowing Al-Qaeda: The Epistemology of Terrorism* (London: Ashgate, 2012).

1 Mondzai, *Image, Icon, Economy*, 152.
2 Mondzain, *Image, Icon, Economy*, 152.
3 Chamayou, "History and Philosophy."
4 Chamayou, "History and Philosophy."
5 Mitchell, *Seeing through Race*.
6 Mondzain, *Image, Icon, Economy*, 149.
7 Agathangelou, "Bodies of Desire."
8 Bellour, "The Double Helix," 175.
9 Gordon, "The Fragile City."
10 Said, *Orientalism*; Shepherd, "Visualising Violence."
11 Mirzoeff, "The Crisis of Visuality," 2; Ghosh, *Global Icons*, 5.
12 Mirzoeff, *The Right to Look*, 478–9.
13 Mirzoeff, *The Right to Look*, 24.
14 Rupert, "Refighting America's Vietnam War."
15 Miller, *Materiality*, 10.
16 Agathangelou, "Bodies to the Slaughter."
17 Beller, "Wagers within the Image," 8.

18 Marriott, *Haunted Life*, 240.
19 Nyquist, "Hobbes, Slavery," 24.
20 Nyquist, "Hobbes, Slavery," 25.
21 Bredekamp, "Thomas Hobbes's Visual Strategies," 38.
22 Bredekamp, "Thomas Hobbes's Visual Strategies," 38.
23 Marx, *Economic and Philosophic Manuscripts of 1844*, 72–3.
24 Fanon, in Marriott, *Haunted Life*, 239–40.
25 Fanon, in Marriott, *Haunted Life*, 239–40.
26 Fanon, in Marriott, *Haunted Life*, 239–40.
27 Tausig, *Defacement*, 3.
28 Aarons, "Cartographies of Capture."
29 Aarons, "Cartographies of Capture."
30 Engle, *Seeing Ghosts*.
31 Chamayou, "History and Philosophy."
32 Agathangelou and Ling, *Transforming World Politics*.
33 Chamayou, "History and Philosophy."
34 Chamayou, "The Manhunt Doctrine."
35 Aarons, "Cartographies of Capture," 4.
36 *New York Post*, 2 May 2011.
37 Said, *Orientalism*, 7.
38 Callahan, "The Cartography," 172.
39 Fanon, in Marriott, *Haunted Life*, 194.
40 Sexton, "Ante–Anti-blackness."
41 Sexton argues: "A living death is a much a death as it is a living. Nothing in afro-pessimism suggests that there is no black (social) life … Black life is not lived in the world that the world lives in, but it is lived underground, in outer space. This is agreed. That is to say, what Moten asserts against afro-pessimism is a point already affirmed by afro-pessimism, is, in fact, one of the most polemical dimensions of afro-pessimism as a project: namely, that black life is not social, or rather that black life is *lived* in social *death*. Double emphasis, on lived and on death. That's the whole point of the enterprise at some level. It is all about the implications of this agreed upon point where arguments (should) begin, but they cannot (yet) proceed." http://lateral.culturalstudiesassociation.org/issue1/content/sexton.html.
42 Kant, *Critique of Judgment*, 9, 54.
43 Mbembe, *On the Postcolony*; Vatter, "Taking Exception to Liberalism."
44 Bellin, "Lessons," 16.
45 Mbembe, *On the Postcolony*, 14–16.

46 Sexton, "Notes on the Afterlife," 37

47 Fanon, *Black Skin, White Masks*.

48 Fanon, *Black Skin, White Masks*, 9.

49 Agathangelou, "Bodies to the Slaughter."

50 Agathangelou, "Bodies to the Slaughter."

51 See "Defend America: US Department of Defense News about the War on Terrorism," where Iraq's fifty-five most wanted are depicted. Accessed 10 January 2014 at http://www.defendamerica.mil/iraq/iraqi55.

52 Ferraris, "What Is There?", 96.

53 Ferraris, "What Is There?", 96–100.

54 Cited in Bowman, *Theorising Bruce Lee*, 102.

55 Bowman, *Theorising Bruce Lee*, 102.

56 Bowman, *Theorising Bruce Lee*, 98.

57 Sutherland, "In You More than You."

58 Cited in Bollyn, "What Does Bin Laden Really Want?"

59 Watts, *The Way of Zen*, 25.

60 For an elaboration of ontological antagonisms, see Agathangelou, "Necro-(neo) Colonizations."

61 Webb, *Ekphrasis, Imagination, and Persuasion*, 20.

62 Farley, "The Black Body as Fetish Object."

63 Hartman, *Scenes of Subjection*; Agathangelou, "Bodies to the Slaughter."

64 Agathangelou, "Bodies of Desire."

65 Chow, *Primitive Passions*, 5.

66 Butler, "Competing Universalities," 154.

67 Dayan, *The Law Is a White Dog*.

68 Judy, *Disforming the American Canon*, 107.

69 Smith, "The Evidence of Lynching Photographs," 23.

70 Wilderson *Red, White, and Black*, 39.

71 Wilderson *Red, White, and Black*, 40–1.

72 This tension is crucial and requires a much longer engagement in another paper.

73 Fanon, *Black Skin, White Masks*.

74 Butler, "Competing Universalities."

75 Butler, "Competing Universalities," 154.

76 Said, *Orientalism*; Butler, "Competing Universalities," 15.

77 Rupert, "Refighting America's Vietnam War," 3.

78 Agathangelou, "Necro-(neo) Colonizations."

79 Agathangelou, "Necro-(neo) Colonizations."

80 Barrett, *Blackness and Value*, 12.

81 Ghosh, *Global Icons*, 8.
82 Lawrence, "Enlightenment, Modernity and War"; Rupert, "Refighting America's Vietnam War."
83 Lawrence, "Enlightenment, Modernity and War."
84 Mamoun Fandy Bin Laden or "Bin Lehman," Al-Arabiya News, 22 September 2011, http://www.alarabiya.net/views/2009/09/22/85709.html.
85 Langlands and Bell had an exhibition on the "House of Osama Bin Laden" at the Imperial War Museum from 10 April to 26 May 2003; David Prudames, "Osama Bin Laden's Lair in London," *Culture* 24, 19 March 2003.
86 Chan, "The Construction and Export," 69.
87 Chan, "The Construction and Export," 70.
88 I am indebted to Kole Kilibarda for this idea.
89 Fanon, *The Wretched of the Earth*, 13.
90 Chow, *Ethics after Idealism*, 12.
91 Bowman, *Theorising Bruce Lee*, 102.
92 Williams and Chrisman, *Colonial Discourse and Post-Colonial Theory*, 122, citing Fanon.
93 Enrique, *Philosophy of Liberation*, cited in Spanos, *America's Shadow*, 206.

24 Viewing Violence in a Far Country: Abu Ghraib and Terror's New Performativities

SUVENDRINI PERERA

A disturbing photograph from Libya, published in the New York Times, shows scores of anonymous arms hoisting cell phones up high to capture the last moments of Muammar Gaddafi. Accentuated against the somber stillness of the photograph with its disembodied assembly of anonymous arms, the luminescent miniature screens throb with imperceptible images, like so many exclamation points. The upraised arms confer a strange unity on the disorder of the crowd, its collective gaze turned toward the unseen. In these moments, outside the field of vision, in the crucial gap between the viewer of the photograph and the cameras of the crowd, Gaddafi is being raped and beaten to death after being dragged out of his hiding place inside a concrete pipe. Facing the crowd in the position of the photographer, a figure casually mirrored, perhaps, in their gaze, I view, not the horrific end of Gaddafi, but the massed array of phone cameras that will bear electronic witness to that visual event.

The crowd wielding their phones up high themselves are not direct witnesses to the killing; rather, they see themselves imaged and multiplied on the screens of other phones: photographer photographed, subject and object, one hand flashing V signs for the camera, camera flashing and pulsing in the other. The photograph prompts a series of questions about the volatility and mobility of contemporary spectacles of violence as they magnify and mutate, implicating viewer and viewed, actor and audience, placing and dis-placing a violence that continues to unfold outside as well as inside the frame.

In *Cloning Terror*, his book on the images of the War on Terror, W.J.T. Mitchell characterizes the post-9/11 era as infected by the viral proliferation of images, a veritable "global plague of images."[1] Mitchell identifies the Abu Ghraib photographs, "and one in particular (the Hooded Man)," as the "central image-event of the epoch."[2] Despite his insistence on the global and epochal significance of the Abu Ghraib images, Mitchell's focus in *Cloning Terror* is on their internal effects within the United States. His "Abu Ghraib archive," comprising secondary documents, analyses and artefacts all centring on the photographs, is a distinctly national one.[3] At the same time, Mitchell recognizes that the Abu Ghraib archive "provides an important case for analysing the role of digital images, digital archives, and their role in contemporary political culture" and is one whose circulation is "unlikely to abate any time soon": "What is the meaning of the Abu Ghraib archive? What are its boundaries? Is it complete or finished? What does it leave out, and what remains to be filled in?"[4]

In this chapter I take up Mitchell's questions about the as yet uncharted boundaries of Abu Ghraib by considering its global circulation and mutation as an image-event. My interest is in the interrelations between the global ramifications of the War on Terror and the visual economies of the digital era – including existing and emergent scopic regimes, representational and aesthetic repertoires, communication and information technologies, mobile media, online circulatory cultures, and networks of social connectivity. How does Abu Ghraib as a cluster of practices, images, discourses, and technologies reappear and resound as it ramifies across diverse geographies and temporalities? Mitchell's term "iconology" refers to "the study of images across media" as both "verbal and visual entities, both metaphors and graphic symbols." The images are understood as "at one and the same time concepts, objects, pictures, and symbolic forms" as well as "becoming operative forces in sociopolitical reality."[5] This is a preliminary iconology of Abu Ghraib in the context of sociopolitical realities that extend beyond the immediate theatres of the War on Terror.

While much has been said about the democratic and liberatory potential of mobile media's new visual economies and the forms of participation, witness, and activism they make possible, their emergence and evolution cannot be separated from contexts of war and militarization. Jenny Terry, in her documentation of Afghanistan battlefield videos posted on YouTube, identifies an "emergent social matrix that brings together cameras, computers, bodies, weapons, sentiments, and ideas."[6] Nicholas Mirzoeff's term, "military-visual complex," references a more specific set of relationships that reaches from 1990s video war games to the deployment of "brilliance" and "shock and awe" as part of the tactics of "rapid dominance" in the 2003 invasion of Iraq.[7] As Mirzoeff elaborates, the military-visual complex consolidated in the early years of the War on Terror leads to the formation of certain kinds of "visual subjectivities" and to an attendant "circulation anxiety" that characterizes "a digital and global culture of hegemonic capitalism."[8] I take "circulation anxiety" to refer to contexts in which the mobility of images goes hand in hand with the confinement of bodies (some more than others) through technologies of surveillance, profiling, biometrics, and other biopolitical practices, even as they are enmeshed in circuits of consumption.[9] What forms of visual subjectivity and modalities of spectatorship does the military-visual complex give rise to, in particular for global and diasporic viewing subjects? Are its new visual economies capable not only of amplifying the effects of violence and terror but also of enabling and facilitating new modalities of violence, terror, and "horrorism" through their distinctive conditions of production, circulation, reception, and consumption?[10] What relations of complicity and responsibility do these in turn engender?

In the Abu Ghraib image-event, the visual and discursive archives of colonial racist violence intersect with the technological possibilities of digital media and the new forms of social connectivity they make possible. At this intersection of terror and technology, I consider the Abu Ghraib images as agents of both incitation and emulation, as operative forces in transnational sociopolitical realities that shape practices and events and their interpretive frames. This chapter considers three disparate scenes of violence at "the intersected place of the viewer and the image in the visual event."[11] The first explores Abu Ghraib's relationship to the project of mainstream feminism and its legacies. In Coco Fusco's *A Field Guide for Female Interrogators*, the Abu Ghraib images are read retrospectively as the (grotesque) outcome of a particular logic of equal opportunity feminism, recasting relations of gender, race, and nation and exposing mainstream feminism's ongoing implication with the nation's violence. The middle section of the chapter considers Abu Ghraib's pedagogical role through the trophy videos and photographs of the final days of the war in Sri Lanka (these were one of the trigger points for the workshop "Violence in a Far Country" on which is based). Finally, I turn to the "Kony 2012" social media campaign, initiated by "the most viral video in history."[12] In each of these digitally circulating global visual events, I foreground questions of situated viewing subjects in relation to the spectacle of violence in a far country.

The Gendered Visual Subject of War

In 2004, Coco Fusco responded to the display of US women soldiers' participation in the torture of Iraqi prisoners at Abu Ghraib by creating the character of an "implacable female interrogator" in the US army and taking her on the road for a series of performances. To develop the character, Fusco conducted extensive research with military officials and interrogators, herself posing as a prospective interrogator. She describes the persona who emerged from this exercise as a little like Shakespeare's Sister, Virginia Woolf's sad exemplar of unfulfilled female potential in *A Room of One's Own*. Unlike Shakespeare's Sister, however, Fusco's interrogator "actually gets the chance to show her stuff."[13] Woolf, "the fairy godmother of so many feminists," is the direct addressee of Fusco's extended reflections on the performance and the questions that prompted it.[14] Fusco identifies the title of her essay "Invasion of Space by a Female" as turning Woolf's best-known title inside out to explore "the dark side of advancing women's rights through warfare" (8). The body of Fusco's work, however, engages less with *A Room of One's Own* than with Woolf's second, far less popular, feminist treatise, *Three Guineas*.

Woolf couches *Three Guineas* in the form of an extended letter to a male interlocutor who has asked for her ideas on how to prevent war (in addition to seeking a financial contribution and inviting her to join an antiwar association). *Three Guineas* was written in 1936–7, in the shadow of the approaching war with Germany and in the face of the then unprecedented brutalities of the Spanish Civil War. Picasso's *Guernica*, one form of visual representation of, and impassioned protest against, the new destructive visual technologies unleashed in that war, also would be completed in 1937. *Guernica* retains such potency that US officials asked for a tapestry of the painting outside the Security Council chamber at UN headquarters to be covered as they made their case for the 2003 invasion of Iraq.[15] *Three Guineas* is framed by another of the formative visual technologies of modernism: the black-and-white photograph. Photographs of atrocities were increasingly circulated during the war, especially within left circles, as part of what we would now describe as a targeted international media strategy. The Spanish Civil War in its mobilization of a politicized transnational subject through visual media bears some overlooked resemblances to the War on Terror in this respect. Photographs of civilian killings lie on the author's desk as she writes *Three Guineas*. The Spanish government sends them, she observes, "with patient pertinacity about twice a week": "This morning's collection [shows] what might be a man's body or a woman's ... But those certainly are dead children, and that undoubtedly is the section of a house."[16] The narrator immediately responds to the photographs as a new form of knowledge from that which is to be found in written histories and biographies. Although conscious of the photographs' role as part of the Spanish government's propaganda campaign, she cannot but apprehend the photographs as unmediated and transparent statements of fact, innocent of the rhetorical manipulability of words:

> Those photographs are not an argument; they are simply a crude statement of fact addressed to the eye. But the eye is connected to the brain; the brain with the nervous system ... When we look at those photographs some fusion takes place within us; however different the education, the traditions behind us, our sensations are the same ... *For now at last we are looking at the same picture*; we are looking with you [our male counterparts] at the same dead bodies, the same ruined houses.[17]

Seeking to explain the seemingly irrefutable address of the photographs, their urgent indexicality, Woolf's narrator understands them as effecting a series of "fusions" between sensory, cognitive, and affective responses, overriding reason, ideology, and location ("argument, education, traditions"). In this account of grappling with the strange effectivity of photographs, and the narrator's attempt to account for the unfamiliar sensations they elicit, is represented the emergence of a new kind of visual subject of war. Her sense of confusion before the address of the photographs, and her barely stated "fear of the force of images," Fusco writes, identify the narrator of *Three Guineas* "as a member of a society whose world views had only recently begun to be shaped by encounters with modern media."[18] Yet difficulties with interpreting visual media and the conflicting emotions aroused by the atrocity photographs are by no means confined to pre–Second World War viewers. These are factors that Angela Davis identifies some seventy years later in her discussion of the Abu Ghraib and Rodney King images:

> Images are very complicated and we haven't promoted ... a visual literacy necessary to critically understand them. To think of the image as an unmediated representation is problematic and often has the effect of producing precisely the opposite of what was expected ... We saw the police beating Rodney King on video, but the prosecutor was able to develop a particular interpretation of that image that bolstered his claim that Rodney King was the aggressor. So I think it is important not to assume that the image has a self-evident relationship to its object. And it is important to consider the particular economy within which images are produced and consumed.[19]

The seemingly incontrovertible address of the atrocity photograph works against the grain of the central argument of *Three Guineas*, namely, the *situatedness* of the gendered subject in its responses to the great national institutions of parliament, church, university, and, especially, the military. To the interpellations of these institutions from which she has been excluded, Woolf argues, the outsider cannot but respond with "indifference." The most famous lines in *Three Guineas* are those of a spokeswoman for the society of outsiders, women situated (limited) like Woolf by class and race, as she responds to the appeal of militarism, patriotism, and what we might today call the notion of the homeland:

> But the outsider ... will ask herself, "What does 'our country' mean to me an outsider?" ... She will inform herself ... how much of "England" in fact belongs to her ... She will reflect that for her there are no "foreigners," since by law she becomes a foreigner if she marries a foreigner ... Probably she will have imbibed, even from the governess, some romantic notion that Englishmen ... are "superior" to the men of other countries. Thus she will consider it her duty to check by comparing ... the testimony of the ruled – the Indians or the Irish, say ... When all these comparisons have been faithfully made by the use of reason, the outsider will find herself in possession of very good reasons for her indifference ... "Our country," she will say, "throughout the greater part of its history has treated me as a slave; it has denied me education or any share in its possessions. 'Our' country still ceases to be mine if I marry a foreigner ... In fact, as a woman, I have no country. As a woman I want no country. As a woman my country is the whole world."[20]

The atrocity photographs, however, effectively represent a turn in this line of argument. Spurred by the evidentiary power and ethical urgency of the photograph, the outsider's critical and informed "indifference" to the call to defend the homeland merges with the desire to end war. The narrator ends by donating a guinea to the society for the prevention of war and signing their petition, although she stops short of joining the society itself. The contribution, however, is contingent on two prior donations, to associations for middle-class women's educational and professional advancement.

In the aftermath of the Abu Ghraib photographs, Fusco identifies in this ambivalent encounter between the privileged white feminist subject and the atrocity photograph the traces of a form of gender politics that would create the conditions for the reception of the contemporary atrocity images of Abu Ghraib. Fusco's letter to Woolf not only challenges the illusion of the female/feminist subject's non-implication in the nation's violence, but also argues that, in the instance of the Abu Ghraib photographs, the claim that women are not implicated in the violence of the nation serves to camouflage or underplay the very forms of torture that the photographs document: "I keep asking myself if there might be some correlation between the relative lack of public outcry against between the Bush administration's attempts to rationalize the use of torture and the prevailing images of its perpetrators as young and naïve white women."[21] Moreover, as the focus on gender became "key to the interpretation of the events depicted" in the photographs, it succeeded in "diverting attention away from the pervasiveness of prisoner abuse by engendering public sympathy for the handful of underlings who bore the brunt of the punishment."[22]

The selective preoccupation with the gender of the women torturers in the Abu Ghraib photographs (e.g., the meaning of Lynndie England's smile as she leads a naked Iraqi on a leash) served to personalize the torturer at the expense of the tortured as the anonymous and abjected object of violence. The identification of the Abu Ghraib perpetrators as "young and naïve white women" submerged their status as soldiers in the US army; their marginal status in the military served to render their actions similarly minor and marginal. At the same time, read through the visual economy of Internet porn and its images of "torture chicks," the enormity of the violence perpetrated against the defenceless prisoners in the photographs is both trivialized and distorted. Most critically, Fusco points out how the focus on the *gender* of the torturers in the photographs served to obscure, distract from, and excuse the practice of torture itself and the ways in which torture was and is central to US war operations, in Iraq and elsewhere.[23] Fusco's *A Field Guide for Female Interrogators* exposes how gendered analyses of the photographs contain and domesticate the violence of Abu Ghraib, for example, through their mobilization into pre-existing internal feminist debates over pornography and women's agency.[24]

Torture and the Trophy Image

The domestication of the Abu Ghraib image-event through a focus on the status and stories of its female perpetrators obscures other ways in which they signify as domestic documents. As Hazel Carby, Angela

Davis, and Joseph Pugliese were among the first to point out, the Abu Ghraib photographs are far from exceptional or unique documents in US domestic histories. Carby's essay "A Strange and Bitter Crop" incisively lays bare how "integral the torture of brown bodies has been to the building of 'the land of the free.'"[25] Moreover, the "symbolic spectacle" of debased and mutilated black and brown bodies," she argues, is "intimately linked with the technologies of photography": "There is a direct, but hidden, line connecting Abu Ghraib, the Rodney King video, and the photographs and 'postcards' of lynchings which circulated widely in the early 20th century." Challenging Susan Sontag's comment that, unlike the lynching postcards, the Abu Ghraib photographs represent a new development in their function as "messages" rather than as trophies or souvenirs, Carby insists that "the importance of spectacles of abuse, the taking of photographs and videos, the preservation and the circulation of the visual image of the tortured/lynched body, the erotic sexual exploitation which produced pleasure in the torturers – all these practices are *continuities* in the history of American racism."[26] The continuities Carby marks were re-enacted in other imperial adventures in the intervening period, an example being the forms of "race pleasure" that Sherene Razack identifies in the images of the Canadian peacekeeping mission in Somalia, with their telling juxtapositions of (powerless) black and (powerful) white bodies.[27]

In his compelling and meticulous analysis of the Abu Ghraib photographs and the shadow archive of US history, Pugliese brings into the frame the entire "historical reservoir of images that functions to construct the enabling conditions for the emergence and cultural intelligibility" of the Abu Ghraib photographs. This archive includes "colonial tableaux; torture; souvenir; news-media event; evidentiary legal document; fetish; pornography; Orientalism; homophobia; misogyny; sadism; carcerality; lynchings; and so on," situated in the context of "a range of aesthetic modalities – including colonial, Orientalist, white supremacist, and penal."[28] The seemingly disparate and disjunctive quality of this inventory, Pugliese argues, indicates the multiple registers and contexts in which photographs signify, a "constitutive polyvalence" that allows them to be used and understood simultaneously in different ways – in this case as both "fetishistic objects of personal pleasure shared amongst the military personnel of the prison and legal documents inscribed with an evidentiary role within the court of law."[29]

In trying to understand the historical continuities and discontinuities of Abu Ghraib as visual event, I am interested in how this "constitutive polyvalence" of the photograph is amplified by the manner of its transmission and (re)circulation through digital media and online circulatory networks. As Carby points out, although the practices of "the preservation and the *circulation* of the visual image of the tortured/lynched body [and] the erotic sexual exploitation which produced pleasure in the torturers – all ... are *continuities* [with the past] ... the digital form in which the Abu Ghraib images circulated is new."[30] How does the digital transmission of the images make them available in new ways, heightening or accentuating specific effects and resignifying their modes of address? More fundamentally, is there a correlation between the infinite communicability of the photographs via networked media and digital transmission and the proliferation of interpretations and alternative versions of their meaning?

Pugliese emphasizes that "despite the fact that the Abu Ghraib photographs are digital and not analogue images, they have, in the context of a so-called post-photography digital culture, lost none of the power or force of the indexicality that characterises the traditional analogue photograph"; rather, "the power of their indexicality – an event took place and it was visually recorded – ... underwrites their evidentiary and testimonial qualities."[31] While the Abu Ghraib images continue to maintain an evidentiary force, the means of their electronic transmission simultaneously intensifies their "constitutive polyvalence." Both the visual economies within which they circulate and their interpretive contexts become increasingly unstable and volatile under the conditions of "communicative capitalism" theorized by Jodi Dean, characterized by a plethora "circulating disintegrated spectacles and opinions."[32] Communicative capitalism, Dean argues, produces an environment in which politics, paradoxically, becomes submerged by the very openness, accessibility, and proliferation of media forms, the "intense circulation of content," and the availability of an infinite array of positions, knowledges and interpretive frames. The conditions created by digital media offer proliferating opportunities to reframe and resignify visual images in particular; they also enable the images to metamorphose and mutate, activating new forms of incitement and excitation as they testify to extremities of terror.

The Killing Fields of Home

The War on Terror often appears to subjects in the West as a singular event, with the United States and its allies as the key protagonists.

There is barely any understanding of how the rhetorics, tactics, and technologies of the war have reverberated through other conflicts. In the third decade of its war in Sri Lanka against the separatist LTTE (Liberation Tigers of Tamil Eelam), the Sri Lankan government was able to reinvent that conflict as a front in the War on Terror, proclaiming its commonalities with the United States and its allies and claiming the mantle of a sovereign state beset by terrorists. Its military victory in 2009 had much to do with this recasting and with the geopolitical realignments of the War on Terror; at the same time, however, the crackdown on transnational Islamist terror networks in the West had reduced support for the LTTE among both foreign governments and diaspora groups.

A disturbing feature of the War on Terror is that the actions and rhetorics of the United States have provided moral legitimation for smaller states that are dealing with real or imagined threats to their authority. To my knowledge, little research has been done regarding the impact of the War on Terror on other wars and conflicts; an account yet remains to be written of the obscene transnational exchanges of torture methods among states in the War on Terror. In the case of Sri Lanka, it is impossible to overestimate how much licence US actions have provided for the continuing perpetration of violence against civilians and captured prisoners. In the context of the transnational adaptability of the rhetorics, tactics, and technologies of the War on Terror, I want to consider, in the context of Sri Lanka, the mobility and communicability of Abu Ghraib across other wars and the ways in which this has given rise to new grammars, repertoires, and technologies of terror.

In 2009, in the final phases of the war in Sri Lanka, verbal accounts of what happened on the battlefield were accompanied by a relatively new form of testimony: visual narratives and battlefield snapshots recorded on mobile phones by both victors and vanquished. These testamentary and trophy videos from the war in Sri Lanka's north circulated internally among diaspora groups before publicly surfacing through YouTube. Eventually they were investigated by human rights groups and independent Western media as well as by the UN. In Britain, the Channel 4 documentary *Sri Lanka's Killing Fields* (2011, followed by sequels in 2012 and 2013) was the outcome of one such investigation. It reconstructed the final weeks and days of the war through the narratives of survivors, NGO and UN officials, and the digital trophy photographs and camera phone videos of the victors.[33] This visual evidence forms a collage of horrific representations, ranging from heaps of dead bodies of brutalized women being mocked by soldiers to excruciatingly detailed recordings of torture and execution.

Trophy photographs have long been a feature of warfare. However, the extensive use of camera phones and social media cannot be isolated from the pervasiveness of this practice at Abu Ghraib or from the global circulation of the Abu Ghraib trophy photographs. In his essay, Pugliese cites Mark Danner's description of the camera as the "ultimate third party" in the multiple acts of torture and violence documented at Abu Ghraib.[34] This third party, as Pugliese shows, is complicit with the actions of the torturer and indeed compounds torture's effects. Visual technologies are omniscient and ever-present third parties that, as they observe and record the torture, ensure its infinite reproduction and continuity. They also serve as communication channels both to survivors and to communities targeted by terror.

The trophy images of the war in Sri Lanka are intimate and public in ways that are at once similar to and different from the frenetic obscenities of Abu Ghraib. Here, Sri Lankan government soldiers, all men, preside over the bodies of the dead at the moment of victory on the battlefield. They address, at times directly, a listener/viewer in a moment framed as one of consolidation, of unquestioned mastery: an act of national affirmation. Yet these horrific images, precisely as forms of performativity, do not mark a terminus in a chain of violence and terror. Rather, through the medium of the photograph, they ensure their own continuity, their indefinite circulation and iteration. For the vanquished, the photographs are intended as messages of warning; for the victor, they speak of the continued exertion of dominance through violence and terror. Sontag writes: "There is the deep satisfaction of being photographed, to which one is now more inclined to respond not with a stiff, direct gaze (as in former times) but with glee. The events are in part designed to be photographed. The grin is a grin for the camera. There would be something missing if, after stacking the naked men, you couldn't take a picture of them."[35]

Sontag's observations on the gleeful torturers of Abu Ghraib resonate as we view smiling Sri Lankan soldiers exchanging banter and sexual innuendo while they stack the bodies, bruised, bloodied, and stripped naked, of young women non-combatants after the Tamil camps have been overrun. Close-ups focus on breasts and thighs as the women are flung, like so many inert bundles, onto the back of a truck. The soldiers speak casually to one another and beyond to the implied audience somewhere off the battlefield. "This one has the best figure," a man comments as he surveys a lifeless body piled on a heap of others like it. It would be a banal statement, except that he is assessing the bodies of dead, most likely raped and tortured, women on a battlefield. What is revealed here is not, or not only, evil's banality, but its relentless performativity. A second soldier declares for the camera, as he throws another dead woman onto the truck, "I'd cut her tits off if no one was looking." As it collapses the distance between the speaker and the photographer/viewer who is looking on as he speaks, the remark draws its audience into silent complicity, compelling a form of identification with the monstrous intentions expressed.

In the Sri Lankan torture and battlefield videos, the Abu Ghraib images reappear, transposed onto new contexts, reformatted, replayed, and marked by the blatant sexualization of the target bodies as well as by a bold and defiant performativity – one that I argue is buttressed and licensed by Abu Ghraib's global visibility. The gender of the perpetrators of these acts is submerged by their status as soldiers of an army asserting its dominance. While Abu Ghraib, as we have seen, can be situated within an archive of colonial and racial violence, it is also a visual event that initiates new repertoires, new grammars, and new modalities of terror that can be performed deliberately in conflicts marked by clear ethno-religious and ethno-cultural divides.

Enabled by the mobilization of digital technologies as third parties, visual events generate new modes for their reception and consumption, addressing and implicating audiences and publics as either targets or supporters of terror. Among supporters of the state, these responses range from excusing, underplaying, or explaining away the violence ("a few rogue soldiers, a few bad apples") to outright denials that the atrocities took place. The authenticity of the Killing Fields videos and of other digital testimonies of military brutality is still bitterly contested by the Sri Lankan government even though the UN as well as mainstream media such as Britain's Channel 4 have confirmed that they are authentic. In the state's version of events, the Killing Fields videos show Tamil LTTE fighters dressed in government uniform. Even more fantastical, the state has attempted to reverse the violence through dubbing so that the perpetrators sound like Tamils. Dean's concept of the "psychotic media" enabled by new communicative technologies is helpful in understanding the positions adopted by the Killing Fields deniers. As Dean argues in the context of 9/11 images, the Internet's "proliferation of contents and voices, sources and alternatives, links and possibilities" enables a landscape of "epistemologically differentiated spaces" and "competing conceptions of the Real"; this landscape then produces the conditions for "psychotic media" to flourish.[36] However, the psychotic media of the Sri Lankan state, which are characterized by an extreme vehemence, certainty, and suspicion, do not exist in isolation. They are mirrored in the psychotic media that continue to be churned out by its enemy, and counterpart, the LTTE. The proliferation of such closed circuits of psychotic media, especially within diaspora groups, since the end of the war represents another destructive and frightening aspect of the formation and consolidation of new digital identities, one that remains to be explored.

Social Media and the White Saviour Industrial Complex

The first phase of the invasion of Iraq demonstrated the arsenal of military-visual technologies at the disposal of the United States and its allies. Beginning with the lethal pyrotechnics of the shock and awe campaign, and including the embedding of journalists, as well as set pieces such as the rescue of Jessica Lynch and the staged demolition Saddam Hussein's statue, this phase culminated in the "Mission Accomplished" Thanksgiving celebration that featured, in Naomi Klein's words, "a fake President dressed as a fake soldier declaring a fake end to combat and then holding up a fake turkey."[37] After this succession of mediatized spectacles, Mirzoeff wrote that he and others who had opposed the war experienced a pervasive depression based on "the realization that the emancipatory promise of digital culture and an emergent networked society in the 1990s had been for nothing."[38]

In the years since, the failure of the "emancipatory promise of digital culture and an emergent networked society" has been compounded by an awareness that the United States and its allies remain mired in the War on Terror. President Obama's pledge to end the detention of prisoners at Guantanamo remains unfulfilled five years after he assumed office. Meanwhile, largely hidden from public view, new military and visual technologies such as armed drones have extended the global reach of US terror. In this context, the "Kony 2012" campaign registers as a tailor-made attempt to re-establish the beneficial possibilities of digital technology and social media and renew faith in the project of human rights, humanitarian action, and global justice. "Kony 2012" can be understood as Abu Ghraib's obverse or antonym: a digitally circulated testament to the US power for good in the world. Against Joseph Kony's history of torture, rape and abuse of children (and, by a chain of unspoken association, the reminders of images of US torture in Iraq and Afghanistan) are arrayed the forces of a networked, concerned, U.S citizenry unequivocally mobilized for the good – one imagined as young, white, and technologically literate.

The "Kony 2012" campaign, in its second phase as I write, aims via its video, released on YouTube and disseminated through social media, to mobilize support for a course of actions that would culminate in Joseph Kony being brought before the International Criminal Court for atrocities committed in Uganda by his Lord's Republican Army (LRA). Produced by the California-based Christian group Invisible Children, "Kony 2012" takes the form of an exchange between the North American founder of the group, Jason Russell, and his baby son. The video aims to educate the viewer – implicitly cast in the role of the unknowing and child-like white subject – about Kony's record of horrific violence. The visual juxtapositions of guilty or abjected black bodies and wholesome, healthy, white ones, and the rhetorical contrasts between the innocence of North American childhood and the horrific violence to which Ugandan children are subjected, all contribute to the implicit race pleasure and civilizational superiority that drives the production. As such, these contrasts reproduce, in an ostensibly benign register, the juxtapositions between bodies at Abu Ghraib.

Launched on 5 March 2012, the campaign succeeded beyond all expectations. Amassing 100 million viewers in six days, "Kony 2012" became "the most viral video in history."[39] Besides garnering an unprecedented audience, it prompted the passing of Congressional resolutions urging increased US efforts to capture Joseph Kony and won support from a number of African state leaders. Simultaneously, however, a series of critiques questioned the ethical, military, and economic ramifications of the campaign and sought to lay bare the "white saviour industrial complex" that underwrote it.[40] In a sequence of devastating Tweets, the Nigerian American author Teju Cole asserted that "Kony 2012" was not about justice, but rather "about having a big emotional experience that validates privilege." As millions of young North Americans bought Stop Kony bracelets and pledged financial support for the campaign, Cole warned of the consequences of increased US military presence in the area and uncritical support for local regimes: "If Americans want to care about Africa, maybe they should consider evaluating American foreign policy, in which they already play a direct role through elections, before they impose themselves on Africa itself ... Let us begin our activism right here: with the money-driven villainy at the heart of American foreign policy."[41]

The deliberate or unwitting self-deceptions that underwrote the phenomenal success of "Kony 2012," among young US citizens in particular, exemplify the workings of Dean's model of "communicative capitalism" in which the "ideals of inclusion and participation in information and entertainment and communicative technologies" in fact have had the effect of "captur[ing] resistance and intensify[ing] capitalism."[42] The "Kony 2012" campaign locates itself within the field of transitional justice, aimed at achieving reconciliation and reparation in war-ravaged "post-conflict" societies. In this regard, Cole's analysis underlines that efforts at transnational justice do not take place in a geopolitical vacuum; rather, they are driven by the interests and investments of dominant powers – in this case, the interests that have also underwritten the wars in Iraq and Afghanistan. Thus, "success for *Kony 2012* would mean increased militarization of the anti-democratic Yoweri Museveni government, which has … played a major role in the world's deadliest ongoing conflict, the war in the Congo … [and who] appears to be a U.S. proxy in its shadowy battles against militants in Sudan and, especially, in Somalia."[43]

The possible implication of the "Kony 2012" campaign in the hidden agendas and proxy wars of the War on Terror suggests that it cannot be dismissed simply as a naive attempt to energize young North American "digital natives."[44] The convergence of humanitarian and military interests in the Kony project underlines not an incidental but a *structural* alignment between the two. Instead of advancing a powerful new force for transnational/transitional justice by mobilizing the latent possibilities of Facebook and YouTube (as the lengthy preamble to "Kony 2012" claims), the campaign reinscribes military interventionism and support for terror at the heart of the digital revolution. Rather than embodying the antithesis of Abu Ghraib, "Kony 2012" can be more accurately understood as its soft power counterpart.

Watching Babylon, Mirzoeff's book of reflections on the new visual subjectivities of the War on Terror, begins with a return to the possibilities for the global visual culture that has characterized the new millennium: "As digital culture interfaced with globalization, the visual turn promised to be the key location for its interpretation. It seemed that the new hybridity of globalization could be represented in … 'the new international visual Esperanto.'"[45] That imagined future of digital media forms capable of generating new polyglot forms of communication across national and racial borders ("the new international visual Esperanto") has largely failed to materialize. Rather, "the visual turn" of the post-Abu Ghraib era appears to include an ever-expanding repertoire of trophy images of violence and torture. Finding a theoretical language adequate to this new visual culture and its effects is a challenge whose dimensions remain to be fully comprehended.

NOTES

Thanks to Inderpal Grewal for the referring me to Jenny Terry's work.
1 Mitchell, *Cloning Terror*, 2.
2 Mitchell, *Cloning Terror*, xv.
3 Mitchell, *Cloning Terror*, 113.
4 Mitchell, *Cloning Terror*, 117.
5 Mitchell, *Cloning Terror*, xvii
6 Terry, "Killer Entertainments."
7 See Ullman and Wade, *Shock and Awe*, 110.
8 Mirzoeff, *Watching Babylon*, 12–13.
9 On biometrics, see Pugliese, *The Biopolitics of Biometrics*.
10 On horrorism, see Caverero, *Horrorism*.
11 Mirzoeff, *Watching Babylon*, 11.
12 Preston, "Sequel to 'Kony 2012' Video."
13 Fusco, *A Field Guide*, 27.
14 Fusco, *A Field Guide*, 17.
15 Dowd, "Powell without Picasso."
16 Woolf, *Three Guineas*, 10–11.
17 Woolf, *Three Guineas*, 11, emphasis added.
18 Fusco, *A Field Guide*, 17.
19 Davis, *Abolition Democracy*, 51.
20 Woolf, *Three Guineas*, 106–7.
21 Fusco, *A Field Guide*, 20.
22 Fusco, *A Field Guide*, 26.
23 See also Razack, forthcoming.
24 For example, see Judith Butler's remarks in *Frames of War*, 88–9, in response to Joanna Burke's Guardian column "Torture as Pornography."
25 Carby, "A Strange and Bitter Crop."
26 Carby, "Strange Fruit."

27 Razack, *Dark Threats and White Knights*, 61.
28 Pugliese, "Abu Ghraib," 251–2.
29 Pugliese, "Abu Ghraib," 251.
30 Carby, "Strange Fruit."
31 Pugliese, "Abu Ghraib," 251.
32 Dean, *Democracy*, 24.
33 See http://nofirezone.org.
34 Danner, cited in Pugliese, "Abu Ghraib," 252.
35 Sontag, "Regarding the Torture of Others."
36 Dean, *Democracy*, 173.
37 Klein, "The Year of the Fake," 10.
38 Mirzoeff, *Watching Babylon*, 83.
39 Preston, "Sequel to 'Kony 2012' Video."
40 Cole, "The White Saviour Industrial Complex."
41 Cole, "The White Saviour Industrial Complex."
42 Dean, *Democracy*, 2.
43 Cole, "The White Saviour Industrial Complex."
44 Perrot, "Kony 2012."
45 Mirzoeff, *Watching Babylon*, 2.

25 Fighting Terror: Race, Sex, and the Monstrosity of Islam

SUNERA THOBANI

Sexual Violence in the Racial Imaginary

Although the initial instruction to US forces to "get" Osama Bin Laden "Dead or Alive" came from President Bush, it was President Obama who, transfixed in his chair in the White House (along with the rest of his team, including Hillary Clinton), oversaw Bin Laden's assassination. The trophy photograph released by the administration reveals the intense fascination – horror and dread tinged with disbelief – marked indelibly on the anxious faces as they witnessed this macabre private screening of the reality show unfolding in Abbottabad, Pakistan. The killing of Bin Laden, US Attorney General Eric Holder was quick to reassure the world, was in keeping with both "U.S. law and values."[1] Bin Laden's murder was thus pronounced to be within the bounds of law *and* a cause for celebration for civilized peoples committed to the defence of Western values. On Fox News, Glenn Beck thanked the US Army on behalf of the American people under the banner headline, "USAMA BIN LADEN Muslim Monster KILLED."[2]

The believing-Muslim-as-potential-terrorist is deemed devoid of ethics and morality within the ideological frame of the War on Terror, as incapable of anything other than murderous envy of the West and irrepressible hatred of women. The turban, the AK-47, and the flowing beard are among the signs that mark out the Muslim male as perverse, a contemporary monster.[3] As for his companion, the Muslim woman, her veiled face masks her fanatic nature, which is capable of vengeful eruption in the diabolic guise of the black widow or the sexually frustrated suicide bomber. Indeed, popular depictions of Muslims – Islamists in particular – routinely portray them as barbaric and monstrous. This

Muslim enemy is considered human only upon her/his transformation into the properly subjugated supplicant to Western power as s/he comes to subscribe to its superior norms and values, particularly with regard to gender. As for the resisting Muslim, his/her fanatic religiosity and deadly propensity for violence mark him/her for elimination.

Feminists have long defined war, terror, and torture as a largely masculinist enterprise, but Abu Ghraib and Guantanamo Bay have complicated such claims about the workings of patriarchy.[4] Abu Ghraib and Guantanamo Bay also undermine feminist theorizing of abjection and monstrosity as tied to the female body within the symbolic order. Indeed, the prisons and torture centres of the War on Terror reveal the complexities of the sexual *and* racial politics engaged in the contemporary production of the Muslim body – male and female – as the site of the monstrous. As Muslim men were smeared in the menstrual blood and other excrements that are defined as signifying sexual difference, their bodies were turned into the sign of a monstrous masculinity by female prison guards and intelligence officers, who defined themselves as defenders of the Western civilized order and as proof of its emancipatory gender politics. In these torture centres, it was white wo/men who covered Muslim men's faces with women's underwear and made the prisoners wear dog collars and crawl on the ground. As they broke male Muslim bodies under torture and turned them into signs of abjection, defilement, and pollution, these women upheld the phallic power of the West. Abjection and monstrosity, it turns out, centre on the *racially* charged politics of the sexual dramas of the West.

The naked Muslim men and the Muslim corpses-turned-props in the photographs taken by/of the white wo/men, who are clearly exulting in their racial pleasures, stand testimony to the powerful desires and fantasies of the women involved in these encounters; the evil filth of the Orient, evident in the excrement smeared on the naked Muslim male bodies, humiliated and ashamed, stands in sharp contrast to the sterile cleanliness and casual mastery of the white wo/men in charge of the scenes being shot. The power of white women in these sites was such that they could penetrate black/brown male Muslim bodies, proof of which was documented by the gaze of the camera. In her choice to be the equal of the white man, here stood the white woman with access to the power to penetrate, possess, and destroy the male Muslim bodies on display. Transgressing the borders between the human (the Western/American body) and the non-human (the evil filth that is the Muslim body) to descend into the nightmare world of Abu Ghraib, white women were critical to the redrawing of the lines between the civilized bodies (who have to resort to violence, even if in entirely unseemly ways) and the bestial (the Muslim male bodies, who remain abject). From this descent into hell to protect Western civilization, American and other Western women soldiers, guards, intelligence officers, mercenaries, and so on have emerged as heroic (even antiwar activists are careful to state their unconditional support for "our" troops), despite being seen as perhaps going too far by being drawn into *doing* evil by the evil that *is* the Muslim enemy.

In his classic study of the fictional and non-fictional narratives of the Freikorps, the volunteer militia that decimated the revolutionary German working class and later became the core of the Nazi SA and the SS, Klaus Theweleit describes how deeply such accounts were informed by the authors' fear of their own sexuality and their hatred of women's bodies.[5] Theweleit argues that the narratives cannot be explained away by recourse to notions of the authors' repressed sexuality; rather, these accounts ought to be considered expressions of the authors' actual violent desires. In this chapter, I draw on Theweleit's insight into what he called "male phantasies" to examine how racial/sexual fantasy-desires for violence are articulated not only by Western men but also by Western women, including feminists, in the cultural politics of the War on Terror.

In a provocative move, Theweleit goes on to claim that the "phantasies and affect" found in the Freikorps narratives were not specific to the particular class of "soldierly" men he was studying: "To make the point even clearer, any male reading the texts of these soldier males – and not taking immediate refuge in repression – might find in them a whole series of traits he recognizes from his own past or present behaviour, from his own phantasies."[6] Be that as it may, the relation between the disciplinary ethos of the hegemonic masculinity that is critical to the effective functioning of the US military in times of war and the "normal" forms of masculinity prevalent in that society has been found to be symbiotic.[7]

What then is the relation of dominant forms of femininity – including feminist – to the war-waging form of hegemonic masculinity and to its monstrous enemy, the Islamist? Reading feminist theorizations of the monstrous in popular culture (fiction and documentary films), my argument here will be that hegemonic forms of femininity in Western society – including feminist – are as implicated as hegemonic masculinity in fashioning an ethos of violence against their monstrous enemy (Islam) and its adherents (believing Muslims).

In an interesting rereading of Theweleit's work, Kevin Amidon and Dan Krier fault him for treating the narratives he examined as *only expressions* of their authors' phantasies and desires; they go on to pointedly note that many of these men had "participated vigorously in the perpetration of violence in the German colonies in Africa during the 1890s and 1900s and in the German imperialist interventions in China during 1900–1, after the so-called Boxer Rebellion."[8] Amidon and Krier further criticize Theweleit for ignoring "the reality of rape as a weapon" in the men's arsenal.[9] The narratives studied by Theweleit, these two scholars conclude, were most likely informed by the actual forms of "annihilating violence," including rape, which the men who subsequently produced this literature had perpetrated in the colonies. Such a reworking of Theweleit's thesis foregrounds coloniality in the forms of violence that German men perpetrated against particular groups of women, thus defining the colony as the staging ground for the working out of the deeply *racialized* sexual violence that was later reproduced upon the men's return to their "homeland." Here, Andrea Smith's contention that sexual violence is how colonialism is "done" in settler societies assumes expanded relevance for understanding its pivotal role in colonial invasion, occupation, and genocide.[10] What role have Western feminists played in such racially sexualized violence against the Enemy, men *and* women, who are defined as emblematic of the barbarity of the non-West?

I reference Theweleit's work here not to argue that the US and other allied forces in Iraq and Afghanistan are contemporary manifestations of the Freikorps; nor do I wish to make the case that the War on Terror reveals the fascist tendencies at work in the US-led Western wars of the early twenty-first century. Others have attempted to make the case for such similarities, and it is not my intention here to engage in a discussion about the merits of such comparison.[11] Theweleit's work remains useful from my perspective because he recognizes that the violence described by the Freikorps was rooted not only in a repressed sexuality resulting from processes of thwarted individuation in early infancy, as the Freudian psychoanalytic tradition would have it, but also in the men's adult experiences, actions, desires, and phantasies.

Indeed, Amidon and Kreir's critique *adds* weight to Theweleit's thesis by pointing to the convergence between the desire and the actuality of racial/sexual violence, as well as to the close links between fantasy, sexual desire, and the violence of colonialism, links that were earlier explored in the case of the Algerian Revolution by the psychiatrist and revolutionary scholar Frantz Fanon.

Moreover, the actions of men such as those of the Freikorps demand attention not only because of the violence they fantasize and enact on particular women's bodies, which shapes their own subject-formation, but also because the violence plays a critical role in processes of state- and nation-formation. Such violence enacts the "state" and "nation" on the ground, so to speak; because they are acting in the name of the nation, these men are allowed to claim the power of the state when enacting the violence of their phantasy-desires. These men, and increasingly women, are clearly indispensible to the state's capacity to enforce its rule over the domains to which it lays claim.

There is another significant aspect of terror and torture that requires attention. In his extensive study of the use of torture by democratic societies, Darius Rejali exposes the myth that torture is a science developed in strictly controlled conditions and then passed on through stern instruction to unwilling intelligence personnel who become reluctant torturers. Instead, Rejali finds that torturers resort to "what is available, what is habitual, what they can get away with, what they have heard from others, what they remember, and what they can learn by imitating others."[12] The daily lives and habitual practices of torturers thus shape the forms of torture they enact, as do the institutional means to power they acquire in the course of their everyday work, such as it is.

Rejali's analysis raises the following question for me: What stock of habitual information is available to Western men – and increasingly women – as they engage in what feminists have defined as purely "masculinist" forms of violence, such as sexual torture and genocidal violence? As I demonstrate in this chapter, feminist theorizations of monstrosity and abjection, and feminist cultural productions depicting monstrous Others, are rich sites for the study of *feminine/ist* phantasy-desires for racial violence; both these sites of knowledge production contribute to the "stock of habitual information" that buttresses, if it does not actually advocate, the forms of terror and violence expended against Muslims as enemy in the War on Terror.

The following sections examine how feminists have theorized the phantasy-desires articulated in the monster genre of popular films. I argue that by identifying sexual difference as singularly constitutive of the monstrous, feminists have obscured the raciality that is central to the sexualization of the figure of the monster within the Western philosophico-legal and politico-psychoanalytic traditions. Such elision reveals feminism's own fraught fantasy-desire for the racially monstrous. Moreover, feminists fuel the paranoia generated by such racial phantasms by inflecting these with gendered and sexualized modalities of violence, thus reinforcing the demonization of the racially monstrous. By defining Woman as the *real* target of aggression of the monstrous enemy, feminists insert themselves as the doubled victim *and* heroine in the Western sexual-political imaginary.

The contemporary racial/sexual phantasies and desires articulated by feminists are not a new phenomenon, nor are the practices described below by which feminists appropriate the experiences and perspectives of Muslim women. Indeed, they use these experiences and perspectives to present themselves as the "true" victims of sexual violence and hence as "real" agents of feminist praxis. These are the stock of habitual responses to which Western women routinely lay claim, and they are entrenched in the store of information/experience from which women fashion their contemporary relations with the West and its Muslim enemy. So powerful are the racially infused *feminist* fantasy-desires for the monstrous enemy that even Muslim feminists are not immune from their seductions. In the final section of this chapter, I demonstrate how such fantasy-desires are rife not only in Western feminist knowledge production but also in the field of Muslim feminist cultural production (documentary and fiction film) about the War on Terror.

The Monster in the Sexual Imaginary

Noting that psychoanalysis and film emerged in the same historical moment, feminist film theorist Barbara Creed has argued that the "subtext" of films corresponds to Freud's concept of the "unconscious," making this medium a particularly productive site for exploring the psychic processes of subject formation, especially those of "repression" and the "workings of desire."[13] One can therefore assume that feminist responses to what they define as the workings of masculinist forms of desire in Western popular culture may well provide an equally productive site for tracing *feminist* workings of phantasies and desires, especially as these relate to the subject of my study, namely, popular constructs of the believing Muslim as enemy of the West.

In her study of Western horror films, Creed argues the genre is "populated" by "the female-as-monster." She rereads Freud's theory of castration anxiety in the primal Oedipal drama to analyse this figure, which she names the "monstrous-feminine."[14] Freudian theorization of male sexuality focuses on the fear of castration experienced by the infant boy as he comes to believe that woman, who does not possess a penis, is likely "castrated." The boy thus comes to see woman as victim by her very nature, and his anxiety over likewise losing his penis and becoming a victim gives rise to a male fear of woman; woman thus reflects back to the male his anxiety about his own (possible) castration.

Creed reworks this Freudian theorization of castration anxiety in her study of the figure of the female monster, arguing that such male fear is articulated through the phantasmic creation of the monstrous woman as a figure who is not already castrated but who *does* the castrating – that is, as the castrating figure. She goes on to argue that since woman is *not* castrated – indeed, she is "intact and in possession of all of her sexual powers" and clearly not mutilated[15] – woman comes to be seen by the male as possessing the sexual power to castrate *him*. Men thus come to fear/phantasize the act of intercourse itself as a form of castration. Reading the "monster" as a quintessentially *female* figure that threatens the male with castration, Creed further argues that this figure also comes to delineate the difference between the human and the non-human. She goes on to identify five main forms in which this castrating "monstrous-feminine" is cast – namely, "the archaic mother; the monstrous womb; the witch; the vampire; and the possessed woman."[16] In contrast to the (castrated) mother of the Oedipal drama, Creed identifies the "archaic" mother as the primal, generative womb defined by her own power and not in relation to the (male) penis.

Interesting as Creed's study of the "monstrous-feminine" is, her insights are significantly distorted by her reproduction of Freudian psychoanalytic theory's staging of gendered subject formation as devoid of racialized articulation, as well as by her curious neglect of the literature on the "monster" as a figure of racial difference, a difference that has long marked the limits of the "human" within the Western tradition. The co-constitutive role of racial difference in the making of the monstrous – a difference integral to its "femininity" *and* "monstrosity" – is thus elided in Creed's reading. I will come back to these two points in the following sections, but for now, back to Creed.

Creed expands on her own formulation of the figure of the "monstrous-feminine" by drawing on Kristeva's theory of abjection and her discussion of borders, particularly with regard to the mother–child relation and the feminine body. Kristeva defines "abjection" as "that which does not 'respect borders, positions, rules,' that which 'disturbs identity, system, order,'" to argue that the "abject" separates the human from the non-human, the "fully formed subject from the partially formed subject."[17] Presenting a constant threat of death and dissolution, the "abject" is "the place where meaning collapses, the place where 'I' am not."[18] Exclusion of the abject becomes key to the defining of the subject, Kristeva argues, but the subject is compelled to "tolerate" the abject, "for that which threatens to destroy life also helps to define life."[19]

Turning her attention to the figure of the mother who imposes her authority over the child in disciplining its bodily functions, Kristeva argues that the mother becomes associated with the abject, with the defilement seen to arise from the bodily functions of excretion, bleeding, and other such im-purifications. Moreover, as the child struggles to separate itself from the mother and to enter the symbolic order where the law of the father prevails, the mother becomes the "abject" yet again, clinging to the child and threatening its suffocation: "Partly consumed by the desire to remain locked in a blissful relationship with the mother and partly terrified of separation, the child finds it easy to succumb to the comforting pleasure of the dyadic relationship," explains Creed.[20] The feminine body, with its cycles of menstruation and other excretions, thus gives woman a "special relationship to the abject," according to both Kristeva and Creed.[21]

Drawing on the psychoanalytic and post-structuralist feminist traditions discussed above, Creed faults other scholars for interpreting the struggles against the monsters that populate horror films as battles between good and evil, between God and the Devil. Instead, she reads these struggles as depicting an epic battle between man and woman, between the masculine and the feminine. But in positing this epic conflict solely in terms of gender, Creed fails to recognize that the monstrous female body she defines as the abject in this epic battle is racialized, that *the raciality of this figure is inseparable from its sexualization*. In other words, it is the *racial* difference of the monster that makes her sexually aggressive: she is phantasized as bent on bewitching, possessing, and destroying the innocent and pure Western subject, be it male or female.

Indeed, Creed's own formulation of the gender of the monstrous, the "monstrous-feminine," is also explicitly racialized so that even as she "fails" to recognize the inextricable coding of racial difference *as* sexual difference in the cinematic texts she studies, she (unconsciously?) reinscribes the racial onto the sexual forms of monstrosities she categorizes. For instance, many of the films she reads as featuring the "classic" female monster – including *Alien, Island of Lost Souls, The Reptile, Captive Wild Woman, The Wolf Man, Jungle Woman,* and *Jungle Captive* – are explicitly forged within the racial/colonial logic of power. Their titles reflect the racial excitements, paranoia, dreads, and desires that permeate the sexual social order within which they were produced and circulated.

More pertinently from my perspective, each of the five tropes of the "monstrous-feminine" identified by Creed – "the archaic mother; the monstrous womb; the witch; the vampire; and the possessed woman"[22] – is a racially coded figure. All five have served for centuries as key markers of the "Oriental" difference in the Western imagination. As Edward Said famously pointed out, the "Orient" was produced by/in the Western imaginary as a quintessentially feminine – albeit dangerous – space, dormant in its desire to be possessed by the civilized Western subject and its superior culture.

How might the theories of "castration anxiety" and "abjection" that inform Creed's analysis be read in the context of the raciality of the Orient, which was, after all, the original site for the European production of "monstrous races" and which remains to this day the home of the "monstrous" religion of Islam and of the Muslim-as-terrorist? The "Orient" was phantasized as feminine in its essence, and the desire to penetrate its "veiled" mysteries guided many an Orientalist's academic enterprise, as noted by Said in his monumental work *Orientalism*.[23] In her reading of Said, Meyda Yeğenoğlu draws attention to the critical distinction he made between "latent" and "manifest" Orientalism. By "manifest" Orientalism, he was referring to opinions, facts, literatures, in short, to the "stated" knowledge produced about the Orient, whereas by "latent" Orientalism he was referring to dreams, images, and phantasies about the Orient. Yeğenoğlu uses this vital theoretical distinction to make a case for psychoanalytic and deconstructive readings of Orientalism that recognize that "the 'Orient' is at once an object of *knowledge* and an object of *desire*."[24]

Since it serves as the elemental sign of dread, possession, and death and as the pre-eminent site of the degenerate and the abject, one could argue that the Orient-as-feminine is the *real* home of the "archaic" mother; indeed, the Orient *is* the archaic mother, appropriated by Creed as the figure of sexual difference that marks the *Western* feminine. As the womb of ancient religions with their vicious hatreds, bloodied homelands, and perverse civilizations, the "Orient" has long been phantasized as containing within its labyrinthine "archaic" cities the degenerate sites (multiple wombs?) of these ancient religions, which threaten to overpower and devour one another. The Orient is also the primal site of carnality, of sex, born in an "original sin" instigated by a serpent such that humanity has been condemned to suffer forever after. As the cradle of human civilization, the "Holy Land," the sacred birthplace of the Judeo-Christian traditions, the womb/manger where the "son-of-God" himself was born, the Orient is said to then have ruthlessly savaged, polluted, and cannibalized all such pure and sacred gifts by birthing Islam, the fake religion of the false Prophet. With the advent of Islam, the Orient offers only defilement, degeneracy, and devilry; it is the "abject" whose pollutions and impurities have leaked into all that was/is pure, good, and civilized about the West, its enlightened rational religions, its noble civilizations.

Moreover, the desire for the Orient, for a return to its hot, throbbing, gory womb, threatens not only to seduce but also to destroy the civilized world; the temptation to "go native" in the sensual, sexual Orient threatens to overwhelm the sovereign Western subject – both male and female – not only with castration (symbolic or otherwise) but also with the oblivion of the self in a delirium of orgiastic passion and barbaric possession. The phantasy of taking over the Orient/al, possessing this Other, feeling with full force its passions and perversions within the Self and experiencing the fullness of its eroticism, has had as strong a hold on the Western psyche as the phantasy of becoming its master and benefactor through colonial tutelage, development, modernization, and humanitarian intervention.

The Race of the Monstrous

The idea of "monstrous races" was prevalent in early modernity; Europeans routinely described the peoples they encountered outside Europe in this manner, relegating them to the status of the "non-human" by way of that classification. It was in relation to the "monstrous" Other that Europeans came to understand themselves as fully human, such that it has been claimed that it was "monsters" who "gave birth to modernity."[25] The association of monstrosity with the sexual perversity of the degenerate primitive body – which Europeans could apparently discern from the normal "human" body – made monstrosity inseparable from raciality, albeit through the prism of sexuality. Feminist theory stubbornly refuses to acknowledge this association. Indeed, in his study of the monster figure in English law, Sharpe points to a challenge that the construction of this figure in legal texts poses for feminist theory: "It is somewhat curious that law's monsters, though informed by human/animal and order/disorder distinctions, are not informed by a body that challenges sexual difference. Indeed, the fact that challenge to the binaries of sex and/or gender failed to register in legal constructions of the category monster might serve as a provocation within feminist legal theory."[26] Sharpe himself refuses to pursue further the implications of this "provocation," despite his referencing of law's *lack of association* of monstrosity with the feminine.

Roman law understood the monster's presence as a sign of divine wrath or as a demonstration of the marvels of God's creation. By contrast, in English law the act of copulation figured large in theories about the creation of monsters. Sharpe notes that law's concern with the conditions of the birth of the monster often focused on the mother's sexuality. Thus, the presence of a monster was viewed as indicative of bestiality: "'Where a woman brings forth a monster' it is because it has been 'procreated perversely, against the way of human kind,'" a "vice that Aquinas placed at the apex of his hierarchy of vices 'contrary to nature.'"[27] So, for example, "copulation between a mother and an animal" resulted in the offspring being classified as a monster, whereas a mother's "intense preoccupation with animals" did not in itself lead to the birth of monsters, nor to the mother being classified as monstrous herself.[28]

Sharpe points out that the early English legal texts (1628–44), especially those written by Cole, included "within the term buggery intercourse between a woman and a beast," recording a case where "a great Lady had committed buggery with a Baboon, and conceived by it."[29] It is notable that the monstrosity in this case was located in the racial transgression (the symbolism of the period associated baboons and apes with black/brown bodies, which would, of course, often have been Muslim bodies); that is, the matter of concern here was the inter-racial nature of this sexual encounter, and not the sex itself, for the "Lady" remained "great" in Cole's estimation, regardless of the racially transgressive sexual act by which she had "produced" a monster. He refrained from considering the Lady herself as monstrous, even if the result of her perverse sexual act had been constituted as such by the law. In his study of the histories of homosexualities, Mondimore points out that "many regarded sex between Christians and Jews or between Christians and Muslims as sodomy – even potentially procreative sex could be forbidden if improper partners were involved. This argument derived from the belief that these 'infidels' were equivalent to dogs and other animals in the eyes of God; intercourse with them was thus unnatural."[30]

Anxieties about inter-racial sex and miscegenation are evident in Cole's narration of this incident. Those anxieties survived in the West well into the twentieth century. For example, Jordan found it pervasive in his study of white attitudes towards black people in the United States: "The supposed affinity between apes and men has as frequently been expressed in sexual as in anatomical terms" so as not to rule out "the possibility of unnatural sexual unions."[31] Most famously, the threat of miscegenation gave rise to the legally enforced "one drop rule" in the United States, which legally defined even one drop of "black" blood as amounting to the racial contamination of whiteness. "Mulattoes are monstrous," declared Henry Hughes, a Mississippi statesman in 1854, and "hybridism is heinous."[32]

Anxieties about the perverse procreation that produced monsters spoke to the perceived dangers of miscegenation in a society obsessed with the question of racial purity. That danger must have been immensely exaggerated by the added fear of the chaste white woman's sexual attraction to the black/brown man's body, an attraction considered characteristic of animalistic sexuality and natural depravity. For example, here is Aphra Behn, writing in the seventeenth century in open admiration of the physique and beauty of Oroonoke, her black male hero: "The most famous Statuary could not form the Figure of a Man more admirably turn'd from Head to Foot … The whole Proportion and Air of his Face was so nobly and exactly form'd, that bating his Colour, there could be nothing in Nature more beautiful, agreeable, and handsome."[33] This public admiration of the Black male body, "from head to foot," by a noted writer and dramatist and early feminist heroine, put into words a desire that would surely have been acceptable to – if not shared by – many in her audience, male and female. In a later age, Frantz Fanon would consider the impact of the hyper-sexualized images of the black man on the white woman: "It is easy to imagine what such descriptions can stimulate in a young girl in Lyons. Horror? Lust? Not indifference, in any case."[34]

It is significant that early English legal texts did not attach the stigma of monstrosity to the white woman herself, nor to her body as proof-in-itself of her perverse nature. These texts derided her *as mother* for having birthed a monster, but she herself was not the monstrosity; copulation with the bestial defined the monstrosity again and again, and it was the "monstrous" offspring, not the English woman, who was legally disinherited.[35] This concern with racial purity was legally proscribed and could be found across the "Christian" world – in the state of Virginia, for example, "white men were scarred by fear of racial intermixture which they equated with Negro insurrection, with free Negroes, with their own freedom, and with their own lack of mastery and self-control."[36] So great was the fear of miscegenation that in the early seventeenth century, free blacks were forced to move out of the state.[37]

If monstrosity was associated with raciality, so too was the Freudian theorization of male sexuality, as David Eng has argued so cogently. In his reading of the Freudian psychoanalytic tradition, Eng pointedly observes that race lies at the heart of its foundational assumptions, such that "from its very inception, psychoanalysis has encoded race as a question of sexual development."[38] Turning to the "pathological" figures of the "primitive" and the "homosexual," Eng notes that in the Freudian corpus, "primitive" sexual practices are related to – and give rise to – the "civilized" forms of "neurosis." In his reading of *Totem and Taboo*, for example, Eng traces the "'dark origins' of the contemporary European psyche" studied by Freud in the practices of "savages" and "half-savages," who are defined as proximate to the "primitive." Although Freud called for more study of these "savages," whom he acknowledged to be his contemporaries, he saw them as "securely positioned as temporally other to modern European man."[39] In other words, argues Eng, the "primitive" was a category of racial difference such that "if, for Freud, ontogeny captures phylogeny, then the development of the individual recapitulated the development of civilized mankind not only through a specifically sexualized form but through a specifically racialized valence."[40] Upholding the idea of European/white "racial progress," Freud further posited that the primitive psyche "had no unconscious to speak of, that his thoughts and motivations are eminently one-dimensional, present and transparent," and that what "marks the primitive psyche as such, beyond all other distinguishing characteristics, is its propensity for sexual impropriety."[41] Freud thus "hypersexualizes the primitive, racialized body," concludes Eng, even as he "links an explicitly psychosexual discourse with a Western anthropological tradition bound to eighteenth and nineteenth-century epistemologies of European dominance and colonial expansionism."[42] With regard to the figure of the "homosexual," Eng notes that Freud links homosexuality to a "stalled and pathological narcissism."[43] Also, Freud views modern nations, classes, and families as founded upon Western heterosexual norms and same-sex desire as the result of "primitive" sexual urges, with the result that "a displaced racial otherness is made legible in the lexicon of pathological (homo)sexuality."[44] Homosexuality and racial difference thus "converge," and there is a "coming together of the homosexual and the primitive as pathological, banished figures within the psychic landscape of the social proper."[45]

As I have discussed above, the "Orient," constituted as archaic, savage, and deadly, serves as the pre-eminent site of primitive defilement and degeneracy in contrast to the purity and modernity of the West. The Orient was/is populated by men monstrous in their sexual indolence and grotesque violence, birthed by equally (if not more) monstrous women. The bewitching Orient was/is replete with djinns, spirits, and zombies. The Orient is also home to the seductive and virginal beauty, who, possessed by a "devilish" religion and imprisoned in a degenerate culture, is compelled to be hostage to the suffocating veil. So, for example, the "devil" who possesses the innocent young white woman in *The Exorcist* (a film analysed by Creed) originates in the Iraqi desert; women in black garb cross the path of the Priest as a sign of the coming evil at the beginning of the film; and the "soundtrack is filled with sounds of hammering, voices babbling, and the chanting of [Muslim?] prayers."[46] Orientalist tropes like this saturate the horror films studied by Creed. As I will discuss below, they also pervade the current crop of "War on Terror" films produced by Muslim feminists.

In the cinematic universe that interests Creed, the "primitive" is the site of origin of the various monstrosities being depicted, but she rewrites this racial difference as sexual difference. In her discussion of *Alien*, for another example, Creed stresses the sexual difference of the creature from space by defining her as the "archaic mother" who is bent on destroying the "mother" (civilized? white?) space station and its human crew. As the crew is killed off one after the other, it is Ripley (played by Sigourney Weaver) who acts the heroine by overpowering and destroying the "alien" monster mother. Creed pays particular attention to a scene at the end of the film that depicts Ripley (uncharacteristically, Creed points out) undressing herself. For Creed, the significance of this act is that it turns Ripley into the reassuring face of the domesticated feminine: "Compared to the horrific sight of the alien as fetish object of the monstrous archaic mother, Ripley's body is pleasurable and reassuring to look at. She signifies the 'acceptable' form and shape of woman."[47] This racial coding of the monstrosity of the alien-as-archaic-mother in relation to the whiteness of Ripley's "pleasurable" female body is left unaddressed.

The deeper significance of the epic encounter between the monstrous archaic mother and Ripley is that it makes possible (even pleasurable) the acceptance of the feminine embodied by Ripley's whiteness, not just her act of undressing. As the aesthetically pleasing body of the civilized Ripley makes itself available to the white fe/male gaze, Ripley completes her mission of destroying the "alien" and of upholding the phallic power of the civilized order she represents and for which she fights to the death. Can this giving up of herself be read as a reassuring act with regard to the racial order? In the self-assertive display of her non-abject white nudity (nothing oozes out of *this* body), Ripley completes her heroic "masculine" role and reveals her body to be female and *white*, her civilized body now available for possession by the likewise civilized (i.e., white like her) gaze. She confirms her willingness to die for a white racial order that marks women's emancipation in the "right" to sexuality, including the right to display female nudity. What makes Ripley's act "pleasurable" and "reassuring" is its dual character: it completes her destruction of the alien racial creature and thus restores the white racial order, *and* it completes her offering of herself (this time, sexually) for possession to the white fe/male civilized gaze. This heroic feminine will fight to the death against possession by the archaic mother as monstrous-feminine but will also willingly deliver herself as equally capable of upholding the phallic order. It is in Ripley's choice to uphold the symbolic order by destroying that of the racially alien and primitive mother that she becomes the reassuring heroic-feminine for her (civilized) audience.

The abject must be repelled, overcome, in the interest of the self-projection of the subject, yet the abject continues to exist as the object of the subject's desire. So Creed argues. In the films she analyses, the abject is repelled by the energies, resources, and labour of the white male and female subject working together to destroy such monstrosity. In this joint venture, the monstrous "archaic" mother is disassociated from any/ every feminine body and firmly associated with the Oriental/alien feminine body. The "monstrous-feminine" cannot be conquered by the white male alone, but by his joining forces with the white female, who, as woman, enters the state of possession or the field of battle; indeed, it is the white woman who experiences and sometimes even embodies (albeit temporarily) the full monstrosity of the "archaic" mother. It is in her act of then overpowering this "evil" that the white woman retrieves her own civilized, innocent, pure self and becomes a sovereign subject like her male counterpart. In this manner, the white female self transforms itself into the "acceptable" and "reassuring" figure of the Western feminine, equally worthy of upholding the law of the father. By turning away in revulsion from the "archaic" m/Other, the white feminine subject transforms herself into the worthy helpmate and trusted companion of the white male subject.

How, then, is the "archaic mother" to be read as anything other than the feminine Orient? For it is not just *any* female body that is constructed as the "monstrous-feminine," to use Creed's memorable term. How can the "innocent" female subject who battles and defeats this "archaic" mother be read as any other kind of subject than the sovereign Western subject, now gendered but still white, who extends and stabilizes the law of the Father in the terror formation that is the colony? The real threat to the symbolic order – to the power of the phallic order – is thus not just any female body, but a very specific female body, that of the black/brown "archaic" m/Other who is the hyper-generative womb, the source of a monstrous plenitude, and who does not define herself in relation to the penis but only with regard to her own regenerative capacity. The threat to the symbolic order can thus be located not in the white feminine body but in that feminine body which wallows in its racial filth and excess, that feminine body which is essentialized-as-evil monstrosity. The feminine body that restores order over chaos is the racially innocent, purified-as-universal, white woman's body. This feminine body slays the black/brown feminine with its overwhelming sexual potency while presenting itself to the masculine subject as also, like him, capable of exorcising the monstrous Other, of exercising the sovereign power of life and death, and thus also, like him, the innocent victim of the racial monster. Her slaying of the "archaic mother" in an act of primal matricide is the *condition* for the white female's inclusion into the symbolic white order. The white feminine body thus turns her back on an alliance with the "archaic" mother, with the monstrous alien/Orient, who is phantasized as attacking the symbolic/civilized order that also belongs to the white heroic woman, not just the white heroic male. Having acquired a stake in the symbolic order, the white feminine body sees little to gain from an alliance with the alien monster. Instead, in turning on the "archaic" mother and neutralizing her as a threat to the white man, the white woman gains entry into t/his order.

It can be no coincidence that many of the horror films featuring the "classic" monster were made in the 1940s and 1950s, a time when the United States was riven by racial conflict at home and faced an external threat from the Soviet Union. Moreover, the unravelling of European empires during those decades enabled the United States to emerge as one of the two global superpowers, staking its claim to the regions of the world that were just then emerging from direct colonial control. US–Soviet rivalries in these decolonizing regions, and the subsequent Cold War, made industrial and military superiority a priority. The US economy's reliance on oil was a key factor in its relations with the "Orient."[48]

With the decline of the Soviet empire, Islamist movements emerged as the strongest challenge to US and other Western states' domination of the Middle East and Central Asia. Those same movements challenged dictatorial regimes that were largely supported by Western powers (and that often had been imposed by those powers). The horror film genre studied by Creed thus included a specifically American brand of Orientalism, one in which, after the fall of the Soviet Union, the Arab world came to be defined in US foreign policy as a threat to, yet also a potential ally of, US interests in the region.

In the wake of the Palestinian liberation struggle, the OPEC oil crisis, and the Iranian revolution, did the earlier fascination inspired by Scheherazade and her passion-filled Arabian-nights-style erotic phantasies give way to the horror and disgust invoked by an insatiable and devouring "archaic" Orient-monster with her terrorizing sons? With the emergence of such threats, could the feminization of the Orient-as-monstrous have paralleled the emergence of the American nation/al as also feminist and heroic after the activism of the 1960s? Feminists could now define themselves as equal rights benefactors who could help "civilize" the Orient with her perverse sons and daughters.

If sexual difference alienated the white woman from the white man, racial affinity helped suture over this sexual difference, masculinizing both as sovereign and imperial subjects – albeit asymmetrically – in relation to the racially dangerous Orient. The "Orient" and the "New" World had earlier been conquered by Europe with the support and willing participation of European women, including European feminists.[49] Not surprisingly then, Western women, including feminists, have been no innocent bystanders in the War on Terror, as I have argued elsewhere.[50] Indeed, so successful has this feminist imaginary been in constructing the monstrous "Other" as incommensurable with civilization that some forms of Muslim feminism (espoused by Muslim women and men) have not been immune to its seductive pleasures; they too have come to stake their claim in slaying the monstrous Other that is the believing Muslim.

Destroying the Monster, Making the Feminist

Since the US invasion of Afghanistan, feminists identifying themselves as Muslims and as insiders to the world of Islam have acquired unprecedented access to international circuits of film production and distribution. This final section is based on my reading of two feature films (*Kandahar* and *Osama*) and one documentary (*Return to Kandahar*). All three were produced by Muslim journalists/filmmakers and are concerned with the status of women in Afghanistan. All three have been distributed widely since 9/11 and have received much international attention and acclaim, especially in the human rights and NGO communities. I have discussed all three films at length elsewhere;[51] here I focus on three particular scenes that contribute directly to the construction of the believing Muslim as a figure of monstrosity.

First, a brief synopsis of *Kandahar* (2000, dir. M. Makhmalbaf), a quasi-documentary based on the experiences of an Afghan Canadian journalist, Nilufer Pazira.[52] Basically, the film depicts a feminist search-and-rescue mission; it traces Pazira's travels/travails in Afghanistan as she sets out to recover her sister, who was inexplicably left behind when the family fled the country after the Soviet withdrawal. The heroine, Nafas (a stand-in for Pazira herself) has received a letter from her sister, who says she intends to kill herself at the last lunar eclipse of the twentieth century. Life is unbearable under the Taliban, she writes, and death is the only release. With the eclipse fast approaching, Nafas/Pazira sets out for Kandahar to save her sister, encountering numerous obstacles along the way. The film ends with Nafas/Pazira still trying to reach Kandahar; the city's outline is visible on the distant horizon. *Return to Kandahar*, the sequel to *Kandahar*, is a documentary made for the CBC that shows Pazira undertaking yet another journey to Afghanistan on the same mission, only this time it is revealed that the sister is actually a friend.

The scene from *Kandahar* I wish to discuss here depicts an incident that occurs soon after Pazira enters Afghanistan via Iran. Leaving behind the Afghan family with whom she has been travelling after they are robbed by Taliban-style bandits, Pazira continues her journey with a young Afghan boy as her guide. The boy loses no opportunity to defraud her, and Nafas/Pazira can barely contain her contempt for him. As she sets out with him, she speaks into the tape recorder she carries with her (it is never clear where the sisterly rescue mission ends and the journalistic adventure begins), describing her experiences and perspectives. She records how she is surrounded by violence wherever she goes, "even in the children's games." She goes on to claim: "Along my journey, everything is at war, dog fights dog, bird fights bird, human fights human." In the chain of signification she sets up, the perversity of "fighting" dogs morphs into that of "fighting" birds, coming to rest in the "fighting" of the Muslim children – dogs-as-humans – who disgust her. Although of Afghan origin herself, Pazira's revulsion at all things Afghan reassures the audience (and presumably herself?) of her own difference from these people – animals really – among whom she finds herself. In other words, using her status as a sometime Afghan to reassure her (mainly Western) audience that she really *knows* how grotesque Afghan Muslims are, she confirms for them what they *already* know about the Muslim world. In this way, her adventures become the telling of "truths" that are always already known by the Westernized subject, a telling that is granted greater authenticity through the deployment of her own identitarian familiarity with the world she is (re)discovering for her audience.

The full measure of the grotesqueness of the Muslim is revealed in the form of the young boy – a child, really – whom Pazira has persuaded to take her to Kandahar. As the two walk through the barren, lifeless landscape that is presented as the "real" Afghanistan, they come upon a skeleton. Nafas/Pazira flees in horror, but the boy goes up to the skeleton and removes a ring from its finger. He then badgers Nafas/Pazira to buy the ring he has retrieved from the skeleton. Pazira's revulsion towards the boy, the skeleton, and the ring merge and becomes more palpable. Here, the living prey on the dead in a zone devoid of life and morality, and the dead reveal the monstrosity of the undead. The young boy, ghoulishly pillaging the spoils from a rotting skeleton in this economy of death and decay, functions as a sign of evil – the evil that is his dead spirit, his dead world, his wretched country, and his thieving people, Muslims. Destructive of all morality, this economy of death is inhospitable to the living, represented here by Nafas/Pazira in her status as outsider, in her Canadian-ness, her Westernization. This scene gives rise to no reflection on a poverty and destitution so desperate that the robbing of corpses, and the hiring out of children to the Western feminists who have come with the invading Western forces, become the only means of survival. Such a reflection might question the calculations of an intrepid heroine who is making a film that exploits the friendship and death of a "sister," or the power of the US dollars she carries with her and hands out to the destitute natives, not in compassion, not in solidarity, not even in exchange for services rendered, but as the means to reveal their venality.

The second scene that interests me for the purpose of this chapter is in *Osama* (2003, dir. Sedigh Barmak), a feature film depicting the struggles of a young Afghan girl who passes as a boy in order to earn a living and support her mother and grandmother during the reign of the Taliban. The scene in question is central to the film's plot, for it features the "outing" of the young boy, "Osama." The Taliban have gathered a group of boys – including Osama – on the streets to recruit them into their ranks ("Bin Laden's training us for war," explains one of the boys). The young recruits are taken to a madrassa, where Osama, undetected as a girl, is made to train with the boys. S/he is unable to keep up with the rigorous physical exercises and draws the suspicions of some of the young boys, as well as the Talibs and the old mullah who control the compound. Made to climb a tree, Osama gets stuck and is unable to sprint down like the boys. As punishment, s/he is swung from a rope into the mouth of a well, and as s/he is drawn up out of the well with the boys crowded around, the camera reveals a stream of menstrual blood running down her legs. Osama's gender identity can no longer be concealed from the men and boys; she is outed in this dramatic fashion before being taken off to prison. She is then forced into marriage with the old mullah, who has several older wives and numerous children.

The young girl Osama, hanging from the rope over the well, attests to the monstrosity of the Talibs and the boys who would punish her in this manner. So does the character of the old, rotund, and wrinkled mullah, who, as a decrepit pedophile, phantasizes about nymphs ("boys who look like girls in heaven"). The degenerating physicality of the old man (shown almost naked as he bathes) stands in stark contrast to the nubile allure of Osama, the young girl forced to marry him. This scene is a stock item in the Orientalist repertoire, entirely predictable in the response (disgust, revulsion) it seeks to elicit from the audience. What interests me about this depiction, however, is the rewriting of the "abject" that it accomplishes, which is contrary to what Kristeva's and Creed's theories might lead one to expect. As the menstrual blood runs down the young Osama's legs, it is not her (leaking) body that is presented as repelling to the viewer. Instead, the menstrual blood running down her legs signifies her young innocence, purity and fragility. Instead of marking the girl as abject, the menstrual blood indicts the men and boys in the compound. Osama is humanized by this flow of blood; it confirms her status as the frail victim of the monstrous (Islamist) males who would destroy her female being. The leaking of the girl's virginal blood serves as alibi – demand even – for the shedding of the blood of the old mullah and the Talibs, who are presented as evil and degenerate like him. Here, the menstruating female body is an incitement to war, for as a Muslim menstruating body, it calls for Western intervention to rescue it and preserve its honour. The abject feminine body is not quite so straightforward to theorize, for in the realpolitik of the global War on Terror, such female abjection has resulted in armies being sent to raze entire communities to the ground. These films demonstrate how the reproduction of the monstrous-as-Muslim relies on feminist approaches that further – rather than contest – the hegemonic constructs of monstrosity as racialized and sexualized, with Muslim men and boys mainly serving in the role of the monstrous. Indeed, the War on Terror has become the occasion for Muslim feminists to partake of the same pleasures as can be found in the Western feminist texts I have discussed above. As the occupation of Afghanistan reveals, feminism is the only terrain on which the claims of Muslims to inclusion into the community of the human can now be made.

The final scene of interest to me here is an eerie echo of the scene from *Alien* that Creed analyses in her reading of the "monstrous-feminine," the scene discussed above in which Sigourney Weaver offers her naked body to the gaze of the audience after slaying the alien mother. The scene features in *Kandahar* and was used repeatedly in television promotions of the film, as well as in the introduction to its celebrated documentary sequel, *Return to Kandahar*.[53] It begins with images of a group of veiled women and girls walking in the distance in the desert landscape of Afghanistan, chanting and singing (babbling?) as they travel to a wedding. The camera then turns to a close-up of Pazira, who turns around to look full face into the camera (and at the group). The embroidered hem of a burqa frames her unveiled face as she turns and stares into the camera. She then hears the women approaching and pulls down the burqa, her face now completely hidden from view. This scene is of particular interest for it is a reversal of the iconic image of the Muslim woman, who is usually depicted with face hidden under the veil, then lifting the veil in a gesture of feminist emancipation. In Pazira's case, the lowering of the burqa signals the harsh imprisonment of the emancipated (Westernized) Muslim woman as she enters the world of Islam and the deathly space to which it is been consigned in the War.

I have argued elsewhere that the reversal of this iconic representation of the veiled Muslim woman serves to laud both Pazira's bravery and her authenticity, propelling her heroic duplicity as covert agent/journalist of the West into the forefront of the gendered and sexualized Islamophobic politics of the War on Terror.[54] Here, I am interested in reading her gesture of veiling herself in the context of Creed's reading of the scene in which the heroine from *Alien* unclothes her body for the gratification of the audience. With the burqa framing her face, Pazira's pre-veiled face serves the same function as Weaver's unclothed body. In this state, Pazira is available for possession by the desiring Western gaze. Her unveiled face is offered as a gesture that signals she can be possessed and is willing to do her duty by the West. Her unveiled face also signals her desire for the "West," a desire to possess its civilizationally superior culture, a desire to give herself up to its embrace as an emancipated woman, an emancipation presented here as valued only by/in the West. This racial desire for the un/veiling of the Muslim woman is deeply sexual, for the veil serves as a signifier of the sexuality of the Muslim woman, as many scholars, including Fanon, have suggested. Fanon once noted of his patients that the tearing away of the veil to make the Muslim woman's body sexually available was a recurring phantasy among the French in Algeria. In the Islamophobic visual logic of *Kandahar,* and in its documentary sequel, the unveiled face signals the sexual availability of the intrepid (Westernized) Muslim woman, who stands on the side of the Western order in its declared global war against its monstrous enemy, Islam and the believing Muslim.

Conclusion

If the "War on Terror" reveals the complexities of the racial in the politics of the sexual, it also reveals the degree to which Westernized women, including feminists, have staked their claim to the racial power of the West through their active participation in – and expansion of – the terrain of violence being waged against the Muslim world. In this chapter, I have argued that the phantasies and desires of racial/sexual domination and subjugation shaping the hegemonic form of Western masculinity that has emerged dominant through the War on Terror are shared and sustained by particular forms of Westernized femininity – even feminisms – that are not wholly inoculated against the quest for sexual power over Muslim men and women. I have also suggested that access to such pleasures is now available to Muslims, but only in the language of feminism. In contrast to the many feminists who have argued that Western women have been manipulated into supporting the War on Terror by the US administration's "hijacking" of feminism, I am more interested in examining why it may be that these women have been duped so readily, why it is that feminism can be hijacked so willingly, if this is indeed the case.

In opening up this question, I have sought to problematize the dominant feminist narrative of women being "used" to serve what are essentially masculinist interests by interrogating whether these women – including the feminists among them – are also not served by such interests, which are not only masculinist but also imperialist. In other words, I have sought to trace how the active engagements and politico-psychic investments of Western women are predicated on an alliance with the forms of Western masculinity that wage predatory violence against invaded and colonized populations. Such investments, I argue, are critical to the transnational spaces that Western/ized women occupy in relation to the Muslim world; these investments are also crucial to the national alliances these women forge in order to occupy their exalted status. These women's claim to the superiority of the West that shapes the geopolitical cultural landscape in the early twenty-first century is grounded in their willingness to extend Western power – through a specifically gendered politic – over the Muslim world by appending to imperialist violence a popular feminist ethos that enables, among other things, the subjugation of the experience of the "Oriental" wo/man. Nor is this alliance a purely utilitarian matter; indeed, it has become central to the very formation of feminist identities and politics in the new millennium. The opportunity for Muslim feminists to now partake of such desires and pleasures can hardly be considered a matter for celebration.

NOTES

1 Williams, "Bin Laden Killing."
2 Beck, "USAMA BIN LADEN Muslim Monster KILLED."
3 Rai, "Of Monsters."
4 See Eisenstein, *Against Empire*; Oliver, "Women as Weapons of War"; Armstrong, *Daughters of Afghanistan*; and so on.
5 Theweleit, *Male Fantasies*.
6 Theweleit, *Male Fantasies*, 89.
7 Enloe, *Maneuvers*, 2000; Brownmiller, *Against Our Will*.
8 Amidon and Krier, "On Rereading," 489.
9 Amidon and Krier, "On Rereading," 490.
10 Smith, *Conquest*.
11 See Woolf, *The End of America*.
12 Rejali, *Torture and Democracy*, 28.

13 Creed, "Film and Psychoanalysis."

14 Creed, *The Monstrous-Feminine*, 1.

15 Creed, *The Monstrous-Feminine*, 6.

16 Creed, *The Monstrous-Feminine*, 7.

17 Creed, *The Monstrous-Feminine*, 8.

18 Kristeva, quoted in Creed, *The Monstrous-Feminine*, 9.

19 Creed, *The Monstrous-Feminine*, 13.

20 Creed, *The Monstrous-Feminine*, 12.

21 Creed, *The Monstrous-Feminine*, 10.

22 Creed, *The Monstrous-Feminine*, 7.

23 Said, *Orientalism*.

24 Yeğenoğlu, *Colonial Fantasies*, 23.

25 Rai, *Of Monsters*.

26 Sharpe, *Foucault's Monsters*, 60.

27 Sharpe, *Foucault's Monsters*, 67.

28 Sharpe, *Foucault's Monsters*, 67.

29 Such inter-racial couplings presented the greatest threat to very notion of "Englishness," which required careful protection against racial contamination and its consequent disintegration of the boundary that separated the English subject as racially pure from the racially degenerate "monster." Sharpe notes that legislation sought to prevent "pollution of the species" and that in the sixteenth century there was a "concern that a distinction between species be maintained." Yet the concern "simultaneously reveal[ed] the fragility of that very distinction." See Sharpe, *Foucault's Monsters*, 77.

30 Mondimore, quoted in Thomas, *The Sexual Demon*, 21.

31 Jordan, *White over Black*, 32.

32 Quoted in Sharpe, *Foucault's Monsters*, 27. Sharpe discusses the complexities of Henry Hughes's own extensive sexual and kinship relations with black slave women, notwithstanding his denouncements of the resulting "monstrosities." See ch. 1 of *Monstrous Intimacies*.

33 Aphra Behn, quoted in Jordan, *White over Black*, 27–8.

34 Fanon, *The Wretched of the Earth*, 170.

35 Sharpe, *Foucault's Monsters*, 72.

36 Jordan, *White over Black*, xiii.

37 Jordan, *White over Black*, xiii.

38 Eng, *Racial Castration*, 6.

39 Eng, *Racial Castration*, 7.

40 Eng, *Racial Castration*, 7.

41 Eng, *Racial Castration*, 8.

42 Eng, *Racial Castration*, 8–9.

43 Eng, *Racial Castration*, 10.
44 Eng, *Racial Castration*, 12.
45 Eng, *Racial Castration*, 13.
46 Creed, *The Monstrous-Feminine*, 33.
47 Creed, *The Monstrous-Feminine*, 14.
48 See Little, *American Orientalism*.
49 Parmar and Amos, "Challenging Imperial Feminism"; A. Smith, *Conquest*; Davis, *Women, Race, and Class*.
50 Thobani, "White Wars."
51 See Thobani, "Imperialist Missions" and "Gender and Empire."
52 *Kandahar* was awarded the Prize of the Ecumenical Jury at Cannes (2001), the Federico Fellini Honour of UNESCO (2001), and a four-star rating by the BBC and *The Guardian* film guides in the UK. Although it is a "semi-documentary," *The Guardian* praised the film as a "historical document." The BBC review described the film as of "unrelenting sadness," concluding that it was "impossible not to emerge from the cinema and wonder about the plight of the Afghan people today." See "Release of Kandahar Film in London," 16 November 2001, http://www.islamfortoday.com/kandahar.htm.
53 The film, produced in 2000, features Ms Nilufer Pazira in the role of the protagonist.
54 See Thobani, "Imperialist Missions" and "Gender and Empire."

Theorizing (at) the Limits of Justice

NASHWA SALEM

The temporalized vision of a homologous human subject as the privileged mode of *being* poses for both Asma Abbas and Denise Ferreira da Silva the specifically modern, onto-epistemic condition that continues to reverberate within humanistic and social scientific modalities of knowledge production and inquiry and that underwrite invocations of justice and self-determination in racial emancipatory programs. In a similar vein, Omeima Sukkarieh challenges the universalizing thrust of a particularist conception of humanity in whose name global warfare is manifest: some lives protected and saved, others denigrated and dehumanized. A fraught conception of humanity, Sukkarieh suggests, that in every instance generates its own citability.

Against privileging the Hegelian logos and its "reasoned" delimitation of what it means *to be*, the following contributions offer what Avery Gordon describes as ghost stories, by dwelling at the site of significative discourse as that which merges "the visible and the invisible, the dead and the living, the past and the present – into the making of worldly relations and into the making of our accounts of the world."[1] In turn, they offer a critical reading practice that begins, most importantly, by accounting for the limitations and violent inscriptions that inhere in modern forms of signification and their fields of representation. Each chapter marks the threshold where force and meaning form the scene of modern signification; each entertains the space of excess as a possibility for understanding otherwise, meditating upon this question: How can the subaltern subject that emerges through violence refuse violence? Central to this exercise is attending to the zones of indistinction that continue to be collapsed in contemporaneous analyses of political subjectivity and action. Differently put, the threshold between fact and fiction, violence and justice, law and force, love and terror, suffering and desire, time and space, is where, albeit slightly differently, Abbas, Silva, and Sukkarieh cite the convergence of epistemology and ontology, the political with the aesthetic, and their production of the human subject as the agent of history and repository of meaning.

Reading love and terror as sensorial attributes of the same significatory plane,[2] Abbas addresses the shortcomings of commentaries on terror that reinstall a "utilitarian morality and structures of sensibility and affect." Produced in turn are life worlds where bodies are relegated to a time-space in anachronistic relation to the historicist subject of Western European provenance and are cast, as Abbas puts it, "in the form of destruction and violence" or as necropolitical figures of "death parading as love." By unpacking love's relationship to terror (a temporal trajectory shared by both "colonial love" and "liberal multicultural love"), Abbas imagines a notion of love (and its relation to time-space) otherwise, as a principle intervention into the ontological and epistemological terrain shaping modern thought.[3]

Silva's piece opens by identifying a disjuncture between racial emancipatory programs and their ascription to a notion of justice that always-already delimits its actualization. Asserting global modernity as the signifying context that simultaneously produces and disavows conditions of affectability/relationality (the bodily and social traces that mark radical otherness in modern social configurations and their subaltern trajectories as citations of these traces[4]) is what renders justice an impossibility so long as it remains tethered to humanist projects or exploratory frames that centre positivist, rationalist, and utilitarian accounts of human experience founded in post-Enlightenment philosophical representations of personhood.

That suffering and desire, love and terror share a discursive terrain is a theme woven throughout Sukkarieh's contribution to this volume. For her, "staying with the violence" means reckoning with the blind spot that permits transnational state violence to masquerade as justice.[5] Blending poetic verse with anecdotes from military and police training modules and playing with the ubiquity of the anti-terror language that shapes our global present, Sukkarieh imaginatively transforms transnational violence into a person and engages him in conversational play. "Do you breathe?" she asks him. "Only without my will," he responds. Breath. Tactical breathing, combat breathing, controlled breathing: a disembodied breath or a breathless life is what Sukkarieh casts as the options for human life in the enduring global War on Terror.

Importantly, Abbas, Silva, and Sukkarieh move us away from the conservation and consumption of meaning as the principle site for intervention towards the thresholds that articulate value and excess in signifying systems. Such a move in turn allows for engagement with and beyond representation: with how productions of the human and of being are obtained in time and space, and with how we can open up the possibility of something different from what we have known.

Given the richness of the following readings, helpful supplements might include Georges Bataille's distinction between restrictive and general economies[6] and Frantz Fanon's reflection on the Hegelian dialectic or, more broadly, his insertion of the sociogenic principle into the calculus of modern power.[7] Achille Mbembe's "Necropolitics" offers a helpful analysis of Hegelian and Bataillean ideas on sovereignty in the context of racial violence.[8]

NOTES

1 Gordon, *Ghostly Matters*, 24.
2 The sensorial attributes of colonialism were central to its Manichean logic, rejecting the possibility of articulating an autonomous subjectivity under its conditions (Mbembe, "The Colony," 30). See especially Fanon, *Black Skin, White Masks*, as well as chapter 5 of *The Wretched of the Earth*: "Because it is a systematized negation of the other, a frenzied determination to deny the other any attribute of humanity, colonialism forces the colonized to constantly ask the question: 'Who am I in reality?' The defensive positions born of this violent confrontation between the colonized and the colonial constitute a structure which then reveals the colonized personality. In order to understand this 'sensibility' we need only to study and appreciate the scope and depth of the wounds inflicted on the colonized during a single day under a colonial regime … A hostile, ungovernable and fundamentally rebellious Nature is in fact synonymous in the colonies with the bush, the mosquitoes, the natives and disease" (182).
3 Take, for instance, where Abbas cites her own ambivalent relationship to ritual processions during Ashura as the effect of a dominant onto-episteme that refuses to assimilate the possibility of a metaphysical relation to the immaterial or otherworldly, vis-à-vis experiences of bodily pain.
4 Silva, "'Bahia Pêlo Negro,'" 327.
5 Drucilla Cornell has written masterfully on this theme; see her chapter "The Violence of the Masquerade," in *The Philosophy of the Limit*.

6 Bataille, *The Accursed Share.*
7 Fanon, *Black Skin, White Masks.* On Hegel's master–slave relation, see specifically chapter 7, "The Black Man and Recognition." The sociogenic principle
   explores the onto-epistemological production of European man and his
   co-emergent others as European cultural productions where historical-racial
   schemas are sutured to the body.
8 Mbembe, "Necropolitics."

27 In Terror, in Love, out of Time

ASMA ABBAS

When terror is pronounced a part of our current global human condition, I take it to mean that terror has come to live with and in us and that we are subjects being wrought in and through that conjugal relation. In the interest of returning politics to lives thus lived, this chapter seeks to comprehend our life with terror in this particular moment, by turning to our genealogies not only of terror but also of love.

How have we loved in order to suffer this way?[1] How might our life in and with terror, and our status as subjects of this terror, be connected with the inherited modalities of love and suffering insinuated in this subjectification? I begin with the premise that the ways in which we suffer and love index our political locations, defined as the spatial *and* temporal coordinates of our existence relative to the bindings of state, society, and ideology. Whether it is these locations that claim or purge us in the name of specific loves, or it is we who struggle to claim or purge those locations for the sake of some other loves, turning to the form and capacities of subjects marked by these locations is what brings politics back into the discussion of our consensus condition of terror, even if only for a moment.

In the post-9/11 era lived away from South Asia, it has become clear to me that the existential-political-reconstructive work to be done from our marginal locations in this time of neoliberal and neocolonial consensus is no longer in the realm of claiming irreducible differences in empirical fact or affect across spaces and cultures. It is necessary to unpack and deconstruct these seemingly unified, globalized, neoliberal, sensual "conditions" and what they mean to those who are *still* very much on different, even irreconcilable, sides of their production, distribution, and consumption. This imperative affirms the inseparability of the epistemological from the ontological, and of the political from the aesthetic, such that wars of political method can no longer be limited to the exposure of truth or the production of objective fact. These wars must be waged at the thresholds where truth is sensed and suffered and where fact collides with the body so as to render it material and actual, disrupting the givenness of the orders of the real, the conceivable, and the perceptible. The identification and reconfiguring of these thresholds opens up one of the few possibilities of dissensus (following Jacques Rancière) and thus of politics itself,[2] a dissensus that, importantly, refuses to delink materialist and anti-colonial imperatives of thought, feeling, and action. The acknowledgment of the lives and loves of terror might unlock a politics whose possibility is premised on shedding the aesthetic and sensual pathologies that are the gift of colonialism, liberalism, and capitalism.

To that end, this chapter posits that our contemporary "condition" of terror manifests itself in a generalized mode of political subjectivity that serves and supports it. The first section puts forward this argument as it begins to stitch together a method for confronting terror intimately and (hence) politically. The second section takes this pursuit to the space and time of the post/colony with which this subject is most intimate and in which this subject of terror seems most familiar. The third section absorbs these methodological conceits and proceeds to examine the construction, affirmation, and negation of the political subjects of terror by transforming the issue of terror into one of love. My turn to terror by way of love and time is in service of bringing closer the subject of terror. A focus on terror as object prevents us from apprehending the forms in which the loves of the subject of terror are cast, and the othering of terror implicit in that focus keeps us from seeing ourselves partaking in those forms of love. Much damage is done when the subject of terror is disavowed and distanced; such a move affirms, even reproduces, its constitutive destruction by allowing it ambient and oblique intimacies and dwellings regardless of our conscious will or conscientious objection. In contrast, I set out to explore where terror has settled in each of us and to inquire into the ways we are intimate with terror. The fourth section turns to the centrality of time in the formation and transformation of these subjects, a conceit folded into the concept of sovereignty. The modern and postcolonial system of states built on a real or wishful monopoly over violence requires a relation of love to the terror that instantiates sovereignty, whether on the state's part or that of the partisan who enters the picture to challenge it.[3] Thus, sovereignty, a temporal claim on space that serves as its limits, already entwines love and terror. I illustrate this using an example from contemporary literature, where the release of time from the death grip of sovereignty, and the subversive plasticity of impelled temporalities and sensibilities in the death hole of the postcolony, instantiates politics *and* possibility.

This chapter is primarily concerned with locating political possibility for lives that are increasingly forced to confront not merely incidences of destruction and terror but their very subjectivities cast in the form of destruction and terror. Articulating such a possibility requires us to reconsider what the times, sites, and senses of politics are; to problematize their normalization within dominant notions of global justice; and to confront them through lenses not only of historical distribution but also, and perhaps more importantly, of historical production and sustenance, of sensibility, life, and the dispensabilities thereof.

The Subjects of Terror: Method and Politics

By terror, I mean a condition wherein the doing and the experiencing of violence meld together inside us and it is difficult to distinguish the fear of what might happen to oneself from the fear of what that self can do. I understand terror to be an emotional state that impacts the aesthetic constitution of political subjectivity in a particular way. When we turn it into "the ultimate fear" or "the unsaid that can only be condemned, never condoned,"[4] terror resembles a sublime we cannot understand: we give it a sense of otherness that keeps it distant and us uninvolved and non-complicit. And then we rely on it to corral us into a collective moment of recognition of the ungodly injustice and incomprehensible insanity of it all.[5] I am concerned here not with terrorism as a tactic but with terror as an emotional state and experience shared by both the doer and the recipient. Terror's specific form in the present moment aligns with the body's increasing pulverizability, disposability, and dislocation.

Beyond the consensus on this condition among radicals and reactionaries alike, opinions diverge regarding the following, among other things: terror's provenance, its uses and consequences, the original terrorist, the political utility of violence, the very existence of anything like (merely) political violence, the novelty of terror for most of the world beyond its most recent and most valuable victims in the West, and its remedy. Yet far from causing any real disruption, these divergences enable deflections and prejudgments that buttress the core consensus and obstruct politics. The consensus on terror and terrorism as object, and on the terrorist as protagonist and subject of interest, amounts to an avoidance of this urgent political question: What form of meaning-making sensuous political subject is generalized, affirmed, and cultivated in order to maintain this consensus? Emerging from this are sensoria shared as never before that cut across the usual lines. Displaced is the form, mode, and capacity of the sensuous subject as the true and effective site of political contention. More deleterious than the wrenching disregard of potentiality ensuing from this rejection of politics and this colonization of embodied spaces of contention, however, is the defacing blindness to the actuality of how different relations to suffering, love, and life itself configure these subjects of terror as well as those subjects that are continually being massaged into being to serve the consensus human condition and its categorical (*sic*) imperatives.

Here is an opportunity to turn to these subjects in a different way, setting aside the fascination with history as consolation, with provenance as a solution to riddles, with the event of terror as climax or catastrophe beyond paltry meaning, and with the blameworthy or pathologized agency of the terrorist as yet another kind of closure. In trying to understand the contemporary political subjects of terror, it is necessary to acknowledge the spatial and temporal, epistemological and ontological, permutations that are made manifest in them, and how those permutations churn out life despite its impossibilities, perhaps life that is illegible or dis-sensual in relation to the normalized understanding of love, terror, and located-ness.

In confronting a new contemporary subject who is "autistic, indifferent, without affective engagement," Slavoj Žižek converses with Catherine Malabou's idea of "destructive plasticity" in an era during which trauma is no longer an interruption but a way of life, so that we have a "new wounded" subject who survives its own destruction, experiences all violence as catastrophe, and is moulded through this trauma rather than merely navigating it. Žižek speaks of destruction today as itself a "form of life."[6] "More precisely," he writes, "the new form is not a form of life, but, rather, a form of death."[7] (Nothing about this is new to anyone who works at the intersection of postcolonialism and feminism, where the issue of our affective encounters with what destroys us is always centre-stage.) For Žižek, today's trauma is that loss itself takes an affirmative form, especially when trauma is said to make the victim into something other than he or she was before, and that we can no longer expect such victims to be human *in the same way*. Thus, he writes, "the true traumatic heart of the matter [is] not the subject's desperate effort to recompense his loss, but the subject of this loss itself, the subject which is the positive form this loss assumes (the disengaged impassive subject)."[8] In other words, the mode in which destruction happens is now so total, so reminiscent of naturalized and normalized catastrophe, that political violence – which I would define as violence that one is compelled to make sense and meaning out of (whether or not one succeeds), or that is connected in any way with the making of meaning (and thus one's own subjectivity) in relation to others – has all but exited the landscape.[9] One can retain the force of the new wounded without indulging in the anti-political gesture of assigning this new trauma to catastrophe beyond politics (which is to say, catastrophe *as* beyond politics). Resisting the incipient idealism of Malabou's psycho-analytic epistemology, two key insights can still inform a materialist political method: plasticity as a way of thinking of a subject's history, and the shift in the temporality of trauma and violence.

Jacques Rancière defines political subjectivity as "an enunciative and demonstrative capacity to reconfigure the relation between the visible and the sayable, the relation between words and bodies: namely 'the partition of the sensible.'"[10] The sensuous, embodied life manifested in love and suffering can be seen to both converge in and diverge from Rancière's understanding. The same is true of our orientations to these, which, over time, sculpt the space for negotiating human relations between necessary materiality and imperative representation. Extending Rancière, political subjectivity need not be limited to the sayable *qua* logos; it can include other forms of enunciation and demonstration as well. Also, instead of being tethered to a determinate aesthetic or perceptual field, the repartitioning of the sensible can be seen as involving a *production and destruction of the sensible*. To take Rancière's logic of politics further, those on the margins, those who truly have no part, may be understood to be structured by relations to space and time that may not be continuous in any way with the dominant logics. If sensuousness is embodied time (as Marx wrote), then these alternative relations constitute alternative sensoria (not only in terms of content but also in terms of form and capacity). Thus, a concern with political subjectivity in a time of terror (one populated by the post-traumatic subject of terror signalled above) has to turn to the capacities in which this manifests itself, capacities that are in turn historical forms with which the present moment's sovereign acts negotiate (in practices *not only* of terror). Thus, in this moment, political subjectivity (even in its supposedly "healthiest" forms) must acknowledge its formative relation to violence, terror, and destruction in order to acknowledge in turn the debt it owes to the violence on which the state and capital have historically depended for their own existence, as well as the terror on which the state and capital now desperately depend for their sustenance.

Contemporary framings of terror and of the fraying of the subject and the social fabric in which the subject it is suspended often rely, on the one hand, on the narrative of people being desensitized to bad things happening, and on the other hand, on a declared consensus that we have nothing to do with it, since as civilized moral beings we are logically, empirically, and practically opposed to it. These framings leave unquestioned, normalized, and static the morality and the structures of sensibility and affect that enable this condition and that sustain the subject at the helm of it and as served by it. I argue that the conundrum we face is not emblematic of *too much* suffering, but of an *inability* to suffer; we are saturated with terror, which ends up installing itself as a discontinuous emotional form, a reality separate from other pathos, sealed from sentiments that perhaps were once known to us or available to us. There is no way out of this form unless the sensible, in Rancièrian terms, is pushed to incur a repartition or reproduction that reclaims the ability to sense presences and absences and to see that we have been suffering, defeated, or grieving. Or, perhaps, where a new relation to this reality supplants or (in Malabou's terms) stretches, disfigures, and refigures the old one – suggesting an acknowledgment of plasticity that must be fundamentally materialist to have any meaning and that must absorb the lessons of the postcolony, the space *and time* thus far reserved, not far away, for the production of suffering and death.

Our Accursed Share

Consanguinity with terror comes easily at a time when the destruction of state and society – as is happening in Pakistan, a country always at war – is inseparable from the rising xenophobia and everyday brutality in the United States and Europe. There are increasing continuities of both sense and structure, even if the empirical phenomena seem different. All of these are examples of societies at war inside and out, and they have been so for a long time. And it is hardly a surprise that signs of social wear and tear, indeed exhaustion and destruction, are ubiquitous for those who can discern them. The wars that wage inside these societies and the wars these polities wage are producing parched, scarce, loveless societies along with subjects to match them in the name of some kind of plentitude, fervour, and love. I say loveless not to suggest any nostalgically positivist conception of love but to allude to the possibilities of love stifled and sullied by a deep anti-politics of those modes of love that are the gifts of our shared colonial pasts and of our shared neoliberal present. There is no way to distance oneself from the loves the possibilities of which are destroyed by this moment and by the tithe taken from other lives as a repercussion of the abstract love for nation, self, property, market, the future, and anything that fits that hole which Rushdie saw as being "god-shaped." I am interested, beyond and away from the narrative of contemporary death of morals or ethics, in how these realities manifest themselves and are worked through to forge political subjectivities in the present. That might be, in this moment, the only approach to take if we are to acknowledge and release the life that is being harnessed to court and foster death.

As this reality intensifies, ordinary negotiations that constitute present-day sensorial life within and across times and spaces – wherever they may be physically mapped – compete as sites of a relentless politics (of unrequited subjects). The narrative of the colonial subject cast as the subject of death need no longer remain sequestered from the more common and generalized subject of terror (wherever it may be found); and neither can be invoked without reference to the margins where a counter-politics and counter-subjectivity are being negotiated and forged, unfortunately often through death. As the form of the subject standardizes across familiar boundaries, exceptions to this exception need to be invoked and provoked. A particular mode of political subjectivity comes to be in the contemporary discourses and dislocations of terror, and I am interested in identifying those capacities and harnessings that might enable a departure from this stifling consensus over politics and subjectivity.

In order to do this work, a conception of political subjectivity is needed that can incorporate and illuminate the impact of a history of colonialism on the sensorial make-up of the "post/colony" not as a cartographic fact but as political experience. Here, with the help of Georges Bataille and Achille Mbembe, I will bring forward into the post/colony the previous section's extraction of the Malabou/Žižek diagnosis of our current trauma and its contact with a Rancièrian notion of political subjectification.[11] Bataille's idea of "the accursed share" offers a way of understanding notions of sacrifice, war, and destruction that may hold some relevance for the sensuous economies of the neoliberal capitalist post/colony. In his book with that title, Bataille speaks of a general economy of human energies by way of which societies channel the excess of their productions into modes of consumption that negate a utilitarian calculus and "succeed" in making true subjects (in acts of sacrifice) out of those who would otherwise become things of use harnessed to the functioning of the normative social order (the restrictive economy).[12] This is certainly a complicated claim with several dubious normative implications. Here, I am interested solely in how this opposition between a general and a restrictive economy plays out not in the realm of labour or even productive activity per se, but at the level of sensuous capacities.[13] Suspicious of the reactionary sanguinity of excess, I propose that we focus on the forms of these capacities and their productions instead of on the discharge of an already-known energy. This will require asking some crucial questions. Is the excess in a relation of active negation of the restrictive economy? Is scarcity still internalized in the mode of excess so that the negation does not quite subvert the scarcity? If these questions are answered yes, we are trapped in a scenario where the state and the market as we know them know this general economy well and exploit it. If, on the other hand, we find that the excess channels different capacities in different forms, we may have a revolutionary politics that is most apposite to the *poeisis* that Rancière attributes to political subjectivity.

Thus, both fanatical destruction and an equally destructive lack of pathos can be understood in terms of the excess that Bataille theorizes. The colonizer and the colonized are now trapped in this general economy. Achille Mbembe's discussion of Fanon and Bataille in relation to the sensorial attributes of the postcolony (which for him is a geographical and historically precise ex-colonial marker) helps with the next step in our methodological journey.[14] Mbembe channels Bataille into thinking about how the postcolony is a debased "mirror" of the colony and is saturated with terror. He reminds us of the necropolitics of the postcolony:[15] excess manifested as death, harnessed by the state in wars that make no sense or by nationalisms and other abstractions, giving over life and its energies to them, offering sacrifices to the nation-state, if not the gods, in confusing erasures and reclamations of the body and subjectivity. The nation-state knows all about this, dependent as it is on violence as a container of this excess economy; it could not exist without violence. To foreground the economic, political, and sensual realities that connect the "centre" of the colony to the "centre" of the metropole, and the "margins" to the "margins," one illuminating the other, we can extend Mbembe's invocation of Fanon and Bataille to the post/colony as a global condition.

To inflect Bataille's "base materialism" with this post/colony, the following element would have to be included: that the colonizer and the colonized have their own pathological modes of escaping the restrictive economy. This is energy in the service of a principle of death parading as a love that has been indentured beforehand. We must take into account, then, the abundance that is needed to counter the brutal scarcities and mortifications of love. For the tired and the exhausted, it is not strong action that is a rebellious departure from a logic, but acts of (and in) abundance that defy those in power and do not serve their purposes. These acts of abundance are acts of love and acts of suffering that defy the imposed logics of the kinds of intimacy, knowledge, and premises that the structure wants from us; they are exceptions to the prescribed modes and unfoldings of love and suffering that do not fit within a liberal utilitarian calculus.[16]

When Mbembe speaks of the accursed share in regimes built around death, of a kind of necropolitics that is lived by the post/colony, one can feel one's way through this darkness by being sensitive to the ways available for negotiating the inheritance of such a curse; the ability to suffer these deaths follows an articulable historical relation to them. The relations among these various ventings of the excess bring to light the disposable body and its compulsion towards death. Who exactly "deserves" to live off (or primitively accumulate) our cultivated terrors? And might this question spur an exit from the spate of self-loathing and self-destruction in which we find ourselves? Those who have never loathed or destroyed themselves (or who have never been aware of it) can stick to their rich, affluent partialities to moderation and to the language of freedom, newness, and compromise, because they have other non-negotiably destructible and disposable bodies on which to premise their own negotiable fears. Yet here, even they may need more love to replace their tyrannical narratives of hope, which are as bloated as their fears and which are no less parasitic and predatory on those "other" bodies. More on this in the following section.

If the general economy is taken to be an economy of form and not merely of content, we may have to be more agnostic about, but also more willing to observe and acknowledge, the modes in which the accursed share manifests itself. This is to say that in apprehending terror, destruction, and wretchedness, not merely the abundance or lack of love and suffering would be evident. We would also find a particular configuration of love and suffering that we may not already know of. In the same way, when faced with the relentless desire to amass wealth and raise fences, we would encounter a different configuration of love and suffering instead of reading into it a known, simplistic calculus of quantity. That violence, art, sex, joy, happen in excess of some limit is certainly noteworthy. But it is the relations *among* those productions that substantiate a framework of political subjectivity in a manner that indexes the trajectory of the form and capacities of the subject in question. Importantly, this augments Rancière's understanding of this process by emphasizing that the nature of political subjectification "as if the colony happened" requires factoring in the destruction and re/production of the aesthetic field beyond politics *qua le partage du sensible.* Only then might we be able to attend to the history of imperial, colonial, and neoliberal policing of the very modes of love and suffering that erupt into a subject.

To sum up, approaching the question of terror politically requires attention to the forms of sensuous life that constitute the mode of political subjectivities that erupt as the form called terror colludes with the forms of love (and suffering, although the latter is not my focus here) in contemporary culture. This requires us to go beyond the empirical cartographies of terror's distribution and appearance and to contend with the question of its production and of one's relation to it as a particular manifestation of the capacities to love and suffer. This question of production must, in turn, be brought into relation with the production of the worlds that suffer, sustain, and make sensible or insensible these destructions and that withstand the production and maintenance of – eruption into and eruption of – the subject of terror. Considering these subjects is inseparable from considering the subject who continues to defer the love on offer, who forms and deforms regimes of times and spaces to which it is forcibly betrothed, and who asks for something different. So I turn to love.

From Terror to Love, with the Puzzling Subject Who Has Survived Its Own Death

At the same time as terror has become normalized in the botched and bloody hometowns of my memory and of the memory of those whom I do not know but whose memory cohabitates with mine in the same sphere as hope, love, regret, torment, and puzzlement, I have come to understand that for those who struggle with the regimes of farcical, murderous, loveless *desire* of "the other" that go by the names of colonialism, liberal multiculturalism, and neoliberal monoculture, love – *and not hope* – is the appropriate double for this suffering.[17] Globalized narratives of progress, redemption, security, salvation, or hope accompany the globalized pronouncements of tragedy and crisis, building on a history of the domestication of suffering that produces victims with scripted relations to their suffering made legible and consumable under the general rubrics of injury and harm. Hope is, in my view, a domestication and commodification of love to match the domestication and commodification of suffering. These domestications of our senses are ultimately primitive accumulations of time; they are the trick that unites capitalism and colonialism.[18] The mediatized deployment of hope is of a piece with the philosophical abstractions and political detachments intrinsic to optimism and nihilism alike, and all of these frenetic performances of homogenized voice and sentimentality are impossible without a dictated translation of, and relation to, suffering and love. Familiar ontologizing epistemes and moralities of life, death, peace, and conflict are deployed against the terrorism that is hinted at by any departure from these, rushing to re-equilibrate, reappropriate, and restore the hegemonic sensorium. As the not-good-enough victims have now become terrorists or potential terrorists, disloyal to the narratives of suffering that unfold in the minds of the good liberal and true fascist alike, it is imperative to speak of the attachment *and* the desire that allow people to suffer as they do. How one is attached and how one desires say much more about how one suffers to become a subject of terror beyond a superficial and generalized relation to the commission of violence and deliverance from it. Thus, how terror lives *with* and *in* us in this moment in history testifies to our inheritances not only of terror, but also of love.

By love, I mean an intense feeling that serves as an adhesive for individuals and groups; it inheres both in desire – understood as a movement and opening towards what one deems beautiful or wants to make proximate – and in attachment – understood as a fastening, fixity, enclosure, and limit. As a natural or conditioned power, capacity, and practice, love is critical to the arrangement of relations within and across bounded collectivities and is significant in determining the nature and possibility of politics. In addition to concerns regarding what brings and holds people together, how different attachments are negotiated by individuals and groups within a polity, who can love and associate with whom, and what kinds of devotions and allegiances are prized within societies, love features in the emotional and corporeal economies that manage the labours and subjectivities performed in society. In the same way that terror is not an object or imperative for my inquiry, I do not treat love as an object or imperative; I want to look at how love and terror live and form inside us in relation to each other, as premises and dynamics of political existence (and non-existence).

The nature of the subject of terror in this moment cannot be separated from the eros and the attachment that produce, foster, validate, necessitate, and mourn it. One possible history of the political subject, the contemporary subject of terror being no exception, can be gleaned from the ways in which the capacities to love and suffer are produced, operationalized, and experienced in different ways across regimes of time and space, including in the production of the experience and act of terror. These capacities are materially interdependent and historically produced, and together they make creation, destruction, and absence present, sensible, and apprehensible. Such a characterization is incompatible with a manner of thinking about affect that places love and terror in a binary or dialectical relation of positing and negation, lack and excess, within a finite and naturalized economy of externalized action and sentiment.

Since it is through loving, desiring, and being attached that one suffers with and for another, becomes available to another as an ethical-political subject, and musters the energy to sustain or interrupt reality, the experience or embodiment of terror cannot be disentangled from the question of love itself. Setting aside hackneyed characterizations of love as inherently violent and of violence as another form of love, it is worth asking which intimacies we are seeking in our relation to terror and which loves permit or compel that seeking. To reverse the unilateral Orientalism observed by Edward Said in the discourses of terrorism,[19] it is important to probe where the Orientalism and the terrorism abide together, and where terror, like violence, needs to be apprehended as a historical form containing significations to things other than itself, such as love.

The empirical cartographies of the distribution and appearance of terror necessarily address only one side of a complex political and sensuous economy that relies foremost on the production of these realities and the ability to make them in/sensible. It is hardly surprising that one's distance from, or closeness to, terror seems to follow the conceits of the same spatial cartographies that are/were set in place by colonialism – cartographies that are now being upheld and even reified in the frenzied erasure of certain boundaries (only to erect new ones). Experiencing this distance and proximity has brought home to me, time and again, the arbitrary nature of the claims to the sublimity or the newness of terror, both of which are essentially temporal qualities converted into spatial ones. For instance, long before the 9/11 "launch" of terror, I used to have nightmares about Karachi around Ashura. Those nightmares were somehow linked to my intimate fear of (mixed with devotion to) the martyrs being commemorated, sympathy for and revulsion to the procession of mourners, and the fact that tragedy was in the air, palpable, hot, repulsive, seductive, all at the same time. Never before coming to the United States had I known a "bystander"; the ontological assumptions that allow any constituent of an experience to be consigned in the categories of victim, perpetrator, and bystander were not natural to me and could only arise from a particular constructed, historical relation to loving and suffering.

Then the film *Cache* left me feeling guilty and embarrassed that I had missed the degree to which the knife, the wielding of it, and the slashing of something with it, came so "naturally" to my people – the consanguinity to which I referred earlier. After all, who could not connect the public slaughter of animals with the release that psychoanalysis reads into women who "cut" themselves, with the video of Daniel Pearl's murder, and with the christening with blood (in name *and* act) of town roundabouts? Think also of the wives of the butchers who went around the neighbourhood dispatching sacrificial animals on Eid, and the wives or mothers or sisters of those who found new ways to flagellate themselves on Ashura (with bunches of small knives) and how they could possibly love them and sleep with them, feed them and wash their clothes. How could I possibly place these "savageries" on the same plane as the savageries of the "civilized," where we could still be invited to conversations about civility in public discourse?

Of course, I *know* better, and I am allergic to any discourse that pathologizes and normalizes at will, that damns and redeems in some mimicry of science, or religion, or theatre, that sets the fantastical table for conversation as long as the self-serving moralities about violence and non-violence are deemed non-negotiable. My allergy is to the anti-politics of these moves – to pre-emptive evacuations of politics, arbitrary demarcations of times and spaces, and the recolonization of that sphere of human thought and action where meanings and limits, indeed entire modes of life, are supposed to be negotiated.[20] All this defiance does not change the fact that I am continually haunted by how my fantasies of love are shaped entirely by my fantasies of terror, not in a formulaic sadomasochism, but because the closeness to the abjection of the martyr and the butcher is what inspires protecting another out of love, where things still have the ability to haunt because they are more material in many ways and sown into all the abstractions thanks to which one lives to see another day. Yes, these *are* my issues, and perhaps it is not accidental that my turn to love in order to address terror is not an act of grace, charity, or transubstantiation, but a thoroughly historical-materialist one that reflects the need not to abandon what is made distant and expunged at will. Love is both my motive and my access to the subject of terror.

Even when the axiomatic regurgitation of colonial violence is our primary way of grasping the very instance of terror, it would be a mistake to forget that colonialism, our history with it, and our overcoming of it, all operate through practices of love and desire that sustain our life worlds. Just as we find in colonialism the roots of the modes of terror that inhabit us today, the collusions of colonialism and liberalism are the roots of our capacities to desire, produce, and attach – our abilities and possibilities of love – that are as much part of the same story. Thus, if politics is to address propensities to want *and* to destroy, the question of murder must be accessed through love rather than the other way around. Even when we seek causal explanations for terror that vary with the chosen points of origin and destination, it behooves us to be honest about what it really is (*about* terror, *about* ourselves) that we are trying to explain, and why and to whom. And in that very question, we might see our complicity with or rejection of the modes of love that are on offer.

Violence relies on intimacy for its meaning, regardless of empirical or physical proximity. No wonder, then, that all too often, understanding postcolonial violence begins with a consensus on some materially borne and seepingly infectious pathology – an intimate relation in itself. There is Bataille's accursed share, there is Mbembe's necropolitics, there is Fanon's misogynist object of the *fidai* woman in a veil, and there is bulimia. There is enough in these frames, and in the idea of a life world pitched at the threshold of necessity and desire, to suggest that even a decrepit and necrophiliac system is not held together solely by mechanistic desire, pleasure, and pain; it needs emotional upkeep through the labour of love and suffering it exacts and manages over time. The forms of inherited and imposed love might be what enable terror, spurred by moralistic invocations of feelings, which then turn into idealized empirical absolutes in discussions of intolerance, violence, terror, and terrorism. In each of these formulations of affect, morality, and experience – utilitarian calculus, ahistorical morality, idealist empiricism, neoliberal securitization – time is enclosed and conscripted in comparable ways, consistent with the temporalities of the colonizer, the nation, the nation-state, religion, and the marketplace. I contend that terror has a politics if (and because) it invokes a counter-temporality in the face of these guardians of a frozen past and a congealed future. Thus, when terror mimics the same temporalities as what it claims to oppose, and affirms the forms of destruction and death that produced it, it has exited politics; if it challenges given regimes of time and sense, it is political. This determination is squarely a matter of political judgment of an intimate kind and might bring some politics back to Malabou's new wounded.

In the Outcast Times of This Post/Colony

In quest of sites that hold any promise for politics by posing a challenge to the given regimes of time and sense, I am ushered to places afforded a "history" by colonialism and capitalism (spaces to which time is brought, and which are brought into time as history, itself spatialized time that temporalizes spaces). These sites continue to sport rhythms of life that deviate from some "normal" tempo. Call them the margins if you will, the enclosures of lived life flaunting a character of its own, irreducible to some tempting objective fact of diagnosed pathology. They are life worlds like any other produced through labours of love and suffering, in need and desire, toggling necessity and freedom. Perhaps colonialism is even a kind of dominant strain of love, to be responded to with a different kind of love.

Nadeem Aslam's *Leila in the Wilderness* (2010) provides glimpses into the temporal palimpsest of terror as life, mediated by love, in the postcolony. It tells the story of a woman, Leila, married off as a child to a feudal lord who contrives the magical construction of a mosque as a ploy to annex the "hallowed" land that surrounds it. That land is at once the site of profuse sacredness for the unloved poor, of Leila's rape by a band of priests, and of her attempted escape by growing wings, which are then cut off and her skin sown back together to prepare her for one man after another. She gives birth to girls whom the husband kills (a few saved by a nanny), and every mishap of the birth of a girl is rewarded by compensatory futuristic impregnating sex. Engirding this story is the story of her lover looking for her with his little music box, and a magnet in his heart like hers.

The story seems ancient, but it is not: there are cellphones around. But that is not the only temporal trick pulled. Temporality is played with not only at the level of narrative/expressive tectonics but also in the normative aspects of subjective experience – certainly old-fashioned, but welcome. In one scene near the end, the two lovers, reunited, and most likely headed to their death at one of the butchers' hands at any moment, return to a room full of dead animals to release them in an act that is not of the scarcity that comes with conventional notions of (bare) survival. Driven home here is that love and the sensuous experience of time are tied to each other. Another retrieval is that, *pace* the modes of interiorized scarcity that shape life today, acts of abundance (what Nietzsche might call life-affirming acts) are not always dizzyingly plentiful (i.e., always in excess out of resentment and reaction). Here, abundance is not to be understood merely in a limited currency of the act itself – that is, how many lives are saved, how much fear overcome, how much self-protection, how much altruism, though those are important too – but as what moves me in the manner in which any act interprets the scarcity on offer and counters it with abundance not merely as compensation, but as if to show the inanity of the very premise of scarcity it comports. In the first case, we prioritize the quantitative economy of action and sentiment as based exclusively on distinct actions relating to one another, counting, countering, and compensating in turn. In the second case, scarcity and abundance are qualities of and orientations to action and experience itself.

In *Leila in the Wilderness*, the temporal schemes of the rulers are defied. Life and death matter differently. There is much life among death, and there are many moments of turning back to save the dead animals, those caught in and by time, as offerings of love, even when every second counts for the escape. Far from indulging in a narrative of hope or of optimism or its absence, the story is silent on these. It is not subservient to any "god-shaped hole" being filled by attachments to new gods, to capital, to nation – a hole that simultaneously draws time in and is exiled from it. The lovers do not give us hope cast in any temporal mould to which religion and its professed secular undoings are beholden.

At moments, this still *might* resemble devotion to an ideology, a god, or a nation, for which one's life or death does not matter. But it is very different from these, because this love is not traumatized by the departure of gods, nor does it ask for something else to fill the hole. Leila and Qes's experience does not constitute a lack of love that lashes out; it is *another* experience of love. Their love's material negotiation with time and space allows it to be a more material principle of action than hope in a conventional sense. The latter assumes a particular relation to time and holds tight to a pit of time that will swallow whole any sacrifice we can give to it; whereas in the former, the question of ends and beginnings, of necessity, is transposed onto that of presence and absence, appearance and disappearance, in time instead of space. De-emphasizing beginnings and ends, the temporality of love rather than hope allows worlds to coexist and not vanquish one another, as long as the lovers can hold the possibility of existences that do not preclude others and that can defy the rationalities that expunge entire worlds at will.[21]

These dissensual claims to outcast time – time that is, oddly enough, both the effluent of sovereignty and the state of emergency – are essential to understanding and making more proximate the terror and the love produced in these spaces. When we recast space as a landscape of time itself, we can see excluded and disjointed spaces for the coagulate dissensual temporalities they are. This is because their incarnation as sites of politics has everything to do with the colonialist and capitalist processes of history and historicizing – bringing history to places, bringing places into history, and spatializing time in order to bring spaces into temporal schemas, so that the production and reproduction of and through bodies is possible (in labour, at war, and so on). When we think of the post/colony, in its various connotations, as defined by alternative temporalities rather than by geopolitical spatial boundaries, we are forced to address the problem of time in the subject's destruction, destructibility, and attachment to terror.

For instance, in understanding "terrorism as political violence" as "the ground upon which sovereignty is in many cases defined in the colonial present,"[22] both "the colonial" and "the present" are noteworthy. The essential link here is of sovereignty to time, not least because sovereignty is iterated in declaring the time of the now, a declaration that already signals (the threat of) its effective (actual or potential) undoing: spaces begin to seem outside of time whether they lie inside or outside the colony; the times of the colony and the metropole increasingly merge (not least through movements of bodies, labour, war); and enclaves of different temporalities develop in the standard sovereign grounds. Perhaps this allows us to read backwards to find exceptions to the colonial present (in terms of experience rather than physical location) in counter-temporalities.

The definition also suggests that the sovereign is sovereign over a moment of time, and not merely within the bounded space of the colony, which is the conventional view. If terrorism institutes sovereignty over time in the colony, we are well-advised not to make the familiar move of seeing the colony as the exception that produces terror; rather, we should see continuities with colonial time as the grounds for all political violence, whether in healthy or "failed" states. This invokes a criterion for separating forms of violence that is more nuanced than just who is deploying it (such as the state versus the partisan or the terrorist), since this distinction is only possible when one can rely on simplistic categories of location, source, and agency. The resulting demarcations suggest that modes of violence are distinguished by the regimes of time to which they adhere, indexed by the relations to love and suffering normalized within them. This allows the form and the relations manifested in a given subject of terror to be more meaningful indicators of the politics of these acts than simply *whose* sovereignty is asserted in them – a rote anarchist and theological fallacy. One might even be able to cite the very emphasis on sovereignty as already a conceit towards a particular temporal relation to spaces that serves to unify authority (a temporal principle) and community (a spatial one), subsuming the latter into the former.

When the states of terror and of emergency are seen as exceptions to time, it is tempting to bring other exceptions to the table. Perhaps, then, seeking exceptions to and ruptures in the sovereign probably should also involve seeking exceptions to and ruptures in the political principle of sovereignty as wielded by subjects. The colony and the margins then appear inhabited and haunted by repeated acts of excepting and excluding, not least in the realms of being, sensing, and meaning. When political theology, for instance, goes in search of the outside of time, for the moment of emergency where law is suspended and can be reinvoked as justice by those who have nothing, this state of emergency carries no surprise for those spaces that are defined *as* states of emergency, margins that are always outside of time of the sovereign state and whose existence is premised on that exclusion. The destruction of the known subject of politics thus rings in a very differently "emergent" register in places where time has always been an effluent to time, and life an effluent to life, and where lives are cast as emergencies to which no one responds except with more violence, be it physical, linguistic, material, or ideal. Here, political subjects are constituted by logics different from those that reassure the healthy and reputable subjects of politics, whose waywardness or destruction is today being lamented. The manner in which we approach and evoke a politics has everything to do with how the question of (in this case) terror must be cast in light of its production and sustenance in the contemporary global subject of terror, beyond the question of its distribution and of the how and who of lives valued or dispensable. Thus, my argument for approaching terror politically via love and time cannot help but be an argument for rejecting an idealized, utilitarian, mystical, or romantic relation to violence as redemptive or remaking (associations that pervade both liberalism and its supposedly terrorizing enemies).

Those spaces that have stood for the "failure" of the post–Second World War project of liberal capitalism need to be looked at not as horror stories but as lenses into the process that has led to the current spate of emergencies. Entire worlds, albeit not always pretty ones, erupt on the margins with new vocabularies of love, devotion, and redemption, or with different material relations to existing vocabularies, and their spatial dis/continuities are much less meaningful here than their temporalities, which coalesce as signals to new politics (or at least different ones). The heartless and loveless economies of fear and brutality apparent in the globalized sensorium of terror can only be challenged and subverted from spaces where the consensus over the body, over anger, over murder, over love, over politics and its promises, is still fluid and occasionally even explodes.

Coda

Between the words love and terror lies a minefield of hauntings, questions, thoughts, and feelings about the awkward self-consciousness of complicit genealogies and consanguine inheritances. I know them too well in a way, and am able to apprehend the repulsions and the attachments that come with them, wondering whether these are an inheritance specific to my religion, my class, my culture, my gender, my city, the colony that I left, or the colony where I have arrived. In this same minefield lies a fascination I have developed with somewhat tragic Bombay gangster films, which offer compelling and radical arguments for love on the margins of time and space and which inspire curiosity about how women love men who kill: Do the wives of soldiers, terrorists, revolutionaries, smell the spilled blood, or do they smell the wounds and deprivations and the prescribed loves that fill those holes that cause the blood to be spilled? And how does love happen on those blurry thresholds between life and death? Amid all of this also lives in me a wish to find a way to salvage acts of destruction, notwithstanding my revulsion towards those acts. And I have an unyielding instinct that the loves on offer to us as a way out of our conundrums are part of what brought us here. I worry that rejecting those loves too harshly might leave none to go around. I cannot bring myself to submit to these, if only to be able to continue to ask for better love that can defy other forms of political subjectivity and life.

My turn to love and to outcast times of the post/colony is made necessary by the fact that as we desire a politics that counters these productions, we cannot separate the forging of forward-looking solidarities from the attachments and capacities to love that have been shaped and conscripted so far, which are connected in turn to the suffering and death produced in the colony. As for being out of time, we can no longer hide behind the urgencies of supposedly progressive or materialist politics that are unapologetically inattentive to the histories of colonized spaces, times, and subjectivities that have produced societies and subjects that are surviving attempts to annihiliate them. As we confront a moment that can ill afford to disavow or ignore the entanglements of colonialism, liberalism, and capitalism, whether in assessing our current "crises," or in articulating interventions in the famed "end times" in which we live, or in addressing the convergent experiences of destruction and grieving on the proliferating margins of colony and metropole alike, there is no way such an intervention can proceed on the ontological or epistemological terms that have been in play so far. Otherwise, all I see in these anxious urgencies, and in these problems of terror and other horrors, are late and unschooled arrivals in the consistent experience of destruction of, and grieving of, societies that have already been sacrificed as precursors to this crisis.

NOTES

1 If Friedrich Nietzsche exclaimed, oh, how we have suffered to suffer this way – a gasp to which I responded in *Liberalism and Human Suffering* – this chapter turns to a part of the story that is only suggested in that response and that needs to be teased out further.

2 Cf. Rancière, *Dissensus: On Politics and Aesthetics*; Rancière, *Chronicles of Consensual Times*.

3 Cf. Weber, "Politics as a Vocation," on the concept of the state. Cf. also Schmitt, *The Concept of the Political*, and Schmitt, *Theory of the Partisan*, for an elaboration on this economy and the figure of the partisan.

4 Boehmer and Morton, *Terror and the Postcolonial*, 6.

5 My inquiry runs counter to the usual move of turning away from terror as if it is a stranger, a monster, or, worse, the sublime, something we do not even want to know (and not "knowing" which outside of a particular con-sensus – which extends in our case to the anxious anti-politics of the positivistic epistemologies of violence and terror that enclose their objects – is our only claim to un-savage humanity). Yet this turning away is disingenuous since all our most familiar consents are evidently laced with terror; at the same time, it cuts to the core of the rampant pathologies of xenophobia, facile cruelty, and the "mindlessness" of terror (in "successful" and "failed" states alike), also showing what these consents and these pathologies have in common. Unfortunately, this turning away, defamiliarizing, distancing, has been the way in which many otherwise friendly thinkers have dealt with the epistemologies of politics. Hannah Arendt is a case in point. For her, this distancing and defamiliarizing is the way for us to understand our complicities, take responsibility, and reinstate the ability and capacity for political judgment. Insofar as she also is building on the aesthetic judgment in Kant to provide some kind of premise for salvaging/conceptualizing political judgment in the twentieth century, my turn to aesthetics inspires the converse as a way of bringing politics back into the picture, and I see these aversions to attachment and familiarity (or sanguinity, one might say) to be anti-political, a luxury that not all of us can afford and that not all of us are moved by. I deal with this in detail elsewhere, but it is important to note the underlying challenge to the usual tricks of political epistemology that my turn to terror via the aesthetics of love is offering: epistemic (and hence ontological, and political) access and desire itself needs to be rethought, reworked, and resensitized, rather than parted with completely or, ironically, salvaged through oblivion. Another thinker is Catherine Malabou, cited in this section, whose notion of "destructive plasticity" also evacuates the politics of this destruction (and the resulting subject), even though hers is a mere diagnosis of how catastrophic and beyond meaning violence and woundedness are today. Her conceptualization also commits the epistemological bungle of ontologizing and renaturalizing in a way that separates the concept from its lived politics – a naming that distances instead of bringing closer (cf. Abbas,

"Damages Inc.," 2). We are so marked by the history of the knowing love that kills that we are compelled to give up the knowing or the love, incapable of imagining an intimate, and differently aesthetic, epistemology and ontology, responsive to its object.

6 Cf. Malabou, *The Ontology of the Accident*; Malabou, *The New Wounded*.

7 Žižek, *Living in the End Times*, 296.

8 Žižek, *Living in the End Times*, 308.

9 By invoking meaning-making in relation to the politics of violence, I want to be careful not to invoke the question that Nietzsche attributes to religion (and to the success of the ascetic priest), "Why do I suffer?" I have in mind more of an ability to remain with, to sense, (merely) understand, make matter, the suffering and violence itself, in a way that allows the how and the who to problematize and politicize the why, and to invoke Tracy Strong, carefully keeps the questions of "Who am I?" and "Who are We?" (and any answers thereof) tied to each other. He writes: "The specialness of politics in our lives come from the fact that in the acknowledgment and recognition that a 'we' is the solution to the problems of the I, we find ourselves required to live in a world which is not incoherent and which places upon us demands that ... we must not fulfill. We, are, however, always tempted to leave the space and time of politics ... for other realms, with clearer boundaries, greater poise, more definition." Strong, *The Idea of Political Theory*, 3.

10 Rancière and Panagia, "Dissenting Words," 115.

11 Post/colony: Not a precise cartographic fact but akin to the "contact zone" (cf. Pratt, *Imperial Eyes*). Pratt defines contact zones as "social spaces where disparate cultures meet, clash, and grapple with each other, often in highly asymmetrical relations of domination and subordination-like colonialism, slavery, or their aftermaths as they are lived out across the globe today." My focus here is that these spaces/times are home to the condition of terror, informed by a history of colonialism and capitalism. In Pierre Bourdieu's or Marcel Mauss's terms, the postcolony would be the field to the habitus of terror.

12 Cf. Bataille, *The Bataille Reader*, 165–98; Carter, *Understanding Religious Sacrifice*, 162–74.

13 This is a distinction that early Marx inherits from Aristotle and that I find worth holding on to. It's discussed in detail elsewhere.

14 Mbembe, "The Colony."

15 Mbembe, "Necropolitics."

16 This calculus proliferates in the mirrors of the metropole, which then spark fissures within the metropole and the post/colony, fissures that bear

no resemblance to the neat faultlines featured in malignantly reificatory idealist projects such as human rights liberalism, nationalism, localism, contemporary forms of utopian socialism or anarchism, and even insistent re-turns to class as stratum and position (a spatial understanding) and not as actuality and principle (more temporal). For instance, "the 99%" and the purist/demographic relation to class as if Du Bois and Fanon never happened.

17 This is also true when it comes to subjects that are undesired, that remain on the margins of state, society, and ideology. Therefore, the issue of love is germane to what binds *and* to what shows a way out of the homogeny of affect that pervades our lives, cutting across colony and metropole in new sense-scapes.

18 Cf. Abbas, *Liberalism and Human Suffering*, chs. 2 and 6.

19 Said, "Punishment By Detail"; Said, "The Essential Terrorist."

20 This includes an uncomplicated resort to even those Fanonian self-analyses of disorder and terror that render the man's body ontologically composed of colonial violence, with the woman's body just an instrument needing a home in that ontology, even when both commit and suffer the same act. This is even more reason to pry into the form of the subject associated with terror, the unravellings of which by many avowed friends often reinstate its constitutive logic.

21 Nadeem Aslam has come of age along with other South Asian writers who can hold the murder and the love together, knowing that the crisis we face is not limited to the liberal frame of the private world and its private anguishes with unwanted political intrusions, and that the phantasmagoria of the world out there is already given to us in the worlds we inhabit in reality or fantasy. At least he is aware that we have to traverse these worlds in our own ways, not serve another's understanding of what they are. Sometimes we have no choice but to navigate these spaces differently, because the margins of the colony and the postcolony are fundamentally deviant from the logics of space *and* time that hold the centre and to which the centre of these projects, as sad mirror and appendage of the metropole, holds.

22 Boehmer and Morton, *Terror and the Postcolonial*, 6.

28 Radical Praxis or Knowing (at) the Limits of Justice

DENISE FERREIRA DA SILVA

Let me begin with Hegel and Fanon:

> Negroes are enslaved by Europeans and sold to America. Bad as this may be, their lot in their own lands is even worse, since there a slavery quite as absolute exists; for it is the essential principle of slavery, that man has not yet attained a consciousness of his freedom, and consequently sinks down to a mere Thing – an object of no value.
>
> G.W.F. Hegel[1]

> It needed more than one native to say "We've had enough"; more than one peasant rising crushed, more than one demonstration put down before we could today hold our own, certain in our victory. As for we who have decided to break the back of colonialism, our historic mission is to sanction all revolts, all desperate actions, all those abortive attempts drowned in rivers of blood.
>
> Frantz Fanon[2]

Everyone knows what happened: a young black man was killed by a police officer. Fires broke out in North, East, and South London and in other English cities, from Leicester to Birmingham.[3] Fires broke out in Watts in 1965 and in Los Angeles in 1992, to recall two other occasions. Every time fires followed justice. These urban revolts are always about justice, yet they cannot be comprehended in ethical-political programs informed by historical materialist, sociological, and postmodern descriptions of social subjugation.

For each of these descriptions presupposes the operation of causality, and thus each explains the event in ways that always already resolve its transformative potential back into objectivity, into facts. Knowing at the limits of justice, refusing to resolve the London revolts – and the others that have preceded it and will follow it – into objectivity (either as raw material, or as results of analysis) requires us to abandon warm and familiar intellectual comforts, such as the methods (calculation, classification, measurement, interpretation) that have characterized modern knowledge since the earliest statements on the how (Bacon's instrumentalism) and why (Descartes' formalism) of certain knowledge. Knowing at the limits of justice must start before representation and must also look beyond it. In this way, the Thing enables the subject, the "I," mediating formulations of the object, the other, and the commodity.

Knowing the limits of justice then requires critique as well as something else. It demands an engagement with what is taken for granted in explanations, or rather in the confusion that ensues when explanations of urban revolts rely on our most precious social categories: Was it black London? Then racism explains the revolts. No, no, it was class – class struggle without class consciousness! It was both! Neither! Thinking the limits of justice does, however, require a plan of sorts, a certain procedure, but one not committed to resolving the conditions it exposes into more effective measures, grids, or accounts that can inform pre-emptive actions or preventive mechanisms. Knowing at the limits of justice is both a kind of knowing and a kind of doing; it is a praxis, one that unsettles what has become but offers no guidance for what has yet to become. Knowing the limits of justice, nonetheless, is an ethical-political praxis, one that acknowledges all the effects and implications as well as the presuppositions that inform our accounts of existing with and in one another. Knowing the limits of justice, as an ethico-political praxis, requires onto-epistemological accounts that begin and end with relationality (affectability) – that anticipate what is to be announced. Perhaps they demand a horizon of radical exteriority, where knowing implicates affection, intention, and attention.

Having started with Hegel and Fanon, I will proceed with a discussion of justice. I will begin not with a plea for its realization but with a consideration of its im/possibility. I do not return to what has happened, the facts, for I am not interested in the meaning(s) – the whys and becauses – of the event. Instead, I consider the dissolution of that which is the basis for any and every explanation of any event. I close with some comments on radical praxis. I will not present a program or a project. Forcing out what sustains prevailing approaches to knowing and doing, I contemplate another horizon, one that has been consistently articulated and disavowed in modern thought: that of affectability/relationality.

For Justice

This chapter is animated by the urban revolts in Britain in the summer of 2011, so my examination of justice is restricted by those particular events and by how I choose to respond to them. The exercise here differs little from Derrida's addressing justice as *droit*.[4] What distinguishes my intervention is that I approach justice as a referent of force (as in Derrida's reading of the law) but also of signification (as legality or rights, as Weber and Foucault, respectively, remind us). Since there is not enough space here to go into the details of this distinction – or rather in/distinction – I will resort to Hegel's civil society to situate my thesis, which is that raciality, precisely because it signifies an im/possible relationship, collapses justice (in the name of law and rights) into violence.

Hegel discusses law enforcement and the administration of justice in the third section of his *Philosophy of Right*.[5] "Civil Society" is where, in his terminology, individuality (which is pure universality in Abstract Rights) finds itself in the realm of the particular just before returning to (a now) True universality in Ethical Life (i.e., the State). When he discusses civil society as the space of differences, and locates there both the police and the administration of justice, Hegel addresses justice (the courts) without requiring that it refer back to a transcendental law. Fully circumscribed in the region of morality, and mediating between the natural/moral ties of the Family and the "transcendental" formal/ethical bounds of the State, Justice – although thoroughly universal – remains in the contingent sphere of Civil Society, the stage of difference. Here, in the juridic, economic, and symbolic domains of Civil Society, is where I find the limits of justice. Limits, not in the sense that Justice cannot go beyond them, but in the sense that it *is/becomes in* them. Justice, when addressed in the registers of the economic and the juridic (in Civil Society), is immanent (it remains within), and as such it is inherently limited and limiting of the relationships it comprehends.

Perhaps it has been so difficult to discuss the limits of justice – economic, juridic, and symbolic – because neither theorists of the social, nor theorists of law, nor theorists of morality seem interested in situating the economic, legal, or moral subject. These figurings of the modern subject retain, as Foucault notes, a transcendental quality, even when approached through biopolitical and disciplinary apparatuses. That is, in each figuring, the subject retains the ontological attributes (interiority/historicity) that ensure that it is inscribed as a thing of reason (of formal understanding or self-unfolding spirit) with self-determination.

To Be Announced

How are we to unsettle this neat assemblage of the theatre of difference, and its stages of Freedom and Necessity? I think it requires a return to The Thing – that is, to Hegel's "object of no value." I cannot even begin to describe the treasures The Thing hides. Let me just say that The Thing hosts the possibility of violence, of that which threatens to undo, because as a mediator, it necessarily unsettles the limits of justice. Remember that social scientific knowledge populated Hegel's stage of difference with objects of *necessitas*, inscribing bodies and territories with formal abstractions that have resisted even the Hegelian resolution of difference as a temporary moment of the trajectory of spirit. *Necessitas* remains in the categories deployed by the knowledge of the human without dissolving self-determination as the privileged onto-epistemological attribute of certain human beings – those whose white bodies locate their origins in the parts of the European space where Hegel found inscriptions of realized spirit. By their nature, as effects of comparison – that is, measurement and classification – social categories pair *self-determined and affectable (outer-determined) subjects*. In doing so, however, those categories do not erase The Thing's promises. For categories hold violence in the subjects of affectability produced by the biopolitical and disciplinary apparatuses that deploy them – in the black other, the female other, the sexual other, in which other possibilities also hide.

Let me try to expose these apparatuses through a three-way conversation about slavery, blackness, and violence between Saidiya Hartman, Lindon Barrett, and Fred Moten. My goal in this invented exchange is to follow violence to find the gifts of The Thing, the "object of no value" that Hegel reads in blackness (of the African Native and the Slave). In *Scenes of Subjection*, Saidiya Hartman refuses to recount the violent scenes – in particular the beating of Fredrick Douglass's Aunt Hester – that have marked the lives of slaves in the colonial and post-colonial United States (and elsewhere in the Americas, for that matter). This refusal to rehearse what she calls the "spectacle of black suffering" is a political-intellectual gesture that, rather than disavowing them, urges us to consider how accounts of suffering do the work of racial subjugation. Here, however, I am interested in other aspects of this de-cision not to recount. I am interested in racial violence as a figuring of excess – which is what justifies otherwise unacceptable events, such as police shooting unarmed persons.[6]

My thesis is that Aunt Hester's black body exhibits the equation "Value + Excess = Racial other", but only in the absence (in representa-tion) of that other figuring of the sexual hosted by the female body. For her body only enters accounts of racial violence as always already in the juridical, economic, and ethical register of Coloniality-Patriarchy-Slavery – that is, in accounts of domination, in bondage, marriage, and rape. My intuition here is that the sexual of the female body refers to a power other than the sovereign's, as Fanon describes in his account of the colonial as the scene of violence and as Bataille describes in his ac-count of erotic expenditure – that power being the sexual that is beyond and before the re/productive capabilities of the fe/male native/slave body.[7] Where it is always already defined in a given – economic and symbolic – productive regime: as object, other, or commodity.

In support of this intuition, I turn to two other black radical intellec-tuals who have confronted blackness as a figuring of value and excess. In Moten and Barrett I find an in/articulation of the radical potential that the juridico-economic figure of the native/enslaved female affords, namely, her sexual body, which insists on signifying Otherwise – The Thing, the mediator, that third (virtual) particle that troubles represen-tation. This radical potential resides precisely in how this excess points to female desire, that which threatens colonial and national juridico-economic goals and has no place in the onto-epistemological grammar that governs post-Enlightenment accounts of existence.

To frame racial violence with the equation "Labouring black body = Value + Excess" is to begin by acknowledging the relationship – as in the "I" and the "other(s)" – that is at the centre of accounts of juridico-political power with regard to the two juridico-politico structures – colony and the polity – that European philosophers developed beginning in the eighteenth century. In these earlier accounts – in Locke and Hobbes, for instance – the human as individual treats this political entity as a thing with reason; later, after Hegel writes reason back into the scene of representation, the human as subject is comprehended as also a product of reason. This is a consequence of Kant's version of rea-son as the transcendental mediator of experience, in both knowledge and morality. But the writing of racial difference to capture universal reason's workings on the human (body and mind) is enabled by yet another move: that which distinguishes a particular mode of being human, the one found in post-Enlightenment Europe (i.e., self-determination), becomes the realization of sovereign reason's design. It is precisely this move that injects Hartman's, Barrett's, Moten's, and Fanon's writings on racial violence into the equation "Black body = Value + Excess".

Let me begin with "Excess = Value + Violence". In his reading of Billie Holiday's *Lady Sings the Blues*, Barrett finds a relationship between the racial "I" and the racial "Other," signified by the white steps of one of the houses Holiday cleaned.[8] With Marx and Baudrillard, and guided by Holiday's overpricing of her non-valued labour (here The Thing works by checking exchange value), Barrett decomposes the differential dimension that the notion of value both presupposes and communicates. Much like Fanon, he disregards the dialectic, perhaps in search of the cracks in an otherwise seemingly stable power configuration. He splits value into "form" and "force" to sustain his notion of "seeing double." In doing so, while acknowledging the hierarchy governing the relationship, he refuses to vanquish blackness by reading "no value" solely as negation. According to Barrett, negotiation – Holiday's exacting of her excess – is possible because the boundary, signified by the white steps that she alone can clean adequately, keeps the "inside" (the white housewife) and the "outside" (the black cleaning lady) in full view of each other ... exposed.

Yet this same move dissolves excess, for the violence of value "as force" is suspended in the proximity it also refigures. The workings of value "as form" and "as force" in racial subjugation, in both the colonial and the national moments of US history, are re-presented in precisely the scenes of subjection that Hartman refuses to retell. For Barrett, however, these figurations of violence do more than spectacularize black suffering because the boundaries they seek to protect, by ex-posing, also refer to the proximity that value (im)poses. I will not follow further Barrett's exposition of the duality of value here; I am more interested in how his working through of this distinction between "value as form" and "value as force" dissolves the excess in the form of value he names – namely, force or violence, which is both more and less than value – into a difference that is of value in itself. My interest is in how, when value becomes both "force" and "form," the very force that destabilizes the form becomes excess – much like sexual desire, which is not represented by the female slave body or the female maid body. This pre-posed excess – that is, the violence that is desire itself and the desire that is violence, that is not subjected to the rules of colonial and patriarchal (re)production – seems to have no place in Fanon's writings or in later writings on colonial and racial subjugation.

For even in works that refuse the liberal version of racial domination (the logic of exclusion) and that describe the scene of violence, the black body is given to representation; it is already the body of violence, the body of the slave, the body of the maid, the body of the lynched black child, female or male. It is always already the black and violated/violent person, victim of the also already valued/protected white Other – that is, a body that can only signify the juridico-economic architectures of slavery, patriarchy, and capitalism. In sum, my point is: The excess that is the never exposed violence, the violence resolved in law, the state, contained in Hegel's civil society, enters into the very constitution of the political categories themselves, in blackness and whiteness, the maid and the housewife, as in the native and the settler.

What if, dismissing value and entertaining excess – that which in figurings of The Thing (object, commodity, or the Other) has "no value" – one stayed with violence? What account of racial subjugation and black response would emerge from this? Recall that here we are presupposing Fanon's description of the colonial space as a product of a particular kind of juridico-economic violence. The distinction between the native's position and the settler's refers to a valuation, which is always already excess. Fanon captures this when he recalls that this distinction is named through the articulation of extreme moral signifiers, namely good and evil, an articulation that allows for only one way to reconfigure the colonial space – that is, is a kind of violence akin to Benjamin's divine violence (the proper figuring of sovereignty?). That being so, I contend that Hartman and Barrett are counter-intuitively tapping into a potential venue for a post-Fanonian plan, a radical praxis, when each, respectively, refuses to write violence onto the racial table so that "black" means suffering and "white" means freedom, or so that "black" means non-value and "white" means value. Moving farther up the road they open, one could with Fanon foreground the violence that constitutes the colonial space in order to set up the explosion of the subject of colonial violence that would enable the obliteration of the settler and his town and the becoming of the "new man." But that would not take us far, because even here, as in Benjamin's critique of violence and in Bataille's writing of the erotic, the subject who emerges through revolutionary and emancipatory excess would refigure what is represented by the male body and the account of desire it signifies: the nation to become, the native as a man, an autonomous collective, alone is liberated. Moving beyond this point, away from self-determination and its limits, in pursuit of a figuring of the sexual (as power) that is hidden in the writing of the female as other, another path would begin with an evocation of the body as excess, the body as a figuring of an unrepresentable/unregulated desire, the body that remains outside the legal-moral order and outside economic and symbolic production – The Thing.

I can anticipate doubts regarding the validity of reading the body in the space of self-determination, the domain the mind has monopolized in modern representation. But I am interested in a frame of intervention that *appreciates* the body as a referent of The Thing, without (outside) modern signification, that is, a referent that exposes precisely that which Hegel's account of sovereign reason has protected in interiority – namely, desire. To be sure, by evoking the body of excess, I do no more than track its disavowal, to indicate how, when desire threatens to become a descriptor of the Other as the subject, the racial subaltern subject – the affectable I – it is immediately returned to the proper place, to the white side of value, from which location authorized violence is meted out in the name of regulated desire.

Not surprisingly, the black subject of violence – as expressed in official accounts of the 2011 revolts – troubles radical black thinking because the tools of racial knowledge, the analytics of raciality, already resolve unauthorized black male violence as pathology, as an expression of Kant's affect, the actualization of the non-self-regulated desire of the black Other. Black radical thinking, I gather, will only be able to dissolve this very consistent effect of raciality when, inhabiting the limits of justice, it begins and stays with excess and embraces violence as a referent of an Other desire, an Other figuration of existence, or an Other mode of being human in the world.

In *In the Break*, Moten does not evoke Fanon as the point of departure for his thinking; he does, however, stay with violence, and he contemplates the emancipatory gifts hidden in the inaccessible excess and in that which it forces into re-presentation without signifying, without value, a sound that is an uncomprehensible expression of affect.[9] Refusing to repeat Hartman's gesture, Moten reproduces Fredrick Douglass's account of the beating of Aunt Hester. Instead of moving to a commentary on her violated black body – which would return violence to the white perpetrator and to the post-Enlightenment political (juridic, economic, ethical) scene, he takes up her utterance, her scream, an expression that is not a response. This evocation of aurality, hovering above the letter and the phoneme, constitutes an acknowledgment of excess that avoids the two writings of racial violence – namely, the one that stays with the account that is solely black, as in Hartman's view of depictions of black suffering, and the one that writes it as always already involving black and white, the latter being the perpetrator, as in Barrett's discussion of value.

Moten reproduces neither. Instead of attending to the violated black body in the regimen of signification of white violence, he listens for past and contemporary reverberations of Aunt Hester's screams. In Douglass's mother-like figure, he traces the moment of emergence of the subject of blackness in resistance, a moment that is a response to torture that does not reduce itself to word – perhaps because doing so would legitimize the power relationship. That is, a plea, a begging, would reinstitute the master's place of power, which Hartman suggests is what rehearsals of black suffering always do. Barrett indicates that here resides, if not black emancipation, at least the possibility of negotiation. If the black subject emerges in a response that is a refusal of representation – without the letter and its signification, before writing yet not in speech – the possibility opens that violence can be contemplated without being immediately resolved in already given blackness and whiteness. The exposure of racial violence might then open up to considerations of the Otherwise of excess, of the no-value of The Thing.

For Moten, becoming black in the exposure of excess, in the refusal to signify in letter and phoneme, is the "resistance of the object." For the body of excess does not need the other to signify; the body of violence is a referent of excess, of that which is constitutive of a particular kind of colonial space, as Fanon describes to us – of that which may be a better name for justice, because it arises from an other account of justice. More importantly, the scream, the expression/exposure without signification – that is, outside signification under the rule of pure reason and its tools (the pure intuitions and categories of the understanding) – makes one wonder. For there is always the possibility that in response to a touch, even one with maximum force, there is no way to state whether the scream refigures pleasure or pain. In that undecidable lies the in/distinction of violence/desire, the one that the body always signifies; and for that reason, modern philosophers have had to work hard to keep it at bay, to deny the body any determining ontological or epistemological role. Tamed, apprehended as a signifier of exteriority, the body in modern Western thought has consistently referred to other ways of existing as human beings, of that which exceeds and hence threatens the accounts of law and morality authorized by sovereign reason. Here I am attending to Moten's invitation to rescue the body from spatiality-exteriority, the signifying moment in which modern philosophy has imprisoned it, but I do so by returning to the very figure, the colonial (native/slave) female, through which he locates the emergence of resisting black su(o)bject – as a referent of The Thing, with no value (not in knowledge, morality, or exchange). The Thing resists as excess.

Conclusion

Whatever a radical praxis may open, following in the steps of black radical thought, getting it/there will take an engagement with The Thing as excess/the abyss. Of course, one could stay with Fanon and hope that a "new man," a new human, will appear as a consequence. As I have said, however, I am not interested in the end point, in grounds, bases, or measures. My concern here is with excess, as exemplified by free radicals, those unpaired electrons that threaten to destroy the very bodies they help constitute. My concern, that is, is with a radical praxis that mimics free radicals – with urban revolts that neither fear nor desire reciprocity, that precisely signify oblivion, an oblivion resolved through racial violence when the state judges/executes without moral or legal justification.

Free radicals, as referents of the excess that always already justifies (renders just) racial violence – are that other possibility, which The Thing, between the I and its objects, others, and commodities, holds and hosts. How is one to recuperate excess? By focusing on the relationship exposed when The Thing is addressed as a mediator and not as a measure. The Thing is no-thing, Hegel tells us. It has no value. Like a virtual particle – without space-time – The Thing signifies the productive immediately/instantaneously registered relationships, violent and otherwise, that constitute our existence. Now this particular statement is kind of out there, but it has company. For many years now, postclassical physics has been challenging us to take relationality and affectability seriously. The major statement in quantum physics, Heisenberg's uncertainty principle, demands a new positioning not only by physicists but also by philosophers. Both the uncertainty principle (i.e., that at subatomic levels, things fail to behave as objects of classical knowledge and insist on behaving in erratic ways) and Schrödinger's wave function collapse theory (i.e., all possibilities are open until measurement is taken) have brought measurement into crisis, along with other producers of value, such as calculation and classification.[10] This undermines prediction, the possibilities celebrated in Bacon's instrumentalist view of knowledge and certainty, which the Cartesian subject of knowledge could rely on because nature itself came to depend on his ability to know it objectively.

A radical praxis would stay with The Thing, releasing free radicals and, by unsettling it – through affect, intention, and attention – expose the relationship, that is, knowledge itself and its effects. Again, I do not pretend to anticipate the many implications of this modality of intervention. I can, however, suggest two possible starting points. First, such radical praxis could begin, as I have done, by assuming that the frame of intervention or detection, the apparatus deployed in the knowledge of human affairs, produces the very results those affairs acquire. Thus, when the tools of racial knowledge are deployed to explain events such as London's recent revolts, they both produce and reproduce the writing of the those living in these urban territories as subjects of violence. However, and this is a crucial point, what knowledge produces, the value it attributes to The Thing to transform it into an object, an Other, or a commodity (as signifier of social relations), is already less and more than everything. It is more or less than any particular thing, more or less than any and every possibility of becoming the "other" indexes. For, because also effects of The Thing, that resists in knowledge, the object, the other, and the commodity are always already excess ... threatening abyss, that is the end of meaning or order or law.

Second, with regard to The Thing, and staying with violence, a radical praxis could not be oblivious to anything – neither to what is already known (in knowledge) nor to what can never be (the virtual particles that constitute the possibility of that which becomes). Intending, affecting/ed, attentive, and attending both to the effects of knowledge and to the possibilities it postpones, the ethical promise that energizes this knowing as a radical praxis refers to that point after attention but before abstraction – where Kant locates confused and unclear impressions. That abstraction will finally resolve itself in concepts (or categories), and reflection will return to the subject of knowledge and to the world itself. Let me end here, at this threshold, before this possible beginning of knowing at the limits of justice.

NOTES

A number of texts, and many conversations, hide in every line and sentence in this text. More particularly, I would like to thank those who read, listened to, and commented on the different versions of this paper

presented at Reading the Damned 50 Years Later (University of Naples
L'Orientale, Naples, 19–20 May 2011); the Centre for Social and Political Thought Research Seminar Series (University of Sussex, Brighton,
19 October 2011); the Radical Politics and Rights Conference (Nùcleo de
Direitos Humanos, Pontófice Universidade Católica, Rio de Janeiro, 10–11
April 2012); and the "Violence in a Far Country: Women Scholars of Colour
Theorize Terror" workshop (OISE, University of Toronto, 18 May 2012), in
particular to Laura Kwak for her comments. An expanded version of this
argument was published in *Social Text* 31 (1–114) (Spring 2013).

1 Hegel, *The Philosophy of History*, 113.
2 Fanon, *The Wretched of the Earth*, 207.
3 The revolts lasted from 6 to 10 August 2011. After a protest in Tottenham
   for the killing of Mark Duggan by a police officer, on 4 August, they
   surged through several London boroughs (especially in east, north, and
   south London) as well as cities like Birmingham, Bristol, Liverpool, and
   Leicester. For coverage of the events and related developments, visit "UK
   Riots 2011" at http://www.guardian.co.uk/uk/london-riots.
4 Derrida, "Force of Law," in *Deconstruction and the Possibility of Justice*, 5–6.
5 Hegel, *Philosophy of Right*, 70.
6 Hartman, *Scenes of Subjection*, 3.
7 Bataille, *The Accursed Share*.
8 Barrett, *Blackness and Value*.
9 Moten, *In the Break*.
10 There are many popular and specialized books and articles on particle
   physics. Since the 1920s, this reconfiguration of physics has animated even
   more complex and counter-intuitive statements than Heisenberg's uncertainty principle. In this paper, I am drawing from what is known as the
   Copenhagen Interpretation of quantum mechanics, which has been identified with Niels Bohr, Werner Heisenberg, Wolfgang Pauli, and Max Born. It
   should be noted that this reference to physics is not recourse to the authority of science, but is actually a reference to particle physics as a domain of
   knowledge, in which the practitioners have been forced to renounce claims
   to any authority. That is, I am more interested in the philosophical open-
   ings that their acknowledgment of the impossibility of certainty provides,
   in particular in the possibility of dismantling Kant's account of knowledge,
   which is still the basis of most social scientific, legal, and commonsense
   views of the advancement of knowledge. See, for instance, Heisenberg,
   Physics and Beyond; Heisenberg, "The Physical Content," in *Quantum
   Theory and Measurement*, ed. Wheeler and Zurek; Bohr, *Atomic Physics and
   Human Knowledge*; and Born, *Natural Philosophy of Cause and Chance*.

29 Unsewing My Lips, Breathing My Voice: The Spoken and Unspoken Truth of Transnational Violence

OMEIMA SUKKARIEH

I am the tears so fragile,
they fall from the sky.
My lips sewn together
with the thread of life.
My hands like leaves,
they shake when it blows.
And my heart it hurts
when there is nowhere to go.
I am the tap that will not stop dripping,
I am the air that cannot be cleared.
I feel the fire that will rage on endlessly.
Is there anything in the world
that will allow me to be real?[1]

I approached transnational violence recently after noticing it was walking around like a zombie and asked it what it was doing. It told me that it was combating stress and its negative effects through tactical breathing and that in law enforcement and military training over the years it was taught controlled breathing, combat breathing, to the point where it feels like it's on autopilot, doing it without thinking. When I asked why it told me that they were combat breathing all the time and only sometimes because it felt like dangerous criminals who were heavily armed were trying to kill it and they wanted to be able to be calm and rational when killing someone or imposing terror on them and that being in combat breathing was not only safe for them but safe for the world and that when they are feeling stress, anxiety or panic this is what they do but they have no choice. When I asked who was trying to kill it, they simply said the walking dead and peace activists.[2]

Breathe in through your nose for a count of four; hold your breath for a count of four (one bomb, two bomb, three bomb, four); exhale through your mouth for a count of four; hold your breath for a count of four (one bullet, two bullet, three bullet, four), and then restart the cycle. Breathe deeply and methodically – completely filling and emptying your lungs during each cycle.

Funnily enough transnational violence told me that when taking a deep breath and when exhaling, I should picture a leaf, slowly, slowly, floating down, lower, and lower until it gently stops and floats and just softly hovers at the height of my belly button. The gentle floating image is intended to enhance the relaxation effects of the deep breath and that since this is usually done initially with your eyes closed, it should only be done in a safe environment. However, *with practice and mastery it can be done quickly, with your eyes open and while maintaining situational awareness.*[3]

Who is the perpetrator? Who is victim? Who is combat breathing and who is not?

Are you dying?
I think I am.
How do you know?
I don't know.
Well, do you feel?
Only in my sleep.
Do you cry?
Only with my eyes.
Do you laugh?
Only with my mouth.
Do you breathe?
Only without my will.
Do you love?
With all my heart.
Then why do you think you're dying?
Because I hate feeling and crying and laughing and breathing and loving.
How do you hate?
Only with my mind.
Then your mind is still working?
Only to whisper in my ears to kiss death.

And do you?
I have this bitter sweet taste in my mouth sometimes, but I don't know.
Could that be life?
Perhaps.
Could that be love?
Perhaps.
But it could be death?
Yes.[4]

Israel, Palestine, the Gaza Flotilla, forged passports, Right of Return, Lebanon, cluster bombs, people smuggling, boat people, terrorism, Australia, Afghanistan, Iraq, one breath, two breaths, three breaths, four.

Transnational state violence effortlessly crosses borders. It is disguised and camouflaged in the blood of propaganda and enslavement of the human soul through nationalist music, development of penal and legal institutions dividing people into the free and imprisoned, the citizen, the asylum seeker, the stateless and the refugee. Detention centres, prison cells, surveillance streets, all fill up with wasted human potential.

What are we breathing when the air is thick with the stench of blood and hate? Whose hands are dirty and who gets to wash them? I ask Transnational Violence who does he think he is and I get only silence!

Then it tells me in a calm voice ...
I could swear someone buried me alive the other day.
"Oumi! Oumi!"
I cried as hard as I could ...
"Mother! Help me Mother! It is getting dark and the sun is fading along with the beats of my heart! Oumi!"
As it got darker I could feel my ribs dislodge slowly from my spine.
It was so painful that my voiceless cries became almost as extinct as the colourful corroborees and rituals of past times.
I am being tortured by the stains of my own flesh and blood.
I am being suffocated in this dark deep hole by the conversations my sweat and tears are having with my tortured soul.
I can't breathe!
Why are you laughing up there ... you who carry the spades and shovels?
Are you laughing at me because I handed them to you?
Why are you holding part of my heart?
Is that the only part that still works?
"Oumi! Oumi!"

I cried as hard as I could …
"Mother! They stole my good heart! They stole the stars in the sky and hid them
behind the disappearing moon and then they stole my heart! Oumi! Oumi!"
Silence!
I must be going mad … am I dead?
Is that why no-one can hear me?
"Tell me before I lay my head to rest while my soul begins its new journey …
Tell me please!"
"Are we all just dispensable human beings just waiting for the day when
we cease to be …?"[5]

I am the state of Israel who has no respect for international borders and states. I am the state of Israel who can go into international waters in the Mediterranean Sea and kill people with environmentally friendly code names like Operation Sea Breeze and Operation Sky Winds.[6] I am threatened by humanitarian aid, medical supplies and women and children who get in my way.

What about the 718 people from 37 countries on board the Flotilla and the 9 people you killed and the many more injured on the Mavi Marmara?[7]

What about the Australian 20-year-old Ahmed Talib who you shot in the leg and forced him to follow his own trail of blood?[8]

An Australian with a name like that? Who cares?

"I looked down and my legs were drowning in blood. I was getting weaker; it was difficult to breathe."[9]

Unmask yourself, Transnational State Violence, so we can see your face?

I am the state of Israel who couldn't care less if a man like Anwar Khalil Balusha suffers from mental health problems after having his five daughters killed during a routine midnight bombing.[10]

Remember, I am the same Israel who laughed at how he and neighbours desperately tried to rescue those five girls with their hands from the rubble of their destroyed home until the sound of their terrifying screams got lower and eventually stopped.

I can counterfeit your passports and the passports of your German, Irish, and French friends, and have them cleared at airports while you wait in line randomly being searched for bombs like a common Arab and by the time you leave the airport I have already used your passport to assassinate who I deem an enemy.[11]

I can enter your homeland and the homeland of your ancestors and in the name of defending myself against terrorism, for 34 days I can kill unabated.[12] Your family, your friends, your neighbours and your hopes and dreams for a better future for your children and theirs are now dead and there is nothing you can do about it because I am transnational violence.

> *... If you had contemplated the victim's face*
> *And thought it through, you would have remembered your mother in the*
> *Gas chamber, you would have been freed from the reason for your rifle*
> *And you would have changed your mind: this is not the way*
> *To find one's identity again.[13]*

It is eight years ago, 14 August 2006, that the UN brokered a cease-fire[14] but after killing almost 1,500 people and making over a million displaced and planting the seeds of cluster bombs to kill Lebanon's future growth and fill the Lebanese body with cancerous diseases, torment, and despair. The seeds of fear and hate keep me going. Transnational violence loves the sound of mothers mourning over their children's nameless body bags.

Did you not learn from your ancestors' horrors and the imposed transnational violence that exterminated them and left scarred generations to come? Are you combat breathing and wanting others to combat breathe also so you don't walk dead alone?

> "I have travelled far" it whispers in my ear.
> "Where?"
> "Almost to the end of the world."

A White Paper, "Transnational Terrorism: The Threat to Australia," was publicly launched by the Minister for Foreign Affairs some few years ago. The paper outlines the Australian government's intention to keep the Australian public fully informed of significant changes to Australia's security environment and the measures being taken by the government to protect Australia's interests, arguing that Australia faces a serious threat from transnational extremist-Muslim terrorism. We are asked to consult the government's online travel advisory service for specific travel advice called "smartraveller." Noting that Australia is at the forefront of international efforts to combat the new terrorist threat, the White Paper provides details of what Australia is doing internationally in our name.[15]

> *Our losses: between two and eight martyrs each day.*
> *And ten wounded.*

And twenty homes.
And fifty olive trees...
Added to this the structural flaw that
Will arrive at the poem, the play, and the unfinished canvas.[16]

Isn't it time we were informed of the truth of what you are doing in our name? How can you name me the terrorist and then say my name in the name of naming the terrorists in my name? How many martyrs are being killed in my name in the name of naming the terrorists by someone else's name? How many homes have you helped destroy or have others destroyed in your name? Australia, are you TSV? Are you still counting your soldiers dead in my name? Are they still counting theirs in yours?

Don't throw your responsibilities to the world! Don't throw it on me!
Just travel smart!
"You mean like you do TSV?"
"Yes, only better!"
"How?"
"Combat breathing, just go in, shoot to kill, kill and but do it while you combat breathing. Even if you don't use bullets, use words, use fear campaigns."
"Really? Like what?"
"Like 'Stop the Boats'."[17]

But if you stop the boats we can't hear the stories of refugees and of people you have helped leave their homeland. We can't hear the stories of the status of refugees and displaced peoples who die when legally stateless and who die on boats coming in search of a new homeland. If we stop the boats we will only hear the screams of 353 women, children and men who drowned almost ten years ago.[18] They are still screaming. What provoked people was that there were no expressions of sympathy about that tragedy. What of others who have died since the Australian Border Protection laws came in? What about the cries of the baby who was born on the first boat you stopped in the name of the Australian Navy who died because you stopped the boat for seven days? Why was this baby's cry silenced by you and your media army? Why was this baby not allowed even to breathe, let alone to combat breathe!

I don't know how long I can last. I used to think I was a dead woman walking, but I don't think that the walking dead cry.

I belong to nowhere, nothing, no one. No home, no heart, no … no. Perhaps my friend was right. Perhaps it is best to belong to nowhere and no one, but rather to not belong is to be free.

> Accept you for who you are.
> But what if I don't know who I am?
> *Find yourself.*
> Where?
> *Deep in your soul.*
> But where do I find that?
> *Just start looking and your Self will find you.*
> But what if I don't like my Self when I find it or it finds me?
> *Then it's not you.*[19]

An amazing young Afghan man, a role model for Australia and for Afghanistan, asks me questions in your name that I cannot answer:

If there are more guns in Afghanistan than we can think of, then why go with more? Why not go with doctors? Where is there time for peace with more warfare? What have you done in the 3,231 days of the so-called war that has been running? The war on Afghanistan has been running for 8 years 10 months 5 days.[20] Did anyone win? How are my grandparents? Did you see my cousins playing in the streets singing happy songs with smiles on their faces? Why don't you spend your billions on imposing less violence on them and better health care on us?

Do you care how much this war has cost in dollars and limbs and litres of blood or are you too busy patting the back of your TSV brothers because this all sounds like B.S to M.E? Why isn't there a "stop the TSVs" campaign? Because if you stop TSVs you could "stop the boats" with no screaming crying babies wishing they were combat breathing instead of being in combat.

Why are you there? Have you ever considered leaving it to see how it survived on its own without the combat breathing?

> Why are you crying so much?
> *Because I have lost happiness.*
> Where?
> *Across the sea somewhere.*
> Then why don't you go find it?
> *Because I can't swim.*
> Does happiness know that you're looking for it?

I don't know, but it threw me in the water in the first place and left me to drown.
Then why do you want to find it?
Because my sorrow is lonely without it.[21]

If you want me to be a smart traveller then stop travelling with me. Let me come back from my own travels narrating the stories of courage and hope of the smiling people who want to give you everything they have left with their smiling faces not to come here combat breathing like a young Afghan girl, a victim of state violence and transnational state violence and in a state of combat breathing herself, writing a poem of her journey to Australia finding herself combat breathing here in a country she was prepared to call home while you were overstaying your welcome in hers.

Faces walk by like models changing clothes
faces appear like time ticking off ...
Seconds pass like years and nights
My body is pilling like a potato on a grill
My heart is dripping like a sponge on a dish...
This was a place I called home
A place where I belonged
I begin my journey with pride
I made an oath for a new beginning
To learn to live like anybody else
been positive and thought of a wish ...
I've been shocked from my dream
I've waken and driven like a river
I feel nothing but pain
I don't feel my soul nor do I feel if am alive or am dead
I can walk on streets, I can smile
My fear for people my fear for hope has made
My mind burn with oil ...
Has made my soul be used to the daily torture like a daily routine
I'm not in piece and nor I belong here again
Am sure am lost between soul and dreams
Why do words play around
Why do faces seem to change like a serial on my daily shows
Judged by looks, judged by culture
Oh boy, help me through my journey
Don't let me shed a tear today
Don't let me finish my breath with tears of pain

Don't let it burn me
I want to reach my destination; I want to make a wish.[22]

Habiba Roshan, like me, writes poetry not to speak on behalf of Palestinians or Tamil or Afghan or Lebanese, or anybody, but to make meaning out of the brutalizing effects of the racialized politics so rampant in the world today.

Habiba makes wishes every day. She makes wishes like I make wishes. Wishes that we will not see or hear of a baby executed with single bullets by snipers while still in the arms of their mothers and parents gunned down as they break a curfew just to go and collect their children's remains, and of families who have to dig through piles of rubble and the stench of hell to find peace in death, to live in a country where not only are we not being affected by you, transnational violence, but that nobody is affected and that one day you and us, us and them, start breathing again, without combat.

Laughter smiles
at despair like a clown with no colour …
Tears whisper
soft words of love
while drowning the heaven
where it has crept from.[23]

We wish that we could change Azmi Bishara's "inequitable distribution of sorrow" where compassion is not contingent on the colour of people's skins where compassion has become a racializing and racialized concept as a result of transnational violence.[24]

In 2006, with a group of helpers in less than three days we made 450 body bags and lined them up in Martin Place with a message that death is not about national identity but about humanity and the desperate cry in a city of the walking dead for people to breathe long enough to have compassion for the sake of having compassion.[25]

NOTES

1 Sukkarieh, "So Fragile."
2 "Combat Breathing," accessed 10 January 2014 at http://www.behindthe blueline.ca/blog/blueline/2009/01/21/combat-breathing.

3 Asken, "The Adrenaline Dump."

4 Sukkarieh, "Untitled."

5 Sukkarieh, "I Cried As Hard As I Could."

6 "Gaza Flotilla Raid," accessed 10 January 2014 at http://en.wikipedia.org/wiki/Gaza_flotilla_raid.

7 Ibid.

8 McGeough, "Australian Student."

9 McGeough, "Australian Student."

10 "OPT: LIFE Partners to Provide a New Home for Gaza Family That Lost 5 Daughters," 15 May 2009, accessed 10 January 2014 at http://www.reliefweb.int/rw/rwb.nsf/db900sid/MUMA-7S46EP?OpenDocument; Musthak Ahmed and Fahad Ansari, "Gaza in the Days after the 22 Day War," 2009, accessed 10 January 2014 at http://www.ihrc.org.uk/file/9781903718599.pdf.

11 Gumuchian, "Ireland Tells Israel."

12 "2006 Lebanon War," http://en.wikipedia.org/wiki/2006_Lebanon_War.

13 From Mahmoud Darwish, "Under Siege," accessed 10 January 2014 at http://www.poemhunter.com.

14 "2006 Lebanon War."

15 "Transnational Terrorism: The Threat to Australia," 2004, accessed 10 January 2014 at http://www.dfat.gov.au/publications/terrorism/introduction.html.

16 From Mahmoud Darwish, "Under Siege."

17 http://www.theage.com.au/federal-election/abbotts-trip-to-fruit-shop-goes-pearshaped-20100720-10iux.html

18 Hutton, "Questions Abound."

19 Sukkarieh, "Untitled."

20 Woodhead, "Why Isn't Afghanistan."

21 Sukkarieh, "Untitled."

22 Roshan, "Untitled."

23 Sukkarieh, "The Illusion of Despair."

24 http://www.international.activism.uts.edu.au/conferences/w_violence/transcripts/abood.html.

25 Baker and Humphries, "Bags of Controversy."

30 Mori Cards: The Body Bags Installation

OMEIMA SUKKARIEH

*Postcards from Omeima
Sukkarieh's Body Bags
installation in Martin Place,
 Sydney, 2006*

In Life and Death Every Human Being is Important!

Body bags make the human tragedy and cruel reality of war visible. By making this reality visible we honour human dignity and humanity regardless of national identity. It took many volunteers, many hours to make hundreds of them. It takes less than a minute to KILL that many human beings.

Remember the often forgotten innocent lives of people killed in wars all over the world.

Death and War do not discriminate. People do!

It could be someone you love... Your Mother. Your Father. Your Son. Your Daughter. Your Brother. Your Sister. Your Best Friend ! It could be the Doctor who could save your life!

There are no winners in War!

Speak Up! Speak Out! Every Voice Counts! Every Body Counts!

A special thanks to the Mori Gallery, Information and Cultural Exchange (ICE) and Auburn Community Development Network (ACDN) and to all those who helped make these body bags and believed in the power to depict the truth.

Installation by Omeima Sukkarieh.

300 makeshift body bags covered Martin Place in Sydney on Sunday 27 August, 2006. These images were taken on that day.

Photographed by Fadia Abboud.

Figure 30.1.

In Life and Death Every Human Being is Important!

Body bags make the human tragedy and cruel reality of war visible. By making this reality visible we honour human dignity and humanity regardless of national identity. It took many volunteers, many hours to make hundreds of them. It takes less than a minute to KILL that many human beings.

Remember the often forgotten innocent lives of people killed in wars all over the world.

Death and War do not discriminate. People do!

It could be someone you love…Your Mother. Your Father. Your Son. Your Daughter. Your Brother. Your Sister. Your Best Friend ! It could be the Doctor who could save your life!

There are no winners in War!

Speak Up! Speak Out! Every Voice Counts! Every Body Counts!

A special thanks to the Mori Gallery, Information and Cultural Exchange (ICE) and Auburn Community Development Network (ACDN) and to all those who helped make these body bags and believed in the power to depict the truth.

Installation by Omeima Sukkarieh.

300 makeshift body bags covered Martin Place in Sydney on Sunday 27 August, 2006. These images were taken on that day.

Photographed by Fadia Abboud.

Figure 30.2.

In Life and Death Every Human Being is Important!

Body bags make the human tragedy and cruel reality of war visible. By making this reality visible we honour human dignity and humanity regardless of national identity. It took many volunteers, many hours to make hundreds of them. It takes less than a minute to KILL that many human beings.

Remember the often forgotten innocent lives of people killed in wars all over the world.

Death and War do not discriminate. People do!

It could be someone you love...Your Mother. Your Father. Your Son. Your Daughter. Your Brother. Your Sister. Your Best Friend ! It could be the Doctor who could save your life!

There are no winners in War!

Speak Up! Speak Out! Every Voice Counts! Every Body Counts!

A special thanks to the Mori Gallery, Information and Cultural Exchange (ICE) and Auburn Community Development Network (ACDN) and to all those who helped make these body bags and believed in the power to depict the truth.

Installation by Omeima Sukkarieh.

300 makeshift body bags covered Martin Place in Sydney on Sunday 27 August, 2006. These images were taken on that day.

Photographed by Fadia Abboud.

Figure 30.3.

In Life and Death Every Human Being is Important!

Body bags make the human tragedy and cruel reality of war visible. By making this reality visible we honour human dignity and humanity regardless of national identity. It took many volunteers, many hours to make hundreds of them. It takes less than a minute to KILL that many human beings.

Remember the often forgotten innocent lives of people killed in wars all over the world.

Death and War do not discriminate. People do!

It could be someone you love…Your Mother. Your Father. Your Son. Your Daughter. Your Brother. Your Sister. Your Best Friend ! It could be the Doctor who could save your life!

There are no winners in War!

Speak Up! Speak Out! Every Voice Counts! Every Body Counts!

A special thanks to the Mori Gallery, Information and Cultural Exchange (ICE) and Auburn Community Development Network (ACDN) and to all those who helped make these body bags and believed in the power to depict the truth.

Installation by Omeima Sukkarieh.

300 makeshift body bags covered Martin Place in Sydney on Sunday 27 August, 2006. These images were taken on that day.

Photographed by Fadia Abboud.

Figure 30.4.

Bibliography

Aarons, Kieran. "Cartographies of Capture." *Theory and Event* 16(2) (2013). *Project MUSE.* Accessed 26 March 2014 at http://muse.jhu.edu.

Abbas, Asma. "Damages Inc.: Making the Sublime Matter." *Politics and Culture* 2 (2005). Accessed 26 March 2014 at http://www.politicsandculture. org/2010/08/17/damages-inc-making-the-sublime-matter-asma-abba-2.

– *Liberalism and Human Suffering: Materialist Reflections on Politics, Ethics, and Aesthetics.* New York: Palgrave Macmillan, 2010.

Abdo, Nahla. "Imperialism, the State, and NGOs: Middle Eastern Contexts and Contestations." *Comparative Studies of South Asia* 30(2) (2010): 238–49.

Abraham, Priya. "Crisis Averted." *World.* 23 July 2005, 21.

– "Deadline on Darfur." *World.* 4 September 2004, 24.

– "Deparation of Temple and State." *World.* 29 May 2004, 20–1.

– "Devotion Quotient." *World.* 9 April 2005, 26–7.

– "Evil Teachings." *Charisma.* December 2004, 25–6.

– "Freedom to Conform." *World.* 2–9 July 2005, 24–5.

– "Justice Denied." *World.* 26 November 2005, 24.

– "Lawyered Over." *World.* 19 May 2007, 25–6.

– "Left Behind." *World.* 3 December 2005, 27–8.

– "Out of the Shadows." *World.* 17 July 2004, 29–30.

– "Remember the Persecuted." *Christianity Today.* 13 November 2004, 30–1.

– "Slave-to-Slave." *World.* 29 January 2005, 24–5.

– "Soft on Saudis." *World.* 14 May 2005, 26–7.

– "Spectator to Genocide." *World.* 2 April 2005, 24–6.

– "Uncovering Deeds of Darkness." *World.* 2 December 2006, 34.

– "Wrist Slap." *World.* 19 November 2005, 20–1.

– "Zeal for the Lost." *World.* 19 May 2007, 25–6.

Abraham, Sara. *Labour and the Multiracial Project in the Caribbean.* New York: Lexington Books, 2007.

Abu-Lughod, Lila. "Do Muslim Women Really Need Saving? Anthropological Reflections on Cultural Relativism and Its Others." *American Anthropologist* 104(3) (2002): 783–90.

– "The Muslim Woman: The Power of Images and the Danger of Pity." *Eurozine*, 2006. Accessed 26 March 2014 at http://www.eurozine.com/articles/2006-09-01-abulughod-en.html.

– *Veiled Sentiments: Honor and Poetry in a Bedouin Society*. Berkeley: University of California Press, 1986.

Abu-Odeh, Lama. "Crimes of Honor and the Construction of Gender in Arab Society." In *Women and Sexuality in Muslim Society*, ed. Pinar Ilkkaracan. Istanbul: Women for Women's Human Rights, New Ways, 2000.

ADC (American-Arab Anti-Discrimination Committee). *1991 Report on Anti-Arab Hate Crimes: Political and Hate Violence against Arab-Americans*. Washington: ADC Research Institute, 1992.

Agamben, Giorgio. *Homo Sacer: Sovereign Power and Bare Life*. Trans. Daniel Heller-Roazen. Stanford: Stanford University Press, 1998.

– *State of Exception*. Trans. Kevin Attell. Chicago: University of Chicago Press, 2005.

Agathangelou, Anna M. "Bodies of Desire, Terror, and the War in Eurasia: Impolite Disruptions of (Neo)Liberal Internationalism, Neoconservatism, and the 'New' Imperium." *Millennium – Journal of International Studies* 38(3) (2010): 1–30.

– "Bodies to the Slaughter: Global Racial Reconstructions, Reconstruction, Fanon's Combat Breath, and Wrestling for Life." *Somatechnics* 1(1) (2011): 209–48.

– "Necro-(neo) Colonizations and Economies of Blackness: Of Slaughters, 'Accidents,' 'Disasters' and Captive Flesh." In *International Relations and States of Exception: Margins, Peripheries, and Excluded Bodies*, ed. Sheila Nair and Shampa Biswas. New York: Routledge, 2010.

– "Neoliberal Geopolitical Order and Value: Queerness as a Speculative Economy and Anti-Blackness as Terror." *International Journal of Feminist Politics*. Special issue, "Murderous Inclusion," 15(4) (2013): 453–76.

Agathangelou, Anna M., and L.H.M. Ling. *Transforming World Politics: From Empire to Multiple Worlds*. New York: Routledge, 2009.

Agier, Michel. "Humanity as an Identity and Its Political Effects (A Note on Camps and Humanitarian Government)." *Humanity* 1(1) (2010): 29–45.

Agnes, Flavia. "Women, Marriage, and the Subordination of Rights.' In *Community, Gender, and Violence: Subaltern Studies XI*. 106–37. Delhi: Permanent Black, 2000.

Ahmad, Eqbal. *Terrorism: Theirs and Ours*. New York: Seven Stories Press, 2001.

Ahmed, Musthak, and Fahad Ansari. "Gaza in the Days after the 22 Day War." Accessed 10 January 2014 at http://www.ihrc.org.uk/file/9781903718599.pdf.

Ahmed, Sara. *The Cultural Politics of Emotion.* Edinburgh: Edinburgh University Press, 2004.

– "The Nonperformativity of Antiracism." *Meridians: Feminism, Race, Transnationalism* 7(1) (2006): 104–26.

"Ahmet Türk: Çözümsüzlüğün Sebebi Başbakan'ın Üslubudur" (Ahmet Türk: The Reason for the Deadlock Is Prime Minister's Style). *Radikal,* 22 June 2012. Accesed 9 January 2014 at http://www.radikal.com.tr/Radikal.aspx?aType=RadikalDetayV3&ArticleID=1091957&CategoryID=78&Rdkref=1.

Ahuja, Neel. "Abu Zubaydah and the Caterpillar." *Social Text* 29(1) (2011): 127–49.

Aikman, David. "A Campaign against Cruelty." *Charisma.* April 1997, 94.

– "China's Crackdown." *Charisma.* February 2005, 79.

– "The Crisis in Darfur." *Charisma.* January 2005, 76.

– "Persecutors, Beware." *Charisma.* December 1998, 110.

– "Religious Freedom Matters." *Charisma.* November 2004, 78.

Ajayi-Soyinka, Omofolabo. "The Fashion of Democracy: September 11 and Africa." *Signs: Journal of Women in Culture and Society* 29(2) (2003): 603–7.

Alexander, M. Jacqui. "Transnationalism, Sexuality, and the State: Modernity's Traditions at the Height of Empire." In *Pedagogies of Crossing: Meditations on Feminism, Sexual Politics, Memory, and the Sacred.* Durham: Duke University Press, 2006.

Alexander, M. Jacqui, and Chandra Mohanty. "Introduction: Genealogies, Legacies, Movements." In *Feminist Genealogies, Colonial Legacies, Democratic Futures,* ed. M. Jacqui Alexander and Chandra Mohanty. xiii. London: Routledge, 1997.

Alford, Deann. "Abducted Pastor Pays His Own Ransom on Installment Plan." *Christianity Today.* 23 October 2000, 23.

– "Caught in the Conflict." *World.* 2 October 1999, 45–6.

– "Character Assassination." *Christianity Today.* December 2005, 24.

– "The CIA Myth." *Christianity Today.* January 2006, 58–9.

– "Death Threats Denied." *Christianity Today.* 8 January 2001, 32.

– "Fragile Accord." *Christianity Today.* March 2005, 22.

– "Imprisoned Evangelicals Dispute Accusations of Terrorism." *Christianity Today.* 9 February 1998, 94–5.

– "Massacre Post-Mortem." *World 1999.* 1999, 31–2.

– "Maximum Security." *World.* 27 March 1999, 22–3.

– "Ministry at the Center of Violence." *Christianity Today.* April 2010, 17–20.

– "New Life in a Culture of Death." *Christianity Today*. February 2004, 48–53.
– "A Peacemaker in Power." *Christianity Today*. 21 May 2001, 26–7.
– "The Truth Is Somewhere." *Christianity Today*. September 2006, 20–1.
– "Values Voters." *Christianity Today*. May 2009, 18.
– "Words against Weapons." *Christianity Today*. 2 March 1998, 66–7.
Alfred, Taiaiake. "Colonial Stains on Our Existence." In Cannon and Sunseri, 3–10.
– "My Grandmother, She Raised Me Up Again: A Tribute, to the Memory of Art Tsaqwassupp Thompson." *Celanen: A Journal of Indigenous Governance* 1(1) (2004). Accessed 26 March 2014 at http://web.uvic.ca/igov/research/journal/articles_taiaiake.htm.
Alonso, Ana Maria. "The Effects of Truth: Re-presentations of the Past and the Imagining of Community." *Journal of Historical Sociology* 1(1) (1988): 33–57.
Al-Sayyad, Ayisha A. "'You're What?': Engaging Narratives from Diasporic Muslim Women on Identity and Gay Liberation." In *Islam and Homosexuality*, ed. Samar Habib. Santa Barbara: Praeger, 2010.
Alsultany, Evelyn. *Arabs and Muslims in the Media: Race and Representation after 9/11*. New York: NYU Press, 2012.
American Bar Association. "Turkey's Anti-Terrorism Law: Protecting the Republic or Violating Children's Rights?" 9 June 2009. Accessed 9 January 2014 at http://www.americanbar.org/content/dam/aba/publishing/criminal_justice_section_newsletter/crimjust_juvjust_newsletterjune09_june09_pdfs_turkey.authcheckdam.pdf.
Amidon, Kevin S., and Dan Krier. "On Rereading Klaus Theweleit's Male Fantasies." *Men and Masculinities* 1(4) (2009): 488–96.
Amin-Khan. *Political Islam*, 3–4.
Amnesty International. *Israel/Lebanon: War Crimes without Accountability*. Vol. MDE 02/001/2007, 2007.
– *Israel/Lebanon under Fire: Hizbullah's Attacks on Northern Israel*. Vol. MDE 02/025/2006, 2006.
– "Partners in Crime: Europe's Role in US Renditions." AI Index: EUR 01/008/2006. June 2006. Accessed 26 March 2014 at http://www.amnesty.org/en/library/info/EUR01/008/2006/en.
– Report: "Below the Radar: Secret Flights to Torture and 'Disappearance.'" 51/051/2006. 4 April 2006. Accessed 9 January 2014 at http://amnesty.org/en/library/info/AMR51/051/2006.
Andaiye. "Making Grassroots Women across Race Visible in the Guyanese Resistance of the 1970s and 1980s.' *Macomere* 12(2) (2010). Accessed 26 March 2014 at http://www.macomerejournal.com/issues/012.html.

Anderson, Chris, and Claude Denis. "Urban Native Communities and the Nation: Before and After the Royal Commission on Aborginal Peoples." In Cannon and Sunseri, 59–67.

Anderson, David. "Giving Hope a Chance." *Christianity Today*. January 2005, 21.

Anderson, Pat, and Rex Wild. *Little Children Are Sacred*. Darwin: Government of Northern Territory, 2007.

Andreasson, Stefan. "Orientalism and African Development Studies: The 'Reductive Repetition' Motif in Theories of African Underdevelopment." *Third World Quarterly* 26(6) (2005): 971–86.

Ankara, Anton. "Hindus Continue to Slaughter Muslims." *Christianity Today*. 10 June 2002, 23.

Anzaldúa, Gloria, ed. *Making Soul, Making Face: Haciendo Caras: Creative and Critical Perspectives by Feminists of Color*. San Francisco: Aunt Lute Books, 1990.

Anzaldúa, Gloria, and Cherríe Moraga. *This Bridge Called My Back: Radical Writings by Women of Color*. Watertown: Persephone Press, 1981.

AP. "US Interrogating at Africa's Secret Prisons: CIA, FBI agents Looking for al-Qaida Militants at Notorious Ethiopian Jails." *MSNBC.com*. 3 April 2007. Accessed 9 January 2014 at http://www.msnbc.msn.com/id/17935971.

"Arabs Outside Middle East to Hear Webcasts." *Christianity Today*. 19 February 2001, 28–9.

Arat-Koç, Sedef. "Annexing the Third World Nation State? Attacks on Third World Sovereignty and the New Racism in International Politics." Presented at Canadian Political Science Association Conference, Concordia University, Montreal, 1–3 June 2010.

– "Human Rights Discourse Fails Palestinian Quest for Justice." *Rabble.ca*. 2 February 2009. http://www.rabble.ca/news/human-rights-discourse-fails-palestinian-quest-justice.

Arce, Luz. *The Inferno: A Story of Terror and Survival in Chile*. Trans. S.A. Skar. Madison: University of Wisconsin Press, 2004.

Archibugi, Daniele. "Cosmopolitical Democracy." *New Left Review* 4 (2000): 137–50.

Arendt, Hannah. *The Origins of Totalitarianism*. New York: Harcourt, 1973.

– *On Violence*. New York: Harcourt, Brace and World, 1969.

Arısoy, Murat. "PKK, KCK, BDP İç İçe." *Hürriyet*. 27 December 2011. Accessed 9 January 2014 at http://www.hurriyet.com.tr/gundem/19546462.asp.

Armstrong, S. *Daughters of Afghanistan*. Documentary produced for CBC. Dir. Robin Benger, 2002.

Arnie, Fiona, Kate McGuiness, and Gary Robinson. "In the Best Interests of the Child? Determining the Effects of the Emergency Intervention on Child Safety and Wellbeing." *Law in Context* 27(2) (2010): 42–57.

Arora, Vishal. "Premeditated Mobs." *Christianity Today*. March 2008, 19.

Asad, Talal. *On Suicide Bombing*. New York: Columbia University Press, 2007.

Asken, Michael. "The Adrenaline Dump: It's More Than Just Breathing." Accessed 10 January 2014 at http://www.policeone.com/training/articles/1271860-The-adrenaline-dump-Its-more-than-just-breathing.

Aslam, Nadeem. "Leila in the Wilderness." *Granta* 112 (2010).

Assensoh, A.B., and Yvette M. Alex-Assensoh. "African Immigrants and the Aftermath of September 11: Historical and Political Lessons." *Signs* 29(2) (2003): 611–14.

Avelar, Idelber. "La Práctica de la Tortura y la Historia de la Verdad." In *Pensar en/la Postdictadura*, ed. Nelly Richard and Alberto Moreiras. Santiago: Cuarto Propio, 2001.

Baca, Judy. "Our People Are the Internal Exiles." In *Making Soul, Making Face: Haciendo Caras: Creative and Critical Perspectives by Feminists of Color*, ed. Gloria Anzaldúa. 256–70. San Francisco: Aunt Lute Books, 1990.

Bacchetta, Paola, et al. "Transnational Feminist Practices against War." *Meridians: Feminism, Race, Transnationalism* 2(2) (2002): 302–8.

Badiou, Alain. 2005. *Metapolitics*. Trans. Jason Barker. London: Verso, 2005.

Bailey, R. "The Muslims Are Coming Here!" *United Evangelical Action*. July–August 1990, 4–7.

Baker, B. "Christians Cleared of Blasphemy." *Christianity Today*. April 2001, 31.

– "Unlocking the Heart of Islam." *Charisma*. January 2003, 37–9.

Baker, Jordan, and David Humphries. "Bags of Controversy over Cenotaph Display." 28 August 2008. Accessed 10 January 2014 at http://www.smh.com.au/news/national/bags-of-controversy-over-cenotaph-display/2006/08/27/1156617213478.html.

Bancel, Nicholas, Pascal Blanchard, and Sandrine Lemaire. "False Memory: Torture in Algeria, Past Acts That Haunt France." *Le Monde Diplomatique*, June 2001.

Barnes, Robert. "Supreme Court: Warrants Needed in GPS Tracking." *Washington Post*. 23 January 2012. Accessed 12 May 2012 at http://www.washingtonpost.com/politics/supreme-court-warrants-needed-in-gps-tracking/2012/01/23/gIQAx7qGLQ_story.html.

Barq, Saad Ullah Jan. "Two Women, Two Stories, Two Points of View." 5 February 2011. Accessed 20 May 2011 at www.pkcolumns.com.

Barrett, Lindon. *Blackness and Value: Seeing Double*. Cambridge: Cambridge University Press, 1998.

Barry, Kathleen. *Unmaking War Remaking Men*. North Melbourne: Spinifex Press, 2010.

Bataille, Georges. *The Accursed Share*. Vols. II and III. Trans. Robert Hurley. New York: Zone Books, 1988.

– *The Bataille Reader*. Ed. Fred Botting and Scott Wilson. New York: Wiley-Blackwell, 1997.

Bathla, Sonia. *Women, Democracy, and the Media: Cultural and Political Representations in the Indian Press*. New Delhi: Sage Publications, 1998.

Bauman, Zygmunt. *Collateral Damage: Social Inequalities in a Global Age*. Malden: Polity Press, 2011.

– *Mortality, Immortality, and Other Life Strategies*. Stanford: Stanford Univesity Press, 1992.

Baxi, P., S. Rai, and S. Ali. "Legacies of Common Law: Crimes of 'Honour' in India and Pakistan." *Third World Quarterly* 27(7) (2006): 1239–53.

Bayefsky, Anne F. "Terrorism and Racism: The Aftermath of Durban." Jerusalem Centre for Public Affairs, *Jerusalem Letter/Viewpoints* no. 468/Tevet 5762. 16 December 2001.

BBC News. "CIA Jails in Europe 'Confirmed.'" 8 June 2007. Accessed 26 March 2014 at http://news.bbc.co.uk/2/hi/6733353.stm.

BBC News [Americas]. "CIA Jail Allegations." 27 June 2006. Accessed 26 March 2014 at http://news.bbc.co.uk/2/hi/americas/4495730.stm.

BBC News [World]. "Poverty 'Fuelling Terrorism.'" 22 March 2002. Accessed 9 January 2014 at http://news.bbc.co.uk/2/hi/1886617.stm.

Beck, Glenn. "USAMA BIN LADEN Muslim Monster KILLED: AMERICA THANKS U.S. ARMED FORCES!!" 2 May 2011. Accessed 31 July 2012 at http://www.youtube.com/watch?v=uovBp-laFWc.

Behrendt, Larissa. "Consent in a (Neo)Colonial Society: Aboriginal Women as Sexual and Legal 'Other.'" *Australian Feminist Studies* 15(33) (2000): 353–67.

– "The Emergency We Had to Have." In *Coercive Reconciliation*, ed. Jon Altman and Melinda Hinkson. Carlton North: Arena Publications, 2007.

Beller, Jonathan. "Wagers within the Image." *Culture Machine* 13 (2012): 93–110.

Bellin, Eva R. "Lessons from the Jasmine and Nile Revolutions: Possibilities of Political Transformation in the Middle East." *Middle East Brief* 50 (May 2011): 1–8.

Bellour, Raymond. "The Double Helix." *In Electronic Culture: Technology and Visual Representation*, ed. Timothy Druckrey. New York: Aperture, 1996.

Belz, Mindy. J. "Baroness for Battle." *World*. 11 December 2004, 34–8.

– "A Complete Lie." *World*. 24 July 1999, 24–5.

– "Count Your Blessings." *World*. 28 November 1998, 16–19.

– "Faces in the Crowd." *World*. 30 November 1996, 12–15.

– "Finding Their Voice." *World*. 3 October 1998, 23–4.

– "First Guns, Then Ballots." *World*. 13 March 2010, 36–7.

– "Improbable Cause." *World*. 31 July 2004, 26.

– "Kidnapped." *World*. 19 May 2007, 22–3.

– "Laying Down the Law." *World*. 20 March 1999, 30–1.

– "Let My People Go." *World*. 3 October 1998, 12–16.

– "Micromanaging Micronesia." *World*. 18 April 1998, 17–19.

– "A Milestone, with Many Miles to Go." *World*. 2 October 1999, 42–4.

– "Missed Opportunity." *World*. 26 January 2008, 56.

– "Name Change." *World*. 18 August 2007, 41.

– "Open and Shut." *World*. 16 April 2005, 30–2.

– "Opening the Safety Valve." *World*. 17 November 2001, 21–2.

– "Plane Truth." *World*. 18 October 2008, 7.

– "Public Disaster." *World*. 21 January 2006, 6.

– "Taking on the Thugs." *World*. 6 November 1999, 16–18.

– "Too Little, Too Late." *World*. 18 August 2007, 42–3.

– "To The Front Lines." *World*. 2 May 1998, 15–17.

Benjamin, Daniel. "5 Myths about Rendition." Brookings Institution. 19 October 2007.

Benjamin, Walter. "Critique of Violence." In *Reflections: Essays, Aphorisms, Autobiographical Writings*, ed. Peter Demetz. 277–336. New York: Schocken Books, 1978.

– "Theses on the Philosophy of History" (1940). In *Illuminations*, ed. Hannah Arendt. Trans. Harry Zohn. 253–64. New York: Schocken Books, 1969.

Bienen, Henry. "State and Revolution: The Work of Amilcar Cabral." *Journal of Modern African Studies* 5(4) (1977): 555–68.

"Bir Tek AKP Suçsuz" (Only the AKP is Innocent). *Sendika.org*. 31 December 2011. http://www.sendika.org/yazi.php?yazi_no=42000.

Bjelajack, Branko. "Evangelical Churches Stoned, Vandalized." *Christianity Today*. 6 August 2001, 28–9.

Bjork, Don. "Foreign Missions: Next Door and Down the Street." *Christianity Today*. 12 July 1985, 17–21.

Blackstock, Cindy. "Why Addressing the Over-Representation of First Nations Children in Care Requires a New Theoretical Approach." *Journal of Social Work Values and Ethics* 6(3) (2009). Accessed 26 March 2014 at http://www.jswvearchives.com/content/view/135/69.

"Blood Money Option Being Studied for Davis's Release." *Dawn* (Lahore). 18 February 2011. Accessed 22 January 2014 at http://www.dawn.com/news/613590/raymond-davis-indicted-in-double-murder.

Blunt, S.H. "Justice before Peace?" *Christianity Today*. May 2009, 16–17.

Bobis, Merlinda. "The Asian Conspiracy: Deploying Voice / Deploying Story." Ed. Leigh Dale. *Australian Literary Studies* 25(3) (2010): 1–19.
– "Border Lover." In *Not Home, But Here: Writing from the Filipino Diaspora*, ed. Luisa A. Igloria. 118–37. Manila: Anvil, 2003.
– "Confounding Light: Subversion and Transnational Sympathy." In *Social Identities: Journal for the Study of Race, Nation, and Culture* 19(2) (March 2013): 145–57. Ed. Pal Ahluwalia and Toby Miller.
– *Fish-Hair Woman*. North Melbourne: Spinifex Press, 2012.
– *A Novel-in-Waiting: Creative Research: Towards Writing Fiction*. Manila: Centre for Intercultural Studies, University of Santo Tomas Publishing House, 2004.
– "Passion to Pasyon: Playing Militarism." In *The Splintered Glass: Facets of Trauma in the Post-Colony and Beyond*, ed. Dolores Herrero and Sonia Baelo Allue. 57–80. Amsterdam: Rodopi, 2011.
– "Storying: Dream and Deployment." In *Living through Terror*, ed. Suvendrini Perera and Antonio Traverso. 81–90. London: Routledge, 2010.
Bobis, Merlinda, and Dolores Herrero. "Sensing and Sensibility: The Late Ripple of Colonisation?" Ed. Anne Collett. *Kunapipi: Journal of Postcolonial Writing and Culture* 32(1–2) (2010): 225–41.
Boehmer, Elleke, and Stephen Morton, eds. *Terror and the Postcolonial: A Concise Companion*. 1st ed. New York: Wiley-Blackwell, 2009.
Bohr, Niels. *Atomic Physics and Human Knowledge*. New York: Dover, 2010.
Bollyn, Christopher. "What Does Bin Laden Really Want?" 11 October 2001. Accessed 10 January 2014 at http://www.whale.to/b/bollyn_oct11.html.
Bonilla, Yarimar. "A Striking Past: Labour and the Politics of History in Guadeloupe." PhD diss., University of Chicago, 2008.
Born, Max. *Natural Philosophy of Cause and Chance*. New York: Dover, 1964.
Bourdieu, Pierre. "The Sentiment of Honor in Kabyle Society." In *Honor and Shame and the Unity of the Mediterranean*, ed. David Gilmore. 121–34. Washington: American Anthropological Association, 1987.
Bourke, Joanna. *What It Means to Be Human: Historical Reflections from 1791 to the Present*. London: Virago, 2011.
Bowman, Paul. *Theorising Bruce Lee*. Vancouver: UBC Press, 2010.
Bredekamp, Horst. "Thomas Hobbes's Visual Strategies." In *The Cambridge Companion to Hobbes's Leviathan*, ed. Patricia Springborg. Cambridge: Cambridge University Press, 2007.
Brigham, Kay. "The Columbus Nobody Knows." *Christianity Today*. 7 October 1991, 26–8.
Brimblecombe, Julie K., et al. "Impact of Income Management on Store Sales in the Northern Territory." *Medical Journal of Australia* 192(10) (2010): 549–54.

Brock, Rita Nakashima, and Rebecca Parker. *Saving Paradise*. Boston: Beacon Press, 2008.

Brohi, Nazish. "At the Altar of Subalternity: The Quest for Muslim Women in the War on Terror: Pakistan after 9/11." *Cultural Dynamics* 20(133) (2008): 133–47.

Brookes, Adrian. "China's Emerging Church." *Charisma*. August 2008, 40–5, 73.

Brooks, Bradley. "US: Bombers Didn't Have Down Syndrome." *USA Today*. 20 February 2008. Accessed 9 January 2014 at http://www.usatoday.com/news/world/2008-02-20-1165634037_x.htm.

Brown, Frank. "Christian Lawyer Battles for Rights of Russian Church." *Charisma*. February 1999, 32–5.

– "Messianic Jews Face Organized Resistance in Russia and Ukraine." *Charisma*. December 2001, 33–4.

– "Opposition Is Mounting as Messianic Jewish Groups Grow in Russia." *Charisma*. September 2000, 34–5.

– "Pentecostals in Former Soviet Republic Face Persecution." *Charisma*. January 2000, 30–2.

Brown, Wendy. "'The Most We Can Hope For …': Human Rights and the Politics of Fatalism." *South Atlantic Quarterly* 103(2–3) (2004): 451–63.

– *Regulating Aversion: Tolerance in the Age of Identity and Empire*. Princeton: Princeton University Press, 2006.

Brownmiller, S. *Against Our Will: Men, Women and Rape*. New York: Bantam Books, 1975.

Bruce, Billy. "Cuban Churches Gain New Freedom." *Charisma*. March 1999, 20–1.

– "Sharing Jesus in the Land of Lenin." *Charisma*. December 2001, 30–7.

Buchan, Alex. "Khmu Christians Arrested." *Christianity Today*. 3 September 2001, 34.

Buğlalılar, Eren. "The Epidemic of Terrorism under Turkey's Mubarak." *MRZine*, 27 December 2011. Accessed 9 January 2014 at http://mrzine.monthlyreview.org/2011/buglalilar271211.html.

Burke, Joanna. "Torture as Pornography." *The Guardian*. 7 May 2004. Accessed 10 January 2014 at http://www.guardian.co.uk/world/2004/may/07/gender.uk.

Bustamente, Paula. "Airlift Rescues Abandoned LA Chihuahuas." AFP. 12 February 2011. Accessed 9 January 2014 at http://www.google.com/hostednews/afp/article/ALeqM5h4LJtByNlHoQT9lwRjDP9BQDamag?docId=CNG.4e201b9124c065f698a3b89b09e38576.101.

Butalia, Urvashi. *The Other Side of Silence: Voices from the Partition of India*. Durham: Duke University Press, 2000.

Butler, Judith. "Competing Universalities." In *Contingency, Hegemony, Universality: Contemporary Dialogues on the Left*, ed. Judith Butler, Jacques Laclau, and Slavoj Žižek. London: Verso, 2000.

– *Frames of War: When Is Life Grievable?* London: Verso, 2009.

– *Gender Trouble: Feminism and the Subversion of Identity*. New York: Routledge, 1990.

– *Precarious Life: The Powers of Mourning and Violence*. London: Verso, 2004.

"The Buzz." *World*. 22 October 2005, 6–7.

Byman, Daniel L. "Extraordinary Rendition, Extraterritorial Detention, and Treatment of Detainees: Restoring Our Moral Credibility and Strengthening Our Diplomatic Standing." Testimony before the Senate Committee on Foreign Affairs. 26 July 2007. Accessed 9 January 2014 at http://www.brookings.edu/testimony/2007/0726terrorism_byman.aspx.

Cagney, M. "Evangelicals Warned against Persecution." *Christianity Today*. 18 May 1998, 20.

– "Senators Champion Rival Bill on Religious Persecution." *Christianity Today*. 18 May 1998, 20–1.

Cainkar, Louise. "Islamic Revival among Second Generation Arab Muslims in Chicago: The American Experience and Globalization Intersect." Presented at the Annual Meeting of the American Sociological Association, 2005.

Cairo, Heriberto. "The Duty of the Benevolent Master: From Sovereignty to Suzerainty and the Biopolitics of Intervention." *Alternatives: Global, Local, Political* 31(3) (2006): 285–311.

Callahan, Timothy. "'Appalling' Persecution." *Christianity Today*. January 2004, 30–1.

Callahan, W.A. "The Cartography of National Humiliation and the Emergence of China's Geobody." *Public Culture* 21(1) (2009): 141–73.

Campbell, Horace. *Global NATO and the Catastrophic Failure in Libya: Lessons for Africa in the Forging of African Unity*. New York: Monthly Review Press, 2013.

Campbell, Timothy. "Bios, Immunity, Life: The Thought of Roberto Esposito." *Diacritics* 36(2) (2006): 2–22.

Canada. *Highlights from the Report of the Royal Commission on Aboriginal Peoples: People to People, Nation to Nation*. Ottawa: Minister of Supply and Services Canada, 1996. Accessed 13 June 2003 at http://www.ainc-inac.gc.ca/ch/rcap/sg/sgmm_e.html.

Cangızbay, Kadir. "İleri Engizisyon" (Advanced Inquisition). *Birgün*, 3 December 2011. Accessed 30 May 2014 at http://www.sendika.org/2011/12/ileri-engizisyon-kadir-cangizbay-birgun/.

– "Yaşasın Medyanın Yeni Düzeni" (Long Live the New Media Order). *Birgün*, 12 November 2011. Accessed 30 May 2014 at http://www.birgunabone.net/politics_index.php?news_code=1321097439&year=2011&month=11&day=12.

Cannon, Martin J., and Lina Sunseri, eds. *Indigeneity in Canada*. Toronto: Oxford University Press, 2011.

Carby, Hazel. "A Strange and Bitter Crop: The Spectacle of Torture." *Open Democracy*. 10 October 2004. Accessed 10 January 2014 at http://www.open-democracy.net/media-abu_ghraib/article_2149.jsp.

Carnes, Tony. "Arrests of Pastor Signal Religious Freedom Setback." *Christianity Today*. 7 February 2000, 28–9.

– "China's New Legal Eagles." *Christianity Today*. September 2006, 106–10.

– "How to Change China." *Christianity Today*. 22 May 2000, 34–5.

– "A Look of Love." *Christianity Today*. February 2005, 71–2.

– "Mixing Oil and Blood." *Christianity Today*. 3 April 2000, 26–7.

– "New China: Same Old Tricks." *Christianity Today*. 11 March 2002, 38–42.

– "The Peoples are Here." *Christianity Today*. February 2003, 76–9.

– "Religious Persecution Bill Drops Trade Sanction Clause." *Christianity Today*. 22 April 2002, 25.

– "Religious Persecution Bill Encounters Stiff Resistance." *Christianity Today*. 5 October 1998, 26.

– "Termites to National Security." *Christianity Today*. October 2004, 21.

– "The Torture Victim Next Door." *Christianity Today*. 6 March 2000, 70–2.

– "The Unlikely Activist." *Christianity Today*. 11 March 2002, 44–5.

– "Walking the Talk after Tsunami." *Christianity Today*. March 2006, 63–6.

Carter, Jeffrey. *Understanding Religious Sacrifice: A Reader*. New York: Continuum, 2003.

Carter, J.W. "Faith Defeats Communism." *Charisma*. January 2000, 72–6.

Castelli, Elizabeth. *Martyrdom and Memory*. New York: Columbia University Press, 2004.

Cavarero, Adriana. *Horrorism: Naming Contemporary Violence*. Trans. William McCuaig. New York: Columbia University Press, 2009.

Cavender, Gray, and Lisa Bond-Maupin. "Fear and Loathing on Reality Television: An Analysis of 'America's Most Wanted' and 'Unsolved Mysteries.'" *Sociological Inquiry* 63(3) (1993): 305–17.

CBC. "The Case of Omar Khadr." *The National*. 19 November 2008. Accessed 9 January 2014 at http://www.cbc.ca/thenational/indepthanalysis/story/2009/11/13/national-thecaseofomarkhadr.html.

Central Bureau of Statistics (CBS). Demographic data for 2010 (in Hebrew). Accessed 10 May 2013 at http://www.cbs.gov.il/reader/?MIval=cw_usr_view_SHTML&ID=629.

Cenzer, Matthew A. "Specters of War: African Chaos Invites Terrorist Exploitation." *Chicago Tribune*, 16 December 2001.

Chabal, Patrick. *Amilcar Cabral: Revolutionary Leadership and the People's War*. New York: Cambridge University Press, 1983.

Chamayou, Gregoire. "History and Philosophy of Traceability." Max-Planck-Institut site, 2003. http://www.mpiwg-berlin.mpg.de/en/research/projects/DeptII_ChamayouGregoire-Traceability.
– "The Manhunt Doctrine." *Radical Philosophy* 169 (September–October 2011): 2–6.
Chambers, S. "Can Christianity and Islam Coexist and Prosper?" *Christianity Today*. 25 October 1999, 22.
Chan, Stephen. "The Construction and Export of Culture as Artifact: The Case of Japanese Martial Arts." *Body and Society* 61(1) (2000): 69–74.
Chandler, David. *From Kosovo to Kabul (and Beyond): Human Rights and International Intervention*. London: Pluto Press, 2002.
Cheah, Peng. "The Limits on Thinking in Decolonial Strategies." November–December newsletter, Townsend Center for the Humanities, UC–Berkeley. Accessed 4 March 2014 at http://townsendcenter.berkeley.edu.
Chenoweth, Gregg. "The Heartless Homeland." *Christianity Today*. October 2004, 44–6.
Children in Military Custody (Report). Accessed 9 August 2012 at http://www.childreninmilitarycustody.org/wp-content/uploads/2012/03/Children_in_Military_Custody_Full_Report.pdf.
Choudhry, D.R. "Feudal Mindset: In the Heart of Darkness." *Deccan Herald*, 1 August 2010, 1.
Chow, Rey. *Ethics after Idealism: Theory, Culture, Ethnicity, and Reading*. Indianapolis: Indiana University Press, 1998.
– *Primitive Passions: Visuality, Sexuality, Ethnography, and Contemporary Chinese Cinema*. New York: Columbia University Press, 1995.
Chowdhry, Prem. *Contentious Marriages, Eloping Couples: Gender, Caste and Class in Northern India*. Delhi: Oxford University Press, 2010.
Chrisjohn, Roland, and Sherri Young. "Among School Children: Psychological Imperialism and the Residential School Experience in Canada." Unpublished paper, 1993.
Christensen, Jon, Janet Schmidt, and Joel Henderson. "The Selling of the Police: Media, Ideology, and Crime Control." *Contemporary Crisis* 6 (1982): 227–39.
Christian Coalition. "Christian Coalition Action Alert." 10 September 2001.
"Christian Woman Sentenced to Death in Blasphemy Case." *Dawn* (Lahore), 2010. Dawn.com.
Christianity Today. "Cartoon Chaos." April 2006, 29.
– "Commission Urges Economic Sanctions." 12 June 2000, 26.
– "Confronting Sudan's Evils." 3 April 2000, 35.
– "Faith Perfected." July 2007, 21.
– "Hindu Radical Fingered in Killing." 6 September 1999, 26.
– "Hotel Sudan Isn't a Film – Yet." May 2005, 26–7.

– "Never Again?" September 2004, 33.
– "Nightmares and Miracles." December 2004, 29.
– "Persecution Is a Holy Word." December 2003, 32–4.
– "Persecution Is Persecution Is Persecution." 9 August 1999, 1.
– "Persecution Panel Appointed." 6 January 1997, 59.
– "See No Evil." October 2008, 22–3.
– "Shaking Hands with Thugs." 3 December 2001, 30–1.
– "Should Christians Continue to Smuggle Bibles into China?" August 2010, 46–7.
– "A Silent Holocaust." 8 February 1999, 28–9.
– "Top Religion Stories of 1996." 6 January 1997, 58.
– "Top Ten News Stories, 2003." January 2003, 22.
– "Top Ten Religion Stories of the Decade." 10 January 2000, 22.
"CIA and Missionaries: More Confusion." *Faith and Freedom*. Spring 1996, 11.
"The CIA's Tentacles: Taking the 'War on Terror' to Africa," *Spiegel International Online*. 13 June 2007. Accessed 9 January 2014 at http://www.spiegel.de/international/world/the-cia-s-tentacles-taking-the-war-on-terror-to-africa-a-488149.html.
Cilliers, Jakkie. "Africa, Root Causes, and the 'War on Terror." *African Security Review* 15(3) (2006): 58–71.
Clark, Ramsey. "Fire and Ice." In *Challenge to Genocide: Let Iraq Live*. 3–32. New York: International Action Center, 1998.
Clarke, Alan. "Holding the Blue Lamp: Television and the Police in Britain." *Crime and Social Justice* 19 (Summer 1983): 44–51.
Cleary, Steve. "Dare to Speak … Dare to Die." *Voice of the Martyrs*. Special Issue, 2005, 4–5.
– "Over the Wall with the Gospel." *Voice of the Martyrs*. December 2004, 6–8.
Clifford, James. *Routes: Travel and Translation in the Late Twenieth Century*. Cambridge: Harvard University Press, 1997.
CNPP (Comisión Nacional sobre Prisión Política y Tortura). *Informe de la Comisión Nacional sobre Prisión Política y Tortura*. Santiago: Ministerio del Interior, 2004.
Coffin, A. "A Different Kind of Horror Movie." *World*. 29 January 2005, 12.
Cole, Teju. "The White Saviour Industrial Complex." *The Atlantic*. 21 March 2012. Accessed 10 January 2014 at http://www.theatlantic.com/international/archive/2012/03/the-white-savior-industrial-complex/254843/2.
Collins, Barrie. "New Wars and Old Wars? The Lessons of Rwanda." In *Rethinking Human Rights: Critical Approaches to International Politics*, ed. David Chandler. 157–75. New York: Palgrave Macmillan, 2002.
Collins, Merle. "Shame Bush." In *Lady in a Boat*. London: Peepal Tree Press, 2003.

– "Tout Moun ka Pléwé." In *Small Axe* 22 (2007): 1–16.

Colson, Charles, and N. Pearcey. "Victory over Napalm." *Christianity Today*. 3 March 1997, 96.

Comfort, Susan. "Counter Memory, Mourning, and History in Toni Morrison's *Beloved*." *Lit: Literature Interpretation Theory* 6(1) (1995): 122–32.

Comisión Etica Contra la Tortura. *Informe de la Comisión Etica Contra la Tortura al Presidente de la Republica, Sr. Ricarco Lagos*. Santiago: CODEPU, 2001.

Compass Direct. "Authorities Crack Down on Churches."*Christianity Today*. January 2003, 28.

– "Highlands Christians Targeted." *Christianity Today*. 9 July 2001, 22.

– "House-Church Christian Dies in Custody." *Christianity Today*. February 2004, 22.

– "7 Christian Executions Suspected."*Christianity Today*. 23 October 2000, 25.

Concerned Australians. *Loss of Rights: The Despair of Aboriginal Communities in the Northern Territory: A Submission to the United Nations Committee on the Elimination of Racial Discrimination*. 2nd ed. Melbourne: Concerned Australians, 2010.

– *This Is What We Said*. Melbourne: Concerned Australians, 2010.

Conlon, Justin. "Sovereignty vs. Human Rights or Sovereignty and Human Rights." *Race and Class* 46(1) (July 2004): 75–100.

Connerton, Paul. *How Societies Remember*. Cambridge: Cambridge University Press, 1989.

– *The Spirit of Mourning: History, Memory, and the Body*. Cambridge: Cambridge University Press, 2011.

Conroy, Scott. "Feds Working in Secret African Prisons." *CBS News*. 4 April 2007. Accessed on 9 January 2014 at http://www.cbsnews.com/stories/2007/04/04/terror/main2647027.shtml.

Cook, Richard. "Behind China's Closed Doors." *Christianity Today*. February 2005, 70–2.

Cooper, John E., and Margaret E. Cooper. *Introduction to Veterinary and Comparative Forensic Medicine*. Oxford: Blackwell, 2007.

Cornejo, Marcela, Rodrigo Rojas, and Francisca Mendoza. "From Testimony to Life Story: The Experience of Professionals in the Chilean National Commission on Political Imprisonment and Torture." *Peace and Conflict* 15 (2009): 111–33.

Cornell, Drucilla. "The Violence of the Masquerade: Law Dressed Up as Justice." In *The Philosophy of the Limit*. 155–69. New York: Routledge, 1992.

Coşkun, Vahap. "Kürt Meselesini Derinleştirmek" (Deepening the Kurdish Issue). *Radikal İki*. 22 July 2012, 3. Accessed 9 January 2014 at http://www.radikal.com.tr/Radikal.aspx?aType=RadikalEklerDetayV3&ArticleID=1095046&CategoryID=42.

"Court Indicts Raymond Davis for Double Murder." *Dawn* (Lahore). 16 March 2011. Accessed 22 January 2014 at http://www.dawn.com/news/613590/raymond-davis-indicted-in-double-murder.

Cox, Caroline. "The Price of a Slave." *Christianity Today*. 8 February 1999, 68–9.

Craige, Tito, and Arnel de Guzman. "Counterinsurgency War in the Philippines and the Role of the US." *Bulletin of Concerned Asian Scholars* 23(1) (1991): 38–47.

Creed, Barbara. "Film and Psychoanalysis." In *Film Studies: Critical Approaches*, ed. John Hill and Pamela Church Gibson. 75–88. Oxford: Oxford University Press, 2000.

– *The Monstrous-Feminine: Film, Feminism, Psychoanalysis*. London: Routledge, 1993.

Cromartie, Michael. "The Jew Who Is Saving Christians." *Christianity Today*. 1 March 1999, 50–5.

Crouch, Andy. "Liberate My People." *Christianity Today*. August 2007, 30–3.

CT Staff. "House-Church Leader Arrested." *Christianity Today*. February 2005, 21.

Curry, Dean. *A World without Tyranny*. Westchester: Crossway Books, 1990.

Dabel, Greg. "Bulldogs, Bodyguards." *World*. 25 April 1998, 19–20.

Dahiya, R.S. "Khap Panchayats: Need to Review Their Role in Society." *Mainstream* 48(36) (2010): 29–32.

Darwish, Mahmoud. "Under Siege." Accessed 10 January 2014 at http://www.poemhunter.com.

Das, Veena. *Critical Events: An Anthropological Perspective on Contemporary India*. New Delhi: Oxford University Press, 1995.

David, S. "Caught on Tape." *Christianity Today*. August 2007, 16–17.

– "Critics Assail Dialogue with Hindu Radicals." *Christianity Today*. 21 May 2002, 33.

Davis, Angela Y. *Abolition Democracy: Beyond Prisons, Torture, and Empire: Interviews with Angela Y. Davis*. New York: Seven Stories Press, 2005.

– *Women, Race, and Class*. New York: Vintage Books, 1983.

Dayan, Colin. *The Law Is a White Dog: How Legal Rituals Make and Unmake Persons*. Princeton: Princeton University Press, 2011.

De Guia, Katrin. "An Ancient Reed of Wholeness – The Babaylan." In *Filipinos and the Call of the Indigenous*, ed. Leny Mendoza Strobel. 90–1. Davao City: Ateneo de Davao University Research and Publications Office, 2010.

De Waal, Frans. *The Age of Empathy*. 2012. Accessed on 8 August 2012 at http://www.emory.edu/LIVING_LINKS/empathy/faq.html.

– *The Age of Empathy: Nature's Lessons for a Kinder Society*. New York: Harmony Books, 2009.

De Witte, Ludo. *The Assassination of Lumumba*. Trans. Ann Wright and Renée Fenby. New York: Verso, [2001]2002.

Dean, Amber. "Public Mourning and the Culture of Redress: Mayerthorpe, Air India, and Murdered or Missing Aboriginal Women." In *Reconciling Canada: Critical Perspectives on the Culture of Redress*, ed. Jennifer Henderson and Pauline Wakeham. 181–97. Toronto: University of Toronto Press, 2013.

Dean, Jamie. "Castes Vote." *World*. 9 May 2009, 48.

– "Looming Storms." *World*. 27 May 2006, 28.

– "No Way Out." *World*. 13 May 2006, 14–18.

Dean, Jodi. *Democracy and Other Neoliberal Fantasies: Communicative Capitalism and the Failure of the Left*. Durham: Duke University Press, 2009.

Debrix, François. "The Hegemony of Tabloid Geopolitics: How America and the West Cannot Think International Relations beyond Conflict, Identity, and Cultural Imposition." Afrasian Centre for Peace and Development, Working Paper Series No. 25. Ryukoku University, Otsu, Shiga, 2007.

Deeb, Lara. *An Enchanted Modern: Gender and Public Piety in Shi'i Lebanon*. Princeton: Princeton University Press, 2006.

– "Hizballah: A Primer." *Middle East Report Online*. 2006. Accessed 21 January 2014 at http://www.merip.org/mero/mero073106.html.

Democracy Now. "Allied with Apartheid: Reagan Supported Racist South African Government." 11 June 2004. Accessed 9 January 2014 at http://www.democracynow.org/2004/6/11/allied_with_apartheid_reagan_supported_racist.

Dempsey, Diane. "Review of *Fish-Hair Woman*." *The Saturday Age*, April 2012. 6–7.

der Derian, James. "9.11: Before, After, and In Between." Social Science Research Council, New York, 18 January 2002. Accessed 9 January 2014 at http://essays.ssrc.org/sept11/essays/der_derian_text_only.htm.

– *Virtuous War: Mapping the Military-Industrial-Media-Entertainment Network*. Boulder: Westview, 2001.

Derrida, Jacques. "Force of Law: The 'Mystical Foundation of Authority.'" In *Acts of Religion*, ed. Gil Anidjar. 228–98. New York: Routledge, 2002. Also in *Deconstruction and the Possibility of Justice*, ed. David Gray Carlson, Drucilla Cornell, and Michael Rosenfeld. New York: Routledge, 1992.

– "Politics and Friendship: A Discussion with Jacques Derrida and Geoffrey Bennington." 1997. Accessed 9 January 2014 at http://www.livingphilosophy.org/Derrida-politics-friendship.htm.

– *The Politics of Friendship*. Trans. George Collins. London: Verso, 1997.

"Details of the Assembly Discussion on Resoultion to Repeal Muslim Family Laws Ordinance." 1963. *Dawn* (Karachi), 4.

Devji, Faisal. "Red Mosque." *Public Culture* 20(1) (2008): 19–26.
– *The Terrorist in Search of Humanity: Militant Islam and Global Politics*. New York: Columbia University Press, 2008.
Dhada, Mustafah. "The Political Thought of Amilcar Cabral." *Monthly Review* 24 (March 1973): 10–21.
Diaz, Vicente, and J. Kehaulani Kauanui. "Native Pacific Cultural Studies on the Edge." *The Contemporary Pacific* 13(2) (2001): 315.
DiManno, Rosie. "Wrong Killer Shown Mercy." *Toronto Star*. 3 October 2012, A2.
Dirlik, Arif. "Place-Based Imagination: Globalism and the Politics of Place." In *Places and Politics in an Age of Globalization*, ed. Roxann Prazniak and Arif Dirlik. 15–51. Lanham: Rowman and Littlefiel, 2001.
Divino, Claudio. "Why Don't They Look Like Us." *Christian Standard*. 5 January 2003, 13–14.
Dixon, Thoma. "In the Shadow of the Mosque." *Charisma*. August 2002, 56–61.
– "Three Christians Martyred in Turkey." *Charisma*. July 2007, 28.
Donnally, E. "Actor Dean Jones Helps Persecuted Christians via New Relief Efforts." *Charisma*. January 2000, 18–20.
Douzinas, Costas. "The Many Faces of Humanitarianism." *Parrhesia* 2 (2007): 1–28. Accessed 9 January 2014 at http://www.parrhesiajournal.org/parrhesia02/parrhesia02_douzinas.pdf.
Dowd, Maureen. "Powell without Picasso." *New York Times*. 5 February 2003. Accessed 10 January 2014 at http://www.nytimes.com/2003/02/05/opinion/powell-without-picasso.html.
Doyle, M. "Faces of Persecution." *Faith Today*. November–December 1999, 24–9.
Drayton, Richard. "British Guiana, American Imperialism, and the Crisis of Independence." In *Yet More Adventures with Britannia: Personalities, Politics, and Culture in Britain*. London: Tauris, 2005.
– "From Kabul to Kingston." *The Guardian*, 14 June 2010. Accessed 9 January 2014 at http://www.guardian.co.uk/commentisfree/2010/jun/14/jamaica-tactics-army-afghanistan.
Duhul, Salad. "Al-Qaida Suspects Still Alive in Somalia: U.S. and Ethiopian Troops Continue Pursuit of Key al-Qaida Suspects in Somalia, Officials Say." *CBS News*, 11 January 2007.
Dustin, Moira, and Anne Phillips. "Whose Agenda Is It? Abuses of Abuses of 'Culture' in Britain." *Ethnicities* 8(3) (2008): 405–24.
Echavez, Sarita. "The Decolonized Eye: Filipino American Art and Performance." 2009.
Ecumenical News International. "'Christian Nation' Label Rings Hollow." *Christianity Today*. 6 March 2000, 29.

Ecumenical News International and Religious News Service. "Will Shari'a Law Curb Christianity?" *Christianity Today*. 23 October 2000, 24.

Eidsmoe, John. *Columbus and Cortez: Conquerors for Christ*. Green Forest: New Leaf Press, 1992.

Eisenstein, Z. *Against Empire: Feminisms, Racism and the West*. London: Zed Books, 2004.

Eliot, T.S. *Selected Poems, 1888–1965*. London: Faber and Faber, 1954.

Elyachar, Julia. *Markets of Dispossession: NGOs, Economic Development, and the State in Cairo*. Durham: Duke University Press, 2005.

Eng, D. *Racial Castration: Managing Masculinity in Asian-America*. Durham: Duke University Press, 2001.

Eng, David L., and David Kazanjian, eds. *Loss: The Politics of Mourning*. Berkeley: University of California Press, 2003.

Engle, Karen. *Seeing Ghosts: 9/11 and the Visual Imagination*. Montreal: McGill-Queen's University Press, 2009.

Enloe, C. *Maneuvers: The International Politics of Militarizing Women's Lives*. Berkeley: University of California Press, 2000.

Enrique, E. Dussel. *Philosophy of Liberation*. Trans. Aquilina Martinez and Christine Morkovsky. Maryknoll: Orbis Press, 1985.

Enriquez, Virgilio. "*Kapwa*: A Core concept in Filipino Social Psychology." *Philippine Social Sciences and Humanities Review* 42 (1978): 1–4.

"Erdoğan: BDP Uludere'yi Istismar Ediyor" (Erdoğan: BDP Is Exploiting the Uludere Issue). *CNN Türk*. 8 February 2012. http://www.cnnturk. com/2012/turkiye/02/08/erdogan.bdp.uludereyi.istismar.ediyor/ 648297.0/index.html.

Esposito, Roberto. *Bíos: Biopolitics and Philosophy*. Trans. Timothy Campbell. Minneapolis: University of Minnesota Press, 2007.

Esposti, Emmanuel Degli. "Pakistan's Blasphemy Law. Timeline." *The Telegraph*, 2 March 2011. Accessed 9 January 2014 at http://www.telegraph. co.uk/news/worldnews/asia/pakistan/8356855/Pakistans-blasphemy-law-timeline.html.

Fabian, Johannes. *Time and the Other: How Anthropology Makes Its Object*. New York: Columbia University Press, 2002.

Falk, Richard. *The Great Terror War*. New York: Olive Branch Press, 2003.

Fanon, Frantz. *Black Skin, White Masks*. Trans. Richard Philcox. New York: Grove Press, 1952/2008.

– "Letter to the Resident Minister." In *Toward the African Revolution*. New York: Grove Press, 1969.

– *The Wretched of the Earth*. Trans. Richard Philcox. New York: Grove Press, 1963/2004.

Farley, Anthony. "The Black Body as Fetish Object." *Oregon Law Review* (1995): 457–535.

Farrell, E. "Mosques on Main Street." *Charisma*. October 1997, 56–8, 66.

Farsoun, Samih K., and Naseer H. Aruri. *Palestine and the Palestinians: A Social and Political History*. 2nd ed. Boulder: Westview, 2006.

Fassin, Didier. "Compassion and Repression: The Moral Economy of Immigration Policies in France." *Cultural Anthropology* 20(3) (2005): 362–87.

Fassin, Didier, and Mariella Pandolfi. *Contemporary States of Emergency: The Politics of Military and Humanitarian Interventions*. New York: Zone Books, 2010.

– "Introduction: Military Humanitarian Government in the Age of Intervention." In Fassin and Pandolfi, 9–25.

Fawzy, Samy. "Christian-Muslim Dialogue in Egypt." *Transformation*. January–March 2000, 34–6.

FBI. "Ten Most Wanted Fugitives 60th Anniversary, 1950–2010." Washington: US Department of Justice. Accessed 24 March 2014 at http://www.fbi.gov/stats-services/publications/ten-most-wanted-fugitives-60th-anniversary-1950-2010/famous_cases.

Feitlowitz, Marguerite. *A Lexicon of Terror: Argentina and the Legacies of Torture*. Oxford: Oxford University Press, 1998.

Feldner, Yotam. "Honor Murders – Why the Perps Get off Easy." *Middle East Quarterly* (December 2000): 41.

Fellows, Mary Louise, and Sherene Razack. "The Race to Innocence: Confronting Hierarchical Relations among Women." *Journal of Gender Race and Justice* 1 (1997): 335–52.

Fergusson, James. *The Anti-Politics Machine: Development, Depoliticization, and Bureaucratic Power in Lesotho*. Minneapolis: University of Minnesota Press, 1994.

– *The World's Most Dangerous Place: Inside the Outlaw State of Somalia*. New York: Da Capo Press, 2013.

Fernando, Ajith. "Bombs Away." *Christianity Today*. 14 June 1999, 76–7.

Ferraris, Maurizio. "What Is There?" In Jacques Derrida and M.A Ferraris, *A Taste for the Secret*. Cambridge: Polity, 2001.

Festa, Lynn. "Humanity without Feathers." *Humanity: An International Journal of Human Rights, Humanitarianism, and Development* 1(1) (2010): 3–28.

Fidler, B. "Infiltrating the Darkness." *Voice of the Martyrs*. Caney: 2005.

Fieguth, Debra. "Persecuted But Not Defeated." *Faith Today*. September–October 2004, 18–21.

Fischbach, Michael R. *Records of Dispossession: Palestinian Refugee Property and the Arab–Israeli Conflict*. Institute for Palestine Studies Series. New York: Columbia University Press, 2003.

Fischer, Michael. "Enemies of the State." *Christianity Today*. 12 June 2000, 26.
– "The Fiery Rise of Hindu Fundamentalism." *Christianity Today*. 1 March 1999, 46–9.
Flinchbaugh, C. Hope. "Christians in the Line of Fire." *Charisma*. October 1999, 72–8.
– "Pakistani Christians Unite in Response to Bloody Attacks." *Charisma*. November 2002, 19–20.
– "Pastor Champions Plight of North Koreans." *Charisma*. January 2007, 24.
Foley, Conor. *The Thin Blue Line: How Humanitarianism Went to War*. London: Verso, 2008.
Ford-Smith, Honor. "Local and Transnational Dialogues on Memory and Violence in Jamaica and Toronto: Staging 'Letters from the Dead' among the Living." *Canadian Theatre Review* 148(1) (2001): 10–17.
Foreman, D. "World Relief." *Charisma*. May 1999, 35–6.
Foucault, Michel. *Discipline and Punish: The Birth of the Prison*. New York: Vintage Books, 1995.
– *The History of Sexuality: An Introduction*. New York: Vintage Books, 1978.
– "Orders of Discourse." *Social Science Information* 10(2) (1971): 7–30.
– "Politics and the Study of Discourses." Trans. Colin Gordon. In *The Foucault Effect: Studies in Governmentality*, ed. Graham Burchell, Colin Gordon, and Peter Miller. 53–72. Chicago: University of Chicago Press, 1991.
– *Power/Knowledge: Selected Interviews and Other Writings, 1972–1977*. Ed. Colin Gordon. Toronto: Random House, 1980.
– *"Society Must Be Defended": Lectures at the College de France, 1975–76*. Trans. David Macey. New York: Picador, 1997.
– "Two Lectures." In his *Power/Knowledge*, 83–8.
Frame, R. "Sanctuary Workers Indicted for Harboring Illegal Aliens." *Christianity Today*. 1 March 1985, 30–1.
"Free China's Church." *Christianity Today*. 7 January 2002, 31.
Freedom House. *In the Lion's Den: A Primer on Mounting Christian Persecution around the World and How American Christians Can Respond*. Washington: Freedom House, 1996.
Friscolanti, Michael. "The Secret Khadr File." *Maclean's Magazine*. 1 October 2012, 16–23.
Fuchs, Cynthia J. "The Buddy Politic." In *Screening the Male: Exploring Masculinities in Hollywood Cinema*, ed. Steven Cohan and Ina Rae Hark. New York: Routledge, 1993.
Füredi, Frank. *The New Ideology of Imperialism*. London: Pluto Press, 1994.
Fusco, Coco. *A Field Guide for Female Interrogators*. New York: Seven Stories Press, 2008.

Gabriel, Karen. *Melodrama and the Nation: Sexual Economies of Bombay Cinema, 1970–2000*. New Delhi: Women Unlimited, 2010.

Gaines, Adrienne. "China Launches New Crackdown on Underground-Church Movement." *Charisma* 29 (2004): 22.

Galli, Mark. "The Chinese Church's Delicate Dance." *Christianity Today*. November 2004, 68–73.

– "A New Day in Vietnam." *Christianity Today*. May 2007, 26–32.

– "Our Geopolitical Moment." *Christianity Today*. March 2008, 44–50.

– "Sometimes Persecution Purifies, Unites, and Grows the Church. Sometimes It Doesn't." *Christianity Today*. 19 May 1997, 16–19.

Ganguly, Keya. *States of Exception: Everyday Life and Postcolonial Identity*. Minneapolis: University of Minnesota Press, 2001.

Gardner, Christine. "Congress Approves Modified Religious Persecution Bill." *Christianity Today*. 16 November 1998, 32–3.

– "Slave Redemption." *Christianity Today*. 9 August 1999, 28–33.

Gaviak, D. "Longing to Be Heard." *Christianity Today*. April 2005, 87–8.

Gbonigi, Emmanuel. "Christians Facing Muslim Authorities in Nigeria." *Transformation*. January–March 2000, 19–20.

Ghamdi, Javid Ahmed. "The Penal Law: Fasad fil-ard (Creating Nuisance in the Land)." *Al Mawrid: A Foundation for Islamic Research and Education*. 2011. Accessed 9 January 2014 at http://www.al-mawrid.org/pages/articles_english_detail.php?rid=1157&cid=304.

Ghosh, Bishnupriya. *Global Icons: Apertures to the Popular*. Durham: Duke University Press, 2011.

Gibson, Paddy. "Working for the BasicsCard in the Northern Territory." Discussion paper, Jumbunna Indigenous House of Learning, University of Technology, Sydney, 2010.

Gilroy, Paul. *The Black Atlantic: Modernity and Double Consciousness*. Cambridge: Harvard University Press, 1993.

Goetz, John, Marcel Rosenbach, and Holger Stark. "Taking the 'War on Terror' to Africa." *Spiegel International Online*. 13 June 2009. Accessed 9 January 2014 at http://www.spiegel.de/international/world/0,1518,488149,00.html.

Goffe, Leslie. "Black Victims of September 11." *New African Magazine*, November 2001, 13.

Goldman, Alvin. "Ethics and Cognitive Science." *Ethics* 103(2) (1993): 337–60.

Gomez-Barris, Macarena. "Torture Sees and Speaks: Guillermo Nunez's Art in Chile's Transition." *Contra Corrientes: A Journal on Social History and Literature in Latin America* 5(1) (2007): 139–59.

Gordon, Avery F. *Ghostly Matters: Haunting and the Sociological Imagination*. Minneapolis: University of Minnesota Press, 2008.

Gordon, Colin. "Governmental Rationality: An Introduction." In *The Foucault Effect: Studies in Governmentality*, ed. Graham Burchell, Colin Gordon, and Peter Miller. 1–53. Chicago: University of Chicago Press, 1991.

Gordon, Joy. *Invisible War: The United States and the Iraq Sanctions*. Cambridge: Harvard University Press, 2010.

Gordon, Lewis R., T. Denean Sharpley-Whiting, and Renee T. White. *Fanon: A Critical Reader*. Oxford: Blackwell, 1996.

Gordon, Mary. "The Fragile City: 'There Were No Sounds of Lamentation.'" *New York Times*, 16 September 2001.

Grady, J. Lee. "God's Moment for India." *Charisma*. February 2009, 26–33, 58–9.

– "Invading the Darkness." *Charisma*. January 2003, 35.

– "Secret Agent Man." *Charisma*. March 2005, 36–42.

– "They Burn Bibles in India." *Charisma*. February 2009, 6.

Grandmaison, Olivier Le Cour. "Violencias Extremas y Campos Totalitarios." In *Politicas y Esteticas de la Memoria*, ed. Nelly Richards. Santiago: Editorial Cuarto Propio, 2000.

Gray, Obika. *Demeaned but Empowered: The Social Power of the Urban Poor in Jamaica*. Kingston: University of the West Indies Press, 2004.

Greer, Susan. "'In the Interests of the Children': Accounting in the Control of Aboriginal Family Endowment Payments." *Accounting History* 14(1–2) (2009): 166–91.

Gregory, Derek. *The Colonial Present: Afghanistan, Palestine, Iraq*. Oxford: Blackwell, 2004.

Grewal, Inderpal. "On the New Global Feminism and the Family of Nations: Dilemmas of Transnational Feminist Practice." In *Talking Visions*, ed. Ella Shohat. 501–30. Cambridge: MIT Press, 1988.

– *Transnational America: Feminisms, Diasporas, Neoliberalisms*. Durham: Duke University Press, 2005.

– "Women's Rights as Human Rights: Feminist Practices, Global Feminism, and Human Rights Regimes in Transnationality." *Citizenship Studies* 3(3) (1999): 337–54.

Grimshaw, Patricia, and Elizabeth Nelson. "Empire, 'the Civilising Mission,' and Indigenous Christian Women in Colonial Victoria." *Australian Feminist Studies* 16(36) (2001): 295–309.

Guilherme, George. "Evangelicals Grow as Political Force." *Christianity Today*. 9 December 2002, 22.

Guillermo, Ramon. "*Pantayong Pananaw*: Exposition, Critique, and New Directions." 2003. Accessed 8 August 2013 at http://kyotoreview.cseas.kyoto-u.ac.jp/issue/issue2/article_260.html.

Gumuchian, Marie-Louise. "Ireland Tells Israel to Withdraw Staffer over Dubai." 15 June 2010. Accessed 10 January 2014 at http://www.reuters.com/article/idUSTRE65E1WL20100615.

Gunning, Jeroen. "A Case for Critical Terrorism Studies." *Governance and Opposition* 42(3) (Summer 2007): 363–93.

Gunst, Laurie. *Born fi' Dead: A Journey through the Jamaican Posse Underworld.* New York: Henry Holt, 1995.

Gunter, Barrie. *Television and the Fear of Crime.* London: John Libbey, 1987.

Gupta, Charu. "Hindu Women, Muslim Men." *Economic and Political Weekly* 44(51) (19–25 December 2009): 13–15.

Guthrie, Stan. "A Crescent for a Cross: Islam Prospers in America." *Christianity Today.* 27 October 1991, 40.

– "Deconstructing Gulags." *Christianity Today.* December 2004, 19.

– "Door to Islam." *Christianity Today.* 9 September 2002, 35–45.

– "A False Cry of Peace." *Christianity Today.* September 2004, 70–1.

– "Keeping Their Heads Low." *Christianity Today.* 18 November 2002, 34–5.

– "Kidnapped Missionaries Reported Safe." *Christianity Today.* 6 August 2001, 28.

– "Muslim Mission Breakthrough." *Christianity Today.* 13 December 1993, 20–6.

– "The Other Side of Church Growth." *Christianity Today.* March 2009, 52–4.

– "Q & A." *Christianity Today.* October 2004, 23.

Gutierrez, David. *Walls and Mirrors: Mexican Americans, Mexican Immigrants, and the Politics of Ethnicity.* Berkeley: University of California Press, 1995.

Haberler.com. "4 Yılda 795 Bin Kişi Gözaltına Alındı" (795 Thousand People Detained in Four Years). 22 September 2012. Accessed 9 January 2012 at http://www.haberler.com/4-yilda-795-bin-kisi-gozaltina-alindi-3957447-haberi.

Hakan, Ahmet. "Şemdinli Neden Halep Olmaz?" (Why Şemdinli Cannot Be Aleppo). *Hürriyet,* 4 August 2012. Accessed 9 January 2014 at http://www.hurriyet.com.tr/yazarlar/21145542.asp.

Halberstam, Judith. *Female Masculinity.* Durham: Duke University Press, 1998.

"Halkın Oturduğu Bir Bölge Değil, Terör Bölgesi" (Not a Region Where People Live, But a Terror Region). *IMC-TV.* 22 May 2012. Accessed 9 January 2014 at http://www.imc-tv.com/haber-halkin-oturdugu-bir-bolge-degil-teror-bolgesi-3221.html.

Hall, Stuart, Chas Critcher, Tony Jefferson, John Clarke, and Brian Roberts. *Policing the Crisis: Mugging, the State, and Law and Order.* London: Macmillan, 2013.

Hall of Shame. *World.* 30 January 2010, 10.

Hammad, Suheir. *Zaatar Diva*. New York: Cypher Books, 2007.

Hansen, Stig Jarle. *Al-Shabab in Somalia: The History and Ideology of a Militant Islamist Group*. Oxford: Oxford University Press, 2013.

Haqqani, Husain. *Pakistan: Between Mosque and Military*. Washington: Carnegie Endowment for International Peace, 2005.

Hardage, Jeanette. "Witnesses amid War." *Christianity Today*. July 2004, 67–8.

Harriot, Anthony, ed. *Understanding Crime in Jamaica: New Challenges for Public Policy*. Kingston: University of the West Indies Press, 2003.

Harrison, Faye V. "The Gendered Politics and Violence of Structural Adjustment." In *Situated Lives: Gender and Culture in Everyday Life*, ed. Louise Lamphere, Helena Ragone, and Patricia Zavella. New York: Routledge, 1997.

Hartman, Saidiya. *Scenes of Subjection*. Oxford: Oxford University Press, 1997.

Hartmann, Heidi. "The Unhappy Marriage of Marxism and Feminism." In *Women and Revolution: A Discussion of the Unhappy Marriage of Marxism and Feminism*, ed. Lydia Sargent. London: Pluto Press, 1981.

Harvey, David. *The New Imperialism*. Oxford: Oxford University Press, 2003.

Haskell, Molly. *From Reverence to Rape: The Treatment of Rape in the Movies*. Chicago: University of Chicago Press, 1987.

Hatem, Mervat F. "How the Gulf War Changed the AAUG's Discourse on Arab Nationalism and Gender Politics." *Middle East Journal* 55(2) (2001): 277–96.

Hawley, Chris. "NYPD Monitored Muslim Students All over the Northeast." *Associated Press*. 18 February 2012. Accessed 8 July 2012 at http://www.ap.org/Content/AP-In-The-News/2012/NYPD-monitored-Muslim-students-all-over-Northeast.

Hawramy, Fazel. "Turkey Would Rather Jail Journalists Than Face the Kurdish Question." *The Guardian*, 14 September 2012. Accessed 9 January 2014 at http://www.guardian.co.uk/commentisfree/2012/sep/14/turkey-jail-journalists-kurdish-question.

Hayes, Jarrod. "Queer Resistance to (Neo-)Colonialism in Algeria." In *Postcolonial, Queer*, ed. John C. Hawley. 79–97. Albany: SUNY Press, 2001.

Healy, Chris. *Forgetting Aborigines*. Sydney: University of New South Wales Press, 2008.

Hegel, G.W.F. *The Philosophy of History*. Kitchener: Batoche Books, 2001.

– *Philosophy of Right*. Oxford: Oxford University Press, 1967.

Heisenberg, Werner. *Physics and Beyond – Encounters and Conversations*. New York: Harper Torchbooks, 1972.

Henderson, Jennifer, and Pauline Wakeham, eds. *Reconciling Canada: Critical Perspectives on the Culture of Redress*. Toronto: University of Toronto Press, 2013.

Hertzke, Allen. *Freeing God's Children*. Lanham: Rowman and Littlefield, 2004.

Herzfeld, Michael. "Honor and Shame: Problems in the Comparative Analysis of Moral Systems." *Man* 15 (1980): 339–51.

Hickey, Marilyn. "A Journey Underground." *Charisma*. January 1997, 39–41.

Hoffman, Derek. "The Risks of Regime Change." *Christianity Today*. April 2005, 77–9.

hooks, bell. *Black Looks: Race and Representation*. Boston: South End Press, 1992.

Horowitz, Michael, and Jeremy Gunn. "Breaking Chains." *Christianity Today*. March 2003, 46–54.

– "Breaking Chains II." *Christianity Today*. April 2003, 88–9.

Hosein, Gus. "Beyond September 11." In *Privacy and Human Rights 2003: Threat to Privacy: An International Survey of Privacy Laws and Developments*." Washington: Electronic Privacy Information Center in association with Privacy International. Accessed 9 January 2014 at http://www.epic.org.

HRCP (Human Rights Commission of Pakistan). Press Release: "Govt–Taliban Deal Worries HRCP." 14 May 2009. http://hrcpblog.wordpress.com/2008/05/22/govt-taliban-deal-worries-hrcp.

– 2010. "Militancy Intensifies Threats to Rights: HRCP." *News Alerts Pakistan*. Accessed 9 January 2014 at http://www.dawn.com/news/589928/militancy-intensifies-threats-to-rights-hrcp.

Hübschle, Annette. "The T-Word: Conceptualizing Terrorism." *African Security Review* 15(3) (2006): 2–18.

Hulsman, Cornelius. "Bad Cops." *Christianity Today*. September 2004, 28.

Human Rights Watch. *Protesting as a Terrorist Offense: The Arbitrary Use of Terrorism Laws to Prosecute and Incarcerate Demonstrators in Turkey*. November 2010. Accessed 9 January 2014 at http://www.hrw.org/sites/default/files/reports/turkey1110webwcover.pdf.

– "'We Are Not the Enemy': Hate Crimes against Arabs, Muslims, and Those Perceived to Be Arab or Muslim after September 11." *Human Rights Watch* 14(6) (2002): 1–42.

Hutton, Marg. "Questions Abound Concerning Agrabinta Asylum Boat Tragedy." 5 October 2013. Accessed 10 January 2014 at http://www.sievx.com.

Hyeok, K. "The Nightmare of North Korea." *Christianity Today*. October 2004, 38–42.

Hyndman, Jennifer. "The Question of 'the Political' in Critical Geopolitics: Querying the 'Child Soldier' in the 'War on Terror.'" *Political Geography* 29 (2010): 247–55.

Hyndman, Jennifer, and Malathi de Alwis. "Bodies, Shrines, and Roads: Violence, (Im)mobility, and Displacement in Sri Lanka.' *Gender, Place, and Culture* 11(4) (2004): 535–57.

Ignatius, David. "'Rendition' Realities." *Washington Post*. 9 March 2005.

IJN (International Justice Network). "Statement By Family Of Dr. Aafia Siddiqui In Response To Guilty Verdict." New York. 3 February 2010.

Ileto, Reynaldo Clemeña. *Pasyon and Revolution: Popular Movements in the Philippines, 1840–1910*. Quezon City: Ateneo de Manila University Press, 1979.

Ilkkaracan, Pinar. "Women, Sexuality, and Social Change in the Middle East and Maghreb." *Social Research* 69(3) (Fall 2002): 753–79.

"Imprisoned Chinese House-Church Leader Admits Guilt." *Charisma*. October 2007, 37.

Incite! Women of Color Against Violence. *The Revolution Will Not Be Funded: Beyond the Non-Profit Industrial Complex*. Cambridge: South End Press, 2007.

Indian and Northern Affairs Canada. *Royal Commission on Aboriginal People*. Vol. IV, ch. 2, 1. 1996. Accessed December 2010 at http://www.ainc-inac.gc.ca/ch/rcap/sg/sj3_e.html.

International Crisis Group. *Turkey: The PKK and a Kurdish Settlement*. Europe Report No. 219, 11 September 2012. Accessed 9 January 2014 at http://www.crisisgroup.org/~/media/Files/europe/turkey-cyprus/turkey/219-turkey-the-pkk-and-a-kurdish-settlement.

Irigiray, Luce. *An Ethics of Sexual Difference*. Trans. Carolyn Burke and Gillian C. Gill. Ithaca: Cornell University Press.

Isais, J. "Mexico: Out of the Salt Shaker." *Christianity Today*. 16 November 1998, 72–3.

Jackson, Michael. *The Politics of Storytelling: Violence, Transgression, and Intersubjectivity*. Copenhagen: Museum Tusculanum Press, 2006.

Jackson, Richard. "The Core Commitments of Critical Terrorism Studies." *European Political Science* 6 (2007): 244–51.

Jahangir, Asma. *Protecting Women*. Lahore: Human Rights Commission of Pakistan, 2010.

Jamal, Amaney A., and Nadine Naber. *Race and Arab Americans before and after 9/11: From Invisible Citizens to Visible Subjects*. 1st ed. Syracuse: Syracuse University Press, 2008.

James, Selma. "Sex, Race, and Class: The New Terms of Unity." Lecture delivered on 26 November 2012, University of Toronto.

Jamoralin, Ella Gajo. "Bayani ng Kababaihang Bikolnon" (Hero of Bikol Women). *Pulang Hamtik*. Sorsogon: Bikol Agency for Nationalist and Human Initiatives, 1997.

Jarmakani, Amira. *Imagining Arab Womanhood: The Cultural Mythology of Veils, Harems, and Belly Dancers in the U.S.* 1st ed. New York: Palgrave Macmillan, 2008.

Jarvis, Lee. "The Space and Faces of Critical Terrorism Studies." *Security Dialogue* 40(1) (2009): 5–27.

Jefferess, David. "Neither Seen nor Heard: The Idea of the 'Child' as Impediment to the Rights of Children." *Topia* 7 (Spring 2002).

Jeffrey, Robin. *Media and Modernity: Communications, Women, and the State in India*. Delhi: Permanent Black, 2010.

Jinnah Institute. "Research Brief: Aasia Bibi's Case." 2012. Accessed 9 January 2014 at http://jinnah-institute.org/research-brief-aasia-bibis-case.

John, Kaleem. "Christians and the Blasphemy Laws in Pakistan." *Transformation*. January-March 2000, 20–3.

Johnson, J. Carter. "Deliver Us from Kony." *Christianity Today*. January 2006, 30–7.

– "Gridlock on Genocide." *Christianity Today*. May 2006, 22–3.

Johnson, Penny, and Eileen Kuttab. "Where Have All the Women (and Men) Gone? Reflections on Gender and the Second Palestinian Intifada." *Feminist Review* 69 (2001): 21–43.

Johnson, Peter. "Foreign Workers Flock to Worship Services in China." *Charisma*. April 2006, 40–1.

– "How One Woman Challenged Oppression." *Charisma*. April 2002, 77–85.

– "The Latinos Are Coming." *Charisma*. March 2003, 58–64.

Jones, Gregg R. *Red Revolution: Inside the Philippine Guerilla Movement*. Boulder: Westview Press, 1989.

Jones, William. *"Is God a White Racist?"* Garden City: Anchor Books, 1973.

Jordan, W.D. *White over Black*. Williamsburg: University of North Carolina Press, 1968.

Joseph, Ammu. *Women in Journalism: Making News*. New Delhi: Konark Publishers, 2000.

Joseph, Ammu, and Kalpana Sharma. "Introduction." In *Whose News? The Media and Women's Issues*, ed. Joseph and Sharma. 5–32. New Delhi: Sage, 1994.

Judy, Ronald. *Disforming the American Canon: African-Arabic Slave Narratives and the Vernacular*. Minneapolis: University of Minnesota Press, 1993.

Kamau, John. "Still Waiting for Compensation." *New African Magazine*, November 2001.

Kamir, Orit. "Law, Society, and Film: *Unforgiven*'s Call to Substitute Honor with Dignity." 40 *Law and Society Review* (2006): 193–235.

Kant, Immanuel. *Anthropology from a Pragmatic Point of View*. Cambridge: Cambridge University Press, 2006.

– *Critique of Judgement* (1790). Trans. J.H. Bernard. New York: Hafner, 1951.

Kaplan, Amy. *The Anarchy of Empire in the Making of U.S. Culture*. Cambridge: Harvard University Press, 2003.

Kaplan, Amy, and Donald Pease, eds. *Cultures of United States Imperialism*. Durham: Duke University Press, 1993.

Kaplan, Caren, and Inderpal Grewal. "Transnational Feminist Cutural Studies: Beyond the Marxism/Postculturalism/Feminism Divides." *Between Woman and Nation: Nationalisms, Transnational Feminism, and the State*, ed. Caren Kaplan, Norma Alarcon, and Minoo Moallem. 349–65. Durham: Duke University Press, 1999.

Kapur, Ratna. "The Tragedy of Victimization Rhetoric: Resurrecting the 'Native' Subject in International/Post-Colonial Feminist Legal Politics." *Harvard Human Rights Journal* 15 (2002): 1–38.

– "Un-Veiling Women's Rights in the War on Terrorism." *Duke Journal of Gender, Law, and Policy* 9(211) (2002): 211–25.

Karstedt, Susanne. "Terror and 'New Wars.'" In *11 September 2001: War, Terror, and Judgment*. London: Cass, 2003.

Keck, Margaret E., and Kathryn Sikkink. *Activists beyond Borders*. Ithaca: Cornell University Press, 1998.

Keen, David. "War without End? Magic, Propaganda, and the Hidden Functions of Counter-Terrorism." *Journal of International Development* 18 (2006): 87–104.

Keener, Craig. "Mutual Mayhem." *Christianity Today*. November 2004, 60–4.

Kennedy, John. "Cuba's Next Revolution." *Christianity Today*. 12 January 1998, 18–25.

Khalidi, Rashid. "Foreword." In *The War on Lebanon: A Reader*, ed. Rashid Khalidi and Nubar Hovsepian. ix–xxiii. New York: Olive Branch Press, 2007.

Khan, Sameera. "When Survivors Become Victims." In *Missing Half the Story: Journalism as if Gender Matters*, ed. Kalpana Sharma. 83–118. New Delhi: Zubaan, 2010.

KHRP (Kurdish Human Rights Project). "Turkey's Anti-Terror Laws: Threatening the Protection of Human Rights." Briefing Paper, 8 August 2008. Accessed 9 January 2014 at http://lib.ohchr.org/HRBodies/UPR/Documents/Session8/TR/KHRP_UPR_TUR_S08_2010_KurdishHumanRightsProject_Annex3.pdf.

Kidd, Rosalind. *The Way We Civilise*. University of Queensland Press, 1997.

Kielburger, Craig. "Omar Khadr: America's Injustice Canada's Shame." In *Omar Khadr, Oh Canada*, ed. Janice Williamson. Montreal: McGill-Queen's University Press, 2012.

– "Omar Khadr, Jean Chretien, and Me." *Toronto Star*. 17 October 2010.

Kim, Jodi. *Ends of Empire: Asian American Critique and the Cold War*. Minneapolis: University of Minnesota Press, 2010.

King, Diane. "The Personal Is Patrilineal: Namus as Sovereignty." *Identities: Global Studies in Culture and Power* 15(3) (2008): 317–42.

King, J. "The Exodus Continues." *Charisma*. November 2000, 77–83.

– "Global March for Jesus in May Focused on the Persecuted Church." *Charisma*. August 1998, 18–22.

King, Thomas. *The Truth about Stories: A Native Narrative*. Toronto: House of Anansi, 2003.

"Kişanak: Türkiye, Kürt özerk Bölgesini İşgal Etmek Isterse Tankların Önüne Geçeriz" (If Turkey Tries to Invade the Autonomous Kurdish Region, We Will Stand in Front of the Tanks). *T24.Com*, 6 October 2012. http://t24.com.tr/haber/kisanak-turkiye-kurt-ozerk-bolgesini-isgal-etmek-isterse-tankla rin-onune-geceriz/214601.

Kisuke, C. "Sudanese Christians Bloody, but Unbowed." *Christianity Today*. 10 August 1998, 24–5.

Klak, Thomas, ed. *Globalization and Neoliberalism: The Caribbean Context*. Lanham: Rowan and Littlefield, 1998.

Klein, Naomi. "The Year of the Fake." *The Nation*, 26 January 2004. Accessed 10 January 2014 at http://www.thenation.com/article/year-fake.

Knippers, D. "A Global Scandal." *Christianity Today*. 1 September 1997, 58–9.

Knockwood, Isabelle. *Out of the Depths: The Experiences of Mi'kmaw Children at the Indian Residential School at Shubenacadie, Nova Scotia*. Lockeport: Roseway Publishing, 1992.

Kosek, Jake. "Ecologies of Empire: On the New Uses of the Honeybee." *Cultural Anthropology* 25(4) (2010): 650–78.

Koshy, Susan. "From Cold War to Trade War: Neocolonialism and Human Rights." *Social Text* 58(17) (1999): 1–32.

Kotef, Hagar. "Objects of Security: Gendered Violence and Securitized Humanitarianism in Occupied Gaza." *Comparative Studies of South Asia, Africa, and the Middle East* 30(2) (2010): 179–91.

Kure, Maikudi, and Josiah Idowu-Fearon. "Evangelism among Muslims." *Transformation*. January–March 2000, 17–19.

Kurst-Swanger, Karel. "Animal Abuse: The Link to Family Violence." In *Encyclopedia of Domestic Violence*, ed. Nicky Ali Jackson. New York: Routledge, 2007.

Lakoff, Andrew. "Two Regimes of Global Health." *Humanity: An International Journal of Human Rights, Humanitarianism, and Development* 1(1) (2010): 59–80.

Landers, M. "Cuban Catholics Make Gains but Protestant Rights Limited." *Christianity Today*. 8 February 1999, 18.

Landrum, Larry. "Instrumental Texts and Stereotyping in *Hill Street Blues*: The Police Procedural on Television." *MELUS* 11(3) (1964): 93–100.

Lane, Gary. "Walking with Christ in Laos." *Voice of the Martyrs*. June 2005, 3–8.

Langton, Marcia. "Aboriginal Sophisticates Betray Bush Sisters." *The Australian* (online). 15 April 2011. Accessed 8 January 2014

at http://www.theaustralian.com.au/national-affairs/opinion/
aboriginal-sophisticates-betray-bush-sisters/story-e6frgd0x-1226039349353.

– "The End of 'Big Men' Politics." *Griffith Review* 22 (2008): 48–73.

– "Trapped in the Aboriginal Reality Show." *Griffith Review* 19 (2007): 1–6.

Laqueur, Thomas. "Mourning, Pity, and the Work of Narrative in the Making of 'Humanity.'" In *Humanitarianism and Suffering: The Mobilization of Empathy*, ed. Richard Ashby Wilson and Richard D. Brown. 31–57. Cambridge: Cambridge University Press, 2009.

Lawrence, Philip. "Enlightenment, Modernity and War." *History of the Human Sciences* 12(1) (1999): 3–4, cited in Amin-Khan, *Political Islam*, 3–4.

Lawrie, Rowena. *Speak Out Speak Strong*. Aboriginal Justice Advisory Council, 2003.

Lawton, Kim. "Evangelicals and Catholics Pledge New Commitment: NCC Stands Aside." *Institute for Religion and Democracy*. Spring 1996, 8–9.

– "Faith without Borders." *Christianity Today*. 19 May 1997, 38–49.

– "The Persecuted Church Stands Faithful." *Christianity Today*. 15 July 1996, 54–64.

Lazreg, Marni. *Torture and the Twilight of Empire: From Algiers to Baghdad*. Princeton: Princeton University Press, 2008.

Le Carré, John. "A War We Cannot Win." *The Nation* 273(16) (2001): 15–17.

Lee, Dan P. "Travis the Menace." *New York*, 23 January 2011, 24–9. http://ny mag.com/news/features/70830/.

Lehman, M. "Death by Sanctions." *Christianity Today*. 2 October 2000, 29.

Lentin, Alana. "Racism and Human Rights: Towards a New Humanism?" *The Voice of the Turtle*, 22 January 2005. Accessed 9 January 2014 at http://www.voiceoftheturtle.org/show_article.php?aid=426.

"Letters." *Christianity Today*. 22 April 2002, 8–10.

– *Christianity Today*. 3 December 2001, 7–13.

Levy, Horace. *They Cry "Respect"! Urban Violence and Poverty in Jamaica*. Kingston: Centre for Population, Community, and Social Change, Department of Sociology and Social Work, University of the West Indies, 1996.

Lichter, Linda S., and Samuel Robert Lichter. *Prime Time Crime*. Washington: Media Institute, 1983.

Lindner, John. "Christians Face New Wave of Violent Attacks in India." *Charisma*. November 2008, 19.

– "Reaching Hidden People." *Charisma*. January 2000, 62–6.

Lira, Elizabeth. "Psicología, Etica y Seguridad Nacional." *Psykhe* 17(2) (2008): 5–16.

Little, Douglas. *American Orientalism: The United States and the Middle East Since 1945*. Chapell Hill: University of North Carolina Press, 2008.

Littleton, S. "Hmong Believers Suffer at Hands of Communist Regime in Vietnam." *Charisma*. February 1999, 30–2.

Lloyd, Maxine. "Politics without Television: The BSP and the Dalit Counter-Public Spheres." In *Television in India: Satellites, Politics, and Cultural Change*, ed. Nalin Mehta. 62–86. Routledge, 2008.

Loconte, Joseph. "The United Nations' Disarray." *Christianity Today*. February 2007, 40–2, 120.

Lombardo, Michelle. "Christians in Sri Lanka Face Attacks, Threats of Anti-Conversion Bills." *Charisma*. August 2005, 28–30.

Lotte, B. "How to Meet the Needs of Immigrants, with a Bonus." *Evangelical Missions Quarterly*. July 1989, 256–60.

Love, Eric Tyrone Lowery. *Race over Empire: Racism and U.S. Imperialism, 1865–1900*. Chapel Hill: University of North Carolina Press, 2004.

Loveland, Ian. *By Due Process of Law: Racial Discrimination and the Right to Vote in South Africa, 1855–1960*. Oxford: Hart Publishing, 1999.

Lowe, Lisa. *Immigrant Acts: On Asian American Cultural Politics*. Durham: Duke University Press, 1996.

Lu, Angela. "Drawn by Grace." *World*. 18 December 2010, 58–60.

Lubold, Gordon. "Africa Command?" *Armed Forces International Journal* 143(5) (December 2004): 22–6.

Lugones, María. "Playfulness, World-Travelling, and Loving Perception." *Hypatia* 2(2) (1987): 3–19.

Lukins, Julia. "Behind the Black Veil." *Charisma*. June 2004, 62–6, 100.

– "When a Nation Is Shaken." *Charisma*. June 2004, 66.

Lumina, Cephas. "Counter-Terrorism Legislation and the Protection of Human Rights: A Survey of Selected International Practice." *African Human Rights Law Journal* 7(1) (2007): 35–67.

– "Terror in the Backyard: Domestic Terrorism in Africa and Its Impact on Human Rights." *African Security Review* 17(14) (2008): 112–32.

Lynch, Sandra. "Aristotle and Derrida on Friendship." *Contretemps* 3 (2002): 98–108.

MacHarg, K. "Death in the Night." *Christianity Today*. 12 June 2000, 30–1.

– "Healing the Violence." *Christianity Today*. 7 August 2000, 30.

– "Twenty-Five Pastors Killed This Year." *Christianity Today*. 4 October 1999, 23.

Mahmood, Saba. "Feminism, Democracy, and Empire: Islam and the War of Terror." In *Women's Studies on the Edge*, ed. Joan Wallach Scott. 81–114. Durham: Duke University Press, 2008.

Mahtani, Minelle. "The Racialized Geographies of News Consumption and Production: Contaminated Memories and Racialized Silences." *GeoJournal* 74(3) (June 2009): 257–64.

– 'Representing Minorities: Canadian Media and Minority Identities.' *Canadian Ethnic Studies* 33(3) (2004): 99–134.

Maira, Sunaina. "Deporting Radicals, Deporting La Migra: The Hayat Case in Lodi." *Cultural Dynamics* 19(1) (2007): 39–66.

– "'Good' and 'Bad' Muslim Citizens: Feminists, Terrorists, and U.S. Orientalisms." *Feminist Studies* 35(3) (2009): 631–56.

– *Missing: Youth, Citizenship, and Empire after 9/11*. Durham: Duke University Press, 2009.

Malabou, Catherine. *The New Wounded: From Neurosis to Brain Damage*. New York: Fordham University Press, 2012.

– *The Ontology of the Accident: An Essay on Destructive Plasticity*. Cambridge: Polity Press, 2013.

Malkki, Liisa. "Children, Humanity, and the Infantilization of Peace." In *The Name of Humanity: The Government of Threat and Care*, ed. Ilana Feldman and Miriam Ticktin. 58–85. Durham: Duke University Press, 2010.

Mallaby, Sebastian. "The Reluctant Imperialist: Terrorism, Failed States, and the Case for American Empire." *Foreign Affairs*, March–April 2002.

Mamdani, Mahmood. "The New Humanitarian Order." *The Nation*, 29 September 2008. Accessed 9 January 2014 at http://www.thenation.com/article/new-humanitarian-order.

– *Saviors and Survivors: Darfur, Politics, and the War on Terror*. New York: Pantheon Books, 2009.

– *When Victims Become Killers: Colonialism, Nativism, and the Genocide in Rwanda*. Princeton: Princeton University Press, 2001.

Mani, Lata. "Contentious Traditions: The Debate on *Sati* in Colonial India." In *Recasting Women: Essays in Colonial History*, ed. Kumkum Sangari and Sudesh Vaid. 88–126. New Delhi: Kali for Women, 1989.

Mann, Eric. *Dispatches from Durban: Firsthand Commentaries on the World Conference against Racism and Post-September 11 Movement Strategies*. Los Angeles: Frontline Press, 2002.

Markon, Jerry. "Tension Grows between Calif. Muslims, FBI after Informant Infiltrates Mosque." 5 December 2010. *Washington Post*. Accessed 9 July 2012 at http://www.washingtonpost.com/wp-dyn/content/article/2010/12/04/AR2010120403710.html.

Marriott, David. *Haunted Life: Visual Culture and Black Modernity*. Piscataway: Rutgers University Press, 2007.

Marshall, Paul. "Correcting the Secular Vision." *Faith and Freedom* 19(2) (2000): 10–11.

Marty, Dick. "Secret Detentions and Illegal Transfer of Detainees Involving Council of Europe Member States: Second Report." Council of Europe Committee on Legal Affairs and Human Rights. 8 June 2007. 1–72.

Marx, Karl. *Economic and Philosophic Manuscripts of 1844*. New York: W.W. Norton, 1978.

Massad, Joseph Andoni. *Desiring Arabs*. Chicago: University of Chicago Press, 2007.

Mathewes-Green, Frederica. "Could We Survive Persecution?" *Christianity Today*. 1 March 1999, 68.

Matthews, G. "Pablo's Prayer." *Decision*. December 2003, 32–3.

Mavhunga, Clapperton Chakanetsa. "Vermin Beings: On Pestiferous Animals and Human Game." *Social Text* 29(1) (Spring 2011): 151–76.

May, Vivian M. "Thinking from the Margins, Acting at the Intersections: Anna Julia Cooper's *A Voice from the South*." *Hypatia* 19(2) (Spring 2004): 74–91.

Mazrui, Ali A. "September 11, 2001 Consequences for Africa." *Horizon* (Dar-es-Salaam), 6–12 June 2007, 10.

Mbembe, Achille. "The Colony: Guilty Secret and Accursed Share." In Boehmer and Morton, 27–54.

– "Necropolitics." *Public Culture* 15(1) (2003): 11–40.

– *On the Postcolony*. California: University of California Press, 2001.

McAdam, L. "Lessons from 9/11." *Evangelical Missions Quarterly*. October 2004, 418–19.

McCannell, Juliet. *The Regime of the Brother*. New York: Routledge, 1991.

McClintock, Anne, Aamir Mufti, and Ella Shohat, eds. *Dangerous Liaisons: Gender, Nation, and Post-Colonial Perspectives*. Minneapolis: University of Minnesota Press, 1997.

McGeough, Paul. "Australian Student Tells of His Flotilla Ordeal." 7 June 2010. Accessed 10 January 2014 at http://www.theage.com.au/national/australian-student-tells-of-his-flotilla-ordeal-20100606-xnbh.html.

McLaren, Peter. "The Dialectics of Terrorism: A Marxist Response to September 11." *Cultural Studies – Critical Methodologies* 2(2) (2002): 169–90.

Meeks, Brian. *Envisioning Caribbean Futures: Jamaican Perspectives*. Kingston: University of the West Indies Press, 2007.

Meetoo, Veena, and Heidi Safia Mirza. "There Is Nothing 'Honourable' about Honour Killings: Gender, Violence, and the Limits of Multiculturalism." *Women's Studies International Forum* 30(3) (May–June 2007): 187–200.

Mei, Xu. "The Price of Protest." *Christianity Today*. October 2006, 23.

Melamed, Jody. *Represent and Destroy: Rationalizing Violence in the New Racial Capitalism*. Minneapolis: University of Minnesota Press, 2011.

Menon, Nivedita. "Embodying the Self: Feminism, Sexual Violence, and the Law." In *Community, Gender, and Violence: Subaltern Studies XI*, ed. Partha Chatterjee and Pradeep Jeganathan. 66–105. Delhi: Permanent Black, 2000.

Menon, Ritu, and Kamala Bhasin. "Abducted Women, the State, and Questions of Honour: Three Perspectives on the Recovery Operation in Post-Partition India." In *Embodied Violence: Communalizing Women's Sexuality in South Asia*, ed. Kumari Jayawardena and Malathi de Alwis. 1–31. London: Zed Books, 1996.

Meral, Z. "Bearing the Silence of God." *Christianity Today*. March 2008, 40–3.

Mercer, Kobena. *Welcome to the Jungle: New Positions in Black Cultural Studies*. New York: Routledge, 1994.

Mernissi, Fatima. "Virginity and Patriarchy." *Women's Studies International Forum* 5 (1982): 183–91.

Mert, Nuray. "The Kurds and the Conservatives." *Hürriyet Daily News*, 28 May 2012. http://www.hurriyetdailynews.com/the-kurds-and-the-conservatives.aspx?pageID=449&nID=21681&NewsCatID=406.

"Mexico." *Rutherford* 3(3) (1994): 16.

Miller, D. "Christians to Help Investigate Crimes." *Christianity Today*. 7 January 2002, 27.

– "Divorcing a Dictator." *Christianity Today*. 5 February 2001, 22—3.

– "Prophet to a Nation." *Charisma*. February 2009, 40–3, 65.

– "Rebels Kill Evangelical Pastors." *Christianity Today*. 9 September 2002, 31.

– "Up from the Ashes?" *Christianity Today*. 18 May 1998, 40–3.

Miller, Daniel. *Materiality*. Durham: Duke University Press, 2005.

Minchakpu, O. "Back to the Basics." *Christianity Today*. November 2004, 62–3.

– "Chronic Violence Claims 2,000 Lives." *Christianity Today*. 7 January 2002, 23.

– "Eye for an Eye for an Eye." *Christianity Today*. July 2004, 17.

– "Moving Toward War?" *Christianity Today*. 24 April 2000, 29.

– "Orphaned and Widowed." *Christianity Today*. 3 September 2001, 34.

– "Religious Riots Displace Nearly 5 Million in Nigeria." *Charisma*. August 2006, 28–30.

"Ministry Impacts Chicago's 'Little India.'" *Charisma*. June 2007, 38.

Mirzoeff, Nicholas. "The Crisis of Visuality / Visualizing the Crisis." *E-mesférica* 7(1) (2011): 2. Accessed 9 August 2014 at http://hemi.nyu.edu/hemi/en/e-misferica-71/mirzoeff.

– *The Right to Look: A Counterhistory of Visuality*. Durham: Duke University Press, 2011.

– "War Is Culture: Global Counterinsurgency, Visuality, and the Petraeus Doctrine." *PMLA* 124(5) (2009): 1737–46.

– *Watching Babylon*. New York: Routledge, 2005.

Mitchell, Anthony. "Police in Kenya Raid Major Media Firm." *Washington Post*, 3 March 2006.

Mitchell, Juliet. *Psychoanalysis and Feminism*. London: Allen Lane, 1974.

Mitchell, Timothy. *Colonising Egypt*. Berkeley: University of California Press, 1991.

– "Society, Economy, and the State Effect." In *The Anthropology of the State: A Reader*, ed. Aradhana Sharma and Akhil Gupta. 169–86. Malden: Blackwell, 2006.

Mitchell, W.J.T. *Cloning Terror: The War of Images, 9/11 to the Present*. Chicago: University of Chicago Press, 2011.

– *Seeing through Race*. Cambridge: Harvard University Press, 2012.

Mitri, T. "Who Are the Christians of the Arab World?" *International Review of Mission*. January 2000, 12–27.

Moallem, Minoo. "Whose Fundamentalism?" *Meridians: Feminism, Race, Transnationalism* 2(2) (2002): 298–301.

Moghissi, Haideh. "Away from Home: Iranian Women, Displacement, Cultural Resistance, and Change." *Journal of Comparative Family Studies* 30(2) (1999): 207–18.

Mohanty, Chandra. "Under Western Eyes: Feminist Scholarship and Colonial Discourses." *Feminist Review* 30 (1988): 61–88.

Mohanty, Chandra Talpade, Minnie Bruce Pratt, and Robin L. Riley, eds. "Introduction: Feminism and U.S. Wars – Mapping the Ground." In *Feminism and War*. London: Zed Books, 2008.

Mojab, Shahrzad, and Amir Hassanpour. "The Politics and Culture of 'Honour Killing': The Murder of Fadime Şahindal." *Atlantis: A Women's Studies Journal*. Special Issue #1 (2003): 56–70.

Mokhtari, Shadi. *After Abu Ghraib: Exploring Human Rights in America and the Middle East*. New York: Cambridge University Press, 2009.

Moll, R. "Four Missionaries Murdered." *Christianity Today*. May 2004, 18.

Mombo, E., and S. Mwaluda. "Relationship and Challenge in Kenya and East Africa." *Transformation*. January–March 2000, 36–41.

Mondzain, Marie-José. *Image, icône, économie. Les sources Byzantines de l'imaginaire contemporain*. Paris: Seuil, 1996. Translated as *Image, Icon, Economy: The Byzantine Origins of the Contemporary Imaginary*. Stanford: Stanford University Press, 2005

Moon, R. "World's Worst Persecutor." *Christianity Today*. December 2008, 19–20.

Moore, A. "Justice Delayed." *Christianity Today*. 12 November 2001, 23–4.

– "US Ally Jails House-Church Leaders." *Christianity Today*. 3 December 2001, 27–8.

Morgan, M. "Black Eye for Freedom." *Christianity Today*. July 2004, 15.

Morgan, T., and David Neff. "The Vulnerable." *Christianity Today*. April 2004, 87–9.

Moritz, Mark. "A Critical Examination of Honor Cultures and Herding Societies in Africa." *African Studies Review* 51(2) (September 2008): 99–117.

Morse, A. "View from the Axis." *World*. 9 March 2002, 20–5.

Moten, Fred. *In the Break: The Aesthetics of the Black Radical Tradition*. Minneapolis: University of Minnesota Press, 2003.

Mouffe, Chantal. "Feminism, Citizenship, and Radical Democratic Politics." In *Feminists Theorize the Political*, ed. Judith Butler and Joan Scott. 369–84. New York: Routledge, Chapman and Hall, 1992.

Moulian, Tomás. *Chile Actual: Anatomía de un Mito*. Santiago, Chile: Arcis-LOM, 1997.

Mueller, John, and Mark G. Stewart. "3 Questions About NSA Surveillance." *Chronicle of Higher Education*, 13 June 2013.

Mugyenzi, S. "Seeking Understanding in Uganda." *Transformation*. January–March 2000, 41–4.

Mu'id, Onaje. "United Nations World Conference against Racism: Disparate Beacon for an Emerging New Humanity under Contest by Racist Detractors." *Socialism and Democracy* 16(1) (2002): 118–23.

Mullings, Beverley. "Neoliberalization, Social Reproduction, and the Limits to Labour in Jamaica." *Singapore Journal of Tropical Geography* 30(2) (2009): 174–88.

Mumper, S. "Where in the World Is the Church Growing?" *Christianity Today*. 11 July 1986, 17–21.

Mundy, David. "Chinese Christian Describes Torture, Coerced Testimony in Labor Camps." *Charisma*. June 2005, 26–7.

– "Muslim–Christian Conflict in Nigeria Claims Thousands of Lives." *Charisma*. October 2004, 19.

– "Secret Government Report Reveals China's Plan to Oppose Christianity." *Charisma*. February 2005, 19.

Naber, Nadine C. *Arab America: Gender, Cultural Politics, and Activism*. New York: NYU Press, 2012.

– "The Rules of Forced Engagement: Race, Gender, and the Culture of Fear among Arab Immigrants in San Francisco Post-9/11." *Cultural Dynamics* 18(3) (2006): 235–67.

– "So Our History Doesn't Become Your Future: The Local and Global Politics of Coalition Building Post September 11th." *Journal of Asian American Studies* 5(3) (2002): 217–42.

– "Transnational Families under Siege: Lebanese Shi'a in Dearborn, Michigan, and the 2006 War on Lebanon." *Journal of Middle East Women's Studies* 5(3) (2009): 145–74.

Nader, Laura. "What the Rest Think of the West – Legal Dimensions." *Global Jurist* 9(1) (2009): Art. 3, 1–7.

Nangiana, Umer. "Militancy Has Cost Pakistan 9,000 Lives, $24 billion." *Express Tribune* (Islamabad), 8 May 2011. Accessed 9 January 2014 at http://tribune.com.pk/story/164274/militancy-has-cost-pakistan-9000-lives-24-billion.

"Nationwide Protests against US Verdict." *Dawn*, 25 September. http://archives.dawn.com/archives/37758.

Neal, Andrew. "Cutting Off the King's Head: Foucault's *Society Must Be Defended* and the Problem of Sovereignty." *Alternative* 29 (2004): 373–98.

Needham, A.D., and R. Sunder Rajan, eds. *The Crisis of Secularism in India.* Durham: Duke University Press, 2007.

Neff, David. "Operation Human Rights." *Christianity Today.* October 2004, 106–7.

– "The Politics of Remembering." *Christianity Today.* 7 October 1991, 28–9.

– "Progress for the Persecuted." *Christianity Today.* 6 October 1997, 19.

Nelson, Dana D. *National Manhood: Capitalist Citizenship and the Imagined Fraternity of White Men.* Durham: Duke University Press, 1998.

Nelson, Jill. "Under Siege." *World.* 25 March 2006, 29.

Nettleford, Rex. *Dance Jamaica: Cultural Definitions and Artistic Discovery; The National Dance Theatre Company of Jamaica, 1962–1983.* New York: Grove Press, 1985.

Nettleton, Todd. "Having Nothing: Yet Having It All." *Voice of the Martyrs.* June 2005, 3–8.

– "My Grace Is Sufficient." *Voice of the Martyrs.* Special Issue, 2004, 5.

Neu, Dean. "Accounting and Accountability Relations: Colonization, Genocide, and Canada's First Nations." *Accounting, Auditing, and Accountability Journal* 13(3) (2000): 268–88.

Newman, Josie. "Egyptian Christian Escapes Death, Seeks to Aid Persecuted Church." *Charisma.* July 2004, 22.

Newman, Saul. "Terror, Sovereignty, and Law: On the Politics of Violence." *German Law Journal* 5(5) (2004): 569–84.

Newman, Saul, and Michael Levine. "War, Politics, and Race." *Theoria* 53(110) (August 2006): 23–49.

"News Briefs." *Charisma.* October 2004, 32.

"News Service Briefs." *Charisma.* June 2002, 34.

"Newsbriefs." *Charisma.* June 2007, 46.

– *Charisma.* April 2007, 36.

– *Charisma.* February 1999, 34.

"News of the Year." *World.* 27 December 2004, 25–37.

Newton, Joshua. "Blockbuster Evangelism." *Christianity Today.* December 2003, 28–30.

– "Dalit Christians Fight for Equal Rights in India." *Charisma.* November 2005, 31.

– "Fending Off Hindutva." *Christianity Today*. June 2003, 26–7.

– "Hindu Extremes." *Christianity Today*. March 2004, 23.

– "Machete Attack on American Alarms Local Christians." *Christianity Today*. March 2003, 30–1.

– "She Chose to Forgive." *Charisma*. September 2004, 56–61.

Nhema, Alfred G., and Tiyambe Zeleza, *The Roots of African Conflict: Costs and Causes*. Oxford: James Currey, 2008.

Nicholson, Alastair, Nicole Watson, and Alison Vivian. *Listening but Not Hearing*. Jumbunna Indigenous House of Learning, University of Technology Sydney, 2012.

Nickles, Beverly. "A Precarious Step Forward." *Christianity Today*. 6 March 2000, 32–3.

Niranjana, Tejaswini. "Nationalism Refigured: Contemporary South Indian Cinema and the Subject of Feminism." In *Community, Gender, and Violence: Subaltern Studies XI*. 138–66. Delhi: Permanent Black, 2000

"No Change to Be Made in Blasphemy Law: PM." *The Nation*, 17 January 2011. Accessed 27 April 2012 at http://www.nation.com.pk/ pakistan-news-newspaper-daily-english-online/politics/17-Jan-2011/ No-plans-to-amend-blasphemy-law-PM.

Noll, Mark. "Early Returns Are Mixed." *Christianity Today*. June 2008, 53–4.

Norton-Taylor, Richard, Stephen Grey, and Vikram Dodd. "M15 Tip-Off to CIA Led to Men's Rendition." *The Guardian*, 28 March 2006.

Nuu-chah-nulth Tribal Council. *Indian Residential Schools: The Nuu-chah-nulth Experience*. Port Alberni: 1996.

NWAC (Native Women's Association of Canada). *Report on the Convention on the Rights of the Child*. Ottawa: NWAC, 1993. Accessed 20 June 2013 at http://www.nwac.ca.

Nyberg, Richard. "Ethnic Cleansing." *Christianity Today* 48(5) (May 2004): 17.

– "Missionaries in Congo Flee." *Christianity Today* 43(2) (February 1999): 24–5.

Nyquist, Mary. "Hobbes, Slavery, and Despotical Rule." *Representations* 106 (2009): 1–33.

Obi, Cyril. "Terrorism in West Africa: Real, Emerging, or Imagined Threats?" *African Security Review* 15(3) (2006): 87–101.

Öğret, Özgür, and Nina Ognianova. "Erdoğan Tells Media Not to Cover Kurdish Conflict." *CPJ Committee to Protect Journalists*. 12 September 2012. Accessed 9 January 2014 at http://cpj.org/blog/2012/09/erdogan-tells-media-not-to-cover-kurdish-conf.php.

Oke, Janette. *Drums of Change: The Story of Running Fawn*. Minneapolis: Bethany House, 1996.

Okite, Odhiambo. "Missionaries or Mercenaries." *Christianity Today*. 24 May 1999, 28.

– "Returning a Tabot: Orthodox Demand That British Give Back All Looted Sacred Items." *Christianity Today* 46(5) (22 April 2002): 22.

Olasky, Marvin. "No es facil." *World*. 1 May 2004, 36–49.

– "The Panda in Winter." *World*. 18 February 2006, 19–21.

– "Touching, Teaching." *World*. 29 May 2004, 48.

– "Wildfire." *World*. 24 June 2006, 16–21.

– "Beyond Wishful Thinking." *World*. 11 December 2004, 56.

Oliver, K. "Women as Weapons of War: Iraq, Sex and the Media." Vanderbilt University, 8 February 2008. Accessed 19 July 2010 at http://www.youtube.com/watch?v=yEkljySp9ds.

Onyeani, Chika. "Africans and the 9/11 Deaths." *African Sun Times*, 15 December 2001, 1.

"Open Doors." *Charisma*. September 2006, 21.

Orford, Anne. "The Passions of Protection: Sovereign Authority and Humanitarian War." In Fassin and Pandolfi, *Contemporary States*, 235–353.

Paisley, Fiona. "Race Hysteria, Darwin 1938." *Australian Feminist Studies* 16(34) (2001): 43–59.

"Pakistan Ranks 3rd on List of Most Dangerous Countries for Women." *Express Tribune* (Karachi), 15 June 2011.

Pandolfi, Mariella. "Laboratory of Intervention: The Humanitarian Governance of the Postcommunist Balkan Territories." In *Postcolonial Disorders*, ed. M.-J.D. Good, S. Hyde, S. Pinto, and B. Good. 157–86. Berkeley: University of California Press, 2008.

Parajon, Gustavo. "One Nicaraguan Christian's Perspective." *Christianity Today*. 3 March 1989, 48.

Parmar, Pratibha, and Valerie Amos. "Challenging Imperial Feminism." *Feminist Review* 17 (1984): 3–19.

"Passages." *Christianity Today*. June 2007, 18.

Pease, Richard. "The Mission Field around Us." *Alliance Witness*. 27 February 1985, 20–1.

Peckham, Elaine. "Speech on Income Management." Delivered at the Northern Territory Council of Social Services Conference, Darwin, April 2011.

Perera, Suvendrini. "The Landscapes of Massacre." In *Torture and the Human Body*, ed. Shampa Biswas and Zahi Zalloua. 215–43. Seattle: University of Washington Press, 2011.

– "Missing in Action." *Borderlands* (forthcoming).

Perrot, Sandrine. "Kony 2012: 100 Million Views for a Non-Event?" *The Independent*. 6 May 2012. Accessed 10 January 2014 at http://www.independent.co.ug/column/comment/5720-kony-2012-100-million-views-for-a-non-event.

"Persecution Watch." *Charisma*. April 2010, 23.

– *Charisma*. June 2008, 27.

– *Charisma*. December 2007, 32.
– *Charisma*. May 2007, 32.
– *Charisma*. March 2007, 29.
– *Charisma*. January 2007, 29.
– *Charisma*. May 2006, 29.
– *Charisma*. January 2006, 21.
– *Charisma*. April 2006, 33.
– *Charisma*. July 2006, 32.
– *Charisma*. August 2006, 30.
– *Charisma*. September 2006, 26.
– *Charisma*. November 2006, 30.
– *Charisma*. February 2005, 26.
– *Charisma*. June 2005, 34.
– *Charisma*. October 2005, 34.
– *Charisma*. September 2005, 27.
– *Charisma*. December 2005, 26.
– *Charisma*. March 2004, 26.
– *Charisma*. April 2004, 26.
– *Charisma*. November 2004, 28.
– *Charisma*. December 2004, 26.

Pettman, Dominic. *Human Error: Species-Being and Media Machines*. Minneapolis: University of Minnesota Press, 2011.

Phelan, Peggy. *Mourning Sex: Performing Public Memories*. New York: Routledge, 1997.

Phiri, Isaac. "Building a Peace beyond Understanding." *Christianity Today*. January 2009, 56–61.

– "Hope in the Heart of Darkness." *Christianity Today*. July 2006, 23–31.

Piepzna-Samarasinha, Leah Lakshmi. 2006. *Consensual Genocide*. Toronto: TSAR Publications.

Pitt-Rivers, Julian. "Honor." In *International Encyclopedia of Social Sciences*, ed. David Sills. VI:503–11. New York: Macmillan, 1968.

Plowman, Edward E. "Motivated by Money." *World Magazine*. 20 March 2004, 27.

Ponniah, Moses. "The Situation in Malaysia." *Transformation*. January–March 2000, 31–4.

Poovey, Mary. *A History of the Modern Fact: Problems of Knowledge in the Sciences of Wealth and Society*. Chicago: University of Chicago Press, 1998.

Portelli, Alessandro. "What Makes Oral History Different." In *The Oral History Reader*, ed. Robert Perks and Alistair Thomson. 2nd ed. London: Routledge, 2006.

Prasad, Nandini. *A Pressing Matter*. New Delhi: Friedrich Ebert Stiftung, 1992.

Pratt, Mary Louise. *Imperial Eyes: Travel Writing and Transculturation*. New York: Routledge, 1992.

Preston, Jennifer. "Sequel to 'Kony 2012' Video Addresses Critics and Outlines Call for Action." *New York Times*. 5 April 2012.

Price, Bess. "Inaugural Peter Howson Lecture." Speech delivered at the Bennelong Society, Sydney, 3 December 2009.

Price, Clive. "It's God's Hour for Iran." *Charisma*. June 2004, 65.

– "Just Call Her Saint Caroline." *Charisma*. August 1997, 68–73.

– "Persecuted Church Takes Spotlight at Human-Rights Gathering in London." *Charisma*. February 2004, 24.

Prudames, David. "Osama Bin Laden's Lair in London." *Culture*, 19 March 2003.

Puar, Jasbir. *Terrorist Assemblages: Homonationalism in Queer Times*. Durham: Duke University Press, 2007.

Puar, Jasbir K., and Amit S. Rai. "Monster, Terrorist, Fag: The War on Terrorism and the Production of Docile Patriots." *Social Text* 20(3) (2002): 117–48.

Pugliese, Joseph. "Abu Ghraib and Its Shadow Archives." *Law and Literature* 19(2) (2007): 247–76.

– "Apostrophe of Empire." *Borderlands e-journal* 8(3) (2009): 1–26.

– *The Biopolitics of Biometrics*. New York: Routledge, 2012.

Pulkkinen, Tuija "Tradition, Gender and Democracy to Come – Derrida on Fraternity." Accessed 23 August 2013 at http://www.jyu.fi/yhtfil/redescriptions/Yearbook%202009/Pulkkinen_2009.pdf.

Pulliam, Sarah. "Costly Commitment." *Christianity Today*. September 2007, 22–3.

Rafter, Nicole. *A Shot in the Mirror: The Crime Film and Society*. Oxford: Oxford University Press, 2006.

Rahman, Tariq. "Can Pakistan End Terrorism?" *Express Tribune* (Islamabad), 16 April 2011. Accessed 9 January 2014 at http://tribune.com.pk/story/150741/can-pakistan-end-terrorism.

Rai, Amit. "Of Monsters: Biopower, Terrorism, and Excess in Genealogies of Monstrosity." *Cultural Studies* 18(4) (July): 538–70.

Rajagopal, Arvind. "The Public Sphere in India: Structure and Transformation." In *The Indian Public Sphere*, ed. Arvind Rajagopal. 1–30. Delhi: Oxford University Press, 2009.

Ramstad, Mans. "Persecution: A Biblical and Personal Reflection." *Evangelical Missions Quarterly*. October 2004, 468–75.

Rancière, Jacques. *Chronicles of Consensual Times*. New York: Continuum, 2010.

– *Dissensus: On Politics and Aesthetics*. New York: Continuum. 2010.

Rancière, Jacques, and Davide Panagia. "Dissenting Words: A Conversation with Jacques Ranciere." *Diacritics* 30(2) (Summer 2000): 113–26.

Rashid, Ahmed. *Taliban: The Story of the Afghan Warlords*. London: Pan Books, 2001.

Rasmussen, K. "Caciques Rule the Highlands of Chiapas." *Indian Life*. May–June 1999, 8.

Ray, Suranjita. "Khap Panchayats: Reinforcing Caste Hierarchies." *Mainstream* 48(36) (2010): 21–7.

Razack, Sherene H. "The Afghan Detainee Scandal: Torture as Pedagogy." In *Empire's Ally: Canada and the War in Afghanistan*, ed. Jerome Klassen and Greg Albo. 367–87. Toronto: University of Toronto Press, 2012.

– *Casting Out: The Eviction of Muslims from Western Law and Politics*. Toronto: University of Toronto Press, 2008.

– *Dark Threats and White Knights: The Somalia Affair, Peacekeeping, and the New Imperialism*. Toronto: University of Toronto Press, 2004.

– "Domestic Violence as Gender Persecution: Policing the Borders of Nation, Race, and Gender." *Canadian Journal of Women and the Law / Revue Femmes et Droit* 8(1) (1995): 45–88.

– "To Essentialize or Not to Essentialize: Is This the Question?" In *Unhomely States: Theorizing English Canadian Postcolonialism*, ed. Cynthia Sugars. 323–31. Peterborough: Broadview Press, 2004.

– "Geopolitics, Culture Clash, and Gender after September 11." *Social Justice* 32(4) (2005): 11–31.

– "How Is White Supremacy Embodied? Sexualized Racial Violence at Abu Ghraib." *Canadian Journal of Women and the Law* 17(2) (2005): 341–63.

– "Imperiled Muslim Women, Dangerous Muslim Men, and Civilized Europeans: Legal and Social Responses to Forced Marriages." *Feminist Legal Studies* 12 (2007): 129–74.

– "Racism, Empire, and Torture." In *Racism Review: Thoughts on Racism, Culture, Society, Politics*. Accessed 28 June 2012 at http://www.racismreview.com/blog/2009/05/22/racism-and-torture.

– "Stealing the Pain of Others: Reflections on the Canadian Humanitarian Responses." *Review of Education, Pedagogy, and Cultural Studies* 29(4) (2007): 375–94.

– "'We Didn't Kill 'em, We Didn't Cut Their Head Off.' Abu Ghraib Revisited." In *Racial Formation in the Twenty-First Century*, ed. Daniel Martinez Hosang, Oneka LaBennett, and Laura Pulido. 217–45. Berkeley: University of California Press, 2012.

– "What Is to Be Gained by Looking White People in the Eye? Culture, Race, and Gender in the Cases of Sexual Violence." *Signs* (Summer 1994): 894–921.

Reapsome, Jim. What's Holding Up World Evangelization?" *Evangelical Missions Quarterly*. January 1989, 18–24.

"Rearing Its Ugly Head." *World*. 6 February 1999, 12–13.

Reddy, Rupa. "Gender, Culture, and the Law: Approaches to 'Honour Crimes' in the UK." *Feminist Legal Studies* (2008): 305–21.

Redfield, Marc. *The Rhetoric of Terror: Reflections on 9/11 and the War on Terror*. New York: Fordham University Press, 2009.

"Rehman Malik Sees Accord on Blasphemy Laws." *Dawn*. 12 March 2011. Accessed 9 January 2014 at http://dawn.com/2011/03/12/rehman-malik-sees-accord-on-blasphemy-laws.

Rejali, Darius. *Torture and Democracy*. Princeton: Princeton University Press, 2007.

Religious News Service. "Priest Killed for 'Illegal' Conversions." *Christianity Today*. 25 October 1999, 25.

– "Three Killed in Christmas Attack on Church." *Christianity Today*. February 2003, 28.

"Religious Parties Threaten Protest in Blasphemy Case." *Dawn* (Lahore). 24 November 2010. Accessed 22 January 2014 at http://www.dawn.com/news/585070/religious-parties-threaten-protest.

Research Media, Ltd. "Dr. Laura Kahn, on the One Health Initiative." *International Innovation*, 27 August 2011. http://www.research-europe.com/index.php/2011/08/dr-laura-kahn-on-the-one-health-initiative.

Reszczynski, Katia, Paz Rojas, and Patricia Barceló. *Torture et Résistance au Chili*. Paris: L'Harmattan, 1984.

Richard, Nelly. *Residuos y Metaforas: Ensayos de critical cultural sobre el Chile de la transicion*. Santiago: Editorial Cuarto Propio, 1998.

Rieff, David. *A Bed for the Night: Humanitarianism in Crisis*. New York: Simon and Schuster, 2003.

Rintoul, Stuart. "Bess Price Takes On Her Critics over NT Intervention." *The Australian* (online). 8 November 2011. Accessed 9 January 2014 at http://www.theaustralian.com.au/national-affairs/indigenous/bess-price-takes-on-her-critics-over-nt-intervention/story-fn9hm1pm-1226188154969.

– "Jenny Macklin Defends Northern Territory Intervention." *The Australian* (online). 29 August 2011. Accessed 9 January 2014 at http://www.theaustralian.com.au/in-depth/aboriginal-australia/jenny-macklin-defends-northern-territory-intervention/story-e6frgd9f-1225767255816.

Robert, Hannah. "Disciplining the Female Aboriginal Body: Inter-Racial Sex and the Pretence of Separation." *Australian Feminist Studies* 16(34) (2001): 68–81.

Robertson, Pat. *The Turning Tide*. Dallas: Word Books, 1993.

Robnett, Belinda. *How Long? How Long? African-American Women in the Struggle for Civil Rights*. New York: Oxford University Press, 2000.

Rogers, Benedict. "Burma's Almost Forgotten." *Christianity Today* 48(3) (March 2004): 52–6.

Rojas, Emilio. *Tejas Verdes: Mis primeros tres minutos*. Santiago: Editora Seminario, 1989.

Roopnaraine, Rupert. "Race and Rebellion: A Personal Interview with the Past – Writing and Making History in Walter Rodney's *History of the Guyanese Working People, 1881–1905*." In his *The Sky's Wild Noise*. London: Peepal Tree Press, 2013.

Roos, John G. "Terrorism Is International: And It Has a Foothold in Africa." *Armed Forces Journal International* 141(12) (July 2004).

Rosaldo, Michelle. "The Use and Abuse of Anthropology: Reflections on Feminism and Cross-Cultural Understanding." *Signs* 5(3) (Spring 1980): 389–418.

Rose, David. "I Helped M15. My Reward: Brutality and Prison." *UK Observer*. 29 July 2007.

Rosenbach, Marcel, and John Goetz. "'Massive and Systematic Violations' of Human Rights." *Spiegel International Online*. 8 June 2007. Accessed 9 January 2014 at http://www.spiegel.de/international/world/0,1518,487325,00.html.

Roshan, Habiba. "Untitled." Unpublished poem. 2010.

Rouse, Shahnaz. *Shifting Body Politics: Gender, Nation, and State in Pakistan*. New Delhi: Women Unlimited, 2004.

Rubenstein, Richard L. "The Bureaucratization of Torture." *Journal of Social Philosophy* 13(3) (2008): 31–51.

Rupert, Mark. "Refighting America's Vietnam War: Populist Militarism and the Paradox of Imperial Consent." Unpublished paper, Syracuse University, 2011.

Sabbagh, Suha. *Sex, Lies, and Stereotypes: The Image of Arabs in American Popular Fiction*. Washington: American-Arab Anti-Discrimination Committee, 1990.

Sackett, Lee. "A Post-Modern Panopticon: The Royal Commission into Aboriginal Deaths in Custody." *Australian Journal of Social Issues* 28(3) (1993): 229–44.

"Safety of Christian Workers Cannot Be Compromised." *NAE Leadership Alert*. 15 December 1996, 1.

Said, Edward. "The Essential Terrorist." *The Nation*. 14 August 2006. Accessed 10 January 2014 at http://www.thenation.com/article/essential-terrorist.

– *Orientalism*. New York: Vintage Books, 1978.

– "Punishment by Detail." *Counterpunch*. 13 August 2002. Accessed 10 January 2014 at http://www.counterpunch.org/2002/08/13/punishment-by-detail.

Said Khan, Nighat. "The Impact of the Global Women's Movement on International Relations: Has It Happened? What Has Happened?" In *Common Grounds or Mutual Exclusions? Women's Movements and International Relations*, ed. Marianne Braig and Sonja Wolte. 35–45. London: Zed Books, 2002.

Saigol, R. "The State and the Limits of Counter-Terrorism: The Case of Pakistan and Sri Lanka." Monograph Series of Council of Social Sciences Pakistan, no. 4 (2006). 1–57.

Salazar, Zeus. *Pantayong Pananaw: Isang Paliwanag* (From Us for Us Theory: An Explanation). Mandaluyong: Palimbagang Kalawakan, 1997.

Sale, Kirkpatrick. *The Conquest of Paradise*. New York: Plume, 1990.

Sanders, Edmund. "Ethiopia's Intervention May Destabilize Region." *Los Angeles Times*. 7 January 2007, A3.

Santos, Paz Verdades M. "Centre of Gravity: The New People's Army in Bikol (A Case Study)." *Primed and Purposeful: Armed Groups and Human Security Efforts in the Philippines*, ed. Soliman Santos and Paz Verdades M. Santos. 43–57. Geneva and Manila: South–South Effort for Non-State Armed Group Engagement and the Small Arms Surveey, 2010.

Saraçoğlu, Cenk. "Islami Muhafazakar Milliyetçiliğin Millet Tasarımı: AKP Döneminde Kürt Politikası" (The Vision of the Nation under Islamic Conservative Nationalism: The Kurdish Policy in the AKP Period). *Praksis* 26 (2011): 31–54.

– *Kurds of Modern Turkey: Migration, Neoliberalism, and Exclusion in Turkish Society*. London: I.B. Tauris, 2011.

Sarkar, Mahua. "Difference in Memory." *Comparative Study of Society and History* (2006): 139–68.

Satterthwaite, Margaret L. "The Legal Regime Governing Transfer of Persons in the Fight Against Terrorism." 2010. New York University Public Law and Legal Theory Working Paper 192, 1–37. Accessed 24 March 2014 at http://lsr.nellco.org/cgi/viewcontent.cgi?article=1192&context=nyu_plltwp.

Sayed, Haneen, and Zafiris Tzannatos. "The Economic and Human Costs of War." *The War on Lebanon: A Reader*, ed. Rashid Khalidi and Nubar Hovsepian. 316–42. New York: Olive Branch Press, 2007.

Scarry, Elaine. *The Body in Pain: The Making and Unmaking of the World*. Oxford: Oxford University Press, 1985.

Schaffer, Sharada J. *Privileging the Privileged: Gender in Indian Advertising*. New Delhi: Promilla, 2006.

Scheper-Hughes, Nancy, and Philippe Bourgois, eds. *Violence in War and Peace: An Anthology*. 236–43. Oxford: Blackwell, 2004.

Schmitt, Carl. *The Concept of the Political*. Chicago: University of Chicago Press, 2007.

– *Theory of the Partisan: Intermediate Commentary on the Concept of the Political*. Candor: Telos Press, 2007.

Schulman, Sarah. *Israel/Palestine and the Queer International*. Durham: Duke University Press, 2012.

Schwartz, Mattathias. "Traces of a Massacre." *The New Yorker*. 12 December 2011. Accessed 9 January 2014 at http://www.newyorker.com/reporting/2011/12/12/111212fa_fact_schwartz.

Scott, Joan. "Experience." In *Feminists Theorize the Political*, ed. Scott and Judith Butler. New York: Routledge, 1992.

– *Gender and the Politics of History*. New York: Columbia University Press, 1988.

Sedgewick, Eve. *Between Men: English Literature and Male Homosocial Desire*. New York: Columbia University Press, 1985.

Seiple, Robert. "Religious Liberty: How Are We Doing?" *Christianity Today*. 22 October 2001, 98–101.

Sellers, Jeff M. "Big, Soft Targets." *Christianity Today*. 4 February 2002, 50–3.

– "To Confront a Theocracy." *Christianity Today*. 8 July 2002, 34–40.

– "Criminal Faith." *Christianity Today*. July 2003, 61.

– "Crushed by a Soviet Relic." *Christianity Today*. 5 August 2002, 54.

– "Crushing House Churches." *Christianity Today*. January 2004, 63.

– "Dumped into Drums." *Christianity Today*. July 2005, 56.

– "Empty Legal Rights." *Christianity Today*. 7 January 2002, 50.

– "Flogged and Deported." *Christianity Today*. 22 April 2002, 82.

– "Forgotten Gulag." *Christianity Today*. 6 August 2001, 62.

– "Hounded, Beaten, Shot." *Christianity Today*. 10 June 2002, 48.

– "Lip Service." *Christianity Today*. April 2004, 95.

– "No Greater Tragedy." *Christianity Today*. 11 June 2001, 95.

– "Ordinary Terrorists." *Christianity Today*. October 2004, 102.

– "Religious Cleansing." *Christianity Today*. April 2003, 98.

– "The Violent Face of Jihad." *Christianity Today*. 23 April 2001, 100.

Sengupta, Nandita. "Death of Two Lovers, 80 Km from Delhi." *The Times of India*. 1 August 2009. Accessed 8 January 2014 at http://blogs.timesofindia.indiatimes.com/mellowdrama/entry/death-of-two-lovers-80.

Sennels, Nicolai. "Muslim Inbreeding: Impacts on Intelligence, Sanity, Health, and Society." *Right Side News*, 10 August 2010. Accessed 9 January 2014 at http://www.rightsidenews.com/2010081111313/life-and-science/culture-wars/muslim-inbreeding-impacts-on-intelligence-sanity-health-and-society.html.

Sexton, Jared. "Ante-Anti-Blackness: Afterthoughts." *Lateral* 1(1) (2012). Accessed 9 January 2014. http://lateral.culturalstudiesassociation.org/issue1/content/sexton.html.
– "People-of-Color-Blindness: Notes on the Afterlife of Slavery." *Social Text* 103(2) (2010): 31–56.
Shah, Natascha, and Kruttika Kallury. "Statutory Warnings." *India Today*. 26 June 2010. Accessed 14 January 2014 at http://indiatoday.intoday.in/site/Story/103097/statutory-warnings.html?complete=1.
Shah, Saeed. "Mainstream Pakistan Religious Organisations Applaud Killing of Salmaan Taseer." *The Guardian*. 5 January 2011. Accessed 9 January 2014 at 2014 at http://www.guardian.co.uk/world/2011/jan/05/pakistan-religious-organisations-salman-taseer.
Shalhoub-Kevorkian, Nadera. "Trapped: The Violence of Exclusion in Jerusalem." *Jerusalem Quarterly* 49 (2012): 6–25.
– *Trapped Bodies and Lives: Military Occupation, Trauma, and the Violence of Exclusion*. Jerusalem: YWCA, 2010.
Sharma, Kalpana. "When Survivors Become Victims." In *Missing Half the Story: Journalism as if Gender Mattered*, ed. Sameera Khan. 83–118. New Delhi: Zubaan, 2010.
Sharpe, A. *Foucault's Monsters and the Challenge of Law*. New York: Routledge, 2010.
Sharpe, Christina. *Monstrous Intimacies: Making Post-Slavery Subjects*. Durham: Duke University Press, 2010.
Shatz, Adam. "The Torture of Algiers." *New York Review of Books*. 21 November 2002.
Shea, Nina. "The Daniel of Religious Rights." *Christianity Today*. September 2005, 52–8.
Sheikh, Wajih Ahmad, and Asif Chaudhry. "Davis Buys His Flight to Freedom." *Dawn* (Lahore). 2011. Accessed 9 January 2014 at http://dawn.com/2011/03/17/davis-buys-his-flight-to-freedom.
– "Sephardim in Israel: Zionism from the Standpoint of Its Jewish Victims." In McClintock et al., 39–68.
Shephard, Michelle. "Canada Not 'Duped' to Take Khadr." *Toronto Star*. 27 July 2012, A14.
Shepherd, L.J. "Visualising Violence: Legitimacy and Authority in the "War on Terror.'" *Critical Studies on Terrorism* 1(2) (2004): 213–26.
Shohat, Ella. "Area Studies, Gender Studies, and the Cartographies of Knowledge." *Social Text* 20(3) (2002): 67–78.
– "Introduction." In *Talking Visions: Multicultural Feminism in a Transnational Age*. Cambridge: MIT Press, 2001.

Shohat, Ella, and Robert Stam. *Unthinking Eurocentrism: Multiculturalism and the Media*. New York: Routledge, 1994.

Siddiqa, Ayesha. *Military Inc.: Inside Pakistan's Military Economy*. London: Pluto Press, 2007.

Siddiqui, Fowzia. "Three Women One Story: In Search of Justice." *Socialist Pakistan News*. 10 May 2011. Accessed 21 May 2013 at http://www.freeaafia.org/index.php?option=com_content&view=article&id=474:three-women-one-story-in-search-of-justice&catid=46:international-news&Itemid=71.

Siebert, Charles. "The Animal-Cruelty Syndrome." *New York Times Magazine*. 11 June 2010. 42–51. Accessed 9 January 2014 at http://www.nytimes.com/2010/06/13/magazine/13dogfighting-t.html?pagewanted=all&_r=0.

Silva, Denise Ferreira da. "'Bahia Pêlo Negro': Can the Subaltern (Subject of Raciality) Speak?" *Ethnicities* 5(3) (2005): 321–42.

– *Toward a Global Idea of Race*. Minneapolis: University of Minnesota Press, 2007.

Silverblatt, Irene. *Modern Inquisitions: Peru and the Colonial Origins of the Civilized World*. Durham: Duke University Press, 2004.

Simon, Bart. "The Return of Panopticism: Supervision, Subjection, and the New Surveillance." *Surveillance and Society* 3(1) (2005): 1–20.

Simon, Roger. "Towards a Hopeful Practice of Worrying: The Problematics of Listening and the Educative Responsibility of Canada's Truth and Reconciliation Commission." In *Reconciling Canada: Critical Perspectives on the Culture of Redress*, ed. Jennifer Henderson and Pauline Wakeham. 129–42. Toronto: University of Toronto Press, 2013.

– "The Pedagogy of Commemoration and Formation of Collective Memories." *Educational Foundations* 8(1) (1994): 5–24.

Singh, Indubala. *Gender Relations and Cultural Ideology in Indian Cinema*. New Delhi: Deep and Deep, 2007.

Singh, Manpreet. "Anti-Conversion Conspiracy." *Christianity Today*. May 2004, 20.

– "Christians Scorn 'China Model.'" *Christianity Today*. 4 December 2000, 28.

– "50,000 Dalits Renounce Hinduism." *Christianity Today*. 7 January 2002, 23.

– "Harassed Kashmir Christians Reach Out to Discreet Muslims." *Christianity Today*. 9 September 2002, 26–7.

– "Hindu Radical Redux." *Christianity Today*. May 2005, 19.

– "Justice Delayed for Dalits." *Christianity Today*. 13 November 2000, 34–5.

– "Militant Hindus Assault Christians." *Christianity Today*. 5 February 2001, 24.

– "Power in Punjab." *Christianity Today*. July 2003, 24–5.

– "Quitting Hinduism." *Christianity Today*. 9 December 2002, 18.

– "Radicals Attack Two Christian Institutions." *Christianity Today*. 9 September 2002, 26.
– "Relief Abuses Rampant." *Christianity Today*. 2 April 2001, 32.
– "Shock and Awesome." *Christianity Today*. July 2004, 15.
– "Under Siege." *Christianity Today*. May 2006, 21–2.
Singh, Rickey. "Guyana's Political Trauma – Tragedies in Linden and a Chief Justice's Budget Ruling." *Guyana Chronicle*, 21 July 2012.
Singh, Uma. *New Woman and Mass Media*. Jaipur: Surabhi Publications, 2001.
Sinha, Mrinalini. "Giving Masculinity a History: Some Contributions from the Historiography of Colonial India." *Gender and History* 11(3) (November 1999): 445–60.
Smith, Andrea. *Conquest: Sexual Violence and American Indian Genocide*. Cambridge: South End Press, 2005.
– "Indigeniety, Settler Colonialism, White Supremacy." *Global Dialogue* 12(2) (2010). Accessed 9 January 2014 at http://www.worlddialogue.org/content.php?id=488.
Smith, Andrea, and J. Kehaulani Kauanui. "'Native Feminisms Engage American Studies.'" *American Quarterly* 60(2) (2008): 241–9.
Smith, Jay. "Deconstructing Islam." *Christianity Today*. 9 September 2002, 37.
Smith, Linda Tuhiwai. *Decolonizing Methodologies: Research and Indigenous Peoples*. New York: Palgrave, 1999.
Smith, Malinda S., ed. *Securing Africa: Post-9/11 Discourses on Terrorism*. Farnham: Ashgate, 2010.
Smith, Shawn Michelle. "The Evidence of Lynching Photographs." In Lynching Photographs, ed. Dora Apel and Shawn Michelle Smith. Berkeley: University of California Press, 2008.
Snyder, Timothy. *Bloodlands: Europe between Hitler and Stalin*. New York: Basic Books, 2010.
Sol Portal. "Diyarbakir Valisi Mustafa Toprak: 'Vatandaşları Korumak İçin Yaptık'" (Diyarbakir Governor Mustafa Toprak: "We Did It to Protect Citizens"). 15 July 2012. Accessed 9 January 2014 at http://haber.sol.org.tr/devlet-ve-siyaset/diyarbakir-valisi-mustafa-toprak-vatandaslari-korumak-icin-yaptik-haberi-57084.
– "Newroz Bilançosu: 659 Gözaltı 71 Tutuklama" (Newroz Balance Sheet: 659 Detentions, 71 Arrests). 23 March 2012. Accessed 9 January 2014 at http://haber.sol.org.tr/devlet-ve-siyaset/newroz-bilancosu-659-gozalti-71-tutuklama-haberi-52976.
Sontag, Susan. "Regarding the Torture of Others." *New York Times*. 23 May 2004. Accessed 10 January 2014 at http://www.nytimes.com/2004/05/23/magazine/regarding-the-torture-of-others.html?pagewanted=all&src=pm.

Spanos, William V. *America's Shadow: An Anatomy of Empire*. Minneapolis: University of Minnesota Press, 1999.

Sparks, Richard. *Television and the Drama of Crime: Moral Tales and the Place of Crime in Public Life*. Buckingham and Philadelphia: Open University Press, 1992.

Spivak, Gayatri Chakravorty. "Can the Subaltern Speak?" In *Marxism and the Interpretation of Culture*, ed. Lawrence Grossberg and Cary Nelson. 271–316. Champaign: University of Illinois Press, 1988. Also in *Colonial Discourse and Postcolonial Theory: A Reader*, ed. Patrick Williams and Laura Chrisman. 66–111. New York: Columbia University Press, 1994.

– *Critique of Postcolonial Reason*. Cambridge: Harvard University Press, 1999.

– "Diasporas Old and New: Women in the Transnational World." *Textual Practice* 10(2) (1996): 245–69.

– "Use and Abuse of Human Rights." *Boundary 2* 32(1) (2005): 131–89.

Sreeprasad, Vidyadar. "Dalits Join Church Amid Persecution." *Charisma*. May 2007, 26.

"Sri Lanka's Killing Fields." Channel 4, UK. Accessed 9 January 2014 at http://srilanka.channel4.com.

St Denis, Verna. "Foreword." In Cannon and Sunseri, vi–ix.

Stafford, Tim. "India Undaunted." *Christianity Today*. May 2004, 28–35.

Stamp, Geoff. "The Church Braves Persecution in Indonesia." *Charisma*. January 2001, 72–8.

Stanley, Elizabeth. "Torture, Silence, and Recognition." *Current Issues in Criminal Justice* 16(1) (2004): 1–25.

Stannard, David E. *American Holocaust*. Oxford: Oxford University Press 1992.

Steffler, Margaret. "The Production and Use of the Globalized Child: Canadian Literary and Political Contexts." *Jeunesse* 1(2) (2009): 117–18.

Steinfels, Peter. "Evangelicals Lobby for Oppressed Christians." *New York Times*. 15 November 1996, 26

Stewart, Frank. *Honor*. Chicago: University of Chicago Press, 1994.

Stewart, Jimmy. "Christians Still Being Enslaved by Muslims in War-Ravaged Sudan." *Charisma*. May 1999, 37–8.

Stoler, Ann Laura. *Along the Archival Grain: Epistemic Anxieties and Colonial Common Sense*. Princeton: Princeton University Press, 2010.

Stoler, Ann Laura, and Karen Strassler. "Castings for the Colonial: Memory Work in 'New Order' Java." *Comparative Study of Society and History* 42 (2000): 4–48.

Stover, Eric. *The Open Secret: Torture and the Medical Profession in Chile: Reports on Medicine and the Prevention of Torture*. Washington: Committee on

Scientific Freedom and Responsibility, American Association for the Advancement of Science, 1987.

Stricherz, Mark. "Better Late than Never." *Christianity Today* 49. November 2005, 19.

Strobel, Leny Mendoza, ed. *Babaylan ('Shaman'): Filipinos and the Call of the Indigenous*. Davao City: Ateneo de Davao University Research and Publications Office, 2010.

Strong, Tracy. *The Idea of Political Theory: Reflections on the Self in Political Time and Place*. Notre Dame: University of Notre Dame Press, 1990.

Sukkarieh, Omeima. "I Cried As Hard As I Could." Unpublished poem. 2006.

– "The Illusion of Despair." Unpublished poem. 1998.

– "So Fragile." In *Bread and Other Stories: A Collection of Writings*, ed. Paula Abood and Latifa Shabnam. Bankstown, NSW: Bankstown Area Multicultural Network , 2001

– "Untitled." In *Auburn Letters*. Auburn: Auburn Community Development Network, 2008.

Sumser, John. *Morality and Social Order in Television Crime Dramas*. Jefferson: McFarland, 1996.

Sutherland, Abena. "In You More than You: D.S. Marriott's *Incognegro*." *Intercapillary Space*. 15 July 2006. Accessed 10 January 2014 at http://intercapillaryspace.blogspot.ca/2007/01/in-you-more-than-you-d-s-mariotts.html.

Tafari-AMA, Imani. *Blood, Bullets, and Bodies: Sexual Politics below Jamaica's Poverty Line*. Kingston: University of the West Indies Press, 2006.

Tausig, Michael T. *Defacement: Public Secrecy and the Labor of the Negative*. Stanford: Stanford University Press, 1999.

Taylor, Diana. *The Archive and the Repertoire: Performing Cultural Memory in the Americas*. Durham: Duke University Press, 2003.

– *Disappearing Acts: Spectacles of Gender and Nationalism in Argentina's "Dirty War."* Durham: Duke University Press, 1997.

Taylor, Greg. "Under Suspicion." *Christianity Today* 44. 22 May 2000, 36.

Tejani, S. *Indian Secularism: A Social and Intellectual History, 1890–1950*. Bloomington: Indiana University Press, 2008.

Tennant, Agnieszka. "The God Who Lives and Works and Plays in Russia." *Christianity Today*. November 2006, 33–41.

– "Long Road." *Christianity Today*. October 2006, 80.

Terry, Jenny. "Killer Entertainments." *Vectors* 3(1) (2007). Accessed 10 January 2014 at http://vectors.usc.edu/projects/index.php?project=86.

Theoharis, Jeanne. "Who Is the Target of NSA Surveillance?" *Chronicle of Higher Education*, 17 June 2013.

Theweleit, Klaus. *Male Fantasies*. Vol. 1. Minneapolis: University of Minnesota Press, 1987.

Thobani, Sunera. "Gender and Empire: Veilomentaries and the War on Terror." In *Global Communications: Towards a Transcultural Political Economy*, ed. Paula Chakravorty and Yuezhi Zhao. 219–42. Lanham: Rowan and Littlefield, 2008.

– "Imperialist Missions: Representing Muslims in the War on Terror." In *The Politics of Nationhood and Belonging*, ed. Meenakshi Thappan. 230–58. Hyderabad: Orient Blackswan, 2010.

– "White Wars: 'Western' Feminisms and the 'War on Terror.'" *Feminist Theory* 8(2) (August 2007): 169–85.

Thomas, Deborah A. *Exceptional Violence: Embodied Citizenship in Transnational Jamaica*. Durham: Duke University Press, 2011.

Thomas, Greg. *The Sexual Demon of Colonial Power: Pan-African Embodiment and Erotic Schemes of Empire*. Bloomington: Indiana University Press, 2007.

Thomas, Robina. *Storytelling in the Spirit of Wise Woman: Experiences of Kuper Island Residential School*. Unpublished MA thesis, School of Social Work, University of Victoria, 2000.

Thyne, Lizie, and Nadje Al-Ali. "An Interview with Kim Longinetto." *Feminist Review* 99 (2011): 25–38.

Ticktin, Miriam. *Casualties of Care: Immigration and the Politics of Humanitarianism in France*. Berkeley: University of California Press, 2011.

– "Policing and Humanitarianism in France: Immigration and the Turn to Law as State of Exception." *Interventions: A Journal of Postcolonial Studies* 7(3) (2005): 347–68.

Timerman, Jacobo. *Prisoner without and Name, Cell without a Number*. Madison: University of Wisconsin Press, 1980.

Todorov, Tzvetan. *Torture and the War on Terror*. Trans. Gila Walker. London: Seagull Books, 2009.

"Tomorrow, North Korea: Hopeful for a Better." *Link* 3 (2004): 1–8.

Trotz, D. Alissa. "Behind the Banner of Culture? Gender, Race, and the Family in Guyana." *New West Indian Guide / Nieuwe West Indische Gids* 77(1–2) (July 2003): 5–29.

– "Between Despair and Hope: Towards an Analysis of Women and Violence in Contemporary Guyana.' *Small Axe* 15 (2004): 1–25.

– "Red Thread: The Politics of Hope in Guyana." *Race and Class* 49(2) (2007): 71–8.

Trouillot, Michel-Rolph. *Silencing the Past: Power and the Production of History*. Boston: Beacon Press, 1995.

Tuğal, Cihan. "Democratic Janissaries? Turkey's Role in the Arab Spring." *New Left Review* 76 (July–August 2012): 5–24.

Turner, Kevin. "Why Isn't the American Church Growing?" *Charisma*. January 2005, 52–9.

Tynes, Robert. "US Counter-Terrorism Policies in Africa Are Counter to Development." *African Security Review* 15(3) (2006): 109–13.

Ullman, Harlan K., and James P. Wade. *Shock and Awe: Achieving Rapid Dominance*. Washington: National Defense University Press, 1996.

"US Interrogates Suspects in Ethiopian Jails." *Spiegel International Online*. 11 June 2007. Accessed 9 January 2014 at http://www.spiegel.de/international/world/0,1518,487893,00.html.

USAF. "Air Force Pamphlet 14- 210: Intelligence." Attachment 7: Collateral Damage, 180. Accessed 14 July 2012 at http://www.fas.org.

Vakil, Sunita. "No Honour in 'Honour' Killings." *Mainstream* 48(17) (2010): 23–9.

Vatter, Harold. *The Rise of Big Government in the United States*. Armonk, NY: M.E. Sharpe, 1997.

Veenker, Jody. "Sanctions Missing the Mark." *Christianity Today* 44. 12 June 2000, 28.

Veith, Gene Edward. "Praying for Persecution." *World*. 1 October 2005, 24.

– "To: Our Chinese Monitor." *World*. 2–9 July 2005, 44.

Velshi, Alykhan, and Howard Anglin. "Who's Really Ignoring the Geneva Conventions?" *National Review Online*. 7 September 2006. Accessed 26 March 2014 at http://www.nationalreview.com/articles/218629/whos-really-ignoring-geneva-conventions/alykhan-velshi.

Villabos-Ruminott, Sergio. "Fin de la Dictadura y Destrabajo del Pensar: Repetición y Catástrofe en Post-Dictadura." In *Pensar en/la Postdictadura*, ed. Nelly Richard and Alberto Moreiras. Santiago: Cuarto Propio, 2001.

Vincent, Lynn. "Shoot First, Ask Questions (Much) Later." *World* 23. 13 December 2008, 13.

Voice of the Martyrs. "Faces of Persecution." *Voice of the Martyrs*. 2000, 1–15.

– "No Time to Lose." *Voice of the Martyrs*. 2006.

Volpp, Leti. "Feminism versus Multiculturalism." *Columbia Law Review* 101(5) (2001): 1181–218.

– "(Mis)Identifying Culture: Asian Women and the Cultural Defense." *Harvard Women's Law Review* 57 (1994): 57–102.

Walcott, Derek. "The Muse of History." In *The Routledge Reader in Caribbean Literature*, ed. Alison Donnell and Sarah Lawson Welsh. 356. London: Routledge, 1996.

Walden, Inara. "'That Was Slavery Days': Aboriginal Domestic Servants in New South Wales in the Twentieth Century." *Labour History* 69 (1995): 196–209.

Walker, Ken. "China's Leaders Critical of 'Clandestine Missions.'" *Christianity Today* 42. 12 January 1998, 64–5.

– "Christians Oppose U.N. Defamation Resolution." *Charisma* 35. January 2010, 17.

Walkom, Thomas. "So-Called 'Secret Evidence' against Omar Khadr Nothing but a Joke." *Guelph Mercury*. 31 July 2012, A9.

– "Tortured Logic on Security Threats." *Toronto Star*. 11 February 2012, A12.

Warnock, Kitty. *Land before Honour*. London: Macmillan, 1990.

Watson, Irene. "Aboriginal Women's Laws and Lives: How Might We Keep Growing the Law?" *Australian Feminist Law Journal* 26 (2007): 95–110.

Watts, Alan. *The Way of Zen*. New York: Pantheon, 1990.

Webb, Ruth. *Ekphrasis, Imagination, and Persuasion in Ancient Rhetorical Theory and Practice*. Burlington: Ashgate, 2009.

Weber, Max. "Politics as a Vocation." In *The Vocation Lectures*. Indianapolis: Hackett, 2007.

Weiss, Anita M. 1986. "Implications of the Islamization Program for Women." In *Islamic Reassertion in Pakistan: The Application of Islamic Laws in a Modern State*, ed. Anita M. Weiss. 97–113. Syracuse: Syracuse University Press, 1986.

Welchman, Lynn, and Sara Hossain, eds. "Introduction." In *Honour: Crimes, Paradigms, and Violence against Women*. New Delhi: Zubaan, 2006.

Welner, Michael. "Omar Khadr and the Jihadism That Lurks in Our Prisons." *National Post*. 19 February 2011. Accessed 9 January 2014 at http://fullcomment.nationalpost.com/2011/02/19/michael-welner-omar-khadr-and-the-jihadism-that-lurks-in-our-prisons.

Wessler, Seth Freed. "Muslim Students Reeling from Shocking News of NYPD's Spying." *Colorlines*. 24 February 2012. Accessed 9 January 2014 at http://colorlines.com/archives/2012/02/first_came_the_shock_then.html.

"What Defines 'Real' Persecution?" *Open Doors Newsbrief* 16. December 2001, 4.

Wheeler, John, and Wojciech H. Zurek, eds. 1983. *Quantum Theory and Measurement*. Princeton: Princeton University Press, 1983.

White, Canon Andrew. "Dampening the Fuse in Iraq." *Christianity Today* 47(7) (2003), 38–40.

White, Sarah. "Thinking Race, Thinking Development." *Third World Quarterly* 23(3) (2002): 407–19.

White, Tom. "Dare to Be Faithful." *Voice of the Martyrs*. Special Issue, 2005, 9–11.

Whitlock, Craig. "Courted as Spies, Held as Combatants: British Resident Enlisted by M15 after September 11 Languish at Guantanamo." *Washington Post.* 2 April 2006.

Wikan, Unni. *In Honor of Fadime: Murder and Shame.* Trans. Anna Paterson. Chicago: University of Chicago Press, 2008.

Wilderson III, Frank B. *Red, White & Black: Cinema and the Structure of U.S. Antagonisms.* Durham, NC: Duke University Press, 2010.

Williams, Patrick, and Laura Chrisman. *Colonial Discourse and Post-Colonial Theory: A Reader.* New York: Columbia University Press, 1994.

Williams, Pete. "Bin Laden Killing Was Legally Justified, Holder Says." *MSNBC.com.* 4 May 2011. Accessed 10 May 2011 at http://www.msnbc.msn.com/id/42900659/ns/world_news-south_and_central_asia/t/bin-laden-killing-was-legally-justified-holder-says.

Williams, Randall. *The Divided World: Human Rights and Its Violence.* Minneapolis: University of Minnesota Press, 2010.

Williams, William A. *Empire as a Way of Life: An Essay on the Causes and Character of America's Present Predicament.* New York: Oxford University Press, 1980.

Wilson, Richard. *The Politics of Truth and Reconciliation in South Africa.* Cambridge: Cambridge University Press, 2001.

Wingfield, Marvin, and Bushra Karaman. "Arab Stereotypes and American Educators." *Social Studies and the Young Learner.* March–April 1995.

Winton, Ezra. "Ismael Beah on Child Soldiers and Hip-Hop & Roméo Dallaire on Corporate Media." *Art Threat.* 17 April 2007. Accessed 9 January 2014 at http://artthreat.net/2007/04/ishmael-beah-on-child-soldiers-and-hip-hop-romeo-dallaire-on-corporate-media.

Wolf, Frank, R. "Inexcusable Silence." *Christianity Today* 44(10) (4 September 2000), 104–5.

Wood, Gail. "Vietnamese Churches Growing under Indigenous Leaders." *Charisma.* August 2001, 34–5.

Woodhead, Jacinda. "Why Isn't Afghanistan an Election Issue?" 13 August 2010. Accessed 10 January 2014 at http://www.abc.net.au/unleashed/stories/s2981357.htm.

Woolf, Naomi. *The End of America: A Letter of Warning to a Young Patriot.* White River Junction: Chelsea Green, 2007.

Woolf, Virginia. *Three Guineas.* London: Harcourt Brace Jovanovich, 1938.

Wunderink, Susan. "Case by Case." *Christianity Today.* November 2008, 15–16.

– "You've Got Jail." *Christianity Today.* March 2009, 16–17.

Wynter, Sylvia. "'Unsettling the Coloniality of Being/Power/Truth/Freedom: Towards the Human, After Man, Its Overrepresentation – an Argument.'" *CR: The New Centennial Review* 3(3) (2003): 257–337.

Yanagisako, Sylvia, and Jane Collier. "Toward a Unified Analysis of Gender and Kinship." In *Gender and Kinship*, ed. J.F. Collier and S.J.Yanagisako. 14–50. Stanford: Stanford University Press, 1987.

Yancey, Philip. "A Dream That Won't Die." *Christianity Today*. March 2009, 96.

– "Holy Subversion." *Christianity Today*. 5 February 1988, 14–19.

– "The Japanese Joseph." *Christianity Today*. July 2005, 64.

– "A Living Stream in the Desert." *Christianity Today*. November 2010, 30–5.

Yeğenoğlu, Meyda. *Colonial Fantasies: Towards a Feminist Reading of Orientalism*. Cambridge: Cambridge University Press, 1998.

Youatt, Rafi. "Counting Species: Biopower and the Global Diversity Census." *Environmental Values* 17 (2008): 393–417.

Young, Robert J.C. "Introduction to Gayatri Chakravorty Spivak's 2001 Oxford Amnesty Lecture, 'Righting Wrongs.'" In *Human Rights, Human Wrongs: The Oxford Amnesty Lectures 2001*, ed. Nicholas J. Owen. 164–7. Oxford: Oxford University Press, 2003.

Young, William. "God and Derrida's Politics: At the Edge of Exemplarity." Accessed 9 January 2014 at http://www.jcrt.org/archives/01.1/young.html.

Yusuf, Huma. 2011. "Fallout of the Davis Case." *Dawn*. 21 February 2011. Accessed 9 January 2014 at http://dawn.com/2011/02/21/fallout-of-the-davis-case.

Zaman. "Yasaklı miting Diyarbakır'ın huzurunu kaçırdı" (The Illegal Demonstration Disturbed Peace in Diyarbakır). 14 July 2012. Accessed 9 January at http://www.zaman.com.tr/haber.do?haberno=1317949&title=yasakli-miting-diyarbakirin-huzurunu-kacirdi.

Zeilig, Leo. *Lumumba: Africa's Lost Leader*. London: Haus Publishing, 2008.

Zembylas, Michalinos. "Bearing Witness to the Ethics of Politics of Suffering: J.M. Coetzee's *Disgrace*, Inconsolable Mourning, and the Task of Educators." *Studies of Philosophy and Education* 28(3) (2009): 223–37.

Zerner, Charles. "Stealth Nature: Biomimesis and the Weaponization of Life." *In the Name of Humanity: The Government of Threat and Care*, ed. I. Feldman and M. Ticktin, 290–324. Durham: Duke University Press, 2010.

Zetter, Kim. "Caught Spying on Student, FBI Demands GPS Tracking Device Back." *Wired*. 7 October 2010. Accessed 9 January 2014 at http://www.wired.com/threatlevel/2010/10/fbi-tracking-device.

Zia, Afiya S. "Faith-Based Politics, Enlightened Moderation, and the Pakistani Women's Movement." *Journal of International Women Studies* 11(1) (2009): 225–45.

Žižek, Slavoj. "Against Human Rights." *New Left Review* 34 (2005): 115–31.

– *Living in the End Times*. New York: Verso, 2011.

– *Welcome to the Desert of the Real*. London: Verso, 2002.

Zunes, Stephen. "Washington's Proxy War." In *The War on Lebanon: A Reader*, ed. Nubar Hovsepian. 93–118. Northampton: Interlink Books, 2008.

Zureik, Elia, David Lyon, and Yasmeen Abu-Laban, eds. *Surveillance and Control in Israel/Palestine: Population, Territory, and Power*, vol. 33. New York: Routledge, 2010.

Zurowski, Tom. "Camel Boy 'Crucified.'" *Voice of the Martyrs*. Special Issue, 2004, 4.

List of Contributors

Asma Abbas is Associate Professor of Politics and Philosophy at Bard College at Simon's Rock in Great Barrington, Massachusetts. She received her doctorate in Political Science and Social Thought from Pennsylvania State University, on the heels of an MA in Liberal Studies from the New School for Social Research and an MBA from the Institute of Business Administration at the University of Karachi. Her research in social and political theory combines continental, historical, feminist, and anti-colonial perspectives and is situated at the intersection of politics, ethics, and aesthetics, addressing the material bases shared by these domains. Her first book was *Liberalism and Human Suffering: Materialist Reflections on Politics, Ethics, and Aesthetics* (2010), and her current book project is tentatively titled *Another Love: Overtures to a Politics of the Unrequited*. She is the translator into English of the memoir of a founding member of the revolutionary left labour movement in Pakistan.

Anna M. Agathangelou teaches in Political Science and Social and Political Thought at York University, Toronto, and is co-director of the Global Change Institute, Nicosia. She is the author of the *Global Political Economy of Sex: Desire, Violence, and Insecurity in Mediterranean Nation-States* (2004); co-author with L.H.M. Ling of *Transforming World Politics: From Empire to Multiple Worlds* (2009); co-editor with Kyle D. Killian of the special issue (December 2011) of *Intensions* subtitled "(De) Fatalizing the Present and Creating Radical Alternatives" (http://www.yorku.ca/intent/cfw.html); and co-editor with Nevzat Soguk of *Arab Revolutions and World Transformations* (2013).

Sedef Arat-Koç is Associate Professor in the Department of Politics and Public Administration and a faculty member of the Yeates School of

Graduate Studies at Ryerson University. Dr Arat-Koç's work and research considers the gendered dimensions of immigration policy and citizenship; the politics of imperialism; racialization and the politics of racism; and the reconfiguration of social and political identities under neoliberal globalization.

Merlinda Bobis is a Filipino-Australian writer, performer, and academic who has published three novels, a collection of short stories, five poetry books, a monograph on creative research, and scholarly essays on creative-critical production, militarism, migration, and the transnational imaginary. She has received various awards for her works, including the Prix Italia (Radio Fiction); the Australian Writers' Guild Award (Radio Play); the Steele Rudd Award for the Best Published Collection of Australian Short Stories; the Philippine National Book Award and Judges' Choice Award; the Carlos Palanca Memorial Award for Literature for her poetry; and the Philippine Balagtas Award, a lifetime award for her fiction and poetry in English, Pilipino, and Bikol. Bobis's plays have been performed/produced, mostly as her one-woman show, in Australia, the Philippines, the United States, Spain, Canada, France, China, Thailand, and the Slovak Republic. She teaches creative writing at the University of Wollongong, Australia. Author's website: http://www.merlindabobis.com.au.

Gulzar R. Charania is a doctoral candidate in the Department of Humanities, Social Sciences, and Social Justice Education at the University of Toronto. Her research interests include critical race and queer theories, women of colour and anti-colonial feminisms, processes of political formation, and the politics of educational policies and practices.

Denise Ferreira da Silva is Professor of Ethics in the School of Business and Management and Director of the Centre for Ethics and Politics, Queen Mary, University of London. Her writings advance a racial/postcolonial critique of modern thought that engages critical legal theory, political theory, historical materialism, feminist theory, critical racial and ethnic studies, and postcolonial/global studies. She is author of *Toward a Global Idea of Race* (2007) and *Notes Towards the End of Time* (2013). She is completing two book projects, *The Critique of Racial Violence* and *Nobodies: Law, Raciality, and Necessity Human, Race, Rights*. She is a co-editor of the Routledge series Law and the Postcolonial: Ethics, Politics, Economy.

Honor Ford-Smith is Associate Professor in the Community and Environmental Arts Practice program in the Faculty of Environmental Studies at York University. Her most recent publication is *3 Jamaican Plays: A Postcolonial Anthology (1977–1987)*, published by Paul Issa Publications, Kingston, Jamaica, in 2010.

Inderpal Grewal is Chair and Professor of the Women's, Gender, and Sexuality Studies Program, Faculty in the South Asia Council and in the Ethnicity, Race and Migration Studies Program, and affiliate faculty in American Studies at Yale University. She is the author of *Home and Harem: Nation, Gender, Empire, and Cultures of Travel* (1996) and *Transnational America: Feminisms, Diasporas, Neoliberalisms* (2005). She is co-editor (with Caren Kaplan) of *Scattered Hegemonies: Postmodernity and Transnational Feminist Practices* (1995), *Introduction to Women's Studies: Gender in a Transnational World* (2001, 2005) and *Theorizing NGOs: Feminism, Neoliberalism, and the State* (with Victoria Bernal, 2014) Her areas of research include feminist theory, cultural studies of South Asia and its diasporas, British and US imperialism, and contemporary feminist transnationalisms.

Roshan A. Jahangeer is completing a PhD in Political Science at York University in Toronto. Her research focuses on the laws against various forms of veiling that have been implemented in France since 2004 and their effects on the education and employment outcomes of French Muslim women. Her research also addresses the debates over veiling that have occurred in Canada at the provincial and federal levels. Her dissertation is tentatively titled "The Politics of (Un)Veiling: Feminism, Secularism, and Citizenship in France and Canada." She has worked with the Canadian Council for Muslim Women (CCMW) and has contributed a case study on secularism in Quebec for an upcoming report on discrimination against Muslims in Canada, to be published by the Islamic Human Rights Commission (IHRC) in Great Britain. She is currently an instructor at Emmanuel College, University of Toronto.

Amina Jamal is an Associate Professor of Sociology at Ryerson University, Toronto. She studies women, gender, Islam, and modernities in South Asia and Canada from a post-structuralist and transnational Muslim feminist location. She has published on the politics of Muslim women's representation, gendered Islamism, and the ongoing discursive struggle of feminism and Islamism in Pakistan. Her forthcoming book on women leaders of Pakistan's Jamaat-e-Islami movement situates these topics within the history of anti-colonial Islamic modernism, postcolonial nation-state formation, recent geopolitical conditions, and the unique mystical dimensions of South Asian Islam.

Laura J. Kwak is a PhD candidate in the Department of Humanities, Social Sciences, and Social Justice Education at OISE/UofT.

Teresa Macias was born in one of the shantytowns on the outskirts of Santiago, Chile, and grew up during the dictatorship of Augusto Pinochet. In her teens, she became an activist, community organizer, and popular educator in some of the many grassroots organizations that emerged to resist the regime. She and her family came to Canada in the late 1980s to escape political persecution. In Canada she attended Ryerson University for her undergraduate degree and then OISE/UofT for her MA and PhD. Her PhD thesis, "On the Pawprints of Terror: The Human Rights Regime and the Production of Truth and Subjectivity in Post-Authoritarian Chile," traces twenty years of history in the development of state policy to deal with human rights abuses. Her work deals with issues of disappearances, torture, truth commissions, and compensation. She is currently conducting research on the Canadian Indian Residential School Truth and Reconciliation Commission. She has taught at the University of Victoria in British Columbia and is currently Assistant Professor at the School of Social Work at York University in Toronto, where she lives with her son.

Sunaina Maira is Professor of Asian American Studies at the University of California, Davis. She is the author of *Desis in the House: Indian American Youth Culture in New York City* and *Missing: Youth, Citizenship, and Empire after 9/11*. She co-edited *Contours of the Heart: South Asians Map North America*, which won the American Book Award in 1997, and *Youthscapes: The Popular, the National, and the Global*. She helped found the South Asian Committee on Human Rights (SACH), which focused on post-9/11 civil and immigrant rights issues in the Boston area. She has also worked with various antiwar, civil rights, and immigrant rights groups in the San Francisco Bay Area.

Nadine Naber is Associate Professor in the American Culture Program and the Department of Women's Studies and an Adjunct Professor in the Department of Anthropology at the University of Michigan, Ann

Arbor. She is author of *Arab America: Gender, Cultural Politics, and Activism* (2012). She is co-editor, with Amaney Jamal, of *Race and Arab Americans* (2008). She is co-editor, with Rabab Abdulhadi and Evelyn Alsultany, of *Arab and Arab American Feminisms: Gender, Violence, and Belonging* (2010). She is co-founder of the Arab Women's Solidarity Association, North America (cyber AWSA), the Arab Movement of Women arising for Justice (AMWAJ), and the Arab Women's Activist Network (AWAN), and a former board member of Incite! Women of Color against Violence, Racial Justice 9/11, and the Women of Color Resource Center.

Suvendrini Perera completed her PhD at Columbia University. She is Professor of Cultural Studies in the School of Media, Culture, and Creative Arts and Deputy Director of the Australia-Asia-Pacific Institute at Curtin University, Australia. She is the author/editor of six books, including *Australia and the Insular Imagination: Beaches, Borders, Boats, and Bodies* (2009), *Our Patch* (2007); *Enter at Own Risk* (co-edited with Graham Seal and Sue Summers, 2010), and *Living through Terror* (co-edited with Antonio Traverso, 2011). Currently she is working on a volume on trophy war videos titled *Old Atrocities, New Media*.

Kendra-Ann Pitt is a PhD candidate in the Department of Humanities, Social Sciences, and Social Justice Education at the University of Toronto. She is also enrolled in the collaborative program in Women and Gender Studies. Her current research examines the significance of discourses of gender, race, class, and sexuality in the provision of domestic violence services in the Caribbean. She holds a BSc in Social Work from the University of the West Indies, St Augustine, and an MSW from York University in Toronto. Her areas of interest include feminist and postcolonial theories, anti-racism studies, and violence and equity in the Caribbean and the diaspora.

Sherene Razack is full Professor in the Department of Humanities, Social Sciences, and Social Justice Education at OISE/UofT. Her books include *Casting Out: The Eviction of Muslims From Western Law and Politics* (2008), *Dark Threats and White Knights: The Somalia Affair, Peacekeeping, and the New Imperialism* (2004), *Looking White People in the Eye: Gender, Race, and Culture in Courtrooms and Classrooms* (1998), and *Canadian Feminism and the Law: The Women's Legal and Education Fund and the Pursuit of Equality* (1991). She co-edited, with Malinda Smith and Sunera Thobani, *States of Race: Critical Race Feminism for the 21st Century* (2010) and edited *Race, Space, and the Law: Unmapping a White Settler Society* (2002). She helped found the feminist and anti-racist network of scholars, Researchers and Academics of Color for Equality (RACE).

Nashwa Salem is a PhD student at the Department of Humanities, Social Sciences, and Social Justice Education and the Women and Gender Studies Institute of the University of Toronto. She locates her work at the interstices of law, history, and postcolonial theory, exploring conditions of the making of the global modern.

Nadera Shalhoub-Kevorkian is Professor at the Faculty of Law, Institute of Criminology, and School of Social Work at the Hebrew University, Jerusalem, and Founding Director of the Gender Studies Program at Mada al-Carmel, the Arab Center for Applied Social Research in Haifa. She is a feminist criminologist and specialist in human rights and women's rights. Her books include *Militarization and Violence against Women in Conflict Zones: A Palestinian Case Study* (2009), *Tribal Justice and Its Effect on Formal Justice in Palestine* (2003), and *Femicide in Palestinian Society* (2001). She is currently working on a new book about security, surveillance, and the political economy of fear. She has worked on examining the limits and the power of law and political economy in conflict zones from a critical race theory perspective, while also looking at the obstacles facing local social policies, international law, and international humanitarian law when violence against women and children is being addressed. She was awarded the 2008 Gruber Women's Rights Prize, which honours individuals who have made significant contributions that advance the human rights of women and girls around the world. She also won the Phenomenal Woman Award from the Gender and Women's Studies Department at California State University, Northridge.

Andrea Smith is an Associate Professor of Media and Cultural Studies at the University of California, Riverside. She is a co-founder of Incite! Women of Color Against Violence and the Critical Ethnic Studies Association. She is also the author of *Native Americans and the Christian Right: The Gendered Politics of Unlikely Alliances* (2008).

Malinda S. Smith is Associate Professor of International Relations and Comparative Politics and the Associate Chair (Graduate Studies) in the Department of Political Science at the University of Alberta. Raised in

The Bahamas, she completed her graduate studies in the United States and Canada. She is the editor of three books on Africa: *Globalizing Africa* (2003), *Beyond the "African Tragedy": Discourses on Development and the Global Economy* (2006), and *Securing Africa: Post-9/11 Discourses on Terrorism* (2010). She is also a co-editor of *Critical Concepts: An Introduction to Politics* (2013), *States of Race: Critical Race Feminism in the 21st Century* (2010) and an e-book, *Beyond the Queer Alphabet: Conversations on Gender, Sexuality, and Intersectionality* (2012). Currently she is Chair of the Equity Committee for the Association of Academic Staff at the University of Alberta and Co-Chair of the Board for the Centre for Race and Culture in Edmonton.

Omeima Sukkarieh is a poet, writer, artist, and cross-cultural community consultant who has been working with communities for over fifteen years. For many years she worked at the Race Discrimination Unit of the Australian Human Rights Commission on projects such as *Isma – Listen: National Consultations on Eliminating Prejudice against Arab and Muslim Australians*, the award-winning *Living Spirit: Muslim Women and Human Rights* national project, and *Unlocking Doors: Muslim Communities and Police Tackling Racial and Religious Discrimination and Hatred*. In 2002, she created controversy for installing more than 450 body bags in the centre of Sydney as an antiwar statement. Most recently, her writing has appeared in the anthology *Auburn Letters*. She is now the Manager and Community Development Officer at the Auburn Community Development Network, an organization that helps empower communities through arts, youth, and community development programs. She believes it can take only one voice to make a difference and that this voice could even be yours.

Sunera Thobani is Associate Professor at the Institute for Gender, Race, Sexuality, and Social Justice at the University of British Columbia. Her research focuses on gender, race, globalization, citizenship, migration, Muslim women, and media representations of the War on Terror. Her book *Exalted Subjects: Studies in the Making of Race and Nation in Canada*, was published in 2007. She co-edited *Asian Women: Interconnections* (2005) and *States of Race: Critical Race Feminist Theory for the 21st Century* (2010). From 1993 to 1996, she was President of the National Action Committee on the Status of Women (NAC), Canada's then largest feminist organization; from 1996 to 2000, she was the Ruth Wynn Woodward Endowed Professor in Women's Studies at Simon Fraser

University. She has helped organize, and spoken at, numerous international conferences, including the NGO Forum at the Fourth UN World Conference on Women in Beijing, the First International Women's Conference on APEC in Manila, and the National Association of Black, Asian, and Ethnic Minority Councillors in Manchester. She helped found the cross-Canada Researchers and Academics of Color for Equity (RACE) network.

Qwul'sih'yah'maht (Robina Thomas) is a member of Lyackson First Nation on Valdez Island (a Gulf Island off of Vancouver Island), British Columbia. She is Associate Professor in the School of Social Work at the University of Victoria. Currently, she also holds the interim position of Co-Chair of the First Peoples' House. She has extensive experience in Indigenous Studies, including an MSW and PhD (in Indigenous Governance) from the University of Victoria. Her MA thesis focused on Kuper Island Residential School, and her PhD dissertation focused on Indigenous Women and Leadership. She is passionate and committed to the work she does at the University of Victoria in teaching courses that highlight Indigenous ways of knowing and being.

Miriam Ticktin is Associate Professor of Anthropology in the New School for Social Research.

D. Alissa Trotz is Associate Professor of Women and Gender Studies and Caribbean Studies at New College, University of Toronto. She is also a member of Red Thread Women's Organization in Guyana and edits a weekly newspaper column, "In the Diaspora," for a Guyanese daily *Stabroek News*.

Hena Tyyebi is a PhD candidate in the Department of Political Science at York University.

Shaira Vadasaria is a doctoral student in the Department of Sociology at York University. Her dissertation research explores formations of carcerality/political imprisonment, settler-colonialism, and community life in Palestine. Her research is inspired and informed by anti-colonial feminism(s), critical race theory, Indigenous theory, and decolonizing methodologies.

Nicole Watson is a member of the Birri Gubba people of central Queensland and the Yugambeh Language Group. She has a Bachelor of Laws from the University of Queensland and a Master of Laws from the Queensland University of Technology. She is a senior research fellow at the Jumbunna Indigenous House of Learning, University of Technology, Sydney.She is currently enrolled in the Doctor of Creative Arts program at the University of Technology, Sydney. She published her first novel, *The Boundary*, in 2011, and she is a regular columnist with the Indigenous current affairs magazine *Tracker*.

Meyda Yeğenoğlu is a Professor of Cultural Studies and Social Sciences at Bilgi University in Istanbul. She has held visiting appointments at Columbia University, Oberlin College, Rutgers University, New York University, the University of Vienna, and Oxford University. She is the author of *Colonial Fantasies; Towards a Feminist Reading of Orientalism* (1998). Her book *Islam, Migrancy, and Hospitality in Europe* was published in 2012. She has published many essays in various edited volumes.